history of the

LATER ROMAN EMPIRE

FROM THE DEATH OF
THEODOSIUS I.
TO THE DEATH OF
JUSTINIAN

by J. B. Bury

In two volumes
Volume One

DOVER PUBLICATIONS, INC., NEW YORK

This new Dover edition first published in 1958 is
an unabridged and unaltered republication of the
first edition. It is published by special arrangement
with St. Martins Press.

Library of Congress Catalog Card Number: 58-11273

Manufactured in the United States of America

Dover Publications, Inc.
180 Varick Street
New York 14, N. Y.

TH! CYZYГΩI MOY

ΡΩMHC ΠΡΕCBYTEPAC TOΔE COI MNHMHION ΈCTΩ

ΉΔE NEAC, ΠΟΛΛΩN KAI CYNOΔOIΠOPIΩN

PREFACE

THE first of these two volumes might be entitled the " German Conquest of Western Europe," and the second the "Age of Justinian." The first covers more than one hundred and twenty years, the second somewhat less than fifty. This disparity is a striking illustration of the fact that perspective and proportion are unavoidably lost in an attempt to tell the story of any considerable period of ancient or early medieval history as fully as our sources allow. Perspective can be preserved only in an outline. The fifth century was one of the most critical periods in the history of Europe. It was crammed with events of great moment, and the changes which it witnessed transformed Europe more radically than any set of political events that have happened since. At that time hundreds of people were writing abundantly on all kinds of subjects, and many of their writings have survived; but among these there is no history of contemporary events, and the story has had to be pieced together from fragments, jejune chronicles, incidental references in poets, rhetoricians, and theologians. Inscribed stones which supply so much information for the first four centuries of the Roman Empire are rare. Nowhere, since the time of Alexander the Great, do we feel so strongly that the meagreness of the sources flouts the magnitude of the events.

Battles, for instance, were being fought continually, but no full account of a single battle is extant. We know much more of the Syrian campaigns of Thothmes III. in the fifteenth century B.C. than we know of the campaigns of Stilicho or Aetius or

Theoderic. The Roman emperors, statesmen, and generals are dim figures, some of them mere names. And as to the barbarian leaders who were forging the destinies of Europe—Alaric, Athaulf, Wallia, Gaiseric, Attila, and the rest—we can form little or no idea of their personalities ; τοὶ δὲ σκιαὶ ἀίσσουσιν. Historians of the Church are somewhat better off. The personalities of Augustine and Jerome, for instance, do emerge. Yet here, too, there is much obscurity. To understand the history of the Ecumenical Councils, we want much more than the official Acts. We want the background, and of it we can only see enough to know that these Councils resembled modern political conventions, that the arts of lobbying were practised, and that intimidation and bribery were employed to reinforce theological arguments.

Although we know little of the details of the process by which the western provinces of the Empire became German kingdoms, one fact stands out. The change of masters was not the result of anything that could be called a cataclysm. The German peoples, who were much fewer in numbers than is often imagined, at first settled in the provinces as dependents, and a change which meant virtually conquest was disguised for a shorter or longer time by their recognition of the nominal rights of the Emperor. Britain, of which we know less than of any other part of the Empire at this period, seems to have been the only exception to this rule. The consequence was that the immense revolution was accomplished with far less violence and upheaval than might have been expected. This is the leading fact which it is the chief duty of the historian to make clear.

When we come to the age of Justinian we know better how and why things happened, because we have the guidance of a gifted contemporary historian whose works we possess in their entirety, and we have a large collection of the Emperor's laws. The story of Justinian's Italian wars was fully related by my friend the late Mr. Hodgkin in his attractive volume on the *Imperial Restoration* ; and, more recently, *Justinian and the Byzantine Civilisation of the Sixth Century* have been the subject of a richly illustrated book by my friend M. Charles Diehl. I do not compete with them; but I believe that in my second volume the reader will find a fuller account of the events of the reign than in any other single work. I have endeavoured to supply the material which will enable him to form his own judgment on Justinian, and to have an opinion on the " question " of Theodora, of whom perhaps the utmost that we can safely say is that she was, in the words used by Swinburne of Mary Stuart, " something better than innocent."

The present work does not cover quite half the period which was the subject of my *Later Roman Empire*, published in 1889 and long out of print, as it is written on a much larger scale. Western affairs have been treated as fully as Eastern, and the exciting story of Justinian's reconquest of Italy has been told at length.

I have to thank my wife for help of various kinds ; Mr. Ashby, the Director of the British School at Rome, for reading the proof-sheets of Vol. I.; and Mr. Norman Baynes for reading those of some chapters of Vol. II. I must also record my obligations, not for the first time, to the readers of Messrs. R. and R. Clark, whose care and learning have sensibly facilitated the progress of the book through the press.

J. B. BURY.

CONTENTS

VOL. I

GENEALOGICAL TABLES—   PAGE

   (1) House of Theodosius xvii

   (2) House of Leo xviii

   (3) Family of Theoderic the Ostrogoth . . . xix

LIST OF EMPERORS xx

   „ BISHOPS OF ROME xxi

   „ PATRIARCHS OF CONSTANTINOPLE . . . xxii

   „ PATRIARCHS OF ALEXANDRIA xxiii

   „ PATRIARCHS OF ANTIOCH xxiv

   „ BISHOPS AND PATRIARCHS OF JERUSALEM . . xxv

CHAPTER I

THE CONSTITUTION OF THE MONARCHY 1

   § 1. The Autocracy 5

   § 2. The Senate, and the Imperial Council . . . 18

CHAPTER II

THE ADMINISTRATIVE MACHINERY 25

   § 1. Civil Administration 25

   § 2. Military Organisation 34

   § 3. Finance 45

   § 4. Compulsory Social Organisation . . . 55

   § 5. Ecclesiastical Organisation 63

CHAPTER III

CONSTANTINOPLE 67

§ 1. Situation. Walls and Harbours . . . 67
§ 2. Topography and Buildings 73
§ 3. Imperial Palaces 78
§ 4. Hippodrome 81
§ 5. The Suburbs. Population 86

CHAPTER IV

THE NEIGHBOURS OF THE EMPIRE AT THE END OF THE FOURTH
CENTURY 89

§ 1. Persia 90
§ 2. The Germans 96
§ 3. The Huns 101
APPENDIX ON THE NUMBERS OF THE BARBARIANS . . 104

CHAPTER V

THE SUPREMACY OF STILICHO 106

§ 1. Stilicho and Rufinus (A.D. 395) . . . 106
§ 2. Stilicho and Eutropius (A.D. 396–397) . . . 115
§ 3. The Rebellion of Gildo (A.D. 397–398) . . . 121
§ 4. Fall of Eutropius, and the German Danger in the East
(A.D. 398–400) 126
§ 5. John Chrysostom 138
§ 6. Alaric's First Invasion of Italy (A.D. 401–403) . . 160
§ 7. Last Years and Fall of Stilicho (A.D. 405–408) . . 166

CHAPTER VI

THE GERMAN INVASIONS UNDER HONORIUS . . . 174

§ 1. Alaric's Second Invasion of Italy. The Three Sieges
of Rome (A.D. 408–410) 174
§ 2. The German Invasions of Gaul and Spain, and the
Tyranny of Constantine III. (A.D. 406–411) . . 185

PAGE

§ 3. The Tyranny of Jovinus and the Reign of Athaulf
in Gaul (A.D. 412–415)   194

§ 4. Settlement of the Visigoths in Gaul, and of the Vandals
and Sueves in Spain (A.D. 415–423) .   .   . 202

§ 5. Elevation and Death of Constantius III. (A.D. 421), and
Death of Honorius (A.D. 423)   .   .   . 209

CHAPTER VII

THEODOSIUS II. AND MARCIAN 212

§ 1. Regency of Anthemius (A.D. 408–414) .   .   . 212

§ 2. Regency of the Empress Pulcheria (A.D. 414–416)   . 214

§ 3. The Usurpation of John in Italy, and Elevation of
Valentinian III. (A.D. 423–425)   .   .   . 221

§ 4. The Empress Eudocia (A.D. 437–444) .   .   . 225

§ 5. The University of Constantinople and the Theodosian
Code   231

§ 6. The Reign of Marcian (A.D. 450–457) .   .   . 235

CHAPTER VIII

THE DISMEMBERMENT OF THE EMPIRE IN THE WEST .   . 240

§ 1. Regency of the Empress Placidia.   The Defence of Gaul
(A.D. 425–430)   240

§ 2. Invasion of Africa by the Vandals (A.D. 429–435)   . 244

§ 3. End of the Regency ; and the Ascendancy of Aetius   . 249

§ 4. Settlement of the Vandals in Africa (A.D. 435–442)   . 254

§ 5. Ravenna   260

CHAPTER IX

THE EMPIRE OF ATTILA   265

§ 1. The Geography of the Balkan Peninsula   .   . 265

§ 2. The Hun Invasions of the Balkan Peninsula (A.D. 441–448) 271

§ 3. The Empire and Court of Attila   .   .   . 276

PAGE

§ 4. Attila's Invasions of Gaul and Italy (A.D. 451, 452), and
the Fall of the Hun Empire (A.D. 454) . . 288

§ 5. Deaths of Aetius (A D. 454) and Valentinian III. (A.D. 455) 298

§ 6. Christian and Pagan Speculations on the Calamities of
the Empire 301

§ 7. Modern Views on the Collapse of the Empire in the West 308

CHAPTER X

LEO I. AND RICIMER'S RULE IN ITALY 314

§ 1. Leo I. (A.D. 457–474) 314

§ 2. Maximus, Avitus, and Majorian (A.D. 455–461) . . 323

§ 3. The War with the Vandals (A.D. 461–468) . . 332

§ 4. Anthemius and Ricimer (A.D. 467–472) . . 337

§ 5. Extension of German Rule in Gaul and Spain . . 341

CHAPTER XI

CHURCH AND STATE 348

§ 1. The Controversies on the Incarnation . . . 349

§ 2. The Controversy on Predestination, and the Growth of
the Papal Power 360

§ 3. Persecution of Paganism 365

§ 4. Persecution of Heresy 378

§ 5. Monasticism 382

CHAPTER XII

THE REIGN OF ZENO, AND THE GERMAN VICEROYALTY IN ITALY 389

§ 1. The Usurpation of Basiliscus (A.D. 475–476) . . 389

§ 2. The Revolts of Marcian and Illus (A.D. 479–488) . 394

§ 3. The Henotikon (A.D. 481) 402

§ 4. The Rise of Odovacar and his Rule in Italy (A.D. 473–489) 404

§ 5. The Ostrogoths in Illyricum and Thrace (A.D. 477–488) 411

§ 6. Theoderic's Conquest of Italy (A.D. 489–493) . . 422

CHAPTER XIII

PAGE

THE REIGN OF ANASTASIUS I. AND THE VICEROYALTY OF THEODERIC   429

§ 1. The Elevation of Anastasius (A.D. 491) and the Isaurian
War   429

§ 2. Church Policy   436

§ 3. Financial Policy   441

§ 4. The Rebellion of Vitalian, and the Death of Anastasius
(A.D. 513–518)   447

§ 5. Italy under Theoderic   453

APPENDIX ON THE PRAETORIAN PREFECTS OF THE EAST   .   470

MAPS AND PLANS

PLAN OF CONSTANTINOPLE   .   .   .   .   *Face page* 67

THE BALKAN PENINSULA   265

GENEALOGICAL TABLE OF THE HOUSE OF THEODOSIUS

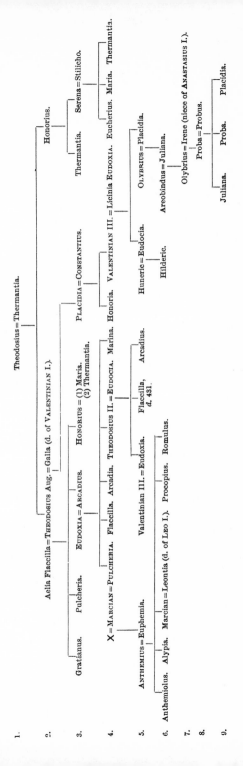

GENEALOGICAL TABLE OF THE HOUSE OF LEO

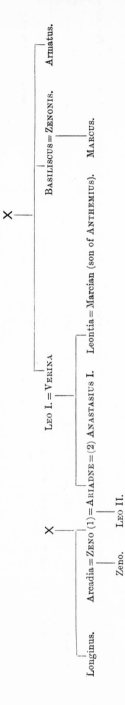

FAMILY OF ANASTASIUS I.

GENEALOGICAL TABLE OF THE FAMILY OF THEODERIC THE OSTROGOTH

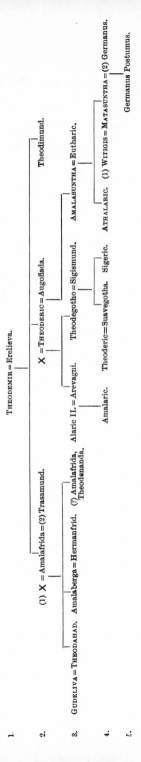

ROMAN EMPERORS [1]

(A.D. 395–565)

IN THE EAST.

		A.D.	A.D.
Arcadius	. . .	395 (Jan. 17) to	408 (May 1).
Theodosius II.	. . .	408 (Jan. 10) „	450 (July 28).
Marcian .	. . .	450 (Aug. 25) „	457 (Jan. 26).
Leo I. .	. . .	457 (Feb. 7) „	474 (Feb. 3).
Leo II. .	. . .	473 (Oct.) „	474 (Nov. 17).
Zeno .	. . .	474 (Feb. 9) „	491 (April 9).
Basiliscus	. . .	475 (Jan.) „	476 (August).
Anastasius I.	. . .	491 (Apr. 11) „	518 (July 8).
Justin I.	. . .	518 (July 10) „	527 (Aug. 1).
Justinian I.	. . .	527 (Apr. 1) „	565 (Nov. 14).

IN THE WEST.

		A.D.	A.D.
Honorius	. . .	393 (Jan. 23) to	423 (Aug. 27).
Constantine III.	. . .	407 „	411 (Sept. 18).
Constantius III.	. . .	421 (Feb. 8) „	421 (Sept. 2).
John	. . .	423 „	425 (May–June).
Valentinian III.	. . .	425 (Oct. 23) „	455 (Mar. 16).
Maximus	. . .	455 (Mar. 17) „	455 (May 31).
Avitus .	. . .	455 (July 10) „	456 (Oct. 17).
Majorian	. . .	457 (Apr. 1) „	461 (Aug. 2).
Severus .	. . .	461 (Nov. 19) „	465 (Aug. 15).
Anthemius	. . .	467 (Apr. 12) „	472 (July 11).
Olybrius .	. . .	472 (April) „	472 (Nov. 2).
Glycerius	. . .	473 (Mar. 5) „	473 (June ?).
Julius Nepos	. . .	473 (June) „	480.
Romulus	. . .	475 (Oct. 31) „	476.

[1] The names of usurpers, and of Emperors who though recognised in Italy were not recognised in the East, are in italics.

BISHOPS OF ROME [1]

	A.D.	A.D.
Siricius	385	to 399 (Nov. 26).
Anastasius I.	399 (Nov. 27)	„ 401 (Dec. 19).
Innocent I.	401 (Dec. 22)	„ 417 (Mar. 12).
Zosimus	417 (Mar. 18)	„ 418 (Dec. 26).
Boniface I.	418 (Dec. 29)	„ 422 (Sept. 4).
Celestine I.	422 (Sept. 10)	„ 432 (July 27).
Sixtus III.	432 (July 31)	,, 440 (Aug. 19 ?).
Leo I. .	440 (Sept. 29)	,, 461 (Nov. 10).
Hilary	461 (Nov. 19)	„ 468 (Feb. 29).
Simplicius	468 (Mar. 3)	,, 483 (Mar. 10).
Felix III.	483 (Mar. 13)	„ 492 (Mar. 1).
Gelasius I.	492 (Mar. 1)	„ 496 (Nov. 21).
Anastasius II.	496 (Nov. 24)	„ 498 (Nov. 19).
Symmachus	498 (Nov. 22)	„ 514 (July 19).
Hormisdas	514 (July 20)	„ 523 (Aug. 6).
John I.	523 (Aug. 13)	,, 526 (May 18).
Felix IV.	526 (July 12)	„ 530 (Sept. 22).
Boniface II.	530 (Sept. 22)	„ 532 (Oct. 17).
John II.	533 (Jan. 2)	„ 535 (May 8).
Agapetus I.	535 (May 13)	„ 536 (April 22).
Silverius	536 (June)	„ 537 (Mar. 11).
Vigilius	537 (Mar. 29)	,, 555 (June 7).
Pelagius I.	555 (April 16)	„ 561 (Mar. 4).
John III.	560 (July 17)	„ 574.

[1] See Preface and Notes to Duchesne's *Liber Pontificalis.*

PATRIARCHS OF CONSTANTINOPLE

	A.D.	A.D.
Nectarius . . .	381	to 397 (Sept. 27).
John I. (Chrysostom) . .	398 (Feb. 26)	„ 404 (June 20).
Arsacius . . .	404 (June 25)	„ 405 (Nov. 11).
Atticus . . .	406 (Feb.)	„ 425 (Oct. 10).
Sisinnius . . .	426 (Feb. 28)	„ 427 (Dec. 24).
Nestorius . . .	428 (April 10)	„ 431.
Maximian . . .	431 (Oct. 25)	„ 434 (April 12).
Proclus . . .	434 (April)	„ 447.
Flavian . . .	447	„ 449 (August).
Anatolius . . .	449 (Nov.–Dec.)	„ 458 (July).
Gennadius . . .	458 (July)	„ 471 (August).
Acacius . . .	471	„ 489.
Fravitta . . .	489.	
Euphemius . . .	489 (Oct.–Nov.)	„ 495 (Nov. ?).
Macedonius II. . .	496 (November)	„ 511 (October).
Timothy . . .	511 (October)	„ 518 (April 5).
John II. . . .	518 (April 17)	„ 520 (Feb.).
Epiphanius . . .	520 (Feb. 25)	„ 535 (June).
Anthimus . . .	535 (June)	„ 536 (Mar. 12).
Menas . . .	536 (Mar. 13)	„ 552 (August).
Eutychius . . .	552 (August)	„ 565 (Jan. 22).
John III. . . .	565 (Feb.–March).	

PATRIARCHS OF ALEXANDRIA [1]

	A.D.	A.D.
Theophilus . .	385	to 412 (Oct. 15).
Cyril . . .	412 (Oct. 18)	„ 444 (June).
Dioscorus . . .	444 (June)	„ 451 (October).
Proterius . . .	452	„ 457 (Mar. 28 or 31).
Timothy II. (Aelurus) .	457 (March)	„ 460 (beginning).
Timothy III. (Salophacialus)	460 (August)	„ 475.
Timothy II. . .	475	„ 477 (July 31).
Timothy III. . .	477	„ 482 (June).
{ John I. (Talaias) . .	482 (June)	„ 482 (August ?).
{ Peter III. (Mongus) .	482	„ 489 (Oct. 29 ?).
Athanasius II. . .	490 (Feb. 7)	„ 496 (Dec. 17).
John II. . .	496 (Sept.)	„ 505 (April 29).
John III. . . .	506 (April 30)	„ 517 (May 22).
Dioscorus II. . .	516 (May)	„ 517 (Oct. 14).
Timothy IV. . .	517 (October)	„ 535 (Feb. 7).
{ Gaian . . .	535 (February)	„ 535 (May).
{ Theodosius . .	535 (February)	„ 536 (end).
Paul . . .	537	„ 542.
Zoilus . . .	542	„ 551.
Apollinarius . .	551 (before Sept.).	

[1] Cp. Krüger, *Monophysiten*, in Hauck's *Realencykl. f. prot. Theologie*, and Brooks in *B.Z.* xii. 494 *sqq.*

PATRIARCHS OF ANTIOCH

(Many of the dates are very uncertain.)

	A.D.	A.D.
Flavian I. . . .	381	to 404 (middle).
Porphyry . . .	404 (middle)	„ 413
Alexander . . .	413	„ 421
Theodotus . . .	421	„ 429
John I. . . .	429	„ 442
Domnus II. . .	442	„ 449 (Aug. 8).
Maximus II. . .	449	„ 455
Basil . . .	456 (Dec. ?)	„ 458
Acacius . . .	458 (before Sept.)	„ 459
Martyrius . . .	460	„ 470
Julian . . .	471	„ 475
Peter (Fullo) . .	476	„ 477
John II. . . .	478	
Stephen II.[1] . .	478	„ 481
Calandio . . .	481 (end)	„ 485 (autumn).
Peter (Fullo) . .	485 (autumn)	„ 489
Palladius . . .	490	„ 498
Flavian II. . . .	498	„ 512
Severus . . .	512 (Nov. 6)	„ 518 (Sept. 29).
Paul II. . . .	519 (May)	„ 521 (May 1).
Euphrasius . . .	521	„ 526 (May).
Ephraim . . .	526	„ 545
Domnus III. . .	546	„ 559
Anastasius I. . .	561	

[1] In the lists of Patriarchs Stephen is divided into two, Stephen II. and Stephen III., but Gelzer has shown that this is probably a mistake (*Zeitschrift f. wiss. Theologie*, xxvi. p. 509, 1883).

BISHOPS AND PATRIARCHS OF JERUSALEM [1]

				A.D.	A.D.
Johannes	.	.	.	388	to 415/6.
Praylius	.	.	.	415/6	„ 421 (? 425).
Juvenal	.	.	.	421	„ 458.
Anastasius		.	.	458 (July)	„ 478 (January).
Martyrius	.	.	.	478	„ 486 (Apr. 13).
Sallustius	.	.	.	486	„ 494 (July 23).
Elias	.	.	.	494	„ 516 (August).
Johannes	.	.	.	516 (Sept. 1)	„ 524 (Apr 20).
Peter	.	.	.	524	„ 552 (October).
Macarius	.	.	.	552 (Oct.–Dec.)	
Eustochius	.	.	.	552 (December)	„ 563/4
Macarius (again)	.	.	.	563/4	„ 575.

[1] Cp. Diekamp, *Origenistische Streitigkeiten*, 15 *sqq.*

CHAPTER I

THE continuity of history, which means the control of the present and future by the past, has become a commonplace, and chronological limits, which used to be considered important, are now recognised to have little significance except as convenient landmarks in a historical survey. Yet there are what we may call culminating epochs, in which the accumulating tendencies of the past, reaching a certain point, suddenly effect a visible transformation which seems to turn the world in a new direction. Such a culminating epoch occurred in the history of the Roman Empire at the beginning of the fourth century. The reign of Constantine the Great inaugurated a new age in a much fuller sense than the reign of Augustus, the founder of the Empire. The anarchy of the third century, when it almost seemed that the days of the Roman Empire were numbered, had displayed the defects of the irregular and heterogeneous system of government which Augustus had established to administer his immense dominion. His successors had introduced modifications and improvements here and there, but events made it clearer and clearer that a new system, more centralised and more uniform, was required, if the Empire was to be held together. To Diocletian, who rescued the Roman world at the brink of the abyss, belongs the credit of having framed a new system of administrative machinery. Constantine developed and completed the work of Diocletian by measures which were more radical and more far-reaching. The foundation of Constantinople as a second Rome inaugurated a permanent division between the Eastern and Western, the Greek and the Latin, halves of the Empire—a division to which events had already pointed—and

1

affected decisively the whole subsequent history of Europe. Still more evidently and notoriously did Constantine mould the future by accepting Christianity as the State religion.

In the present work the history of the Roman Empire is taken up at a point about sixty years after Constantine's death, when the fundamental changes which he introduced have been firmly established and their consequences have emerged into full evidence. The new system of government has been elaborated in detail, and the Christian Church has become so strong that no enemies could prevail against it. Constantinople, created in the likeness of Rome, has become her peer and will soon be fully equipped for the great rôle which she is to play in Europe and Hither Asia for more than a thousand years. She definitely assumes now her historical position. For after the death of Theodosius the Great, who had ruled alone for a short time over a dominion extending from Scotland to Mesopotamia, the division of the Empire into two geographical portions, an eastern and a western, under two Emperors, a division which had been common during the past century, was finally established. This dual system lasted for eighty-five years, and but for the dismemberment of the western provinces by the Germans might have lasted indefinitely. In the constitutional unity of the Empire this arrangement caused no breach.

Again, the death of Theodosius marks the point at which the German danger, long imminent over the Empire, begins to move rapidly towards its culmination. We are on the eve of the great dismemberment of Roman dominion which, within seventy years, converted the western provinces into Teutonic kingdoms. The fourth century had witnessed the settlement of German peoples, as *foederati*, bound to military service, on Roman lands in the Balkan peninsula and in Gaul. Through the policy of Constantine Germans had become a predominant element in the Roman army, and German officers had risen to the highest military posts and had exercised commanding political influence. Outside, German peoples were pressing on the frontiers, waiting for opportunities to grasp at a share of the coveted wealth of the Roman world. The Empire was exposed to the double danger of losing provinces to these unwelcome claimants who desired to be taken within its border, and of the growing ascendancy

of the German element in the army.[1] The East was menaced
as well as the West, and the great outstanding fact in the
history of the fifth century is that the East survived and
the West succumbed. The success of the Eastern government
in steering through these perils was partly due to the fact
that during this critical time it was on good terms, only
seldom and briefly interrupted, with Persia, its formidable
neighbour.

The diminished Roman Empire, now centering entirely in
Constantinople, lasted for a thousand years, surrounded by
enemies and frequently engaged in a struggle for life or death,
but for the greater part of that long period the most powerful
State in Europe. Its history is marked by distinct ages of
expansion, decline, and resuscitation, which are easily remembered
and help to simplify the long series of the annals of Byzantium.[2]
Having maintained itself in the fifth century and won its way
through the German peril, it found itself strong enough in the
sixth to take the offensive and to recover Africa and Italy.
Overstrain led to a decline, of which Persia took advantage, and
when this danger had been overcome, the Saracens appeared as
a new and more formidable force and deprived the Empire of
important provinces in Asia, while at the same time European
territory was lost to the Bulgarians and the Slavs (seventh
century). Then a period of resuscitation in the eighth and
ninth centuries led to a new age of brilliance and expansion
(ninth to eleventh centuries). When the Saracens had ceased
to be formidable, the Seljuk Turks appeared, and the Empire
found it difficult to hold its own against this foe as well as against
the western powers of Europe, and the barbarians of the north.
This period ends with the disaster of 1204, when Constantinople
fell into the hands of the Crusaders, who treated the city with
more barbarity than the barbarian Alaric had treated Rome eight
hundred years before. After this the cycle begins anew ; first,
the period of revival at Nicaea, which became the temporary
capital ; then the recovery of Constantinople (1261), followed
by a period in which the Empire could assert its power ; finally,
from the middle of the fourteenth century, the decline, and the

---

[1] The Roman fear of barbarisation
is marked by a law of A.D. 370 or
373, which forbade marriages between
provincials and barbarians on pain of

death. *C. Th*. iii. 14. 1.

[2] Cp. Bury, Appendix 9 to Gibbon,
vol. v.

last death-struggle with the Ottomans, ending in the capture of the city in 1453.

The State which maintained itself in unbroken continuity throughout the vicissitudes of more than a thousand years is proverbial for its conservative spirit. It was conservative in its constitution and institutions, in the principles and the fashions of its civilisation, in its religion, in its political and social machinery. It may be conjectured that this conservatism is partly to be attributed to the influence of the legal profession.[1] Lawyers are always conservative and suspicious of change, and it would be difficult to exaggerate their importance and the power of their opinion in the later Empire. It was natural and just that their influence should be great, for it has well been observed that it was to the existence of a " judicial establishment, guided by a published code, and controlled by a body of lawyers educated in public schools, that the subjects of the Empire were chiefly indebted for the superiority in civilisation which they retained over the rest of the world." [2] But the conservatism of Byzantium is often represented as more rigid than it actually was. The State could not have survived if it had not been constantly adapting its institutions to new circumstances. We have seen how its external history may be divided into periods. But its administrative organisation, its literature, its art display equally well-defined stages.

One more introductory remark. The civilisation of the later Empire, which we know under the name of Byzantine, had its roots deep in the past. It was simply the last phase of Hellenic culture. Alexandria, the chief city of the Hellenic world since the third century B.C., yielded the first place to Byzantium in the course of the fifth century. There was no breach in continuity ; there was only a change of centre. And while the gradual ascendancy of Christianity distinguished and stamped the last phase, we must remember that Christian theology had been elaborated by the Greek mind into a system of metaphysics which Paul, the founder of the theology, would not have recognised, and which no longer seemed an alien product.

---

[1] This point may be illustrated by the interesting section on *L'Esprit légiste* in de Tocqueville's *De la démo-* *cratie en Amérique* (part ii. chap. viii.).

[2] Finlay, *Hist. of Greece*, i. 411.

§ 1. *The Autocracy*

The Roman Empire was founded by Augustus, but for three centuries after its foundation the State was constitutionally a republic. The government was shared between the Emperor and the Senate ; the Emperor, whose constitutional position was expressed by the title Princeps, was limited by the rights of the Senate. Hence it has been found convenient to distinguish this period as the Principate or the Dyarchy. From the very beginning the Princeps was the predominant partner, and the constitutional history of the Principate turns on his gradual and steady usurpation of nearly all the functions of government which Augustus had attributed to the Senate. The republican disguise fell away completely before the end of the third century. Aurelian adopted external fashions which marked a king, not a citizen ; and Diocletian and Constantine definitely transformed the State from a republic to an autocracy. This change, accompanied by corresponding radical reforms, was, from a purely constitutional point of view, as great a break with the past as the change wrought by Augustus, and the transition was as smooth. Augustus preserved continuity with the past by maintaining republican forms ; while Constantine and his predecessors simply established on a new footing the supreme Imperial power which already existed in fact, discarding the republican mask which had worn too thin.

The autocracy brought no change in the principle of succession to the throne. Down to its fall in the fifteenth century the Empire remained elective, and the election rested with the Senate and the army. Either the Senate or the army could proclaim an Emperor, and the act of proclamation constituted a legitimate title. As a rule, the choice of one body was acquiesced in by the other ; if not, the question must be decided by a struggle. Any portion of the army was considered, for this purpose, as representing the whole army, and thus in elections at Constantinople it was the troops stationed there with whom the decision lay. But whether Senate or army took the initiative, the consent of the other body was required ; and the inauguration [1] of the new Emperor was not complete till he had

---

[1] The term ἀναγόρευσις, proclamation, was used for all the proceedings of the inauguration. In the case of Carus the Senate played no part. Mommsen, *Staatsrecht*, ii. 843.

been acclaimed by the people.   Senate, army, and people, each had its place in the inaugural ceremonies.

But while the principle of election was retained, it was in actual practice most often only a form.   From the very beginning the principle of heredity was introduced indirectly.   The reigning Emperor could designate his successor by appointing a co-regent. In this way Augustus designated his stepson Tiberius, Vespasian his son Titus.   The Emperors naturally sought to secure the throne for their sons, and if they had no son, generally looked within their own family.   From the end of the fourth century it became usual for an Emperor to confer the Imperial title on his eldest son, whether an adult or an infant.   The usual forms of inauguration were always observed ; but the right of the Emperor to appoint co-regents was never disputed.   The consequence was that the succession of the Roman Emperors presents a series of dynasties, and that it was only at intervals, often considerable, that the Senate and army were called upon to exercise their right of election.

The co - regent was a sleeping partner.   He enjoyed the Imperial honours, his name appeared in official documents ; but he did not share in the actual government, except so far as he might be specially authorised by his older colleague.   This, at least, was the rule.   Under the Principate the senior Imperator distinguished his own position from that of his colleague by reserving to himself the title of Pontifex Maximus.   Marcus Aurelius tried a new experiment and shared the full sovranty with Lucius Verus.   This division of the sovranty was an essential part of the system of Diocletian, corresponding to the geographical partition of the Empire which he introduced.   From his time down to A.D. 480, the Empire is governed by two (or even more) sovran colleagues, who have all equal rights and competence, and differ only in seniority.   Sometimes the junior Emperor is appointed by the senior, sometimes he is elected independently and is recognised by the senior.   Along with these there may be co-regents, who exercise no sovran power, but are marked out as eventual successors.   Thus the child Arcadius was for nine years co-regent with the Emperors Valentinian II. and Theodosius the Great.   No formal title, however, raised the sovran above the co-regent, though the latter, for the sake of distinction, was often called " the second his elder son Arcadius. But it is to be observed that this measure was not taken till after the death of the Western Emperor Valentinian II., and that its object was to provide two sovrans, one for the East and one for the West. If the division of the Empire had not been contemplated, Honorius would not have been created Augustus in A.D. 393. To avoid a struggle between brothers, the obvious policy was to confer the supreme rank on only one. Before the reign of Basil I. in the ninth century, there were few opportunities to depart from this rule of expediency, and it was only violated twice, in both cases with unfortunate consequences.[1]

But the Caesarship was not the only method employed to signalise an eventual successor. In the third century it became usual to describe the Caesar, the Emperor's adopted son, as *nobilissimus*. In the fourth, this became an independent title, denoting a dignity lower than Caesar, but confined to the Imperial family. On two occasions we find nobilissimus used as a sort of preliminary designation.[2] But it fell out of use in the fifth century, and apparently was not revived till the eighth, when it was conferred on the youngest members of the large family of Constantine V.[3] In the sixth century Justinian introduced a new title, Curopalates, which, inferior to Caesar and nobilissimus, might serve either to designate or simply to honour a member of the Imperial family. We find it used in both ways.[4] It was a less decided designation than the Caesarship, and a cautious or suspicious sovran might prefer it.

The principle of heredity, which was thus conciliated with the principle of election, gradually gave rise to the view that not only was the Emperor's son his *legitimate* successor, but that if he had no male issue, the question of succession would be most naturally and satisfactorily settled by the marriage of a near female relative—daughter, sister, or widow,—and the election of her husband, who would thus continue the dynasty.[5] There

---

[1] By Heraclius and by Constans II.

[2] Jovian conferred it on his infant son Valerian, and Honorius on his child-nephew Valentinian III.

[3] Cp. Bury, *Imp. Adm. System*, 35.

[4] As designation, of Justin II. by his uncle Justinian, of Domentziolus by his uncle Phocas. As an honour it was conferred by Maurice and Heraclius on their brothers; by Leo III. and Nicephorus I. on their sons-in-law. It was not confined to the Imperial family after the tenth century. Cp. Bury, *ib.* 34.

[5] In the fifth century we have two cases: Pulcheria (450) and Ariadne (491).

Emperor," or, if he was a child, " the little Emperor." [1]   W
towards the end of the fifth century the territorial partition
the Empire came to an end, the system of joint sovranty ceas
and henceforward, whenever there is more than one August
only one exercises the sovran power.[2]

But the Emperor could also designate a successor, witho
elevating him to the position of co-regent, by conferring on h
the title of Caesar. This practice, which since Hadrian w
usual under the Principate,[3] and was adopted by Constanti
is not frequent in the later Empire.[4] If the Emperor has so
he almost invariably creates his eldest son Augustus. If n
he may signify his will as to the succession by bestowing t
dignity of Caesar. The Caesarship may be considered a pr
visional arrangement. The Emperor before his death migl
raise the Caesar to the co-regency.[5] If he died without havir
done this, the Caesar had to be elected in the usual way by tl
Senate and army. This method of provisional and revocabl
designation was often convenient. An Emperor who had n
male issue might wish to secure the throne to a son-in-law, fo
instance, in case of his own premature death. If he conferre
the Caesarship and if a male child were afterwards born to
him,[6] that child would be created Augustus, and the Caesar'
claim would fall into abeyance.

When the Emperor had more than one son, it was usual to
confer the title of Caesar on the younger.[7] Constitutionally
this may be considered a provision for the contingency of the
death of the co-regent. Practically it meant a title of dignity
reserved for members of the Imperial family. Sometimes the
co-regency was conferred on more than one son. Theodosius
the Great raised Honorius to the rank of Augustus as well as

---

[1] Ὁ δεύτερος βασιλεύς, ὁ μικρὸς β. In later times the actual sovran was sometimes distinguished as the αὐτοκράτωρ, but the plural, οἱ αὐτοκράτορες, was used to designate all the Augusti.

[2] There are indeed one or two exceptional cases.

[3] Mommsen, *Staatsrecht*, ii. 1139 *sqq.*

[4] Bury, *Imp. Adm. System*, 36.

[5] So Justin II. created the Caesar Tiberius Augustus, shortly before his death in 578 ; similarly Tiberius created his son-in-law Maurice Caesar, and on his death-bed caused him to

be proclaimed Augustus.

[6] This occurred in the ninth century in the case of Theophilus. His children were daughters ; he bestowed the rank of Caesar on his son-in-law Musele, and a son, who succeeded him as Michael III., was born later. The Caesarship conferred on Bardas by his nephew Michael III. is also a case in point.

[7] The only cases which occur before 800 are the three younger sons of Heraclius, and the second and third sons of Constantine V.

was a general feeling of attachment to a dynasty, and the history of the Later Empire presents a series of dynasties, with few and brief intervals of unsettlement. During the four centuries between 395 and 802, we have five dynasties, which succeed one another, except in two cases,[1] without a break. Though there was no law excluding women from the succession, yet perhaps we may say that up to the seventh or eighth century it would have been considered not merely politically impossible, but actually illegal, for a woman to exercise the sovran power in her own name. The highest authority on the constitution of the early Empire affirms that her sex did not exclude a woman from the Principate.[2] But the title Augusta did not include the proconsular Imperium and the tribunician potestas, which constituted the power of the Princeps, and it is not clear that these could have been conferred legally on a woman or that she could have borne the title Imperator. It is said, and may possibly be true, that Caligula, when he was ill, designated his favourite sister Drusilla as his successor[3]; but this does not prove that she could legally have acted as Princeps. Several Empresses virtually shared the exercise of the Imperial authority, bore themselves as co-regents, and enjoyed more power than male co-regents; but their power was *de facto*, not *de jure*. Some were virtually sovrans, but they were acting as regents for minors.[4] Not till the end of the eighth century do we find a woman, the Empress Irene, exercising sovranty alone and in her own name.[5] This was a constitutional innovation. The experiment was only once repeated,[6] and only in exceptional circumstances would it have been tolerated. There was a general feeling against a female reign, both as inexpedient and as a violation of tradition.[7] Between the fourth and the eighth centuries, however, two circumstances may have combined

---

[1] Phocas, between the dynasty of Justin and that of Heraclius; and the period of anarchy between the Heraclian and Isaurian dynasties.

[2] Mommsen, *Staatsrecht*, ii. 788. The evidence he adduces is not convincing.

[3] Suetonius, *C. Caligula*, 24.

[4] Pulcheria; Placidia; Martina.

[5] If the eligibility of a woman had been recognised, the principle would probably have been applied in the case of the Augusta Pulcheria (who had considerable experience of government, and enjoyed the respect and confidence of the Empire) in A.D. 450.

[6] In the eleventh century, when Zoe and Theodora reigned together. There would have been another instance if Stauracius, in 811, had succeeded in procuring the succession for his wife Theophano (Bury, *Eastern Roman Empire*, p. 18).

[7] This feeling was strongly expressed towards Martina in A.D. 641.

to make it appear no longer illegal. The Greek official term for Imperator was Autokrator, and in the course of time, when Latin was superseded by Greek, and Imperator fell out of use and memory, Autokrator ceased to have the military associations which were attached to its Latin equivalent, and the constitutional incompatibility of the office with the female sex is no longer apparent. In the second place, female regencies prepared the way for Irene's audacious step. When a new Emperor was a minor, the regency might be entrusted to his mother or an elder sister, whether acting alone or in conjunction with other regents. Irene was regent for her son before she grasped the sole power for herself.

The title of Augusta was always conferred [1] on the wife of the Emperor and the wife of the co-regent, and from the seventh century it was frequently conferred on some or all of the Emperor's daughters. The reigning Augusta might have great political power. In the sixth century, Justinian and Theodora, and Justin II. and Sophia, exercised what was virtually a joint rule, but in neither case did the constitutional position of the Empress differ from that of any other consort.

The diadem was definitely introduced by Constantine,[2] and it may be considered the supreme symbol of the autocratic sovranty which replaced the magistracy of the earlier Empire. Hitherto the distinguishing mark of the Emperor's costume had been the purple cloak of the Imperator ; and " to assume the purple " continued to be the common expression for elevation to the throne. The crown was an importation from Persia, and it invested the Roman ruler with the same external dignity as the Persian king. In Persia it was placed on the king's head by the High Priest of the Magian religion.[3] In theory the Imperial crown should be imposed by a representative of those who conferred the sovran authority that it symbolised. And in the fourth century we find the Prefect Sallustius Secundus crowning Valentinian I., in whose election he had taken the most prominent part. But the Emperor seems to have felt some hesitation in

[1] In the East, from the time of Arcadius. The wives of Honorius were not Augustae.

[2] See W. Sickel, *B.Z.* vii. 513 *sqq.* According to Victor, *Epit.* 35. 5, it was already worn by Aurelian ; according to John Lydus, *De mag.* i. 4, by Diocletian. The diadem was a white browband, set with pearls.

[3] The rest of this paragraph is borrowed from my *Constitution of the L.R.E.*

receiving the diadem from the hands of a subject, and the selection of one magnate for the office was likely to cause jealousy. Yet a formality was necessary. In the fifth century the difficulty was overcome in an ingenious and tactful way. The duty of coronation was assigned to the Patriarch of Constantinople. In discharging this office the Patriarch was not envied by the secular magnates because he could not be their rival, and his ecclesiastical position relieved the Emperor from all embarrassment in receiving the diadem from a subject. There is, as we shall see, some evidence that this plan was adopted in A.D. 450 at the coronation of Marcian, but it seems certain that his successor Leo was crowned by the Patriarch in A.D. 457. Henceforward this was the regular practice. But it was only the practice. It was the regular and desirable mode of coronation, but was never legally indispensable for the autocrat's inauguration. The last of the East Roman Emperors, Constantine Palaeologus, was not crowned by the Patriarch ; he was crowned by a layman.[1] This fact that coronation by the Patriarch was not constitutionally necessary is important. It shows that the Patriarch in performing the ceremony was not representing the Church. It is possible that the idea of committing the office to him was suggested by the Persian coronations by the High Priest. But the significance was not the same. The chief of the Magians acted as representative of the Persian religion, the Patriarch acted as representative of the State. If he had specially represented the Church, his co-operation could never have been dispensed with. The consent of the Church was not formally necessary to the inauguration of a sovran.

This point is further illustrated by the fact that when the Emperor appointed a colleague, the junior Augustus was crowned not by the Patriarch but by the Emperor who created him.[2]

When Augustus founded the Empire, he derived his Imperial authority from the sovranty of the people ; and the essence of this principle was retained throughout the duration not only of the Principate but also of the Monarchy ; for the Imperial office remained elective, and the electors had the right of deposing the Emperor. But though these rights were never abrogated,

---

[1] Nicephorus Bryennius (eleventh century) crowned himself. Anna Commena, *Alexiad*, i. 4.

[2] See Const. Porph. *De cer.* i. 38,

p. 194. Sometimes he might commit the office to the Patriarch, who then acted simply as his delegate.

there was a tendency, as time went on, to regard the majesty
and power of the monarch as resting on something higher than
the will of the people. The suggestion of divinity has constantly
been the device of autocrats to strengthen and enhance their
power ; and modern theories of Divine Right are merely a substitute for the old pagan practice of deifying kings. Augustus
attempted to throw a sort of halo round his authority by designating himself officially *Divi Filius*. But the glow of this
consecration faded, and disappeared entirely with the fall of
the Julio-Claudian dynasty. With Aurelian, who foreshadows
the new Monarchy, the suggestion of divinity again appears.[1]
Diocletian and his colleague Maximian are designated as gods
and parents of gods.[2] The official deification of the Emperor,
which seemed in sight at the beginning of the fourth century, was
precluded by Christianity ; but the consecration of the ruler's
person was maintained in the epithets *sacred* and *divine*; and
the Emperors came to regard themselves rather as vicegerents of
God than as rulers set up by their people. Justinian, in one of
his laws, speaks of the Emperor as sent down by God to be a
living law.[3] In the ninth century Basil I. tells his son, " You
received the Empire from God." [4]

Under the Monarchy, the Emperor appropriated the full
right of direct legislation, which had not belonged to him under
the Principate.[5] The Princeps possessed the right of initiating
laws to be passed by the comitia of the people, but from the time
of Tiberius legislation was seldom effected in this way, and after
the first century it was exclusively in the hands of the Senate.
The Emperor, communicating his instructions in the form of an
oratio to the Senate, could have his wishes embodied in senatorial
decrees (*senatus consulta*). But indirectly he possessed virtual
powers of legislation by means of edicts and constitutions, which,
though technically they were not laws, were for practical purposes
equivalent.[6] The edict, unlike a law, did not necessarily contain

---

[1] On his coins, Eckhel, *Doct. num.*
7, 482.

[2] *Diis genitis et deorum creatoribus,*
C.I.L. iii. 710.

[3] *Nov.* 81. 4. At the Council of
Chalcedon, Marcian was acclaimed
as " priest and Emperor," τῷ ἱερεῖ καὶ
βασιλεῖ (Mansi, vii. p. 177).

[4] *Paraenesis ad Leonem*, in *P.G.*

107, p. xxv., cp. p. xxxii.

[5] In one particular class of cases,
namely the bestowal of civil rights
on individuals and municipal rights
on corporations, the Princeps had the
power *leges dare* without the co-operation of the comitia. Mommsen,
Staatsrecht, ii. 888 *sqq.*

[6] See Mommsen, *ib.* 905 *sqq.*

a command ; it was properly a public communication made by a magistrate to the people. But the legislative activity of the early Emperors was chiefly exercised in the form of constitutions, a term which in the stricter sense applied to decisions which were only brought to the notice of the persons concerned.[1] This term included the Imperial correspondence and especially the mandates, or instructions addressed to officials. These " acts " had full validity, and the magistrates every year swore to observe them.[2] But when an act required a dispensation from an existing law, the Imperial constitution was valid only during the lifetime of its author.

The power of dispensing from a law properly belonged to the Senate, and the earlier Emperors sought from the Senate a dispensation when necessary. Domitian began to encroach on this privilege. But the principle remained that the Princeps, who was constitutionally a magistrate, was bound by the laws ; and when lawyers of the third century speak of the Princeps as *legibus solutus*, they refer to laws from which Augustus had formally obtained dispensation by the Senate.[3]

Under the Monarchy the Emperors assumed full powers of legislation, and their laws took the form occasionally of an *oratio* to the Senate, but almost always of an edict. The term edict covered all the decisions which were formerly called constitutions, mandates, or rescripts, provided they had a general application.[4] And the Emperor not only legislated ; he was the sole legislator, and reserved to himself the sole right of interpreting the laws.[5] He possessed the dispensing power. But he always considered himself bound by the laws. An edict of A.D. 429 expresses the spirit of reverence for law, as something superior to the throne itself, which always animated the Roman monarchs. " To acknowledge himself bound by the laws (*alligatum legibus*) is, for the sovran, an utterance befitting the majesty of a ruler. For the truth is that our authority depends on the authority of law. To submit our sovranty to the laws is verily a greater

---

[1] *Constitutiones* is sometimes used in a wider sense to include *leges* and *senatus consulta*.

[2] Pomponius (*Dig.* i. 2. 2. 14) : *est principalis constitutio ut quod ipse princeps constituit pro lege servetur.*

[3] Mommsen, *ib.* 751, *n.* 3.

[4] *C.J.* i. 14. 3 (A.D. 426).

[5] *C.J.* i. 14. 12 (A.D. 529): *si enim in praesenti leges condere soli imperatori concessum est, et leges interpretari solum dignum imperio esse oportet.* Cp. *ib.* 1.

thing than Imperial power." [1]   Deep respect for the rules of
law, and their systematic observance characterised the Roman
autocracy down to the fall of the Empire in the fifteenth century,
and was one of the conditions of its long duration.   It was
never an arbitrary despotism, and the masses looked up to the
Emperor as the guardian of the laws which protected against
the oppression of nobles and officials. [2]

The laws, then, were a limitation on the power of the autocrat ;
and soon another means of limiting his power was discovered.
In the fifth century, the duty of crowning a new Emperor at
Constantinople was, as we saw, assigned to the Patriarch.   In
A.D. 491 the Patriarch refused to crown Anastasius unless he
signed a written oath that he would introduce no novelty into
the Church.   This precedent was at first followed perhaps only
in cases where a new Emperor was suspected of heretical tendencies, but by the tenth century [3] an oath of this kind seems to
have been a regular preliminary to coronation.   The fact that
such capitulations could be and were imposed at the time of
election shows that the autocracy was limited.

The essence of an autocracy is that no co-ordinate body
exists which is able constitutionally to act as a check upon
the monarch's will.   The authority of the Senate or the Imperial
Council might constitute a strong practical check upon an
Emperor's acts, but if he chose to disregard their views, he
could not be accused of acting unconstitutionally.   The ultimate
check on any autocracy is the force of public opinion.   There
is always a point beyond which the most arbitrary despot
cannot go in defying it.   In the case of a Roman Emperor,
public opinion could exert this control constitutionally, by an
extreme measure.   The Emperor could be deposed.   The right
of deposition corresponded to the right of election.   The deposition was accomplished not by any formal process, but by the
proclamation of a new Emperor.   If any one so proclaimed
obtained sufficient support from the army, Senate, and people,
the old Emperor was compelled to vacate the throne by *force*

---

[1] *Ib.* 4. So the Lawbook of the
ninth century lays down that general
laws are valid against the Emperor,
and forbids rescripts which contradict
them.   *Basilica* ii. 6. 9.

[2] Finlay has frequently insisted on
this. Compare his remarks, and his
comparison with the Saracen empire,
in *Hist. of Greece*, ii. 23-24.

[3] Constantine Porph. *De adm.
imp.* p. 84.

was regarded as the legitimate
ne was proclaimed ; the pro-
ı expression of the general will.
owerful following to render the
s suppressed, he was treated as
uggle and before the catastrophe,
a portion of the army had proclaimed
ptive constitutional status which the
m or annul.   The method of deposition
on ; and we are accustomed to regard
tion as something essentially unconstitutional, an appeal
from law to force ; but under the Imperial system it was not
unconstitutional ; the government was, as has been said,[1] " an
autocracy tempered by the legal right of revolution." [2]

The transformation of the Principate into the Autocracy
was accompanied by changes in the titular style of the Emperors,
in their dress, in the etiquette of the court, which showed how
entirely the old tradition of the republic had been forgotten.

The oriental conception of divine royalty is now formally
expressed in the diadem ; and it affects all that appertains to the
Emperor.   His person is divine ; all that belongs to him is
" sacred."   Those who come into his presence perform the act
of adoration [3] ; they kneel down and kiss the purple.   It had
long been the habit to address the Imperator as *dominus,*
" lord " ; in the fourth century the sovrans begin to use it of
themselves and *Dominus Noster* appears on their coins.[4]

Since the first century we can trace the use of *Basileus* to
designate the Princeps, and *Basileia* to describe the Imperial
power, in the eastern provinces of the Empire.[5]   Dion Chrysostom wrote a discourse on the Basileia ; Fronto calls Marcus
Aurelius " the great Basileus, ruler of land and sea."   Basileus
was the equivalent of Rex, a title odious to Roman ears ; but
by the fourth century the Greek name had long ceased to wound

[1] By Mommsen.
[2] I have borrowed the last few
sentences from my *Constitution of the
L.R.E.* 8-9.
[3] Cp. Victor, *Caes.* 39 (of Diocletian).   See Godefroy's Comm. on
C. Th. vol. ii. p. 83.
[4] Mommsen, *Staatsrecht,* ii. 760 *sqq.*
He observes that the terminological
transition from princeps to dominus

is a measure of the constitutional
development towards autocracy. D.N.
appears on brick-stamps towards end
of 2nd cent. : *C.I.L.* xv. pp. 204-5.—
Probus, the consul of 406, in his
consular ivory diptych preserved at
Aosta (*C.I.L.* v. 6836) could describe
himself as the *famulus* of Honorius.
[5] Bréhier, " L'Origine des titres im-
périaux à Byzance," *B.Z.* xv. 161 *sqq.*

any susceptibilities ; it became the term regularly employed by Greek writers and in Greek inscriptions, and the Emperors began to employ it themselves. Usage soon went further. *Basileus* was reserved for the Emperor and the Persian king,[1] and *rex* was employed to designate other barbarian royalties.

The Imperial Chancery was conservative, and it was not till the seventh century that the Emperor designated himself as Basileus in his constitutions and rescripts.[2] The official Greek equivalent of *Imperator* was *Autokrator*, which was similarly used as a praenomen.[3] The mint of Constantinople continued to inscribe the Imperial coins with Latin legends till the eighth century.[4] The earliest coins with Greek inscriptions have *Basileus* and *Despotes*.

The general use of Despotes is one of the most characteristic oriental features of the new Empire. It denoted the relation of a master to his slaves, and it was regularly used in addressing the Emperor from the time of Constantine to the fall of the Empire. Justinian expected this form of address. The subject spoke of himself as " your slave." But this orientalism was a superficial etiquette ; the autocrat seldom forgot that his subjects were freemen, that if he was a *dominus*, he was a *dominus liberorum*.

A few words may be said here about the unity of the Empire. From the reign of Diocletian to the last quarter of the fifth century, the Empire is repeatedly divided into two or more geographical sections—most frequently two, an Eastern and a Western—each governed by its own ruler. From A.D. 395 to A.D. 476, or rather 480, the division into two realms is practically continuous ; each realm goes its own way, and the relations between them are sometimes even hostile. It has, naturally

---

[1] Bréhier (p. 170) omits to note this important exception. The Abyssinian king seems to have been another. Cp. Bury, *op. cit.* p. 20.

[2] This change was introduced by Heraclius.

[3] Justinian's style was : Imperator Iustinianus (or Imp. Caesar Flavius Iust.) pius felix inclitus victor ac triumphator semper Augustus (A.D. 529, *De Iust. cod. conf.*, at beginning of *C.J.*). In A.D. 534, this is expanded by a number of honourable epithets glorifying victories (Alamanicus,

Gothicus, etc.) inserted immediately after Iustinianus. The Greek equivalent of the above is : αὐτοκράτωρ (Καῖσαρ Φλ.) Ἰουστινιανός, εὐσεβής, εὐτυχής, ἔνδοξος, νικητής, τροπαιοῦχος, ἀεισέβαστος Αὐγοῦστος (*C.I.G.* iii. 8636). Cp. Bréhier, p. 171.

[4] The style is, *e.g.* D(ominus) N(oster) Arcadius P(ius) F(elix) Aug(ustus). In the reign of Leo I., PP (or Perp) = Perpetuus was substituted for PF, and this was normal till the beginning of the eighth century.

enough, proved an irresistible temptation to many modern writers to speak of them as if they were different Empires. To men of the fourth and fifth centuries such a mode of speech would have been unintelligible, and it is better to avoid it. To them there was and could be only one Roman Empire ; and we should emphasise and not obscure this point of view. But it is not merely a question of constitutional theory. The unity was not only formally recognised ; it was maintained in practical ways. In the first place, the Imperial colleagues issued their laws under their joint names, and general laws promulgated by either and transmitted for publication to the chancery of his associate were valid throughout the whole Empire.[1] In the second place, on the death of either Emperor, the Imperial authority of the surviving colleague was constitutionally extended to the whole Empire until a successor was elected. Strictly speaking, it devolved upon him to nominate a new colleague. After the fall of the Theodosian House, some of the Emperors who were elected in Italy were not recognised at Constantinople, but the principle remained in force.

The unity of the Empire was also expressed in the arrangement for the nomination of the annual Consuls. Each Emperor named one of the two consuls for the year. As a general rule the names were not published together. The name of the Western consul was not known in the East, nor that of the Eastern in the West, in time for simultaneous publication.[2]

Many passages in our narrative will show that the Empire throughout the fifth century was the one and undivided Roman Empire in all men's minds. There were " the parts of the East," and " the parts of the West," [3] but the Empire was one.[4] No one would speak of two or more Roman Empires in the days of the sons of Constantine ; yet their political relation to one another was exactly the same as that of Arcadius to Honorius or of Leo I. to Anthemius. However independent of each other

[1] *C. Th.* i. 1. 5.
[2] There are exceptions to this rule. Occasionally the two Emperors held the consulship together, and this was prearranged. It also sometimes happened that one of them resigned his right of nomination to the other, and in this case the two names were published together. *E.g.* in A.D. 437

Valentinian III. nominated Aetius and Sigisvultus. The whole subject of the consulship in the fifth century and in the Ostrogothic period has been elucidated by Mommsen in *Ostgothische Studien*, in *Hist. Schr.* iii.
[3] *Partes orientis et occidentis.*
[4] *Coniunctissimum imperium, C.Th.* i. 1. 5.

or even unfriendly the rulers from time to time may have been, the unity of the Empire which they ruled was theoretically unaffected. And the theory made itself felt in practice.

§ 2. *The Senate. The Imperial Council*

Although the dyarchy, or double government of Emperor and Senate, had come to an end, and autocracy, as we have seen, was established without reserve or disguise, the Senate remained as an important constitutional body, with rights and duties, and, though it was remodelled, it maintained many of its ancient traditions. The foundation of Constantinople had led to the formation of a second Senate, modelled on that of Rome—a great constitutional innovation. Constantine himself had not ventured upon this novelty. He did found a new senate in Byzantium, but his foundation seems rather to have resembled the senates of important cities like Antioch than the august Senatus Romanus.[1] His son Constantius raised it from the position of a municipal to that of an Imperial body.[2]

The principles that senatorial rank was hereditary and that the normal way of becoming a member of the Senate itself was by holding a magistracy still remained in full force. The offices of aedile and tribune had disappeared, and by the end of the fourth century the quaestorship was on the point of disappearing. Hence the praetorship remained as the portal through which the sons of senators could enter the Senate. They not only could, but they were obliged. The sole duty of the Praetor now was to spend money on the exhibition of games or on public works. There were eight praetors in the East ; the expenses were divided among them ; and the Senate, which had the duty of designating them, named them ten years in advance, in order to enable them to economise or otherwise collect the necessary funds, as the cost of holding the office was extremely heavy.[3] The burden of the consulship

---

[1] Cp. the (contemporary) Anon. Vales. (Part 1) 6. 30 *senatum constituit secundi ordinis, claros vocavit.*

[2] The exaltation of the senate by Constantius is touched on in the Presbeutic speech of Themistius addressed to the Emperor at Rome (*Or.* 3).

[3] *C. Th.* vi. 4. 13, § 2. Olympiodorus, *fr.* 44, mentions some sums spent on Praetorian games at Rome (£184,000 ; £92,000 ; £55,200). These were evidently quite exceptional. The expenses of a consul on the spectacles which he exhibited during the first week of the new year might amount to over £92,000, but were largely defrayed by the Imperial treasury, at least in the sixth century. Procopius, *H.A.* 26, p. 159.

was not so severe, but that supreme dignity was bestowed only on men who were already senators.

Men who were not born in the senatorial order could be admitted to the Senate in various ways, whether by a decree of the Senate itself or by the Emperor, who might confer either upon an individual or upon a whole class of persons an order of rank which carried with it a seat in the Senate. Persons thus co-opted by the Senate were liable to the burden of the praetorship, and likewise those whom the Emperor ennobled, unless special exemption were granted.

Exemption was granted frequently, and it took the form of *adlectio*.[1] This was the term used in the early Empire for the process by which the Emperor could introduce into the Senate a candidate of his own and make him a member of the aedilician, for instance, or of the praetorian class, though he had never filled the corresponding magistracy. In the fourth century these classes disappeared and were replaced by the three orders of *illustres*, *spectabiles*, and *clarissimi*, in each of which there were certain subdivisions. The Emperor could confer these orders of rank on any one,[2] and a person to whom he granted the clarissimate became thereby a member of the lowest order of the Senate, and belonged to the *adlecti* who were exempt from the praetorship. Further, under the new administrative system which will be described in the following chapter, all the important offices carried with them the title *illustris*, or *spectabilis*, or *clarissimus*, and thus secured to their occupants eventually, if not immediately,[3] seats in the Senate. And in some cases, though by no means in all, this admission by virtue of office carried with it exemption. Again, there were many classes of subordinate functionaries who received, when they retired from office, the clarissimate or perhaps one of the higher titles, thus becoming senators, and these as a rule enjoyed exemption.

To resume : the Senate was recruited from men of senatorial origin, that is, sons of senators, and from men who, born outside the senatorial class, were ennobled by elevation to office, or

---

[1] Lécrivain, *Le Sénat romain*, 15-23, gives a lucid account.

[2] It was done by means of a brief or patent of rank (*codicilli*). The older rank of *perfectissimus*, which did not carry senatorial rank, still survived, soon to disappear.

[3] *C.J.* iii. 24. 3 (law of Zeno) seems to imply that the *quaestor s. pal.*, the *mag. off.*, the *praepositus s. cub.* did not belong to the Senate, although they were *illustres*, till after they had laid down their offices.

on retiring from office, or occasionally by a special act of the Emperor or of the Senate. The praetorship was the front gate for entering the Senate, but there was also a back gate, adlection, of which the Emperor held the key, and a large and increasing number of the second section entered by this way.

One of Constantine's administrative reforms was the opening to senators of all the official posts, which hitherto had been confined to the equestrian order, so that the careers open to a young man of senatorial birth were far more numerous and varied. The equestrian order gradually disappeared altogether. On the other hand, men of the lowest origin might rise through the inferior grades of the public service to higher posts which carried with them the right of admission to the Senate. Thus an aristocracy was formed, which was recruited every year by men whose fathers had not belonged to it, and was divided into grades depending on office or special Imperial favour, not on birth.[1] Ancient tradition was so far preserved that those who had discharged the functions of consul (including honorary consuls) had the most exalted rank.[2] Next to the consuls came Patricians, a new order instituted by Constantine, not connected with any office, and conferred—at first very sparingly—by the Emperor on men highly distinguished for their services to the State.[3]

A large number of senators preferred living on their estates in the country to residence in the capitals, and of those who actually attended the meetings of the Senate[4] it is probable

---

[1] Within the ranks of the three grades *illustres*, *spectabiles*, and *clarissimi* precedence was determined by office. Thus a Praetorian Prefect was superior to a Master of Soldiers; both were illustrious. A man who was created a *spectabilis* might be assimilated to a proconsul, a vicarius, or a dux, all of whom were *spectabiles*, but in descending rank. All these were superior to the *viri consulares*, who were practically coincident with the class of *clarissimi* (cp. *C.J.* xii. 17. 2). These *viri consulares* must be carefully distinguished from men who had held the consulship or had received the honorary consulship, and who were in the highest class of the *illustres*.

[2] But among the consuls, a Praetorian Prefect was superior to one who had not held that office, etc.

(*C. Th.* vi. 6. 1).

[3] In the fifth and sixth centuries the patriciate was bestowed more freely. By a law of Zeno (*C.J.* xii. 3. 3) it could be conferred only on a man who had been Consul, Praetorian Prefect, Prefect of the City, Master of Soldiers, or Master of Offices. In later times, most ministers who would formerly have had the illustrious rank were patricians.

[4] The quorum for a meeting of the Senate in A.D. 356 was fixed at 50. There was no limit to the number of Senators. Themistius speaks of 2000 in his time (*Or.* 34, *ed. Dindorf*, p. 456). At the beginning of our period there were no Senators who had not the right to sit in the Senate. But there were some persons who had the clarissimate and yet were not Senators (*C. Th.* xvi. 5. 52)—

that the greater number were men who held official posts and that simple senators were few. We may conjecture that the highest and smallest class, the Illustrious, came to form the majority of the active members of the Senate, and that this fact caused the Emperors before the middle of the fifth century to permit the two inferior classes, the Spectabiles and the Clarissimi, to live wherever they pleased.[1] A few years later all members of these classes who lived in the provinces were relieved from the Praetorship, and were graciously recommended to stay at home and enjoy their dignities.[2] This meant that while they belonged to the senatorial class and paid the senatorial taxes, they were expressly discouraged from sitting in the Senate. The next step was to exclude entirely the two lower classes and confine the right of deliberating in the Senate to Illustres, and by the end of the fifth century this seems to have been the rule.[3]

The functions of the Senates of Rome and Constantinople were both municipal and Imperial. As the funds contributed by the praetors were exclusively applied for the benefit of the capital cities, the nomination of these magistrates and the control exercised over the distribution of the funds belonged to the municipal part of their duties. The Prefect of the City acted as chief of the Senate and as its executive officer, and conducted all its communications with the Emperor.[4] He was the guardian of the rights of senators [5]; and that body acted with him as an advisory council on such matters as the food supply of the capital, or the regulation of the public instruction given by professors and rhetors.

We have already seen the constitutional importance of the Senate when a vacancy on the throne occurred. It could pass resolutions (*senatus consulta*) which the Emperor might adopt and issue in the form of edicts.[6] It could thus suggest Imperial

---

apparently those who received this dignity without *adlectio* and had not discharged the office of *praetor*. Cp. Lécrivain, *op. cit.* 12.

[1] *C.J.* xii. 1. 15.

[2] *Ib.* 2. 1 (A.D. 450).

[3] Cp. Lécrivain, *op. cit.* 66. Add to his references *Digest*, i. 9. 12.

[4] Illustrated by the *Relationes* of Symmachus, Praef. urb. Cp. Cassiodorus, *Var.* vi. 4. Under the Prefect was a staff of *censuales*, who kept the lists, investigated the incomes of the

senators, and managed the financia business. Cp. *C. Th.* vi. 4. 13 and 26.

[5] Symmachus, *Rel.* 48 *praefecturae urbanae proprium negotium est senatorum iura tutari.*

[6] This is obviously the case with Valentinian III., *Nov.* 14 ; possibly with Theodosius II., *Nov.* 15 (as Lécrivain has suggested). The Senate of Rome retained in theory the right *leges constituere*; but this perhaps never belonged to the Senate of New Rome

legislation, and it acted from time to time as a consultative body
in co-operation with the Imperial Council. Some of the Imperial
laws took the form (we do not know on what principle) of
" Orations to the Senate," and were read aloud before that
body.[1] Valentinian III., in A.D. 446, definitely formulated a
legislative procedure which granted to the Senate the right of
co-operation. When any new law was to be promulgated, it
was first to be discussed at meetings of the Senate and the
Council ; if agreed to, it was to be drafted (by the Quaestor),
and then submitted again to the same bodies, after which it was
to be confirmed by the Emperor.[2] This regulation points to the
probability that it was already the habit frequently to consult
the Senate.[3]

The Senate might act as a judicial court, if the Emperor so
pleased, and trials for high treason were sometimes entrusted to
it.[4] For ordinary crimes, Senators were judged by a court
consisting of the Prefect of the City and five Senators chosen
by lot.[5]

There were two Senate-houses at Constantinople, one, built
by Constantine, on the east side of the Augusteum, close to the
Imperial Palace [6] ; the other on the north side of the Forum
of Constantine.[7] It is not clear why two houses were required.[8]
But in the sixth century we are told that the Senate had ceased
to meet in its own place and used to assemble in the Palace.[9]
This change was probably connected with its co-operation with
the Imperial Council.

Important decisions as to legislation and public policy were
not usually taken by the Emperor on the single advice of the

[1] *E.g. C. Th.* viii. 18. 9, 10; 19. 1.
Cp. Symmachus, *Ep.* x. 2.

[2] *C.J.* i. 14. 8. We cannot be sure
whether this procedure was adopted
in the East, though it is included in
Justinian's Code.

[3] For instance cp. *C. Th.* vi. 24. 11 ;
Marcian, *Nov.* 5, *ad in.*

[4] John Lydus, *De mag.* iii. 10 τῶν
βασιλέων ἅμα τῇ βουλῇ δίκας ἀκροωμένων,
referring apparently to the time of
Arcadius. *Ib.* 27, a reference of an
appeal case to the Senate for revision
is mentioned.

[5] *Quinquevirale iudicium, C. Th.* ix.
1. 13, ii. 1. 12.

[6] *Not. Urbis Cpl.* p. 231. Sozomen,
ii. 3 ; Zosimus, v. 24 ; Procopius,

Aed. i. 10.   σενάτον is the Greek for
Senate-house.

[7] First referred to in connexion
with Theodosius II. : Παραστάσεις,
ed. Preger, 50. It was burnt down
in the reign of Leo I. Cedrenus, i.
pp. 610 and 565.

[8] Cedrenus, i. 610 (= Zonaras iii.
125) says that the Emperor, when he
assumed the consulship, was invested
with the consular robes in the Senate-
house in the Forum. He also mentions in the same passage another
house, used for senatorial deliberations,
in the Forum of Taurus. Of this we
do not hear elsewhere.

[9] John Lydus, *De mag.* ii. 9.

minister specially concerned. He was assisted by the Consistorium or Imperial Council, which was constantly summoned to deliberate on questions of moment, and we must always remember that, while the Emperor was officially and legally sole author of all laws and responsible for acts of state, the deliberations of the Imperial Council had a large share in the conduct of public affairs. The Consistorium was derived from the legal Consilium of Hadrian, enlarged in its functions and altered in its constitution by Diocletian and Constantine.[1] It acted as a high Court, before which important cases, such as treason, might be tried. It was consulted generally on matters of legislation and policy. The Quaestor was its president. It included the two financial Ministers and the Master of Offices ; and probably the Praetorian Prefect and the Masters of Soldiers who were in residence at the capital generally attended. We have very little information about its size or its constitution ; nor do we know how often it met. We have good reason to suppose that it met at stated times, and not merely when convened for a special purpose.[2] That the transaction of a considerable amount of ordinary business devolved upon it may be inferred from the fact that it disposed of a large bureau of secretaries and officials known as Tribunes and Notaries. These clerks, who had their office in the Palace, drafted the proceedings and resolutions of the Consistorium, and were sometimes employed to execute missions in pursuance of its decisions.[3]

Among the ordinary duties of the Council was that of receiving deputations from the provinces.[4] But the most important part

---

[1] Diocletian changed the old name *consilium* to *consistorium*, because, under the new autocracy, the members stood (*consistere*) in the Emperor's presence. Hadrian's consilium had no permanent members ; those who assisted at each meeting were summoned *ad hoc*. Constantine instituted permanent members, with the title of *comites consistoriani*, and included military as well as legal members. *Comites* was an appropriate name, as the Council accompanied the Emperor as he moved about from camp to camp, or city to city. Constantine bestowed the title of *comes* (of first, second, or third class) as an honorary distinction, and it was attached to many offices. It corresponded in

some ways to our Privy Councillor. Cp. Seeck, *Untergang*, ii. 76 *sqq.*

[2] *Nov. Theod. 11.* xxiv. (A.D. 443). A report concerning the strength of the military forces on the frontiers is to be made *quotannis mense Ianuario in sacro consistorio.*

[3] A certain number of the *tribuni et notarii* were appointed to special duties as legal secretaries of the Emperor and were often employed on special missions. They were called *referendarii.* For their functions and appointment see Bury, *Magistri scriniorum,* etc.

[4] *C. Th.* xii. 12. 6-10. In these constitutions the Consistorium is called *comitatus noster* and *sacrarium nostrum.*

of its regular work seems to have been judicial. In serious cases, senators who did not belong to the Council were frequently called to assist.[1] The technical term for a meeting of the Council was *silentium* ; a meeting in which the Senate took part was called *silentium et conventus*.[2] But the words *et conventus* were frequently dropped [3] ; and thus it becomes difficult to say in a given case whether a *silentium* means the Council only or the Council and Senate.[4]

It would seem that, while the Senate and Council continued to be formally distinct, the Senate came virtually to be a larger Council and met in the great hall of Council, the Consistorium in the Palace. The Emperor, at his discretion, referred political questions either to this larger body or to a smaller body of functionaries which corresponded to the old Imperial Council. The chief occasions on which the Senate could exercise independent political action were when a vacancy to the throne occurred ; but some cases are recorded in which it seems to have taken the initiative in recommending political measures.

[1] See the law of Justinian *De ordine senatus*, *Nov.* 62. 1 (A.D. 537).

[2] *Ib.* John Malalas, p. 438 γενομένου σιλεντίου κομβέντου (to try a patrician for libelling the Emperor Justinian). Peter Patr. *apud* Const. Porph. *Cer.* i. 92, p. 422, 95, p. 433, σιλέντιον καὶ κομέντον (where we should read κοβέντον).

[3] Justinian, *Nov. cit.*, *Etsi non addatur conventus vocabulum.* Thus in Theophanes, p. 246. 14 (ἐπὶ σελεντίου) a *silentium et conventus* is meant, as is shown by the words παρουσίᾳ τῆς συγκλήτου below (l. 24).

[4] In connexion with the relations of Council and Senate it is worth noticing that the words *in amplissimo et venerabili ordine* (*sc.* the Senate) in a law of Theodosius II., *C. Th.* vi. 23. 1, are replaced in *C.J.* xii. 16. 1 by *in nostro consistorio.*

CHAPTER II

WE pass from the constitution of the monarchy to the bureaucratic system of government which it created. This system, constructed with the most careful attention to details, was a solution of the formidable problem of holding together a huge heterogeneous empire, threatened with dissolution and bankruptcy, an empire which was far from being geographically compact and had four long, as well as several smaller, frontiers to defend. To govern a large state by two independent but perfectly similar machines, controlled not from one centre but from two foci, without sacrificing its unity was an interesting and entirely new experiment. These bureaucratic machines worked moderately well, and their success might have been extraordinary if the monarchs who directed them had always been men of superior ability. Blots of course and defects there were, especially in the fields of economy and finance :

sed delicta tamen quibus ignouisse uelimus.

The political creation of the Illyrian Emperors was not unworthy of the genius of Rome.

§ 1. *Civil Administration*

The old provinces had been split up by Diocletian into small parts, and these new provinces placed under governors whose powers were purely civil. A number of adjacent provinces were grouped together in a circumscription which was called a Diocese (resembling in extent the old province), and the Diocese was under the control of an official whose powers were likewise purely civil. The Dioceses in turn were grouped in four vast

25

circumscriptions,[1] under Praetorian Prefects, who were at the head of the whole civil administration and controlled both the diocesan and the provincial governors. This system, it will be observed, differed from the previous system in three principal features : military and civil authority were separated ; the provincial units were reduced in size ; and two higher officials were interposed between the Emperor and the provincial governor. Perhaps we should add a fourth ; for the Praetorian Prefect (whom Constantine had shorn of his military functions) possessed, so far as civil administration was concerned, an immensely wider range of power than any provincial governor had possessed under the system of Augustus.

At the end of the fourth century, then, the whole Empire, for purposes of civil government, was divided into four great sections, distinguished as the Gauls, Italy, Illyricum, and the East (*Oriens*). *The Gauls*, which included Britain, Gaul, Spain, and the north-western corner of Africa, and *Italy*, which included Africa, Italy, the provinces between the Alps and the Danube, and the north-western portion of the Illyrian peninsula, were subject to the Emperor who resided in Italy. *Illyricum*, the smallest of the Prefectures, which comprised the provinces of Dacia, Macedonia, and Greece, and *the East*, which embraced Thrace in the north and Egypt in the south, as well as all the Asiatic territory, were subject to the Emperor who resided at Constantinople. Thus each of the Praetorian Prefects had authority over a region which is now occupied by several modern

---

[1] During the fourth century, the number of Prefectures was sometimes four, sometimes three ; for at times, Italy and Illyricum were under one Prefect. The division of the Empire in 395 stereotyped the quadruple division. Cp. Mommsen, *Hist. Schr.* iii. 284 *sqq.*—For the administrative fabric of the fourth and fifth centuries a main source is the *Notitia dignitatum*, which consists of two distinct documents, the *Not. in partibus Orientis*, and the *Not. in partibus Occidentis*. It was the function of a high official, the *primicerius notariorum*, to prepare and issue the codicilli or diplomas of their appointments to all the higher officials of the Empire from Praetorian Prefects to provincial governors. The insignia of the office were represented on the codicil, for instance in the case of a Master of Soldiers the shields of the regiments which were under his command. For this purpose the primicerius of the West, and the primicerius of the East, had each a list (*laterculum maius*) of all the officials in order of precedence, with information as to their staffs and subordinates. The text which we by a lucky chance possess is derived from the lists which were probably in the hands of the primicerius of the West in A.D. 427 or not much later. The *Not. Or.* did not strictly concern him, but it was useful for reference, and a copy brought up to date had been sent to him from Constantinople. Compare Bury, *The Notitia dignitatum*, in *J.R.S.* x.

States. The Prefecture of *the Gauls* was composed of four Dioceses : Britain, Gaul, Viennensis (Southern Gaul), and Spain ; *Italy* of three : Africa, the Italies,[1] and Illyricum ; *Illyricum* of two : Dacia and Macedonia ; *the East* of five : Thrace, Asiana, Pontus, Oriens, and Egypt. Each of the diocesan governors had the title of *Vicarius*,[2] except in the cases of Oriens where he was designated *Comes Orientis*, and of Egypt where his title was *Praefectus Augustalis*.[3] It is easy to distinguish the Prefecture of the Oriens from the Diocese of Oriens (Syria and Palestine) ; but more care is required not to confound the Diocese with the Prefecture of Illyricum.

The subordination of these officials to one another was not complete or strictly graded. A comparison of the system to a ladder of four steps, the Emperor at the top, the provincial governor at the foot, with the Prefect and the Vicarius between, would be misleading. For not only were the relations between the provincial governor and the Prefect direct, but the Emperor might communicate directly both with the governor of the diocese and with the governor of the province. Two provinces had a special privilege : the proconsuls of Africa and of Asia [4] were outside the jurisdiction either of Vicarius or of Prefect, and were controlled immediately by the Emperor.[5]

The Praetorian Prefect of the East, who resided at Constantinople, and the Praetorian Prefect of Italy were in rank the highest officials in the Empire ; next to them came respectively the Prefect of Illyricum, who resided at Thessalonica, and the Prefect of the Gauls. The functions of the Prefect embraced a wide sphere ; they were administrative, financial, judicial,

---

[1] The Italies were divided into two districts, under two Vicarii : the V. urbis Romae, whose district comprised all Italy south of Tuscany and Umbria (inclusive) with Sardinia, Corsica, and Sicily ; the V. Italiae, who was over the rest of Italy and Raetia.

[2] There was no Vicarius of Dacia ; it was directly subject to the Prefect.

[3] Egypt had been part of the Diocese of the East till about A.D. 380-382, when it was made a distinct Diocese, and the praefectus Aegypti received the title of Augustalis. Cp. M. Gelzer, *Studien zur byz. Verw. Ägyptens*, 7. The Augustalis seems to have acted at the same time as

praeses of the province of Egypt.

[4] Under the proconsul of Asia were two provinces, Hellespontus and Insulae (the islands along the coast of Asia Minor) : *Not. Or.* xx.

[5] The governor of one other province, Achaia, bore the old title of proconsul ; the others were *consulares* or *correctores* or *praesides*. The governor had judicial as well as administrative powers. His court was the court of first instance in his province ; but an appeal lay either to the court of the Vicarius or to that of the Prefect. He had also the duty of supervising the collection of taxes.

and even legislative. The provincial governors were appointed
at his recommendation, and with him rested their dismissal,
subject to the Emperor's approval. He received regular reports
of the administration throughout his prefecture from the Vicarii
and from the governors of the provinces. He had treasuries
of his own, and the payment and the food supplies of the army
devolved upon him. He was also a supreme judge of appeal ;
in cases which were brought before his court from a lower
tribunal there was no further appeal to the Emperor. He could
issue, on his own authority, praetorian edicts, but they concerned
only matters of detail. The most important Imperial enactments were usually addressed to the Prefects, because they
were the heads of the provincial administration, and possessed the machinery for making the laws known throughout the
Empire.

The exalted position of the Praetorian Prefect was marked
by his purple robe, or *mandyes*, which differed from that of
the sovran only in being shorter, reaching to the knees instead
of to the feet. His large silver inkstand, his pen-case of gold
weighing 100 lbs., his lofty chariot, are mentioned as three
official symbols of his office. On his entry all military officers
were expected to bend the knee, a survival of the fact that
his office was originally not civil but military.

Rome and Constantinople, with their immediate neighbour-
hoods, were exempt from the authority of the Praetorian Prefect
and under the jurisdiction of the Prefect of the City.[1] The
Prefect of Constantinople had the same general powers and
duties as the Prefect of Rome, though in some respects the
arrangements were different. He was the head of the Senate,
and in rank was next to the Praetorian Prefects. While all
the other great officials, even though their functions were purely
civil, had a military character, in token of which they wore
military dress and the military belt, the Prefect of the City
retained his old civil character and wore the toga. He was the
chief criminal judge in the capital. For the maintenance of
further order the Roman Prefect had under his control a force
of city cohorts, as well as police. We hear nothing of any
institution at Constantinople corresponding to the city cohorts,
but the police (*vigiles*) were organised as at Rome under a

----

[1] Ὁ ἔπαρχος τῆς πόλεως.

praefectus vigilum,[1] subject to the Prefect. For the care of the aqueducts and the supervision of the markets the Prefect was responsible. One of his most important duties was to superintend the arrangements for supplying the city with corn.[2] He had also control over the trade corporations (*collegia*) of the capital.

The supreme legal minister was the Quaestor of the Sacred Palace. His duty was to draft the laws, and the Imperial rescripts in answer to petitions. A thorough knowledge of jurisprudence and a mastery of legal style were essential qualifications for the post.[3]

The post of Master of Offices (*magister officiorum*) had grown from small beginnings and by steps which are obscure into one of the most important ministries.[4] It comprised a group of miscellaneous departments, unrelated to each other, and including some of the functions which had belonged to the pre-Constantinian Praetorian Prefects. *Officium* was the word for the body of civil servants (*officiales*) who constituted the staff of a minister or governor, and the Master of Offices was so called from the authority which he exercised over the civil service, but especially over the secretarial departments in the Palace.

There were three principal secretarial bureaux (*scrinia*), which had survived from the early Empire, and retained their old names : *memoriae*, *epistularum*, and *libellorum*.[5] At Constantinople the second bureau had two departments, one for Latin and one for Greek official correspondence. The secretarial business was conducted by *magistri scriniorum*,[6] who were in direct touch with the Emperor and were not subordinate to any higher official. They were not, however, heads of the

---

[1] Νυκτέπαρχος. The page of the *Not. dig.* appertaining to the Prefect of Constantinople is unfortunately lost.

[2] In Rome there was a subordinate official, *praefectus annonae*, who presided over this department ; and there was a *praefectus annonae* in Africa, who was under the Praetorian Prefect. At Constantinople there was no *pr. ann.*, but the *pr. ann.* at Alexandria, where the corn was shipped, seems to have been under the Prefect of the City.

[3] His functions in regard to

petitions involved co-operation with the *Magistri scriniorum*, and the *Scrinia* supplied him with assistants ; he had no special staff of his own.

[4] In the *Not. dig.* he precedes in rank the Quaestor, but this was only a temporary arrangement. Μάγιστρος, when unqualified, in Greek writers always means the *Mag. Off.*

[5] See Karlowa, *op. cit.* i. 834 *sqq.* ; Schiller, *op. cit.* ii. 102 *sqq.* ; Bury, *Magistri Scriniorum*, etc.

[6] The Greek title was ἀντιγραφῆς, Bury, *ib.* 24 *sqq.*

bureaux, but the bureaux, which were under the control of the Master of Offices, supplied them with assistants and clerks.[1]

With the three ancient and homogeneous *scrinia* was associated a fourth,[2] of later origin and at first inferior rank, the *scrinium dispositionum*, of which the chief official was the *comes dispositionum*. His duty, under the control of the Master of Offices, was to draw up the programme of the Emperor's movements and to make corresponding arrangements.

The Master of Offices was responsible for the conduct of court ceremonies, and controlled the special department [3] which dealt with ceremonial arrangements and Imperial audiences. The reception of foreign ambassadors thus came within his scope, and he was the head of the corps of interpreters of foreign languages.   In the Roman Empire the administrations of foreign and internal affairs were not sharply separated as in modern states, but the Master of Offices is the minister who more than any other corresponds to a Minister of Foreign Affairs.   As director of the State Post (*cursus publicus*) [4] he made arrangements for the journeys of foreign embassies to the capital.

One of his duties was the control of the *agentes in rebus*, a large body of officials who formed the secret service of the State and were employed as Imperial messengers and on all kinds of confidential missions.   As secret agents they were ubiquitous in the provinces, spying upon the governors, reporting the misconduct of officials, and especially vigilant to secure that the state post was not misused.   Naturally they were open to bribery and corruption.   The body or *schola* of *agentes* was strictly organised in grades, and when they had risen by regular

---

[1] The *Magister memoriae* drafted brief Imperial decisions (*adnotationes*, on the margin of documents), answered petitions, and probably threw into their final form many of the documents emanating from the offices of the other magistri.   The *Magistri epistularum* and *epistularum Graecarum* dealt with answers to communications from foreign powers and to deputations from the provinces ; examined the questions addressed to the Emperor by officials ; and also dealt with petitions.   The duties of the *Magister libellorum* were concerned chiefly with appeal cases (*cognitiones*) and petitions which involved specifically legal questions.   We have not sufficient information to draw a sharp line between the functions of these three ministers, which seem at many points to have overlapped and involved constant co-operation.   They must also have been in constant touch both with the Master of Offices and with the Quaestor.

[2] They are sometimes grouped together as *sacra scrinia nostra*.

[3] *Officium admissionum* under a *magister*.

[4] It had been under the control of the Praet. Prefect, who still retained the right of issuing passes or orders for its use.   The change was made in A.D. 396 ; see below, p. 115.

promotion, they were appointed to be heads (*principes*) of the official staffs of diocesan and provincial governors, and might rise to be governors themselves. Their number, in the East, was over 1200.[1]

The Scholarian bodyguards, organised by Constantine,[2] were subject to the authority of the Master of Offices, so that in this respect he may be regarded as a successor of the old Praetorian Prefect. He also possessed a certain control over the military commanders in frontier provinces.[3] He became (in A.D. 396) the director of the state factories of arms. In the Eastern half of the Empire there were fifteen of these factories (*fabricae*), six in the Illyrian peninsula, and nine in the Asiatic provinces.

One of the most striking features of the administrative system was the organisation of the subordinate officials, who were systematically graded and extremely numerous.[4]

Our use of the words " office " and " official " is derived from the technical meaning of *officium*, which, as was mentioned above, denoted the staff of a civil or military dignitary.[5] Most ministers, every governor, all higher military commanders, had an officium, and its members were called *officiales*. Theoretically, the civil as well as the military officials were supposed to be soldiers of the Emperor ; their service was termed *militia*, its badge was the military belt, which was discarded when their term of service expired, and their retirement from service was called in military language "honourable dismissal " (*honesta missio*). But these usages were a mere survival, and the state service was really divided into military, civil, and palatine offices. The term palatine in this connexion meant particularly the staffs of the financial ministers, the Counts of the Sacred Largesses and the Private Estates.

---

[1] They are often called *magistriani* (as under the authority of the *Mag. Off.*). In 430 there were more than 1174 (*C. Th.* vi. 27. 23) ; in the reign of Leo I. the number was 1248 (*C.J.* xii. 20. 3.

[2] See below, p. 37.

[3] See *C.J.* xii. 59. 8 ; *Nov. Theodosii* 24. Perhaps he inherited this duty from the Praet. Pref. in A.D. 396.

[4] A short survey of this compli-

cated subject will be found in Karlowa, *Röm. Recht*, i. 875 *sqq.*

[5] In Greek, τάξις was used as well as ὀφφίκιον, and, for the members, ταξεῶται as well as ὀφφικιάλιοι. *Apparitores* (used in the early Empire for officials) is sometimes applied to members of the more important, *cohortalini* to those of the least important, offices. In the military *officia* the posts were confined to soldiers.

The number of subalterns in each office was fixed. To obtain a post an Imperial rescript was required, and advancement was governed by seniority. Those who had served their regular term in the higher offices became eligible for such a post as the governorship of a province and might rise to the highest dignities in the Empire.

Offices, such as those of a Praetorian Prefect, a vicar, or a provincial governor, were divided into a number of departments or bureaux (*scrinia*), each under a head. On these permanent officials far more than on their superior, who might only hold his post for a year, the efficiency of the administration depended. The bureaux differed in nature and name according to the functions of the ministry. Those in the office of the Praetorian. Prefecture differed entirely from those of the financial ministries or those of the Master of Offices. But the offices of all the governors who were under the Praetorian Prefect reproduced in their chief departments the office of the Prefect himself. Each of these had a *princeps*,[1] who was the right hand of the chief and had a general control over all departments of the office.

The State servants were paid originally (like the army) both in kind and coin, but as time went on the *annona* or food ration was commuted into money. They were so numerous that their salaries were a considerable item in the budget. We have no information as to the total number of State officials; but we have evidence which may lead us to conjecture that the civil servants in the Prefectures of the East and Illyricum, including the staffs of the diocesan and provincial governors, cannot

---

[1] The princeps of the Prefect, the vicars, and the proconsuls was selected from the *agentes in rebus*. Strictly speaking he was outside the officium, though he is included in it in the *Not. dig.* The officium consisted of the *cornicularius*, who assisted the chief in administering justice; a criminal department under a *commentariensis*, who brought the accused to trial, drew up the acts of the process, executed judgment, superintended prisons; a section of accountants (*numerarii*), who dealt with fiscal business; the *adiutor* (βοηθός), and some others. Outside the officium there were attached a number of organised bodies (*scholae*) of clerks and assistants of various kinds, who were at the disposal of the officials, especially the school of *exceptores* or shorthand writers, the most expert of whom formed an inner college of *augustales* (cp. John Lydus, *De mag.* iii. 9). Other schools were the *chartularii*; the *singulares* (employed as messengers to the provinces); the *scriniarii*. From these the chief officials selected their clerks, who then became members of the officium.— The military staffs had a *princeps* and a *commentariensis*, but as they had no jurisdiction in civil cases they did not require a *cornicularius* or *adiutor*.

have been much fewer than 10,000.[1] To this have to be added the staffs of the military commanders, of the financial and other central ministries.

It was a mark of the new monarchy that the eunuchs and others who held posts about the Emperor's person and served in the palace should be regarded as standing on a level of equality with the State officials and have a recognised position in the public service. The Grand Chamberlain (*praepositus sacri cubiculi*), who was almost invariably a eunuch, was a dignitary of the highest class. In the case of weak sovrans his influence might be enormous and make him the most powerful man in the State ; in the case of strong Emperors who were personally active he seldom played a prominent part in politics. It is probable that he exercised a general authority over all officers connected with the Court and the Imperial person, but this power may have depended rather on a right of co-operation than on formal authority.[2] At Constantinople the Grand

---

[1] The offices of the provincial governors in Illyricum consisted of about 100 persons (*C.J.* xii. 57. 9); the maximum number in the vicariates was fixed at 300 (*ib.* i. 15. 5, cp. 12. A.D. 386), but that of the vicariate of Asia was 200, and that of the Count of the East 600 (*ib.* i. 15. 13 ; i. 13. 1). A calculation based on these figures for the dioceses and provinces of the Orient and Illyricum, as enumerated in *Not. dig.* would give about 8000, to which we must add probably more than 1000 for the offices of the Prefects. Justinian's ordinance (*C.J.* i. 27. 1), creating the Pr. Prefecture of Africa in the sixth century, gives the numbers and salaries of the officials both of the Prefect and of the provincial governors. There were 396 in the bureaux of the Prefect's office (including the scholae), and each of the seven civil governors had a staff of 50. Including the salaries of the Prefect and the governors, the total cost amounted to nearly £11,000. The salary of the Prefect was 7200 solidi (£4500), that of a governor, 448 (£280). The staffs of the five military governors (dukes) were paid at a higher rate than those of the civil and the total cost of their establishments was £7050. The incomes of the subordinate officials,

who handled legal matters, were considerably increased by fees ; the salaries of all the subalterns were miserable.

[2] The pages relating to the *praepositus* in the *Not. dig.* (both *Or.* and *Occ.*) are lost. The *primicerius sacri cubiculi*, chief of the staff of the bed-chamber, may have been nominally or partially independent of the *praepositus* ; he was a *spectabilis* ranking immediately after the Counts of the Domestics. It is not clear what the relations of the *praepositus* were to the *castrensis sacri palatii*, who appears to have controlled many of the servants of the Great Palace at Byzantium, besides supervising stewards and caretakers in the various Imperial residences (*curae palatiorum*). Imperial rescripts were sometimes addressed to him. The Count of the Wardrobe (*com. sacrae vestis*) was probably under the *prae-positus*, as were also the decurions and the *silentiarii*, ushers who kept guard at the doors during meetings of the Imperial Council and Imperial audiences.—The Empress had a staff of cubicularii of her own ; and there was a *praepositus sacri cubiculi Augustae*, at least in the reign of Anastasius I. (*C.J.* xii. 5. 3 and 5).

Chamberlain had a certain control over the Imperial estates in Cappadocia which supplied the Emperor's privy purse.[1] We have already seen [2] that all the higher officials in the Imperial service belonged to one or other of the three classes of rank, the illustres, spectabiles, and clarissimi,[3] and were consequently members of the senatorial order. The heads of the great central ministries, the commanders-in-chief of the armies,[4] the Grand Chamberlain, were all illustres. The second class included proconsuls, vicars, the military governors in the provinces, the *magistri scriniorum*, and many others. The title clarissimus, which was the qualification for the Senate, was attached *ex officio* to the governorship of a province, and to other lesser posts. It was possessed by a large number of subaltern civil servants and was bestowed on many after their retirement. The liberality of the Emperors in conferring the clarissimate gradually detracted from its value. In consequence of this it was found expedient to raise many officials, who would formerly have been clarissimi to the rank of spectabiles ; and this in turn led to a cheapening of the rank of illustres. The result was that before the middle of the sixth century a new rank of gloriosi [5] was instituted, superior to that of illustres, and the highest officials are henceforward described as gloriosi.

§ 2. *Military Organisation*

The principal features in which the military establishment of the fourth century [6] differed from that of the Principate were the existence of a mobile field army, the organisation of the

---

[1] See below, p. 52.

[2] See above, p. 19.

[3] Ἰλλούστριοι, περίβλεπτοι, λαμπρό-τατοι were the official equivalents in Greek. Between A.D. 460 and 550 all illustres seem to have also a right to be addressed by the title of *magnificus*, μεγαλοπρεπής. See Koch, *Die byzantinischen Beamtentitel*, 51 (a book which must be used with caution).

[4] Also the *Comites domesticorum*.

[5] Also *gloriosissimi*. In Greek, ἐνδοξότατοι (also ἔνδοξοι). The *gloriosissimi senatores* are clearly marked off from the *illustres* in Justinian, *Nov.*

43. 1 (A.D. 537).

[6] Mommsen, *Das röm. Militärwesen seit Diocletian* (*Hist. Schr.* iii. 206 *sqq.*) is the principal work on the subject. A summary of the reorganisation by Reid will be found in *C. Med. H.* i. 44 *sqq.* It is treated very fully in Grosse, *Röm. Militärgeschichte.*— Recent investigation has shown that Gallienus initiated changes, especially in regard to the organisation of the cavalry, that prepared the way for the reforms of Diocletian. Cp. Homo, "L'Empereur Gallien," in *Rev. Hist.* 1 *sqq.*, 225 *sqq.*, 1913 ; Ritterling, "Zum röm. Heerwesen," in *Festschr. f. O. Hirschfeld*, 1903.

cavalry in bodies independent of the infantry, and the smaller size of the legionary units.

Diocletian had created, and Constantine had developed, a field army which the Emperor could move to any part of his dominion that happened to be threatened, while at the same time all the frontiers were defended by troops permanently stationed in the frontier provinces. The military forces, therefore, consisted of two main classes : the mobile troops or *comitatenses*, which accompanied the Emperor in his movements and formed a " sacred retinue " (*comitatus*) ; and the frontier troops or *limitanei*.

The strength of the old Roman legion was 6000 men. The legion of this type was retained in the case of the *limitanei* ; but it is broken up into detachments of about 1000 (corresponding to the old cohort), which are stationed in different quarters, sometimes in different provinces. And these detachments are no longer associated with a number of foot-cohorts and squadrons of horse, as of old, when the legatus of a legion commanded a body of about 10,000 men. The cavalry and the cohorts are under separate commanders.[1]

The field army consisted of two classes of troops, the simple *comitatenses* and the *palatini*.[2] The palatini, who took the place of the old Praetorian guards, were a privileged section of the comitatenses and retained the special character of Imperial guards, in so far as most of them were stationed in the neighbourhood of Constantinople or in Italy.[3] The infantry of the field army was composed of small legions of 1000, and bodies of light infantry known as *auxilia* which were now mainly recruited from Gauls, and from Franks and other Germans. The cavalry, under a separate command, consisted of squadrons, called *vexillationes*, 500 strong.

Each of these units,—the legion, the *auxilium*, the *vexillatio*

[1] There were cohorts as a rule among the frontier troops, but on the Danube, where there were *auxilia*, cohorts are exceptional. The cavalry squadron, *ala*, is generally 600 strong. Other classes of the cavalry of the *limitanei* were known as *cunei equitum* and *equites*.

[2] Constantine, who formed the Palatini, increased the field army and withdrew many troops from the frontier provinces for the purpose.

These new bodies were called *pseudo-comitatenses* (18 legions in the west, 20 in the east).

[3] Of the 12 palatine legions in the west, 8 were in Italy, 3 in Africa, 1 in Gaul. Of the 13 in the east, 12 were near Constantinople, 1 in Illyricum. Of the 65 *auxilia* in the west, 21 were in Italy ; of 43 in the east, 35 were near the capital. So the *Not. dig.* See Mommsen, *op. cit.* 235.

of the comitatenses, the legionary detachment, the cohort of the limitanei,—was as a rule under the command of a tribune, in some cases of a praepositus.[1] The tribune corresponded roughly to the modern colonel.

All these armies were under the supreme command of Masters of Soldiers, *magistri militum.* The organisation of this command in the east, as it was finally ordered by Theodosius I., differed fundamentally from that in the west. In the east there were five Masters of Horse and Foot. Two of these, distinguished as Masters in Presence (*in praesenti*, in immediate attendance on the Emperor), resided at Constantinople, and each of them commanded half of the Palatine troops. The three others exercised independent authority over the armies stationed in three large districts, the East, Thrace, and Illyricum.[2]

It was otherwise in the west. Here instead of five co-ordinate commanders we find two masters *in praesenti*, one of infantry and one of cavalry. The Master of Foot was the immediate commander of the infantry in Italy and had superior authority over all the infantry of the field army in all the dioceses, and also over the commanders of the limitanei. In the dioceses the commanders of the comitatenses had the title of military counts.[3]

According to this scheme the Master of Horse *in praesenti* was co-ordinate with the Master of Foot. But this arrangement was modified by investing the Master of Foot with authority over both cavalry and infantry ; he was then called Master of Horse and Foot, or Master of Both Services, *magister utriusque militiae*, and had a superior authority over the Master of Horse. In the last years of Theodosius the command of the western armies was thus centralised in the hands of Stilicho, and throughout the fifth century this centralisation, giving enormous power and responsibility to one man, was, as we shall see, the rule.

The limitanei were under the command of dukes, the successors of the old *legati pro praetore* of the Augustan system. In the west the duke was subordinate to the Master of Foot ;

---

[1] Cp. Grosse, on tribune, praepositus praefectus. *op. cit.* pp. 143-151.

[2] The *magistri in praes.* had precedence over the others, and seem to have exercised some slight control (cp. *C. I.* xi. 55. 18), but n t so as to viola.. the principle of co-ordination.

[3] *Comites rei militaris.*—The comi-

tatenses in Africa were under the immediate command of the *duces* of the limitanei. In regard to the titles *comes* and *dux* it is to be observed that every *dux* had the rank of *comes*, but usually of the second class. When he was a *comes* of the first class he was called *comes et dux*, and then simply *comes*.

in the east to the Master of Soldiers in the military district to which his province belonged.[1]

The Palatine legions were the successors of the old Praetorian guards, but Constantine or one of his predecessors organised guard troops who were more closely attached to the Imperial person.[2] These were the Scholae, destined to have a long history. We associate the name of School with the ancient Greek philosophers, who gave leisurely instruction to their schools of disciples in Athenian porticoes. It was applied to Constantine's guards because a portico was assigned to them in the Palace [3] where they could spend idle hours waiting for Imperial orders. The Scholarians were picked men, and till the middle of the fifth century chiefly Germans ; mounted, better equipped and better paid than the ordinary cavalry of the army. There were seven schools at Constantinople, each 500 strong [4] and commanded by a tribune who was generally a count of the first rank.[5] We have already seen that the whole guard was under the control of the Master of Offices. Closely associated with the Scholarians was a special body of guards, called *candidati* from the white uniforms which they wore.

While the Scholarians and Candidates were in a strict sense bodyguards of the Imperial person and never left the Court except to accompany the Emperor, there was another body of guards, the Domestici, consisting both of horse and foot, who as a rule were stationed at the Imperial Court, but

---

[1] *E.g.* the *dux* of Osroene to the *mag. mil. per orientem.* There were 12 dukes in the west ; 13 in the east, where there were also two of superior rank, the count of the *limes* of Egypt and the count of Isauria. The province of Isauria was treated exceptionally like frontier provinces on account of the wild, insubordinate character of its uncivilised mountaineers. For the same reason the civil powers were invested in the military governor ; the count was also the *praeses*. Other exceptions to the rule of separating civil from military functions were Arabia and Mauretania Caesariensis. The union of functions was sometimes temporarily introduced, *e.g.* in Sardinia (*C. Th.* ix. 27. 3, A.D. 382), Tripolitana (*ib.* xii. 1. 133, A.D. 393). Before A.D. 450 the

duke of the Thebaid, which had been divided into two provinces, was *praeses* of the upper province (cp. Gelzer, *Byz. Verw. Agyptens*, p. 10) : and on some occasions the Augustal Prefect of Egypt was invested with military powers.

[2] Cp. Babut, *La Garde impériale,* § xi. p. 262, who thinks that they replaced the Equites singulares Augusti.

[3] Procop. *H.A.* 14.

[4] *Not. dig.*, Or. 11. Five in the west (*Occ.* 9) and this was perhaps the original number.

[5] *C. Th.* vi. 13. 1 ; *Nov. Theod.* ii. 21. The title tribune was dropped in the course of the fifth century ; and these officers were known till late times as Counts of the Schools (κόμητες σχολῶν).

might be sent elsewhere for special purposes.[1] They were under the command of Counts (*comites domesticorum*) who were independent of the Master of Soldiers.[2] It will be observed that most of the new military creations of the third and fourth centuries had names indicating their close relation to the autocrat, comitatenses, soldiers of the retinue ; palatines, soldiers of the palace ; domestics, soldiers of the household.

The army of this age had a large admixture of men of foreign birth, and for the historian this perhaps is its most important feature. In the early Empire the foreigner was excluded from military service ; the legions were composed of Roman citizens, the *auxilia* of Roman subjects. Every able-bodied citizen and subject was liable to serve. Under the autocracy both these principles were reversed. The *auxilia* were largely recruited from the barbarians outside the Roman borders ; new troops were formed, designated by foreign names ; and the less civilised these soldiers were the more they were prized.[3] Some customs and words [4] illustrate the influence which the Germans exercised in the military world. The old German battle-noise, the *barritus*, was adopted as the cry of the Imperial troops when they went into battle. The custom of elevating a newly-proclaimed Emperor on a shield was introduced by German troops in the fourth century. It would be interesting to know how many Germans there were in the army. The fact that most of the soldiers whom we know to have held the highest posts of command in the last quarter of the fourth century were of German origin speaks for itself.

[1] *C. Th.* vi. 24. 3 where *praesentales* are distinguished from *non in praes.* The full title of the domestics was *protectores et domestici.*—The question of the *protectores* is difficult. We have to distinguish the Protectors who formed the Schola prima scutariorum in the Scholarian Guards from the Protectors who belonged to a sort of school for officers and were under the orders of the Masters of Soldiers. The discussion of Babut, *op. cit.*, has not definitely cleared up the questions connected with the Protectors. See also Grosse, *op. cit.* 138 *sqq.*

[2] In the *Not. dig.* we find two comites, a *comes equitum* and a *comes peditum*, in both east and west, but it seems probable that the command was not always thus divided. For the evidence see Seeck, *sub* "Comites" in *P.-W.* col. 548.

[3] Mommsen, *ib.* 247.

[4] *Drungus* (δροῦγγος), a body of infantry in close formation (cp. Vegetius, *Ep. r. mil.* iii. 16) is Germanic, and so is *bandum* (βάνδον), which the Greeks used as the regular term for military standard (σημεῖον). It may be noted here that in the fourth and fifth centuries the standard of the legion and the legionary detachment seems to have been the dragon. Though the eagle, the standard of the old legion, is sometimes mentioned, it probably went out of use gradually. See Grosse, *op. cit.* 230 *sqq.*

The legions continued to be formed from Roman citizens ; but the distinction between citizens and subjects had disappeared since the citizenship had been bestowed, early in the third century, upon all the provincials, and it was from the least civilised districts of the Empire, from the highlands of Illyricum, Thrace, and Isauria, from Galatia and Batavia, that the mass of the citizen soldiers was drawn. From a military point of view highly civilised provinces like Italy and Greece no longer counted. The legions and citizen cavalry ceased to have a privileged position. For instance, the *auxilia* on the Danube frontier, who were chiefly of barbarian race, were superior in rank to the legionary troops under the same command.

It was a natural consequence of this new policy, in which military considerations triumphed over the political principle of excluding foreigners, that the other political principle of universal liability to service should also be relinquished. It was allowed to drop. In the fifth century it had become a dead letter, and Valentinian III. expressly enacted that " no Roman citizen should be compelled to serve," except for the defence of his town in case of danger.[1]

A third ancient principle of the Roman State, that only freemen could serve in the army, was theoretically maintained,[2] and though it was often practically evaded and occasionally in a crisis suspended,[3] it is probable that there were never many slaves enrolled.

If we examine the means by which the army was kept up, we find that the recruits may be divided into four classes. (1) There were the numerous poor adventurers, Roman or foreign, who voluntarily offered themselves to the recruiting officer and received from him the *pulveraticum* (" dust-money," or travelling expenses), the equivalent of the King's shilling. (2) There were the recruits supplied by landed proprietors from among their serf-tenants. This was a State burden, but it fell only on the estates in certain provinces.[4] (3) The son of a soldier was bound to follow his father's profession. But this hereditary military

---

[1] *Nov.* 5.
[2] *C. Th.* vii. 13. 8; *Digest,* xlix. 16. 11.
[3] Mommsen, 250-51. In the danger of Italy, invaded by barbarians, in A.D. 406 slaves were invited to serve for the reward of liberty, *C. Th.*

vii. 13. 16.
[4] *C. Th.* vii. 13. 2 *per eas provincias a quibus corpora flagitantur.* In other provinces the proprietors could make a money payment instead of furnishing the men.

service fell into abeyance before the time of Justinian. (4) The settlements of foreign barbarians within the Empire were another source of supply. These foreigners (*gentiles*), incorporated in the Empire but not enjoying the personal rights of a Roman,[1] were chiefly Germans and Sarmatians, and they were organised in communities under the control of Roman officers. They are found in Gaul, where they had the special name of *laeti*,[2] and in the Alpine districts of Italy.

The Imperial army was democratic in the sense that the humblest soldier, whatever his birth might be, might attain to the highest commands by sheer talent and capacity. The first step was promotion to the posts of *centenarius* and *ducenarius*, who discharged the duties of the old centurions and our non-commissioned officers.[3] Having served in these ranks the soldier could look forward to becoming a tribune, with the command of a military unit,[4] and the efficient tribune would in due course receive the rank of *comes*.

In order to follow the history of the fifth century intelligently and understand the difficulties of the Imperial government in dealing with the barbarian invaders it would be of particular importance to know precisely the strength of the military forces at the death of Theodosius.

The strength of the Roman military establishment at the beginning of the third century seems to have been about 300,000. It was greatly increased under Diocletian ; and considerable additions were made in the course of the fourth century. The data of the *Notitia dignitatum* would lead to the conclusion that about A.D. 428 the total strength considerably exceeded 600,000.[5]

---

[1] For instance, such a foreigner could not marry a Roman woman. See Mommsen, *Hist. Sch.* iii. 168.

[2] *C. Th.* vii. 20. 12 *laetus Alamannus Sarmata* ; in *Not. Occ.* we meet *laeti Franci, l. gentiles Suebi, Sarmatae et Taifali gentiles*.

[3] Cp. Vegetius, *op. cit.* ii. 8.

[4] Before becoming a tribune, it was usually necessary perhaps to serve in the school of protectors. The three ranks *protector, tribunus, comes* (*et tribunus*) appear *e.g.* in Ammian. xxx. 7. 3; Vegetius, iii. 10, and can be illustrated by inscriptions. But I do not think that Babut (*op. cit.*) is right in regarding the *protectors* as equivalent to the centurions under a new name and organisation.

[5] Mommsen's estimate (*op. cit.* 263) based on the *Notitia* is : Limitanei (infantry 249,500, cavalry 110,500) 360,000 ; Comitatenses (infantry 148,000, cavalry 46,500) 194,500. Total, 554,500. But to this have to be added the limitanei of Italy, Africa, Gaul, and Britain, and they must have amounted to not much less than 100,000. If we estimate them at 90,000 we should get the figure 645,000, which according to Agathias (v. 13) ought to represent the total force of the Empire. Agathias must have derived this figure from some document of the fourth century. John Lydus (*De*

We have, however, to reckon with the probability that the legions and other military units enumerated in the *Notitia* were not maintained at their normal strength and in some cases may have merely existed on paper. We may conjecture that if the army once actually reached the number of 650,000 it was not after the death of Theodosius, but before the rebellions of Maximus and Eugenius, in which the losses on both sides must have considerably reduced the strength of the legions. But if we confine ourselves to the consideration of the field army, there seems no reason to doubt that in A.D. 428 it was nearly 200,000 strong. It was unequally divided between east and west, the troops assigned to the west being more numerous. In Italy there were about 24,500 infantry and 3500 cavalry.[1]

The military organisation of Rome, as it existed at the end of the fourth century, was to be completely changed throughout the following hundred years. We have no material for tracing the steps in the transformation ; of the battles which were fought in this period not a single description has come down to us. But we shall see, when we come to the sixth century, for which we have very full information, that the military forces of the Empire were then of a different character and organised on a different system from those which were led to victory by Theodosius the Great. These changes partly depended on a change in military theory. The conquests of Rome had always been due to her infantry, the cavalry had always been subsidiary, and, down to the second half of the fourth century and the successful campaigns of Julian on the Rhine, experience had consistently confirmed the theory that battles were won by infantry and that squadrons of horse were only a useful accessory arm. The battle of Hadrianople, in which the East German horsemen rode down the legions, shook this view, and the same horsemen who had defeated Valens showed afterwards in the battles which they helped Theodosius to win, how effective might be large bodies of heavy cavalry, armed with lance and

mens. i. 27) states that under Dio-cletian the strength of the army was 389,074, and that Constantine doubled it (the latter part of the statement is certainly an exaggeration). We are told that it was further increased by Valentinian I. (Zosimus iv. 12. 1) but declined under Theodosius (με-μείωτο, *ib.* 29. 1).

[1] The distribution of the troops in the west *c.* 428 is given in *Not. Occ.* vii. ; there is no corresponding section in *Or.* In Africa there were 11,500 infantry, 9500 cavalry ; in Spain 10,500 infantry ; in western Illyricum 14,000 infantry; in Gaul 39,000 infantry, 5500 cavalry. Cp. Bury, *Not. Dig.*

sword. The lesson was not lost on the Romans, who during
the following generations had to defend their provinces against
the inroads of East German horsemen, and the leading feature
of the transformation of the Imperial army was the gradual
degradation of the infantry until it became more or less subsidiary
to the cavalry on which the generals depended more and more
to win their victories. In the sixth century we shall see that
the battles are often fought and won by cavalry only. It is
obvious that this revolution in tactics must have reacted on
the organisation and carried with it a gradual modification of
the legionary system. Another tactical change was the increased
importance of archery, brought about by the warfare on the
eastern frontier.

Rome did not depend only on her own regular armies to
protect her frontiers. She relied also on the aid of the small
Federate States which lay beyond her provincial boundaries
but within her sphere of influence and under her control. The
system of client states goes back to the time of the Republic.
The princes of these peoples were bound by a definite treaty
of alliance—*foedus*, whence they were called *foederati*—to defend
themselves and thereby the Empire against an external foe,
and in return they received protection and were dispensed from
paying tribute. In the later period with which we are concerned
the treaty generally took a new form. The client prince received
from the Emperor a fixed yearly sum,[1] supposed to be the pay
of the soldiers whom he was prepared to bring into the field.
We shall meet many of these federates, such as the Abasgians
and Lazi of the Caucasus, the Saracens on the Euphrates, the
Ethiopians on the frontier of Egypt. It was on the basis of a
contract of this kind that the Visigoths were settled south of the
Danube by Theodosius the Great, and it was by similar contracts
that most of the German peoples who were to dismember the
western provinces would establish, in the guise of Federates, a
footing on Imperial soil.

It may be added that " federation " was extended so as to
facilitate and regulate the practice of purchasing immunity

---

[1] *Annonae foederaticae* ($\sigma\iota\tau\dot{\eta}\sigma\epsilon\iota\varsigma$).
Perhaps at first it was paid in kind.
The subject of the frontier Federates
has been clearly and briefly elucidated
by Mommsen, *Hist. Sch.* iii. 225 *sqq.*

from foreign foes, such as the Huns and Persians, a device to which the rulers of the Empire as its strength declined were often obliged to resort. The tribute which was paid for this purpose was designated by the same name (*annonae*) as the subsidies which were allowed to the client princes.

While the Federate system was continued and developed, a new class of troops began to be formed in the fifth century to whom the name Federates was also applied, and who must be carefully distinguished. These troops were drawn indifferently from foreign peoples ; they were paid by the government, were commanded by Roman officers, and formed a distinct section of the military establishment. We shall see that, in the course of the sixth century, these mixed Federate troops had come to be the most important and probably the most efficient soldiers in the Imperial army.

The origin of another class of fighting men who were to play a considerable part in the wars of the sixth century goes back to much the same time as that of the Federates. These were the Bucellarians, or private retainers.[1] It became the practice of powerful generals, and sometimes even civilians, to form an armed retinue or private bodyguard.[2] These soldiers were called *bucellarii*, from *bucella*, the military biscuit. Such private armed forces were strictly illegal, but notwithstanding Imperial prohibitions [3] the practice increased, the number of retainers was limited only by the wealth of their master, and officers of subordinate rank had their private armed followers. In the sixth century Belisarius had a retinue of 7000 horse, and these private troops formed a substantial fraction of the fighting strength of the Empire. When they entered the service of their master they took an oath of loyalty to the Emperor.

If the expense of maintaining the army formed a large item

---

[1] Olympiodorus fr. 7. (It was also used as an official term, for in the *Not. dig., Or.* 7, we find a squadron of *comites catafractarii bucellarii iuniores*.) The bucellarians were largely drawn from Goths, Isaurians, and Galatians. Cp. Mommsen, *op. cit.* 241 *sqq.* ; Benjamin, *De Iust. imp. aet.* 18 *sqq.*

[2] We have the cases of Rufinus (Claudian, *In Ruf.* ii. 76) ; Stilicho (Zosimus v. 11 ; on the other hand, cp. Claudian, *In cons. Stil.* 220 *sqq.*) :

Aetius (Prosper, *sub a.*, 455) ; Aspar (Malalas, frag. in *Hermes*, vi. p. 369, where Patzig has shown that the words οὒς ἐκάλεσε φοιδεράτους are not genuine, see *Unerkannt und unbekannt gebliebene Malalasfragmente*, 13). The *bucellarii* are recognised as a regular institution in Spain in the laws of Euric (*Leges Visigotorum*, p. 13). It is generally supposed that this custom was adopted by the Romans from the Germans.

[3] *C.J.* ix. 12. 10 (A.D. 468).

in the annual budget the navy cost little. It would be almost
true to say that the Empire at the period had no naval arma-
ments. There were indeed fleets at the old naval stations which
Augustus had established at Misenum and Ravenna, and another
squadron (classis Venetum) was maintained at Aquileia. But
it is significant that the prefects of these fleets, which were
probably very small, were under the control of the Master of
Soldiers in Italy.[1] There was no independent naval command.
In the east we find no mention of fleets or naval stations [2] with
the exception of the small flotillas which patrolled the Lower
Danube under the direction of the military commanders on
that frontier. For centuries the Mediterranean had been a
Roman lake, and it was natural that the navy should come to
be held as an almost negligible instrument of war. In the
third century it had been neglected so far as even to be inadequate
to the duty of policing the waters and protecting the coasts
against piracy. An amazing episode in the reign of Probus
illustrates its inefficiency.[3] A party of Franks, settled on the
shores of the Black Sea, seized some vessels, sailed through the
Propontis, plundered Carthage, Syracuse, and other cities, and
then passing into the Atlantic safely reached the mouths of
the Rhine. Yet in the contest between Constantine and Licinius
navies played a decisive part, and the two adversaries seemed
to have found many useful vessels in the ports of Greece, Syria,
Egypt, and Asia Minor. The fleet of Licinius numbered 350
ships and that of Constantine 200, some of which he built for
the occasion. It is not clear what the status of these ships was.
In the fifth century the Empire was to feel the want of an
efficient navy, when the Mediterranean ceased to be an entirely
Roman sea and a new German power in Africa contested the

---

[1] Under him, too, were flotillas on
Lake Como, Lake Neuchâtel, and on
the Loire and Seine. Those on the
Middle Danube, Lake Constance, and
in the British channel were under the
local military commanders. The
Britannic fleet was important in the
fourth century, but in the fifth we
find instead a classis Sambrica,
stationed apparently at Étaples (cp.
Lot, Les Migrations sax. p. 5), and
under the duke of Belgica Secunda.
The care of the government is no
longer to protect the coasts of Britain
but to protect the other side of the

channel. On all these fleets and flotillas see Fiebiger, art. "Classis" in
P.-W. John Lydus (loc. cit.) says
that in Diocletian's time the number
of sailors employed in the fleets both
on sea and rivers was 45,000 and that
Constantine increased it.

[2] The classis Carpathia, the classis
Alexandrina, and the classis Seleuciae
(C.J. xi. 2. 4 and 13. 1) were merely
fleets of transports,—the former two
being part of the service for conveying
the grain supplies from Egypt to
Constantinople.

[3] Zosimus i. 71.

supremacy of its waters. But the failures and defeats which marked the struggle with the Vandals did not impress the government of Constantinople with the need of building up a strong navy. The sea forces continued to be regarded as subsidiary, and in overseas expeditions the fleets which convoyed the transports were never placed under an independent naval command. Not until the seventh century, when the Empire had to fight for its very existence with an enemy more formidable than the Vandals, was a naval establishment effectively organised and an independent Ministry of Marine created.

§ 3. *The Financial System*

There are three things which it is important to know about the finances of the Empire. The first is, the sources of revenue, and how they were collected ; the second is the total amount of the revenue ; the third is the total amount of the normal expenditure. As to the first we are fairly well informed ; we know a good deal, from first-hand sources, about the system of taxation and the financial machinery. As to the second and third we are in the dark. No official figures as to the annual budget at any period of the later Roman Empire have been preserved, and all attempts to calculate the total of either income or outgoings are guess work, and are based on assumptions which may or may not be true. The utmost that can be done is to fix a minimum.

The financial, like every other department of administration under the autocracy, differed in its leading features from that of the Principate. In raising the revenue the ideal aimed at was equalisation and uniformity ; to treat the whole Empire alike, to abolish privileges and immunities. Italy, which had always been free from the burdens borne by the provinces, was largely deprived of this favoured position by the policy of Diocletian.[1] The ideal was not entirely attained ; some anomalies and differences survived ; but on the whole, uniformity in taxation is the striking characteristic of the new system in contrast with the old. Another capital difference had been gradually brought about. The device of committing the collection of the revenue to middlemen, the publicans, who

---

[1] Aurelius Victor, *Caes.* 39.

realised profits altogether disproportionate to their services, was superseded partly by the direct collection of the taxes by Imperial officials, partly through the agency of the local magistracies of the towns. Moreover, when we survey the sources of revenue at the end of the fourth century, we find that many of the old imposts of the Principates have disappeared, that new taxes have taken their place, and that the modes of assessment have been changed.

The most important and productive source of revenue was the tax on land and agricultural labour. This tax consisted of two distinct parts, the ground tax proper, which represented the old *tributum* imposed on conquered territories, and the *annona*. The tribute was paid only by those communities and in those districts which had always been liable ; it was not extended to those which had been exempted under the Principate. It was paid in coin. The annona which was paid in kind was universal, and was a much heavier burden ; no land was exempt ; the Imperial estates and the domains of ecclesiastical communities had to pay it as well as the lands of private persons.

Originally the annona [1] was an exceptional tax imposed on certain provinces in emergencies, especially to supply Rome with corn in case of a famine, or to feed the army in case of a war. The amount of this extraordinary burden, and its distribution among the communities which were affected by it, were fixed by a special order of the Emperor, known as an indiction. During the civil wars of the third century indictions became frequent. The scarcity of the precious metals and the depreciation of the coinage led to a change in the method of paying the soldiers. They no longer received their wages in coin. Money donations were bestowed on them from time to time, but their regular salary consisted in allowances of food. This practice was systematically organised by Diocletian. The supply of provisions,—consisting of corn, oil, wine, salt, pork, mutton—necessary to feed a soldier for a year, was calculated, and was called an annona.[2] In the course of the fourth century

---

[1] Much light has been thrown on the history of the *annona* by Seeck in *Die Schatzungsordnung Diocletians*, (see Bibliography, ii. 2, C) and *Gesch. des Untergangs der antiken Welt*, ii.

[2] This annona was a unit ; the officers received, according to their rank, so many annonae. There was also an allowance for horses (*capitum*). For the distribution of the *annona militaris* (ῥόγα) in the sixth cent. cp. *Pap. Cairo*, ii. 67145.

the principle was extended and civil officials received salaries in kind.

This new method of paying the army was the chief consideration which determined the special character of Diocletian's reform in taxation. He made the annona a regular instead of an extraordinary tax, and he imposed it, as was perfectly fair, on all parts of the Empire. But he did not fix it at a permanent amount. It was still imposed by an indiction ; only an indiction was declared every year. Thus it could be constantly modified and varied, according to the needs of the government or the circumstances of the provinces ; and it was intended that it should be revised from time to time by a new land survey.[1]

The valuation of the land was the basis of the new system. All the territory of the Empire was surveyed, and landed property was taxed not according to its mere acreage but with reference to its value in producing corn or wine or oil. Thus there was a unit (*iugum*) of arable land, and the number of acres in the unit might vary in different places according to the fertility of the soil ; there were units for vineyards and for olives ; and the tax was calculated on these units.[2] The unit was supposed to represent the portion of land which one able-bodied peasant (*caput*) could cultivate and live on. Thus a property of a hundred *iuga* meant a property of a hundred labourers or *capita*, human heads.[3]

Apart from Imperial estates, the greater part of the soil of the Empire belonged to large proprietors (*possessores*). In country

[1] Seeck has made it probable that a survey or census of the Empire was made every five years, beginning with A.D. 297 (then 302, 307, 312, etc.). See his article " Die Entstehung des Indictionencyclus," in *Deutsche Zeitschrift f. Geschichtswissenschaft*, xii. In later times a cycle of 15 indictions came to be used officially as a method of chronological reckoning. This cycle is usually counted as starting with A.D. 312, but it comes to the same thing if it is supposed to begin with A.D. 297.

[2] In Syria there were seven classes of land ; the same tax was paid on 5 acres of vineyard as on 20 of the best kind of tilled land and as on 225 of the best kind of olive land. The tax on the seventh class, mountain and pasture, was fixed according to the actual profits. See Bruns and Sachau, *Syro-römisches Rechtsbuch* (1880), pp. 37, 287. The unit of the *iugum* was not universal. In Italy there was a larger unit, the *millena*. In Africa the unit was the centuria = 100 acres, and no distinction was made between different classes of land.

[3] That the *iugatio* and the *capitatio* were not two different taxes (as Savigny held and Seeck and others still hold) but the same land tax seems to me to have been proved by Piganiol in his *L'Impôt de capitation*. In most cases the terms could be applied indifferently ; but in the case, for instance, mentioned in the text, of a proprietor reserving a part of his estate the term capitation would be inappropriate, as there were no *capita* (colons).

districts they were generally of the senatorial class ; in the neighbourhood of the towns they were probably more often simple curials, members of the local municipal senate. Their lands were parcelled out among tenants who paid a rent to the proprietor and defrayed the land tax. The tenants were known as *coloni* and, as we shall see later, were practically serfs. Their names and descriptions were entered in the public registers of the land tax, and hence they were called *adscriptitii*.[1] As a rule, the proprietor would reserve some part of his estate as a domain for himself, to be cultivated by slaves, and for the tax on the *iuga* of this domain he would, of course, be directly liable.

Besides the large proprietors there were also small peasants who owned and cultivated their own land, and were distinguished from the serfs on the great estates by the name of plebeians. The tax which they paid was known as the *capitatio plebeia*. The meaning of the term has been much debated, but there seems little doubt that it is simply the land tax, assessed on the free peasant proprietors on the same principles as it was assessed on large estates.[2]

The Imperial domains and the private estates of the Emperors, let on leases whether perpetual or temporary, and their cultivators, were liable to the universal annona or capitation, and it was the same with lands held by monastic communities. As to the amount of the land taxes we have hardly any information.[3]

The ground-tax proper, or tribute, which was a trifle compared with the annona, seems to have been always paid in money,

---

[1] That is, *censibus adscripti*. The Greek is, ἐναπόγραφοι. Fragments of a tax roll for the island of Thera have been preserved in which the various denominations of land, the cattle, asses, sheep, slaves, and colons are all enumerated. *C.I.G.* iii. 8656 = *I.G.* xii. fasc. 3, 343-349 (1898).

[2] This has been shown by Piganiol, *op. cit.* 33 *sqq.* The *capitatio humana* —another term which has caused much discussion—was probably (in the fifth century) a tax on slaves, paid by their owners, like the *capitatio animalium* which is usually associated with it in the laws. *Ib.* 68 *sqq.*

[3] When Julian went to Gaul, the tribute on each *caput* was 25 solidi. He reduced it to 7, including all the burdens (on the text of Ammian. xvi.

5, 14 cp. Seeck, *Rheinisches Museum*, xlix. 630). In Illyricum it appears that the amount required by provincial governors for their own supplies was at one time a solidus on 120 capita, and was increased, illegally, so that the same sum was paid on 60 capita, and finally on 13. This flagrant case drew a rescript from the Emperor in A.D. 412, *C. Th.* vii. 4. 32.—It was the duty of the Praetorian Prefect to send to the provinces lists of the dues for which the taxpayers were liable every year, and on him principally rested the responsibility of deciding whether the ordinary taxation was sufficient to cover the expenses or an addition (*superindictio*) would be required which could only be imposed with the consent of the Emperor.

except in Africa and Egypt, which were the granaries of Rome and Constantinople. It was fixed on the basis of the same survey and was entered in the same book as the annona, but, as we have seen, it was not paid in the privileged territories which had always been exempt. As the currency gradually became established, after Constantine's reforms, the annona too was under certain conditions commuted into a money-payment, and this practice gradually became more frequent.[1]

In the town territories the body of the decurions or magistrates of the town were responsible for the total sum of the taxes to which the estates and farms of the district were liable. The general control of the taxation in each province was entirely in the hands of the provincial governor, but the collection was carried out by officials appointed by the decurions of each town.[2] These collectors handed over their receipts to the *compulsor*, who represented the provincial governor, and he brought pressure to bear upon those who had not paid.[3]

Heavy taxes fell upon all classes of the population when a new Emperor came to the throne and on each fifth anniversary of his accession. On these occasions it was the custom to distribute a donation to the army, and a large sum of gold and silver was required.[4] The senators contributed an offertory (*aurum oblaticium*).[5] The decurions of every town had to scrape together gold which was presented originally in the form of crowns (*aurum coronarium*). Finally a tax was imposed on all profits arising from trade, whether on a large or a petty scale. This burden, which was known as the Five-yearly Contribution (*lustralis collatio*) or Chrysargyron (" Gold and Silver ") fell upon prostitutes as well as upon merchants and shopkeepers, and was

---

[1] *Adaeratio* was the technical term for the commutation of *species* into *pretia*. Its extension in the fifth century can be traced in *C. Th.* vii. 4. (cp. 28, 31, 32, 35, 36).

[2] The *exactor*, whose duty was to make known the financial ordinances of the provincial governor and to see that they were executed, in his community ; the *susceptores* (=*procuratores* = ἐπιμελῆται) who actually received the taxes.

[3] Cp. *Nov. Majoriani*, vii. 14. The procedure is briefly summed up in *C. Th.* i. 14. 1, *omnia tributa exigere suscipere postremo conpellere iubemus.*

Egyptian documents afford a good deal of illustration, see Gelzer, *Studien zur byz. Verw. Ägyptens*, 42 *sqq.*

[4] Each common soldier seems to have received more than £6. Seeck (*Untergang*, ii. 281) calculates that the quinquennial donation, including presents to senators and others, must have cost the Emperor $3\frac{1}{2}$ millions sterling at least. But before the sixth century the amount per soldier seems to have been reduced to 5 solidi (about 3 guineas); Procopius, *H.A.* 2 A.

[5] The amount presented to Valentinian II. in A.D. 385 was 1600 lbs. = about £73,000 (Symmachus, *Rel.* 13).

felt as particularly oppressive. It is said that parents sometimes sold their children into slavery or devoted their daughters to infamy to enable them to pay it.[1]

The chief immunity which senators enjoyed was exemption from the urban rates. Besides the *aurum oblaticium*, and the obligation of the wealthier of their class to fill the office of consul or of praetor, they were liable to a special property tax paid in specie. It was commonly known as the *follis* [2] and was scaled in three grades (1 lb., ½ lb., and ¼ lb. of gold) according to the size of the property. Very poor senators paid seven solidi [3] (£4, 8s. 6d.).

The senators, however, were far from being overtaxed. Most of them were affluent, some of them were very rich, and proportionally to their means they paid less than any other class. In Italy the income of the richest was sometimes as high as £180,000, in addition to the natural products of their estates which would fetch in the market £60,000. Such revenues were exceptional, but as a rule the senatorial landed proprietors, who had often estates in Africa and Spain as well as in Italy, varied from £60,000 to £40,000.[4]

---

[1] Libanius, *Or.* xlvi. 22 (vol. iii. p. 389); Zosimus, ii. 38; *C. Th.* xiii. 1; and see below, chap. xiii. § 3. It was collected at the end of every four years, and yielded in the case of Edessa, a town of moderate size, about £450 a year.

[2] The official name was *collatio glebalis*; it was also called *gleba*, and *descriptio*. See *C. Th.* vi. 2; Zosimus, ii. 38; Hesychius, *fr.* 5; Seeck, *Collatio glebalis* in P.-W. The *follis* was originally a bag of small coins. It was probably sealed at the mint and contained 3125 double denarii = 1 lb. gold, and was used in making large payments. The senatorial tax was known as *follis* because, as instituted by Constantine, the amount was fixed as so many bags. Popular usage transferred the name from the bag to the coin, and the double denarius itself was known as follis.

[3] The *magister census*, who was subordinate to the Prefect of the City, decided (on the basis of the *annona* registers) at which rate each senator should be liable.

[4] Olympiodorus, *fr.* 44, gives these figures. Probus, *c.* A.D. 424, spent £52,000 on his praetorship; Symmachus and Maximus £80,000 and £180,000 respectively on the praetorships of their sons. Symmachus had estates in Mauretania and in Italy (where he had 15 country houses); the Sallustii had estates in Spain; the domains of the Probi were in all parts of the Empire.—The reader may be reminded that the real value, or purchasing power, of gold was far greater then than it is to-day. It is generally reckoned that a gold coin in the sixteenth or seventeenth century was as useful as five of the same weight, say, in 1900. It is safe to assume that the proportion, 1 : 3, is not excessive for a practical comparison, in regard to the purchasing power of money in the nineteenth with the fourth and following centuries. In other words the purchasing power of a solidus approached that of £2 in 1900. This of course does not apply to every commodity, but to labour and commodities all round. Compare the useful remarks of Tenney Frank, *Economic History of Rome* (1920), pp. 80-83.

Besides the yield of all these taxes, which ultimately fell on agricultural labour, the Emperor derived a large revenue from custom duties,[1] mines, state factories, and extensive Imperial estates. We have no figures for conjecturing the amount of their yield.

The central treasury, which represented the fisc of the early Empire, was presided over by the Count of the Sacred Largess.[2] All the senatorial taxes, the *aurum oblaticium*, the *collatio lustralis*, the custom duties, the yield of the mines and of the public factories, that portion of the land-tax which represented the old tributum, the land-tax which was paid by the colons on the Imperial domains,[3] all flowed into this treasury. The Count of the Largess administered the mint, the customs, and the mines.

Besides the central treasury, at the Imperial residence in each half of the Empire, there were the chests (*arcae*) of the Praetorian Prefects. These ministers, though they had lost their old military functions, were paymasters of the forces. They were responsible not only for regulating the amount but also for the distribution of the annona. As much of the annona collected in each province as was required for the soldiers stationed there was handed over immediately to the military authorities ; the residue was sent to the chest of the Praetorian Prefect.[4] These chests seem also to have paid the salaries of the provincial governors and their staffs.

The administration of the Imperial domains, which were extensive and were increased from time to time by the confiscation of the property of persons convicted of treason, demanded a separate department and a whole army of officials. At the head of this department was the Count of the Private Estates.[5]

---

[1] In the early Empire custom duties (*vectigalia*) varied in different places, and were nowhere very high. In the east, at least, they were raised in the fourth century, and an apparently uniform tariff of $12\frac{1}{2}$ per cent (*octavae*) was imposed (*C. Th.* iv. 61. 7 and 8). As no alteration was made in subsequent laws, this rate probably continued. For the whole volume of trade, we have no figures except Pliny's estimate of imports from the east in the first century A.D. (see below,

p. 54). These imports were undoubtedly the largest item.

[2] *Comes sacrarum largitionum*, so called because when the office was first instituted the chief duty of the comes was to arrange the largess for the soldiers. The Greek equivalent is κόμης λαργιτιώνων or τῶν θείων θησαυρῶν.

[3] Cp. *C. Th.* v. 16. 29.

[4] *C. Th.* vii. 4. Zosimus, ii. 33.

[5] *Comes rerum privatarum*, κόμης τῶν πριβάτων.

The Private Estate (*res privata*) had originally been organised by Septimius Severus, who determined not to incorporate the large confiscated estates of his defeated rivals in the Patrimony but to have them separately administered.[1] In the fourth century the Patrimony and the Private Estate were combined and placed under a minister of illustrious rank. His officials administered the domains and collected the rent from the colons. The greater part of the Imperial lands were treated as State property of which the income was used for public purposes. But certain domains were set aside to furnish the Emperor's privy purse. Thus the domains in Cappadocia were withdrawn from the control of the Count of Private Estates and placed under the control of the Grand Chamberlain.[2] And in the same way, in the west, certain estates in Africa (*fundi domus divinae per Africam*) were appropriated to the personal disposition of the Emperor, although they remained under the control of the Count.

What were the relations between the fisc or treasury of the Count of the Sacred Largess on one hand, and the chests of the Praetorian Prefects and the treasury of the Count of the Private Estates on the other ? We may conjecture that the Prefects paid out of the treasuries directly the salaries of all the officials, both central and provincial, who were under their control ; that in the same way the Count of the Private Estates paid out of the monies that came in from the domains all the officials who were employed in their administration ; and that all that remained over, after the expenses of the departments had been defrayed, was handed over to the treasury of the Count of the Sacred Largess.[3] This was the public treasury which had to supply the money required for all purposes with the four exceptions of the Emperor's privy purse, the upkeep of the administration

[1] Cp. Platnauer, *Lucius Septimius Severus*, pp. 183-184. Stein, *Stud. z. Gesch. d. byz. Reiches*, p. 169.

[2] Stein (*op. cit.* 171) is certainly right in pointing out that this transference meant the appropriation of the Cappadocian domains to the privy purse. In A.D. 379 these domains were under the *comes r. p.* (*C. Th.* vi. 30. 2). I should conjecture that the change was made in the first years of Arcadius while the powerful Eutropius was Chamberlain. The section on *praepositus s. cub.* in the west in the *Not. dig., Occ.* is lost, but there is no evidence that a corresponding change was ever made in the west, or that the Imperial domains in Africa were ever under the *praepositus*. Stein's view that the change was common to both parts of the Empire, and that in the west the *domus divina* in Africa was restored to the *comes r. p.* before A.D. 409, seems to me to be unnecessary.

[3] Or, if not handed over, that the accounts were submitted to him so that he knew the surplus on which he could draw.

of the Imperial domains, the maintenance of the civil service under the Praetorian Prefects, and the payment of the army.

It has already been observed that no figures are recorded either for the annual revenue or for the annual expenditure. We have no data to enable us to conjecture, however roughly, the yield of the mines or of the rents of the Imperial domains. There is some material for forming a minimum estimate of the money value of the land-tax in Egypt, but even here there is much uncertainty.[1] Turning to expenditure, we find that the evidence points to 500,000 or thereabouts as the lowest figure we can assume for the strength of the army in the time of Theodosius the Great. The soldiers were paid from the annona. When this payment in kind was commuted into coin, it was valued at 25 or 30 solidi a year for each soldier.[2] The annual value of the annona must then have exceeded $12\frac{1}{2}$ million solidi or nearly 8 million sterling. Of the salaries paid to the civil and military officials and their staffs we can only say that the total must have exceeded, and may have far exceeded, £400,000.[3]

From the general consideration that the population of the Empire at the lowest estimate must have been 50 millions, we might assume as the minimum figure for the revenue 50 million solidi, on the ground that in a state which was severely taxed the taxation could not have been less than 1 solidus per head.[4]

---

[1] For instance the figures as to the corn sent to Constantinople in Justinian, *Edict* 13 ; and to Rome, in the time of Augustus, in Victor, *Epitome*, c. 1 ; as to the amount of corn and of money taxes paid by Antaeopolis in the sixth century, in *Pap. Cairo*, i. No. 67057 ; and other data furnished by papyri. A figure which has been overlooked is the incidental statement in a later document, but which may come from a sixth century source, that the annual money taxes of Egypt amounted to 36,500 pounds of gold = 2,508,000 solidi ; see Διήγησις περὶ τῆς ἁγ. Σοφίας, § 25 (cp. below, Vol. II. Chap. XV. § 6).

[2] 25 solidi (*C. Th.* vii. 7. 13), 30 solidi (*Nov. Valentin.* vi. 3) were the sums which, in A.D. 397 and 443 respectively, persons liable to the furnishing of recruits might pay instead. In *Pap. Brit. Mus.* iii. 985, we have a soldier's receipt for his

pay, 30 solidi.

[3] Based on various figures given in laws of Justinian (sixth century, but rates of pay were probably much the same). Cp. above, p. 33, n. 1. We have no material for conjecturing the cost of the numerous officials subordinate to the *mag. off.* and the financial ministers ; and the chamberlains and staff of the Palaces are left entirely out of account. Bouchard (*Étude sur l'admin. des finances de l'empire romain*, p. 49) calculated that the *civil* service cost less than £250,000. Sundwall (*Weström. Studien*, p. 156) has much higher figures which seem precarious. He thinks the cost of paying the civil officials in Gaul and Italy amounted to £2,000,000. He calculates the revenue from land-taxes under Honorius as about £13,200,000 (p. 155).

[4] To illustrate this, in 1760 the population of England and Wales was over $6\frac{1}{2}$ millions, and the revenue

That would be about £31,250,000. It is probably much under the mark.

Of the financial problems with which Diocletian and Constantine had to deal, one of the most difficult was the medium of exchange. In the third century the Empire suffered from scarcity of gold. The yield of the mines had decreased ; and a considerable quantity of the precious metals was withdrawn from circulation by private people, who during that troubled period buried their treasures. But the chief cause of the scarcity was the drain of gold to the east in exchange for the Oriental wares which the Romans required. In the first century A.D. the annual export of gold to the east is said to have amounted (at the least) to a million pounds sterling.[1] The Emperors resorted to a depreciation of the coinage, and up to a certain point this perhaps was not particularly disadvantageous so far as internal trade was concerned, since the value of the metals had risen in consequence of the scarcity. When Diocletian came to the throne there was practically nothing in circulation but the double denarius, which ought to have been a silver coin (equivalent to about 1s. 9d.), but was now made of copper, with only enough silver in it to give it a whitish appearance, and worth about a halfpenny. Both Aurelian and Diocletian made attempts to establish a stable monetary system, but the solution of the problem was reserved for Constantine. The Constantinian gold *solidus* or *nomisma* remained the standard gold coin and maintained its proper weight, with little variation, till the eleventh century. Seventy-two solidi went to the pound of gold, so that its value was about twelve shillings and sixpence.[2] But the solidus was not treated as a coin in the proper sense ; and it was not received as interchangeable into so many silver or copper pieces. The pound of gold was really the standard, and, when solidi were used in ordinary transactions, they were weighed. In the payment of taxes they were accepted at their nominal value, but for other

from taxes amounted in 1762 to £6,711,000. This was about £1 a head, and the country, which was still mainly agricultural, was not overburdened. The taxation would necessarily have been much higher but for the happy expedient of the Public Debt.

[1] 100,000,000 sesterces (Pliny, *N.H.* xii. 18, § 84), of which 55,000,000 went to India. The Emperor Gratian, about A.D. 374, legislated against the export of gold, *C.J.* iv. 63. 2.

[2] The legend CONOB, which appears on solidi minted at Constantinople (till the reign of Leo III.) is an abbreviation of the name of the mint and of the word *obryzum*, refined gold.

purposes they were pieces of metal, of which the purity, not the weight, was guaranteed by the mint.[1]

§ 4. *Compulsory Social Organisation*

Diocletian and Constantine had to seek solutions not only of political but also of more difficult economic problems. The troubles of the third century, the wars both domestic and foreign, the general disorder of the State, had destroyed the prosperity of the Empire and had rapidly developed sinister tendencies, which were inherent in ancient civilisation, and legislators whose chief preoccupation was the needs of the public treasury applied methods which in some ways did more to aggravate than to mitigate the evils. We find the State threatened with the danger that many laborious but necessary occupations would be entirely abandoned, and the fields left untilled for lack of labourers. The only means which the Emperors discovered for averting such consequences was compulsion. They applied compulsion to the tillers of the soil, they applied compulsion to certain trades and professions, and they applied it to municipal service. The results were serfdom and hereditary status. The local autonomy of the municipal communities,[2] the cities and towns

---

[1] The siliqua was a silver coin $= \frac{1}{24}$th of the solidus ; but the silver coin most in use was the half-siliqua known as the *nummus decargyrus*. The silver miliarense ($= \frac{1}{1000}$ lb. gold) was, according to Babelon, in the fifth and sixth centuries a *monnaie de luxe* (cp. Justinian, *Nov.* 105. 2) ; 12 (not 14) went to the solidus. The ratio between gold and silver in A.D. 397 is given in *C. Th.* xiii. 2. 1 as 1 lb. silver $= 5$ solidi $= \frac{5}{72}$ lb. gold, and in A.D. 422, 1 lb. silver $= 4$ solidi $= \frac{1}{18}$ lb. gold (*ib.* viii. 4. 27). Thus in these 25 years the ratio changed from $1 : 14\frac{2}{5}$ to $1 : 18$, a considerable depreciation of silver. On the silver and copper coins of the fourth and fifth centuries see Babelon, *Traité des monnaies grecques et romaines*, vol. i. (1901) 566 *sqq.*, and 612 *sqq.*—It may be noted here that the ordinary rate of interest in the fourth and early fifth century was from 4 to 6 per cent. 12 per cent (the *centesima*) was the maximum allowed by law, but it would be an error to infer from the fulminations of Ambrose and Chrysostom against it that it was normal or typical in business transactions. It was only exacted in cases where there was no good security. See Billeter, *Gesch. des Zinsfusses*, 236 *sqq.* It was possibly due to clerical influence that senators were forbidden towards the end of the fourth century to lend on interest. The law was, of course, evaded and (after the fall of Chrysostom) they were allowed to receive interest up to 6 p.c. (See *C. Th.* ii. 33. 3 and 4, with the commentary of Gothofredus, vol. i. p. 274-275).

[2] J. S. Reid, *Municipalities of the Roman Empire* (1913). The early Roman Empire may be regarded " as an organisation based upon a federation of municipalities forming an aggregate of civic communities enjoying a greater or less measure of autonomy, and having certain characteristics derived from an age when state and city were convertible terms " (p. 3).

which were the true units in the structure of the Empire, had
been undermined in some ways under the Principate, but before
Diocletian no attempt had been made to impose uniformity,
and each community lived according to its own rules and
traditions. The policy of uniform taxation, which Diocletian
introduced, led to the strict control of the local bodies by the
Imperial Government. The senates and the magistrates became
the agents of the fisc ; the municipalities lost their liberties and
gradually decayed.

(1) For some centuries there had been a general tendency
to substitute free for servile labour on large estates. The
estate was divided into farms which were leased to free tenants,
coloni, on various conditions, and this system of cultivation
was found more remunerative.[1] But towards the end of the
third century the general conditions of the Empire seem to have
brought about an agrarian crisis. Many colons found themselves
insolvent. They could not pay the rent and defray the heavy
taxes. They gave up their farms and sought other means of
livelihood. Proprietors sometimes sold their lands, and the
tenants declined to hold their farms under the new owners.
Thus land fell out of cultivation and the fiscal revenue suffered.
Constantine's legislation, to solve this agrarian problem, created
a new caste. He made the colons compulsory tenants. They
were attached to the soil, and their children after them. They
continued to belong legally to the free, not to the servile, class ;
they had many of the rights of freemen, such as that of acquiring property. But virtually they were unfree and were regarded
as chattels. Severe laws prevented them from leaving their
farms, and treated those who ran away as fugitive slaves. The
conception of a colon as the chattel of his lord comes out clearly
in a law which describes his flight as an act of theft ; " he steals
his own person." [2] But the Emperors, whose principal aim in
their agrarian legislation was to guard the interests of the
revenue, protected the colons against exorbitant demands of
rent on the part of the proprietors. And if a proprietor sold
any part of his estate, he was not allowed to retain the tenants.[3]

---

[1] For the origins and history of the
colonatus, see M. Rostowzew, *Studien
zur Geschichte des römischen Kolonates*
(1910).

[2] *C.J.* xi. 48. 3, *sese . . . furari*

intelligatur. The oppression of the
colons is graphically described by
John Chrysostom, *Homilia in Matth.*
61, 31 (*P. G.* 58, 591).

[3] *C. Th.* xiii. 10. 3.

At the same time the condition of rustic slaves was improved. The government interfered here too, for the same reason, and forbade masters to sell slaves employed on the land except along with the land on which they worked.[1] This limitation of the masters' rights tended to raise the condition of the slave to that of the colon.

The proprietor's power over his tenants was augmented by the fact that the State entrusted him with the duties of collecting the taxes for which each farm was liable,[2] and of carrying out the conscription of the soldiers whom his estate was called upon to furnish. He also administered justice in petty matters and policed his domains. Thus the large proprietors formed an influential landed aristocracy, with some of the powers which the feudal lords of western Europe exercised in later times. They were a convenient auxiliary to the Government, but they were also a danger. The custom grew up for poor freemen to place themselves under the protection of wealthy landowners, who did not scruple to use their influence to divert the course of justice in favour of these clients, and were able by threats or bribery to corrupt the Government officials. Such patronage was forbidden by Imperial laws, but it was difficult to abolish it.[3]

It had long been the custom for public bodies to grant the land which they owned on a perpetual lease, subject to the payment of a ground-rent (*vectigal*). It was on this principle that Rome had dealt with conquered territory. The former proprietors continued to possess their land, but subject to the ownership (*dominium*) of the Roman people and liable to a ground-rent. In the fifth century this form of land tenure coalesced with another form of perpetual lease, *emphyteusis*, which had its roots not in Roman but in Greek history. *Emphyteusis* meant the cultivation of waste land by planting it with olives or vines or palms.[4] To encourage such cultivation a special kind of tenure had come into use. The *emphyteutes* bound himself by contract to make certain improvements on the land ; he paid a small fixed rent ; his tenure was perpetual

---

[1] *C.J.* xi. 48. 7.

[2] *C. Th.* xi. 1. 14.

[3] The evils of patronage (προστασία) are portrayed in the oration of Libanius Περὶ τῶν προστασιῶν ad-

dressed to Theodosius I. in A.D. 391 or 392 (*Or.* xlvii. ed. Förster). Cp. F. de Zulueta, *De patrociniis vicorum* (*Oxford Studies in Legal and Social History*, ed. by Vinogradoff, 1909).

[4] Cp. Rostowzew, *op. cit.* 105, 267.

and passed to his heirs, lapsing only if he failed to fulfil his contract. In the course of time, all kinds of land, not only plantation land, might be held by emphyteutic tenure. Legally this agreement did not answer fully to the Roman conception either of a lease or of a sale, and lawyers differed as to its nature. It was finally ruled that it was neither a sale nor a lease, but a contract *sui generis*.[1] This kind of tenancy was the rule on the Imperial domains. But it was also to be found on the estates of private persons.

(2) The trades to which the method of compulsion was first and most harshly applied were those on which the sustenance of the capital cities, Rome and Constantinople, depended, the skippers who conveyed the corn supplies from Africa and Egypt, and the bakers who made it into bread. These trades, like many others, had been organised in corporations or guilds (*collegia*), and as a general rule the son probably followed the father in his calling. It was the most profitable thing he could do, if his father's capital was invested in the ships or in the bakery.[2] But this changed when Diocletian required the skippers to transport the public food supplies, and made their property responsible for the safe arrival of the cargoes. They had to transport not only the supplies for the population of the capital, but the annonae for the soldiers. This was a burden which tempted the sons of a skipper to seek some other means of livelihood. Compulsion was therefore introduced, and the sons were bound to their father's calling.[3] The same principle was applied to the bakers, and other purveyors of food, on whom the State laid public burdens. In the course of the fourth century the members of all the trade guilds were bound to their occupations. It may be noticed that the workmen in the public factories (*fabricae*) were branded, so that if they fled from their labours they could be recognised and arrested.

(3) The decline of municipal life, and the decay of the well-to-do provincial citizen of the middle class, is one of the important social facts of the fourth and fifth centuries. The

---

[1] By Zeno, *C.J.* iv. 66. 1. See Justinian, *Instit.* 3, 24. This law provided that if part of an emphyteutic property became unproductive, the loss fell on the tenant; but if the whole, the owner was responsible.

[2] Seeck, *Untergang*, ii. 311.

[3] *C. Th.* xiii. 5. For the regulations about the *navicularii* see E. Gebhardt, *Das Verpflegungswesen von R. und C.* Their services in transporting corn were remunerated by 4 per cent of the cargo (*C. Th.* xiii. 5. 7).

beginnings of this process were due to general economic conditions, but it was aggravated and hastened by Imperial legislation, and but for the policy of the Government might perhaps have been arrested.

The well-to-do members of a town community, whose means made them eligible for membership of the curia or local senate and for magistracy, formed the class of *curiales*.[1] The members of the senate were called *decuriones*. But in the period of decline these terms were almost synonymous. As the numbers of the curials declined, there was not one of them who was not obliged at some time or other to discharge the unwelcome functions of a decurion. In former times it had been a coveted honour to fulfil the unpaid duties of local administration, but the legislation of the Emperors, from the end of the third century onward, rendered these duties an almost intolerable burden. The curials had now not only to perform their proper work of local government, the collection of the rates, and all the ordinary services which urban councils everywhere discharge. They had also to do the work of Imperial officials. They had to collect the land-taxes of the urban district. And they were made responsible for the full amount of taxation, so that if there were defaulters, they were collectively liable for the deficiency.[2] They had also to arrange for the supply of horses and mules for the Imperial post, the upkeep of which, though its use was exclusively confined to Government officials, was laid upon the provincials and was a most burdensome *corvée*.

The burdens laid upon the curials became heavier as their numbers diminished. Diocletian's reorganisation of the State

---

[1] For the history and organisation of the curial bodies, see Kübler's article *Decurio* in P.-W.

[2] This seems to have been the rule, though the Emperors sometimes legislated otherwise; cp. *C.J.* xi. 59. 16, *C. Th.* vii. 22. 1. The decuriones themselves seem, so far as they could, to have made those whom they appointed to collect the taxes, liable for deficiencies. The results were not only cruel to the individual, but calamitous for the community. One of the forms of patronage, described by Libanius (*op. cit.*) illustrates the difficulties of the tax - collector. Villages in the district of an urban community would place themselves under the protection of soldiers quartered in the district, who, in return for gifts in kind or corn, would help them to defy the taxgatherer and drive him out of the village. The unfortunate man might have to sell his property to make up the sum which he was required to produce. And thus the number of curials was reduced. Βουλευτὴς βουλῆς ἐξαλείφεται . . . ταῦτ' ἐλάττους ποιεῖ τὰς βουλὰς ἀντὶ μειζόνων (*ib.* 10). See also Libanius, *Or.* ii. 33-36 for the decline of the senates.

service, with innumerable officials, invited the sons of well-to-do
provincial families, who in old times would have been content
with the prospect of local honours, to embrace an official career
by which they might attain senatorial rank; and senatorial
rank would deliver them from all curial obligations.

In course of time the plight of the middle-class provincials,
who were generally owners of small farms in the neighbourhood
of their town and suffered under the heavy taxation, became so
undesirable that many of them left their homes, enlisted in the
army, took orders in the Church, or even placed themselves
under the patronage of rich proprietors in the country. The
danger was imminent that the municipal organisation would
entirely dissolve. Here again the Emperors resorted to compulsion. The condition of the curial was made a hereditary
servitude.[1] He was forbidden to leave his birthplace; if he
wanted to travel, he had to obtain leave from the provincial
governor. His sons were bound to be curials like himself;
from their birth they were, in the expressive words of an Imperial
law, like victims bound with fillets.[2] He could only escape
from his lot by forfeiting the whole or a part of his property.
Restrictions were placed on his ordinary rights, as a Roman
citizen, of selling his land or leaving it by will at his own discretion. Nothing shows the unenviable condition of the curial
class more vividly than the practice of pressing a man into the
curia as a punishment for misdemeanours.[3]

The power of the local magistrates had been diminished in
the second century by Trajan's institution of the *curator civitatis*,
whose business was to superintend the finances of the munici-
pality. The curator was indeed a townsman, but as a State
servant he had ceased to belong to the curial order and he was
appointed by the provincial governor. By the middle of the
fourth century his prestige had declined because the right of
appointing him had been transferred to the curia itself. He was
overshadowed by the new office of *defensor* instituted by Valentinian I. to protect the interests of the poorer classes against

---

[1] The principle is laid down in *C.
Th.* xii. 1. 22 (A.D. 336). This long
Title, *de decurionibus*, is a monument
of merciless despotism. The decay
of the curials is very fully treated by
Dill, *Roman Society*, Book iii. chap. ii.

[2] *Ib.* 122 *veluti dicati infulis mys-*
terium perenne custodiant. Men born
in the curial class, who entered the
army or the civil service, were sternly
" restored " to their municipal
duties, *ib.* 137, 139, 146.

[3] The practice is forbidden *ib.* 66
and 108.

the oppression of the powerful.[1] The defensor was to be appointed by the Praetorian Prefect, and he was to be a man who filled some not unimportant post in the State service. But the institution did not prove a success. It was difficult to get the right sort of people to undertake the office, and it was soon bestowed for corrupt reasons on unsuitable persons. Theodosius the Great sought to remedy this by transferring the appointment of the defensor to the curials.[2] The prestige of the office at once declined, and the defensorship like the curatorship became one more burden imposed upon the sorely afflicted curial class, without any real power to compensate for the duties which it involved. The influence of all the urban magistracies, which had become anything rather than an honour, was soon to be overshadowed by that of the bishop. And this reminds us of another feature in the decline of municipal life which deserves to be noticed.

That much-abused expression " age of transition " has a real meaning when some fundamental change forces a society to adapt itself slowly and painfully to new conditions. The period of the industrial transformation, brought about by the invention of machinery, in modern states is an example of a true age of transition. The expansion and triumph of Christianity in the third and fourth centuries rendered that period a genuine age of transition in the same sense, and the transition was marked by distress and destruction. Roman and Greek municipal life was inextricably bound up with pagan institutions—temples, cults, games. The interests and habits of the town communities were associated with these institutions, and when Christianity suppressed them, municipal life was deprived of a vital element. For the Church did not succeed in bringing her own institutions and practices into the same intimate connexion with municipal organisation.[3] With the passing of paganism something went out of the vitality of ancient town life which could never be restored.

(4) The principle of compulsion was extended to military service. The sons of veterans were obliged to follow the

---

[1] *C. Th.* i. 29. See Seeck's art., *Defensor civitatis*, in P.-W. Constantius had instituted (A.D. 361) *defensores senatus* in the provinces to protect members of the senatorial order against official oppression. *C. Th.* i. 28.

[2] *C. Th.* i. 29. 6.

[3] Cp. the excellent remarks of Vinogradoff, in *C. Med. H.* i. 554-555.

profession of their fathers, with the uninviting alternative of being enrolled in the class of decurions. They were definitely debarred from a career in the civil service. The sons of civil servants too were expected to follow the career of their fathers.[1]

We might better understand the economic conditions which the Emperors sought to regulate by tyrannical legislation if we possessed some trustworthy statistics of the population of the Empire and its various provinces. In the eighteenth century, even after Hume had exploded the old delusion that the ancient states in Europe were far more populous than the modern, Gibbon estimated the population of the Empire in the time of Claudius as 120,000,000. It is now generally agreed that this figure is far too high. Any estimate rests on a series of conjectures, but perhaps half this figure would be nearer the truth. According to a recent calculation, which is probably below rather than over the mark, the population at the death of Augustus amounted to 54,000,000, of which 26,000,000 are assigned to the western provinces including the Danubian lands, and 28,000,000 to the Greek and Oriental provinces.[2] By the beginning of the fourth century there seems some reason to suppose that the population had increased. This would be the natural result of the development of city life in Spain and Gaul, and the gradual civilisation of the Illyrian and Danubian provinces. On this basis of calculation, which, it must be repeated, involves many possibilities of error, we might conclude that in the time of Constantine the population of the Empire may have approached 70,000,000.

We have indeed some definite evidence that in the fourth century the government was not alarmed by the symptoms of a decline in numbers which had confronted the Emperor Augustus. It may be remembered that among the measures which Augustus adopted to arrest the fall in the birth-rate of Roman citizens he penalised bachelors by rendering them incapable of inheriting, and married people who were childless by allowing them to take only half of an inheritance which if they had children would

---

[1] See *C. Th.* vii. 22. 3.

[2] Beloch, *Die Bevölkerung der griechisch-römischen Welt* (cp. the Table, p. 507). His numbers for the Danubian lands are 2,000,000; for Greece, 3,000,000; for Spain, 6,000,000; for Narbonensis, 1,500,000; for the other Gallic provinces, 3,400,000. E. A. Foord has attempted to prove that in A.D. 395 the population was 120,000,000 (*Byzantine Empire*, p. 10).

fall to them entirely. It is significant that Constantine removed this disability from bachelors,[1] while Theodosius II. abrogated the law of Augustus with regard to the childless. This repeal of a law which had been so long in force may fairly be taken as an indication that in the fourth century no fears of a decline in population troubled the Imperial Government.

§ 5. *Ecclesiastical Organisation*

While in all ancient monarchies religion and sacerdotalism were a political as well as a social power, the position of the Christian Church in the Roman Empire was a new thing in the world, presenting problems of a kind with which no ruler had hitherto been confronted and to which no past experience offered a key. The history of the Empire would have been profoundly different if the Church had remained as independent of the State as it had been before Constantine, and if that Emperor and his successors had been content to throw the moral weight of their own example into the scale of Christianity and to grant to the Church the same freedom and privileges which were enjoyed by pagan cults and priesthoods. But heresies and schisms and religious intolerance on one side, and the despotic instinct to control all social forces on the other, brought about a close union between State and Church which altered the character and spirit of the State, and constituted perhaps the most striking difference between the early and the later Empire. The disorders caused by violent divisions in the Church on questions of doctrine called for the intervention of the public authorities, and rival sects were only too eager to secure the aid of the government to suppress their opponents. Hence at the very beginning Constantine was able to establish the principle that it devolved upon the Emperor not indeed to settle questions of doctrine at his own discretion, but to summon general ecclesiastical Councils for that purpose and to preside at them. The Council of Arles (A.D. 314) was convoked by Constantine, and the Ecumenical Council of Nicaea exhibited the full claim of the Emperor to be head of the Church. But in this capacity he stood outside the ecclesiastical hierarchy ; he

---

[1] *C. Th.* viii. 16. 1 (A.D. 320). In A.D. 410 Theodosius II. abrogated the law of Augustus with regard to the childless ; this applied only to the eastern half of the Empire. *Ib.* viii. 17. 2.

assumed no title or office corresponding to that of Pontifex
Maximus. Historical circumstances decided that this league
of Church and State should develop on very different lines in
the east and in the west. In the west it was to result in the
independence and ultimately in the supremacy of the Church ;
in the east the Church was kept in subordination to the head
of the State, and finally ecclesiastical affairs seem little more
than a department of the Imperial Government. Even in the
fourth century the bishop of Rome has a more independent
position than the bishop of Constantinople.

At the beginning of our period the general lines of ecclesiastical
organisation had been completed. The clergy were graded in
a hierarchical scale of seven orders—bishops, priests, deacons,
subdeacons, acolytes, exorcists, and readers. In general, the
ecclesiastical divisions closely correspond to the civil.[1] Every
city has its bishop. Every province has its metropolitan, who
is the bishop of the metropolis of the province. And above the
provincial metropolitans is the exarch, whose jurisdiction corresponds to the civil diocese. A synod of bishops is held annually
in each province.

But among the more important sees, four stood out pre-
eminent—Rome, Constantinople, Alexandria, and Antioch. Of
these Rome was acknowledged to be the first, but there was
rivalry for the second place. Besides these the See of Jerusalem
had, by virtue of its association with the birth of Christianity,
a claim to special recognition. By the middle of the fifth century
the positions of these great sees were defined, and their jurisdiction fixed. Their bishops were distinguished as Patriarchs,[2]
though the bishop of Rome did not assume this title. The
ecclesiastical map shows five great jurisdictions or Patriarchates.
The authority of Rome extended over the whole western or
Latin half of the Empire, and included the Praetorian Prefecture
of Illyricum.[3] The Patriarchate of Constantinople ultimately

---

[1] In the east this seems to have
strictly prevailed.

[2] In early times the name Patriarch
was sometimes given to simple
bishops ; cp. *J. H. S.* vi. 346 (archbishop of Hierapolis in Phrygia). See
also Cassiodorus, *Var.* ix. 15 ; and
cp. the " Patriarchate " of Aquileia.
Duchesne, *Églises séparées*, 262.

[3] The bishop of Thessalonica acted

as Vicar of the Pope in Illyricum. The
Patriarchs of Constantinople sometimes contested the Papal rights in
this prefecture ; *e.g.* Atticus, who
doubtless prompted the law of
Theodosius II., in *C. Th.* xvi. 2. 45
(A.D. 421), claiming the jurisdiction
for the Patriarch. On the whole
subject see Duchesne, *op. cit.* 229
sqq.

embraced the civil dioceses of Thrace, Pontus, and Asia.[1] The Patriarchate of Alexandria, third in precedence, corresponded to the Diocese of Egypt. The Patriarchate of Antioch comprised the greater part of the Diocese of the East; the small Patriarchate of Jerusalem the three Palestinian provinces. The autocephalous Church of Cyprus stood apart and independent.[2]

The development of a graded hierarchy among the bishops revolutionised the character of the Church. For three centuries the Christian organisation had been democratic. Its union with the monarchical state changed that. The centralised hierarchical system enabled the Emperors to control it in a way which would have been impossible if the old democratic forms had continued.

Constantine and his successors knew how to attach to themselves the powerful organisation of which they had undertaken the direction. Valuable privileges were conceded to the clergy and the churches. Above all, the clergy, like the pagan priests, were exempted from taxation,[3] a privilege which attracted many to their ranks. The churches had an unrestricted right of receiving bequests, and they inherited from the pagan temples the privilege of affording asylum.[4] The bishops received the right of acting as judges in civil cases which the parties concerned agreed to bring before them, and their decisions were without appeal.[5] It was the Imperial policy to make use of the ecclesiastical authorities in local administration, and as the old life of the urban communities declined the influence of the bishops increased. The bishop shared with the *defensor civitatis* the duty of protecting the poor against the oppression of the powerful and the exactions of government officials, and he could bring cases of wrongdoing to the ears of the Emperor himself. Ultimately he was to become the most influential person in urban administration.

The first century of Christianity in its new rôle as a state religion was marked by the development of ecclesiastical law. The canons of the Council of Nicaea formed a nucleus which was enlarged at subsequent councils. The first attempt to codify canon law was made at the beginning of the fifth century.

[1] This was settled at the Council of Chalcedon, A.D. 451.
[2] Its independence of Antioch was decreed by the Council of Ephesus A.D. 431.
[3] *C. Th.* xvi. 2. 1. 2; xi. 1. 1.
[4] *Ib.* xvi. 2. 4; *C.J.* i. 12. 2.
[5] *C. Th.* i. 27, *episcopalis audientia.*

The legislation of councils was of course only binding on the Church as such, but as time went on it became more and more the habit of the Emperors to embody ecclesiastical canons in Imperial constitutions and thus make them part of the law of the state.   It is, however, to be noticed that canon law exerted little or no effect upon the Roman civil law before the seventh century.

CONSTANTINOPLE

BOSPORUS

SYCAE
(GALATAi)

COSMEDION

GOLDEN HORN

PROPONTIS

Ch. of S. Mary
Palace of Blachernae
Gate of Xylokerkos
Gate of Chorsius
S. Saviour of Chora
Cistern
Military Gate 5
Cistern of Mocius
Gate of Romanus
Military Gate 4
Gate of Rhegium
Military Gate 3
Gate of the Pege or Selymbria
Ch. of S. Mary of the Pege
Military Gate 2
Ch. of John Baptist Studion
Golden Gate
Gate of Psamathia
Ch. of S. Diomed

Gate of the Phanar
Ch. of S. Laurentius
Ch. of the Holy Apostles
Aqueduct
Column of Marcian
Forum of Theodosius
Forum of Bous
Forum of Arcadius
Harbour of Theodosius
Gate of S. Aemilianus
Golden Gate

Gate of S. Barbara
Column of Claudius
Kynegion
Gate of Eugenius
Strategion
Gate of Neorion
Gate of Perama
Harbour of Prosphorion
Mangana
Ch. of S. Irene
Topi
ACROPOLIS
Ch. of S. Mary-Hodegetria
S. Sophia
Augusteum
Palace of Hormisdas
Harbour of Hormisdas
Great Palace
Hippodrome
S.S. Sergius and Bacchus
Basilica
Forum of Constantine
Mese
Ch. of S. Anastasia
Iron Gate
Ch. of S. Thomas
Ch. of Kontoscalion
Gate of Julian
Harbour of Julian
Amastrianus
Mese
Lycus
Wall of Constantine
Wall of Theodosius

English Miles

0   ¼   ½   ¾   1   1½

Kilometres

0   ½   1   1½   2

Emery Walker Ltd. sc.

CHAPTER III

CONSTANTINOPLE

§ 1. *Situation, Walls, and Harbours*

THE history of a thousand years approved the wisdom of
Constantine in choosing Byzantium for his new capital. A
situation was needed from which the Emperor could exercise
imminent authority over south-eastern Europe and Asia, and
could easily reach both the Danube and the Euphrates. The
water passage where Asia and Europe confront each other was
one of the obvious regions to be considered in seeking such a
central site. Its unique commercial advantages might have
been alone sufficient to decide in its favour. It was the natural
meeting-place of roads of trade from the Euxine, the Aegean,
and northern Europe. When he determined to found his city by
this double-gated barrier between seas and continents, there were
a few sites between which his choice might waver. But there
was none which in strategical strength could compare with the
promontory of Byzantium at the entrance of the Bosphorus.
It had indeed some disadvantages. The prevailing winds are
north-easterly, and the arrival of sea-borne merchandise was often
seriously embarrassed, a fact which the enemies of Constantine
did not fail to insist on.[1] The frequency of earthquakes [2] was
another feature which might be set against the wonderful
advantages of Byzantium as a place for a capital of the Empire.

While the whole trend of the passage through which the
waters of the Euxine reach the Aegean is from east to west,
the channel of the Bosphorus runs from north to south.[3] At

---

[1] Eunapius, *Vit. Aedes.* p. 23.

[2] Thirteen are recorded between
395 and 565. The most serious were
those of 447, 480, and 558.

[3] Dethier (*Der Bosphor und Cpel.*
p. 65) gives the length of the Bosphorus
as exactly 27 kils. and the narrowest
breadth between Rumili and Anatoli
Hissar as 550 metres

the point where it widens into the Propontis, the European shore is broken by a deep narrow inlet which penetrates for more than six miles and forms the northern boundary of a hilly promontory, on which Byzantium was built. This inlet or harbour was known as the Golden Horn, and it is the feature which made the fortune of Constantine's city.

The shape of Constantinople is a trapezium, but the eastern side is so short that the city may be described as a triangle with a blunted apex. On three sides, north, east, and south, it is washed by water. The area of the city " is about four miles long and from one to four miles wide, with a surface broken up into hills and plains. The higher ground, which reaches an elevation of some 250 feet, is massed in two divisions—a large isolated hill at the south-western corner of the promontory, and a long ridge, divided, more or less completely, by five cross valleys into six distinct eminences, overhanging the Golden Horn." These two masses of hill " are separated by a broad meadow through which the stream of the Lycus flows athwart the promontory into the Sea of Marmora." [1]

Constantine found the town [2] as it had been left by the Emperor Septimius Severus, who had first destroyed and then restored it. The area enclosed by his wall occupied only a small portion of the later city, lying entirely to the east of a line drawn southward from the modern bridge.[3] The central place in old Byzantium was the Tetrastoon, north of the Great Hippodrome which Severus built but left incomplete. In the

[1] Van Millingen, *Byzantine Cple.* p. 2.

[2] Besides the miscellaneous notices in histories and chronicles, the chief sources for the topography of the city are : (1) *Notitia urbis Constantinopolitanae*, an inventory of the principal buildings and monuments in each of the fourteen regions. The author says in his preface that he describes it in its perfect completion, as it has been transformed and adorned by the labours of Theodosius II. (*invicti principis*) ; and we can fix the date of its composition to A.D. 447–450, as the *double* wall of Theodosius is mentioned (p. 242 ed. Seeck). See Bury, *Eng. Hist. Review*, xxxi. p. 442 (1916). (2) The Πάτρια Κωνσταντινοπόλεως, a work of the end of the tenth century, first published by Banduri, and known as the Anonymus Banduri, but recently edited critically by Preger. The *Antiquities* of Codinus is only a corrupt copy of this work. (3) The treatise *De cerimoniis* of Constantine Porphyrogennetos (10th century). (4) Petrus Gyllius, *De topographia Constantinopoleos* (16th century). Much information is also derived from the descriptions of other foreign visitors, in the later Middle Ages, which need not be enumerated here. Of modern books the older are of little value now, except Ducange's *Constantinopolis Christiana*. For the more recent see Bibliography, II. 2, E.

[3] The wall of Severus appears not to have reached the southern coast of the promontory but to have turned eastward, south of the Hippodrome.

north-east corner rose the fortified Acropolis, on which stood
the chief temples. Against the eastern side of this hill, close
to the shore, were a theatre and amphitheatre (Kynêgion) ; on
the north a Stadion, for foot-races ; on the north-west, the
Stratêgion, an open space for military drill.

The area of Constantine's city was about four times as large.
He built a wall across the promontory from the Propontis to
the Golden Horn, about two miles to the west of the wall of
Severus. Of this wall of Constantine nothing is left, and its
course can only be traced approximately ; for within a century
the city was enlarged, a new land fortification was built, and
the founder's wall was allowed to fall into decay and gradually
disappeared.[1]

The New Rome, as Constantinople was called, dissimilar as
it was from the Old in all its topographical features, was nevertheless forced to resemble it, or at least to recall it, in some
superficial points. It was to be a city of seven hills and of
fourteen regions. One of the hills, the Sixth, lay outside
the wall of Constantine, on the Golden Horn, and had a fortification of its own. This was the Fourteenth Region. The
Thirteenth Region lay on the northern side of the Horn (in
Galata) and corresponded to the Region beyond the Tiber in
Rome.[2]

Constantine was more successful perhaps than he had hoped
in attracting inhabitants to his eastern capital. Constantinople
was dedicated in A.D. 330 (May 11),[3] and in the lifetime of two
generations the population had far outgrown the limits of the
town as he had designed it. The need of greater space was met
partly by the temporary expedient of filling up the sea, here
and there, close to the shore, and a suburban town was growing

[1] One of the gates, the Porta Aurea
(also called Old Gate), survived the
Turkish conquest and was destroyed
by an earthquake in 1508. The Turks
knew it as Isa Kapussi. Van Millingen,
ib. 21, 30.
[2] Other points of resemblance were
the proximity of the Great Palace to
the Hippodrome, recalling that of the
Circus Maximus to the palaces of the
Palatine ; and the erection of a
building called the Capitolium on the
Second Hill. The Milion in the
Augusteum corresponded to the Mil-

iarium in the Roman Forum. As
Rome had a hieratic name, Flora, so
the personified city of Constantinople
had a corresponding secret name
Anthûsa (Flowering). See John Lydus,
De mens. iv. 25, 50, 51 ; Stephanus
Byz. *s.v.* Συκαί ; Paulus Silent. *Hagia
Sophia*, v. 156 χρυσοχίτων 'Ανθοῦσα.
In *Chron. Pasch.*, *s.a.* 328, it is said
that the Tyche or personification of
the city was named Anthusa.
[3] The Encaenia of the city were
celebrated annually on this date. Cp.
Hesychius, *Patria*, p. 154.

up outside the Constantinian wall.[1]   The desirability of enlarging
the city was forced upon the government,[2] and early in the
reign of Theodosius II. the matter was taken in hand.   Anthemius, Praetorian Prefect of the East and pilot of the State
during the Emperor's minority, may be called, in a sense, the
second founder of Constantinople ; the stones of his great wall
still stand, an impressive monument of his fame.

The new line of circuit was drawn about a mile to the west
of the old.   The Anthemian wall did not extend the whole way
from sea to sea.   It was planned so as to take advantage of the
fortification round the Sixth Hill, within which the Palace of
Blachernae stood, but this north-western quarter of the city
has been so changed, partly by subsequent constructions and
partly by demolition, that it is impossible, at least without
systematic excavation, to determine how the line of defence
ran in the fifth century.[3]

The wall which was constructed under the auspices of Anthemius (A.D. 413) [4] sustained extensive damages from an earthquake in A.D. 447.   It was then restored and strengthened by
the exertions of the Praetorian Prefect Constantine, and a new
outer wall was erected.[5] At this time the city might have been
exposed at any moment to an attack of the Huns, and the
whole work was executed with incredible rapidity in the course
of a few months.

The fortification, thus completed and enlarged, was never
afterwards structurally altered.   It consists of five parts.   The
inner wall, which was the main defence, had a mean thickness
of about 14 feet, and was strengthened by ninety-six towers,
60 feet high, about 60 yards apart.   Each tower had two
chambers, of which the upper, entered from the parapet of the
wall, contained munitions, and was always occupied by watch-

---

[1] Cp. Himerius, *Or.* vii. 7, p. 522
(reign of Julian).   For the growth of
the population in the fourth century
compare Zosimus 2, 35 ; Eunapius,
Vit. Aedes, p. 22 ; Sozomen, ii. 3.

[2] Themistius said (*Or.* 18, p. 223),
in A.D. 384, that "if the city goes on
growing as it has recently, it will
require next year a new circuit of
wall."

[3] See the interesting discussion in
van Millingen, *op. cit.* chap. viii.

[4] Cp. *C. Th.* xv. 1. 51 ; Socrates,
H.E. vii. 1.

[5] The building of the wall in sixty
days is recorded in inscriptions, of
which two, one in Latin, the other in
Greek hexameters, are still to be read
on the Porta Rhegii.   The Latin runs :

Theodosii iussis, gemino nec mense peracto,
Constantinus ouans haec moenia firma
     locauit.
tam cito tam stabilem Pallas uix conderet
     arcem.

See van Millingen, *op. cit.* p. 47.

men. Between the inner and the outer wall was a terrace (*peribolos*) from 50 to 64 feet broad. The outer wall was only 2 to 6½ feet thick, and it was built for the most part in arches; it too had ninety-six towers, varying from 30 to 35 feet in height. Outside the wall was an embankment,[1] 61 feet broad; and outside the embankment a ditch, of varying depth,[2] also 61 feet broad, and divided by low dams.

The fortification was pierced by ten gates, of which five were exclusively for military purposes. The two sets, civil and military, were arranged alternately. The chief and most famous entrance, nearest to the Sea of Marmora, was the Golden Gate. It may have been erected by Theodosius the Great as a triumphal arch in memory of his victory over the rebel Maximus. This imposing structure was pierced by three archways and was built of huge square blocks of polished marble. Above the central archway, on either front, it bore the following inscription in metal:

> haec loca Theudosius decorat post fata tyranni.
> aurea saecla gerit qui portam construit auro.[3]

This designation of the arch as a gate suggests that Theodosius may have already contemplated the enclosure of the city by a new wall.[4]

The other four public gates were those known by the names of Melantias, Rhegion, St. Romanus, and Charisius.[5] The stretch of wall descending from the Gate of St. Romanus into the valley

---

[1] Τὸ ἔξω παρατείχιον.

[2] It is still 22 feet deep in front of the Golden Gate.

[3] The legend is quoted by Sirmond in the fifteenth century, and has recently been confirmed by the discovery of holes in the stones, in which the metal letters were fixed, by Strzygowski; see *Jahrb. des k. deutschen arch. Instituts*, Bd. viii. (1893).

[4] Against the view (of Strzygowski) stated in the text, E. Weigand (*Das Goldene Tor*, in *Ath. Mitt.* xxxix. 1 *sqq.*) has argued that *Theudosius* is Theodosius II. and the tyrant John (see below, p. 222), that *decorat*, *construit auro*, mean gilding, not building, and that the structure was originally built as a gate of the Anthemian wall.

[5] The road issuing from the Porta Melantiados led to Melantias and Selymbria. In later times it was called the Gate of Selybria and is now known as Selivri Kapussi. Since the later fifth century it was also known as the Gate of the Pêgê, from a holy well close at hand. The Gate of Rhegion (named from the town on the Marmora at Kuchuk Chekmeje) was also known as Porta Rusia (a reference to the Red Faction of the circus). The Gate of Romanus is that known to the Turks as Top Kapussi (Cannon Gate). The most northerly gate, that of Charisius, was also called the Gate of Polyandrion from the cemetery which lay outside the city near this point. The traveller to Hadrianople would quit the city by this egress, and it is called by the Turks the Gate of Hadrianople (Edirne Kapussi).

of the Lycus, and then ascending to the Gate of Charisius, was known as the Mesoteichion or Middle Wall, and when the city was attacked the enemy usually selected it as the most vulnerable portion of the defences. The gates divided the wall into six sections, each of which had its own division of the garrison, distinguished as the First, the Second, and so on. In each section, except in the short one between the Golden Gate and the sea which was manned by the First division, there was a military gate giving access to the terrace, and these gates were distinguished by the number of the division. Thus the military gate between the Porta Aurea and the Porta Melantiados was known as the gate of the Second.[1] The gate of the Sixth, north of the Porta Charisii, was called the gate of the Xylokerkos, from a wooden circus which was near it.

It was twenty-five years after the completion of the wall of Anthemius that the sea-walls of the Constantinian city were extended along the Golden Horn and the Marmora to join the new line of fortification. This work seems to have been carried out under the direction of Cyrus, Prefect of the city, in A.D. 439.[2]

The Thirteenth Region, beyond the Golden Horn, known as Sycae, and subsequently as Galata,[3] was not fortified, and, though formally a part of the city, it was virtually a suburb. The regular communication with this region was by ferry,[4] but the Golden Horn was also crossed by a wooden bridge of which the southern end was at Blachernae.[5] In the sixth century this was replaced by a bridge of stone.

The Golden Horn itself was the great port of Constantinople. But there were also small harbours on the Propontis. At the end of the fourth century there were two : the Harbour of Eleutherius or of Theodosius,[6] and farther east the Harbour of Julian, also known as the New Harbour, and after the sixth

---

[1] 'Η πύλη τοῦ δευτέρου. It is convenient in modern languages to call these gates the Second, Third, etc., military gate ; but the true nomenclature prevents us from asking the question, where was the First ?

[2] *Chron. Pasch.*, *sub a*. Cyrus was afterwards credited with the subsequent additions to the land wall which were due to the Prefect Constantine, and has even been identified with him. Cp. van Millingen, p. 48.

[3] We do not meet this, the modern name of the region, before the eighth century. See Theophanes, A.M. 6209 (A.D. 717).

[4] The ferry started close to the Arsenal, near the modern outer bridge. A gate in the sea wall at this point was called the Gate of the Ferry (τοῦ περάματος).

[5] *Pontem sublicium siue ligneum*, *Not. urb. Cpl.* p. 241. The stone bridge was built by Justinian, *Chron. Pasch.*, *sub a*. 528.

[6] At Vlanga Bostan.

century as the Harbour of Sophia.[1] At these wharves the corn-
ships from Egypt were probably unloaded, for between them
were situated the Alexandrine grain magazines.[2] In the fifth
century the Harbour of Eleutherius, which Theodosius the Great
had improved and honoured with his own name, was filled up and
disused, but a small new harbour was built near it known as the
Portus Caesarii.[3] It was probably not till a later period, but
before the end of the sixth century, that the port of Hormisdas
(afterwards known as that of Bucoleon) was constructed.[4] These
small harbours on the Propontis were a great convenience, indeed
a necessity. For the frequently prevailing north winds often
rendered it very difficult for ships to round the promontory and
enter the Golden Horn. In that gulf the chief landing-place
was the Portus Prosphorianus, also called the Bosporion, under
the Acropolis and close to the Arsenal.

§ 2. *Topography and Buildings*

In founding a new city, one of the first things which the
practical Romans provided was an abundant supply of water.
The construction of aqueducts was a branch of engineering which
they had brought to perfection, and it was a task of little difficulty
to bring in water from the northern hills. A ruined bit of the
old aqueduct is still a striking object in the centre of the city.[5]
Many reservoirs and cisterns, both open and covered, supplied
the inhabitants with water ;[6] and, a hundred years after the

---

[1] At Kadriga Limani.

[2] *Horrea Alexandrina*, also the *Horreum Theodosianum*, in the Ninth Region.

[3] Perhaps in the reign of Leo I. Van Millingen would identify this harbour with that which in later times was called Heptaskalon (seven piers), *op. cit.* 301 *sqq.*

[4] Another harbour, the Konto-skalion (short-pier), is first mentioned in the eleventh century. Van Millingen locates it between the harbours of Caesarius and Julian.

[5] An extension built by Valens A.D. 368.

[6] The remains of the cisterns have been studied in full detail by Strzygowski and Forchheimer, *Die Wasser-behälter Cpels.* Strzygowski has identified the Cisterna Modestiaca (A.D.

369) with Sarrâdshchane, near the aqueduct of Valens. The Cist. Aetii (*c.* A.D. 368) was on the Sixth Hill near the Tekfur Serai; the Cist. Theodosiana near the mosque of Valideh. The Cist. Asparis (A.D. 459) is probably Kara Gumrûk, in north-west of the city, outside the Constantinian wall. The Cist. S. Mocii is Exi Marmara (see plan).

All these were open reservoirs. Of the covered may be mentioned Cist. Maxima, in the Forum of Constantine, and Cist. Philoxeni, near this Forum, neither of which has been discovered ; Cist. Basilica (built by Justinian), adjoining the Basilica, identified (with certainty) with the Yeri Batan Serai; and Cist. Illi (A.D. 528), identified with Bin Bir Derek (=1001 pillars), W. of the Hippodrome.

foundation of the city, there were eight public baths (*thermae*), and 153 private baths in the fourteen Regions.[1]

Constantine accorded to the citizens of his new capital the same demoralising privilege which Rome had so long enjoyed, a free supply of bread at the public expense. The granaries of Africa were still appropriated to the needs of Rome ; the fruitful lands of the Nile supplied Constantinople. There were five corn-stores ; there were twenty public bakeries, and 117 " steps," from which the bread was distributed to the people, in different parts of the city.[2]

A visitor to Constantinople soon after its foundation would have been struck by the fact that there was no public sign of pagan worship. The gods of Greece and Rome were conspicuously absent. If he were a pagan, he might walk to the Acropolis and gaze sadly on the temples of Apollo, Artemis, and Aphrodite, in which the men of old Byzantium had sacrificed, and which Constantine had dismantled but allowed to stand as relics of the past.[3] From its very inauguration the New Rome was ostensibly and officially Christian.[4] Nor did the statue of the founder, as a sun-god, compromise his Christian intention. In the centre of the oval Forum, which he laid out on the Second Hill just outside the wall of old Byzantium, he erected a high column with porphyry drums, on the top of which he placed a statue of Apollo, the work of an old Greek master, but the head of the god was replaced by his own. It was crowned with a halo of seven rays, and looked towards the rising sun.[5] The column, blackened by time and fire, and injured by earthquakes, still stands,[6] the one monument of the founder which has survived. Within the pedestal beneath Constantine is said to have placed the Palladium of Rome and several Christian relics.

Lofty columns, as Imperial monuments, were a feature of

[1] See *Not. urb. Cpl.*

[2] 80,000 loaves were distributed daily. Socrates, ii. 13.

[3] John Malalas, xiii. p. 324. Theodosius I. turned the temple of Aphrodite into a coachhouse for the chariot of the Praet. Prefect, *ib.* 345.

[4] Augustine, *De civ. Dei*, v. 25 ; Eusebius, *Vit. Const.* iii. 48. There is, however, no reason to reject the statement that Constantine consulted the advice of astronomers in laying out the city (John Lydus, *De mens.* iv. 25).

[5] Constantine Rhodios (in his poem on the Church of the Apostles, 71 *sqq.*, in *Revue des Études grecques*, ix.) quotes four verses, as an inscription on this column, dedicating the City to Christ. But they are certainly not of the Constantinian epoch.

[6] It is commonly known as the Burnt Column. The Turks call it Chemberli Tash, hooped pillar.

Constantinople as of Rome. Theodosius the Great, Arcadius, Marcian, Justinian, all had their memorial pillars like Trajan and Marcus Aurelius. That of Marcian, the least interesting, still towers in the centre of the city ; [1] and the site of the sculptured column of Arcadius, erected by his son, is marked by the ruins of its high pedestal.

The Tetrastoon (Place of the Four Porticoes), on the First Hill, was the centre of old Byzantium. Constantine laid it out anew, and renamed it the *Augusteum* in honour of his mother, the Augusta Helena, whose statue he set up here.[2] Around it were grouped the buildings which played a principal part in the political life and history of the city. On the north side was the Great Church dedicated to St. Sophia, the Holy Wisdom, which was perhaps founded by Constantine, and certainly completed by his son Constantius.[3] On the east was the Senate-house, a basilica with the customary apse at the eastern end. On the south was the principal entrance to the Imperial Palace, and near it the Baths of Zeuxippus.[4] The Augusteum was entered from the west, and here was the Milion (Milestone), a vaulted monument, from which the mileage was measured over the great network of roads which connected the most distant parts of the European provinces with Constantinople.[5]

---

[1] South of the Mosque of Mohammad the Conqueror. Incisions on the pedestal have made it possible to recover the inscription :

principis hanc statuam Marciani cerne
    torumque
Tercius vovit quod Tatianus opus.

The column which stands near the N.E. shore of the promontory, under the Acropolis, probably commemorated the victory of Claudius Gothicus over the Goths. It bears the inscription *Fortunae reduci ob devictos Gothos*.

[2] *Chron. Pasch.*, *sub a.* 328 ; Hesychius, *Patria*, 40, 2. The site of the Augusteum is the place which the Turks call Aya Sofia Atmeïdan.

[3] Dedicated in 360, Socrates, *H.E.* ii. 43. For the later sources ascribing the foundation to Constantine, see Antoniades, Ἔκφρασις τῆς ἁγ. Σοφίας, i. 3. Close to St. Sophia was St. Irene, which was certainly built by Constantine, Socrates, i. 16, ii. 16.

[4] Built by Severus, improved and adorned with statues by Constantine.

The Zeuxippus was between the Augusteum and the Hippodrome, but did not touch the Hippodrome, as we know that there was a house, and therefore probably a passage, between. See the epigram of Leontius, *Anth. Pal.* ix. 65. It seems likely that this passage is meant by the Diabatika of Achilleus, through which the Hippodrome could be reached from the Palace gate. The Achilleus was probably a statue (Bieliaev, *Byzantina*, i. p. 132), not a bath as some have supposed. The Zeuxippus was in the Augusteum, for acc. to *Chron. Pasch.*, *sub* 197, it was in the middle of the Tetrastoon. Ebersolt places it outside the Aug. on his plan ; but p. 20 places it " between the Chalkê and the Milion."

[5] Ebersolt supposes that the Augusteum was entered through gates (*Le Grand Palais*, p. 15). But the evidence relates only to a very late period (Nicolaus Mesarites, ed. Heisenberg, p. 21 ; beginning of thirteenth century).

Passing the Milion one entered the great central thoroughfare of the city, the Mesê or Middle Street, which led, through the chief Fora and public places, direct to the Golden Gate.   Descending the First and ascending the Second Hill, it passed on the right the palace of the rich eunuch Lausus,[1] which was a museum of art, and on the left the Praetorium, where the Prefect of the city administered justice.[2]   Then it reached the oval Forum of Constantine, generally known as " the Forum," on the north side of which was the second Senate-house.   Continuing our way westward we reach the Forum of Taurus, adorned with the column of Theodosius the Great, which could be ascended by an interior staircase.   In close proximity to this space was the Capitolium, in which, when a university was established, lecture-rooms were assigned to the professors.[3]   Just beyond the Forum was a monument known as the Philadelphion,[4] perhaps an archway, where an important main street branched off, leading to the Church of the Holy Apostles and to the Gate of Charisius. Following Middle Street one passed through a place called the Amastrianos, and then bearing south-westward reached the Forum of Bous, so named from an oven shaped like an ox, in which calumnious legend said that Julian the Apostate had burned Christians.[5]   The street soon ascended the Sixth Hill and, passing through the Forum of Arcadius,[6] reached the old Golden Gate in the wall of Constantine.   Just outside this gate was the Exakionion, perhaps a pillar with a statue of Constantine, which gave its name to the locality.[7]   Farther on, before reaching the Golden Gate of Theodosius, a street diverged leading to the Gate of Pêgê.

Many streets must have diverged from this thoroughfare, both northwards and southwards, but only for three have we direct evidence : the two already mentioned leading one to the Pêgê

---

[1] He lived in the reign of Theodosius II.

[2] The section of the street between the Augusteum and the Forum was called the Regia (Royal Street). The colonnades on either side had been built by Constantine and were adorned with statues and marbles.   *Chron. Pasch.*, *sub a.* 328. There seem to have been colonnades (ἔμβολοι) along the whole length of the Mesê.

[3] See below, p. 231.

[4] It is said to have been so called from a representation, apparently plastic, of the meeting of the three sons of Constantine after their father's death.   See *Patria*, p. 177.

[5] *Ib.* 180.

[6] Now called the Evret Bazaar. The Sixth Hill was known as the Xerolophos.

[7] " The Exakionion was a land wall built by the great Constantine. . . . Outside it stood a pillar with a statue of C. ;   hence the name," *Patria*, p. 180.

Gate, the other to the Church of the Apostles, and a third close to the Augusteum, which conducted to the Basilica and the quarter of the Bronzesmiths (Chalkoprateia),[1] where the Empress Pulcheria built a famous church to the Mother of God. The site of the Basilica or law-court can be determined precisely, for the Emperor Justinian constructed beside it an immense covered cistern, which is still preserved,[2] a regular underground pillared palace, well described by its Turkish name Yeri Batan Sarai. Julian had endowed the Basilica with a library of 150,000 books, and it was the haunt of students of law.[3] The proximity of the cistern seems to have inspired an anonymous writer to pen the following epigram : [4]

> This place is sacred to Ausonian law ;
> Here wells a spring abundant, here a rill
> Of legal lore, that all who run may draw
> And studious throngs of youth may drink their fill.

The Church of the Holy Apostles stood in the centre of the city, on the summit of the Fourth Hill.[5] It was built in the form of a basilica by Constantine, and completed and dedicated by his son Constantius.[6] Contiguous to the east end Constantine erected a round mausoleum, to receive the bodies of himself and his descendants.[7] He placed his own sarcophagus in the centre, and twelve others (the number was suggested by the number of the Apostles) to right and left. This mausoleum remained intact till the Turkish conquest, and many emperors were laid to rest in it ; but the church itself was rebuilt in the sixth century. In its new form it was the most magnificent ecclesiastical building in Constantinople, next to St. Sophia, but it was less fortunate than its greater rival. After the Turkish conquest it was destroyed to make room for the mosque of Mohammad the

---

[1] Cp. Bury, *The Nika Riot*, p. 111.

[2] Technical description in Forchheimer and Strzygowski, *op. cit.* 212 *sqq.*

[3] Cp. Agathias, iii. 1.

[4] *Anth. Pal.* ix. 660.

[5] This hill was called Μεσόλοφον (central hill), and hence popularly Μεσόμφαλον (navel), *Patria*, p. 219.

[6] It is described by Eusebius, *Vit. Const.* iv. 58. See Heisenberg, *Apostelkirche*, 99, 110.

[7] The mausoleums of Diocletian at Salona, of Augustus and Hadrian at Rome, would have naturally suggested the idea. Cp. Schultze, *Konstantinopel*, 13, 15. Heisenberg (*op. cit.* 100, 116), however, thinks that Constantine only contemplated his own burial in the rotunda, that the other twelve sarcophagi were meant as cenotaphs of the Apostles, and that Constantius converted the building into an Imperial mausoleum. The question is difficult, and depends on the interpretation of some phrases in Eusebius, *loc. cit.*

Conqueror, and no vestige remains of it or of the imperial
burying-place.

§ 3. *The Imperial Palaces*

The Great Palace lay east of the Hippodrome. Ultimately it
was to occupy almost the whole of the First Region, extending
over the terraced slopes of the first hill down to the sea-shore.[1]
Thus gradually enlarged from age to age it came to resemble the
mediæval palaces of Japan or the Kremlin at Moscow,[2] and
consisted of many isolated groups of buildings, throne rooms,
reception halls, churches, and summer houses amid gardens and
terraces. But the original palace which was designed for Constantine, and to which few or no additions were made till the
sixth century, was of more modest dimensions. It was on the
top and upper slopes of the hill, and was perhaps not much
larger than the fortified residence which Diocletian built for himself at Salona.[3] It is reasonable to suppose that the two palaces
resembled each other in some of their architectural features; but
the plan of the palace at Salona can hardly serve as a guide for
attempting to reconstruct the palace at Constantinople ; [4] for not
only were the topographical conditions different, but the arrangements requisite in the residence of a reigning sovereign could not
be the same as those which sufficed for a prince living in retirement. It is indeed not improbable that Constantine's palace, like
Diocletian's, was rectangular in form. It was bounded on the
west by the Hippodrome, on the north by the Augusteum, and
on this side was the principal entrance.[5] This gate was known
as the Chalkê, called so probably from the bronze roof of the
vestibule. Immediately inside the entrance were the quarters
of the Scholarian guards, and here one may notice a resemblance
to the palace of Diocletian, in which the quarters of the guards

---

[1] Its northern limit near the shore
was marked by the Topoi, a place
which has been identified by a tier
of seats. See van Millingen, *op. cit.*
p. 256.

[2] Or the Turkish Seraglio which
replaced it.

[3] For the construction and plan of
this palace see Hébrard and Zeiller,
Spalato.

[4] Ebersolt was influenced by the
plan of Spalato in his conjectural plan

of Constantine's Palace, but I have
shown that his reconstruction does
not conform to our actual data (see
B.Z. 21, 210 *sqq.*). He has also
sought analogies at the palace of
Mschatta in Syria.

[5] Over this entrance was a painting
representing the triumph of Christianity. Constantine with a cross
above his head was depicted with
his sons, and at their feet a dragon
pierced by a dart sank into the abyss.

were close to the chief entrance, the Porta Aurea.[1] On the
western side of the enclosure, towards the Hippodrome, was a
group of buildings specially designated as the Palace of Daphne,
of which the two most important were the Augusteus, a throne
room, on the ceiling of which was represented a large cross
wrought in gold and precious stones,[2] and the Hall of the Nineteen
Akkubita, which was used for ceremonial banquets.[3] It is
possible that the Tribunal, a large open terrace, lay in the centre
of the precincts.   On the eastern side were the Consistorium,[4] or
Council Chamber, the Chapel of the Lord,[5] and the quarters of
the Candidati and the Protectors.[6]

If all these buildings, with other apartments and offices,[7] were,
as seems not improbable, arranged symmetrically in a rectangular
enclosure, there was outside this enclosure another edifice contiguous and in close communication, which might be regarded
either as a separate palace or as part of the Great Palace.   This
was the Magnaura.[8] It was situated on the east side of the
Augusteum, close to the Senate-house, and the passage which
connected the Great Palace with the precincts of the Magnaura
was near the Chapel of the Lord.

On the sea-shore to the south of the Palace was the House of

---

[1] On the right side of the entrance.
At Constantinople the Scholarian
quarters were in front of the entrance
and were traversed in order to reach
the interior of the Palace.

[2] The Augusteus is referred to by
Eusebius in *Vit. Const.* iii. 49, and
iv. 66.

[3] But this hall consisted of two
parts, probably separated by curtains,
one on a higher level in which the
banquets were held, and the other a
reception hall (triklinos). The building is ascribed to Constantine in
Patria, p. 144.

[4] Probably a rectangular building
like the Consistorium at Mschatta.
It was used not only for meetings of
the Council but also for the reception
of embassies and other functions.
In later times there was also a smaller
Consistorium for use in winter.

[5] Ὁ Κύριος. Ascribed to Constantine
(*Patria*, p. 141). It contained relics of
the true cross.

[6] These porticoes (*Chron. Pasch.*,
loc. cit.) were probably replaced in the
same area by the Halls of the Ex-

cubitors and the Candidati after
A.D. 532.

[7] Ebersolt has not made due
allowance in his plan for the private
apartments of the Emperor and of
the Empress, or for the quarters of
the Chamberlains and numerous
palace officials.   The Master of
Offices must have had a bureau in
the Palace; likewise the two ministries
of finance and the treasuries were
doubtless within the precincts.   He
tacitly assumes that the Palace of
Constantine as a whole remained
intact when later additions were
made and the Imperial family ceased
to reside in Daphne. This assumption
seems to be unwarranted.   It is
probable that many of Constantine's
constructions were removed in later
times to make way for others.

[8] See *Patria*, p. 144.   The great
Hall of the Magnaura was a basilica
with three naves.   In the tenth
century it was a very magnificent
building, but we cannot be sure that
the descriptions of it apply to earlier
times.

Hormisdas, which Constantine the Great is said to have assigned as a dwelling to Hormisdas, a Persian prince who had fled to him for protection. In later times this house was enclosed within the grounds of the Great Palace.[1] The sea-shore and the lower slopes of the hill, for a long time after the foundation of the city, were covered with the private houses of rich senators, which were destined gradually to disappear as the limits of the Imperial residence were extended.[2]

There was another Imperial Palace at Blachernae, in the north-west of the city. We know little of it in early times, but in the thirteenth century it superseded the Great Palace as the home of the Emperors.[3]

Much more important in the fourth and fifth centuries was the Palace of Hebdomon on the shore of the Propontis not far from the Golden Gate. The place has been identified with Makri Keui, which is distant exactly seven Roman miles from the Augusteum.[4] Here there was a plain suitable for a military encampment, and it was called, in reminiscence of Rome, the Campus Martius. The Emperor Valens built a Tribune [5] for the use of the Emperor when he was reviewing troops, and to him we may probably attribute the foundation of the palace which was afterwards enlarged or rebuilt by Justinian. The place was sanctified by several churches, especially that of the Prophet Samuel containing his remains, and that of John the Baptist which Theodosius I. built to receive the sacred relic of the saint's head.[6] All the emperors who were elevated at New Rome from Valens to Zeno and Basiliscus were crowned and acclaimed at the Hebdomon. The Campus Martius was to witness many historical scenes, and more than once when the city was visited by earthquakes the panic-stricken populace found it a convenient refuge.

[1] The façade of the House of Hormisdas on the sea-shore is still preserved (generally known as the House of Justinian, who resided there before his accession). About 100 yards from here there were till recently remains of another imperial edifice. Both buildings doubtless formed parts of the Palace of Bucoleon. See van Millingen, p. 275 *sqq.*

[2] The author of the *Notitia* of Constantinople describes the First Region as *regiis nobiliumque domiciliis clara*, and enumerates 118 mansions.

[3] It is mentioned in the *Notitia*. For the position of the palace see van Millingen, 128 *sq.*

[4] See van Millingen, chap. xix. ; Bieliaev, *Byzantina*, iii. p. 57 *sqq.*

[5] Van Millingen takes it for granted (p. 326) that the harbour was the little bay east of Makri Keui, but Bieliaev thinks that it was at Makri Keui itself, houses and gardens now covering the place where were once the waters and quays of the port.

[6] Sozomen, vii. 24.

§ 4. *The Hippodrome*

The site of the Hippodrome corresponds to the modern Atmeïdan, which is the Turkish equivalent of the word, and its orientation (N.N.E. to S.S.W.) is exactly marked by three monuments which lay in its axis and still stand in their original positions. Of its general structure and arrangements we can form an idea from what we know of the Circus Maximus at Rome, which seems to have served as its model when it was designed and begun by Septimius Severus before the end of the second century.[1] But it was of smaller dimensions,[2] and, completed by Constantine, it had many peculiarities of its own. As there was not enough level ground on the hill, the southern portion, which terminated in a semicircle (the *sphendone*), was suspended on massive vaults, which can still be seen. The nature of the site determined an important difference from the arrangement of the Circus Maximus. There the main entrances were at the semicircular extremity ; here this was impossible, and the main entrances (if there was more than one) were on the western side.

At the northern end, as at Rome, were the *carceres*, stalls for the horses and chariots, and storehouses for all the appurtenances of the races and spectacles. But above this structure, which was an indispensable part of all Roman racecourses, arose the Kathisma, the unique and characteristic feature of the Hippodrome of Constantinople. This edifice, apparently erected by Constantine, was a small " palace " with rooms for the accommodation of the Emperor, communicating with the Great Palace by a spiral staircase.[3] In front of it was the Imperial " box,"

---

[1] Descriptions of the building will be found in Labarte and Oberhummer, *opp. citt.* ; in Murray's *Handbook to Constantinople* (the part written by van Millingen), pp. 39 *sqq.* ; in Grosvenor's *Constantinople*, i. 319 *sqq.* (a minute reconstruction, of which many details cannot be substantiated); in Paspatès, *Great Palace*, 38 *sqq.*

[2] The dimensions of the Circus are given by Pollack (*Circus Maximus*, in Pauly-Wiss.) as follows : length of course = 590 metres (2000 Roman feet) ; length of building including *carceres* and semicircle = 635 mm. ; breadth of arena = 80 mm. ; breadth of building = 150 mm. Van Millingen estimates the Hippodrome as " be-

tween 1200 and 1300 feet in length and about half as wide." Grosvenor makes it longer and narrower (1382 feet long, 395 feet wide). Van Millingen has probably exaggerated the width, but it is not unlikely that the area occupied by the seats was larger in the Hippodrome than in the Circus Maximus.

[3] The earliest mention of the staircase (κοχλίας) is in *Chron. Pasch., s.a.* 380. It is not clear whether the door of Decimus, which is connected with it here, was at the bottom or the top. The Kathisma could also be reached from the Hippodrome itself, as is clear from the story of the Nika riot in A.D. 532.

from which the Emperors watched the races—the *Kathisma* or seat which gave its name to the whole building. Immediately below the palace there was a place, probably raised above the level of the course and known as the *Stama*,[1] which was perhaps occupied during the spectacles by Imperial guards.

Down the middle of the racecourse ran the *spina* (backbone), a long low wall at either end of which were the goals round which the chariots had to turn. The length of a race was generally seven circuits, and it is probable that the same device was used at Constantinople as at Rome for helping the spectators to remember at any moment the number of circuits already accomplished. At one extremity of the *spina* seven dolphins were conspicuously suspended, at the other seven eggs—emblems respectively of Neptune and of Castor and Pollux, deities associated with horses. As the foremost chariot passed the turning-point, an attendant removed a dolphin or an egg. The *spina* was adorned by works of art, and three of these ornaments have survived the Turkish conquest. An ancient Egyptian obelisk of Thothmes III., which had been brought from Heliopolis, was placed at the central point of the *spina* by Theodosius the Great, on a pedestal with bas-reliefs representing the Emperor and his family witnessing races.[2] The choice of the position for this monument was doubtless suggested by the fact that Augustus had placed in the centre of the *spina* of the Roman Circus the obelisk which now stands in the Piazza del Popolo. South of the memorial of Theodosius is a more illustrious relic of history, the bronze pillar shaped of three serpents whose heads had once supported the gold tripod which the Greeks dedicated to Apollo at Delphi after the great deliverance of Plataea. Constantine had carried it off from Delphi when he despoiled Hellas to adorn

[1] Also known as the Pi. See Constantine Porph. *Cer.* i. 69, pp. 310, 338; 92, p. 423.

[2] The obelisk is 60 feet high. The bas-relief on the north side represents (1) below—the erection of the obelisk; (2) above—the Kathisma with upper and lower balconies; Theodosius with his two sons is seated in the upper, on either side are courtiers and guards. On the east: (1) above—Kathisma, as before; Theodosius holds crown for the victor in a race, and in the lower balcony are a number of persons, including musicians; (2) below—a Latin inscription recording the erection of the obelisk. On the south: (1) above—Kathisma, Imperial family in upper balcony, courtiers in the lower; in front on steps two *mandatores*, addressing the people for the Emperor; (2) below—a chariot race. On the west: (1) above—Kathisma, Imperial family in upper balcony, barbarians bringing tribute in lower; (2) below—a Greek inscription on the erection of the obelisk. These reliefs supply some material for a conjectural construction of the front of the Kathisma.

his new capital. The third monument, which stands farther south, is a column of masonry, which originally rose to the height of 94 feet and was covered with plates of gleaming bronze. The bronze has gone, and the upper half of the pillar.[1] There were many statues and works of art, not only along the *spina*, but in other parts of the Hippodrome, especially in the long promenade which went round the building above the tiers of seats. The façade of the Kathisma was decorated with the four Horses of Lysippus,[2] in gilt bronze, which were carried off to Venice by the Doge Dandolo, after the capture of the city by the brigands of the Fourth Crusade, and now adorn the front of San Marco.

The accommodation for spectators may have been larger than in the original Circus Maximus, where, according to a recent calculation, there may have been room for 70,000 or 80,000.[3] The tiers of seats rose higher ; it appears that there were over thirty rows. Special seats, probably on the lowest row, were reserved for senators,[4] and it was customary for members of the Blue Faction to sit on the west side of the building, to the right of the throne, and those of the Green on the east.

The spectators entered the Hippodrome from the west. We know that there was one main entrance close to the Kathisma, and it was probably known as the Great Gate.[5] We may consider it likely that there was another ingress farther south, though its existence is not expressly recorded.[6] The only other issue of which we hear in early times was the Dead Gate, which, from its name, is supposed to have been used for carrying out corpses. It seems to have been somewhere in the eastern wall

[1] As to its date we only know from the inscription which remains on the pedestal that by the reign of Constantine VII. in the tenth century it had suffered from the injuries of time (χρόνῳ φθαρέν) and required restoration. Paspatês (*op. cit.* p. 42) gives the distance from the Egyptian obelisk to the bronze pillar as 94 paces.

[2] It is said that they were brought from Chios by Theodosius II.

[3] In the time of Augustus ; in that of Constantine, perhaps it was more than double (Hülsen, in Jordan, *Top. d. S. Rom.* I. iii. 137). Paspatês calculates

that the Hippodrome accommodated 60,000, Grosvenor 80,000.

[4] Marcellinus, *Chron., s.a.* 528.

[5] Const. Porph. *Cer.* i. 68, p. 307. The existence of a principal gate here is generally admitted. The position of the entrances is discussed by Labarte, *loc. cit.* His assumption, on grounds of symmetry, that there were gates on the E. side exactly opposite to those on the W. is arbitrary. The question of the gates is important in connexion with the Nika riot of A.D. 532. See below, Vol. II. Chap. XIV.

[6] It is assumed by Labarte, and is probable on grounds of convenience (to avoid congestion).

of the building.[1]   In later times there was a gate into the Palace
near the Kathisma, but in the fifth and sixth centuries the only
passage from the Hippodrome to the Daphne Palace was through
the Kathisma itself and the winding stair which has been mentioned.[2]

Since the establishment of the Empire, chariot-races had been
a necessity of life for the Roman populace.   Inscriptions, as well
as literary records, of the early Empire abundantly illustrate the
absorbing interest which was found by all classes in the excitement of the Circus, and this passion, which Christianity did
nothing to mitigate, was inherited by Constantinople.   Theologians might fulminate against it, but their censures produced
no greater effect than the declamations of pagan satirists.   In
the fifth and sixth centuries, charioteers were as wealthy a class
as ever ;   Porphyrius was as popular an idol in the days of Anastasius as Scorpus and Thallus had been in the days of Domitian,
or Diocles in those of Hadrian and Antoninus.   Emperors, indeed,
did not follow the unseemly example of Nero, Commodus, and
other dissolute princes, and practise themselves the art of the
charioteer, but they shared undisguisedly in the ardours of
partisanship for one or other of the Circus Factions, which
played a far more conspicuous part at Constantinople for a
couple of centuries than they had ever played at Rome.

The origin of the four Factions, named after their colours, the
Blues, Greens, Reds, and Whites, is obscure.   They existed in the
last age of the Republic,[3] and they were perhaps definitely
organised by contractors who supplied the horses and chariots
when a magistrate or any one else provided a public festival.
The number of the rival colours was determined by the fact that
four chariots generally competed in a race, and there consequently arose four rival companies or Factions, requiring considerable staffs of grooms, mechanics, and messengers, and sup-

---

[1] Labarte placed it near the Sphendone, but there is no evidence.   If
conjecture is permissible, it may have
been in the centre of the eastern wall,
where the Skyla gate was afterwards
constructed (probably by Justinian II.).

[2] The absence of any entrance here
may be inferred from the circumstances of the suppression of the Nika
riot.   I have shown that in the
seventh and eighth centuries there

was a covered hippodrome on the
E. side of the great Hippodrome (and
about half as long) between it and
the Palace grounds ;   but there is
no evidence that it existed in the
fifth or sixth century.   See Bury,
Covered Hippodrome, 113-115.

[3] The Reds and Whites, at least ;
some think that the Blues and Greens
(*Veneti* and *Prasini*) arose under the
Empire.

ported by what they received from the givers of the festivals, who paid them according to a regular tariff.[1]

In every class of the community, from the Emperor down, people attached their sympathies to one or other of the rival factions. It would be interesting to know whether this partisanship was, like political views, frequently hereditary. In the fourth century a portion of the urban populations, in the greater cities of the east, was officially divided into partisans of the four colours, and used for purposes which had no connexion with the hippodrome. They were organised as quasi-military bodies, which could be used at need for the defence of the city or for the execution of public works.[2] In consequence of this official organisation, embracing the *dêmos* or people, the parties of the hippodrome came to be designated as the demes,[3] and they were placed under the general control of demarchs, who were responsible to the Prefect of the city. We do not know on what principle the members of the demes were selected from the rest of the citizens, most of whom were attached in sympathy to one or other of the colours ; but we may assume it to be probable that enrolment in a deme was voluntary.[4]

Like the princes of the early Empire, the autocrats of the fifth and sixth centuries generally showed marked favour towards one of the parties. Theodosius II. was indulgent to the Greens,[5] Marcian favoured the Blues, Leo and Zeno the Greens, while Justinian preferred the Blues. These two parties had risen into such importance and popularity that they completely overshadowed the Reds and Whites, which were gradually sinking into insignificance [6] and were destined ultimately, though they

---

[1] Friedländer, *Roman Life and Manners*, ii. 27.

[2] The part taken by the demes in restoring and extending the walls of Theodosius II. at Cple. is recorded in Πάτρια, p. 150. See van Millingen, *Byz. Cple.* pp. 44, 79. The name of the 3rd military gate, Rusion, may refer to its construction by the Red deme. In later times we have cases of the demes defending the walls. For the organisation at Alexandria, cp. M. Gelzer, *Studien*, p. 18.

[3] Δημότης was used to designate the member of a deme, and δημοτεύω was used in two senses—(1) neuter, to be a δημότης ; (2) trans., to arm δημόται for

military service (Theophanes, A.M. 6051). μέρη was the ordinary word for the circus parties.

[4] There is abundant evidence to show that the demes included only a portion of the urban population (see Rambaud, *De Byz. Hippodromo*, pp. 87, 88 ; Reiske, *Comm. ad Const. Porph. de Cer.* pp. 28, 29).

[5] He changed the seats of the Greens from the right to the left of the Kathisma (John Mal. xiv. p. 351).

[6] Thus in an important passage of Theophylactus Simocatta (who wrote early in the seventh century), *Hist.* viii. 7. 11, only two parties are recognised, εἰς δύο γὰρ χρωμάτων ἐφέσεις τὰ τῶν

retained their names, to be merged in the organisations of the Greens and Blues respectively.

While the younger Rome inherited from her elder sister the passion for chariot races,[1] the Byzantine hippodrome acquired a political significance which had never been attached to the Roman circus. It was here that on the accession of a new Emperor the people of the capital acclaimed him and showed their approval of his election. Here they criticised openly his acts and clamoured for the removal of unpopular ministers. The hippodrome was again and again throughout later Roman history the scene of political demonstrations and riots which shook or threatened the throne, and a modern writer has described the *spina* which divided the racecourse as the axis of the Byzantine world.[2] It may be said that the hippodrome replaced, under autocratic government, the popular Assembly of the old Greek city-state.

§ 5. *The Suburbs. Population*

The Romans whom Constantine induced to settle in his new city found in its immediate neighbourhood as favourable conditions as they could desire for the *villeggiatura* which for hundreds of years had been a feature of Roman life. From Rome they had to travel up to Tibur or Tusculum or Lanuvium, or drive to the seaside resorts of Antium and Terracina, if they did not fare further and seek the attractions of the bay of Naples. At Constantinople their villas were in the suburbs near the seashore and could easily be reached by boat. We may divide the suburbs into three principal groups : the western, extending from the Theodosian Wall to Hebdomon ; the banks of the Bosphorus ; and the Asiatic coast from Chrysopolis (Skutari) south-eastward to Karta Limên (Kartal). The suburb and palace of Hebdomon have already been described.

On the European side of the Bosphorus, outside Galata, was the suburban quarter of St. Mamas, where the Emperors had a

Ῥωμαίων καταπέκτωκε πλήθη. — The history of the demes has been investigated in the important article of Uspenski, *Partii Tsirka i Dimy v Kplie* in *Viz. Vrem.* i. 1 *sqq.*

[1] The popularity of the circus with the Romans of the sixth century is noted in Cassiodorus, *Var.* iii. 51, 11 : *illic supra cetera spectacula fervor animorum inconsulta gravitate rapiatur. transit prasinus, pars populi maeret : praecedit venetus et ocius turba civitatis affligitur.* Cp. Salvian, *De gub. Dei,* vi. 20-26.

[2] Rambaud, *op. cit.* p. 19 *quidam axis fuit quo Byzantinus orbis universus nitebatur.*

house, which in the eighth and ninth centuries they often fre-
quented.[1] Farther north was one of the two places specially
known as the Anaplûs—a confusing term, which was also used in
the more general sense of the whole European bank of the straits.
This, the southern Anaplûs, corresponds to the modern Kuru-
Chesme ; the other is at Rumili Hissar. Between these places
were the suburbs of Promotus and Hestiae (Arnaut Keui), where
there was a famous church of St. Michael, founded by Constantine
and rebuilt by Justinian. This must not be confused with
another church of the Archangel at Sosthenion, of which the name
is preserved in Stenia, about two miles north of Rumili Hissar.
On the Asiatic side, opposite Stenia and in the neighbourhood
of Kanlija, were the suburbs of Boradion and Anthemius.

Opposite Constantinople itself were the towns of Chrysopolis,
beautifully situated on the western slopes of a hill, and Chalcedon,
now Kadi Keui. South of Chalcedon the coast turns and trends
south-eastward, to form the bay of Nicomedia. Here were the
suburbs of Hieria (Fanar Bagche), Drys, the "Oak" (Jadi Bostan),
Satyros, Bryas (Mal-tepe), and Karta Limên. At Drys was
Rufinianae, the estate of the Praetorian Prefect Rufinus, where
he built a monastery and a mansion ; confiscated after his death
it became imperial property, and we find the palace sometimes
occupied by members of the Imperial family. At Hieria, Justinian built a famous palace as a summer retreat, and in the
ninth century Theophilus chose Bryas for the same purpose.
These suburbs look across to the group of the Princes' Islands,
so admirably suited by their climate for villa-life ; but in the
days of the Empire they were not to Constantinople what Capri
and Ischia are to Naples and what they were to become in
modern times ; they were covered with convents and were used
as honourable and agreeable prisons for fallen princes.

All these suburban quarters in both continents formed a
greater Constantinople connected by water-roads. If we suppose
that the population of the city itself and all these suburbs
approached a million, we shall probably not be much over the

[1] That there was an imperial house
here in the fifth century seems to
follow from the fact that in 469, on
the occasion of the great fire, Leo I.
stayed at St. Mamas for six months.
He constructed a harbour and portico
(*Chron. Pasch.*, *sub a.*). The question
as to the locality was cleared up by
the late J. Pargoire, who has definitely
identified many of the more important
suburbs in his valuable articles (see
Bibliography, ii. 2, E).

mark. There are no data for a precise calculation. A writer of the fifth century declares that it was generally admitted that the new city had outstripped Rome in numbers as well as in wealth.[1] But unfortunately the population of Rome at this time, and indeed throughout the Imperial period, is highly uncertain ; recent computations vary from 800,000 to 2,000,000.[2] They vary from 500,000 to 1,000,000 for Constantinople ; the probability is that in the fifth century its population was little less than a million.[3]

[1] Sozomen, *H.E.* ii. 3. Chrysostom (*In Acta Ap. Hom.* xi. 3) gives 100,000 as the number of Christians and 50,000 as the number of poor (*sc.* Christians) who need public assistance. But we can base no conclusion on figures which are clearly Chrysostom's own guesses. How wildly he guessed is shown by his estimate of the wealth of Constantinople in the same passage. He reckons the value of all the real and personal property to be a million pounds of gold (*i.e.* over £45,000,000), " or rather *twice or thrice as much.*"

[2] Beloch and Lanciani respectively. There have been many estimates, based on area, the corn distribution, the number of houses and *insulae* (apartment-houses), etc.

[3] It would be too long to go into the evidence, which has been thoroughly sifted and criticised by A. Andreades in his articles Περὶ τοῦ πληθυσμοῦ and *De la population de Cple* (see Bibliography, ii. 2, C), in which he has refuted the arguments of E. A. Foord (*The Byzantine Empire*, 1911) that the population was 500,000. His conclusion is that the population was between 800,000 and 1,000,000

at the end of the fifth century. I may observe that the number of *domus* given in the *Not. Urb. Const.* is 4388 ; the *domus* are the palaces and houses of the rich. The number of the *insulae* or apartment-houses in which the poorer lived is not given. Now in Rome, in the time of Constantine, the number of *domus* was about 1790, and the number of *insulae* more than 4400. It is reasonable to suppose that the number of *insulae* in Constantinople, though not more than double (like that of the *domus*) the number of *insulae* in Rome, was at least considerably over 2000 ; and this would bear out Sozomen's statement (see penultimate note) that the new city was more populous than Rome.—As to the population of Alexandria the available evidence tends to show that from the early period of the Empire down to the seventh century it was not less than 600,000. For Antioch, Libanius (*Epp.* 1137) gives 150,000, which is much too small. Acc. to John Malalas (Bk. xvii. p. 420) 250,000 perished in the earthquake of A.D. 526. He was an Antiochene and a contemporary.

CHAPTER IV

THE NEIGHBOURS OF THE EMPIRE AT THE END OF THE
FOURTH CENTURY

IT was the mature judgment of the founder of the Empire that
Roman dominion had then reached the due limit of its expansion,
and it was a corollary of this opinion of Augustus that all the
future wars of Rome should be wars in which defence and not
aggression was the motive. His discernment was confirmed by
the history of nearly fifteen hundred years. Throughout the
long period of its duration, there were not many decades in which
the Roman Empire was not engaged in warfare, but with few
exceptions all its wars were waged either to defend its frontiers
or to recover provinces which had been taken from it. The only
clear exception was the conquest of Britain.[1] For the motive
of Trajan's conquest of Dacia and of the lands beyond the
Tigris (which were almost immediately abandoned) was not the
spirit of aggression or territorial greed or Imperial vanity, so
much as the need of strengthening the defences of the Illyrian
and eastern provinces. After Trajan there were few cases even
of this kind. Diocletian's acquisitions on the Tigris were mainly
designed for security, and if any war can be described as a war
of self-defence it was that which carried Heraclius into the heart
of Persia. There were, indeed, wars of conquest, in which the
Roman government took the first step, but they were all to
recover lands which had formerly belonged to Rome for centuries.
If we regard unprovoked aggression against neighbours as the
most heinous crime of which a state can be guilty, few states

[1] Yet in this case too the motive
was that the complete Romanisation
of the Celts of Gaul could not be
accomplished so long as the Celts of
Britain, with whom they were in
constant communication, remained
free.

have a cleaner record than the later Roman Empire. But it was a crime which there was neither the temptation nor the power to commit. There was little temptation, because there was no pressure of population demanding more territory for expansion ; and the Empire was seldom in a position to plan conquests, for all its available forces were required for self-preservation. As in the days of Augustus, there were perpetually two enemies to be faced :

> hinc mouet Euphrates, illinc Germania bellum.

In the east, Parthian was succeeded by Persian, Persian by Saracen, Saracen by Turk. In the west, after the German invasions had reduced the Empire to half its size and the Teutonic kingdoms had been shaped, the Roman rulers had to confront the Frank after the Lombard, the Norman after the Frank, and then the Crusaders. But this was not all. New enemies appeared in the north in the shape of Asiatic nomads and Slavs.

In this chapter we will glance at the three enemies with whom the Empire had to reckon in the fifth century, the Persians, the Germans, and the Huns.

§ 1. *Persia*

When the Parthian power was overthrown by the revolution of A.D. 226, the Iranian state was renewed and strengthened under a line of monarchs who revived the glories of the ancient Achaemenids, of whom they considered themselves the true successors. Persia under the Sassanid dynasty was recognised by the Roman Empire as a power of equal rank with itself, a consideration which it showed to no other foreign state and had never accorded to the Parthian. The rise of the new dynasty occurred when the Empire was about to enter on a period of internal trouble which shook it to its foundations, and nothing shows more impressively the efficacy of the reforms which were carried out at the end of the third century than the fact that for the following three hundred years the Romans (notwithstanding the perpetual struggles which claimed their energy in Europe) were able to maintain their eastern frontiers, without any serious losses, against this formidable and well-organised enemy.

The two most conspicuous features of the Persian state were

the hereditary nobility and the Zoroastrian church. The first was a point of sharp contrast, the second of remarkable resemblance, to the Roman Empire. The highest nobility were known as " the people of the Houses," [1] and probably all of them possessed large domains in which they exercised princely rights. But the soundest part of the nation seems to have been the inferior nobility, also landed proprietors, who were known as the Dikhāns. Relations of a sort which may be called feudal are supposed to have existed between the two classes of nobility, and the organisation of the army seems to have been connected with the feudal obligations. Some of the high offices of state were restricted by law to certain families, and the power of the great nobles was frequently opposed to the authority of the kings.

To admirers of ancient Greece and Rome one of the most pleasing features of their condition, compared with that of the subjects of the great Iranian monarchy which threatened them in the east, was the absence of a jealous religion controlled by a priesthood possessing immense power in the state and exerting an extreme conservative influence incompatible with the liberty which the city-states of Europe enjoyed. The establishment of Christianity brought Rome into line with Persia. Henceforward both states were governed by jealous gods. Both realms presented the spectacle of a powerful priesthood organised as a hierarchy, intolerant and zealous for persecution. Each district in a Persian province seems to have been under the spiritual control of a Magian high priest (corresponding to a bishop), and at the head of the whole sacerdotal hierarchy was the supreme Archi-mage.[2] In some respects the Magian organisation formed a state within a state. The kings often chafed under the dictation of the priests and there were conflicts from time to time, but the priests generally had the moral support of the nobility behind them. They might be defied for a few years, but their power inevitably reasserted itself.

Although both governments discouraged private peaceable intercourse between their subjects, following a policy which reminds us of China or mediaeval Russia, and the commerce

---

[1] Or " of the seven Houses." On the seven families, which included the royal, see Nöldeke, Excurs 3 to *Tabari*, p. 437.

[2] The Magian high priest was called Mobedh; the supreme head, Mobedhan-mobedh.

between the two countries was carried on entirely on the frontiers, the influence of Persia on Roman civilisation was considerable. We have seen how the character of the Roman army was affected by the methods of Persian warfare. We have also seen how the founders of the Imperial autocracy imitated, in however modified a form, the royal ceremonial of the court of Ctesiphon ; and from this influence must ultimately be derived the ceremonial usages of the courts of modern Europe. In the diplomatic intercourse between the Imperial and Persian governments we may find the origin of the formalities of European diplomacy.

It is a convention for modern sovrans to address each other as " brother," and this was the practice adopted by the Emperor and the King of kings.[1] Whatever reserves each might make as to his own superiority, they treated each other as equals, and considered themselves as the two lights of the world—in oriental figurative language, the sun of the east and the moon of the west.[2] When a new sovran ascended either throne it was the custom to send an embassy to the other court to announce the accession,[3] and it was considered a most unfriendly act to omit this formality. The ambassadors enjoyed special privileges ; their baggage was exempt from custom duties ; and when they reached the frontier, the government to which they were sent provided for their journey to the capital and defrayed their expenses. At Constantinople it was one of the duties of the Master of Offices to make all the arrangements for the arrival of an ambassador, for his reception and entertainment, and, it must be added, for supervising his movements.[4] For all important negotiations men of high rank were chosen, and were

[1] Amm. Marc. xvii. 5. 10 *victor terra marique Constantius semper Augustus fratri meo Sapori regi salutem plurimam dico.* Cp. Kavad's letter in John Mal. xviii. p. 449; etc. The Empress Theodora addressed the Persian queen as her sister (*ib.* p. 467). The Emperor never gave the title βασιλεὺς βασιλέων (*shahan-shah*) to the king ; always simply βασιλεύς. The king called him Kaisar i Rūm.

[2] Malalas, *ib.* p. 449. Cp. Peter Patr. *fr.* 12, *De leg. gent.* ὡσπερανεὶ δύο λαμπτῆρες. Theophylactus Sim. iv. 11. See Güterbock, *Byzanz und Persien*, for a detailed study of the diplomatic forms.

[3] Κατὰ τὸ εἰωθός, Menander, *fr.* 15 *De leg. Rom.* p. 188. Several particular instances are recorded.

[4] The arrangement for the journey from Daras to Constantinople and the reception ceremonies in the sixth century are described by Peter the Patrician (*apud* Const. Porph. *De Cer.* i. 89, 90). The journey was very leisurely, 103 days were allowed. Five horses and thirty mules were placed at the envoy's disposal, by an agreement concluded " in the Praetorian Prefecture of Constantine " (*ib.* p. 400). Perhaps this refers to Constantine who was Pr. Pr. in A.D. 505.

distinguished as "great ambassadors" from the envoys of inferior position who were employed in matters of less importance.[1]

Of the details of the procedure followed in concluding treaties between ancient states we have surprisingly little information. But a very full account of the negotiations which preceded the peace of A.D. 562 between Rome and Persia, and of the manner in which the treaty was drafted, has come down to us, and illustrates the development of diplomatic formalities.[2]

We may conclude with great probability that it was the intercourse with the Persian court that above all promoted the elaboration of a precise system of diplomatic forms and etiquette at Constantinople. Such forms were carefully adhered to in the relations of the Emperor with all the other kings and princes who came within his political horizon. They were treated not as equals, like the Persian king, but with gradations of respect and politeness, nicely regulated to correspond to the position which they held in the eyes of the Imperial sovran. This strict etiquette, imposed by Constantinople, was the diplomatic school of Europe.

In the fourth century the eastern frontier of the Empire had been regulated by two treaties, and may roughly be represented by a line running north and south from the borders of Colchis on the Black Sea to Circesium on the Euphrates.

Jovian had restored to Persia, in A.D. 363, most, but not all, of the territories beyond the Tigris which Diocletian had conquered;[3] and the new boundary followed the course of the Nymphius, which flows from the north into the upper Tigris, then a straight line drawn southward between Nisibis and Daras to the river Aborras, and then the course of the Aborras, which joins the Euphrates at Circesium. Thus of the great strongholds

---

[1] Cp. *ib.* p. 398 ; Menander, *fr.* 13 *De leg. Rom.* p. 200 ; etc.

[2] See below, Vol. II. Chap. XVI.

[3] There has been a confusion in the identification of the provinces recorded to have been conquered (Peter Patr.) and those recorded to have been surrendered (Amm. Marc. xxv. 7, 9). The question has been recently discussed by Adonts, *Armeniia v epokhu Iustiniana*, pp. 43, 44. Diocletian conquered the five provinces Arzanene, Zabdicene, Corduene, Sophene, and Ingilene (or Angilene). The first three were restored, the last two retained, in 363. The two districts which Ammian enumerates as also restored, Moxoene and Rehimene, were portions respectively of Arzanene and Zabdicene. Sophene means Little Sophene (N.W. of Anzitene), and is to be distinguished from Great Sophene = Sophanene (S.E. of Anzitene), of which Ingilene was a portion.

beyond the Euphrates, Nisibis and Singara were Persian ; Amida and Martyropolis, Edessa, Constantia, and Resaina were Roman.[1]

The treaty of A.D. 387 [2] between Theodosius and Sapor III., which was negotiated by Stilicho, partitioned Armenia into two client states, of which the smaller (about one-fifth of the whole) was under a prince dependent on the Empire, the larger under a vassal of Persia. The Roman client, Arsaces, died in A.D. 390, leaving the government in the hands of five satraps. The Emperor gave him no successor, but committed the supervision of the satrapies to an official entitled the Count of Armenia, and this arrangement continued till the sixth century.[3]

The Roman system of frontier defence, familiar to us in Britain and Germany, was not adopted in the east, and would hardly have been suitable to the geographical conditions. In Mesopotamia, or in the desert confines of Syria, we find no vestiges of a continuous barrier of vallum and foss, such as those which are visible in Northumberland and Scotland and in the Rhinelands. The defensive works consisted of the modern system of chains of forts. The Euphrates was bordered by castles, and there was a series of forts along the Aborras (Khabur), and northward from Daras to Amida.[4]

The eastern frontier of Asia Minor followed the Upper Euphrates (the Kara-Su branch), and the two most important bases were Melitene in the south and Satala (Sadagh) in the north.[5] Melitene was equally distant from Antioch and Trebi-

---

[1] It will be convenient to enumerate here the following identifications of places mentioned in the eastern campaigns : Amida = Diarbekr ; Apamea = Kalaat al - Mudik ; Batnae = Seruj ; Beroea = Aleppo ; Carrhae = Harran ; Chalcis = Kinnesrin ; Constantia = Uerancher ; Edessa = Urfa ; Emesa = Hims ; Epiphania = Hama ; Hierapolis = Kara Membij ; Marde = Mardin ; Martyropolis = Mayafarkin ; Melitene = Malatia ; Resaina (Theodosiopolis) = Ras al-Aïn ; Samosata = Samsat ; Singara = Sinjar ; Theodosiopolis (in Armenia) = Erzerum.

[2] Faustus, vi. 1. The correct date has been established by Güterbock (*Römisch-Armenien*, in *Festgabe* of the Juristic Faculty at Königsberg in honour of J. Th. Schirmer, 1900). It is accepted by Baynes and Hübschmann. For the circumstances and

the history of Armenia between 363 and 387, see Baynes, "Rome and Armenia in the Fourth Century," in *E.H.R.* xxv., Oct. 1910. This article proves the value and trustworthiness of the history of Faustus.

[3] Procopius, *De aed.* iii. 1 ; *C.J.* i. 29. 3. Cp. Chapot, *La Frontière de l'Euphrate*, p. 169.

[4] The best account of the defences of the eastern frontier will be found in Chapot, *op. cit.*

[5] Roads from Melitene led westward (1) to Arabissus (Yarpuz), (2) to Caesarea (Kaisariyeh), and (3) to Sebastea (Sivas). Roads from Satala : (1) westward to Sebastea and Amasea ; (2) northward to the coast ; (3) eastward to Erzerum ; while Colchis was reached by the Lycus (Chorok) valley.

zond, and it could be reached from Samosata either by a direct road or by a longer route following the right bank of the Euphrates. Beyond the Euphrates lay Roman Armenia (as far as a line drawn from Erzerum to the Nymphius), which in itself formed a mountain defence against Persia.

The great desert which stretches east of Syria and Palestine to the Euphrates, and the waste country of southern Mesopotamia, were the haunt of the Nabatean Arabs, who were known to the Romans as Saracens or Scenites (people of the tents). They had no fixed abode, they lived under the sky, and a Roman historian graphically describes their life as a continuous flight : *vita est illis semper in fuga*.[1] They occupied all the strips of land which could be cultivated, and otherwise lived by pillage. They could raid a Roman province with impunity, for it was useless to pursue them into the desert. Vespasian used their services against the Jews. In the third century some of their tribes began to immigrate into Roman territory, and these settlements, which may be compared to the German settlements on other frontiers, were countenanced by the government. Beyond the frontier they remained brigands, profiting by the hostilities between Rome and Persia, and offering their services now to one power and now to the other. In the south many were converted to Christianity in the fourth and fifth centuries, through the influence of the hermits who set up their abodes in the wilderness.[2] These converts belonged chiefly to the tribe of Ghassan, and we shall find the Ghassanids acting, when it suited them, as dependents of the Empire ; while their bitter foes, the Saracens of Hira,[3] who had formed a powerful state to the south of Babylon, are under the suzerainty of Persia. These barbarians, undesirable either as friends or foes, played somewhat the same part in the oriental wars as the Red Indian tribes played in the struggle between the French and English in North America.

The defence of Syria against the Saracens of the waste was a chain of fortresses from Sura on the Euphrates to Palmyra, along an excellent road which was probably constructed by

---

[1] Amm. Marc. xiv. 4. 1. He describes them as *nec amici nobis umquam nec hostes optandi*.

[2] Socrates iv. 36 · Sozomen. vi. 38.

Duchesne, *Églises séparées*, 336 *sqq.*

[3] Hira was close to the site of the later Arabic foundation of Kufa.

Diocletian.[1] Palmyra was a centre of routes leading southward to Bostra, south-westward to Damascus, westward to Emesa, and to Epiphania and Apamea.[2]

The long fierce wars of the third and fourth centuries, in the course of which two Roman Emperors, Valerian and Julian, had perished, were succeeded by a period of 140 years (A.D. 363–502) in which peace was only twice broken by short and trifling interludes of hostility. This relief from war on the eastern frontier was of capital importance for the Empire, because it permitted the government of Constantinople to preserve its European provinces, endangered by the Germans and the Huns. This protracted period of peace was partly at least due to the fact that on the Oxus frontier Persia was constantly occupied by savage and powerful foes.

§ 2. *The Germans*

The leading feature of the history of Europe in the fifth century was the occupation of the western half of the Roman Empire by German peoples. The Germans who accomplished this feat were not, with one or two exceptions, the tribes who were known to Rome in the days of Caesar and of Tacitus, and whose seats lay between the Rhine and the Elbe. These West Germans, as they may be called, had attained more or less settled modes of life, and, with the exception of those who lived near the sea-coast, they played no part in the great migrations which led to the dismemberment of the Empire. The Germans of the movement which is known as the Wandering of the Peoples were the East Germans, who, on the Baltic coast, in the lands between the Elbe and the Vistula, had lived outside the political horizon of the Romans in the times of Augustus and Domitian and were known to them only by rumour. The evidence of their own traditions, which other facts seem to confirm, makes it probable that these peoples—Goths, Vandals, Burgundians, Lombards,

[1] Diocletian organised a systematic defence of the frontier from Egypt to the Euphrates. John Mal. xii. p. 308.

[2] From Apamea a north road followed the valley of the Orontes to Antioch ; while the north road from Epiphania ran by Chalcis and Beroea to Batnae (Chapot, 332 *sqq.*). From Batnae an east road reached the Euphrates at Caeciliana (Kalaat al-Najim) via Hierapolis. In north Syria the principal east highway was that from Antioch to Zeugma. Another led via Cyrrhus (Herup-Pshimber, cp. Chapot, *op. cit.* p. 340) to Samosata.

and others — had originally lived in Scandinavia and in the course of the first millennium B.C. migrated to the opposite mainland.

It was in the second century A.D. that the East German group began to affect indirectly Roman history. When the food question became acute for a German people, as a consequence of the increase of population, there were two alternatives. They might become an agricultural nation, converting their pasture-lands into tillage, and reclaiming more land by clearing the forests which girdled their settlements and which formed a barrier against their neighbours ; or they might migrate and seek a new and more extensive habitation. The East German barbarians were still in the stage in which steady habits of work seem repulsive and dishonourable. They thought that laziness consisted not in shirking honest toil but in " acquiring by the sweat of your brow that which you might procure by the shedding of blood." [1]   Though the process is withdrawn from our vision, we may divine, with some confidence, that the defensive wars in which Marcus Aurelius was engaged against the Germans north of the Danube frontier were occasioned by the pressure of tribes beyond the Elbe driven by the needs of a growing population to encroach upon their neighbours. Not long after these wars, early in the third century, the Goths migrated from the lower Vistula to the northern shores of the Black Sea. This was the first great recorded migration of an East German people. In their new homes they appear divided into two distinct groups, the Visigoths and the Ostrogoths, each of which was destined to have a separate and independent history. How the Visigoths severed themselves from their brethren, occupied Dacia, and were gradually converted to Arian Christianity is a story of which we have only a meagre outline. They do not come into the full light of history until they pour into the Roman provinces, fleeing in terror before the invasion of the Huns, and are allowed to settle there as Federates by the Roman government. The battle in the plains of Hadrianople, where a Roman army was defeated and a Roman Emperor fell, foretold the nature of the danger which was threatening the Empire. It was to be dismembered, not only or chiefly by the attacks of professed enemies from without, but by the self-assertion of the barbarians

---

[1] Tacitus, *Germ.* c. 14.

who were admitted within the gates as Federates and subjects. The tactful policy of Theodosius the Great restored peace for a while. We shall see how soon hostilities were resumed, and how the Visigoths, beginning their career as a small federate people in a province in the Balkan peninsula, founded a great independent kingdom in Spain and Gaul.

Of the other East German peoples who made homes and founded kingdoms on Imperial soil, nearly all at one time or another stood to Rome in the relation of Federates. This is a capital feature of the process of the dismemberment of the Empire. Another remarkable fact may also be noticed. Not a single one of the states which the East Germans constructed was permanent. Vandals, Visigoths, Ostrogoths, Gēpīds, all passed away and are clean forgotten ; Burgundians and Lombards are remembered only by minor geographical names. The only Germans who created on Roman territory states which were destined to endure were the Franks and Saxons, and these belonged to the Western group.

It is probable that the dismemberment of the Empire would have been, in general, a far more violent process than it actually was, but for a gradual change which had been wrought out within the Empire itself in the course of the third and fourth centuries, through the infiltration of Germanic elements. It is to be remembered in the first place that the western fringe of Germany had been incorporated in the Germanic provinces of Gaul. Cöln, Trier, Mainz were German towns. In the second place, many Germans had been induced to settle within the Empire as farmers (colons), in desolated tracts of country, after the Marcomannic Wars of Marcus Aurelius. Then there were the settlements of the *laeti*, chiefly in the Belgic provinces, Germans who came from beyond the Rhine, and received lands in return for which they were bound to military service. Towards the end of the fourth century we find similar settlers both in Italy and Gaul, under the name of *gentiles*, but these were not exclusively Germans.[1] Further there was a German population in many of the frontier districts. This was not the result of a deliberate policy ; Germans were not settled there as such. Lands were assigned to the soldiers (*milites limitanei*) who protected the frontiers, and as the army became more and more

[1] See above, p. 40.

German, being recruited extensively from German colons, the frontier population became in some regions largely German.

In the third century German influence was not visible. The army had been controlled by the Illyrian element. The change begins in the time of Constantine. Then the German element, which had been gradually filtering in, is rising to the top. Constantine owed his elevation as Imperator by the army in Britain to an Alamannic chief ; he was supported by Germans in his contest with the Illyrian Licinius ; and to Germans he always showed a marked favour and preference, for which Julian upbraids him. Thus within the Empire the German star is in the ascendant from the end of the first quarter of the fourth century. We notice the adoption of German customs in the army. Both Julian and Valentinian I. were, on their elevation, raised on the shields of soldiers, in the fashion of German kings. Henceforward German officers rise to the highest military posts in the State, such as Merobaudes, Arbogastes, Bauto and Stilicho, and even intermarry with the Imperial family. An Emperor of the fifth century, Theodosius II., has German blood in his veins.

At the death of Theodosius the Great the geography of the German world, so far as it can roughly be determined, was as follows. On the Rhine frontier there were the Franks in the north, and the federated group of peoples known as Alamanni in the south. The Franks fell into two distinct groups : the Salians, the future conquerors of Gaul, who were at this time Federates of the Empire, and dwelled on the left bank of the Rhine in the east of modern Belgium ; and the Ripuarians, whose abodes were beyond the middle Rhine, extending perhaps as far south as the Main, where the territory of the Alamanni began. Behind these were the Frisian coast dwellers, in Holland and Frisia ; the Saxons, whose lands stretched from the North Sea into Westphalia ; the Thuringians, in and around the forest region which still bears their name. Neighbours of the Alamanni on the Upper Main were the Burgundians.[1] More remote were the Angles near the neck of the Danish peninsula, the Marcomanni in Bohemia, the Silings (who belonged to the Vandal nation) in Silesia, to which they seem to have given its name. The Asdings, the other great section of the Vandals, were still on the Upper Theiss, where they had been settled since the end of the

---

[1] Somewhere in this neighbourhood too were a portion of the Silings.

second century, and not far from them were the Rugians. Another East German people, the Gēpīds (closely akin to the Goths), inhabited the hilly regions of northern Dacia. Galicia was occupied by the Scirians; and on the north coast of the Black Sea were the Ostrogoths, and beyond them the Heruls, who in the third century had left Sweden to follow in the track of the Goths.[1] The Pannonian provinces were entirely in the hands of barbarians, Huns, Alans, and a section of the Ostrogoths, which had moved westward in consequence of the Hunnic invasion. Dacia was in the power of the Huns, whose appearance on the scene introduced the Romans to enemies of a new type, from whom European civilisation was destined to suffer for many centuries.

It must not be thought that the inhabitants of central and northern Europe were so numerous that each of the principal peoples could send a host of hundreds of thousands of warriors to plunder the Empire. " The irregular divisions and the restless motions of the people of Germany dazzle our imagination, and seem to multiply their numbers." [2] Fear and credulity magnified tenfold the hosts of Goths and Vandals and other peoples who invaded and laid waste the provinces. A critical analysis of the evidence suggests that of the more important nations the total number may have been about 100,000, and that the number of fighting men may have ranged from 20,000 to 30,000.

The period of the invasions of the Empire by the East German peoples, from the middle of the fourth century till the middle of the sixth, was the " heroic age " of the Teutons, the age in which minstrels, singing to the harp at the courts of German kings, created the legendary tales which were to become the material for epics in later times, and passing into the Norse Eddas, the Nibelungenlied, and many other poems, were to preserve in dim outline the memory of some of the great historical chieftains who played their parts in dismembering the Empire.[3] It has been the fashion to regard with indulgence these German leaders, who remade the map of Europe, as noble and attractive

---

[1] A portion of them migrated to the neighbourhood of the Lower Rhine, where they appear in A.D. 286. In the following century they furnished *auxilia* to the Roman armies on the Rhine. Schmidt, *Deutsche Stämme*, i. 344.

[2] Gibbon, *Decline*, c. ix. *ad fin.* The evidence as to the numbers is discussed in an appendix to this chapter.

[3] The facts are collected, ordered, and illuminated in Chadwick's *The Heroic Age*, 1912.

figures ; some of them have even been described as chivalrous.
This was the " propaganda " of the nineteenth century. When
we coldly examine their acts, we find that they were as barbarous,
cruel, and rapacious as in the days of Caesar's foe, Ariovistus,
and that the brief description of Velleius still applies to them,
in summa feritate uersutissimi natumque mendacio genus.

§ 3. *The Huns*

The nomad hordes, known to history as the Huns, who in the
reign of Valens appeared west of the Caspian, swept over southern
Russia, subjugating the Alans and the Ostrogoths, and drove
the Visigoths from Dacia, seem to have belonged to the Mongolian
division of the great group of races which includes also the Turks,
the Hungarians, and the Finns.[1] It is probable that for many
generations the Huns had established their pastures near the
Caspian and Aral lakes.   It is almost certain that political
events in northern and central Asia, occasioning new movements
of nomad peoples, drove them westward ; and the rise of the
Zhu-zhu, who were soon to extend their dominion from Corea to
the borders of Europe, about the middle of the fourth century, is
probably the explanation. As rulers of Tartar Asia, the Zhu-zhu
succeeded the Sien-pi, and the Sien-pi were the successors of
the Hiung-nu.   It is supposed that the name *Huns* is simply a
Greek corruption of Hiung-nu ; and this may well be so.   The
designation (meaning " common slaves ") was used by the
Chinese for all the Asiatic nomads.   But the immediate events
which precipitated the Huns into Europe had nothing directly
to do with the collapse of the Hiung-nu power which had occurred
in the distant past.[2]

The nomad life of the Altaic peoples in central Asia was

[1] Cp. the classification of the Ural-
Altaic languages in Peisker's brilliant
chapter, "The Asiatic Background,"
in *C. Med. H.* i. p. 333.   The *Uralic*
group includes the three classes, (1)
Finnish : Fins, Mordvins, etc. ; (2)
Permish ; (3) Ugrian : Hungarians,
Voguls, Ostyaks ; the *Altaic* includes
(1) Turkish, (2) Mongolian, (3) Manchu-
Tungusic. Peisker's chapter, to which
I would refer, supersedes all previous
studies of the Asiatic nomads.

[2] Our knowledge of these revolutions

is derived from the Annals of China ;
De Guignes, *Histoire des Huns,* 4 vols.,
1756–1758 ; E. H. Parker, *A Thousand
Years of the Tartars,* 1895 (cp. his
article on the " Origin of the Turks "
in *E.H.R.* xi. 1896) ;   L. Cahun,
Introduction à l'histoire de l'Asie,
1896 ; F. Hirth's article in *S.-B.* of
Bavarian Academy, *Phil. - Hist. Kl.*
ii. 245 *sqq.,* 1899 ; Drouin, *Notice sur
les Huns et Hioung-nu,* 1894 (he dates
the destruction of the Hiung-nu
empire by the Sien-pi to *c* 221 A.D.).

produced by the conditions of climate. The word nomad, which etymologically means a grazer, is often loosely used to denote tribes of unsettled wandering habits. But in the strict and proper sense nomads are pastoral peoples who have two fixed homes far apart and migrate regularly between them twice a year, like migratory birds, the nomads of the air. In central Asia, northern tracts which are green in summer supply no pasturage in winter, while the southern steppes, in the summer through drought uninhabitable, afford food to the herds in winter. Hence arises the necessity for two homes. Thus nomads are not peoples who roam promiscuously all over a continent, but herdsmen with two fixed habitations, summer and winter pasture-lands, between which they might move for ever, if they were allowed to remain undisturbed and if the climatic conditions did not change.[1] Migrations to new homes would in general only occur if they were driven from their pastures by stronger tribes.

The structure of Altaic society was based on kinship. Those who lived together in one tent formed the unit. Six to ten tents formed a camp, and several camps a clan. The tribe consisted of several clans, and the highest unit, the *il* or people, of several tribes. In connexion with nomads we are more familiar with the word horde. But the horde was no ordinary or regular institution. It was only an exceptional and transitory combination of a number of peoples, to meet some particular danger or achieve some special enterprise ; and when the immediate purpose was accomplished, the horde usually dissolved again into its independent elements.

Milk products are the main food of most of these nomad tribes. They may eke out their sustenance by fishing and hunting, but they seldom eat the flesh of their herds. Their habits have always been predatory. Persia and Russia suffered for centuries from their raids, in which they lifted not only cattle but also men, whom they sent to the slave markets.

The successive immigrations of nomads into Europe, of the ancient Scythians, of the Huns, and of all those who came after them, were due, as has already been intimated, to the struggle for existence in the Asiatic steppes, and the expulsion of the

---

[1] Peisker (*op. cit.* 327-328) shows that "the main cause of the nomad invasions of Europe is not increasing aridity but political changes."

weakest. Those who were forced to migrate " with an energetic
Khan at their head, who organised them on military lines, such
a horde transformed itself into an incomparable army, compelled
by the instinct of self-preservation to hold fast together in the
midst of the hostile population which they subjugated ; for
however superfluous a central government may be in the steppe,
it is of vital importance to a conquering nomad horde outside it." [1]
These invading hordes were not numerous ; they were esteemed
by their terrified enemies far larger than they actually were.
" But what the Altaian armies lacked in numbers was made up
for by their skill in surprises, their fury, their cunning, mobility,
and elusiveness, and the panic which preceded them and froze
the blood of all peoples. On their marvellously fleet horses they
could traverse immense distances, and their scouts provided
them with accurate local information as to the remotest lands
and their distances. Add to this the enormous advantage that
among them even the most insignificant news spread like wildfire
from *aul* to *aul* by means of voluntary couriers surpassing any
intelligence department, however well organised." [2] The fate
of the conquered populations was to be partly exterminated,
partly enslaved, and sometimes transplanted from one territory
to another, while the women became a prey to the lusts of the
conquerors. The peasants were so systematically plundered
that they were often forced to abandon the rearing of cattle and
reduced to vegetarianism. This seems to have been the case
with the Slavs.[3]

Such was the horde which swept into Europe in the fourth
century, encamped in Dacia and in the land between the Theiss
and Danube, and held sway over the peoples in the south Russian
steppes, the Ostrogoths, Heruls, and Alans.[4]

For fifty years after their establishment north of the Danube,
we hear little of the Huns. They made a few raids into the
Roman provinces, and they were ready to furnish auxiliaries,
from time to time, to the Empire. At the time of the death
of Theodosius they were probably regarded as one more barbarian

[1] Peisker, *op. cit.* p. 350.

[2] *Ib.*

[3] *Op. cit.* p. 348.

[4] Also over the Scirians in Galicia ;
probably over the Slavs in the Pripet
region ; perhaps already over the
Gepids ; and presently over the
Rugians, who soon after 400 occupied
the regions on the Upper Theiss
vacated by the Asdings (cp. Schmidt,
op. cit. p. 327).

enemy, neither more nor less formidable than the Germans who threatened the Danubian barrier. We may conjecture that the organisation of the horde had fallen to pieces soon after their settlement in Europe.[1] No one could foresee that after a generation had passed Rome would be confronted by a large and aggressive Hunnic empire.

APPENDIX

ON THE NUMBERS OF THE BARBARIANS

THE question of the numbers of the German invaders of the Empire is so important that it seems desirable to collect here some of the principal statements of our authorities, so as to indicate the character of the evidence. These statements fall into two classes.

(1) Large numbers, running into hundreds of thousands.

a. Eunapius appears to say that the fighting forces of the Visigoths when they crossed the Danube in A.D. 376 numbered 200,000, *fr.* 6, *De leg. gent.* p. 595. The text of the passage, however, is corrupt.

β. The mixed host of barbarians who invaded Italy in A.D. 405–406 is variously stated to be 400,000, 200,000, or more than 100,000 strong. See below, Chap. V. § 7. It is to be observed that the lowest of these figures is given (by Augustine) in an argument where a high figure is effective.

γ. Two widely different figures are recorded for the number of those who fell (on both sides) in the battle of Troyes in A.D. 451, 300,000 and 162,000. See below, Chap. IX. § 4.

δ. 150,000 is given (by Procopius) as the number of the Ostrogoths who besieged Rome in A.D. 537. This can be shown, from the circumstances, to be incredible. See below, Chap. XVIII. § 5.

ϵ. The Franks are made to boast, in A.D. 539, that they could send an army of 500,000 across the Alps (Procopius, *B.G.* ii. 28, 10) Then they were a great power and had many subjects. A few months before, one of their kings had invaded Italy with 100,000 men (*ib.* 25, 2) ; but the number is highly suspicious.

(2) Small numbers.

a. It is difficult to forgive Ammian, who was a soldier and well versed in military affairs, for not stating the number of the forces engaged on either side in the battle of Hadrianople in A.D. 378. The one indication he gives is that the Roman scouts by some

---

[1] It is uncertain whether Uldin, the Hun king whom we meet in the reign of Arcadius, was king of all the Huns or only of a portion.

curious mistake reported that the Visigothic forces numbered only 10,000. It is difficult to believe that this mistake could have been made if the Goths, with their associates, had had anything like 50,000 to 100,000 men (Hodgkin's estimate for the army of Alaric), much less the 200,000 of Eunapius. So far as it goes, the indication points rather to a host of not more than 20,000.

β. After Alaric's siege of Rome in 408, it is stated that his army, reinforced by a multitude of fugitive slaves from Rome, was about 40,000 strong. See below, Chap. VI. § 1.

γ. The total number of the Vandal people (evidently including the Alans who were associated with them), not merely of the fighting forces, is stated to have been 80,000 in A.D. 429 (see below, Chap. VIII. § 2). They were then embarking for Africa and it was necessary to count them in order to know how many transport ships would be needed. This figure has, therefore, particular claims on our attention.

δ. The facts we know about the Vandalic and Ostrogothic wars in the sixth century, as related by Procopius, consistently point to the conclusion that the fighting forces of the Vandals and the Ostrogoths were to be counted by tens, not by hundreds, of thousands. Procopius does not give figures (with the exception of one, which is a deliberate exaggeration, see above, (1) δ), but the details of his very full narrative and the small number of the Roman armies which were sent against them and defeated them make this quite clear.

ε. The total number of the warriors of the Heruls, who were a small people, in the sixth century was 4500 (Procopius, *B.G.* iii. 34, 42-43).

Intermediate between these two groups, but distinctly inclining towards the first, is the statement of Orosius, *Hist.* vii. 32. 11, that the armed forces of the Burgundians on the Rhine numbered more than 80,000. If the figure has any value it is more likely to represent the total number of the Burgundian people at the beginning of the fifth century.

Schmidt has observed (*Gesch. der deutschen Stämme*, i. 46 *sqq.*) that certain numbers in the enumerations of German forces by Roman writers constantly recur (300,000, 100,000, 60,000, etc.) and are therefore to be suspected.

Delbrück (*Gesch. der Kriegskunst*, ii. 34 *sqq.*) discusses the density of population in ancient Germany and concludes that it was from four to five to the square kilometre.

CHAPTER V

§ 1. *Stilicho and Rufinus* (A.D. 395)

THE Emperor Theodosius the Great died at Milan on January 17, A.D. 395. His wishes were that his younger son, Honorius, then a boy of ten years, should reign in the west, where he had already installed him, and that his elder son, Arcadius, whom he had left as regent at Constantinople when he set out against the usurper Eugenius, should continue to reign in the east.[1] But Theodosius was not willing to leave his youthful heirs without a protector, and the most natural protector was one bound to them by family ties. Accordingly on his deathbed he commended them to the care of Stilicho,[2] an officer of Vandal birth, whom he had raised for his military and other talents to the rank of Master of Both Services in Italy,[3] and, deeming him worthy of an alliance with his own house, had united to

---

[1] Flavius Arcadius was born in 377–378, created Augustus Jan. 19, 383, at Constantinople, and was consul in 385. Honorius, born Sept. 9, 384, was created Augustus Jan. 10, 393. As to the succession, we are told that before his death Theodosius had made all the necessary arrangements : Ambrose, *De obitu Theod.* 5.

[2] Ambrose in the funeral oration he pronounced in the presence of Honorius says : *liberos praesenti commendabat parenti* (*ib.*). We must reject the statement of Olympiodorus, fr. 2, that Theodosius appointed Stilicho legal guardian (ἐπίτροπος) of his sons. The relation of guardian and ward had no existence in constitutional law. Cp. Mommsen, *Hist. Schr.* i. p. 516.

[3] Originally serving in the Pro-

tectors, he had been raised to the post of Count of Domestics. Then he married Serena and was appointed *magister equitum praesentalis* (c. 385). After the victory in 394 over Eugenius and Arbogastes, he succeeded the latter as *mag. utriusque militiae*, and held this supreme command till his death. We do not know who succeeded him as *mag. equitum* in Italy, but in 401–402 the post was held by one Jacobus, whose name happens to be recorded because he did not admire Claudian's verses (Claudian, *Carm. min.* 2). That Stilicho's mother was a Roman may be inferred from Jerome's description of him as *semibarbarus* (*Epp.* 123). His son Eucherius was named after the uncle, his daughter Thermantia after th mother, of Theodosius.

his favourite niece, Serena. It was in this capacity, as the husband of his niece and a trusted friend, that Stilicho received the last wishes of the Emperor ; it was as an elder member of the same family that he could claim to exert an influence over Arcadius. Of Honorius he was the natural protector, for he seems to have been appointed regent of the western realm during his minority.

Arcadius was in his seventeenth or eighteenth year at the time of his father's death. He was of short stature, of dark complexion, thin and inactive, and the dulness of his wit was betrayed by his speech and by his sleepy, drooping eyes.[1] His mental deficiency and the weakness of his character made it inevitable that he should be governed by the strong personalities of his court. Such a commanding personality was the Praetorian Prefect of the East, Flavius Rufinus, a native of Aquitaine, who presented a marked contrast to his sovran. He was tall and manly, and the restless movements of his keen eyes and the readiness of his speech, though his knowledge of Greek was imperfect, were no deceptive signs of his intellectual powers. He was ambitious and unprincipled, and, like most ministers of the age, avaricious, and he was a zealous Christian. He had made many enemies by acts which were perhaps more than commonly unscrupulous, but we cannot assume that all the prominent officials [2] for whose fall he was responsible were innocent victims of his malice. But it is almost certain that he had formed the scheme of ascending the throne as the Imperial colleague of Arcadius.

This ambition of Rufinus placed him at once in an attitude of opposition to Stilicho,[3] who was himself suspected of enter-

---

[1] He was educated first by his mother Aelia Flaccilla, then by Arsenius a deacon, and finally by the pagan sophist Themistius. His personal appearance and that of Rufinus are described by Philostorgius (*H.E.* xi. 3), who lived at Constantinople and must have known them both by sight. That Arcadius seldom appeared outside the Palace has been inferred from the mention in Socrates, vi. 23, of the crowds which flocked to see him when on one occasion he did appear in the streets (Seeck, *Gesch. d. Untergangs*, v. 545).

[2] Promotus, Tatian, and Proclus

(Zosimus, v. 51, 52). Rufinus had become Master of Offices in 388 (cp. Seeck, *Die Briefe des Libanius*, 256-257) ; he was consul in 392, and in the same year became Praet. Pref. He was on friendly terms with the pagan sophist Libanius (Lib. *Epp.* 784, 1025). His sister Salvia is remembered as one of the early pilgrims to the Holy Land (Palladius, *Hist. Laus.* 142).

[3] The antagonism was of older date. Theodosius, at the instance of Rufinus, had forbidden Stilicho to punish the Bastarnae who had slain Promotus, whom Rufinus had caused to be exiled. Claudian, *De laud. Stil.* i.

taining similar schemes, not however in his own interest, but
for his son Eucherius. He certainly cherished the design of
wedding his son to the Emperor's stepsister, Galla Placidia.[1]
The position of the Vandal, who was connected by marriage
with the Imperial family, gave him an advantage over Rufinus,
which was strengthened by the generally known fact that
Theodosius had given him his last instructions. Stilicho, moreover, was popular with the army, and for the present the great
bulk of the forces of the Empire was at his disposal; for the
regiments united to suppress Eugenius had not yet been sent
back to their various stations. Thus a struggle was imminent
between the ambitious minister who had the ear of Arcadius,
and the strong general who held the command and enjoyed the
favour of the army. Before the end of the year this struggle
began and ended in a curious way; but we must first see how
a certain scheme of Rufinus had been foiled by an obscurer but
wilier rival nearer at hand.

It was the cherished project of Rufinus to unite Arcadius
with his only daughter; once the Emperor's father-in-law he
might hope to become an Emperor himself. But he was
thwarted by a subtle adversary, Eutropius, the lord chamberlain
(*praepositus sacri cubiculi*), a bald old eunuch, who with oriental
craftiness had won his way up from the meanest services and
employments. Determining that the future Empress should be
bound to himself and not to Rufinus, he chose Eudoxia, a girl
of singular beauty, who had been brought up in the house of
the widow and sons of one of the victims of Rufinus.[2] Her
father was Bauto, a Frank soldier who had risen to be Master
of Soldiers, and for a year or two the most powerful man in
Italy, in the early years of Valentinian II.[3] Her mother had
doubtless been a Roman, and she received a Roman education,
but she inherited, as a contemporary writer observes, barbaric

---

94-115. It may be noted that Zosimus,
at the beginning of Book V., represents
Rufinus and Stilicho as ethically on
a level; but when his source is no
longer Eunapius, but Olympiodorus,
his tone towards Stilicho changes.
Cp. Eunapius, *fr.* 62, 63 ἄμφω τὰ
πάντα συνήρπαζον ἐν τῷ πλούτῳ τὸ
κράτος τιθέμενος. Eunapius was also
the source of John Ant., *frr.* 188-190
(*F.H.G.* iv. p. 610).

[1] This is unmistakably conveyed
in Claudian, *De cons. Stil.* ii. 352-361,
and hinted at again in *De vi. cons.
Honorii*, 552-554.

[2] Promotus. His sons had been
playmates of Arcadius. Zosimus, v. 3.

[3] Ambrose, *Epp.* i. 24 *Bauto qui
sibi regnum sub specie pueri vindicavit*
(words quoted from the tyrant
Maximus). In 385 Bauto was consul,
as colleague of Arcadius.

traits from her German father.[1] Eutropius showed a picture of
the maiden to the Emperor, and so successfully enlarged upon her
merits and her charms that Arcadius determined to marry her ;
the intrigue was carefully concealed from the Praetorian Prefect ; [2]
and till the last moment the public supposed that the bride for
whose Imperial wedding preparations were being made was the
daughter of Rufinus. The nuptials were celebrated on April
27, A.D. 395. It was a blow to Rufinus, but he was still the
most powerful man in the east.

The event which at length brought Rufinus into collision
with Stilicho was the rising of the Visigoths. They had been
settled by Theodosius in the province of Lower Moesia, between
the Danube and the Balkan mountains, and were bound in
return for their lands to do battle for the Empire when their
services were needed. They had accompanied the Emperor
in his campaign against Eugenius, and had returned to their
homes sooner than the rest of the army. In that campaign
they had suffered severe losses, and it was thought that Theodosius deliberately placed them in the most dangerous post
for the purpose of reducing their strength.[3] This was perhaps
the principal cause of the discontent which led to their revolt,
but there can be no doubt that their ill humour was stimulated
by one of their leaders, Alaric (of the family of the Balthas or
Bolds), who aspired to a high post of command in the Roman
army and had been passed over. The Visigoths had hitherto
had no king. It is uncertain whether it was at this crisis [4] or
at a later stage in Alaric's career that he was elected king by
the assembly of his people. In any case he was chosen leader

---

[1] Philostorgius, xi. 6 ἐνῆν αὐτῇ τοῦ
βαρβαρικοῦ θράσους οὐκ ὀλίγον.

[2] It is difficult to understand how
Rufinus could have been so completely hoodwinked, unless the
machinations of Eutropius were
carried out during the absence of the
Prefect from the court, and he was
confronted on his return by a *fait
accompli*. We are entitled to conclude
from the account of Zosimus (source,
Olympiodorus) that Rufinus was
absent at Antioch just before the
marriage, having gone thither in order
to punish Lucian, the Count of the
East, for an offence which he had
offered to an uncle of the Emperor.

Seeck has argued that this visit to
Antioch is wrongly dated by Zosimus
and belongs to A.D. 393 (*op. cit.* p.
447), but his reasoning is not convincing. Rufinus did visit Antioch
in 393 (as letters of Libanius show),
and was in a hurry, but he may have
gone there again in 395.

[3] See Sievers, *Studien*, 326 ;
Schmidt, *Deutsche Stämme*, i. 191.

[4] Jordanes, *Get.* 146 ; Isidore, *Hist.
Goth.* (*Chron. min.* ii.) p. 272. But
contemporary writers do not use
the word *king*, and Schmidt (*ib.* 192)
thinks that Alaric was on this occasion
only nominated commander-in-chief.

of the whole host of the Visigoths, and the movements which
he led were in the fullest sense national.

Under the leadership of Alaric, the Goths revolted and spread
desolation in the fields and homesteads of Thrace and Macedonia.
They advanced close to the walls of Constantinople. They
carefully spared certain estates outside the city belonging to
Rufinus, but their motive was probably different from that
which caused the Spartan king Archidamus to spare the lands
of Pericles in the Peloponnesian war. Alaric may have wished,
not to draw suspicions on the Prefect, but to conciliate his friendship and obtain more favourable terms. Rufinus went to the
Gothic camp, dressed as a Goth.[1] The result of the negotiations
seems to have been that Alaric left the neighbourhood of the
capital and marched westward.

At the same time the Asiatic provinces were suffering, as we
shall see, from the invasions of other barbarians, and there were
no troops to take the field against them, as the eastern regiments
which had taken part in the war against Eugenius were still in
the west. Stilicho, however, was already preparing to lead
them back in person.[2] He deemed his own presence in the east
necessary, for, besides the urgent need of dealing with the
barbarians, there was a political question which deeply concerned
him, touching the territorial division of the Empire between the
two sovrans.

Before A.D. 379 the Prefecture of Illyricum, which included
Greece and the central Balkan lands, had been subject to the
ruler of the west. In that year Gratian resigned it to his new
colleague Theodosius, so that the division between east and
west was a line running from Singidunum (Belgrade) westward
along the river Save and then turning southward along the
course of the Drina and reaching the Hadriatic coast at a point
near the lake of Scutari. It was assumed at Constantinople
that this arrangement would remain in force and that the
Prefecture would continue to be controlled by the eastern

---

[1] Claudian, *In Rufin.* ii. 78 *sqq.*
Alaric must have moved very early
in the spring ; for it was still early
in the year when Stilicho marched
from Italy, *ib.* 101.—It has been suggested (Seeck, *Gesch. des Untergangs*,
v. 274) that the zeal of Rufinus
against heretics (especially the Eunomians), displayed in a series of four

edicts (*C. Th.* xvi. 5. 25, xxvi. 28, 29),
was dictated by a superstitious belief
that the calamities of the time were
due to the anger of Heaven at laxity
in the suppression of heresy.

[2] He had been occupied with the
task of driving out bands of German
marauders who had invaded Pannonia
and Noricum.

government. But Stilicho declared that it was the will of
Theodosius that his sons should revert to the older arrangement,
and that the authority of Honorius should extend to the confines of Thrace, leaving to Arcadius only the Prefecture of the
East.[1] Whether this assertion was true or not, his policy
meant that the realm in which he himself wielded the power
would have a marked predominance, both in political importance and in military strength, over the other section of the
Empire.

It would perhaps be a mistake to suppose that this political
aim of Stilicho, of which he never lost sight, was dictated by
mere territorial greed, or that his main object was to increase
the revenues. The chief reason for the strife between the two
Imperial governments may have lain rather in the fact that
the Balkan peninsula was the best nursery in the Empire for
good fighting men.[2] The stoutest and most useful native troops
in the Roman army were, from the fourth to the sixth century,
recruited from the highlands of Illyricum and Thrace. It might
well seem, therefore, to those who were responsible for the defence
of the western provinces that a partition which assigned almost
the whole of this great recruiting ground to the east was unfair
to the west ; and as the legions which were at Stilicho's disposal
were entirely inadequate, as the event proved, to the task of
protecting the frontiers against the Germans, it was not unnatural that he should have aimed at acquiring control over
Illyricum.

It was a question on which the government of New Rome,
under the guidance of Rufinus, was not likely to yield without
a struggle, and Stilicho took with him western legions belonging
to his own command as well as the eastern troops whom he was
to restore to Arcadius. He marched overland, doubtless by the
Dalmatian coast road to Epirus, and confronted the Visigoths in
Thessaly, whither they had traced a devastating path from the
Propontis.[3]

Rufinus was alarmed lest his rival should win the glory of
crushing the enemy, and he induced Arcadius to send to Stilicho

---

[1] Olympiodorus, *fr.* 3. Cp. Mommsen, *op. cit.* 517.

[2] This aspect of the question has
hitherto been overlooked.

[3] Alaric had experienced a repulse
at the hands of garrison soldiers in
Thessaly—perhaps in attempting the
pass of Tempe. See Socrates, *H.E.*
vii. 10, a confused passage of which
little can be made.

a peremptory order to dispatch the troops to Constantinople and depart himself whence he had come. The Emperor was led, legitimately enough, to resent the presence of his relative, accompanied by western legions, as an officious and hostile interference. The order arrived just as Stilicho was making preparations to attack the Gothic host in the valley of the Peneius. His forces were so superior to those of Alaric that victory was assured ; but he obeyed the Imperial command, though his obedience meant the delivery of Greece to the sword of the barbarians. We shall never know his motives, and we are so ill-informed of the circumstances that it is difficult to divine them. A stronger man would have smitten the Goths, and then, having the eastern government at his mercy, would have insisted on the rectification of the Illyrian frontier which it was his cherished object to effect. Never again would he have such a favourable opportunity to realise it. Perhaps he did not yet feel quite confident in his own position ; perhaps he did not feel sure of his army. But his hesitation may have been due to the fact that his wife Serena and his children were at Constantinople and could be held as hostages for his good behaviour.[1] In any case he consigned the eastern troops to the command of a Gothic captain, Gaïnas, and departed with his own legions to Salona, allowing Alaric to proceed on his wasting way into the lands of Hellas. But he did not break up his camp in Thessaly without coming to an understanding with Gaïnas which was to prove fatal to Rufinus.

Gaïnas marched by the Via Egnatia to Constantinople,[2] and it was arranged that, according to a usual custom,[3] the Emperor and his court should come forth from the city to meet the army in the Campus Martius at Hebdomon. We cannot trust the statement of a hostile writer that Rufinus actually expected to be created Augustus on this occasion, and appeared at the Emperor's side prouder and more sumptuously arrayed than

[1] Cp. Mommsen, *ib.* 521. See Claudian, *In Rufin.* ii. 95 and *Laus Serenae*, 232 (Serena kept Stilicho informed by letters of what was going on in the East).—The chronology presents a difficulty. Stilicho had set out in the spring, yet Gaïnas and the army did not reach Constantinople till November (see below).

[2] Claudian, *In Rufin.* ii. 291—

percurritur Hebrus,
deseritur Rhodope Thracumque per ardua
    tendunt,
donec ad Herculei perventum nominis
    urbem.

The city of Herculean name, Heraclea, is the ancient Perinthus.

[3] Zosimus, v. 7. 5 ταύτης γὰρ τῆς τιμῆς ἠξιῶσθαι τοὺς στρατιώτας ἔλεγε σύνηθες εἶναι.

ever ; we only know that he accompanied Arcadius to meet
the army. It is said that, when the Emperor had saluted the
troops, Rufinus advanced and displayed a studied affability
and solicitude to please even towards individual soldiers. They
closed in round him as he smiled and talked, anxious to secure
their goodwill for his elevation to the throne, but just as he felt
himself very nigh to supreme success, the swords of the nearest
were drawn, and his body, pierced with wounds, fell to the
ground (November 27, A.D. 395).[1] His head, carried through
the streets, was mocked by the people, and his right hand,
severed from the trunk, was presented at the doors of houses
with the request, " Give to the insatiable ! "

There can be no reasonable doubt that the assassination of
Rufinus was instigated by Stilicho, as some of our authorities
expressly tell us.[2] The details may have been arranged between
him and Gaïnas, and he appears not to have concerned himself
to conceal his complicity. The scene of the murder is described
by a gifted but rhetorical poet, Claudius Claudianus, who now
began his career as a trumpeter of Stilicho's praises by his poem
Against Rufinus.[3] He paints Stilicho and Rufinus as two oppos-
ing forces, powers of darkness and light : the radiant Apollo,
deliverer of mankind, and the terrible Pytho, the scourge of the
world. What we should call the crime of Stilicho is to him a
glorious deed, the destruction of a monster, and though he does
not say in so many words that his hero planned it, he does not
disguise his responsibility. Claudian was a master of violent
invective, and his portrait of Rufinus, bad man though he unquestionably was, is no more than a caricature. The poem
concludes with a picture of the Prefect in hell before the tribunal
of Rhadamanthys, who declares that all the iniquities of the
tortured criminals are but a fraction of the sins of the latest
comer, who is too foul even for Tartarus, and consigns him to an
empty pit outside the confines of Pluto's domain.

[1] Πλήθους ὁπλιτεύοντος ἀθρόᾳ κινήσει
περιπεσών, Asterius of Amasea, in his
Λόγος κατηγορικὸς τῆς ἑορτῆς τῶν
καλανδῶν, *P.G.* xl. 224.

[2] Zosimus (source certainly Eunapius), *ib.* 3. Philostorgius, xi. 3. It
is remarkable that Claudian does not
mention Gaïnas, whose part in the
affair we find in Zosimus.—On the

confiscation of the large property of
Rufinus see *C. Th.* ix. 42. 14 ; Symmachus, *Epp.* vi. 14.

[3] See Claudian, *Carm. min.* xli.
vv. 13-16, which seem to imply that
he came to Italy in the consulship of
Probinus (and Olybrius), A.D. 395.
Cp. Prosper, *Chron., sub a.*

Tollite de mediis animarum dedecus umbris.
adspexisse sat est. oculis iam parcite nostris
et Ditis purgate domos. agitate flagellis
trans Styga, trans Erebum, vacuo mandate barathro
infra Titanum tenebras infraque recessus
Tartareos ipsumque Chaos, qua·noctis opacae
fundamenta latent ; praeceps ibi mersus anhelet,
dum rotat astra polus, feriunt dum litora venti.

It was not only the European parts of the dominion of
Arcadius that were ravaged, in this year, by the fire and sword
of barbarians. Hordes of trans-Caucasian Huns poured through
the Caspian gates, and, rushing southwards through the Armenian
highlands and the plains of Mesopotamia, carried desolation into
Syria. St. Jerome was in Palestine at this time, and in two of
his letters we have the account of an eye-witness. " As I was
searching for an abode worthy of such a lady (Fabiola, his friend),
behold, suddenly messengers rush hither and thither, and the
whole East trembles with the news, that from the far Maeotis,
from the land of the ice-bound Don and the savage Massagetae,
where the strong works of Alexander on the Caucasian cliffs keep
back the wild nations, swarms of Huns had burst forth, and,
flying hither and thither, were scattering slaughter and terror
everywhere. The Roman army was at that time absent in consequence of the civil wars in Italy. . . . May Jesus protect the
Roman world in future from such beasts ! They were everywhere, when they were least expected, and their speed outstripped the rumour of their approach ; they spared neither
religion nor dignity nor age ; they showed no pity to the cry
of infancy. Babes, who had not yet begun to live, were forced
to die ; and, ignorant of the evil that was upon them, as they
were held in the hands and threatened by the swords of the
enemy, there was a smile upon their lips. There was a consistent and universal report that Jerusalem was the goal of the
foes, and that on account of their insatiable lust for gold they
were hastening to this city. The walls, neglected by the carelessness of peace, were repaired. Antioch was enduring a blockade. Tyre, fain to break off from the dry land, sought its ancient
island. Then we too were constrained to provide ships, to stay
on the seashore, to take precautions against the arrival of the
enemy, and, though the winds were wild, to fear a shipwreck
less than the barbarians—making provision not for our own

safety so much as for the chastity of our virgins." [1]   In another
letter, speaking of these " wolves of the north," he says : " How
many monasteries were captured ?   the waters of how many
rivers were stained with human gore ?   Antioch was besieged and
the other cities, past which the Halys, the Cydnus, the Orontes,
the Euphrates flow.   Herds of captives were dragged away ;
Arabia, Phoenicia, Palestine, Egypt were led captive by fear." [2]

§ 2. *Stilicho and Eutropius* (A.D. 396–397)

After the death of Rufinus, the weak Emperor Arcadius
passed under the influence of the eunuch Eutropius, who in
unscrupulous greed of money resembled Rufinus and many other
officials before and after, and, like Rufinus, has been painted
blacker than he really was.   All the evil things that were said
of Rufinus were said of Eutropius ; but in reading of the
enormities of the latter we must make great allowance for the
general prejudice existing against a person with his physical
disqualifications.

The ambitious eunuch naturally looked on the Praetorian
Prefects of the East, the most powerful men in the administration next to the Emperor, with jealousy and suspicion.   To his
influence we are probably justified in ascribing an innovation
which was made by Arcadius.   The administration of the *cursus
publicus*, or office of postmaster-general, and the supervision of
the factories of arms, were transferred from the Praetorian Prefect
to the Master of Offices. [3]

It has been supposed that a more drastic arrangement was
made for the purpose of curtailing the far-reaching authority of
the Praetorian Prefect of the East.   There is evidence which
has been interpreted to mean that during the three and a half
years which coincided with the régime of Eutropius there were
two Prefects holding office at the same time and dividing the
spheres of administration between them.   If this was so, it
would have been a unique experiment, never essayed before or

---

[1] *Epp.* lxxvii. 8. These Huns were
doubtless the Sabeiroi, whom we shall
meet again. Their seats were between
the Caspian and the Euxine. See
below, p. 432, note.

[2] *Epp.* lx. 16. Jerome is dwelling
on the miseries of human society

(*temporum nostrorum ruinas*), which
he also illustrates by the ravages
of Alaric in Europe, and by the
fates of Rufinus, Abundantius, and
Timasius. The letter was written in
396.

[3] John Lydus, *De mag.* iii. 40.

since. But the evidence is not cogent, and it is very difficult to believe that some of the contemporary writers would not have left a definite record of such a revolutionary change.[1]

The Empire was now falling into a jeopardy, by which it had been threatened from the outset, and which it had ever been trying to avoid. There were indeed two dangers which had constantly impended from its inauguration by Augustus to its renovation by Diocletian. The one was a cabinet of imperial freedmen, the other was a military despotism. The former called forth, and was averted by, the creation of a civil service system, to which Hadrian perhaps made the most important contributions, and which was elaborated by Diocletian, who at the same time met the other danger by separating the military and civil administrations. But both dangers revived in a new form. The danger from the army became danger from the Germans, who preponderated in it ; and the institution of court ceremonial tended to create a cabinet of chamberlains and imperial dependents. This oriental ceremonial, so notorious a feature of " Byzantinism," meant difficulty of access to the Emperor, who, living in the retirement of his palace, was tempted to trust less to his eyes than his ears, and saw too little of public affairs. Diocletian himself appreciated this disadvantage, and remarked that the sovran, shut up in his palace, cannot know the truth, but must rely on what his attendants and officers tell him. Autocracy, by its very nature, tends in this direction ; for it generally means a dynasty, and a dynasty implies that there must sooner or later come to the throne weak men, inexperienced in public affairs,

[1] The evidence consists in the circumstance that in the Theodosian Code we find laws addressed to Caesarius Pr. Pr. from Nov. 30, 395, throughout 396 and 397, and on July 26, 398, and at the same time four laws addressed to Eutychianus Pr. Pr. in 396, six laws addressed to him in 397, and six in the first half of 398. Hence Seeck has argued that Caesarius and Eutychianus were colleagues in the Prefecture of the East during these years. The natural explanation is that the dates of some of the constitutions are wrong (viz. six Eutychianus dates in 396 and 397, and one Caesarius date in 398) and that while Caesarius succeeded Rufinus Dec. 395, Eutychianus suc- ceeded Caesarius between July 13 (*C. Th.* viii. 15. 8) and Sept. 4 (*ib.* vi. 3. 4) 397. Eutychianus held office till the fall of Eutropius in August 399. Seeck thinks that this series of errors is improbable (*Gesch. des Untergangs*, v. 551), but errors of date are very common, and in these years alone we find Caesarius addressed as Pr. Pr. in June 395 ; Aurelian in Oct. 396 (iv. 2. 1 and v. 1. 5) and Jan. 399 ; and Eutychianus in Dec. 399 (when Aurelian was Prefect). On the general question see Mommsen, *Hist. Schr.* iii. p. 290 ; Seeck, in *Philologus*, 52, p. 449. The list of the laws which are concerned will be found in Mommsen's ed. of *C. Th.* i. pp. clxxv-vi.

reared up in an atmosphere of flattery and illusion, at the mercy of intriguing chamberlains and eunuchs. In such conditions aulic cabals and chamber cabinets are a natural growth.

The greatest blot on the ministry of Eutropius (for, as he was the most trusted adviser of the Emperor, we may use the word ministry), was the sale of offices, of which the poet Claudian gives a vivid and exaggerated account.[1] This was a blot, however, that stained other powerful men in those days as well as Eutropius, and we must view it rather as a feature of the times than as a peculiar enormity. Of course, the eunuch's spies were ubiquitous ; of course, informers of all sorts were encouraged and rewarded. All the usual stratagems for grasping and plundering were put into practice. The strong measures that a determined minister was ready to take for the mere sake of vengeance, may be exemplified by the treatment which the whole Lycian province received at the hands of Rufinus. On account of a single individual, Tatian, who had offended that minister, all the provincials were excluded from public offices.[2] After the death of Rufinus, the Lycians were relieved from these disabilities ; but the fact that the edict of repeal expressly enjoins " that no one henceforward venture to wound a Lycian citizen with a name of scorn " shows what a serious misfortune their degradation was.[3]

The eunuch won considerable odium in the first year of his power (A.D. 396) by bringing about the fall of two soldiers of distinction, whose wealth he coveted—Abundantius, to whose patronage he owed his rise in the world, and Timasius, who had been the commander-general in the East. The arts by which Timasius was ruined may illustrate the character of the intrigues that were spun at the Byzantine court.[4]

Timasius had brought with him from Sardis a Syrian sausage-seller, named Bargus, who, with native address, had insinuated himself into his good graces, and obtained a subordinate command in the army. The prying omniscience of Eutropius discovered that, years before, this same Bargus had been forbidden

---

[1] *In Eutrop.* i. 198 *instilor imperii, caupo famosus honorum,* etc.

[2] Probably in A.D. 394. Tatian had been Praetorian Prefect of the East 389–393 and Consul in 391. His son Proclus was Prefect of the City 389–392. Both incurred the jealousy of Rufinus, who procured their arrest and condemnation. Proclus was beheaded, Tatian exiled to Lycia. Cp. Asterius, *op. cit. ib.*

[3] *C. Th.* ix. 38. 9 ; Claudian, *In Ruf.* i. 232.

[4] Zosimus, v. 8.

to enter Constantinople for some misdemeanour, and by means of this knowledge he gained an ascendency over the Syrian, and compelled him to accuse his benefactor Timasius of a treasonable conspiracy and to support the charge by forgeries. The accused was tried,[1] condemned, and banished to the Libyan oasis, a punishment equivalent to death ; he was never heard of more. Eutropius, foreseeing that the continued existence of Bargus might at some time compromise himself, suborned his wife to lodge very serious charges against her husband, in consequence of which he was put to death.

It seems probable that a serious plot was formed in the year 397, aiming at the overthrow of Eutropius. Though this is not stated by any writer, it seems a legitimate inference from a law [2] which was passed in the autumn of that year, assessing the penalty of death to any one who had conspired " with soldiers or private persons, including barbarians," against the lives " of *illustres* who belong to our consistory or assist at our counsels," or other senators, such a conspiracy being considered equivalent to treason. Intent was to be regarded as equivalent to crime, and not only did the person concerned incur capital punishment, but his descendants were visited with disfranchisement. It is generally recognised that this law was an express protection for chamberlains ; but we must suppose it to have been suggested by some actual conspiracy, of which Eutropius had discovered the threads. The mention of *soldiers* and *barbarians* points to a particular danger, and we may suspect that Gaïnas, who afterwards brought about the fall of Eutropius, had some connexion with it.

During this year, Stilicho was engaged in establishing his power in Italy and probably in courting a popularity which he had so far done little to deserve. He found time to pay a hurried visit [3] to the Rhine provinces, to conciliate or pacify the federate

---

[1] The general feeling in favour of Timasius, a man of the highest character, was so great that the Emperor gave up his first intention of presiding at the trial. The letter of Jerome (lx.—quoted above, p. 114), which was written in 396, proves that Abundantius and Timasius were exiled in that year. Abundantius had been consul and *mag. utr. mil.*, Timasius consul and *mag. mil.* Their fates are referred to by Asterius, *ib.* (cp. M. Bauer, *Asterios Bischof von Amaseia*, 1911, p.

12 *sqq.*). See also Sozomen, viii. 17.

[2] Sept. 4 ; *C. Th.* ix. 14. 3.

[3] Cp. Claudian, *De cons. Stil.* i. 218 *sqq.* Perhaps it was at this time that the military administration on the Rhine frontier was reorganised by the institution of two new high commands, that of the dux Mogontiacensis (*Not., Occ.*, xli.) and that of the comes Argentoratensis (*ib.* xxvii.), who had their seats at Mainz and Strassburg respectively. Cp. Seeck, art. *Comites*, in P.-W.

Franks and other German peoples on the frontier, and perhaps to collect recruits for the army. We may conjecture that he also made arrangements for the return of his own family to Italy. He had not abandoned his designs on Eastern Illyricum, but he was anxious to have it understood that he aimed at fraternal concord between the courts of Milan and Byzantium and that the interests of Arcadius were no less dear to him than those of Honorius. The poet Claudian, who filled the rôle of an unofficial poet-laureate to Honorius, was really retained by Stilicho who patronised and paid him. His political poems are extravagant eulogies of the powerful general, and in some cases we may be sure that his arguments were directly inspired by his patron. In the panegyric for the Third Consulate of Honorius (A.D. 396) which, composed soon after the death of Rufinus, suggests a spirit of concord between East and West, the writer calls upon Stilicho to protect the two brethren :

> geminos dextra tu protege fratres.

Such lines as this were written to put a certain significance on Stilicho's policy.

For Stilicho was preparing to intervene again in the affairs of the East. We must return here to the movements of Alaric who, when the Imperial armies retreated from Thessaly without striking a blow, had Greece at his mercy. Gerontius, the commander of the garrison at Thermopylae, offered no resistance to his passage ; Antiochus, the pro-consul of Achaia, was helpless, and the Goths entered Boeotia, where Thebes alone escaped their devastation.[1] They occupied Piraeus but Athens itself was spared, and Alaric was entertained as a guest in the city of Athene.[2] But the great temple of the mystic goddesses, Demeter and Persephone, at Eleusis was plundered by the barbarians ; Megara, the next place on their southward route, fell ; then Corinth, Argos, and Sparta. It is possible that Alaric entertained

---

[1] For the invasion, besides Zosimus, see Socrates vii. 10. It is noticed also by Eunapius, *Vita Maximi* (i. p. 52), and *Vita Prisci* (i. p. 67).

[2] The walls of Athens had been restored in the reign of Valerian (Zosimus, i. 29), and Alaric was amenable to terms. The legend was that he saw Athene Promachus standing on the walls, and Achilles in front of them (*ib.* v. 6). Philostorgius says that Alaric " took Athens " (xii. 2) but he meant Piraeus. The mischief wrought by the Goths in Greece has often been exaggerated (see Gregorovius, *Gesch. der Stadt Athen*, i. 35 *sqq.* ; Bury, App. 13 to Gibbon, vol. iii.).

the design of settling his people permanently in the Peloponnesus.[1]
However this may be, he remained there for more than a year,
and the government of Arcadius took no steps to dislodge him
or arrange a settlement.

Then in the spring of A.D. 397,[2] Stilicho sailed across from
Italy, and landing at Corinth marched to Elis where he confronted
Alaric. There was some fighting—enough to give the general's
poet a pretext for singing of the slaughter of skin-clad warriors
(*metitur pellita iuventus*).[3] But the outcome was that the Gothic
enemy was spared in Elis much as he had been spared in Thessaly.
The Eastern government seems to have again intervened with
success.[4] But what happened is unknown, except that Stilicho
made some agreement with Alaric,[5] and Alaric withdrew to
Epirus, where he appears to have come to terms with Arcadius
and perhaps to have received the title he coveted of Master of
Soldiers in Illyricum.[6]

That Stilicho had set out with the purpose of settling the
question of Illyricum cannot be seriously doubted. That he
withdrew for the second time without accomplishing his purpose
was probably due to the news of a dangerous revolt in Africa
to which the government of Arcadius was accessory. We can
easily understand the indignation felt at Constantinople when it
was known that Stilicho had landed in Greece with an army.
It was natural that the strongest protest should be made, and
Eutropius persuaded the Emperor and the Senate to declare him
a public enemy.[7]

Of this futile expedition, Claudian has given a highly misleading

---

[1] So Schmidt, *ib.* 197.

[2] Since Koch's article in *Rh.
Museum*, xliv. (1889), it has generally
been recognised that Stilicho's second
expedition to Greece must be placed
in 397 (not 396). See Birt, *Praef.* to
Claudian, p. xxxi; Gibbon, *Decline*,
iii. editor's App. 12. The spring of
the year must be inferred from
Claudian, *De c. Stil.* i. 174 *sqq.* That
Elis was the scene of operations is
proved by *Pholoe* in Zos. v. 7. 2, and
more than one reference to the
Alpheus in Claudian. The second Book
In Rufinum was not published till
after this campaign (see *Praef.* 9 *sqq.*).

[3] *De iv. cons. Hon.* 466. Cp. *De cons.
Stil.* 186 *Alpheus Geticis angustus
acervis.*

[4] See Claudian, *B. Got.* 517 *sub
nomine legum proditio regnique favor
texisset Eoi.*

[5] Claudian *ib.* 496 seems to imply
that Alaric undertook not to cross
the frontiers of the territory of
Honorius.

[6] Cp. *ib.* 535-539 and *In Eutrop.* ii.
216. Was this a breach of the agreement with Stilicho (cp. *foedera rumpit,
ib.* 213) ?—It may have been during
this absence of Stilicho that Serena
embellished with marble the tomb of
St. Nazarius at Milan as a vow for
his safe return, *C.I.L.* v. 6250, unless
it were rather in the Raetian campaign of 401-402.

[7] Zosimus, v. 11.

account in his panegyric in honour of the Fourth Consulate of Honorius (A.D. 398), which no allowance for conventional exaggeration can excuse. He overwhelms the boy of fourteen with the most extravagant adulations, pretending that he is greater—vicariously indeed, through the deeds of his general— than his father and grandfather. We can hardly feel able to accord the poet much credit when he declares that the western provinces are not oppressed by heavy taxes nor the treasury replenished by extortion.[1]

§ 3. *The Rebellion of Gildo* (A.D. 397–398)

Eighteen years before an attempt had been made by the Moor Firmus to create a kingdom for himself in the African provinces (A.D. 379), and had been quelled by the armies of Theodosius, who had received valuable aid from Gildo, the brother and enemy of Firmus. Gildo was duly rewarded. He was finally appointed Count of Africa with the exceptional title of Master of Soldiers, and his daughter Salvina was united in marriage to a nephew of the Empress Aelia Flaccilla.[2] But the faith of the Moors was as the faith of the Carthaginians. Gildo refused to send troops to Theodosius in his expedition against Eugenius, and after the Emperor's death he prepared to assume a more decided attitude of independence and engaged many African tribes to support him in a revolt. The strained relations between the two Imperial courts suggested to him that the rebellion might assume the form of a transference of Africa from the sovranty of Honorius to that of Arcadius ; and he entered into communication with Constantinople, where his over- tures were welcomed. A transference of the diocese of Africa to Arcadius seemed quite an appropriate answer to the proposal of transferring the Prefecture of Illyricum to Honorius. But the Eastern government rendered no active assistance to the rebel.[3]

---

[1] 496 *sqq.* Claudian is at his finest in his eulogies of Theodosius *avus*, the hero of Africa and Britain, and Theodosius *pater*, the Great.

[2] Nebridius. Salvina was after- wards a friend of John Chrysostom.

[3] Zosimus, *ib.* It appears that embassies on the subject passed between Italy and Constantinople (Symmachus, *Epp.* iv. 5 ; Claudian, *B. Gild.* 236 *sqq.*, 279 *De cons. Stil.* i. 295 ; Orosius, vii. 36), and that Arcadius went so far as to issue edicts menacing any one who should attack Gildo, see Claudian, *De cons. Stil.* i. 275 *sqq.*—

> hoc Africa saevis cinxerat auxiliis, hoc coniuratus alebat insidiis Oriens. illinc edicta meabant corruptura duces.

For Rome and the Italians a revolt in Africa was more serious than rebellions elsewhere, since the African provinces were their granary. In the summer of A.D. 397 Gildo did not allow corn ships to sail to the Tiber; this was the declaration of war. The prompt and efficient action of Stilicho prevented a calamity; corn supplies were obtained from Gaul and Spain sufficient to feed Rome during the winter months. Preparations were made to suppress Gildo, and Stilicho sought to ingratiate himself with the Senate by reverting to the ancient usage of obtaining its formal authority.[1] The Senate declared Gildo a public enemy, and during the winter a fleet of transports was collected at Pisa. In the early spring an army of perhaps 10,000 embarked.[2] Stilicho remained in Italy, and the command was entrusted to Mascezel, a brother of Gildo who had come to the court of Honorius to betray Gildo as Gildo had betrayed Firmus. The war was decided, the rebel subdued, almost without bloodshed, in the Byzacene province on the little river Ardalio between Tebessa and Haïdra. The forces of Gildo are said to have been 70,000 strong, but they offered no resistance. We may suspect that some of his Moorish allies had been corrupted by Mascezel, but Gildo himself was probably an unpopular leader. He tried to escape by ship, but was driven ashore again at Thabraca and put to death.[3]

Returning to Italy, Mascezel was welcomed as a victor, and might reasonably hope for promotion to some high post. But his swift and complete success was not pleasing to Stilicho, who desired to appropriate the whole credit for the deliverance of Italy from a grave danger; perhaps he saw in Mascezel a possible rival. Whether by accident or design, the Moor was removed from his path. The only writer who distinctly records the event, states that while he was crossing a bridge he was thrown into a river by Stilicho's bodyguards and that Stilicho gave the sign for the act.[4] The evidence is not good enough to justify us in

---

[1] Claudian, *De cons. Stil.* i. 326 *sqq.*—

non ante fretis exercitus adstitit ultor
ordine quam prisco censeret bella senatus
neglectum Stilicho per tot iam saecula morem
rettulit, etc.

[2] So Seeck (*Forsch. zur d. Geschichte*, 24, 175 *sqq.*), who identifies the troops (chiefly auxilia palatina) named by Claudian, *B. Gild.* 418-423. Orosius, vii. 36, says 5000 (*ut aiunt*).

[3] Claudian, *De cons. Stil.* i. 359, ii.

258; *In Eutrop.* i. 410; *De vi. cons. Hon.* 381. The date was July 31, *Fasti Vind. pr.*, *sub a.* 398 (*Chron. min.* i. p. 398). According to Zosimus (v. 11) Gildo took his own life.

[4] Zosimus, v. 11. Orosius (*ib.*), who represents the Moor's death as a punishment for profaning a church, does not tell how it occurred; but *occisus est* means a violent end.

bringing in a verdict of murder against Stilicho ; Mascezel may have been accidentally drowned and the story of foul play may have been circulated by Stilicho's enemies.   But if the ruler of Italy was innocent, he assuredly did not regret the capable executor of his plans.   The order seems to have gone out that the commander of the expedition against Gildo was to have no share in the glory,[1] and the incomplete poem of Claudian on the *Gildonic War* tells the same tale.

This poem, which will serve as an example of Claudian's art, begins with an announcement of the victory and was probably composed when the first news of the success arrived in Italy. *Redditus imperiis Auster,* " the South has been restored to our Empire ; the twin spheres, Europe and Libya, are reunited ; and the concord of the brethren is again complete." *Iam domitus Gildo,* the tyrant has already been vanquished, and we can hardly believe that this has been accomplished so quickly.

Having announced the glad tidings, Claudian goes back to the autumn and imagines Rome, the goddess of the city, in fear of famine and disaster, presenting herself in pitiable guise before the throne of Jupiter and supplicating him to save her from hunger.   Are the labours and triumphs of her glorious history to be all in vain ?   Is the amplitude of her Empire to be her doom ?   *Ipsa nocet moles.*   " I am excluded from my granaries, Libya and Egypt ; I am abandoned in my old age."

> Nunc quid agam ?   Libyam Gildo tenet, altera [2] Nilum.
> ast ego, quae terras umeris pontumque subegi,
> deseror ; emeritae iam praemia nulla senectae.

The supplications of Rome are reinforced by the sudden appearance of Africa, who bursts into the divine assembly with torn raiment, and in wild words demands that Neptune should submerge her continent rather than it should have to submit to the pollution of Gildo's rule.

> Si mihi Gildonem nequeunt abducere fata,
> me rape Gildoni.

Jupiter dismisses the suppliants, assuring them that " Honorius will lay low the common enemy," and he sends Theodosius the

---

[1] Cp. *C.I.L.* vi. 1730 (see below, p. 125).   The question is discussed by Crees, *Claudian* 102 *sqq.*   The inscription found in the Roman Forum,

armipotens Libycum defendit Honoriu[s orbem],

may refer to the Gildonic War, *C.I.L.* vi. 31256.

[2] I.e. *altera Roma*, Constantinople.

Great and his father, who are both deities in Olympus, to appear
to the two reigning Emperors in the night. Arcadius is
reproached by his father for the estrangement from his brother,
for his suspicions of Stilicho, for entertaining the proposals of
Gildo ; and he promises to do nothing to aid Gildo. Honorius
is stimulated by his grandfather to rise without delay and smite
the rebel. He summons Stilicho and proposes to lead an expedition himself. Stilicho persuades him that it would be unsuitable
to his dignity to take the field against such a foe, and suggests
that the enterprise should be committed to Mascezel. This is
the only passage in which Mascezel is mentioned, and Claudian
does not bestow any praise on him further than the admission
that he does not resemble his brother in character (*sed non et
moribus isdem*), but dwells on the wrongs he had suffered, and
argues that to be crushed by his injured brother, the suppliant
of the Emperor, will be the heaviest blow that could be inflicted
on the rebel.

The military preparations are then described, and an inspiriting
address to the troops, about to embark, is put into the mouth
of Honorius, who tells them that the fate of Rome depends on
their valour :

> caput insuperabile rerum
> aut ruet in vestris aut stabit Roma lacertis.

The fleet sails and safely reaches the African ports, and the first
canto of the poem ends.[1]

It is all we have ; a second canto was never written. Claudian
evidently intended to sing the whole story of the campaign as
soon as the story was known. The overthrow of " the third
tyrant," whom he represents as the successor of Maximus and
Eugenius, deserved an exhaustive song of triumph. But it
would have surpassed even the skill of Claudian to have told the
tale without giving a meed of praise to the commander who
carried the enterprise through to its victorious end. We need
have little hesitation in believing that the motive which hindered
the poet from completing the *Gildonic War* was the knowledge
that to celebrate the achievements of Mascezel would be no service
to his patron.[2]

[1] In the MSS. it is described as
Liber primus.

[2] The complications which resulted
in Africa from the despotism of Gildo,
and the efforts to right wrongs and
restore property, lasted for many
years. The large property which
Gildo had amassed required a special

While the issue of the war was still uncertain, in the spring of A.D. 398,[1] Stilicho's position as master of the west was strengthened by the marriage of his daughter Maria with the youthful Emperor. Claudian wrote an epithalamium for the occasion, duly extolling anew the virtues of his incomparable patron. We may perhaps wonder that, secured by this new bond with the Imperial house, and his prestige enhanced by the suppression of Gildo,[2] Stilicho did not now make some attempt to carry out his project of annexing the Prefecture of Illyricum. The truth is that he had not abandoned it, but he was waiting for a favourable opportunity of intervention in the affairs of the east. It seems safe to infer his attitude from the drift of Claudian's poems, for Claudian, if he did not receive express instructions, had sufficient penetration to divine the note which Stilicho would have wished him to strike. In the *Gildonic War* he had announced the restoration of concord between east and west : *concordia fratrum plena redit* ; it was the right thing to say at the moment, but the strain in the relations between the two courts had only relaxed a little. The discord broke out again, with more fury than ever, in the two poems in which he overwhelmed Eutropius with rhetoric no less savage than his fulminations against Rufinus four years before. The first was written at the beginning of A.D. 399, protesting against the disgrace of the Empire by the elevation of Eutropius to the consulate, the second in the summer, after the eunuch's fall. The significant point is that in both poems the intervention of Stilicho in eastern affairs is proposed.[3] Stilicho did not overtly intervene ; but it seems probable that he had an understanding with Gaïnas, the German commander in the east, who had been his instrument

official to administrate it, entitled *comes Gildoniaci patrimonii.* See *C. Th.* vii. 8. 7, and *Notit. Occ.* xi.

[1] Claudian, *De cons. Stil.* i. 1-5.

[2] An inscription in honour of Stilicho on a marble base, found at Rome (*C.I.L.* vi. 1730), celebrates the " deliverance " of Africa :

Fl(avio) Stilichoni inlustrissimo viro, magistro equitum peditumque, comiti domesticorum, tribuno praetoriano et ab ineunte aetate per gradus clarissimae militiae ad columen gloriae sempiternae et regiae

adfinitatis evecto, progenero divi Theodosi, comiti divi Theodosi Augusti in omnibus bellis adque victoriis et ab eo in adfinitatem regiam cooptato itemque socero d. n. Honori Augusti Africa consiliis et provisione et liberata.

There is also an inscription to the two Emperors, belonging to some memorial erected by the Senate and Roman people, *vindicata rebellione et Africae restitutione laetus* ; *C.I.L.* vi. 31256. This is the *titulus perennis* of Claudian, *De vi. cons. Hon.* 372. Cp. also *C.I.L.* ix. 4051.

[3] *In Eutrop.* i. 500 *sqq.*, ii. 591 *sqq.*

in the assassination of Rufinus.   It is a suggestive fact that in
describing the drama which was enacted in the east Claudian
brings the minor characters on the stage but does not even
pronounce the name of Gaïnas, who was the principal actor,
or betray that he was aware of his existence.   We must now
pass to the east and follow the events of that drama.

§ 4.   *Fall of Eutropius and the German Danger in the East*
(A.D. 398–400)

In these years, in which barbarians were actively harrying
the provinces of the Illyrian peninsula and the eastern provinces
of Asia Minor, concord and mutual assistance between east and
west were urgently needed.   Unfortunately, the reins of government were in the hands of men who for different reasons were
unpopular and in all their political actions were influenced
chiefly by the consideration of their own fortunes.   The position
of Eutropius was insecure, because he was a eunuch ; that of
Stilicho, because he was a German.   So far as the relation
between the two governments was concerned the situation had
been eased for a time after the fall of Rufinus, and it was doubtless
with the consent and perhaps at the invitation of Eutropius
that Stilicho had sailed to Greece in A.D. 397.   For the eastern
armies were not strong enough to contend at the same time
against Alaric and against the Huns who were devastating in
Asia.   The generals who were sent to expel the invaders from
Cappadocia and the Pontic provinces seem to have been incompetent, and Eutropius decided to take over the supreme
command himself.   It was probably in A.D. 398 that he conducted a campaign which was attended with success.   The
barbarians were driven back to the Caucasus and the eunuch
returned triumphant to Constantinople.[1]   His victory secured
him some popularity for the moment, and he was designated
consul for the following year.

The brief understanding between the courts of Milan and

---

[1] Claudian, *In Eutr.* i. 234-286.   We
can read clearly through the jeers
and sarcasms of the poet that the
martial adventure of Eutropius was
a distinct success.   It is not proved
that he assumed the office and title
of a Master of Soldiers, as Birt thinks

(*Preface*, xxxiv.) ; but, however this
may be, Birt is certainly wrong in
his view that Eutropius ever filled
the office of Praetorian Prefect.   The
expressions of Claudian which he
cites (*ib.* xxx.) are far from proving
it.

Byzantium had been broken as we saw by the attitude of the
eastern government during the revolt of Gildo. There was
an open breach. When the news came that Eutropius was
nominated consul for A.D. 399, the Roman feelings of the Italians
were deeply scandalised. A eunuch for a consul—it was an
unheard-of, an intolerable violation of the tradition of the
Roman Fasti.

Omnia cesserunt eunucho consule monstra

wrote Claudian in the poem in which, at the beginning of the
year, he castigated the minister of Arcadius.[1] The west refused
to recognise this monstrous consulship.[2] It was perhaps hardly
less unpopular in the east.

The Grand Chamberlain, confidently secure through his
possession of the Emperor's ear, had overshot the mark. His
position was now threatened from two quarters. Gaïnas, the
German officer who under the direction of Stilicho had led the
eastern army back to Constantinople, had risen to the office
of a Master of Soldiers.[3] It is probable that he maintained
communications with Stilicho, and his first object was to compass
the downfall of Eutropius.

Less dangerous but not less hostile was the Roman party,
which was equally opposed to the bedchamber administration
of Eutropius and to the growth of German power. It consisted
of senators and ministers attached to Roman traditions, who
were scandalised by the nomination of the eunuch to the consulship in A.D. 399 and alarmed by the fact that some of the highest
military commands in the Empire were held by Germans. The
leader of the party was Aurelian, son of Taurus (formerly a
Praetorian Prefect of Italy), who had himself filled the office
of Prefect of the City.

Gaïnas had some supporters among the Romans. The most
powerful of his friends was an enigmatical figure, whose real
name is unknown but who seems to have been a brother of

---

[1] *In Eutropium liber I.* (cp. Birt,
ib. xl.).

[2] After this year, the practice was
introduced of publishing the eastern
and western consuls successively, in
each part of the Empire. Simultaneous publication only occurred
when the consuls had been fixed
before Jan. 1 by special arrangement,
as when two Emperors assumed the
office together. Mommsen, *Hist. Schr.*
iii. 367.

[3] Socrates, vi. 6 στρατηλάτης ‘Ρωμαίων
ἱππικῆς τε καὶ πεζικῆς, *i.e. Mag. mil.
in praesenti*; Philostorgius, xi. 8 ὁ
στρατηγός, cp. Sozomen, viii. 4 *ad
init.* Cp. Tillemont, *Histoire*, v.
p. 783.

Aurelian. Of this dark person, who played a leading part in the events of these years, we derive all we know from a historical sketch which its author Synesius of Cyrene cast into the form of an allegory and entitled *Concerning Providence or the Egyptians*. This distinguished man of letters, who was at this time a Platonist —some years later he was to embrace Christianity and accept a bishopric—was on terms of intimacy with Aurelian and was at Constantinople at this time.[1] The argument is the contest for the kingship of Egypt between the sons of Taurus, Osiris and Typhos. Osiris embodies all that is best in human nature. Typhos is a monster, perverse, gross, and ignorant. Osiris is Aurelian ; Typhos cannot be identified,[2] and we must call him by his allegorical name ; the kingship of Egypt means the Praetorian Prefecture of the east.

In the race for political power Typhos allied himself with the German party, who welcomed him as a Roman of good family and position. Synesius dwells much on his profligacy, and on the frivolous habits of his wife, an ambitious and fashionable lady. She was her own tirewoman, a reproach which seems to mean that she was inordinately attentive to the details of her toilet.[3] She liked public admiration and constantly showed herself at the theatre and in the streets. Her love of notoriety did not permit her to be fastidious in her choice of society, she liked to have her salon filled, and her doors were not closed to professional courtesans. Synesius contrasts her with the modest wife of Aurelian, who never left her house, and asserts that the chief virtue of a woman is that neither her body nor her name should ever cross the threshold. This is a mere rhetorical flourish ; the writer's friend and teacher, Hypatia the philosopher,

---

[1] He was there for three years (A.D. 399–402): *Hymns*, iii. 430-434 ; he went home during the great earthquake of 402. *Epp.* 61, p. 1404. Cp. Seeck, in *Philologus* 52, p. 458.

[2] On the interpretation of the allegory see Sievers, *Studien*, 387 *sqq.*, Seeck, 442 *sqq.*, and *Untergang*, v. 314 *sqq.*, Mommsen, *Hist. Schr.* iii. 292 *sqq.* Thebes is Constantinople, and the high priest (p. 1268) is Arcadius. Seeck has endeavoured to prove that Typhos is Caesarius, who succeeded Rufinus as Pr. Prefect of the east in 395 and held that office till 397, in which year he was consul (see

laws in *C. Th.* ed. Mommsen, i. p. clxxv., Philostorgius xi. 5). Mommsen has given cogent reasons for rejecting this view. If Typhos is Caesarius, it ought to have been mentioned that he had already held the office of king, but Synesius says (p. 1217) that he was ταμίας χρημάτων, which would naturally mean *comes rei privatae* (Seeck interprets it as Praet. Pr., but Synesius describes it as a διάθεσις ἐλάττων), and then apparently a governor of part of the Empire (perhaps a *vicarius*).

[3] P. 1240 ἑαυτῆς κομμώτρια, θεάτρου καὶ ἀγορᾶς ἄπληστος κτλ.

whom he venerated, certainly did not stay at home. He was probably thinking of the piece of advice to women which Thucydides placed in the mouth of Pericles.

The struggle against the German power in the east began in the spring of A.D. 399. It was brought on by a movement on the part of Ostrogoths in Phrygia, but we have no distinct evidence to show that it was instigated by Gaïnas.[1] These Ostrogoths had been established as colons[2] by Theodosius the Great in fertile regions of that province (in A.D. 386), and contributed a squadron of cavalry to the Roman army. The commander, Tribigild, bore Eutropius a personal grudge, and he excited his Ostrogoths to revolt. The rebellion broke out just as Arcadius and his court were preparing to start for Ancyra, whither he was fond of resorting in summer to enjoy its pleasant and salubrious climate.

The barbarians were recruited by runaway slaves and spread destruction throughout Galatia, Pisidia, and Bithynia. Two generals, Gaïnas and Leo, a friend of Eutropius—a good-humoured, corpulent man who was nicknamed Ajax—were sent to quell the rising.

It was at this time that Synesius, the philosopher of Cyrene, who had come to the capital to present a gold crown to Arcadius on behalf of his native city, fulfilled his mission and used the occasion to deliver a remarkable speech " On the office of King." [3] It may be regarded as the anti-German manifesto of the party of Aurelian [4] with which Synesius had enthusiastically identified himself. The orator urged the policy of imposing disabilities on the Germans in order to eradicate the German element in the State. The argument depends on the Hellenic but by no means Christian principle that Roman and barbarian are different in kind and therefore their union is unnatural. The soldiers of a state should be its watchdogs, in Plato's phrase, but our armies are full of wolves in the guise of dogs. Our homes are full of German servants. A state cannot wisely give arms to

---

[1] Tribigild had visited the capital at the beginning of 399 to pay his respects to Eutropius the new consul, who on this occasion slighted him. It is possible that he arranged the plan of campaign with Gaïnas before he returned to Phrygia. But their complicity may have begun only after the fall of Eutropius.

[2] Claudian, *In Eutrop.* ii. 153, *Ostrogothis colitur mixtisque Gruthungis Phryx ager.* Gruthungis is only another name for Ostrogoths.

[3] Περὶ βασιλείας, *Opera* p. 1053 *sqq.*

[4] Cp. Sievers, *Studien*, p. 379, and Güldenpenning, *Gesch. d. oström. Reiches*, p. 106.

any who have not been born and reared under its laws ; the shepherd cannot expect to tame the cubs of wolves. Our German troops are a stone of Tantalus suspended over our State, and the only salvation is to remove the alien element.[1] The policy of Theodosius the Great was a mistake. Let the barbarians be sent back to their wilds beyond the Danube, or if they remain be set to till the fields as serfs. It was a speech which if it came to the ears of Gaïnas was not calculated to stimulate his zeal against the Germans he went forth to reduce.

The rebels, seeking to avoid an engagement with Leo's army, turned their steps to Pisidia and thence to Pamphylia, where they met unexpected resistance.[2] While Gaïnas was inactive and writing in his reports to Constantinople that Tribigild was extremely formidable, Valentine, a landowner of Selge, gathered an armed band of peasants and slaves and laid an ambush near a narrow winding pass in the mountains between Pisidia and Pamphylia. The advancing enemy were surprised by showers of stones from the heights above them, and it was difficult to escape as there was a treacherous marsh all around. The pass was held by a Roman officer, and Tribigild succeeded in bribing him to allow his forces to cross it. But they had no sooner escaped than, shut in between two rivers, the Melas and the Eurymedon, they were attacked by the warlike inhabitants of the district. Leo meanwhile was advancing, and the insurrection might have been crushed if Gaïnas had not secretly reinforced the rebels with detachments from his own army. Then the German troops under his own command attacked and overpowered their Roman fellow-soldiers, and Leo lost his life in attempting to escape.[3] Gaïnas ánd Tribigild were masters of the situation, but they still pretended to be enemies.

Gaïnas, posing as a loyal general, foiled by the superior power of the Ostrogoths, despatched a message to the Emperor urging him to yield to Tribigild's demand and depose Eutropius from power. Arcadius might not have yielded if a weightier influence had not been brought to bear upon him. The Empress Eudoxia, who had owed her fortune to the eunuch, had become jealous of the boundless power he had secured over her husband's

---

[1] 'Εκκρῖναι δἐ δεῖ τἀλλότριον, p. 1089.

[2] Zosimus, v. 16.

[3] Claudian, writing to put him in a ridiculous light, pretends that he was killed by fright—*ualuit pro uulnere terror* (*In Eutr.* ii. 453). Leo was doubtless one of the two Masters of Soldiers *in praesenti*.

mind ; there was unconcealed antagonism between them ; and one day Eudoxia appeared in the Emperor's presence, with her two little daughters,[1] and made bitter complaint of the Chamberlain's insulting behaviour.

Eutropius realised his extreme peril when he heard of the demand of Gaïnas and he fled for refuge to the sanctuary of St. Sophia.[2] There he might not only trust in the protection of the holy place, but might expect that the Patriarch would stand by him in his extremity when he was deserted by his noonday friends. For it was through him that John Chrysostom, a Syrian priest of Antioch, had been appointed to the see of Constantinople in the preceding year. And the Patriarch's personal interference was actually needed. Arcadius had determined to sacrifice him, and Chrysostom had to stand between the cowering eunuch and those who would have dragged him from the altar. This incident seems to have occurred on a Saturday, and on the morrow, Sunday, there must have been strange excitement in the congregation which assembled to hear the eloquence of the preacher. Hidden under the altar, overwhelmed with fear and shame, lay the old man whose will had been supreme a few days before, and in the pulpit the Patriarch delivered a sermon on the moral of his fall, beginning with the words, " Vanity of vanities, all is vanity." [3] While he mercilessly exposed the levity and irreligion of Eutropius and his circle, he sought at the same time to excite the sympathy of his hearers.

The church was again entered by soldiers, and again Chrysostom interposed. Then Eutropius allowed himself to be removed on condition that his life was spared. He was deprived of his patrician rank, banished to Cyprus, and his property was confiscated. The imperial edict which pronounced this sentence is profuse of the language of obloquy.[4] The consulship " befouled and defiled by a filthy monster " has been " delivered

---

[1] Flaccilla, born June 17, 397, and Pulcheria, born Jan. 19, 399 (*Chr. Pasch., sub annis*). We never hear of Flaccilla again, she probably died in girlhood. The third child, Arcadia, was born April 3, 400 ; the youngest daughter, Marina, Feb. 11, 403.

[2] The fall of Eutropius is recounted by the ecclesiastical historians, and by Zosimus (v. 18).

[3] Ὁμιλία εἰς Εὐτρόπιον, *P.G.* 52. 391 *sqq.* Asterius refers to the eunuch's fall in his sermon on the Calends (*P.G.* 40. 225), delivered Jan. 1, 400 (Bauer, *Asterios*, p. 21). He mentions the enormous landed property the eunuch had acquired, ἐκτήσατο γῆν ὅσην οὐδὲ εἰπεῖν εὔκολον.

[4] *C. Th.* ix. 40. 17, addressed to Aurelian Pr. Pr., but wrongly dated.

from the foul stain of his tenure and from the recollection of his name and the base filth thereof," by erasing his name from the Fasti. All statues in bronze or marble, all coloured pictures set up in his honour in public or private places, are to be abolished " that they may not, as a brand of infamy on our age, pollute the gaze of beholders."

The fall of Eutropius involved the fall of Eutychian, the Praetorian Prefect of the east, who was presumably one of his creatures. There was a contest between the two brothers, Aurelian and Typhos, for the vacant office, which Synesius in his allegory designated as the kingship of Egypt. But though Gaïnas had succeeded in overthrowing the eunuch, he failed to secure the appointment of Typhos. The post was given to Aurelian, and this was a triumph for the anti-German party.[1] Aurelian was a man of considerable intellectual attainments ; he was surrounded by men of letters such as Synesius, Troilus the poet, and Polyaemon the rhetor. His success was a severe blow to Typhos and his friends, and especially to his wife, who had been eagerly looking forward to the Prefecture for the sake of the social advantage of it. Synesius gives a curious description of the efforts of the profligate to console himself for his disappointment. He constructed a large pond in which he made artificial islands provided with warm baths, and in these retreats he and his friends, male and female, used to indulge in licentious pleasures.[2]

But if Aurelian's elevation was a blow to Typhos it was no less a blow to Gaïnas, who now threw off the mask and, openly declaring his true colours, acted no longer as a mediator for Tribigild, but as an adversary bargaining for terms. Tribigild and he met at Thyatira and advanced to the shores of the

---

[1] The last constitution addressed to Eutychian is dated July 25, 399 (*C. Th.* ix. 40. 18), the first to Aurelian, Aug. 27 (*ib.* ii. 8. 23). This gives limits for the fall of Eutropius, which may be placed in August.—There are many errors in the dates of the laws in *C. Th.* from 395 to 400. The solution certainly does not lie in Seeck's theory that Caesarius and Eutychian held the Pr. Prefecture conjointly in 396 and 397. The dates of the six laws addressed to Eutychian between Feb. 26, 396 and April 1, 397 ; as well as that to Caesarius on July 26, 398, are simply false. See above, p. 128, n. 2. The succession was Caesarius, Nov. 395 to July or August 397 ; Eutychian, to July or August 399 ; Aurelian, Aug. 399 to Oct. 6 at least (*C. Th.* iv. 21 ; v. 1. 5) ; Typhos (no laws) ; Aurelian again, 400, perhaps continuing to 402, if we accept Seeck's corrections in *C. Th.* iv. 2. 1 and v. 1. 5 of *Arc. A.* v. (for IIII) *et Honor. A.* v. (for III) *conss.*, *i.e.* 402 (for 396) ; Eutychian again 403-405. Cp. Seeck and Mommsen, *opp. citt.*

[2] *Egyptians*, p. 1245.

Propontis, plundering as they went. Gaïnas demanded and obtained an interview with the Emperor himself at Chalcedon. An agreement was made that he should be confirmed in his post as Master of Soldiers *in praesenti*,[1] that he and Tribigild might cross over into Europe, and that three hostages should be handed over to him, Aurelian, Saturninus, one of Aurelian's chief supporters, and John, the friend (report said the lover) of the Empress. This meant the deposition of Aurelian from the Prefecture and the succession of Typhos. For the moment Gaïnas was master of the government of the east (end of A.D. 399).

The demand for the surrender of Aurelian had been prearranged with Typhos,[2] and the intention seems to have been to put him to death. The Patriarch went over to Chalcedon to intercede for the lives of the three hostages, and Gaïnas contented himself with inflicting the humiliation of a sham execution and banishing them. He then entered Constantinople with his army.[3] The rule of Gaïnas seems to have lasted for about six months (to July A.D. 400). But he was evidently a man of no ability. He had not even a definite plan of action, and of his short period of power nothing is recorded except that he tried to secure for the Arians a church of their own within the city, and failed through the intolerant opposition of the Patriarch ; and that his plans to seize the Imperial Palace, and to sack the banks of the money-changers, were frustrated.

This episode of German tyranny came to an abrupt end early in July. The Goth suddenly decided to quit the capital. We know not why he found his position untenable, or what his intentions were. Making an excuse of illness he went to perform his devotions in a church about seven miles distant, and ordered his Goths to follow him in relays. Their preparations for departure frightened the inhabitants, ignorant of their plans, and the city was so excited that any trifle might lead to serious consequences. It happened that a beggar-woman was standing at one of the western gates early in the morning asking for alms. At the unusual sight of a long line of Goths issuing from the

---

[1] Synesius describes the intrigues carried on by the wife of Typhos and the wife of Gaïnas, p. 1245. The Gothic lady is described as a βάρβαρος γραῦς καὶ ἀνόητος.

[2] Sozomen, viii. 4 ; Tillemont, v. 461.

[3] Tribigild disappears entirely from the scene ; he perished soon afterwards.

gate she thought it was the last day for Constantinople and prayed aloud. Her prayer offended a passing Goth, and as he was about to cut her down a Roman intervened and slew him. The incident led to a general tumult, and the citizens succeeded in closing the gates, so that the Goths who had not yet passed through were cut off from their comrades without. There were some thousands of them [1] but not enough to cope with the infuriated people. They sought refuge in a church (near the Palace) which had been appropriated to the use of such Goths as had embraced the Catholic faith. There they suffered a fate like that which had befallen the oligarchs of Corcyra during the Peloponnesian war. The roof was removed and the barbarians were done to death under showers of stones and burning brands (July 12, A.D. 400).[2]

The immediate consequence of this deliverance was the fall of Typhos [3] and the return of Aurelian, who at once replaced him in the Prefecture. The conduct of Typhos was judicially investigated, his treasonable collusion with the Germans was abundantly exposed, and he was condemned provisionally to imprisonment. He was afterwards rescued from the vengeance of the mob by his brother. His subsequent fate is as unknown to us as his name. Aurelian, who had been designated for the consulship of the year 400, but had been unable to enter upon it in January, seems now to have been invested with the insignia,[4] and the name of whatever person had been chosen to fill it by Typhos and Gaïnas was struck from the Fasti.

Gaïnas, in the meantime, a declared enemy, like Alaric three years before, marched plundering through Thrace. But he won little booty, for the inhabitants had retreated into the strong places which he was unable to take. He marched to the Hellespont, intending to pass over into Asia. But when he reached

---

[1] Synesius says they numbered 7000, rather more than one-fifth of the whole army of Gaïnas; which has hence been reckoned by modern writers as 30,000 strong. The number is probably much too high. In any case the church could not have been large enough to hold 7000.

[2] These events are related by Synesius, p. 1261 *sqq.*, Zosimus, v. 19, Philostorgius, xi. 8, Socrates, vi. 6, Sozomen, viii. 4. Socrates had the poems of Eusebius and Ammonius (see below) before him. For date see *Chron. Pasch., sub a.*

[3] From Synesius we know that his tenure of the office was less than a year, p. 1256 : οὐ γὰρ ἐνιαυτοὺς ἀλλὰ μῆνας ἔφη τοὺς εἱμαρτοὺς εἶναι.

[4] This seems to be the meaning of Synesius, p. 12 μετὰ συνθήματος μείζονος. Zosimus, v. 18. 8, is inaccurate.

the coast opposite Abydos he found the Asiatic shore occupied by troops, who were supported by warships. These forces were under the command of Fravitta, a loyal pagan Goth who in the last years of Theodosius had played a considerable part in the politics of his own nation as leader of the philo-Roman party. He had since served under Arcadius, had been promoted to be Master of Soldiers in the east, and had cleared the eastern Mediterranean of pirates from Cilicia to Syria and Palestine.[1] The Goths encamped on the shore, but when their provisions were exhausted they resolved to attempt the crossing and constructed rude rafts which they committed to the current. Fravitta's ships easily sank them, and Gaïnas, who had remained on shore when he saw his troops perishing, hastened northwards, beyond Mount Haemus, even beyond the Danube, expecting to be pursued. Fravitta did not follow him, but he fell into the hands of Uldin, king of the Huns, who cut off his head and sent it as a grateful offering to Arcadius (December 23, A.D. 400). History has no regrets for the fate of this brutal and incompetent barbarian.

It was significant of the situation in the Empire that a Gothic enemy should be discomfited by a Goth. Fravitta enjoyed the honour of a triumph, and was designated consul for A.D. 401. Arcadius granted him the only favour he requested, to be allowed to worship after the fashion of his fathers.

Thus the German danger hanging over the Empire was warded off from the eastern provinces. Stilicho could no longer hope to interfere in eastern affairs through the Goths of the eastern army. The episode was a critical one in Roman history, and its importance was recognised at the time. It was celebrated in two epic poems [2] as well as in the myth of Synesius. Scenes from the revolt were represented in sculpture on the pillar of Arcadius which was set up in A.D. 403 in the Forum named after him.[3]

The year 400, which witnessed the failure of the German bid

---

[1] Zosimus, v. 20. 2. The article in Suidas, *s.v.* Φράβιθος, may come from Eunapius (see Müller, *F.H.G.* iv. 49).

[2] The *Gaïnia* of Eusebius (a pupil of Troilus, Aurelian's friend) and a poem of Ammonius (recited in 437), of which two lines are preserved in the *Etymologicum genuinum*, 588. 4—

ἤδη δ' ὑψιτενής τε Μίμας ὑπελείπετ' ὀπίσσω,
λείπετο δ' ὑψικάρηνον ἔδος Πιμπληΐδος ἄκρης,

which seem to come in the description of a voyage along the coast of Asia Minor.

[3] See Strzygowski, in *Jahrb. des kais. arch. Instituts*, viii. 203 *sqq.* (1893); C. Gurlitt, *Antike Denkmalsäulen in Konstantinopel* (1909).

for ascendancy at Constantinople, was the year of Stilicho's first consulship. Claudian celebrated it in a poem which was worthy of a greater subject:

> quem populi plausu, procerum quem voce petebas,
> adspice, Roma, virum. . . .
> . . . hic est felix bellator ubique
> defensor Libyae, Rheni pacator et Histri.

The hero's services to the Empire in war and peace outshine the merits and glories of the most famous figures in old Roman history. The poet himself aspired to be to Stilicho what Ennius had been to Scipio Africanus. *Noster Scipiades Stilicho*—a strange conjunction of names; but we forgive the poet his hyperboles for his genuine sense of the greatness of Roman history. The consulship of the Vandal general inspired him with the finest verses he ever wrote, a passage which deserves a place among the great passages of Latin literature—the praise of Rome, beginning—

> proxime dis consul, tantae qui prospicis urbi
> qua nihil in terris complectitur altius aether.[1]

He has expressed with memorable eloquence the Imperial ideal of the Roman State:

> haec est in gremium victos quae sola recepit
> humanumque genus communi nomine fovit
> matris, non dominae ritu, civesque vocavit
> quos domuit nexuque pio longinqua revinxit.[2]

The approaching disruption of the Empire was indeed hidden from Claudian and all others at the end of the fourth century. The Empire still reached from the Euphrates to the Clyde. Theodosius, who ruled a larger realm than Augustus, had steered it safely through dangers apparently greater than any which now menaced, and Stilicho was the military successor of Theodosius. The sway of Rome, if the Roman only looked at the external situation, might seem the assured and permanent order of the world:

> nec terminus umquam
> Romanae dicionis erit.

Yet there was a very uneasy feeling in these years that the end of Rome might really be at hand. It was due to supersti-

---

[1] *De cons. Stil.* iii. 130-160.
[2] The weak point in these verses is the monotonous succession of the verb at the end of each line.

tion. The twelve vultures that appeared to Romulus had in ages past been interpreted to mean that the life of Rome would endure for twelve centuries, and for some reason it was thought that this period was now drawing to a close :

> tunc reputant annos interceptoque volatu
> vulturis incidunt properatis saecula metis.[1]

The ancient auspice seemed to be confirmed by exceptional natural phenomena—the appearance of a huge comet in the spring of A.D. 400 [2] and three successive eclipses of the moon. Before these signs appeared, Honorius and Stilicho had allowed the altar of Victory which had been removed from the Senate-house by Theodosius to be brought back, a momentary concession to the fears of the Roman pagans. And it is very probably due to superstitious fears that the work of restoring the walls of Rome was now taken in hand.[3]

When Stilicho went to Rome to enter upon his consulship,[4] Claudian accompanied him, and his verses richly deserved the statue which was erected at the instance of the senate in the Forum of Trajan " to the most glorious of poets," although (the inscription runs) " his written poems suffice to keep his memory eternal." [5]

---

[1] Claudian, *B.G.* 265. Cp. Censorinus, *De die natali*, xvii. 36, ed. Hultsch.

[2] Claudian, *ib.* 243 *sqq.* The comet is also referred to by eastern writers (*e.g.* Socrates, vi. 6), and its appearance is recorded in Chinese annals. In the same passage, 233 *sqq.*, are mentioned the eclipses which occurred in Dec. 17, 400, June 12 and Dec. 6, 401.

[3] Seeck, *Untergang*, v. 329.

[4] A fine consular diptych is preserved in the Cathedral of Monza, which is probably Stilicho's (whether to be associated with his first consulship in 400 or with his second in 405). The consul is represented on the left leaf, a bearded man standing with a lance in his left hand. On the right leaf is a lady (Serena) with pearl earrings and necklace, and an oriental turban like a wig (we see similar coiffures on coins), holding a boy (Eucherius) by the hand. See Molinier, *Catal. des ivoires.* The robe of state (*trabea*) which Stilicho wears is embroidered with pictures of his wife and son, according to the custom of the time, and it is interesting to find that Claudian in his *De cons. Stil.* describes such a trabea, on which scenes of Stilicho's family life (including the birth of Maria, Eucherius practising horsemanship) were represented (iii. 340 *sqq.*). A good reproduction will be found in the Album (vol. i. pl. 1) to the *Histoire des arts indust.* of Labarte, who thought that it was a diptych of Aetius, with Placidia and Valentinian III. It was the custom for the consul of the year to present to senators these ivory diptychs (two pieces of ivory joined by hinges), to commemorate his year of office. They were generally inscribed with the consul's name and titles, and many specimens of them have survived from the fifth and sixth centuries.

[5] *C.I.L.* vi. 1710, from which we learn that Claudian was a *tribunus et notarius.* A distich in Greek is appended to the inscription :

εἰν ἑνὶ Βιργιλίοιο νόον καὶ μοῦσαν Ὁμήρου,
Κλαυδιανὸν Ῥώμη καὶ βασιλῆς ἔθεσαν.

§ 5. *John Chrysostom*

It was during the interlude in which Gaïnas and Typhos were supreme that Eudoxia, who had borne Arcadius two daughters, was crowned Augusta (January 9, A.D. 400).[1] Notwithstanding her German descent, she had no sympathies with the German party, though she had independently helped them to compass the fall of Eutropius. It is significant that of the hostages whom Gaïnas had demanded, John was notoriously her favourite and Saturninus was the husband of her intimate friend Castricia. The Empress was a woman of forceful character and impulsive temper,[2] and after the eunuch's fall she won unbounded influence óver her weak and sluggish husband. Her historical importance centres in the conflict into which she was drawn with Chrysostom, a drama which was to settle the future relations between the Imperial and the Patriarchal authority. No critical collision had occurred before. With the exception of Valens no Emperor had resided constantly at Constantinople before Arcadius, who never left the capital except for a summer holiday at Ancyra. Moreover, the see had only recently attained to the first rank in the Eastern Empire (A.D. 381), and its primacy was hotly disputed by Alexandria. That the collision between Emperor and Patriarch occurred at this time was due principally to the aggressive and uncompromising character of Chrysostom.

John, the " golden-mouthed " preacher, was in his forty-sixth or forty-seventh year when he became bishop of Constantinople (February 26, A.D. 398).[3] He was an independent and austere man, who in his own habits carried asceticism to excess, and his ways were rough and uncourtly. At Constantinople he found himself confronted by a superb court under the sway of Eudoxia. There is no reason to suppose that it was particularly vicious,

---

[1] Copper coins of Ael. Eudoxia Aug., with *Gloria Romanorum* on the reverse, are ascribed by De Salis (*Coins of the Eudoxias*) to A.D. 400, 401, before the coronation of the child Theodosius (in Jan. 402), and her gold coins with *Salus Reipublicae* and a seated Victory holding the monogram of Christ (and copper coins with same legend) to the period after that event.

[2] Compare above, p. 109, n. 1, and Zosimus, v. 24 πέρα τῆς φύσεως αὐθαδιζομένη.

[3] Besides the monographs of Thierry, Stephens, Ludwig, Puech (see Bibliography), there is a good article by E. Venables in the *Dict. of Christian Biography*. The chief sources for his life are his own letters and sermons, the *Dialogue* of Palladius (a very partial work), and the *Histories* of Socrates and Sozomen.

but it was at least frivolous and embodied for him the pride of life and the pomps and vanities of the world.

Chrysostom stands alone among the great ecclesiastics of the later Empire in that his supreme interest lay not in controversial theology but in practical ethics. His aim was the moral reformation of the world, and as his work lay in two rich cities, Antioch and Constantinople, he conceived it to be one of his chief duties to strive against the flaunting luxury of the rich classes, and denounce the lavish expenditure of wealth on personal gratification, wealth which in his eyes should have been devoted to alleviating the lot of the poor. Thus we learn from his sermons, whether at Constantinople or at Antioch, many details as to the luxurious life of the higher classes. Many rich nobles possessed ten or twenty mansions and as many private baths ; a thousand, if not wellnigh two thousand, slaves called them lord, and their halls were thronged with eunuchs, parasites, and retainers.[1] In their gorgeous houses the doors were of ivory, the ceilings lined with gold, the floors inlaid with mosaics or strewn with rich carpets ; the walls of the halls and bedrooms were of marble, and wherever commoner stone was used the surface was beautified with gold plate. Nude statues, to the scandal of strict ecclesiastics, decorated the halls. Spacious verandahs and baths adjoined the houses, which were surrounded by gardens with fountains. The beds were made of ivory or solid silver, or, if on a less expensive scale, of wood plated with silver or gold. Chairs and stools were usually of ivory, and the most homely vessels were often of the most costly metal ; the semicircular tables or sigmas, made of gold or silver, were so heavy that two youths could hardly lift one. Oriental cooks were employed ; and at banquets the atmosphere was heavy with all the perfumes of the East, while flute girls, whose virtue was as easy as in the old days of Greece and Rome, entertained the feasters.

To Chrysostom the contrast between the life of the higher classes and the miseries of the toiling populace was such a painful spectacle, that he was almost a socialist. If he inveighs against the men for their banquets, he is no less severe on the women for their sumptuous mule-cars, their rich dresses, their jewellery,

[1] For the description of such houses see the *Homily* on *Ps.* 48. 17, *P.G.* 55. 510.511.

their coquettish toilettes.[1] Their extravagance often involved their husbands in expenses which they could not afford. He denounces the use of silk and brocade. All the " evils " which Chrysostom describes are characteristic—allowance being made for difference of environment—of all wealthy societies, pagan or christian. His passionate denunciations of the rich have the same import and value as the denunciations of modern European plutocrats by socialists.

The problem of marriage interested him, and he preached the unpopular doctrine that the two partners in marriage are equal, the woman having the same rights against an unfaithful husband as the man against an unfaithful wife. We should hardly require the express evidence which Chrysostom supplies, to know that marriages for money were frequent. He complains that children were excessively indulged, and that their fathers too often gave their sons the worst possible moral education.[2] It is interesting to learn from his homilies that the treatment of slaves was still often marked by much of the old brutality. People passing in the street might often hear the furious outbreaks of an angry mistress beating her maid. Chrysostom describes vividly how a wife summoned her husband to aid her in punishing an offending servant.[3] The girl is stripped, tied to the foot of the bed, whipped by the master, while the mistress exhausts her vocabulary of abuse. The offence was probably quite trivial, perhaps an awkwardness in assisting at the mistress's toilette.[4] The condition of domestic slaves had in some respects changed little more than human nature since the days of Juvenal. But harsh and brutal treatment was not more universal than in those days. There were many masters (as other passages of Chrysostom show) who took the deepest interest in the well-being of their slaves. And there was also another side to the question. The servants were often trying and maleficent, slandering and spying upon their owners. The troubles which were caused by the lying tongues of maidservants are actually urged by Chrysostom as an argument against marriage.

---

[1] See also the verses of Gregory Naz. Κατὰ γυναικῶν καλλωπιζομένων (*Carmina*, I. sect. ii. 29, *P.G.* 37. 884).

[2] *Ep. 1 ad Tim., Hom.* 9, *P.G.* 64. 546.

[3] *Ep. ad Ephes., Hom.* 15, *P.G.* 64. 109.

[4] Cp. Juvenal vi. 490 *sqq.*; Martial ii. 66.

Christianity had not yet succeeded in abolishing all the old pagan customs from the celebrations of funerals and marriages. In the reign of Arcadius the usage was still maintained of hiring female mourners to sing dirges over the dead. Chrysostom considered it idolatry, and even threatened to excommunicate those who practised it. He also stigmatised the pagan practice of ablutions after the funeral ceremony, which were intended to purify from contact with the dead. The expense and ostentation which marked the funerals of the rich also earned his censure. More scandalous in the eyes of austere Christians were the survivals of pagan manners on the occasion of weddings. The Church had introduced an ecclesiastical ceremony in the presence of the bishop, but as soon as this was completed, the wedding was celebrated in the old way. The bride was conducted in procession at nightfall from the house of her father to that of the bridegroom. The procession was followed by troops of actors and actresses and dancing-girls, who were admitted to the house, where they danced indecently and sang indelicate songs. The epithalamia and the odes which Claudian composed on the occasions of the marriages of Honorius may give some idea of the licence which was still fashionable.

Chrysostom fought not only against the extravagance of the rich but also against the sensuality, gluttony, and avarice of the clergy and the monks, to whom his austerity was, in the words of his biographer, " as a lamp burning before sore eyes." Women were introduced into the monasteries or shared the houses of priests as " spiritual sisters," a practice which if often innocent was always a snare.[1] Deaconesses, unable to adopt the meretricious apparel that had become the mode, arranged their coarse dresses with an immodest coquetry which made them more piquant than professional courtesans.[1]

The Patriarch had his own devoted female admirers. The most distinguished was the deaconess Olympias, a rich lady, who in her early girlhood had been a favourite of Gregory Nazianzene. Her bounty to the poor won the heart of Chrysostom, to whom she proved a most unselfish and devoted friend. Another of his friends was Salvina, daughter of the Moor Gildo, whom Theodosius had given in marriage to Nebridius his

---

[1] See the vivid picture of such a ménage in the sermon *Contra eos qui subintroductas habent virgines*, c. 9.

wife's nephew.   In " A Letter to a Young Widow " Chrysostom
contrasts the peaceful happiness of her life at Constantinople
with the unrest of her father's turbulent career.   A deacon
named Serapion was the Patriarch's trusted and devoted
counsellor, but his influence was not always wisely exerted.   He
had no judgment, and instead of trying to restrain the impetuous
temper of Chrysostom, encouraged or incited him to rash acts.

With the common people the Patriarch enjoyed great
popularity.   He was no respecter of persons, and he interpreted
Christianity in a socialistic sense which has not generally been
countenanced or encouraged by the Church.   Though it was not
political but social inequality that he deprecated, and nothing
was further from his thoughts than to upset the established
order of things, the spirit of his teaching certainly tended to
set the poor against the rich.   On the occasion of an earthquake
he said publicly that " the vices of the rich caused it, and the
prayers of the poor averted the worst consequences."   It was
easy for his enemies to fasten upon utterances like this and
accuse him of " seducing the people."   His friendships with
Olympias and other women whom he sometimes received alone
supplied matter for another slander.   Having ruined his digestive
organs by excessive asceticism, he made a practice of not dining
in company, and in consequence of this unsocial habit he was
suspected of private gluttony.

For three years Chrysostom and Eudoxia were on the best
of terms.   Chrysostom owed his see, Eudoxia her throne, to
Eutropius, and they both refused to be his creatures.   But early
in A.D. 401 she did something which evoked a stern rebuke from
the Archbishop, and the consequence of his audacity was that
he was not received at Court.   We learn of this in connexion
with an episode which reveals Eudoxia herself in an amiable light.

Porphyrius, the bishop of Gaza, with other clergy of that
diocese, visited Constantinople in the spring of A.D. 401, to
persuade the government to take strong measures for the suppression of pagan practices.   For the citizens of Gaza still obstinately held to the worship of their old deities, Aphrodite, the Sun,
Persephone, and above all Marnas, the Cretan Zeus.   When the
clergy reached the capital and secured lodgings, their first act
was to visit Chrysostom.   " He received us with great honour
and courtesy, and asked us why we undertook the fatigue of

the journey, and we told him. And he bade us not to despond but to have hope in the mercies of God, and said, ' I cannot speak to the Emperor, for the Empress excited his indignation against me because I charged her with a thing which she coveted and robbed. And I am not concerned about his anger, for it is themselves they hurt and not me, and even if they hurt my body they do the more good to my soul. . . . To-morrow I will send for the eunuch Amantius, the *castrensis* (chamberlain) of the Empress, who has great influence with her and is really a servant of God, and I shall commit the matter to him.' Having received these injunctions and a recommendation to God, we proceeded to our inn. And on the next day we went to the bishop and found in his house the chamberlain Amantius, for the bishop had attended to our affair and had sent for him and explained it to him. And when we came in, Amantius stood up and did obeisance to the most holy bishops, inclining his face to the ground, and they, when they were told who he was, embraced him and kissed him. And the archbishop John bade them explain orally their affair to the chamberlain. And Porphyrius explained to him all the concernment of the idolaters, how licentiously they perform the unlawful rites and oppress the Christians. And Amantius, when he heard this, wept and was filled with zeal for God, and said to them, ' Be not despondent, fathers, for Christ can shield His religion. Do ye therefore pray, and I will speak to the Augusta.'

" The next day the chamberlain Amantius sent two deacons to bid us come to the Palace, and we arose and proceeded with all expedition. And we found him awaiting us, and he took the two bishops and introduced them to the Empress Eudoxia. And when she saw them she saluted them first and said, ' Give me your blessing, fathers,' and they did obeisance to her. Now she was sitting on a golden sofa. And she said to them, ' Excuse me, priests of Christ, on account of my situation, for I was anxious to meet your sanctity in the antechamber. But pray God on my behalf that I may be delivered happily of the child which is in my womb.' And the bishops, wondering at her con-descension, said, ' May He who blessed the wombs of Sarah and Rebecca and Elizabeth, bless and quicken the child in thine.' After further edifying conversation, she said to them, ' I know why ye came, as the castrensis Amantius explained it to me.   But if you are fain to instruct me, fathers, I am at your service.'   Thus bidden, they told her all about the idolaters, and the impious rites which they fearlessly practised, and their oppression of the Christians, whom they did not allow to hold a public office nor to till their lands 'from whose produce they pay the dues to your Imperial sovereignty.'   And the Empress said, ' Do not despond ; for I trust in the Lord Christ, the Son of God, that I shall persuade the Emperor to do those things that are due to your saintly faith and to dismiss you hence well treated.   Depart, then, to your privacy, for you are fatigued, and pray God to co-operate with my request.'   She then commanded money to be brought, and gave three handfuls of money to the bishops, saying, ' In the meantime take this for your expenses.'   And the bishops took the money and blessed her abundantly and departed.   And when they went out they gave the greater part of the money to the deacons who were standing at the door, reserving little for themselves.

  " And when the Emperor came into the apartment of the Empress, she told him all touching the bishops, and requested him that the heathen temples of Gaza should be pulled down. But the Emperor was put out when he heard it, and said, ' I know that city is devoted to idols, but it is loyally disposed in the matter of taxation and pays a large sum to the revenue. If then we overwhelm them with terror of a sudden, they will betake themselves to flight and we shall lose so much of the revenue.   But if it must be, let us afflict them partially, depriving idolaters of their dignities and other public offices, and bid their temples be shut up and be used no longer.   For when they are afflicted and straitened on all sides they will recognise the truth ;   but an extreme measure coming suddenly is hard on subjects.'   The Empress was much vexed at this reply, for she was ardent in matters of faith, but she merely said, ' The Lord can assist his servants the Christians, whether we consent or decline.'

  " We learned these details from the chamberlain Amantius. On the morrow the Augusta sent for us, and having first saluted the bishops according to custom, she bade them sit down.   And after a long spiritual talk, she said, ' I spoke to the Emperor, and he was somewhat displeased.   But do not despond, for, God willing, I cannot cease until ye be satisfied and depart, having succeeded in your pious purpose.' And the bishops made obeisance. Then the sainted Porphyrius, moved by the spirit, and recollecting the word of the thrice blessed anchoret Procopius, said to the Empress : ' Exert yourself for the sake of Christ, and in recompense for your exertions He can bestow on you a son whose life and reign you will see and enjoy for many years.' At these words the Empress was filled with joy, and her face flushed, and new beauty beyond that which she already had passed into her face ; for the outward appearance shows what passes within. And she said, ' Pray, fathers, that according to your word, with the will of God, I may bear a male child, and if it so befall, I promise you to do all that ye ask. And another thing, for which ye ask not, I intend to do with the consent of Christ ; I will found a church at Gaza in the centre of the city. Depart then in peace, and rest quiet, praying constantly for my happy delivery ; for the time of the birth is near.' The bishops commended her to God and left the Palace. And prayer was made that she should bear a male child ; for we believed in the words of Saint Procopius the anchoret.

"And every day we used to visit John, the archbishop, and had the fruition of his pious discourse, sweeter than honey and the honey comb. And Amantius the chamberlain used to come to us, sometimes bearing messages from the Empress, at other times merely to pay a visit. And after a few days she brought forth a male child [April 10], and he was called Theodosius after his grandfather Theodosius, the Spaniard, who reigned along with Gratian. And the child Theodosius was born in the purple, wherefore he was proclaimed Emperor at his birth. And there was great joy in the city, and men were sent to the cities of the Empire, bearing the good news, with gifts and bounties.

"But the Empress, who had only just been delivered, sent Amantius to us with this message : ' I thank Christ that God bestowed on me a son, on account of your holy prayers. Pray, then, fathers, for his life and for my lowly self, in order that I may fulfil those things which I promised you, Christ himself again consenting through your holy prayers.' And when the seven days of her lying-in were fulfilled, she sent for us and met us at the door of the chamber, carrying in her arms the infant in the purple robe. And she inclined her head and said, ' Draw nigh, fathers, unto me and the child which the Lord granted to me through your holy prayers.' And she gave them the child that they might seal it (with God's signet). And the bishops sealed both her and the child with the seal of the cross, and, offering a prayer, sat down. And when they had spoken many words full of edification, the lady says to them, ' Do ye know, fathers, what I resolved to do in regard to your affair ? ' [Here Porphyrius related a dream which he had dreamed the night before ; then Eudoxia resumed :] ' If Christ permit, the child will be privileged to receive baptism in a few days. Do ye then depart and compose a petition and insert in it all the requests ye wish to make. And when the child comes forth from the baptismal rite, give the petition to him who holds the child in his arms ; and I shall instruct him what to do.' Having received these directions we blessed her and the infant and went out. Then we composed the petition, inserting many things in the document, not only as to the overthrow of the idols but also that privileges and revenue should be granted to the holy Church and the Christians ; for the Church was poor.

" The days ran by, and the day on which the young Emperor Theodosius was to be baptized arrived. And all the city was crowned with garlands and decked out in garments made of silk and gold jewels and all kind of ornaments, so that no one could describe the adornment of the city. One might behold the inhabitants, multitudinous as the waves, arrayed in all manner of garments. But it is beyond my power to describe the brilliance of that pomp ; it is a task for those who are practised writers, and I shall pursue my true history. When the young Theodosius was baptized and came forth from the church to the Palace, you might behold the magnificence of the multitude of the magnates and their dazzling raiment, for all were dressed in white, and you would have thought they were covered with snow. The patricians headed the procession, with the *illustres* and all the other ranks, and the military contingents, all carrying wax candles, so that the stars seemed to shine on earth. And close to the infant, which was carried in arms, was the Emperor Arcadius himself, his face cheerful and more radiant than the purple robe he was wearing, and one of the magnates carried the infant in brilliant apparel. And we marvelled, beholding such glory. . . .

" And we stood at the portal of the church, with our petition, and when he came forth from the baptism we called aloud, saying, ' We petition your Piety,' and held out the paper. And he who carried the child seeing this, and knowing our business, for the Empress had instructed him, bade the paper be showed to him, and when he received it halted. And he commanded silence, and having unrolled a part he read it, and folding it up, placed his hand under the head of the child and cried out, ' His majesty has ordered the requests contained in the petition to be ratified.' And all having seen marvelled and did obeisance to the Emperor, congratulating him that he had the privilege of seeing his son an emperor in his lifetime ; and he rejoiced thereat. And that which had happened for the sake of her son was announced to the Empress, and she rejoiced and thanked God on her knees. And when the child entered the Palace, she met it and received it and kissed it, and holding it in her arms greeted the Emperor, saying, ' You are blessed, my lord, for the things which your eyes have beheld in your life-time.' And the king rejoiced thereat. And the Empress, seeing him in good humour, said, ' Please let us learn what the petition contains that its contents may be fulfilled.' And the Emperor ordered the paper to be read, and when it was read, said, ' The request is hard, but to refuse is harder, since it is the first mandate of our son.' "

The petition was granted, and Eudoxia arranged a meeting between the quaestor, the minister on whom it devolved to draft the Imperial rescripts, and the bishops, that all the wishes of the latter might be incorporated in the edict. The execution of it, which was invidious and required a strong hand and will, was intrusted to Cynegius, and the bishops returned to Palestine, having received considerable sums of money from the Empress and Emperor, as well as the funds which the Empress had promised for the erection of a church at Gaza.

This narrative gives us an idea of the kind of little dramas that probably lay behind many of the formal decrees and rescripts preserved in the Imperial Codes. The wonder of the provincial bishops at the splendid apparel of the great of the earth, their edifying spiritual conversations with the Empress, with the eunuch, and with the archbishop, the ruse of Eudoxia to compass the success of the petition, all such details help us to realise the life of the time ; while the hesitation of the pious Arcadius to root out the heathen " abominations " because the heathen were respectable taxpayers shows that even he, when the ghostly and worldly policies of the Empire clashed, was more inclined to be Emperor than churchman.

To return to Chrysostom. When he performed the ceremony of baptizing the Emperor's son and heir, there must have been a reconciliation with the court, but Eudoxia could not forget the incident, and henceforward she would be at least disposed to lend a patient ear to his enemies. And his enemies were many, both in clerical and in secular circles. Among the fashionable ladies who were particularly offended by his castigations of female manners were three who were intimate friends of the Empress—Marsa, wife of Promotus, in whose house Eudoxia had been brought up ; Castricia, the wife of Saturninus, whom Chrysostom had helped to rescue from the vengeance of Gaïnas ; and Eugraphia, whose house was a centre for all those who detested him.[1] It is easy to imagine how easily they could continue to poison Eudoxia's mind against a priest who was exceptionally tactless by twisting his invectives against the foibles of women into personal attacks upon herself.

But the agitation of irresponsible enemies might not have shaken his position, if he had not committed indiscretions in the domain of ecclesiastical policy. Antoninus, the bishop of Ephesus, had been accused of simony and other offences, and Chrysostom was appealed to. He determined to investigate the matter on the spot, and set out in the winter of A.D. 401.[2] The inquiry disclosed abuses in many of the churches of western Asia Minor, and Chrysostom acted with more zeal than wariness. He deposed and replaced at least thirteen bishops, exceeding the rights of his jurisdiction, and, it was said, not giving a fair hearing to the cases. Naturally he stirred up many new enemies.

He was absent five months from Constantinople. He had deputed an eloquent Syrian, Severian, bishop of Gabala, to act for him during his absence. Severian seems to have joined the league of his enemies, and there was an open rupture between him and Serapion the deacon. When the Patriarch returned he found his own See disorganised, and a local council was held

---

[1] See Palladius, c. 4, c. 8. The author describes Eugraphia as ἀμφι-   μανής τις, τὰ δὲ λοιπὰ αἰδοῦμαι καὶ λέγειν.

[2] Cp. Seeck, *Untergang*, v. p. 577.

to hear the charges which Serapion brought against Severian.
When Severian, who felt sure of support in high quarters, resisted
the efforts of the bishops to induce him to be reconciled with the
deacon, Chrysostom told him that it would be well for him to
return to the see of Gabala which he had so long neglected.
Severian, who seems to have entertained the ambition of replac-
ing Chrysostom on the Patriarchal throne, now saw that he had
gone too far, and he left the city. At Chalcedon he was recalled.
The Empress had herself implored the Patriarch to reconcile
himself with Severian. Throughout the quarrel popular opinion
had been on Chrysostom's side, but it may be questioned whether
his conduct was altogether creditable.[1] He yielded to Eudoxia's
prayers, but it was necessary to tranquillise popular feeling,
for which purpose he preached a pacific sermon which ended
with the words, " Receive our brother Severian the bishop." [2]
Severian responded by a sermon of which the note was likewise
peace. But the peace was hollow.

A new storm from another quarter was soon to burst over
Chrysostom. Theophilus, the archbishop of Alexandria, bore no
goodwill to the eloquent preacher who occupied the great see
which had now precedence over his own. Theophilus, whose
principal claim to be remembered is the destruction of the
Serapeum, the famous stronghold of paganism at Alexandria,
seems, so far as we can judge from his acts, to have been a
domineering and unscrupulous prelate. He had probably been
spoiled by the enjoyment of power. He is described as " naturally impulsive, bold and precipitous in action, extraordinarily
quarrelsome, impatient and determined in grasping at any
object he had set his mind on." [3] He had hoped to secure for
a candidate of his own the archiepiscopal chair of Constantinople
after the death of Nectarius, and had not forgiven Chrysostom
his disappointment ; which was rendered particularly humiliating by the fact that Eutropius had forced him to take part in
Chrysostom's consecration. Theophilus had held the heretical
opinion of Origen, who rejected the anthropomorphic conception
of the Deity which is suggested by many passages in the Hebrew
Scripture. The same opinion was held in a monastic settlement

---

[1] The silence of Palladius is significant (cp. Seeck, *op. cit.* 577).

[2] Text in Papadopulos-Kerameus,
Ἀναλ. ἱεροσολ. σταχυολογίας, i. 15 *sqq.* ;

Latin translation in Migne, *P.G.* 52,
423 *sqq.*

[3] Palladius, c. 9.

in the desert of Nitria in Upper Egypt, over which four monks presided who were known, from their remarkable stature, as the Tall Brothers.[1] Theophilus, however, changed his view on the theological point and (A.D. 401) issued a Paschal letter condemning Origen and his disciples. He then convoked a synod, which anathematised Origen and condemned the Nitrian monks. He had other reasons for desiring the destruction of the Tall Brothers, and he obtained troops from the augustal Prefect of Egypt to arrest them. The habitations of the monks were sacked and pillaged, and the Tall Brothers with their followers, clad in sheepskins, made their way to Palestine, where the bishops, admonished by letters from Theophilus, refused them shelter. Unable to find rest for the soles of their feet, they took ship for Constantinople to place themselves under the protection of Chrysostom. He received them kindly, but would not communicate with them until their cause had been examined, and he lodged them in the church of St. Anastasia,[2] where their wants were ministered to by his deaconesses.

The piety and virtues of the Tall Brothers were well known by repute at Constantinople, and the Empress was eager to exert herself in their behalf. Meeting one of them as she was driving through the city, she stopped her carriage, asked him to pray for her, and promised to arrange that a synod should be convoked and Theophilus summoned to attend it. The monks then drew up a petition to the Emperor, setting forth their charges against their archbishop, and an Imperial messenger was sent to Alexandria to compel Theophilus to come to Constantinople and answer for his conduct at a synod to be held there.

Theophilus had already instigated Epiphanius, bishop of Constantia in Cyprus, who was an authority on heresies, to convene a synod of the Cypriote bishops to condemn the opinion of Origen, and to circulate its decisions to the sees of the Church. This had been done, and Theophilus, finding himself in an awkward position by the peremptory summons to appear as a defendant in the capital, urged Epiphanius to go in person to Constantinople and obtain Chrysostom's signature to the decree of the Cypriote council. Epiphanius, persuaded by the crafty

---

[1] Ammonius, Dioscorus (whom Theophilus made bishop of Hermupolis), Eusebius, and Euthymius.

[2] On this church see Du Cange, *Cplis Christiana*, bk. iv. pp. 98-99 ; Paspates, Βυζ. μελέται, 368 *sqq.*

flatteries of the Alexandrian prelate that a crisis in the Church
depended on his intervention, sailed for Constantinople (early
in A.D. 403). But he was not a strong ally ; he was out of place
and bewildered amid the intrigues of the capital. Finally he
became acquainted with the Tall Brothers, and when they told
him that they had read his books [1] with admiration, and re-
monstrated with him for condemning their writings, which he
was obliged to confess he only knew from hearsay, he came to
the conclusion that he had made a mistake and allowed himself
to be used as a tool by Theophilus. Disgusted and dejected he
set sail for home, but the fatigue and excitement had overtaxed
his failing strength and he died on the voyage (May 12).

About a month later (in June) Theophilus arrived with a
large retinue of bishops who came to support him from Egypt,
Syria, and Asia Minor. He had been summoned to appear as
an accused man before an ecclesiastical tribunal over which
Chrysostom would preside, but he was determined to invert
the parts, and be himself the judge, with Chrysostom at the bar.
That he succeeded in his plan was due entirely to Chrysostom's
indiscretions. The Empress had interested herself in the affair
of the Tall Brothers, and it was due to her influence that Theophilus had been forced to come to answer for his conduct. If
Chrysostom, who in that affair had shown admirable caution,
had now exercised ordinary tact and self-restraint, he could have
had Eudoxia entirely on his side and might have defied all the
arts and intrigues of his Alexandrian rival. Eudoxia had shown
her veneration for the saintly bishop Epiphanius, by asking him
to pray for her infant son who was ill, and Chrysostom, offended
by her graciousness towards a bishop who had been openly
hostile to himself, preached a violent sermon against women,
in which the word Jezebel was pronounced. The congregation
interpreted it as allusive to the Empress, and the matter was
soon brought to her ears.[2] She was furious at the insult, and
prepared to exert all her influence to support the party which
was planning the ruin of the archbishop. Theophilus, rejecting
the hospitality which Chrysostom offered him, established himself in the palace of Placidia, close to the Great Palace, and his

---

[1] For his works on heresies, the
Panarion and the *Ancoratus*, see the
article on him by R. A. Lipsius in
Dict. of Chr. Biography.

[2] Socrates, vi. 15, combined with
Palladius, c. 8. Cp. below.

bribes, banquets, and flatteries drew thither all the ecclesiastics and fashionable ladies whom Chrysostom had offended.

Chrysostom seems hardly to have realised the danger of his position. Instead of attempting to turn away the wrath of the Empress, he adopted a weak and conciliatory attitude towards the archbishop of Alexandria. The question of the Tall Brothers, though it was now a secondary consideration, had to be disposed of before Theophilus could take any open steps against Chrysostom, and Chrysostom was invited by the Emperor to preside over an investigation into the charges they had preferred against Theophilus. But he declined on the ground that such an inquiry into things which had occurred in another diocese would be illegal. This decision at once freed Theophilus from his position as an accused person, and the board was clear for him to organise his attack on Chrysostom. A list of charges was drawn up, sufficient to move the Emperor, under his wife's influence, to summon a council to inquire into them. Witnesses were procured to substantiate the accusations.

Popular feeling ran so high in favour of Chrysostom that the authorities were afraid to hold the synod within the precincts of the city, and it met across the water in the palace of the Oak, which had been built by the Praetorian Prefect Rufinus in the suburbs of Chalcedon. Chrysostom refused to appear before a body which was packed with his enemies. The majority of the bishops present were Egyptians, prepared to do whatever their archbishop told them. The chief accuser of Chrysostom was John, his archdeacon. Among the numerous charges that were formulated for the synod to investigate were these : that he had sold the marble which Nectarius had set aside for decorating the church of St. Anastasia ; that he had reviled the clergy as corrupt ; that he had called Epiphanius a fool and a demon ; that he had intrigued against Severian ; that he received visits from women by themselves after he had sent every one else out of the room ; that a bath was heated for him alone, and that after he had bathed Serapion emptied the bath so that no one else might use it ; that he ate gluttonously alone, living like a Cyclops.[1] The accusations which really demanded an inquiry

---

[1] The proceedings of the synod are known from a summary of the Acts in Photius, *Bibliotheca*, 59. It sat for about a fortnight (there were 13 sessions), and there were 45 members. Palladius, c. 3, gives the number as 36, of whom 29 were Egyptians. Bishops friendly to

concerned his conduct in deposing bishops in Asia and ordaining
others without due investigation of their characters.

As Chrysostom, repeatedly summoned, refused to appear
and plead, he was condemned, not as guilty of the crimes which
were alleged against him, but because he refused to appear,
and he was formally deposed from his see. A report of the result
was communicated to the Emperor, with the suggestion that it
was for him and not for the Council to deal with the charge
that the archbishop had spoken treasonably of the Empress.[1]
Arcadius confirmed the decree in a rescript which pronounced
the sentence of banishment. To the archbishop's enemies the
penalty may have seemed too lenient, but it roused the indignation of the people, who would not have their idol removed by
the act of a small packed assembly like the Synod of the Oak.
Loud clamours were raised for the assembling of a general
Council of the Church. Flocking round St. Sophia and the
archiepiscopal palace, the populace made it impossible for the
Imperial officers to seize Chrysostom and expel him from the
city for three days. He delivered two discourses in the church,
in which he referred to the Empress as a Jezebel or a Herodias.
" One day she called me the thirteenth apostle, and now her
name for me is Judas." [2] But he had no intention of defying
the Emperor or causing a sedition. He stole out from his palace
at night, surrendered himself, was taken across to the Asiatic
coast, and withdrew to Praenetus near Nicomedia.

When it was discovered that he had departed, the fury of
the people burst out. The city was in an uproar. The populace
clamoured for the recall of their pastor, and an earthquake

Chrysostom did not attend. The
date of the synod may probably be
fixed to the end of June, or July.
As Epiphanius died on May 12 (ASS.
iii. 36) on his voyage to Cyprus, he
must have left the city early in May.
A short time elapsed before the arrival
of Theophilus (οὐ πολὺς ἐν μέσῳ χρόνος,
Socrates, vi. 15), who spent three
weeks in organising the opposition to
Chrysostom (τρεῖς ἐβδομάδας ἡμερῶν,
Pallad. c. 8). This gives the middle
of June as the earliest date for the
opening of the synod, and the beginning of July as the earliest date for
Chrysostom's exile. On the other
hand, the synod cannot be placed later
than some time in July. This accords

with the indication of Palladius, in
c. 9, παρίππασαν μῆνες ἐννέα ἢ δέκα,
sc. from the first exile of Chrysostom
to Lent or Easter 404, as the context
shows. Cp. Tillemont, Mém. ecc. xi.
p. 601.

[1] By calling her Jezebel. See
Palladius, c. 8. This charge was not
formally included in the list of charges
presented to the synod, and did not
appear in the Acta.

[2] Homilia ante exilium, P.G. 52,
437 ; the other text, 427 sqq., seems
to be a second version of the same
discourse. As Seeck has observed,
it was doubtless taken down in shorthand (ὑπὸ τῶν ὀξυγράφων, Socrates,
vi. 4).

which at this crisis shook the city and the Great Palace was interpreted to mean that the voice of the people was the voice of God.[1] The Empress herself, who was very superstitious, was panic-stricken, and she sent one of her chamberlains with a letter to Chrysostom imploring him to return. In this conciliatory letter she disclaimed all responsibility for his exile. " Let not your Holiness suppose," she wrote, " that I was privy to what has been done. I am innocent of thy blood. Wicked and corrupt men devised this plot ; God to whom I sacrifice is witness of my tears. I remember that my children were baptized by thy hands. I touched the knees of the Emperor and besought him : ' We have lost the priest, let us bring him back. Unless we restore him there is no hope for the Empire.' " Chrysostom accepted her overtures and returned. When he was back in his palace, Eudoxia sent him a verbal message : " My prayer has been fulfilled. My success is a crown more precious than my Imperial diadem. I have received the priest, restored the head to the body, the pilot to the ship, the shepherd to the flock, the bridegroom to the bridal chamber." She was generous in her amends, and the archbishop, not to be outdone in generosity, paid an extravagant tribute to her in a triumphant sermon he preached the next day in St. Sophia [2] (July). His eulogy of the Empress, who seems to have been very popular, was loudly applauded.

Chrysostom desired to regularise his position by a general Council which should inquire into his case and the proceedings of the Synod of the Oak. Theophilus began to spin new intrigues, and there were bloody frays between the populace and his partisans. Not having the countenance of the court, he did not dare to remain any longer in the city, and sailed with his followers back to Egypt.[3] If Chrysostom had now been able to control

---

[1] The earthquake is recorded only by Theodoret, v. 34, 5 σεισμοῦ δὲ μεγίστου νύκτωρ γεγενημένουκ αἱ δείματος τὴν βασιλίδα κατεσχηκότος, and has been generally supposed to explain the vague words of Palladius, c. 9 *ad init.*, θραῦσίν τινά γενέσθαι ἐν τῷ κοιτῶνι. Seeck (*op. cit.* p. 582) questions the earthquake and conjectures that the θραῦσις was the death of one of the Imperial children (Flaccilla). I cannot think that such an occurrence would have been re- ferred to in this way.

[2] See the Homily after his return, *P.G.* 52, 443 *sqq.*

[3] Socrates, vi. 17, whose story shows that Theophilus remained some time in the capital or its neighbourhood after Chrysostom's return. From Palladius, c. 9 *ad init.*, and from Chrysostom's letter to Innocent (*apud Pallad.* c. 2), one would suppose he had sailed almost immediately, but these narratives are very condensed. Sozomen, viii. 19, dates his departure

his temper, his reconciliation with the court might have been
permanent, and all might have gone smoothly. But a trivial
incident occurred which betrayed him into gross impoliteness
towards the Empress.

Some months after his return,[1] a silver image of Eudoxia on
a tall porphyry column was erected by Simplicius, Prefect of
the City, in the middle of the Augusteum, and thus close to the
vestibule of St. Sophia.[2] The inaugural ceremonies were of a
pagan character, and accompanied by dancing and music, and
the loud noise of the merriment interrupted the service in St.
Sophia. Chrysostom complained to the Prefect in no measured
terms, and his denunciation of the heathenish rites was taken
by the Empress as a personal affront. She was an impulsive
woman, and she was now ready to side with his enemies, Severian
of Gabala and the rest, who were lurking for an opportunity of
vengeance. Chrysostom poured fuel on the flame by a sermon
which began: "Again Herodias is furiously raging, again she is
dancing, again demanding the head of John on a charger."[3]

Chrysostom had demanded a general Council;[4] the sum-
monses had been sent out; but Eudoxia was now eager that
the Council should be so packed with his opponents that its
result would be not to rescind but to confirm the decree of the
Synod of the Oak. At Christmas she and the Emperor refused
to communicate with the pastor whom she had so warmly welcomed on his return, until the approaching Council should have
tried his case. Theophilus refused to attend; his experiences
at Constantinople did not encourage a second visit. But many

---

at the beginning of winter, and Seeck
has therefore dated the Synod of the
Oak to September (*op. cit.* p. 584),
which contradicts the other evidence.
I take Sozomen's statement to be an
error.

[1] Palladius, *ib.*, says that μετὰ δύο
μῆνας πάλιν his enemies began to
recover and seek new means of
deposing him. He says nothing of
Eudoxia's statue, so that this incident
which is related by Socrates (vi. 18)
may have occurred somewhat later
than September.

[2] The stylobate was discovered in
1848, with the inscriptions, on one side,
*D N Aeliae Eudoxiae semper Augustae
vir clarissimus Simplicius Prf. U.
dedicavit*; on the other the hexameters

κίονα πορφυρέην καὶ ἀργυρέην βασίλειαν
δέρκεο, ἔνθα πόληι θεμιστεύουσιν ἄνακτες.
οὔνομα δ' εἰ ποθέεις, Εὐδόξια· τίς δ' ἀνέθηκεν;
Σιμπλίκιος, μεγάλων ὑπάτων γένος, ἐσθλὸς
ὕπαρχος.

See *C.I.L.* iii. 736; Paspates, Βυζ.
ἀνάκτορα, p. 97. Cp. Marcellinus,
Chron., *sub a.*

[3] Socrates, *ib.* The homily which
is preserved containing these words
(*P.G.* 59, 485) is generally considered
a fabrication, but Seeck defends it
(*op. cit.* p. 583).

[4] His position had been provisionally regularised by a meeting or synod
of about 60 bishops, who declared his
condemnation illegal (Sozomen, viii.
19).

of his bishops went, and he instructed them to make use of the
canon of the Council of Antioch of A.D. 341, which laid down
that if a bishop who had been deposed by a synod should then
appeal to the secular power his deposition should be final
and irrevocable. The Council met early in A.D. 404, but many
supporters of Chrysostom were present ; and his enemies, who
did not propose to investigate the charges against him but to
condemn him by virtue of the canon of Antioch, found themselves in an awkward position. For the Council of Antioch was
deeply tainted with Arianism, and the canon was aimed at
Athanasius. When it was suggested to them in the Emperor's
presence that if the canon was to be accepted as authoritative
they must subscribe to the acts of the Council in question, they
were taken aback, but for very shame they promised to subscribe.
It was a promise they could not possibly fulfil, for the Council
was notoriously heretical. And so the matter hung fire, while
Chrysostom continued to perform his ordinary duties. But
Easter (April 17) was now approaching, and representations
were made to the Emperor that it was impossible to allow the
ceremonies of that high festival to be celebrated by a man who
had been deposed and excommunicated by a synod. He was
ordered to remain in his palace and not to enter the church, but
he refused to comply unless he were compelled by force.

Easter Eve was the great day for the baptism of converts,
and in this year there were three thousand candidates. Large
multitudes assembled in St. Sophia, many having come in from
the neighbouring towns. At night the church was crowded,
when a body of soldiers entered and scattered the congregation.
Women and children fled shrieking through the streets, but the
clergy succeeded in reassembling the congregation in the Baths
of Constantine, and preparations were made to celebrate the
services there. But the flock was again dispersed by soldiers.
On Easter Day the devoted followers of Chrysostom would not
attend the services in St. Sophia, and celebrated Easter in an
open field beyond the walls.

For two months longer Chrysostom was allowed to remain in
his palace, but was prevented from leaving it. Arcadius felt
some compunction about proceeding to extremities. But at
length he yielded to the pressure of Severian and the other bishops,
who were urging him to tranquillise the city by removing the

cause of scandal and disturbance, and on June 20 an Imperial mandate was delivered to Chrysostom, ordering him to leave the city. He submitted, and allowed himself to be conducted stealthily to one of the harbours and conveyed in a boat to the Bithynian coast.

On the same night a fire broke out in St. Sophia. It began at the chair of the archbishop and, flaming upwards, caught the roof and turned round the building like a serpent. There was a high wind, and the flames, blown southward, caught the senate-house. Both buildings were destroyed, but the destruction of the senate-house was the greater misfortune, because it was a museum of precious works of classical art. The statues of the nine Muses were burned, but the Zeus of Dodona and the Athene of Lindus escaped.[1]

The cause of the conflagration was made a matter of judicial inquiry. Some attributed it to Chrysostom himself, others to his friends. It was made a pretext for a bitter and cruel persecution of all his adherents.[2] The deaconess Olympias was treated with great harshness ; she fell ill and withdrew to Cyzicus. Many persons were punished for refusing to communicate with Arsacius,[3] the new archbishop, who was installed a few days later (June 26). He was a brother of Chrysostom's predecessor Nectarius, and was a gentle old man, whom Chrysostom's admirers described as muter than a fish and more inert than a frog. Partaking of the communion with him was a sort of test for discovering Johannites, as the followers of Chrysostom were called.

Chrysostom lived in exile for three years, at first in Cucusus on the borders of Cappadocia and Armenia, then at Arabissus.[4]

---

[1] Zosimus, v. 24. 6. He (*i.e.* Eunapius) considers the party of Chrysostom responsible for the fire.

[2] The investigation was conducted by Studius, Prefect of the City, and he acted with great severity. See Socrates, vi. 18, 19 ; Sozomen, viii. 23, 24 ; Palladius, c. 20. Tigrius, a presbyter, was tortured till his bones were dislocated ; Serapion was cruelly beaten, and his teeth knocked out. Olympias was harshly treated and withdrew to Cyzicus. Socrates seems to be wrong in ascribing the cruelties to Optatus, who was a pagan and succeeded Studius not before September ; but Optatus may have afterwards sought to force the clergy to communicate with Arsacius. As the inquisition led to no results the imprisoned clergy were released at the end of August (*C. Th.* xvi. 2. 37).

[3] His tenure of the see was brief. He died Nov. 11, 405, and was succeeded by Atticus in March 406.

[4] In common with the inhabitants of these regions he endured considerable distress and anxiety from the depredations of the Isaurians, who wasted the villages round Cucusus, and slaughtered the villagers. We learn about their doings in his letters.

From these places he conducted an active correspondence with his friends and admirers in all parts of Christendom, and his influence was so great that his enemies thought it prudent to procure his removal to a more remote spot, Pityus on the Euxine coast. On the way thither he died from exhaustion (September 14, A.D. 407).

The treatment of Chrysostom caused fresh trouble between the courts of Constantinople and Ravenna. Theophilus had first apprised Pope Innocent I. of his deposition : letters from Chrysostom himself and his clergy, delivered a few days afterwards, probably convinced him that the proceedings had been extremely irregular, and this conviction was confirmed when he received from Theophilus a memorandum of the acts of the Synod of the Oak. He decided that the matter should be brought before a general Council, and meanwhile declined to desist from communion with the Patriarch, to whom he sent a letter of consolation. An Italian Synod was summoned, and declared the condemnation of Chrysostom illegal and demanded a general Council at Thessalonica.

Honorius had already written twice to Arcadius,[1] deploring the tumults and conflagrations which had disgraced Constantinople, and criticising the inconvenient haste with which the sentence against the condemned had been carried out before the decision of the head of the Church had been ascertained. He wrote under the influence of Innocent, and definitely asserted the doctrine that " the interpretation of divine things concerns churchmen, the observation of religion concerns us (the Emperors)." After the meeting of the Italian Synod he wrote a third letter,[2] to be carried by a deputation of bishops and priests, who were to inform his brother of the opinion of the Italian Church. The envoys had reason to repent of their expedition. Escorted by soldiers from Athens to Constantinople, they were not permitted to land in that city, but were thrown into a Thracian fortress, forcibly deprived of the letters they bore, and at last hardly allowed to return to Italy (A.D. 406). As they had

----

[1] One of these letters is preserved, *Coll. Avell.*, *Ep.* 38 (or Mansi, iii. 1122), probably written in July 404. He refers in it to the criticisms which the Imperial honours conferred on Eudoxia had evoked : *quamvis super imagine muliebri novo exemplo per provincias circumlata et diffusa per universum orbem obtrectantium fama litteris aliis commonuerim,* etc.

[2] Quoted in Palladius, c. 3.

been specially recommended by Honorius himself to Arcadius, the outrageous treatment they received was a grievous affront to the western court. The Eastern Emperor took no notice whatever of the proposal to summon a general Council, and the Imperial brothers seem never again to have held any communications. Honorius and Innocent could do no more ; they had to abandon Chrysostom to his fate.[1]

The Empress Eudoxia did not live to see the later phase of the episode in which she had played a considerable part, though rather as the instrument of unscrupulous ecclesiastics than as the directress of a conspiracy against a man whose probity she certainly respected. She died on October 6, A.D. 404, of a miscarriage.[2]

Arcadius slumbered on his throne for three and a half years after her death, and died on May 1, A.D. 408. During this time the reins of power seem to have been in the hands of Anthemius, the Praetorian Prefect of the East, who was afterwards to prove himself an able minister.[3] One of the principal concerns of the government during these years was the condition of the southern and eastern provinces of Asia Minor, exposed to the savagery of the Isaurian brigands. Their devastations continued from A.D. 404 to 407.[4] We hear of the failure of a general to suppress them

---

[1] Theophilus wrote an Apologia for his own conduct, with violent invectives against Chrysostom. He sent it to Jerome, who translated it into Latin (*Epp.* 113, 114), and we have some extracts from it in the *Pro defensione trium capit.* of Facundus. Chrysostom is denounced as a sacrilegious persecutor, not a Christian, but "worse than Belshazzar," a blasphemer against Christ who delighted the Arians ; in the next world he will suffer eternal punishment. Theophilus probably was genuinely convinced that his adversary was a very bad man.

[2] Eunapius, *apud* Photium, *Bibl.* 77, Date : *Chron. Pasch., sub a.* A few days before her death, there was a terrible shower of hail at Constantinople (*ic.*), which the populace said was a mark of divine displeasure at the persecution of Chrysostom (Socrates, vii. 19) ; perhaps it also alarmed Eudoxia. This particular hailstorm may have been in the mind of Philostorgius when he wrote xi. 7.

It seems probable that it was just after these occurrences that an amnesty was granted to the Johannites. The date depends on a passage in Synesius, *Ep.* 66 τουτὶ μὲν ἔτος τρίτον ἐξήκει μετὰ τὴν ἀμνηστίαν. Seeck has given reasons for dating the letter to the end of 407, and drawn the inference (*op. cit.* 585-586).

[3] He was already Prefect on July 10, 405 (*C. Th.* vii. 10. 1), and had been raised to the rank of Patrician before April 28, 406 (*ib.* ix. 34. 10). He was grandson of Philippus, Praet. Pr. in 346. He had been *comes sacr. larg.* in 400, then *mag. off.*, and was consul in 405.

[4] For 404 and the campaign of Arbazacius see Zosimus, v. 25, who says that this incompetent commander escaped punishment by bribing Eudoxia; Eunapius, *frr.* 84, 86 ; Marcellinus, *Chron., sub* 405; Sozomen, viii. 25 (all the cities between Caria and Phoenicia devastated). Philostorgius, xi. 8, says that they subdued Cyprus. During the following years

at the beginning of the movement, but we are not told how this civil war was brought to an end. Anthemius had also to keep a watchful eye on Alaric and Stilicho. To them we must now return.

§ 6. *Alaric's First Invasion of Italy* (A.D. 401–403)

We saw how Alaric and his Visigoths had withdrawn from the Peloponnesus into the province of New Epirus in A.D. 397, and that Alaric had been appointed to some Imperial post, probably that of Master of Soldiers in Illyricum. For four years we hear nothing of him except that he took advantage of his official position to equip his followers with modern arms from the Roman arsenals in the Dacian diocese.[1] Then suddenly he determined to invade Italy. Perhaps it was the defeat of the attempt of Gaïnas to establish a German ascendancy at Constantinople that averted his covetous eyes from the Balkan lands and moved him to seek a habitation for his people in the realm of Honorius. It can hardly have been his hope to establish a permanent kingdom in Italy itself.[2] We may take it that his intention was rather to frighten Honorius into granting him lands and concessions in the Danube provinces. An opportune moment came when, towards the end of A.D. 401, a host of Vandals and other barbarians under a savage leader named Radagaisus had broken into Noricum and Raetia.[3] Alaric passed the Italian Alps in November,[4] and advanced to Aquileia, which he appears to have captured.[5] The Italians were in consternation, and not least Honorius himself, who thought of fleeing to Gaul, and was with difficulty persuaded that he was safe behind the walls of Milan.[6]

their ravages can be traced in Chrysostom's letters ; see Clinton, *F.R. sub annis.*—For the Armenian Arbazacius cp. *C.I.L.* vi. 31978. He may be the same as the Ἀρταβάζακος in Synesius, *Epp.* 134. — Isaurians on vessels in the Cilician ports are vividly described by Ammianus, xiv. 2. 1.

[1] Claudian, *B. Goth.* 537 *sqq.* Zosimus, who omits the Italian campaigns of 402 and 403, and passes from 397 to 405, as though Alaric had remained eight years quiet in Epirus, says (v. 26) : τὸ παρὰ Στελίχωνος ἀνέμενε σύνθημα τοιόνδε πως ὅν, namely τῇ Ὀνωρίου βασιλείᾳ τὰ ἐν Ἰλλυρίοις ἔθνη πάντα προσθεῖναι

with Alaric's help. From this point Zosimus follows Olympiodorus instead of Eunapius.

[2] This, indeed, is Schmidt's view, *Deutsche Stämme*, i. 204.

[3] Radagaisus was a German, as his name shows; he is called a "Scythian" in the sources.

[4] *Fast. Vind. pr., sub a.* (*Chron. min.* i. 299).

[5] Jerome, *C. Rufin.* iii. 21. Claudian's words *deploratumque Timavo vulnus* may refer either to the capture of the city or to a battle in the neighbourhood.

[6] Claudian, *ib.* 296. Prudentius has briefly described the invasion, *C. Symm.* ii. 696 *sqq.*

During the next two months the cities of Venetia opened their gates to the Goths, and Alaric was ready to march on Milan, where he hoped to seize the Emperor's sacred person.

At the moment Italy was defenceless, because Stilicho had led his mobile troops across the Alps to drive back Radagaisus and the invaders of Raetia. This winter campaign was successful. The barbarians were checked, and Stilicho induced them to furnish him with auxiliaries against the Goths.[1] Reinforced by this accession and also by troops hastily summoned from the Rhine frontier and from Britain, he came down to relieve Milan and deliver Italy (about the end of February, A.D. 402).[2] Alaric abandoned the siege and marched westward to Hasta (Asti), which he failed to take, and then went on to Pollentia (Pollenzo) on the river Tanarus, where he decided to make a stand against the forces of Stilicho who marched in pursuit. According to the poet who celebrated this campaign, a council was held in the Gothic camp, and one of the veterans who feared the issue of a trial of strength with Stilicho besought the king to withdraw from Italy while there was yet time. Alaric indignantly refused ; he was confident that he was destined to capture Rome ; and he assured the assembled warriors that a clear voice had come to him from a grove, saying *penetrabis ad Urbem*, " thou shalt penetrate to the City."

The battle was fought on Easter-day (April 6). Neither side could claim a decisive victory,[3] but the Romans occupied the Gothic camp, and Alaric's family among other captives fell into their hands. The Goths descended to the Ligurian coast and marched along the coast road in the direction of Etruria.[4]

---

[1] Claudian, *ib.* 279 *sqq.*, 321 *sqq.*, 364 *sqq.*, 414. Cp. Hodgkin, *Italy and her Invaders*, i. 711 *sqq.*, and Bury, App. 15 to Gibbon, vol. iii.

[2] Symmachus, *Ep.* vii. 13. Stilicho seems to have marched to Raetia by the Splügen pass (Claudian, *ib.* 320) and returned by the Brenner (*ib.* 488) ; see Seeck, *Ges. d. Untergangs*, v. 573. For the forces summoned from Gaul and Britain see Claudian, *ib.* 416 *sqq.* The Rhine was left defended *solo terrore.* The Britannic legion came from the north-west,

uenit et extremis legio praetenta Britannis
quae Scotto dat frena truci ;

probably it was a detachment of the old IInd legion. Cp. Bury, *The Not. Dig.*, in *J.R.S.* x.

[3] Prosper, *sub a.*, *vehementer utriusque partis clade pugnatum est.* Cp. Prudentius, *ib.* 717-720. Crees, *Claudian*, 175-180, argues for 403 as the year of the battle.

[4] Alaric's goal was Rome. Cp. Claudian, *De VI. cons. Hon.* 483. The verses of Prudentius, *l.c.*, reflect the profound relief felt in Rome at the success of Stilicho. An illustration of this is possibly to be found in an early Christian missal, where deliverance from a foe at Eastertide is referred to. See Grisar, i. 37.

Stilicho did not attempt to overtake and crush them.   He opened negotiations and Alaric agreed to leave Italy, but we do not know what conditions were made.[1]

When he retired from Italian soil in accordance with this treaty, he remained near the borders of the peninsula, dissatisfied with a bargain which perhaps the captivity of his wife and children had chiefly moved him to accept.   At the end of a year, during which Stilicho strengthened the military forces in Italy, probably at the expense of the defences of Gaul, he crossed the Italian frontier again in the early summer (A.D. 403) and attacked Verona.[2]   Here defeated by Stilicho, and almost captured himself, he took the northward road to the Brenner pass, pursued by the Romans.   The army of the Goths suffered from hunger and disease, and seems to have been entirely at the mercy of the Roman general.   But Stilicho acted once more as he had acted in Thessaly, in the Peloponnesus, and in Liguria.[3]   He came to an understanding with Alaric and allowed him to take up his quarters in the border districts between Dalmatia and Pannonia, where he was to hold himself in readiness to help Stilicho to carry out the plan of annexing Eastern Illyricum.[4] Here he seems to have remained for some time and then to have moved again into Epirus.

The story of these two critical years in Italy can hardly be said to be known.   The slight chronicle which we can construct of Alaric's invasions is drawn from rhetorical poets and the scrappy notices of chroniclers.   They do not tell us the things that would enable us to judge the situation.   They do not tell us the number of the Gothic warriors, or the number and composition of the Imperial forces which opposed them ; they do not tell us anything of the actual course of the fighting or the tactics employed at Pollentia or at Verona ; and they are silent as to the precise conditions on which Stilicho spared Alaric. We know enough, however, to see that if another than this German general had been at the head of affairs, if the

[1] Schmidt (*ib.* 206) is mistaken in thinking that Alaric was now created a western Mag. mil., citing Sozomen, viii. 25.   This passage refers to a later date (406-407 ?).

[2] This second invasion used to be placed in 402, but Birt (*Praef.* to his ed. of Claudian, liii. *sqq.*) determined the true date as 403.   Cp. Mommsen,

Hist. Sch. i. 525, *n.* 4 ;   Bury, App. 18 to Gibbon, vol. iii.   The sole source is Claudian, *ib.* 201 *sqq.*

[3] Orosius (vii. 37) notes these repeated releases of Alaric : *taceo de Alarico . . . saepe victo saepeque concluso semperque dimisso.*

[4] Zosimus, v. 26 (Olympiodorus).

defence of the provinces had been in the hands of a Roman
commander possessing the ability and character of Theodosius
or Valentinian I., the Visigoths and their king would have
been utterly crushed, and many calamities would have been
averted, which ensued from the indulgent policy of the
Vandal to whom Theodosius had unwisely entrusted the destinies of Rome.

The Emperor Honorius celebrated the repulse of the invader
by a triumphal entry into Rome.[1] It was probably in the summer
or autumn of A.D. 402 that, menaced by Alaric's proximity, he
had moved his home and court from Milan to Ravenna,[2] and,
as future events were to prove, he could not have chosen a safer
retreat. But he could now venture to Rome, which he had never
visited before, enjoy the celebration of a triumph,[3] reside in the
palace of the Caesars on the Palatine Hill, and enter upon his
sixth consulship (A.D. 404) in the presence of the Senate and the
Roman people. For the Romans, the triumphal entry of the
Emperor was an event. Rome, which had not witnessed a
triumph for more than a hundred years, had in certain ways
changed much since the days of Diocletian. In external appearance the transformation from ancient into medieval Rome had
already begun. Christian basilicae had been built in all parts
of the city. Most of the great churches that still exist, though
rebuilt, enlarged, or restored, had been founded in the fourth
century. St. John in the Lateran, the basilica of Liberius on the
Esquiline which was soon to become Sta. Maria Maggiore, and
outside the walls St. Peter beyond the Tiber, and St. Paul on
the road to Ostia, were all probably visited by Honorius.[4] The
temples of the gods stood still unharmed, but derelict ; more
than twenty years before the altar of Victory had been removed
from the Senate-house. Some distinguished senatorial families
had been converted from their errors, like the Anicii and the

---

[1] The walls, towers, and gates of
Rome had been renovated and
fortified, at the instance of Stilicho,
in 402. This is recorded in the
identical inscriptions over the Portae
Portuensis, Praenestina, and Tibur-
tina, where statues of the Emperors
were placed ; these inscriptions
(*C.I.L.* 1188-1190) are prior to Feb. or
March 402, as the name of Theodosius,
who was created Augustus on Jan. 10,
does not appear. See Seeck,
Symmachus, p. clxxxviii.

[2] The earliest extant rescript issued
at Ravenna is dated Dec. 6, 402
(*C. Th.* vii. 13. 15).

[3] Claudian, *ib.* 523 *sqq.* Prudentius,
ib. 726 *sqq.*

[4] St. Paul's and the baptistery of
St. Peter's are described by Prudentius
in the *Peristephanon,* xii.

Bassi,[1] but the greater number of the senators were still devoted
to paganism and would have welcomed a new Julian on the
Imperial throne. Of these pagans the most distinguished was
Symmachus, who had been their eloquent spokesman when they
vainly pleaded with Theodosius and Valentinian II. to permit
the restoration of the altar of Victory. And now during the
visit of Honorius to Rome the Christian poet Prudentius took
occasion to compose a poem confuting the arguments of
Symmachus and exulting over the discomfiture of his cause.[2]
He affected to believe that the senators had freely and joyfully
proscribed the pagan idols, and that there were few pagans left—
ingenia obtritos aegre retinentia cultus. " The Fathers," he says,
" the luminaries of the world, the venerable assembly of Catos,
were impatient to strip themselves of their pontifical garment,
to cast the skin of the old serpent, to assume the snowy robes
of baptismal innocence, and to humble the pride of the consular
forces before the tombs of the martyrs." [3]

Prudentius concluded his work with an appeal to the Emperor
to suppress gladiatorial shows : [4]

> tu mortes miserorum hominum prohibeto litari,
> nullus in urbe cadat cuius sit poena voluptas.

This appeal probably expressed a considerable volume of public
opinion, and if it was not in this year that exhibitions of gladiators
were finally forbidden, it must have been soon afterwards.
Possibly it is not a mere legend that the immediate occasion
of the abolition of these spectacles was the act of an aged monk
named Telemachus, who rushed into the arena of the Colosseum
to separate two combatants and was killed by the indignant
populace with showers of stones.[5]

The occasion of the Imperial visit to Rome was celebrated by
Claudian with his unflagging enthusiasm. He had already,
in a poem on the *Gothic War*, sung the repulse of Alaric at
Pollentia—

> o celebranda mihi cunctis Pollentia saeclis !—

---

[1] Also the Paullini and the Gracchi.
Prudentius eagerly enumerates them,
and the shortness of his list shows
that they were in a small minority.

[2] *Contra Symmachum*, in 2 Parts.

[3] *Ib.* i. 546 *sqq.* Gibbon's Para-
phrase (vol. iii. chap. xxviii.). If

Claudian read the verses of Prudentius
he must have smiled at the liberties
which that writer takes with the
quantities of Greek words (*e.g. idŏla,
hĕresis, cătholicus*).

[4] ii. 1114 *sqq.*

[5] Theodoret, *H.E.* v. 26.

and united the name of Stilicho with that of Marius as the
protectors of Italy, imagining the bones of Cimbrians and Goths
laid under a common trophy with the inscription

    ' hic Cimbros fortesque Getas, Stilichone peremptos
    et Mario claris ducibus, tegit Itala tellus.
    discite uesanae Romam non temnere gentes.'

The campaign of Verona was celebrated in the poem which he
composed at the end of the year for the *Sixth Consulship of
Honorius*, immediately after the triumph. This was his last
work. Our records are silent as to his fate, but the most probable
conjecture is that death cut short his career and that he did not
live to see the second consulship of his patron (A.D. 405), a theme
which he could not have neglected.[1]

    Great allowances as the historian has to make for·Claudian's
partiality and rhetoric, he owes him an appreciable debt and
would give much to have his guidance for the last obscure and
critical five years of Stilicho's career. But apart from the
information which he gives us, his poetry is one of the most
interesting facts of the age. He was born at Alexandria,[2] and
his earliest literary work was in Greek, but we may take it that
he had learned Latin as a child. He saturated himself in the
poetical literature of Rome from Ennius to Juvenal, and his
verses abound in echoes and reminiscences. His Roman feeling
for Roman traditions is not compromised or embarrassed by any
allegiance to the new religion ; and the statement of his contemporary Augustine that he was a stranger to the name of
Christ [3] is borne out by his poems, from which, if they were the
sole monument of the time, we should not suspect the existence
of Christianity.[4] In talent and technical skill he is incomparably

---

[1] Seeck's view is that in 404 he
was accused of pagan practices, and
thrown into prison by the Praetorian
Prefect of Italy, Rufus Synesius
Hadrianus (a man of Egyptian birth,
who had been *com. s. larg.* in 395,
mag. off. 397–399, and was Pr. Pr. 400–
405 and again 413–416), who owed him
a grudge for a biting epigram (*Carm.
min.* xxi.) ; his friends were tortured
and banished ; and in prison Claudian
wrote an appeal to the Prefect for
mercy, the *Deprecatio ad Hadrianum*
(*Carm. min.* xxii.). Stilicho basely
withdrew his protection. This theory
depends on the interpretation of the

Deprecatio, which Birt (Preface, xi.,
xii.) has otherwise explained.

[2] Suidas, *s.v.* ; Claudian, *Carmina
minora*, xix. 3 (*nostro Nilo*), xxii. 58.
His identity with the author of the
Greek *Gigantomachy*, of which fragments remain, and seven Greek
epigrams is generally admitted, and
explains *Carm. min.* xli. (*ad Probinum*)
14 *et Latiae accessit Graia Thalia togae.*

[3] *De civ. Dei*, v. 26.

[4] With the exception of the short,
perfunctory production, *De Salvatore*
(*Carm. min.* xxxii.), which stands
alone curiously out of place in the
collection.

superior to the Christian poets of the day, Prudentius and
Paulinus, and through his genuine feeling for the dignity and
majesty of the Empire he has succeeded in shedding a certain
lustre over the age of Stilicho and Alaric.

§ 7. *Last Years and Fall of Stilicho* (A.D. 405–408)

The provinces of the Upper Danube, Raetia, Noricum, and
Pannonia, were at this time still under the effective control of
Roman governors, and the principal towns still flourishing centres
of Roman civility.   In Pannonia indeed considerable districts
had been occupied by Ostrogoths, Huns, and Alans, whom
Gratian and Theodosius had settled after their victories over
the Gothic invaders of A.D. 380.   Of these the Ostrogoths had
perhaps been settled in the north-western of the four Pannonian
provinces, Pannonia Prima,[1] and it is probable that the north-
eastern, Valeria, was occupied by the Huns.[2]

The line of division between Pannonia and Noricum ran from
the neighbourhood of Tulln on the Danube to Pettau, while the
course of the Aenus (Inn) formed the western boundary of
Noricum, separating it from Raetia.[3]   The most northerly point
in the course of the Danube, which was the northern border
of Raetia, was marked by Batava Castra (Ratisbon), and the
province extended westward to the source of that river.[4]   The

[1] Cp. Schmidt, *Gesch. der deutschen
Stämme*, i. 115.   Alaric's wife belonged to one of the Ostrogothic
families of this colony.

[2] Pannonia at this time consisted
of four provinces : (1) the north-
western, Pannonia Prima, including
the towns of Vindobona (Vienna) and
Carnuntum (Petronell), Savaria (Stein-
am-Anger), Scarpantia (Odenburg) ;
(2) the south-western, Savia : chief
town, Siscia on the Save ; (3) the
north-eastern, Valeria, bounded on
north and east by the Danube and
including Sopianae, Aquincum (Alt-
Ofen), Brigetio (O-Szöny), and Inter-
cisa (Dunapentele) ; and (4) the south-
eastern, Pannonia Secunda, including
the regions of the lower Drave, in
which the chief towns were Sirmium,
Mursa (Eszeg), Ciballae (Vinkovce).
Noricum was divided into two provinces, (1) Noricum Ripense : chief
towns, Lauriacum and Commagenae

(near Tulln) on the Danube, Juvavum
and Ovilava (Wels) ; (2) Noricum
Mediterraneum : Teurnia (near Spittal),
Virunum, Aguntum, Celeia, and
Poetovio.   Both Noric provinces and
Pannonia I were governed by prae-
sides ; Pannonia II by a consular,
Savia by a corrector.

[3] In *Not. dig.* Valeria has no civil
governor.   The Huns remained in
Pannonia for 45 years or more (380
to 426 or 427); see Marcellinus, *Chron.
sub* 427.

[4] For the western boundary of
Raetia see Jung, *Römer und Romanen*,
p. 30.   There were two Raetian
provinces : (1) Prima, the southern :
chief town, Curia (Chur) ; (2) Secunda,
the northern :   chief town, Aug.
Vindelicorum.   Each had both a civil
and a military governor, a praeses
and a dux.   On all these Danubian
lands see Jung, *op. cit.*, and Zeiller,
Les Origines chrét. dans les prov. dan.

most important highway from Italy to Raetia was the Via Claudia Augusta, which led through the Tirol by Meran and Vintschgau to Augusta Vindelicorum (Augsburg) ; the Brenner road was less used. Aquileia was the great centre of roads leading from Italy into Noricum, Pannonia, and the Balkan lands. The traveller to Pannonia would proceed from Aquileia to Celeia (Cilly) and Poetovio (Pettau), whence the high road continued to Savaria (Stein-am-Anger) where several roads met, one leading northward to Carnuntum (Petronell), a second northeastward, and a third south-eastward to Sopianae (Fünfkirchen). Three roads led from Aquileia over the Julian Alps : (1) to Aguntum (near Lienz) ; (2) to Virunum (Maria Saal near Klagenfurt), whence roads led to Juvavum (Salzburg) and to Lauriacum (Lorsch) and other places on the Danube, and (3) to Emona (Laibach), which belonged administratively to Venetia and was itself connected by a road over the mountains to Virunum. Here at Emona the two roads met of which one led into northern Pannonia, as we saw, by Celeia, and the other through southern Pannonia along the valley to the Save, by Siscia (Siszek) to Sirmium (Mitrovica) and Singidunum (Belgrade), and thence to Constantinople. It should be observed that Pannonia was bounded on the south by the province of Dalmatia, for Dalmatia then included not only the coastlands of the Hadriatic as far south as Alessio, but also the lands which were afterwards to be known as Bosnia and Herzegovina, and a part of Istria, west of the river Arsia.

During the early years of Honorius, the defence of the Pannonian frontier was almost abandoned, and the Pannonian provinces suffered both from the barbarians who were within,[1] and from those who were without. Of all this devastation we have no regular story ; we have only the vague complaints and hints of contemporary writers.[2] But the alarm, even in those much tried lands, must have been great when in the last months of A.D. 405 a vast host of Germans, principally Ostrogoths, descended upon Italy.[3] They were led by the adventurer

---

[1] Jerome, *Epp.* 123. 15 *hostes Pannonii.*

[2] *Id. Epp.* 60. 16 (A.D. 396); Prudentius, *C. Symm.* ii. 716; Claudian, *In Ruf.* ii. 45 ; *De cons. Stil.* ii. 191 *sqq.*

[3] The chief sources are Olympiodorus, fr. 9 ; Zosimus, v. 26 ; Augustine, *De civ. Dei,* v. 23 : Orosius, vii.

37 ; Paulinus, *Vit. Ambrosii,* 50. We may conjecture that the number of the invaders did not exceed 50,000. The huge figures of Zosimus and Orosius, 400,000 and 200,000, are absurd ; Augustine's " more than 100,000 " must also be a gross exaggeration.—With Gothofredus and Seeck, I have followed *Fast. Vind. pr.*

Radagaisus, who had been repulsed from Raetia by Stilicho a few years before.   As the home of the Ostrogothic people was still in the neighbourhood of the river Dniester, they had a long march by whatever route they came, and it may be presumed that they crossed the Danube on the Pannonian frontier. We are told nothing of their doings in the Danubian provinces, or by what roads they reached Aquileia, and it seems probable that Radagaisus, wishing to surprise Italy, did not tarry on his way to plunder the cities of Pannonia and Noricum.   But we are told that the inhabitants of the districts through which they passed fled before them, seeking the refuge of Italy.[1]   Italy was entered without resistance, and the barbarian host overran the northern provinces.   After some time it is said that they divided into three companies,[2] of which the chief under Radagaisus attacked Florence.   Stilicho, who had collected his forces at Ticinum, numbering perhaps less than 20,000 *comitatenses*,[3] reinforced by Alans and Huns from beyond the Danube,[4] compelled him to withdraw to Fiesole.   The Romans were able to cut off the supplies of the barbarians and then massacre them at their pleasure.[5]   Radagaisus was captured and executed (Aug. 23, A.D. 406), and the victory, which was fondly declared to have extinguished the Gothic nation for ever, was celebrated by a triumphal arch in Rome.[6]   But Italy must have suffered terribly, for the barbarians had been six months in the land.

It is clear from the meagre records of this invasion that when Radagaisus surprised Italy, the field army at the disposal of

p. 299 and Marcellinus *sub* 406 in placing the invasion in 405 and the defeat in 406, contrary to the general view, which, on the authority of Prosper, places them a year earlier. The later date supplies the motive of the two constitutions issued at Ravenna in April 406 (*C. Th.* vii. 13. 16 and 17), calling for volunteers to defend the provinces against invaders in an emergency (*pro imminentibus necessitatibus*).   Gothofredus, *C. Th.* ii. 389.

[1] Cp. *C. Th.* x. 10. 25.

[2] We hear nothing of the other two.

[3] 30 ἀριθμοί (Zos. *ib.*) The numerus might vary between 300 and 900 men.

[4] Huns under Uldin, whose seat was north of the lower Danube.

[5] Augustine declares that not a single Roman was wounded.   Probably the work was done by the Huns.

[6] *C.I.L.* vi. 1196.   The arch was adorned with the statues of the Emperors (*toto orbe victoribus*) and trophies *ad perenne indicium triumphorum quod Getarum nationem in omne aevum docuere extingui.*   In another inscription the services of Stilicho were recorded, but his name was erased after his fall (*ib.* 31987 ; cp. 31988).   It was perhaps in the Jan. of this year, while the Goths were wasting Italy, that Paulinus of Nola wrote his *Poema* xxvi.   For the date of the victory see *Consul. Ital.* (*Chr. min.* i. 299).   According to Olympiodorus (*fr.* 9) Stilicho enrolled 12,000 Goths in the Roman army. Probably they did not belong to the band which attacked Florence.

Stilicho was so small that he could not venture on a battle with
the superior forces of the enemy until he had obtained help
from the Huns. It is possible that some of the troops which
had come from Gaul and Britain to oppose Alaric had been sent
back, but, if so, the Gallic legionaries of the Rhine frontier must
have again been summoned to fight against Radagaisus, and must
have been retained. For the Rhine was virtually undefended at
the end of A.D. 406, when hosts of Germans crossed the river
and began a progress of destruction through Gaul. This event
was decisive for the future history of Western Europe, though the
government of Ravenna had little idea what its consequences
would be. But Stilicho was at least bound to hasten to the rescue
of the Gallic provincials. Instead of doing this, he busied himself (A.D. 407) with his designs on Illyricum which the invasion
of Radagaisus had compelled him to postpone. The unfriendli-
ness which had long existed between the eastern and western
courts came to a crisis when the ecclesiastics whom Honorius
had sent to remonstrate with his brother on the treatment of
Chrysostom were flung into prison.[1] It was a sufficient pretext
for Stilicho to close the Italian ports to the ships of the subjects
of Arcadius and break off all intercourse between the two realms.[2]
Alaric was warned to hold Epirus for Honorius; and Jovius
was appointed, in anticipation, Praetorian Prefect of Illyricum.[3]
Stilicho was at Ravenna, making ready to cross the Hadriatic,
when a report reached him that Alaric was dead. It was
false, but it caused delay; and then came the alarming
news that a certain Constantine, a soldier in Britain, had been
proclaimed Emperor and had crossed over to Gaul. Once
again the design of Stilicho was thwarted. He might look with
indifference on the presence of barbarian foes in the provinces
beyond the Alps, but he could not neglect the duty of devising
measures against a rebel.[4]

Alaric cared not at all for the difficulties of his paymaster,
and chafed under the intolerable delay. Early in A.D. 408,
threatened perhaps by preparations which the eastern government was making to defend Illyricum,[5] he marched northwards,

---

[1] See above, p. 158.
[2] The measure is referred to in
C. Th. vii. 16. 1.
[3] Sozomen, viii. 25 = ix. 4.
[4] The course of events in Gaul will

be related in the following chapter.
[5] Cp. *C. Th.* xi. 17. 4 (April 11,
408) = xv. 1. 49 (April 9, 412, false
date) Cp. Seeck's conjectures, *op.
cit.* v. 591.

and followed the high road from Sirmium to Emona. He halted there, and instead of marching across the Julian Alps to Aquileia and Italy, he turned northwards by the road which led across the Loibl Pass to Virunum.[1] Here in the province of Noricum he encamped, and sent an embassy to Rome demanding compensation for all the trouble he had taken in the interest of the government of Honorius. 4000 pounds of gold (£180,000) was named. The Senate assembled, and Stilicho's influence induced it to agree to the monstrous demand ; but many were dissatisfied with a policy which played into the hands of the barbarians, and one senator bolder than the rest exclaimed, " That is not a peace ; it is a compact of thraldom." Such, however, was the power of the Emperor's father-in-law, and such the awe in which he was held, that the rash speaker after the dissolution of the assembly deemed it prudent to seek refuge in a church. The money was paid to Alaric, and he was retained in the service of Honorius. Perhaps he might be employed against the usurper in Gaul.

But Stilicho's position was not so secure as it seemed. His daughter, the Empress Maria, was dead, but Honorius had been induced to wed her sister Aemilia Materna Thermantia,[2] and Stilicho might think that his influence over the Emperor was impregnable and still hope for the union of his son with Placidia. But any popularity he had won by the victory over Gildo, by the expulsion of Alaric from Italy, by the defeat of Radagaisus was ebbing away. The misfortunes in Gaul, which had been occupied by a tyrant and was being plundered by barbarians, were attributed to his incapacity or treachery, and his ambiguous relations with Alaric had only resulted in a new danger for Italy. It was whispered that his design on Eastern Illyricum only covered the intention of a triple division of the Empire, in which his own son Eucherius should be the third Imperial colleague. Both he and his wife Serena were detested by the pagan families of Rome who still possessed predominant influence in the capital. Nor

---

[1] Cp. Jung, *Römer und Romanen*, p. 120.

[2] Early in 408. Zosimus, v. 28 ; Olympiodorus, *fr.* 2. For her full name see *C.I.L.* xv. 7152. The marriage was arranged through the efforts of Serena. We do not know when Maria died. She seems to have been buried at Rome in a porphyry sarcophagus, in St. Peter's. A remarkable golden bulla was found in the sarcophagus with the inscription :

Honori, Maria, Stelicho, Serena vivatis ! Stelicho, Serena, Thermantia, Eucheri vivatis !

See Dessau, 800.

was his popularity with the army secure.   While he and Honorius were at Rome in the spring of A.D. 408, a friend warned him that the spirit of the troops stationed at Ticinum was far from friendly to his government.

Honorius had reached Bononia, on his way back to Ravenna, when the news of his brother's death arrived (May).   He entertained the idea of proceeding to Constantinople to protect the interests of his child nephew Theodosius, and he summoned Stilicho for consultation.   Stilicho dissuaded him from this plan, urging that it would be fatal for the legitimate Emperor to leave Italy while a usurper was in possession of Gaul ; and he undertook to travel himself to the eastern capital ; during his absence there would be no danger from Alaric, if he were given a commission to march against Constantine.   The death of Arcadius had presented to Stilicho too good an opportunity for prosecuting his design on Illyricum to be lost.   Honorius agreed, and official letters were drafted and signed, to Alaric instructing him to restore the Emperor's authority in Gaul, and to Theodosius regarding Stilicho's mission to Constantinople.

The Emperor then proceeded to Ticinum, and there a plot was woven for the destruction of the powerful and unsuspicious minister.   Olympius, a palace official, who had opportunities of access to Honorius on the journey, let fall calumnious suggestions that Stilicho was planning to do away with Theodosius and place his own son on the eastern throne.   At Ticinum he sowed the same suspicions among the troops, who were discontented and mutinous.   His efforts brought about a military revolution, in which nearly all the highest officials who were in attendance on the Emperor, including the Praetorian Prefects of Italy and Gaul, were slain (August 13).[1]

The first thought of Stilicho, when the confused story of these alarming occurrences reached him at Bononia and it was doubtful whether the Emperor himself had not been killed, was to march at the head of the barbarian troops who were with him and punish the mutineers.   But when he was reassured that the Emperor was safe, reflexion made him hesitate to use the barbarians against Romans.   His German followers, conspicuous

---

[1] The list is : Limenius, Pr. Pr. of Gaul (who had come to Italy to escape from Constantine) ; the Master of Offices, the Quaestor, the Comes s. larg., the Comes r. priv., the two comites domest., and Longinianus, Pr. Pr. of Italy (Zos. v. 32).   Date : *Cons. Ital.* p. 300.

among them Sarus the Goth, were eager to act and indignant at the change of his resolve. He went himself to Ravenna, probably to assure himself of the loyalty of the garrison ; but Honorius, at the instigation of Olympius, wrote to the commander instructions to arrest the great Master of Soldiers. Stilicho under cover of night took refuge in a church, but the next day allowed himself to be taken forth and imprisoned on the assurance that the Imperial order was not to put him to death, but to detain him under guard. Then a second letter arrived, ordering his execution. The foreign retainers of his household, who had accompanied him to Ravenna, attempted to rescue him, but he peremptorily forbade them to interfere and was beheaded (August 22, A.D. 408). His executioner, Heraclian, was rewarded by the post of Count of Africa. His son Eucherius was put to death soon afterwards at Rome, and the Emperor hastened to repudiate Thermantia, who was restored a virgin to her mother. The estates of the fallen minister were confiscated as a matter of course. There had been no pretence of a trial, his treason was taken for granted, but after his execution there was an inquisition to discover which of his friends and supporters were implicated in his criminal designs. Nothing was discovered ; it was quite clear that if Stilicho meditated treason he had taken no one into his confidence.[1]

The fall of Stilicho caused little regret in Italy. For thirteen and a half years this half-Romanised German had been master of western Europe, and he had signally failed in the task of defending the inhabitants and the civilisation of the provinces against the greedy barbarians who infested its frontiers. He had succeeded in driving Alaric out of Italy, but he had not prevented him from invading it. He had annihilated the host of Radagaisus, but Radagaisus had first laid northern Italy waste. It was while the helm of state was in his hands that, as we have yet to see, Britain was nearly lost to the Empire, and Gaul devastated far and wide by barbarians who were presently to be lords in Spain and Africa. The difficulties of the situation were indeed enormous ; but the minister who deliberately provoked and prosecuted a domestic dispute over the government of Eastern Illyricum, and allowed his

---

[1] Stilicho's designs for the advantage of his son were not necessarily treasonable, but the suspicion of treason is not confuted by the fact that Eucherius only held insignificant posts. Cp. Zos. v. 34. 7.

policy to be influenced by jealousy of Constantinople, when all his
energies and vigilance were needed for the defence of the frontiers,
cannot be absolved from responsibility for the misfortunes which
befell the Roman state in his own lifetime and for the dismemberment of the western realm which soon followed his death.   Many
evils would have been averted, and particularly the humiliation
of Rome, if he had struck Alaric mercilessly—and Alaric deserved
no mercy—as he might have done more than once, and as a
patriotic Roman general would not have hesitated to do.   The
Roman provincials might well feel bitter [1] over the acts and
policy of this German, whom the unfortunate favour of Theodosius
had raised to the supreme command.   When an Imperial law
designated him as a public brigand who had worked to enrich
and to excite the barbarian races, the harsh words probably
expressed the general opinion.[2]

The death of the man who had been proclaimed a public
enemy at Constantinople altered the relations between the two
Imperial governments.   Concord and friendly co-operation succeeded coldness and hostility.   The edict which Stilicho had
caused Honorius to issue, excluding eastern traders from western
ports, was rescinded.   The Empire was again really as well as
nominally one.[3]   The Romans of the west, like the Romans of
the east, had shown that they did not wish to be governed by
men of German race, and the danger did not occur again for
forty years.

---

[1] Orosius, *H.E.* vii. 37 and 38.
Here (as in *Chron. Gall.* 55, p. 652)
Stilicho is accused of having stirred
up the barbarians against Gaul.
The charge must be rejected, but it
illustrates the general feeling that
his policy was to blame for many of
the disasters of the time.   The
fiercest attack on Stilicho is that of
Rutilius Namatianus, *De reditu suo,*
ii. 41 *sqq.*, who designates him as
proditor arcani imperii, but sees his
chief crime in the burning of the

Sibylline Books, *aeterni fatalia pignora
regni*.   The poet consigns him to
Nero's place in Tartarus:

omnia tartarei cessent tormenta Neronis,
    consumat Stygias tristior umbra faces.

[2] *C. Th.* ix. 42. 22 (Nov. 22, 408).

[3] The fact that after 396 Arcadius
and Honorius never assumed the consulship together is significant, and
illustrates the bad relations between
the two courts.

CHAPTER VI

THE GERMAN INVASIONS UNDER HONORIUS

§ 1. *Alaric's Second Invasion of Italy. The Three Sieges of Rome* (408–410)

THE fall of Stilicho was the signal for the Roman troops to massacre with brutal perfidy the families of the barbarian auxiliaries who were serving in Italy. The foreign soldiers, 30,000 of them, straightway marched to Noricum, joined the standard of Alaric, and urged him to descend on Italy.[1] Among the few who remained faithful to Honorius were the Goth Sarus and his followers.

The general conduct of affairs was now in the hands of Olympius, who obtained the post of Master of Offices. He was faced by two problems. What measures were to be taken in regard to Constantine, the tyrant who was reigning in Gaul ? And what policy was to be adopted towards Alaric, who was urgently demanding satisfaction of his claims, in Noricum ? The Goth made a definite proposal, which it would have been wise to accept. He promised to withdraw into Pannonia if a sum of money was delivered to him and hostages were interchanged. The Emperor and Olympius declined, but took no measures for defending Italy against the menace of a Gothic invasion.[2]

---

[1] The number 30,000 is open to some suspicion. For if this army joined Alaric's forces (say 15,000 or 20,000) in invading Italy, the invaders would have been at least 45,000 strong ; and we are told that Alaric, when he was reinforced by fugitive slaves after the siege of Rome (see below, p. 177), was 40,000 strong. Possibly 30,000 does represent the total of the barbarian troops, but only some of them joined Alaric. In any case these numbers are useful in illustrating the strength of the Visigothic host (see above, p. 105).

[2] For the following events the chief sources are Olympiodorus, frags. 3, 4, 6, 8, 10, 13 ; Zosimus, v. 36 *sqq.* ; Sozomen, ix. *sqq.* (both these writers used Olympiodorus) ; Philostorgius, xii. 3 ; Orosius, vii. 38-40.

Alaric acted promptly. In the early autumn of A.D. 408 he crossed the Julian Alps, and entered Italy for the third time. He marched rapidly and unopposed, by Cremona, Bononia, Ariminum, and the Flaminian Way, seldom tarrying to reduce cities,[1] for this time his goal was Rome itself. The story was told that a monk appeared in his tent and warned him to abandon his design. Alaric replied that he was not acting of his own will, but was constrained by some power incessantly urging him to the occupation of Rome. Here we have, in another form, the same *motif* of Alaric's belief in his destiny to capture the City— *penetrabis ad Urbem*—to which Claudian ascribed his resolve to risk battle at Pollentia.

At length he encamped before the walls of Rome [2] and hoped soon to reduce by blockade a city which had made no provision for a siege. His hopes were well founded. The Senate was helpless and stricken with fear. One of their first acts shows the extremity of their panic. Serena, the widow of Stilicho, lived in Rome, and, as Stilicho's collusive dealings with Alaric were well known, it was suspected that she had an understanding with the Goth and might betray the city. They decided to put her to death, calculating that Alaric, learning that he had no ally within to open the gates to him, would abandon the siege. The fact that she was the niece of the great Theodosius did not save her ; she was strangled ; and it is said that her cousin, the Emperor's sister, Galla Placidia, approved of the cruel act, which was based on the merest, and perhaps unfounded, suspicion.[3] The pagan historian who records it acquits Serena of any thought of treachery, but regards her fate as a divine punishment for a sacrilege which she had committed many years before. The story is that when Theodosius closed the temples of Rome, Serena, moved by curiosity, visited the temple of the Great Mother,[4] and seeing a necklace on the neck of the goddess took it off and hung it round her own. An aged Vestal virgin who had accompanied her cried shame on the impiety, and when

---

[1] Narnia is the only case recorded (see below). As this town blocked the Flaminian Way, and Alaric failed to take it, we may guess that, having turned off from that road, he approached Rome by the Via Salaria.

[2] Probably in October, as Seeck argues (*op. cit.* v. 593-594). For

Honorius was still at Milan on Sept. 24 (*C. Th.* ix. 42. 10), but at Ravenna during the siege (Zosimus, v. 37).

[3] Should we assign to this year the bronze tablet with *D. n. Gallae Placidiae n. p.* (i.e. *nobilissimae puellae*) ? *C.I.L.* xv. 7153.

[4] It was on the Palatine.

Serena ordered her to be removed imprecated curses upon her, her husband, and children. To the pagans it seemed a fitting retribution that the neck which had worn the necklace of Rhea should feel the cord of the executioner.

The death of Serena did not change the plans of Alaric. He hindered provisions from coming up the Tiber from Portus, and the Romans were soon pressed by hunger and then by plague. The streets were full of corpses. Help had been expected from Ravenna, and as none came the Senate at length decided to negotiate. There was a curious suspicion abroad that the besieging army was led not by Alaric himself, but by a follower of Stilicho who was masquerading as the Gothic king. In order to assure themselves on this point, the Senate chose as one of the envoys John, the chief of the Imperial notaries, who was personally acquainted with Alaric. The envoys were instructed to say that the Romans were prepared to make peace, but that they were ready to fight and were not afraid of the issue. Alaric laughed at the attempt to terrify him with the armed populace of Rome, and informed them that he would only desist from the siege on the delivery of all the gold, silver, and movable property in the city and all the barbarian slaves. " What will be left to us ? " they asked. " Your lives," was the reply.

The pagan senators of Rome attributed the cruel disaster which had come upon them to the wrath of the gods at the abandonment of the old religion. The blockade, continued a few days longer, would force them to accept Alaric's cruel terms ; the only hope lay in reconciling the angry deities, if perchance they might save the city. Encouraging news arrived at this moment that in the Umbrian town of Narnia, to which Alaric had laid siege on his march, sacrifices had been performed and miraculous fire and thunder had frightened the Goths into abandoning the siege. The general opinion was that the same means should be tried at Rome. The Prefect of the City, Pompeianus, thought it well that the Christians should share in the responsibility for such a violation of the laws and he laid the matter before the bishop, Innocent I.[1] The Pope is said to have " considered the safety of the city more important than his own opinion, and to have consented to the *secret* performance of the necessary rites. But the priests said that the rites would not avail unless they

[1] A.D. 402–417.

were celebrated publicly on the Capitol in the presence of the
Senate, and in the Forum.   Then the half-heartedness of the
Roman pagans of that day was revealed.   No one could be found
with the courage to perform the ceremonies in public.[1]

After this futile interlude, nothing remained but, in a chastened
and humble spirit, to send another embassy to Alaric and seek
to move his compassion.   After prolonged negotiations he granted
tolerable terms.   He would depart, without entering the city, on
receiving 5000 pounds of gold (about £225,000), 30,000 of silver,
4000 silk tunics, 3000 scarlet-dyed skins, and 3000 pounds of
pepper, and the Senate was to bring pressure to bear on the
Emperor to conclude peace and alliance with the Goths.   As the
treasury was empty, and the contributions of the citizens fell
short of the required amount of gold and silver, the ornaments
were stripped from the images of the gods, and some gold and
silver statues were melted down, to make up the ransom of the
city.   Before delivering the treasure to Alaric, messengers were
despatched to Ravenna to obtain the Emperor's sanction of the
terms and his promise to hand over to Alaric some noble hostages
and conclude a peace.   Honorius agreed, and Alaric duly received
the treasures of Rome.   He then withdrew his army to the
southern borders of Etruria to await the fulfilment of the Emperor's promise (December A.D. 408).   The number of his followers was soon increased by the flight from Rome of a multitude
of the barbarian slaves, whose surrender he had formerly demanded.   They flocked to his camp, and it is said that his host,
thus reinforced, was 40,000 strong.

The year came to an end, Honorius entered upon his eighth
consulship,[2] and through the influence of Olympius, who was
engaged in tracking down the friends and adherents of Stilicho,
nothing was done to carry out the engagements to Alaric.   The
Goth grew impatient, Rome feared another attack, and the
Senate sent three distinguished men to Ravenna to urge the
government to send the hostages demanded by Alaric and

---

[1] Zosimus v. 40.   Sozomen does
not refer to the alleged consent of
Innocent.   The statement in the *Vit.
Melaniae iun.*, published by Surius,
I. p. 769, that a Prefect was slain by
the people *praetextu penuriae panis*
at a time when barbarians were
devastating the neighbourhood is
referred by Tillemont (*Hist.* v. 569)
to Pompeianus.   The incident is not
mentioned in the older *Life* (*Anal.
Boll.* viii. p. 34), but the arrival of
Alaric at Rome shortly after Melania
departed for Africa is noticed.

[2] His colleague was his nephew, the
Emperor Theodosius II.

compose a peace. One of these envoys was Priscus Attalus,[1] who belonged to a family of Ionia. The embassy was unsuccessful, but Attalus was appointed to the post of Count of the Sacred Largesses, and his colleague Caecilian to that of Praetorian Prefect of Italy (January 16-20, A.D. 409).[2] It was recognised, however, that something must be done to protect Rome, and a force of six thousand men were brought over from Dalmatia and sent to serve as a garrison in the menaced city. On the march thither they were intercepted by Alaric and almost all killed or captured. Attalus, who accompanied them, escaped. The Senate then sent another embassy, including as the principal delegate the bishop of Rome himself.

Before the siege of Rome Alaric had sent a message to his wife's brother, Athaulf, who was then in Pannonia, to join him in Italy. Athaulf with a force of Goths and Huns now crossed the Alps and marched to Etruria. Olympius collected some troops and sent them to intercept the new-comers. There was an engagement near Pisa, in which 300 Huns were said to have slain 1100 Goths, losing themselves only 17 men. But the success was not followed up, and the failure to hinder Athaulf from joining Alaric gave the enemies of Olympius, among whom were the eunuchs of the Palace, an opportunity to compass his fall. He fled to Dalmatia, and Jovius, his most formidable opponent, was created a patrician and appointed to the office of Praetorian Prefect of Italy.[3] The first thing to be done was to induce the Emperor to remove adherents of Olympius who were in command of the military forces, and Jovius brought this about by secretly organising a meeting of the soldiers at Classis. The mutineers clamoured for the heads of the Masters of Soldiers, and Honorius was terrified into superseding them.[4]

[1] Attalus was a pagan and had been a friend of Symmachus ; eleven short letters addressed to him are preserved in the correspondence of Symmachus (*Epp.* vii. 15-25). Seeck (Symm. *Opp.* p. clxxi.) thinks that he was son of the Ampelius who was Prefect of Rome in 370-372. The portrait of Attalus on his medallions confirms his Greek origin.

[2] The date is from *C. Th.* xvi. 5. 46, and ix. 2. 5.

[3] Feb. or March 409. Jovius was Pr. Pr. before April 1 (*C. Th.* ii. 8. 25), but not before Feb. 1 (*C.J.* ii. 4 7).

[4] The changes in the military commands between August 408 and April 409 seem to have been as follows. After the death of Stilicho *mag. utr. mil.*, Varanes became *mag. ped.*, and Turpilio *mag. equit.* ; while Vincentius and Salvius *comites domesticorum equit. et ped.* (see Mommsen, *Hist. Schr.* i. 552, *note* 1, on the interpretation of Zos. v. 32) were succeeded by Vigilantius and Valens. In the following months there was a rearrangement : Varanes is deposed and succeeded by Turpilio ; whose place is taken by Vigilantius,

Jovius, who had been a guest friend of Alaric, was anxious to bring about peace, and for this purpose he arranged an interview at Ariminum. The Goth demanded that the provinces of Venetia, Istria, Noricum, and Dalmatia should be ceded to him and his people as foederati, and that a certain annual supply of corn and a money stipend should be granted. In his report of these demands to Honorius, Jovius suggested that Alaric might relax their severity if the honorary rank of Master of Both Services were conferred on him. But Honorius would not entertain the idea of bestowing on the barbarian or any of his kin an Imperial dignity ; and he refused to grant the lands in which the Goths desired to settle.

Jovius opened the Emperor's answer in the presence of the king and read it aloud. The German deeply resented the language in which it was couched, and rising up in anger he ordered his barbarian host to march to Rome to avenge the insult which was offered to himself and all his kin. But in the meantime the government had been engaged in military preparations, and a large body of Huns had come to their assistance. And the food of the Goths was running short. Considering all things, Alaric thought it worth while to offer more moderate terms. Innocent, the bishop of Rome, which the Goths again threatened, was sent as an envoy to Ravenna, to press the Emperor to pause ere he exposed the city which had ruled the world for more than four hundred years to the fury of a savage foe. All that Alaric asked now was the two Noric provinces ; he did not ask for Venetia nor yet for Dalmatia. Give the Goths Noricum and grant them annual supplies of grain ; in return, they will fight for the Empire, and Italy will be delivered of their presence. Hard as it would have been to have had these barbarians so close to the threshold of Italy, it might have been better to have accepted these conditions. But Jovius, instead of advising peace, which he had desired before, advised a firm refusal. It appears that Honorius had taken him to task for his disposition to yield to Alaric at Ariminum, and that, fearing

and his by Hellebich. Finally in March 409 Valens replaces Turpilio, and Hellebich Vigilantius. See Mendelssohn on Zos. v. 47, p. 288. Shortly afterwards, apparently Hellebich is removed, and Valens becomes, like Stilicho, *mag. utr. mil.* (Olympiodorus,

fr. 13). Just after the fall of Stilicho it was an obvious measure of policy to restore the old system of two *co-ordinate* magistri. Mommsen, however (*ib.* 557), questions the accuracy of the statements of Zosimus.

for his personal safety, he had leaped to the other extreme, and swore, and made others swear, by the head of the Emperor—a most solemn oath [1]—to war to the death with Alaric. Honorius himself swore to the same effect.

Having met with this new refusal, Alaric marched to Rome (towards the end of A.D. 409) and called upon the citizens to rally to him against the Emperor. When this invitation was declined, he occupied Portus and blockaded the city for the second time. The corn stores lay at Portus, and he threatened that if the Senate did not comply with his demands he would use them for his own army. The Romans had no desire to submit again to the tortures of famine and they decided to yield. Alaric's purpose was to proclaim a new Emperor, who should be more pliable to his will than Honorius. He selected Priscus Attalus, the Prefect of the City,[2] who was ready to play the part, and the Senate consented to invest him with the purple and crown him with the diadem. Attalus permitted himself to be baptized into the Arian religion by a Gothic bishop, but he had no thought of playing the part of a puppet. He and Alaric hoped each to use the other as a tool.[3]

It was evidently a condition of the arrangement that Alaric should receive a military command. He was appointed Master of the Foot,[4] while the Mastership of the Horse was entrusted to a Roman. His brother-in-law Athaulf was appointed Count of the Domestics.[5] Lampadius, the same senator who had in the days of Stilicho protested in the Senate-house against the " compact of servitude " with Alaric, now accepted the Praetorian Prefecture.[6] And it is significant that he and Marcian, who became Prefect of the City, and Attalus himself, had in old days all belonged to the circle of Symmachus, the great pagan senator.[7] We are told that the inhabitants of Rome were in high spirits,

---

[1] More binding, Jovius asserted, than an oath by Heaven, Zos. v. 50.

[2] Attalus was appointed to this post at the time of the fall of Olympius.

[3] He seems to have given hostages to Alaric, one of whom perhaps was Aetius. See Merobaudes, *Panegyr.* ii. 127 *sqq.* (*pignusque superbi foederis et mundi pretium fuit*) and *Carm.* iv. 42 *sqq.* ; Renatus Frigeridus, in Gregory of Tours, *H.F.* ii. 8 *tribus annis Alarico obsessus.*

[4] But with the title Master of Both Services, Sozomen, ix. 8. See Zos. vi. 7.

[5] *Sc.* of the cavalry. His colleague, too, was probably a Roman.

[6] He had been Prefect of Rome in 398.

[7] As observed by Seeck (Symmachus, *Opp.* p. cci.) ; Tertullus, a member of the same group, was nominated consul in 410.

because the new ministers were well versed in the art of government.

The first problem which presented itself to Attalus and Alaric was how they were to act in regard to Africa, which was held by the count Heraclian, who was loyal to Honorius. They were not safe so long as they did not possess the African provinces, on which Rome depended for her supplies of corn. Alaric advised that a Gothic force should be sent to seize Africa ; but Attalus would not consent, confident that he could win Carthage without fighting a battle. He sent thither a small company of Roman soldiers under Constans, while he himself marched with Alaric against Ravenna.

Honorius was overwhelmed with terror at the tidings that a usurper had arisen in Italy, and that Rome had given him her adhesion. He made ready ships in Classis, which, if it came to the worst, might bear him to the shelter of New Rome, and he sent an embassy, including Jovius and other ministers, to Attalus, proposing a division of the Empire. But Attalus had such high hopes that he would not consent to a compromise ; he agreed to allow the legitimate Augustus to retire to an island and end his days as a private individual. So probable did it seem that the tottering throne of Honorius would fall, and so bright the prospects of his rival, that Jovius, who had sworn eternal enmity to Alaric, went over to the camp of the usurper. The policy of Jovius was ever, when he adopted a new cause, to go to greater lengths than any one else. And now, when he joined the side of Attalus, he went further than Attalus in hostility to Honorius, and recommended that the Emperor, when he was dethroned, should be deformed by bodily mutilation.[1] But Attalus is said to have chidden him for this proposal ; he did not guess that it was to be his own fate hereafter.

It seemed probable that Honorius would flee. But at this juncture the Eastern came to the assistance of the Western government, and Anthemius, the Praetorian Prefect of the East, sent about four thousand soldiers to Ravenna (end of A.D. 409). With these Honorius was able to secure the city of the marshes against the hostile army, and await the result of the operations of Constans, the emissary of Attalus in Africa. If Heraclian

---

[1] So Olympiodorus. Philostorgius (xii. 3) attributes the proposal of *acroteriasm* to Attalus himself.

maintained the province loyally against the usurper, the war might be prosecuted in Italy against Alaric and Attalus ; if, on the other hand, Africa accepted a change of rule, Honorius determined to abandon Italy.

The news soon arrived that Constans had been slain.   At this point, the opposition between the ideas of Attalus and the ideas of Alaric began to reveal itself openly.   Alaric wished to send an army to Africa ; and Jovius supported the policy in a speech to the Roman Senate.   But neither the Senate nor Attalus were disposed to send barbarians against a Roman province ; such a course seemed *indecent* [1]—unworthy of Rome.

Jovius, the shifty Patrician, decided, on account of the failure in Africa, to desert his allegiance to Attalus, and return to his allegiance to Honorius ; and he attempted to turn Alaric away from his league with the Emperor whom he had created. But Alaric would not yet repudiate Attalus.   He had said that he was resolved to persist in the blockade of Ravenna, but the new strength which Honorius had obtained from Byzantium seems to have convinced him that it would be futile to continue the siege.   He marched through the Aemilian province compelling the cities to acknowledge the authority of Attalus, and, failing to take Bononia, which held out for Honorius, passed on to Liguria, to force that province also to accept the tyrant.

Attalus meanwhile returned to Rome, which he found in a sad plight.   Count Heraclian had stopped the transport of corn and oil from the granary of Italy, and Rome was reduced to such extremities of starvation, that some one cried in the circus, *Pretium impone carni humanae,* " set a price on human flesh." The Senate was now desirous to carry out the plan which it had before rejected with Roman dignity, and to send an army of barbarians to Africa ; but Attalus again refused to consent to such a step.

Accordingly Alaric determined to pull down the tyrant whom he had set up ; he had found that in Attalus, as well as in Honorius, the Roman temper was firm, and that he too was keenly conscious that the Visigoths were only barbarians. An arrangement was made with Honorius, who consented to pardon the usurper and those who had supported him.   Near Ariminum Attalus was discrowned and divested of the purple

---

[1] Zosimus, vi. 9 ἀφεὶς πρὸς αὐτὴν [the Senate] ἀπρεπῆ τινα ῥήματα.

robe with ceremonious solemnity (summer, A.D. 410) ; but Alaric provided for his safety, and retained him in his camp.[1]

Alaric could now approach Honorius with a good chance, as he thought, of concluding a satisfactory settlement. Leaving his main army at Ariminum he had a personal interview with the Emperor a few miles from Ravenna (July, A.D. 410).[2] At this juncture the Visigoth Sarus appeared upon the scene and changed the course of history. He had been a rival of Alaric and a friend of Stilicho, and had deserted his people to enter the Roman service. Hitherto he had taken no part in the struggle between the Romans and his own nation, but had maintained a watching attitude in Picenum, where he was stationed with three hundred followers. He now declared himself for Honorius, and he resolved to prevent the conclusion of peace. His motives are not clear, but he attacked Alaric's camp. Alaric suspected that he had acted not without the Emperor's knowledge, and enraged at such a flagrant violation of the truce, he broke off the negotiations and marched upon Rome for the third time.

Having surrounded the city and once more reduced the inhabitants to the verge of starvation, he effected an entry at night through the Salarian Gate, doubtless by assistance from within,[3] on August 24, A.D. 410.[4] This time the king was in no humour to spare the capital of the world. He allowed his followers to slay, burn, and pillage it at will. The sack lasted for two or three days.[5] It was confessed that some respect was

---

[1] Along with his son Ampelius (*ib.* 12). For date see Schmidt, *op. cit.* i. 215.

[2] The chronology of the events between spring 409 and August 410 cannot be determined with any precision. Attalus can hardly have been elevated before the last months of 409. The hunger in Italy, due to the measures of Heraclian, was probably felt before the beginning of 410 ; and probably affected the loyalty of the followers of Attalus, who had begun to desert to Honorius before Feb. 14 (see *C. Th.* ix. 38. 11, cp. Schmidt, *op. cit.* i. 214). The deposition of Attalus must have been later than the beginning of April (as it was not known at Constantinople on April 24 ; *C. Th.* vii. 16. 2, where *tyrannici furoris et barbaricae feritatis* refer to Attalus and Alaric), perhaps in May or June (Schmidt, *ib.* 215).

[3] Sozomen, ix. 9 προδοσίᾳ. One of the stories told in Procopius, *B.V.* i. 2, is that Anicia Faltonia Proba was the culprit. Unable to endure the sight of the sufferings of the people, she admitted the foe. The story, generally rejected, is accepted by Seeck (*op. cit.* 413). Proba was the cousin and wife of Sextus Petronius Probus, who had a long and distinguished career recorded in many inscriptions. She was mother of three consuls. Cp. *C.I.L.* vi. 1754-5, and the genealogical tree of the Anicii in Seeck's edition of Symmachus, p. xci.

[4] The day is recorded in one MS. of Prosper's chronicle (*Chron. min.* i. 466, cp. 491), in the *Excerpta Sangallensia* (*ib.* 300, where 9 should evidently be read for 19 *Kal. Sept.*), and Theophanes, *Chron.* A.M. 5903.

[5] Orosius, ii. 19. 13 ; vii. 39. 15.

shown for churches, and stories were told to show that the violence of the rapacious Goths was mitigated by veneration for Christian institutions.[1] There is no reason to suppose that all the buildings and antiquities of the city suffered extensive damage. The palace of Sallust, in the north of the city, was burnt down, and excavations on the Aventine, then a fashionable aristocratic quarter, have revealed many traces of the fires with which the barbarians destroyed the houses they had plundered.[2] A rich booty and numerous captives, among whom was the Emperor's sister, Galla Placidia, were taken.

On the third day, Alaric led his triumphant host forth from the humiliated city, which it had been his fortune to devastate with fire and sword. He marched southward through Campania, took Nola and Capua, but failed to capture Naples. He did not tarry over the siege of this city, for his object was to cross over to Africa, probably for the purpose of establishing himself and his people in that rich country. Throughout their movements in Italy the food-supply had been a vital question for the Goths, and to seize Africa, the granary of Italy, whether for its own sake, or as a step to seizing Italy itself, was an obvious course. The Gothic host reached Rhegium ; ships were gathered to transport it to Messina, but a storm suddenly arose and wrecked them in the straits. Without ships, Alaric was forced to retire on his footsteps, perhaps hoping to collect a fleet at Naples. But his days were numbered. He died at Consentia (Cosenza) before the end of the year (A.D. 410) ; his followers buried him in the Basentus, and diverted its waters into another channel, that his body might never be desecrated.[3] It is related that the men

[1] Alaric issued special orders that the churches of St. Peter and St. Paul were not to be violated. We hear that the silver tabernacle over the altar of the Lateran Basilica was stolen (*Lib. Pont.* i. 233) ; cp. Grisar, i. 85. For the sack see (besides Orosius, and Sozomen) Augustine, *De civ. Dei*, i. 7 (and cp. the following chapters) ; *De urbis excidio* (*P.L.* 40) ; Jerome, *Epp.* 127, 128, 130 ; *Prolog.* to Bks. i. and iii. of *Comm. in Ezechielem.*

[2] Marcellinus, *Chron. sub* 410, says that Alaric burned part of the city. The palace of the Valerii on the Caelian hill was partly burned, *Vit. Melan. iun.* c. 14. The devastation

in Rome and Italy is referred to in *C. Th.* vii. 13. 20, which is to be dated to Feb. 411 (not 410), as Seeck has shown (*Regesten*, p. 73). See further Lanciani, *Destruction of Ancient Rome*, and A. Merlin, *L'Aventin dans l'antiquité*, pp. 430-433.

[3] Cp. Olympiodorus, *fr.* 10. The same writer (*fr.* 15) relates the legend that Alaric was hindered from crossing the straits by the miraculous warning of a statue. The story was suggested by an actual statue at Catona (near Reggio), the place of embarkation for Sicily, which was known as *ad fretum ad statuam*, *C.I.L.* x. 6950. See Pace, *I Barb. e Biz.* p. 6.

who were employed on the work were all massacred, that the
secret might not be divulged.[1]

Alaric's Ostrogothic brother-in-law Athaulf was elected by
the Visigoths to succeed him as their king.[2] They must have
remained for some time in southern Italy, perhaps still con-
templating an invasion of Africa, but they finally abandoned
the idea and marched northward along the west coast, to seek
their fortunes in Gaul. Of their doings in Italy during the
thirteen or fourteen months which elapsed between Alaric's
death and their entry into Gaul we hear almost nothing. It is
hardly probable that they visited Rome and plundered it again,[3]
but they laid Etruria waste. Five years later a traveller from
Rome to Gaul preferred a journey by sea to traversing Tuscany
devastated by Gothic sword and fire.

> Postquam Tuscus ager postquamque Aurelius agger
> perpessus Geticas ense vel igne manus
> non silvas domibus, non flumina ponte cohercet,
> incerto satius credere vela mari.[4]

Athaulf crossed the Alps early in A.D. 412, perhaps by the
pass of Mont Genèvre,[5] to play a leading part in the troubled
politics of Gaul. But to explain the situation which confronted
him we must go back to A.D. 406 and follow the course of events
of six years which were of decisive importance for the future
histories of Gaul, Spain, and Britain.

§ 2. *The German Invasion of Gaul and Spain, and the Tyranny of Constantine III.* (A.D. 406–411)

On the last day of December A.D. 406 vast companies of
Vandals, Suevians, and Alans began to cross the Rhine near
Moguntiacum and pour into Gaul.[6]

---

[1] Jordanes, *Get.* 158.
[2] Alaric had children in 402, and
Theoderic I. was his grandson (see
below, p. 205). They may have died
since or perhaps were girls. Athaulf
was marked out by his capacity, and
may have been the nearest surviving
and eligible relative of Alaric.
[3] As alleged by Jordanes, *Get.* 159.
[4] Rutilius Nam. i. 39 *sqq.*
[5] *Chron. Gall.* 87, p. 654 ; Schmidt,
op. cit. i. 223. If the Goths had taken
the coast-road, they would have had

to do with Constantius, who was at
Arles.
[6] The sources for the events related
in this section are Olympiodorus, *frs.*
12, 14, 16 ; Zosimus, v. 27. 31, 32,
43, vi. 1-6, 9, 13, and Sozomen, ix.
11-15 (both dependent on Olympiodorus) ; Orosius, vii. 38, and 40-42 ;
Prosper ; *Consularia Italica* ; and
Hydatius ; Jerome, *Ep.* 123 (*ad
Ageruchiam*, A.D. 409) ; Renatus
Profuturus Frigeridus *apud* Gregory
of Tours, *H.F.* ii. 9 ; Orientius,

The Asding Vandals, who, as we saw, invaded Raetia in A.D. 401, were finding their lands on the Theiss insufficient to support their growing numbers,[1] and joining with the Alans, who were living in Pannonia, and with Suevians, who probably represent the ancient Quadi, they migrated northward to the Main. We may conjecture that this movement had some connexion with the unsettled conditions beyond the Middle Danube, which caused Radagaisus and his followers to invade Italy ; and that the smaller German peoples who lived in those regions found themselves pressed and harried by their more powerful neighbours the Huns and the Ostrogoths. The idea of wandering into Gaul was naturally suggested by the fact that the Rhine frontier was no longer adequately defended. A large number of the Roman troops stationed there had been withdrawn recently by Stilicho, for the defence of Italy. On the Main, the host was joined by the Siling Vandals, who lived there with the Burgundians, to the east of the Alamanni.

The Alans were the first to reach the Rhine. They were led by two kings, Goar and Respendial, but here Goar separated himself from his fellows and offered his services to the Romans. The Asdings, under their king Godegisel, were some distance behind, when their march was interrupted by the appearance of an army of Franks,[2] who as federates had undertaken the duty of protecting the Rhine for Rome. Godegisel was slain, and the Vandals would have been utterly destroyed had not Respendial returned to their aid. His Alans changed the fortunes of the battle, the Franks were defeated, and the invaders crossed the Rhine. Their first exploit was to plunder Mainz and massacre many of the inhabitants, who had sought refuge in a church. Then advancing through Germania Prima they entered Belgica, and following the road to Trier they sacked and set fire to that Imperial city. Still continuing their westward path they crossed the Meuse and the Aisne and wrought their will on Reims. From here they seem to have turned northward. Amiens,

---

Common. ii. 165 *sqq.* ; Paulinus (his identity is uncertain), *Epigramma* 10 *sqq.* ; Prosper, *De prov. Dei*, 15 *sqq.* ; Salvian, *De gub. Dei*, vi. 15, vii. 12. The most useful modern studies are Freeman's essay on *Tyrants of Britain, Gaul, and Spain* (*E.H.R.* i., Jan. 1886 ; reissued in *Western Europe in the Fifth Century*), and Schmidt's *Gesch. der Wandalen*, 17 *sqq.*

[1] Procopius, *B.V.* i. 22. 3 λιμῷ πιεζόμενοι (perhaps the tradition of the Vandals themselves).

[2] Obviously the Ripuarian Franks, whose seats were along the Rhine north of the Alamanni (whose territory extended from the Main southward to the Lake of Constance).

Arras, and Tournay were their prey ; they reached Térouanne,[1] not far from the sea, due east of Boulogne, but Boulogne itself they did not venture to attack. After this diversion to the north, they pursued their course of devastation southward, crossing the Seine and the Loire into Aquitaine, up to the foot of the Pyrenees. Few towns could resist them. Toulouse was one of the few, and its successful defence is said to have been due to the energy of its bishop Exuperius.

Such, so far as we can conjecture from the evidence of our meagre sources, was the general course of this invasion, but we may be sure that the barbarians broke up into several hosts and followed a wide track, dividing among them the joys of plunder and destruction. Pious verse-writers of the time, who witnessed this visitation, painted the miseries of the helpless provinces vaguely and rhetorically, but perhaps truthfully enough, in order to point a moral.

> Uno fumavit Gallia tota rogo.

The terror of fire and sword was followed by the horror of hunger in a wasted land.

In Eastern Gaul too some famous cities suffered grievously from German foes. But the calamities of Strassburg, Speier, and Worms were perhaps not the work of the Vandals and their associates. The Burgundians seem to have taken advantage of the crisis to push down the Main, and at the expense of the Alamanni to have occupied new territory astride the Rhine. And it is probably these two peoples, especially the Alamanni dislodged from their homes, who were responsible for the havoc wrought in the province of Upper Germany.[2]

It may have been in the early summer of A.D. 407 that the situation was changed by the arrival of Roman legions not from Italy but from Britain. That island had the reputation of being a fertile breeder of tyrants, and before the end of the previous year the Britannic soldiers had denounced the authority of Honorius and set up an Emperor for themselves in the person of a certain Marcus. We have no knowledge of their reason for this step, but we may conjecture that the revolt was due to discontent with the rule of the German Stilicho, just as the revolt of Maximus had been aimed at the German general

---

[1] Teruanna, the town of the Morini.   [2] Cp. Schmidt, *op. cit.* 2 A.

Merobaudes. There was a certain Roman spirit alive among
the legionaries, jealous of the growth of German influence.
And we can well understand that they were impatient of the
neglect of the defence of the Britannic provinces by the central
government. One of the legions which guarded the island had
been withdrawn in A.D. 401 [1] for the defence of Italy, but we
are not informed whether it was sent back. In any case the
troops in the island were probably not kept up to their nominal
strength and were insufficient to contend against the constant
inroads of the Picts and the expeditions of the Irish from beyond
their channel, as well as the raids of Saxon freebooters from the
continent. To subdue these enemies had been a task which
had demanded all the energy of Theodosius himself. A victory
over the Picts seems to have been gained in the early years of
Honorius, but it was not of great account, [2] and when events
in the south forced Stilicho to denude the Rhine of its defenders,
little thought can have been taken at Rome or Ravenna for
the safety of remoter Britain. It was a favourable opportunity
for such an expedition as that which Irish Annals record to
have been led against the southern coasts of Britain by the
High King of Ireland in A.D. 405. [3] In such circumstances we
can easily conceive that the troops longed for a supreme responsible authority on the spot.

Marcus was not a success. Soon after his elevation he was
pronounced unfit and slain, to make way for Gratian, who
reigned for four months (A.D. 407) and then met the fate of
Marcus. The third tyrant was a private soldier who bore the
auspicious name of Constantine, and was to play a considerable
part for a few years on the stage of western Europe.

The first act of Constantine was to cross with an army into
Gaul. It has been supposed that he feared an invasion of
Britain by the German hordes, who had indeed approached the
Channel, and that he went forth to meet the danger. It seems
more probable that he was following the example of Magnus
Maximus, who had in like manner crossed over to the continent
to wrest Gaul and Spain from Gratian. He landed at Boulogne.
It appears to be commonly supposed that he took with him all

[1] See above, p. 161.
[2] Claudian, *In Eutrop.* i. 393 *fracto
secura Britannia Picto.*   Had the
success been considerable, Claudian

would have made more of it.

[3] Cp. Bury, *Life of Saint Patrick*,
p. 331.

the forces in Britain, not only the field army, but also the garrisons of the frontiers. This is highly improbable. For we cannot imagine that he did not intend to retain his hold on the island, and it has been inferred from the evidence of a coin that he set up a colleague before he sailed.[1] But he must have been accompanied by the whole field army, which was not very large, or the greater part of it.

Gaul sorely needed a Roman defender at the head of Roman legions, and the Gallic legions went over to Constantine. He inflicted a severe defeat on the barbarians, we know not where, and he is said to have guarded the Rhine more efficiently than it had been guarded since the reign of Julian—a statement which comes from a pagan admirer of the Apostate. The representatives of Honorius fled to Italy when Constantine passed into the Rhone valley and the south-eastern districts, which had escaped the ravages of the Germans. He seems to have made agreements with some of the intruders,[2] which they perfidiously violated. But we know nothing definite as to his dealings with them. " For two years," writes a modern historian,[3] " they and he both carry on operations in Gaul, each, it would seem, without any interruption from the other. And when the scene of action is moved from Gaul to Spain, each party carries on its operations there also with as little of mutual let or hindrance. It was most likely only by winking at the presence of the invaders and at their doings that Constantine obtained possession, so far as Roman troops and Roman administration were concerned, of all Gaul from the Channel to the Alps. Certain it is that at no very long time after his landing, before the end of the year 407, he was possessed of it. But at that moment no Roman prince could be possessed of much authority in central or western Gaul, where Vandals, Suevians, and Alans were ravaging at pleasure. The dominion of Constantine must have consisted of a long and narrow strip of eastern Gaul, from the Channel to the Mediterranean, which could not have differed very widely from the earliest and most extended of the many uses of the word Lotharingia. He held the imperial city on the Mosel, the home of Valentinian and the earlier Constantine."

---

[1] See A. J. Evans, *Numismatic Chronicle*, 3rd series, vii. 191 *sqq.*, 1887 ; Bury, App. 19 to Gibbon, vol. iii.

[2] Probably with Alamanni and Burgundians. See Orosius, vii. 40.

[3] Freeman, *op. cit.*

When Constantine obtained possession of Arelate (Arles), then the most prosperous city of Gaul, it was time for Honorius and his general to rouse themselves. We saw how Stilicho formed the design of assigning to Alaric the task of subduing the adventurer from Britain, who had conferred upon his two sons, Constans, a monk, and Julian, the titles of caesar and nobilissimus respectively. But this design was not carried out. A Goth indeed, and a brave Goth, but not Alaric, crossed the Alps to recover the usurped provinces ; and Sarus defeated the army which was sent by Constantine to oppose him. But he failed to take Valentia, and returned to Italy without having accomplished his purpose (A.D. 408).

The next movement of Constantine was to occupy Spain.[1] We need not follow the difficult and obscure operations which were carried on between Spanish kinsmen of Honorius and the troops which the Caesar Constans and his lieutenant Gerontius led across the Pyrenees.[2] The defenders of Spain were overcome, and Caesaraugusta (Zaragoza) became the seat of the Roman Caesar. Thus in the realm of Constantine almost all the lands composing the Gallic prefecture were included ; he might claim to be the lord of Britain ; the province of Tingitana, beyond the straits of Gades, was the only province that had obeyed Honorius and did not in theory obey Constantine.

Constans, however, was soon recalled to Gaul by his father, and elevated to the rank of Augustus. But Constantine himself meanwhile, possessing the power of an Emperor, was not wholly content ; he desired also to be acknowledged as a colleague by the son of Theodosius, and become legitimised. He sent an embassy for this purpose to Ravenna (early in A.D. 409), and Honorius, hampered at the time by the presence of Alaric, was too weak to refuse the pacific proposals.[3]   Thus

---

[1] Zosimus, vi. 4. Terentius was appointed *mag. mil.*, Apollinaris (grandfather of Sidonius the poet) Praetorian Prefect (*ib.*), and Decimius Rusticus Master of Offices (Greg. of Tours, ii. 9, quoting from Renatus Frigeridus).

[2] Freeman has shown that we are not justified in accepting the version of the story which states that the representatives of the Theodosian house were engaged in defending the northern frontier of the peninsula

against the Vandals and their fellow-plunderers before Constantine attempted to occupy it.

[3] Constantine assumed the consulship in 409 in his dominions, as colleague of Honorius. See Liebenam, *Fasti consulares*, p. 41. Captives of the Theodosian house, who had been taken in the Spanish expedition, were in the hands of Constantine, and a hope of their release seems to have been one of the motives of Honorius in sending the purple robe to the

Flavius Claudius Constantinus was recognised as an Augustus and an Imperial brother by the legitimate Emperor ; but the fact that the recognition was extorted and soon repudiated, combined with the fact that he was never acknowledged by the other Augustus at New Rome, might justify us in refusing to include the invader from Britain who ruled at Arelate in the numbered list of Imperial Constantines.   Some time afterwards another embassy, of whose purpose we are not informed, arrived at Ravenna, and Constantine promised to assist his colleague Honorius against Alaric, who was threatening Rome.   Perhaps what Honorius was to do in return for the proffered assistance was to permit the sovran of Gaul to assume the consulship. In any case it was suspected that Constantine aspired to add Italy to his realm as he had added Spain, and that the subjuga-tion of Alaric was only a pretext for his entering Italy, as it might have been said that the subjugation of the Vandals and their fellow-invaders had been only a pretext for his entering Gaul.   Hellebich, Master of Soldiers (*equitum*), was also sus-pected of favouring the designs of the usurper, and the suspicion, whether true or false, cost him his life ; Honorius caused him to be assassinated.   When this occurred Constantine was already in Italy, and the fact that when the news reached him he im-mediately recrossed the mountains, strongly suggests that the suspicion was true, and that he depended on this general's treason for the success of his Italian designs.

Constans had left his general, Gerontius, a Briton, in charge of Spain.   Barbarian federates, known as Honorians, had been used for the conquest of Spain by Constans, and to these was entrusted the defence of the passes of the Pyrenees.   It was an unfortunate measure.   The Spanish regular troops, who now acknowledged the authority of Constantine, thought that the charge ought to have been entrusted as before to the national militia, and they revolted.[1]   The Honorians betrayed or neglected their trust.   It was the autumn of A.D. 409, and on a Tuesday, either September 28 or October 5, the host of barbarians who had been oppressing western Gaul for more than two years—the

---

usurper ; but before the embassy was sent the captives had been put to death.   For the coinage of Constan-tine and Constans see Cohen, viii. 198 *sqq.*

[1] For the troops stationed there in the fifth century see *Not. dig., Occ.* xlii. 25-32.   One legion (septima gemina) and four cohorts in Gallicia, and one cohort at Veleia in Tarraconensis.

Asdings under King Gunderic, the Silings, the Sueves, and the Alans—crossed the mountains and passed into Spain.[1]

Constans imputed the troubles in Spain to the incapacity of Gerontius, and he returned from Gaul to supersede him and restore order. But Gerontius was not of a spirit to submit tamely. He seems to have come to terms with the legions, and he made some sort of league with the barbarians, by which a large part of the land was abandoned to them.[2] He renounced the authority of Constantine, and though he did not assume the purple himself, he raised up a new Emperor, a certain Maximus, who was perhaps his own son.

Thus at the beginning of A.D. 410 there were six Emperors, legitimate and illegitimate, acknowledged in various parts of the Empire. Besides Honorius and his nephew Theodosius, there was Attalus at Rome, there were Constantine and Constans at Arles, and there was Maximus at Tarragona.

Constans soon fled before Gerontius and his barbarian allies to Gaul, and after some time—the chronology is very obscure—Gerontius, leaving Maximus to reign in state at Tarragona, marched into Gaul against the father and son who had once been his masters. It was apparently in A.D. 411 that Constans was captured and put to death at Vienne, and then his father Constantine was besieged at Arles.

But Honorius, now that Alaric was dead, although the Goths were still in Italy, was able to bethink him of the lands he had lost beyond the Alps, and he sent an army under two generals, Constantius and Ulfila, to do what Sarus had failed to do and win back Gaul. Constantius was an Illyrian, born at Naissus, the birthplace of Constantine the Great, and for the next ten years the fortunes of Honorius were to depend upon him as before they had depended upon Stilicho. We may consider it certain that when he led the troops of Italy to Gaul he had already been raised to the post of Master of Both Services.[3] We have a slight portrait of his appearance and manners. He had

[1] The alternative dates are given by the Spanish chronicler Hydatius. They may have followed (as Schmidt thinks, *op. cit.* 26) the main road from Bordeaux to Pampluna.

[2] The sources give confused and contradictory accounts as to the order of events, and uncertainty may be felt whether the revolt of Gerontius preceded the entry of the Vandals into Spain, as there is a suggestion in some writers that they were invited by him.

[3] In succession to Valens. Prosper describes him as *mag. mil.*, *sub* 412, as *patricius*, *sub* 415. What post Ulfila held and who was *mag. equitum* is unknown.

large eyes, a broad head, and a long neck ; he leaned low over the
neck of his horse, and as his eyes shot swift glances right and
left he seemed to beholders a man who might one day aim at
the throne. On public occasions his look was stern, but in
private, at table and at wine-parties, he was genial and agreeable. He was superior to the temptations of money, though at
a later stage of his career he was to fall into the vice of avarice.
His ambition was associated with love. He was passionately
attached to the Emperor's step-sister Galla Placidia, who was
now a captive in the hands of the Goths.

When Constantius and his Gothic subordinate Ulfila advanced
along the coast road of Provence against Arles, the blockading
army of Gerontius fled before the representatives of legitimacy.
Gerontius returned to Spain and there his own troops turned
against him. The house in which he took refuge was besieged ; he and his Alan squire fought long and bravely for
their lives ; then the house was set on fire, and at length in
despair he slew his squire and his wife at their own request
and then stabbed himself.[1] Maximus fled to find safety
among some of the barbarian invaders who had supported
his throne.

Meanwhile Constantine, with his second son Julian, was
being besieged in Arles by the army of Italy which had replaced
the army of Spain. The siege wore on for three months, and
the hopes of the legitimised usurper depended upon the arrival
of his general Edobich, who had been sent beyond the Rhine
to gain reinforcements from the Alamanni and Franks. Edobich
at length returned with a formidable army, but a battle, fought
near the city, resulted in a victory for the besiegers. Edobich
was slain by the treachery of a friend in whose house he sought
shelter, and Constantine, seeing that his crown was irrecoverably
lost, thought only of saving his life. He stripped off the Imperial
purple and " fled to a sanctuary, where he was ordained priest,
and the victors gave a sworn guarantee for his personal safety.
Then the gates of the city were thrown open to the besiegers,
and Constantine was sent with his son to Honorius. But that
Emperor, cherishing resentment towards them for his cousins,
whom Constantine had slain, violated the oaths and ordered

[1] The story is given in great detail
by Sozomen (ix. 4), who praises
Nunechia (she was a Christian) for
imploring her husband to kill her.

them to be put to death, thirty miles from Ravenna "[1] (September, A.D. 411).

§ 3. *The Tyranny of Jovinus and the Reign of Athaulf in Gaul* (A.D. 412–415)

It was not long after the fall of Constantine that a new tyrant was elevated in Gaul. Jovinus, a Gallo-Roman, was proclaimed at Moguntiacum. This city, which had been wrecked by the barbarians five years before, was now in the power of the Burgundians, and it was their king, Gundahar, and Goar, the Alan chief (who, it will be remembered, had been enlisted in the service of Honorius), to whom Jovinus owed the purple. Constantius and Ulfilas, having done their work in overthrowing the tyrant of Arles, had returned to Italy, and the subjugation of Jovinus was reserved for the Visigoths.

It has already been related that the Visigoths, under the leadership of King Athaulf, crossed the Alps early in A.D. 412. They took with them their captive Galla Placidia and the deposed Emperor Attalus. They had come to no agreement with Ravenna ; if any agreement had been made, the restoration of Placidia would have been a condition. Athaulf was probably more inclined to side with Jovinus against Honorius than with Honorius against Jovinus. Circumstances decided him to champion the cause of legitimacy.

Attalus, from some motive which is not clear, persuaded him to offer his services to Jovinus. But it appears that the arrival of this unexpected help was not welcome to the tyrant. Perhaps his Burgundian friends did not look with favour on the coming of a people into Gaul who might prove rivals to themselves. Perhaps the terms which Athaulf proposed seemed exorbitant. Then Sarus, the Visigoth who had been in the service of Honorius, and who was the mortal enemy of Athaulf as he had been the mortal enemy of Alaric, appeared on the scene with about a score of followers to attach himself to the fortunes of Jovinus, because Honorius had refused to grant him justice for the murder of a faithful domestic. Athaulf was incensed when he heard of his approach, and advanced with ten thousand

[1] Olympiodorus, *fr.* 16.

to crush twenty men.   Sarus did not shirk fighting against such appalling odds, and having performed deeds of marvellous heroism he was taken and put to death.   This incident did not tend to smooth the negotiations with Jovinus, and when the tyrant proclaimed his brother Sebastian Augustus, against Athaulf's wishes,[1] the Visigoth entered into communication with Dardanus the Praetorian Prefect, the only important official in Gaul who had not deserted the cause of Honorius.   Envoys were sent to Ravenna, and Honorius accepted the terms of Athaulf, who promised to send him the heads of the two tyrants. Sebastian was defeated and slain immediately, and Jovinus fled to Valence, which, so recently besieged by Gerontius, was now to undergo another siege.   It seems to have been taken by storm ; Jovinus was carried to Narbonne and executed by the order of Dardanus (autumn, A.D. 413).[2]   For the moment the authority of Honorius was supreme in Gaul.

It may be wondered why Constantius having suppressed Constantine did not return to Gaul to deal with Jovinus.   The explanation probably is that his presence in Italy was required to prepare measures for dealing with another tyrant who had arisen in Africa.   The revolt of the count Heraclian, the slayer of Stilicho, was instigated, we are told, by the examples of tyranny which he had observed in Gaul.[3]   So infectious was " tyranny " that the man who three years before resisted the proposals of Attalus and the menaces of Alaric, loyally standing by the throne of Honorius, and who had been rewarded by the consulship,[4] now threatened his sovran without provocation. He did not wait to be attacked in Africa.   With a large fleet,

---

[1] The reason of his objection is not stated.   Schmidt (*op. cit.* i. 224) says that Athaulf aspired himself to be the colleague of Jovinus.   That sounds incredible.   I suggest that Athaulf's scheme was the elevation of Attalus and the division of Gaul between him and Jovinus.

[2] Olympiodorus says that the heads of the two tyrants were exposed Καρθαγένης ἔξωθεν, as those of Constantine and Julian had been (two years before).   Καρθαγένη might mean either Carthage or New Carthage (Carthagena) in Spain.   It is generally explained to mean Carthage.   I am inclined to think that Olympiodorus

confused the two cities, and that while the heads of the earlier tyrants were exhibited at Carthagena, those of the later pair were taken to Carthage (in view of the revolt of Heraclian).   Coins of Sebastian (silver) were issued during what must have been a very brief reign at Arles and Trier.   For these and those of Jovinus see Cohen, viii. 202-203.

[3] See Philostorgius, xii. 6, where Heraclian's name has been rightly restored.

[4] Heraclian's consulship in 413 shows that his revolt began in that year (not in 412 as Hydatius, 51, suggests).

of which the size was grossly exaggerated at the time,[1] he landed in Italy, intending to march on Rome, but was almost immediately defeated,[2] and fled back to Africa in a single ship to find that the African provinces would have none of him. He was beheaded in the Temple of Memory at Carthage (summer, A.D. 413).[3] His consulship was declared invalid, and his large fortune was made over to Constantius, who was designated consul for the following year.

This revolt affected the course of events in Gaul. Honorius, whose mind did not travel far beyond his family and his poultry-yard, was bent on recovering his sister Placidia from the hands of the Visigoth, and this desire was ardently shared by Constantius, who aspired to the hand of this princess. Athaulf had agreed to restore her when the bargain had been made that in return for his services in crushing Jovinus he and his people should be supplied with corn and receive a Gallic province as Federates of the Empire. But Africa was the corn-chamber of Italy, and when Heraclian stopped the transport of supplies [4] it became impossible to fulfil the engagement with Athaulf. There was hunger in the Gothic camp. Athaulf therefore refused to carry out his part of the compact and surrender Placidia. He made an attempt to take Marseilles, which he hoped might fall by treachery, but it was defended by " the most noble " Boniface, an officer who was afterwards to play a more conspicuous and ambiguous part in Africa. Athaulf himself was severely wounded by a stroke which the Roman dealt him. But he was more fortunate at Narbonne. He captured this town and made it his headquarters, and he also seized the important cities of Bordeaux and Toulouse.[5]

Having established himself in Narbonensis and Aquitaine,

---

[1] 3700 ships acc. to Orosius, vii. 42 and one of the two best MSS. of Marcellinus (*sub* 413 ; the other gives 700 ships and 3000 soldiers).

[2] The words of Orosius, *ib.*, suggest that he landed at the mouth of the Tiber and was defeated near the coast on his way to Rome (so Gibbon). But our other Spanish authority, Hydatius, 56, states that the battle was fought at Otricoli and 50,000 were slain. Otricoli is the first place where the Via Flaminia crosses the Tiber, after the Pons Mulvius.

[3] The edict annulling the acts of Heraclian and obliterating his name (*C. Th.* xv. 14. 13) is dated Aug. 3.

[4] Orosius, *ib.*

[5] *Capta Tolosa*, Rutil. Namat. i. 496 ; *nostra ex urbe* [*sc.* Burdigala] *Gothi, fuerant qui in pace recepti*, Paulinus Pell. *Eucharisticos*, 312. The notice in *Chron. Gall.* p. 654, *Aquitania Gothis tradita*, relates to A.D. 414, but seems to be a mistaken anticipation of the settlement of 418 (cp. Schmidt, *op. cit.* i. 226).

Athaulf determined to give himself a new status by allying himself in marriage to the Theodosian house. Negotiations with Ravenna were doubtless carried on during his military operations, but he now persuaded Placidia, against the will of her brother, to give him her hand. The nuptials were celebrated in Roman form (in January, A.D. 414)[1] at Narbonne, in the house of Ingenius, a leading citizen, and the pride of Constantius, who had just entered upon his first consulship, was spoiled by the news that the lady whom he loved was the bride of a barbarian. We are told that, arrayed in Roman dress, Placidia sat in the place of honour, the Gothic king at her side, he too dressed as a Roman. With other nuptial gifts Athaulf gave his queen fifty comely youths, apparelled in silk, each bearing two large chargers in his hands, filled one with gold, the other with priceless gems— the spoils of Rome. They had an ex-Emperor, Attalus, to conduct an epithalamium. The marriage festivities were celebrated with common hilarity by barbarians and Romans alike.

A contemporary writer[2] has recorded words said to have been spoken by Athaulf, which show that, perhaps under the influence of Placidia, he had come to adopt a new attitude to the Empire. " At first," he said, " I ardently desired that the Roman name should be obliterated, and that all Roman soil should be converted into an empire of the Goths ; I longed that Romania should become Gothia[3] and Athaulf be what Caesar Augustus was. But I have been taught by much experience that the unbridled licence of the Goths will never admit of their obeying *laws*, and without laws a republic is not a republic. I have therefore chosen the safer course of aspiring to the glory of restoring and increasing the Roman name by Gothic vigour ; and I hope to be handed down to posterity as the initiator of a Roman restoration, as it is impossible for me to change the form of the Empire."

We can hardly be wrong in ascribing this change in the spirit and policy of Athaulf to the influence of Placidia, and conjecturing

---

[1] The description comes from Olympiodorus, *fr.* 24. Philostorgius (xii. 4) compares the marriage to the union of pottery with iron (the fourth empire symbolised by the iron legs of the image in Daniel ii. was explained as the Roman, see Sulpicius Severus, *Chron.* ii. 3). See the note of Bidez, *ad loc.* Hydatius, 57, saw in it the fulfilment of Daniel's prophecy (xi. 6) that the queen of the south would marry a king of the north.

[2] Orosius, vii. 42.

[3] *Romania, ut vulgariter loquar.* This early use of Romania for the territory of the Roman Empire deserves notice.

that his conversion to Rome was the condition of her consent to the marriage. We know too little of the personality of this lady who was to play a considerable part in history for thirty years. She was now perhaps in her twenty-sixth year, and she may have been younger.[1] Her personal attractiveness is shown by the passion she inspired in Constantius, and the strength of her character by the incidents of her life. She can have been barely twenty years of age when she approved of the execution of her cousin Serena at Rome, and in her defiance of her brother's wishes in uniting herself to the Goth she displayed her independence. She was in later years to become the ruler of the West.

The friendly advances which were now made to Honorius by the barbarian, who had been forced upon him as a brother-in-law, were rejected. Athaulf then resorted to the policy of Alaric. He caused the old tyrant Attalus to be again invested with the purple. Constantius, the Master of Soldiers, went forth for a second time to Arles to suppress the usurper and settle accounts with the Goths. He prevented all ships from reaching the coast of Septimania, as the territory of Narbonensis was now commonly called. The Goths were deprived of the provisions which reached Narbonne by sea, and their position became difficult. Athaulf led them southward to Barcelona, probably hoping to establish himself in the province of Tarraconensis (early in A.D. 415). But before they left Gaul, the Goths laid waste southern Aquitaine and set Bordeaux on fire.[2] Attalus was left behind and abandoned to his fate, as he was no longer of any use to the Goths. Indeed his elevation had been a mistake. He had no adherents in Gaul, no money, no army, no one to support him

---

[1] Theodosius married her mother Galla in 387 (Zos. iv. 43 ; so Gibbon, Clinton, Güldenpenning ; in 386 acc. to Marcellinus *sub a.*, so Tillemont, Sievers) towards the end of the year ; so that Placidia may have been born in 388. Theodosius went to the west in that year and did not return to Constantinople, where Galla had remained during his absence, till Nov. 391, where he remained till the day after Galla's death in May 394. Galla died in childbirth, and the child died. It follows from these dates that Placidia might have been born in 392–393. Of the two alterna-

tives 388 appears to me to be the more probable.

[2] We learn of these events from the *Eucharisticos*, the poem of Paulinus of Pella, already cited (308 *sqq.*). He describes the siege of Vasatae (Bazas), of which he was a witness. It was attacked by Goths and Alans, and was saved by the success of Paulinus in inducing the Alans to go over to the side of the Romans, *ib.* 329 *sqq.* The king of the Alans, an old friend of his, was probably Goar, whom we have already met (so Tillemont, Freeman, Schmidt).

except the barbarians themselves.[1] He escaped from Gaul in
a ship, but was captured and delivered alive to Constantius.[2]
In A.D. 417, the eleventh consulship of Honorius and the second
of Constantius, the Emperor entered Rome in triumph with
Attalus at the wheels of his chariot. He punished the inveterate
tyrant by maiming him of a finger and thumb, and condemning
him to the fate which Attalus had once been advised to inflict
upon himself. He had not forgotten how the friend of Alaric
had demanded with an air of patronising clemency that the son
of Theodosius should retire to some small island, and he banished
his prisoner to Lipara.

At Barcelona a son was born to Athaulf and Placidia. They
named him Theodosius after his grandfather, and the philo-
Roman feelings of Athaulf were confirmed. The death of the
child soon after birth was a heavy blow ; the body was buried,
in a silver coffin, near the city.[3] Athaulf did not long survive
him. He had been so unwise as to take into his service a certain
Dubius, one of the followers of Sarus, who avenged his first by
slaying his second master. The king had gone to the stable,
as was his custom, to look after his own horses, and the servant,
who had long waited for a favourable opportunity, stabbed him
(September, A.D. 415).[4] He did not die till he had time to
recommend his brother, who he expected would succeed to the
kingship, to send Placidia back to Italy. But his brother did
not succeed him. Singeric, the brother of Sarus—who probably
had been privy to the deed of Dubius—seized the royalty and
put to death the children of the dead king by his first wife,
tearing them from the arms of the bishop Sigesar to whose
protection they had fled for refuge. Placidia he treated with
indignity and cruelty, compelling her to walk on foot for twelve

---

[1] Paulinus, who was grandson of the
poet Ausonius and son of Hesperius,
Praet. Prefect of Gaul in 379, accepted
from Attalus the post of keeper of the
privy purse, *comes privatae largitionis*
(the title of an official subordinate to
the *comes r. priv.*, see *Not. dig.*, *Occ.*
xii. 4)—a post, says Paulinus (*Euchar.*
296),

> quam sciret nullo subsistere censu,
> iamque suo ipse etiam desisset fidere regno,
> solis quippe Gothis fretus male iam sibi notis
> quos ad praesidium uitae praesentis habere,
> non etiam imperii poterat, per se nihil ipse
> aut opibus propriis aut ullo milite nixus.

(This is a specimen of the doggerel
written by the grandson of Ausonius.)
Coins show that Attalus had obtained
some recognition at Trier.

[2] He was captured in 416 (*Chron.
Pasch.*, *sub a.*). Cp. Prosper, *sub* 415,
and Orosius, vii. 42. Philostorgius
(xii. 4) says he was surrendered by
the Goths, after Athaulf's death.

[3] Olympiodorus, *fr.* 27.

[4] The news of his death reached
Byzantium on Sept. 24 (*Chron. Pasch.*,
sub a.) and was the occasion of games
and rejoicings.

miles in the company of captives. But the reign of the usurper (for he had seized the power by violence without any legal election) endured only for seven days ; he was slain, and Wallia was elected king.

For the moment Gaul was free from the presence of German invaders, with the exception of one region. The Burgundians, who had crossed the Rhine and occupied the province of Germania Superior, had been confirmed in their possession by the tyrant Constantine. After the fall of Jovinus, whom they had supported, Honorius was in no position to turn them out. He accepted them as Federates of the Empire ; [1] they were bound to guard the Rhine against hostile invaders. Thus in A.D. 413 was founded the first Burgundian kingdom in Gaul, the kingdom of Worms (Borbetomagus). It is the Burgundy of the Nibelungenlied, which also preserves the name of the king, Gundahar (Gunther), who had gained for his people a footing west of the Rhine.

The island of Britain, when many of the troops were withdrawn by Constantine in A.D. 407, was left to defend itself as best it could against Picts, Scots, and Saxons. For a while the Vicar of the Diocese and the two military commanders of the frontier forces, the Count of the Saxon Shore in the south-east, and the Duke of the Britains in the north, were doubtless in communication with Constantine and taking their orders from him. When a great Saxon invasion devastated the country in A.D. 408,[2] the Emperor in Gaul was in no position to send troops to the rescue, and the inhabitants of Britain renounced his authority, armed themselves, and defended their towns against the invaders.[3] The news reached Italy, and Honorius seized the opportunity of writing, apparently to the local magistrates, authorising them to take all necessary measures for self-defence.[4] We have no information as to the attitude of the Imperial garrisons and their commanders to the revolution. It is possible

---

[1] Prosper, *sub* 413.

[2] *Chron. Gall.* 62 (p. 654). Here there are two successive entries : 61, *hac tempestate praevaletudine (praevalente hostium multitudine,* Mommsen) *Romanorum vires attenuatae* ; 62, *Britanniae Saxonum incursione devastatae.* Freeman (*op. cit.* p. 149) was misled by the bad text of Roncalli's edition.

[3] Zosimus, vi. 5. 2 ὅπλα ἐνδύντες : this was a violation of a Lex Julia.

[4] *Ib.* 10. 2 'Ονωρίου δὲ γράμμασι πρὸς τὰς ἐν ᾿Βρεταννίᾳ χρησαμένου πόλεις φυλάττεσθαι παραγγέλλουσι. It may be noted that in the reign of Honorius, Anderida (Pevensey) on the Saxon Shore was repaired and a new fort built at Peak on the Yorkshire coast (Haverfield, *C. Med. H.* i. 379).

that they sympathised with the provincials and shared in it ; most of these troops had the tradition of association with Britain for centuries. In any case, when Constantine fell, and the tyrant Jovinus had been crushed and Honorius was again master in Gaul, there can be little doubt that he and Constantius took measures to re-establish his power in Britain.[1] In the first place, it is not probable that the provincials would have been able to hold out against the Saxon foe for fifteen or sixteen years without regular military forces, and we know that the Saxon did not begin to get any permanent foothold in the island before A.D. 428.[2] And, in the second place, we have definite evidence that in or not long after that year there was a field army there under the Count of the Britains.[3] At this time the Empire

---

[1] This is contrary to the ordinary view. Cp. Sagot, *La Bretagne romaine*, 251 *sqq.* ; Lot, *Les Migrations saxonnes*, 11-13. For the condition of Britain in the last period of Roman rule see Haverfield, *Romanization of Roman Britain*, and his article on *Britain (Roman)* in *Encyclopœdia Britannica* (Ed. 11) ; and *C. Med. H.* i.

[2] This is the British tradition. See Nennius, *Historia Brittonum*, 31 and 66 (*Chron. min.* iii. pp. 171-209). The Saxon tradition, recorded in the *Saxon Chronicle*, places the coming of the Saxons as permanent settlers in 449. *Chron. Gall.* 126, p. 660, has the following entry : *Britanniae usque ad hoc tempus variis cladibus eventibusque latae (late vexatae*, Mommsen) *in dicionem Saxonum rediguntur.* The date given is the 19th year of the joint rule of Theodosius and Valentinian = A.D. 442-443. (The argument of Freeman, *ib.* p. 158, is spoiled by his reckoning it as the 18th year of Theodosius after the death of Arcadius.) A little later we have the appeal of the Britons for help to Aetius in Gaul recorded by Gildas (*De excidio Britanniae*, c. 20), *Agitio ter consuli gemitus Britannorum.* A.D. 446 was the third consulship of Aetius. These notices taken together look as if the Saxons, having gained some footholds about 428, during the following fourteen years extended their power, and then about 442 Roman rule definitely disappeared. See Bury, *The Not. dig.*, J.R.S. x. Cp. also W. M. F. Petrie, *Neglected British*

History, 1917. It is to be noted that communications between Britain and the continent were not broken off during the fifth century. Germanus, bishop of Auxerre, who had been sent there by the Pope in 429 to contend with the Pelagian heresy (Prosper, *sub a.*), and is said to have gained a bloodless victory over the Saxons and Picts near St. Albans (Constantius, *Vit. Germ.* c. 17), visited the island a second time probably about 440 (*ib.* c. 25). See Levison, " Bischof Germanus von Auxerre," in *Neues Archiv*, xxix. (1903). We have evidence too of communications in 475 (Sidonius Apoll. *Epp.* ix. 9. 6).

[3] The fact that the Imperial officials in Britain are all recorded in the *Not. dig., Occ.* (c. A.D. 428) would not be decisive, as they might not have been erased unless Britain had been definitely handed over by treaty to another power. But there is one section, vii. (*Distributio numerorum*), which has been brought up to date, and here we find, under the *comes Britanniarum*, three numeri of infantry and six vexillationes, of which at least four and probably more are not recorded in the lists of the field forces which are under the supreme commands of the *mag. ped.* and the *mag. eq. praes.* (in sections v. and vi.). This must mean that these forces had been sent to Britain comparatively recently and had been entered under vii. but not under v. and vi. See Bury, *op. cit.*

was hard set to maintain its authority in Gaul and Spain and Africa, and it could not attempt to reinforce or keep up to strength the regiments in Britain. But there is no reason to suppose that during the last ten years of the reign of Honorius, and for some time after, Roman government in Britain was not carried on as usual. Its gradual collapse and final disappearance belong to the reign of Valentinian III.

In these years of agony many British provincials fled from the terror-stricken provinces and sought a refuge across the sea in the north-western peninsula of Gaul. Maritime Armorica received a new Celtic population and a new name, Brittany, the lesser Britain.[1]

§ 4. Settlement of the Visigoths in Gaul, and of the Vandals and Sueves in Spain (A.D. 415–423)

The Visigoths were far from sharing in the philo-Roman proclivities of Athaulf. Their new king Wallia was animated by a national Gothic spirit and was not disposed at first to assume a pacific attitude towards Rome. A Spaniard two years later [2] informs us that " he was elected by the Goths just for the purpose of breaking the peace, while God ordained him for the purpose of confirming it." Circumstances forced him into becoming a Federate of Rome, for he found his position in Spain untenable. The other barbarians had occupied most of the peninsula except Tarraconensis, and the Visigoths were unable to settle there because Roman ships blockaded the ports and hindered them from obtaining supplies. They were threatened by famine. To Wallia now, as to Alaric before, Africa seemed the solution of the difficulty, and he marched to the south of Spain (early in A.D. 416). But it was not destined that the Goths should set foot on African soil. As the fleet of Alaric had been wrecked in the straits of Sicily, even so some of the ships which Wallia had procured were shattered in the straits of Gades, and whether from want of transports or from

---

[1] See Freeman, op. cit. 162 sqq. We do not know whether any of the German invaders who crossed the Rhine in 406 had penetrated to Armorica. The enemies from whom we are told that Armorica suffered in the days of Constantine III. were probably the Saxon pirates who infested the Channel and the western coast of Gaul. The Armoricans like the Britons resorted to self-help. Zosimus, vi. 5. 2.

[2] Orosius, vii. 43.

superstitious fear he abandoned the idea. He decided that the best course was to make peace, and he entered into negotiations with Constantius.

Placidia, though still retained as a hostage, had been well treated, and her brother and lover were willing to treat with Wallia as they would not have treated with Athaulf. An agreement was concluded by which the Emperor undertook to supply the Goths with 600,000 measures of corn, and Wallia engaged to restore Placidia and to make war in the name of the Empire against the barbarians in Spain (before June, A.D. 416).

These engagements were carried out. After five years spent among the Goths, as captive and queen, Placidia returned to Italy,[1] and she was persuaded, against her own wishes, to give her hand to the Patrician Constantius. They were married on January 1, A.D. 417, the day on which he entered on his second consulship.[2]

Wallia set about the congenial task of making war on the four barbarian peoples who had crossed the Pyrenees seven years before and entered the fair land of Spain, rich in corn and crops, rich in mines of gold and precious stones. For two years they seem to have devastated it far and wide. Then they settled down with the intention of occupying permanently the various provinces. The Siling Vandals, under their king Fredbal, took Baetica in the south ; the Alans, under their king Addac, made their abode in Lusitania, which corresponds roughly to Portugal ;[3] the Suevians, and the Asding Vandals, whose king was Gunderic, occupied the north-western province of Gallaecia north of the Douro. The eastern provinces of Tarraconensis and Carthaginiensis, though the western districts may have been seized, and though they were doubtless constantly harried by raids, did not pass under the power of the invaders.

---

[1] She was escorted by Euplutius, an *agens in rebus* who had conducted the negotiations. Olympiodorus, *fr.* 31.

[2] He was consul again in 420, and in that year Symmachus the Prefect of Rome put up some monument in his honour, of which the dedicatory inscription is preserved (*C.I.L.* vi. 1719). He is there described as *reparatori reipublicae et parenti invictissimorum principum—comiti et magistro utriusque militiae, patricio et tertio* *cons. ordinario.* At Trier is preserved a memorial of his second consulship : an inscription copied on stone (in the twelfth century) probably from one of his consular ivory diptychs (*C.I.L.* xiii. 3674), *Fl. Constantius v. c. comes et mag. utriusq. mil. atq. patricius et secundo consul ordinarius.*

[3] Hydatius, our chief authority for Spain in these years, says *Lusitaniam et Carthaginiensem* ; but we may question whether *Carth.* was occupied as a whole.

Wallia began operations by attacking the Silings in Baetica. Before the end of the year he had captured their king by a ruse and sent him to the Emperor. The intruders in Spain were alarmed, and their one thought was to make peace with Honorius, and obtain by formal grant the lands which they had taken by violence. They all sent embassies to Ravenna. The obvious policy of the Imperial Government was to sow jealousy and hostility among them by receiving favourably the proposals of some and rejecting those of others.[1] The Asdings and the Suevians appear to have been successful in obtaining the recognition of Honorius as Federates, while the Silings and Alans were told that their presence on Roman soil would not be tolerated. Their subjugation by Wallia was a task of about two years.[2] The Silings would not yield, and they were virtually exterminated. The king of the Alans was slain, and the remnant of the people who escaped the sword of the Goths fled to Gallaecia and attached themselves to the fortunes of the Asding Vandals. Gunderic thus became " King of the Vandals and Alans," and the title was always retained by his successors.

After these successful campaigns, the Visigoths were recompensed by receiving a permanent home. The Imperial government decided that they should be settled in a Gallic not a Spanish province, and Constantius recalled Wallia from Spain to Gaul. A compact was made by which the whole rich province of Aquitania Secunda, extending from the Garonne to the Loire, with parts of the adjoining provinces (Narbonensis and Novempopulana), were granted to the Goths. The two great cities on the banks of the Garonne, Bordeaux and Toulouse, were handed over to Wallia. But Narbonne and the Mediterranean coast were reserved for the Empire. As Federates the Goths had no

---

[1] I infer this from what actually happened, combined with the naïve statement of Orosius (vii. 43) that all the barbarian kings had made representations to Honorius that he should allow them to fight it out in Spain, as their mutual slaughter would be to the interest of the Empire : *tu cum omnibus pacem habe omniumque obsides accipe ; nos nobis confligimus, nobis perimus, tibi vincimus, immortali vero quaestu reipublicae tuae, si utrique pereamus.* When Orosius was writing this last chapter of his work (for which see below, Chap. IX. § 6), the war was still raging between the Visigoths and their foes, and the latest news was that Wallia was strenuously working for the establishment of peace, apparently early in 418. He was writing in Africa.

[2] Sidonius Apollinaris, celebrating Wallia's grandson Ricimer, writes (*Carm.* ii. 363) :

Tartesiacis avus huius Vallia terris
Vandalicas turmas et iuncti martis Halanos
stravit et occiduam texere cadavera Calpen.

authority over the Roman provincials, who remained under the control of the Imperial administration. And the Roman proprietors retained one-third of their lands; two-thirds were resigned to the Goths. Thus, from the point of view of the Empire, south-western Gaul remained an integral part of the realm; part of the land had passed into the possession of Federates who acknowledged the authority of Honorius; the provincials obeyed, as before, the Emperor's laws and were governed by the Emperor's officials. From the Gothic point of view, a Gothic kingdom had been established in Aquitaine, for the moment confined by restraints which it would be the task of the Goths to break through, and limited territorially by boundaries which it would be their policy to overpass. Not that at this time, or for long after, they thought of renouncing their relation to the Empire as Federates, but they were soon to show that they would seize any favourable opportunity to increase their power and extend their borders.

This final settlement of the Visigoths, who had moved about for twenty years, in the three peninsulas of the Mediterranean, to find at last a home on the shores of the Atlantic, was a momentous stage in that process of compromise between the Roman Empire and the Germans which had been going on for many years and was ultimately to change the whole face of western Europe. Constantius was doing in Gaul what Theodosius the Great had done in the Balkans. There were now two orderly Teutonic kingdoms on Gallic soil under Roman lordship, the Burgundian on the Rhine, the Visigothic on the Atlantic.

Wallia did not live to see the arrangements which he had made for his people carried into effect. He died a few months after the conclusion of the compact, and a grandson of Alaric [1] was elected to the throne, Theoderic I. (A.D. 418). Upon him it devolved to superintend the partition of the lands which the Roman proprietors were obliged to surrender to the Goths. It must have taken a considerable time to complete the transfer. The Visigoths received the lion's share. Each landlord retained one-third of his property for himself and handed over the remaining portion to one of the German strangers.[2] This arrange-

---

[1] See Sidonius, *Carm.* vii. 505. There seems no reason why *avus* should not be understood literally, if we assume that Alaric was born c. 360 A.D.

[2] See the fragments of laws of Euric in *Leges Visig. ant.* p. 3.

ment was more favourable to the Goths than arrangements of the same kind which were afterwards made in Gaul and Italy, as we shall see in due course, with other intruders. For in these other cases it was the Germans who received one-third, the Romans retaining the larger share. And this was the normal proportion. For the principle of these arrangements was directly derived from the old Roman system of quartering soldiers on the owners of land. On that system, which dated from the days of the Republic, and was known as *hospitalitas*, the owner was bound to give one-third of the produce of his property to the guests whom he reluctantly harboured. This principle was now applied to the land itself, and the same term was used ; the proprietor and the barbarian with whom he was compelled to share his estate were designated as host and guest (*hospites*).

This fact illustrates the gradual nature of the process by which western Europe passed from the power of the Roman into that of the Teuton. Transactions which virtually meant the surrender of provinces to invaders were, in their immediate aspect, merely the application of an old Roman principle, adapted indeed to changed conditions. Thus the process of the dismemberment of the Empire was eased ; the transition to an entirely new order of things was masked ; a system of Federate States within the Empire prepared the way for the system of independent states which was to replace the Empire. The change was not accomplished without much violence and continuous warfare, but it was not cataclysmic.

The problem which faced the Imperial Government in Gaul was much larger than the settlement of the Gothic nation in Aquitaine. The whole country required reorganisation, if the Imperial authority was to be maintained effectively as of old in the provinces. The events of the last ten years, the ravages of the barbarians, and the wars with the tyrants had disorganised the administrative system. The lands north of the Loire, Armorica in the large sense of the name, had in the days of the tyrant Constantine been practically independent, and it was the work of Exuperantius to restore some semblance of law and order in these provinces.[1] Most of the great cities in the south and

---

[1] Rutilius Nam., writing in 417, says (*De rel. suo*, i. 213) :

cuius Aremoricas pater Exuperantius oras
nunc postliminium pacis amare docet.

leges restituit, libertatemque reducit
et servos famulis non sinit esse suis.

Freeman suggested that Exuperantius was Praet. Pref. Germanus, who

east had been sacked or burned or besieged. We saw how Imperial Trier, the seat of the Praetorian Prefect, had been captured and plundered by the Vandals ; since then it had been, twice at least, devastated by the Franks with sword and fire.[1] The Prefect of the Gauls translated his residence from the Moselle to the Rhone, and Arles succeeded to the dignity of Trier.

What Constantius and his advisers did for the restoration of northern Gaul is unknown, but the direction of their policy is probably indicated by the measure which was adopted in the south, in the diocese of the Seven Provinces. On April 17, A.D. 418, Honorius issued an edict enacting that a representative assembly was to meet every autumn at Arles, to debate questions of public interest. It was to consist of the seven governors of the Seven Provinces,[2] of the highest class of the decurions,[3] and of representatives of the landed proprietors. The council had no independent powers ; its object was to make common suggestions for the removal of abuses or for improvements in administration, on which the Praetorian Prefect might act himself or make representations to the central government. Or it might concert measures for common action in such a matter as a petition to the Emperor or the prosecution of a corrupt official.[4]

Such a council was not a new experiment. The old provincial assemblies of the early Empire had generally fallen into disuse in the third century, but in the fourth we find provincial assemblies in Africa, and diocesan assemblies in Africa and possibly in Spain.[5] Already in the reign of Honorius a Praetorian Prefect, Petronius, had made an attempt to create a diocesan assembly in Southern Gaul, probably in the hope that time and labour might be saved, if the affairs of the various provinces

became in 418 bishop of Auxerre, seems to have been in the preceding years *Dux tractus Armoricani et Nervicani*, a military command which extended over five provinces (the two Aquitaines, and 2nd, 3rd, and 4th Lugdunensis). This is the natural identification of his ducatus (Constantius, *Vit. Germ.* i. c. i. p. 202), since his authority ran in Sens and Auxerre which were in Lugd. Quarta.

[1] Apparently about A.D. 410–412. Renatus Frigeridus (in Greg. Tur. *Hist. Fr.* ii. 9) : *Treverorum civitas a Francis direpta incensaque est secunda*

irruptione ; Salvian, *De gub. Dei*, vi. c. 15, *ter excisa*, but vii. c. 2, *quadruplici eversione prostrata*.

[2] It is provided that the governors (*iudices*) of Aquitania Sec. and Novempopulana, on account of their distance from Arles, might send deputies.

[3] *Honorati*, retired decurions.

[4] We shall meet an instance in the prosecution of Arvandus : below, Chap. XI. § 4.

[5] See *C. Th.* xii. 12. 1 and 9 ; Guiraud, *Les Assemblées provinciales dans l'empire romain*, p. 228.

were all brought before him in the same month of the year.
The Edict of A.D. 418 was a revival of this idea, but had a wider
scope and intention.   It is expressly urged that the object of
the assembly is not merely to debate public questions, but also
to promote social intercourse and trade.   The advantages of
Arles—a favourite city of Constantine the Great, on which he
had bestowed his name, Constantina—and its busy commercial
life are described.   " All the famous products of the rich Orient,
of perfumed Arabia and delicate Assyria, of fertile Africa, fair
Spain, and brave Gaul, abound here so profusely that one might
think the various marvels of the world were indigenous in
its soil.   Built at the junction of the Rhone with the Tuscan
sea, it unites all the enjoyments of life and all the facilities of
trade." [1]

It must also have been present to the mind of Constantius
that the Assembly, attracting every year to Arles a considerable
number of the richest and most notable people from Aquitania
Secunda and Novempopulana, would enable the provincials,
surrounded by Visigothic neighbours, to keep in touch with the
rest of the Empire, and would help to counteract the influence
which would inevitably be brought to bear upon them from the
barbarian court of Toulouse.

The prospect of a return to peace and settled life in Spain
seemed more distant than in Gaul.   Soon after the Visigoths had
departed, war broke out between Gunderic, king of the Vandals,
and Hermeric, king of the Suevians.   The latter were blockaded
in the Nervasian mountains, but suddenly Asterius, Count of the
Spains,[2] appeared upon the scene, and his operations compelled
the Vandals to abandon the blockade.   At Bracara a large
number were slain by the Roman forces.   Then the Vandals and
Alans, who now formed one nation, left Gallaecia and migrated
to Baetica.   On their way they met the Master of Soldiers,

---

[1] The edict is addressed to Agrippa,
the Pr. Pr. of Gaul.   It was not included in the Theodosian Code, but has
been preserved as a separate document
in several MSS.   The text will be
found in Sirmond's ed. of Sidonius
Apollinaris (ed. 2, 1659, p. 241), in
Hänel's *Corpus legum* (p. 238), and
other collections ; and also in Carette,
*Les Assemblées prov. de la Gaule
romaine*, p. 460 (in this book a very

full discussion will be found).

[2] The military command in Spain,
with the title *comes Hispaniarum*, was
new and must have been established
after the invasion of the barbarians
in 409.   The first mentions of it are
in *Not. Occ.* vii. 118 and in Hydatius
74.   Asterius was created a Patrician
in reward for his success (Renatus, in
Gregory of Tours, *H.F.* ii. 9).

Castinus,[1] who had come from Italy to restore order in the peninsula. He had a large army, including a force of Visigothic Federates, but he suffered a severe defeat, partly through the perfidious conduct of his Gothic allies. The Vandals established themselves in Baetica, but it does not appear whether the recognition they had received in Gallaecia as a Federate people vas renewed when they took up their abode in the southern province (A.D. 422).[2]

§ 5. *Elevation and Death of Constantius III.* (A.D. 421), *and Death of Honorius* (A.D. 423)

When the Patrician Constantius had been virtual ruler of the western provinces of the Empire for ten years and had been for four a member of the Imperial family as the Emperor's brother-in-law, Honorius was persuaded, apparently against his own wishes, to co-opt him as a colleague. On February 8, A.D. 421, Flavius Constantius was crowned Augustus,[3] and immediately afterwards the two Emperors crowned Galla Placidia as Augusta. Two children had already been born to Constantius, the elder Justa Grata Honoria (A.D. 417 or 418) and the younger Placidus Valentinianus (July 3, A.D. 419).[4]

But the achievement of the highest dignity in the world was attended by a bitter mortification. The announcement of his elevation and that of Placidia was sent in the usual way to Constantinople, but Theodosius and his sister Pulcheria refused to recognise the new Augustus and Augusta. Their reasons for this attitude are not clear. Perhaps they had never forgiven Placidia for her marriage with Athaulf, and perhaps they had some idea of reuniting the whole Empire under the sway of Theodosius when his uncle died, and saw in Placidia's son Valentinian, on

---

[1] Castinus is designated as *mag. mil.*, not as *mag. utr. mil.*, in the sources. This may mean that after the elevation of Constantius in 421 (see below) Castinus was appointed *mag. ped. praes.*, along with a co-ordinate *mag. equit. praes.* We find in 423 Crispinus *mag. equit.* in *C. Th.* ii. 23. 1 (where Seeck and Sundwall are surely wrong in reading *Castino*). In 419, or 420, Castinus was Count of

the Domestics and led a campaign against the Franks (Renatus, *ib.*).

[2] For these events see Hydatius 77 and Prosper *sub* 422.

[3] The day of the month of his elevation, and that of his death, come from Theophanes, A.M. 5913.

[4] Marcellinus, *sub a.* Honoria was called Justa Grata after her mother's maternal aunts, sisters of Galla.

whom the title of *nobilissimus* was bestowed,[1] an obstacle to this project. Constantius, writhing under this insult, thought of resorting to arms to force the eastern court to recognise him.[2] In other ways too he found the throne a disappointment. The restraints surrounding the Imperial person were intolerably irksome to him ; he was not free to go and come as he used when he was still in a private state. His popularity, too, had dwindled, for during the last few years he had grown grasping and covetous. His health failed, and after a reign of seven months he died (September 2).[3]

After his death, Honorius, who had always been fond of his step-sister, displayed his affection by kisses and endearments which were embarrassing for her and caused considerable scandal. The love, however, was presently turned into hatred through the machinations of Placidia's attendants ; [4] and the estrangement between the Emperor and his sister led to frays in the streets of Ravenna between the parties who espoused their causes. Goths who had accompanied the widow of Athaulf from Spain and remained in her service, and retainers of her second husband, fought for her name and fame. Castinus, the Master of Soldiers, was her enemy ; we may conjecture that he hoped to succeed to the power and authority of Stilicho and Constantius. The breach widened, and at length Placidia, with her two children, was banished from Ravenna, and sought refuge with her kindred at Constantinople (A.D. 423).[5] There was a rumour that Honorius suspected her of appealing to an enemy power to come to her assistance.[6] If there is any truth in this, we may guess that the " enemies " to whom she appealed were the Visigoths.

The reign of Honorius came to an end a few months later. He died of dropsy [7] on August 15, A.D. 423. His name would be forgotten among the obscurest occupants of the Imperial throne were it not that his reign coincided with the fatal period

[1] Honorius reluctantly yielded to the pressure of Placidia to confer the title, whether before or after the death of Constantius. For the conjecture as to the project of Theodosius see Güldenpenning, *op. cit.* 240.

[2] Olympiodorus, *frs.* 34, 38, 39, is our source for the last years of Constantius.

[3] Olympiodorus adds that after his death petitions came in from all sides complaining of unjust acts he had committed to extort money.

[4] Her old nurse Elpidia, a maid Spadusa, and Leonteus her curator or intendant, are mentioned. Olymp. *fr.* 40.

[5] Prosper, *sub a.*

[6] Cassiodorus, *Chron., sub a.*

[7] Philostorgius, xii. 13 ; *Narr. de imp. dom. Val.* p. 630.

in which it was decided that western Europe was to pass from the Roman to the Teuton. A contemporary, who was probably writing at Constantinople,[1] observed that many grievous wounds were inflicted on the State during his reign. Rome was captured and sacked ; Gaul and Spain were ravaged and ruined by barbarian hordes ; Britain had been nearly lost. It was significant of the state of the times that a princess of the Imperial house should be taken into captivity and should deign to marry a barbarian chieftain.[2] The Emperor himself did nothing of note against the enemies who infested his realm, but personally he was extraordinarily fortunate in occupying the throne till he died a natural death and witnessing the destruction of the multitude of tyrants who rose up against him.

[1] *Ib.* The writer was an admirer of Theodosius II. and probably wrote soon after the death of Honorius.

[2] The curious expression used of Placidia's marriage, *statum temporum decolorat*, indicates the criticism which her act evoked in the east.

CHAPTER VII

§ 1. *The Regency of Anthemius* (A.D. 408–414)

WHEN Arcadius died his son Theodosius was only seven years old.[1] Anthemius, the Praetorian Prefect of the East, acted as regent,[2] while Antiochus, a palace eunuch, was entrusted with the care of the young prince. The guidance of the State through the first critical years of the new reign showed the competence of the regent. The measures which were passed during the six years in which he held the power exhibit an intelligent and sincere solicitude for the general welfare. The name of Anthemius is chiefly remembered for its association with the great western land wall of Constantinople, which was built under his direction and has been described in an earlier chapter.[3] But this was only one of many services that he performed for the Empire. Harmony was established between the courts of Constantinople and Ravenna and, while this was rendered possible by the death of Stilicho, it must be ascribed largely to the efforts and policy of Anthemius. A new treaty was made which secured peace on the Persian frontier.[4] An invasion of Lower Moesia by Uldin, the king of the Huns, who had executed Gaïnas, seemed at first serious and menacing, but was successfully repelled.[5] An

---

[1] Born April 10, 401; crowned Augustus Jan. 10, 402. For the children of Arcadius see the genealogical table of the house of Theodosius. On the will of Arcadius, under which the Persian king Yezdegerd is said to have been appointed guardian of Theodosius, see below, Chap. XV. § 1.

[2] We do not know by what legal form this was arranged or whether others were associated in the regency. For Anthemius see above, p. 159. In 408 he was made a Patrician. Chrysostom wrote to congratulate him on the Praetorian Prefecture, saying that the office was more honoured by his tenure than he by the office (*Ep.* 147).

[3] See Chap. III.

[4] *C.J.* iv. 63. 4.

[5] Sozomen, ix. 5.

immense horde of Sciri were in the Hun's host, and so many were taken prisoners that the government had some trouble in disposing of them. They were given to large landowners in Asia Minor to be employed as serfs. In order to secure the frontier against future invasions of Hun or German barbarians, Anthemius provided for the improvement of the fleet stationed on the Danube ; many new ships were built to protect the borders of Moesia and Scythia, and the old crafts were repaired.[1]

Constantinople depended on Egypt for its bread, and it sometimes happened that there was a lack of transport ships at Alexandria and the corn supplies did not arrive at the due time.[2] This occurred in A.D. 408, and there was famine in the city. The populace was infuriated, and burned the house of Monaxius, the Prefect of the City, whose duty it was to distribute the corn.[3] Anthemius and the Senate did their utmost to relieve the distress by procuring corn elsewhere,[4] and then Anthemius made permanent provision for a more efficient organisation of the supplies from Egypt.[5] He also took measures to revive the prostrate condition of the towns of the Illyrian provinces, which had suffered sorely through the protracted presence of Alaric and his Visigoths.[6] Towards the close of his tenure of office, all the fiscal arrears for forty years (A.D. 368–407) were remitted in the provinces of the eastern Prefecture.[7] It is interesting to observe that the most intimate friend and adviser of Anthemius is said to have been Troilus, a pagan sophist of Side, who seems to have been the leader of a literary circle at Constantinople.[8]

[1] *C. Th.* vii. 17. 1 (Jan. 28, 412). The Danube boats were called *lusoriae.* The flotillas are enumerated in *Not. dig., Or.* For the Sciri see *C. Th.* v. 4. 3.

[2] Sometimes a dishonest skipper sold his cargo at some remote place. See *C. Th.* xiii. 5. 33.

[3] Marcellinus, *Chron.*, *sub* 409. *Chron. Pasch.*, *sub* 407.

[4] *C. Th.* xiv. 16. 1.

[5] A.D. 409. The responsibility was transferred from the *navicularii* or naval collegia, to the *summates* of the fleets, whose recompense for their trouble was increased by the addition of a small remuneration. The island of Carpathus was the half-way station

between Alexandria and Byzantium, and thus the care of the corn supplies now devolved conjointly on the Prefect of the City, the Prefect of Egypt, and the *praeses insularum* (the governor of the Islands along the coast of Asia Minor ; he was subordinate to the Proconsul of Asia). *C. Th.* xiii. 5. 32 (Jan. 19).

[6] *C. Th.* xii. 1. 177 (A.D. 412).

[7] A.D. 414, April 9. *C. Th.* xi. 28. 9.

[8] Socrates, vii. 1. Anthemius was celebrated by Theotimus, a pagan poet (Synesius, *Epp.* 49). Synesius calls Anthemius τοῦ μεγάλου (*Epp.* 73; addressed to Troilus) and cp. *C.I.L.* iii., 737 *magno Anthemio.*

§ 2. *Regency of the Empress Pulcheria* (A.D. 414–416)

In her sixteenth year Pulcheria was created Augusta (July 4, A.D. 414),[1] and assumed the regency in the name of her brother, who was two years younger than herself. Anthemius soon disappeared from the scene ; we may conjecture that death removed him ; and he was succeeded in the Prefecture of the East by Aurelian, who in the preceding reign had been the leader of the Roman party in resisting the designs of Gaïnas.[2] It seems probable that he was the chief adviser of Pulcheria.

One of her first acts was to remove from the court the eunuch Antiochus,[3] who had been her brother's tutor. She super-intended and assisted in the education of Theodosius. It is said that she gave him special instruction in deportment ; and she sought to protect him from falling under the influence of intriguing courtiers to which his weak character might easily have rendered him a prey. The new mode of palatial life, established in the reign of Arcadius, enabled women to make their influence increasingly felt in public affairs. The example had been set by Eudoxia, and throughout the whole space of the fifth and sixth centuries we meet remarkable ladies of the imperial houses playing prominent parts. The daughters of Eudoxia were unlike their mother, and the court of Theodosius II. was very different from that of Arcadius. The princesses Pulcheria, Arcadia, and Marina, and the young Emperor inherited the religious temperament of their father, with which Pulcheria combined her grandfather's strength of character. The court, as a contemporary says, assumed the character of a cloister, and pious practices and charitable works were the order of the day. Pulcheria resolved to remain a virgin, and prevailed upon her sisters to take the same resolution, in which they were confirmed by their spiritual adviser, the Patriarch Atticus, who wrote for them a book in praise of virginity.

---

[1] Coins of Ael. Pulcheria, with *salus reipublicae* on the reverse, belong to the years 414–421, before her brother's marriage. They may have been struck in 415 when Theodosius celebrated his third quinquennalia and issued coins with *Gloria reipublicae vot.* xv. *mult.* xx. (Cp. de Salis, *Coins of the Eudoxias.*)

[2] According to the date of *C. Th.* viii. 4. 26, Anthemius was still Prefect on Feb. 17, 415. But according to *Chron. Pasch.*, *sub a.*, he was succeeded by Aurelian before Dec. 30, 414.

[3] Cp. Theophanes, A.M. 5905. Antiochus is said to have been sent to Constantinople by King Yezdegerd, in order to fulfil the duties of guardian which he had accepted under the will of Arcadius. See below, Chap. XV. § 1.

Theodosius had studious tastes, and he formed a remarkable collection of theological books,[1] but he was also interested in natural science including astronomy. He was of a gentle and kindly nature, and it is recorded that he was reluctant to inflict capital punishment.[2] He seems to have possessed none of the qualities of a capable ruler either in peace or war.[3]

To an unprejudiced observer in the reign of Arcadius it might have seemed that the Empire in its eastern parts was doomed to a speedy decline. One possessed of the insight of Synesius might have thought it impossible that it could last for eight hundred years more when he considered the threatening masses of barbarians who encompassed it, the oppression of the subjects, and all the evils which Synesius actually pointed out. The beginning of the fifth century was a critical time for the whole Empire. At the end of the same period we find that while the western half had been found wanting in the day of its trial, the eastern half had weathered the storm; we find strong and prudent Emperors ruling at New Rome. The improvement began in the reign of Theodosius. The truth is that this Emperor, though weak like his father, was far more intelligent, and had profited more by his education. Throughout the greater part of his reign the guidance of affairs seems to have been in the hands of prudent ministers who maintained the traditions of Anthemius and Aurelian. In the chronicles we do not hear much about the Senate; everything is attributed to Pulcheria or Theodosius. But it seems probable that the Senate exercised considerable influence on the policy of the rulers. The State was not threatened in this reign by the danger of a military dictatorship, and it was only towards its close that an unworthy eunuch enjoyed undue political power.

Soon after her accession to the responsibilities of government the young Empress was called upon to deal with serious troubles which had arisen in Egypt. The old capitals, Alexandria and Antioch, although they had been overshadowed by the greatness of Byzantium, were far from degenerating into mere provincial towns. They retained much of their old importance and all their old characteristics. In Alexandria, in the fifth century,

---

[1] See Socrates, vii. 22, who devotes a chapter to his virtues.

[2] John Ant. *fr.* 71, in *Exc. de Virt.* p. 204.

[3] Tillemont has some just remarks on the defects in his character, *Hist. des Empereurs*, vi. 23 *sqq.*

with its population of perhaps 600,000 citizens,[1] life was as busy, as various, and as interesting as ever. The Romans had found no city in the Empire so difficult to govern as that of the quick-witted and quick-tempered Alexandrians ; the streets were continually the scene of tumults between citizens and soldiers, and revolts against the Augustal Prefects. " While in Antioch, as a rule, the matter did not go beyond sarcasm, the Alexandrian rabble took on the slightest pretext to stones and cudgels. In street uproar, says an authority, himself Alexandrian, the Egyptians are before all others ; the smallest spark suffices here to kindle a tumult. On account of neglected visits, on account of the confiscation of spoiled provisions, on account of exclusion from a bathing establishment, on account of a dispute between the slave of an Alexandrian of rank and the Roman foot-soldier as to the value or non-value of their respective slippers, the legions were under the necessity of charging among the citizens of Alexandria." [2]

Instead of healing the discords and calming the intractable temper of this turbulent metropolis by diffusing a spirit of amity and long-suffering, Christianity only gave the citizens new things to quarrel about, new causes for tumult, new formulae and catchwords which they could use as pretexts for violence and rioting.

The troubles which agitated Alexandria, when Pulcheria became regent, were principally due to the bigotry and ambition of the Patriarch. In this office, Theophilus, whom we met as the enemy of Chrysostom, had been succeeded (A.D. 412) by his nephew Cyril, who was no less ambitious to elevate the prestige of his see and was even more unscrupulous in the arts of intrigue. In the first years of his pontificate his chief objects were to exalt his own authority above that of the civil governor of Egypt, the Augustal Prefect, and to make Alexandria an irreproachably Christian city by extirpating paganism which still flourished in its schools, and by persecuting the Jews who for centuries had formed a large minority of the population. He was an ecclesiastical tyrant of the most repulsive type,

---

[1] 300,000 is the number of the citizens given for the time of Augustus (Diodorus, xvii. 52). It excludes slaves and foreigners. Güldenpenning (p. 225) thinks it must have been nearly twice as much in the fifth century. Cp. above, Chap. III. § 5, p. 88.

[2] Mommsen, *Hist. of Rome*, v. (ii. 264 Eng. tr.).

and the unfortunate Hypatia was the most illustrious of his victims.

Hypatia was the daughter of Theon, a distinguished mathematician,[1] who was a professor at the Museum or university of Alexandria. Trained in mathematics by her father, she left that pure air for the deeper and more agitating study of metaphysics, and probably became acquainted with the older Neoplatonism of Plotinus [2] which, in the Alexandrian Museum, had been transmitted untainted by the later developments of Porphyrius and Iamblichus. When she had completed her education she was appointed to the chair of philosophy, and her extraordinary talents, combined with her beauty, made her a centre of interest in the cultivated circles at Alexandria, and drew to her lecture-room crowds of admirers. Her free and unembarrassed intercourse with educated men and the publicity of her life must have given rise to many scandals and backbitings, and her own sex doubtless looked upon her with suspicion, and called her masculine and immodest. She used to walk in the streets in her academical gown ($\tau\rho\iota\beta\omega\nu$, the philosopher's cloak) and explain to all who wished to learn, difficulties in Plato or Aristotle.[3] Of the influence of her personality on her pupils we have still a record in some letters of Synesius

---

[1] His most important studies were on Euclid, Aratus, and Ptolemy, Nearly all our MSS. of the geometry of Euclid are based on his critical recension, and the *scholia* on Aratus, whom he exalted as an astronomer above Eudoxus, are derived from him. The character of his work has been elucidated by Heiberg and Maass. Hypatia wrote three mathematical books, (1) a memoir on Diophantus (who wrote a standard work on arithmetic of which about half is extant); (2) a commentary on the Conic Sections of Apollonius; (3) a commentary on the astronomical Canon ($\kappa\alpha\nu\omega\nu$ $\beta\alpha\sigma\iota\lambda\epsilon\iota\omega\nu$) of Ptolemy. See the article on Ὑπατία in Suidas, which is largely based on the Life of Isidore by Damascius (for the reconstruction of which see the study of J. Asmus in *B.Z.* xviii. 424 *sqq.*, xix. 265 *sqq.*). The statement of Suidas that Hypatia was the wife of Isidore was due to a misunderstanding of his source. Palladas, the contemporary Alexandrian poet, wrote the following

very poor verses on Hypatia (*Anth. Pal.* ix. 400):

ὅταν βλέπω σε, προσκυνῶ, καὶ τοὺς λόγους,
τῆς παρθένου τὸν οἶκον ἀστρῷον βλέπων·
εἰς οὐρανὸν γάρ ἐστι σοῦ τὰ πράγματα,
Ὑπατία σέμνη, τῶν λόγων εὐμορφία,
ἄχραντον ἄστρον τῆς σοφῆς παιδεύσεως·

[2] Plotinus and his master Ammonius Sacas belonged to the university, while the later Neoplatonists were not connected with it. This point— Hypatia's affiliation to Plotinus—is due to W. A. Meyer, whose careful little tract, *Hypatia von Alexandria* (1886), has thrown much light on the subject. Hoche (in his article in *Philologus*, xv. 439 *sqq.*, 1860) showed that the supposed journey of Hypatia to Athens is based on a mistranslation of Suidas. The date of her birth was probably about 370.

[3] I follow Meyer's translation of a passage in Suidas. The most pleasing passage in Socrates is that in which he speaks with admiration of Hypatia (*H.E.* vii. 15).

of Cyrene, who, although his studies under her auspices did not hinder him from adopting Christianity, always remained at heart a semi-pagan, and was devotedly attached to his instructress. That some of her pupils fell in love with her is not surprising,[1] but Hypatia never married.

The cause of the tragic fate, which befell her in March A.D. 415, is veiled in obscurity. We know that she was an intimate friend of the pagan Orestes, the Prefect of Egypt; and she was an object of hatred to Cyril, both because she was an enthusiastic preacher of pagan doctrines and because she was the Prefect's friend.

The hatred of the Jews for the Patriarch brought the strained relations between Cyril and Orestes to a crisis. On one occasion, seeing a notorious creature of Cyril present in an assembly, they cried out that the spy should be arrested, and Orestes gratified them by inflicting public chastisement on him. The menaces which Cyril, enraged by this act, fulminated against the Jews led to a bloody vengeance on the Christian population. A report was spread at night that the great church was on fire, and when the Christians flocked to the spot the Jews surrounded and massacred them. Cyril replied to this horror by banishing all Hebrews from the city and allowing the Christians to plunder their property, a proceeding which was quite beyond the Patriarch's rights, and was a direct and insulting interference with the authority of Orestes, who immediately wrote a complaint to Constantinople. At this juncture 500 monks of Nitria, sniffing the savour of blood and bigotry from afar, hastened to the scene. These fanatics insulted Orestes publicly, one of them hitting him with a stone; in fact the governor ran a serious risk of his life.[2] The culprit who hurled the missile was executed, and Cyril treated his body as the remains of a martyr.

---

[1] One of her pupils is said to have declared his passion for her, and the tale went that she exorcised his desire by disarranging her dress and displaying τὸ σύμβολον τῆς ἀκαθάρτου γεννήσεως : " This, young man," she said, " is what you are in love with, and nothing beautiful." This story, recorded by Suidas, was without doubt a contemporary scandal, and indicates what exaggerated stories were circulated about the independence and perhaps the free-spokenness of Hypatia. Seven letters of Synesius to " the philosopher Hypatia " are preserved. He addresses her (*Ep.* 16) as " mother, sister, and teacher."

[2] It is to be remembered that the Aug. Prefect did not possess military powers. Subsequently some Prefects united civil and military functions (Florus under Marcian, Alexander under Leo I.), but these cases were exceptional. Cp. M. Gelzer, *Byz. Verw. Ägyptens*, p. 19.

It was then that Hypatia fell a victim in the midst of these infuriated passions. One day as she was returning home she was seized by a band of *parabalani*[1] or lay brethren, whose duty it was to tend the sick and who were under the supervision of the Patriarch. These fanatics, led by a certain Peter, dragged her to a church and, tearing off her garments, hewed her in pieces and burned the fragments of her body.[2] The reason alleged in public for this atrocity was that she hindered a reconciliation between Orestes and Cyril; but the true motive, as Socrates tells us, was envy. This ecclesiastical historian does not conceal his opinion that Cyril was morally responsible.

There can be no doubt that public opinion was deeply shocked not only in Alexandria but also in Constantinople. Whatever Pulcheria and Atticus may have thought, the Praetorian Prefect Aurelian, who was the friend of her friend Synesius, must have been horrified by the fate of Hypatia. It would seem that the Empress found it impossible to act on the partial and opposite reports which were received from Orestes and Cyril, and a special commissioner, Aedesius, was sent to Alexandria to investigate the circumstances and assign the guilt. We have no direct information concerning his inquiry, but it would appear that it was long drawn out and it was publicly recognised that the parabalani were dangerous. The government consequently reduced the numbers of their corporation, forbade them to appear at games or public assemblies, and gave the Prefect authority over them.[3] But within little more than a year the influence of Cyril at the pious court of Pulcheria elicited a new decree, which raised the number of the parabalani from 500 to 600 and restored them to the Patriarch's authority.[4] If condign punishment had been inflicted on the guilty we should probably have heard of it. The obscure murderers may have escaped, but " the murder of Hypatia has imprinted an indelible stain on the character and religion of Cyril of Alexandria." [5] He was an

---

[1] We find the form παραβαλανεῖς in Mansi, vi. p. 828.

[2] ὀστράκοις ἀνεῖλον (Socrates, vii. 14), killed her with either sharp sherds or mussel shells. Gibbon (v. 117) misunderstood ἀνεῖλον when he interpreted, " her flesh was scraped from her bones." Philostorgius (viii.

9) says that she was torn in pieces (διασπασθῆναι) by the Homousians.

[3] C. Th. xvi. 2. 42, A.D. 416, Sept. 29. It was suspected that Aedesius was bribed by Cyril and his party, Suidas, s.v. Ὑπατία.

[4] C. Th. ib. 43, A.D. 418, Feb. 3.

[5] Gibbon, ib.

able theologian and we shall next meet him in the stormy scene
of an ecumenical Council.

We are not told at what time the regency of Pulcheria formally
came to an end. Perhaps we may suppose that on reaching the
age of fifteen Theodosius was declared to have attained his
majority. But for several years after his assumption of the
supreme authority his sister continued to be the presiding spirit
in affairs of state. The most influential minister during these
years was probably Monaxius, who succeeded Aurelian as
Praetorian Prefect of the East.[1]

Pulcheria chose a wife for her brother when he was twenty
years of age. She seems to have been confident that her own
influence would not be endangered. The story of the Athenian
girl who was selected to share the throne of Theodosius was
romantic.[2] Athenais was the daughter of Leontius, a pagan
philosopher, and had been highly educated by her father in the
pagan atmosphere of Athens. When he died, she had a dispute
with her brothers about the inheritance of her father's property
and she came to Constantinople to obtain legal redress. Her
beauty and accomplishments won the notice and patronage of
the Empress, who chose her as a suitable bride for the Emperor.
She took the name of Eudocia and embraced Christianity. The
marriage was celebrated on June 7, A.D. 421, and was followed
by the birth of a daughter, who was named Eudoxia after her
grandmother.[3] In A.D. 423 (January 2) she was created Augusta.

---

[1] Before August 416 ; he held the
post till 420.

[2] Gregorovius made *Athenais* the
subject of an interesting monograph
(1882).

[3] A.D. 422. Her full name was
Licinia Eudoxia. It appears on those
of her coins which were minted in
Italy, after her marriage. She was
created Augusta in her infancy, for
she is so designated in Placidia's
dedicatory inscription (see below, p.
262), which belongs probably to c.
426–428. From the same inscription
we learn that Eudocia had a son
named Arcadius (born 423–425 ?), who
must have died very young ; and
Dessau is doubtless right (*Insc. Lat.*
818) in holding that this child is the
minor Arcadius mentioned in the
Preface (l. 13) to the *Cento* of Proba,
a copy of which the writer of the

Preface seems to have presented to
Theodosius II. A second daughter
was born later, Flaccilla, who died
in 431 (Marcellinus, *Chron., sub a.* ;
Nestorius, Πραγμ. 'Ηρακλ., tr. Nau,
p. 331).—Coins of Ael. Eudocia Aug.
are preserved which must have been
issued soon after her coronation in
Jan. 423, as the reverse legend is *vot.* xx
mult. xxx. They correspond closely
to coins of Theodosius, Pulcheria, and
Honorius. As Theodosius kept his
third quinquennalia in 415 (*Chron.
Pasch., sub a.*), the presumption is
that he celebrated his vicennalia in
420, and that in that year were issued
these coins of himself, Pulcheria, and
Honorius at Constantinople. The
design of the reverse (a standing
winged Victory holding a cross) on
the coins of Eudocia differs from the
others by having a star. We have

Though she was sincerely loyal to her new faith, wrote religious poems, and learned to interest herself in theology, she always retained some pagan leanings, and we may be sure that, when her influence began to assert itself, the strict monastic character of the court was considerably alleviated.

§ 3. *The Usurpation of John at Ravenna, and Elevation of Valentinian III.* (A.D. 423–425)

It was about this time that the Empress Placidia with her two children, driven from Ravenna by Honorius, came to Constantinople and sought the protection of their kinsfolk.[1] Then the news arrived that Honorius was dead, and the first care of the government was to occupy the port of Salona in Dalmatia.[2] The event was then made public, and for seven days the Hippodrome was closed and Constantinople formally mourned for the deceased Emperor. The intervention of Theodosius at this crisis in the destinies of the west was indispensable, and two courses were open to him. He might overlook the claims of his cousin, the child Valentinian, son of the Augustus whom he had refused to recognise as a colleague, and might attempt to rule the whole Empire himself as his grandfather had ruled it without dividing the power. Or he might recognise those claims, and act as his cousin's protector. In either case there was fighting to be done, for a usurper, whose name was John, had been proclaimed Emperor at Ravenna. Theodosius and Pulcheria decided to take the second course and support the cause of Placidia and her son. It was an important decision. The eastern government was not blind to its own interests, and a bargain seems to have been made with Placidia that the boundary between the two halves of the Empire should be rectified by the inclusion of Dalmatia and part of Pannonia in the realm of Theodosius.[3] The measure of occupying Salona had been taken with a view

also similar coins of Ael. Placidia Aug., with the star, evidently minted in 423 or 424, soon after her arrival at Constantinople (see below). Cp. de Salis, *Coins of the Eudoxias.*

[1] See above, p. 200.

[2] Socrates, vii. 23. Epigraphic evidence indeed suggests that Salona was under Constantinople in 414–415, see Jung, *Römer und Romanen,* 186, n. 2.

[3] The words *patrui mei* in *C. Th.* xi. 20. 5 need not point to the definite transference of the administration of Dalmatia in A.D. 424, for in that year Theodosius was sole Emperor. But the change was not regarded as definitely settled till the marriage of Valentinian and Eudoxia in 437. See below, p. 226.

to this change. It is probable that at the same time it was arranged that the future Emperor of the west should marry the infant daughter of the Emperor of the east. In any case Theodosius could contemplate a closer union between his own court and that of Ravenna, a union in which he would have the preponderating influence for about a dozen years to come during the minority of his cousin and the regency of his aunt ; while he would have no direct responsibility for any further misfortunes which the western provinces might sustain from the rapacity of the German guests whom they harboured.

John, who had assumed the purple at Rome, was an obscure civil servant who had risen to the rank of *primicerius notariorum*.[1] It is evident that he owed his elevation to the party which was adverse to Placidia, and certain that he had behind him the Master of Soldiers Castinus, who had failed to win laurels in Spain,[2] and was probably partly responsible for her exile. His envoys soon arrived at Constantinople to demand his recognition from the legitimate Emperor, and the answer of Theodosius was to banish them to places on the Propontis.[3] Placidia was now recognised as Augusta, her son as nobilissimus [4]—titles which Constantinople had refused to acknowledge when they had been conferred by Honorius ; and the dead Constantius was posthumously accepted as a legitimate Augustus.[5] A large army was prepared against the usurper and placed under the command of Ardaburius, an officer of Alan descent, and his son Aspar. Placidia and her children accompanied the army, and at Thessalonica Valentinian was raised to the rank of Caesar (A.D. 424).[6] When they reached Salona, the infantry under Ardaburius embarked and sailed across to the coast of Italy, and Aspar with the cavalry proceeded by land to Sirmium and thence over the Julian Alps to the great city of the Venetian march, Aquileia, of which they made themselves masters.[7] Here Placidia remained to await the issue of the struggle.

---

[1] Renatus Frigeridus, in Gregory of Tours, *H.F.* ii. 8. Was he the same John who was sent to negotiate with Alaric in 408 ? (above, p. 176).

[2] See above, p. 209.

[3] Philostorgius, xii. 11.

[4] Olympiodorus, *fr.* 46 ; Marcellinus, *sub* 424.

[5] This is shown by the fact that some laws issued in his name with Honorius and Theodosius were published in *C. Th.* (*e.g.* iii. 16. 2) ; cp. Mommsen, *C. Th.* p. ccxcvii.

[6] Probably towards the end of the year. Valentinian was designated consul (Flavius Placidus Valentinianus Caesar) as colleague of Theodosius for 425. John assumed the consulship in the west. See *Fast. Cons.*, *sub a.*

[7] Philostorgius, *ib.*, Olympiodorus, *ib.*, and Socrates, vii. 23 are the chief sources.

Of the situation in Italy and the attitude of the Italians to the Emperor who had established himself at Ravenna we know nothing, except the fact that he was not acknowledged at Rome,[1] although it was at Rome that he had assumed the purple. Castinus, whom one might have expected to play the leader's part, remained in the background; we are only told that he was thought to have connived at John's elevation.[2] But two younger men, whose names were to become more famous than that of the Master of Soldiers, were concerned in the conflict of parties. Boniface, an able soldier, who was perhaps already Count of Africa in A.D. 422, had been ordered to co-operate with Castinus in the ill-fated expedition against the Vandals in Spain, but he had quarrelled with the commander and returned to Africa.[3] We next find him espousing the cause of Placidia when she was banished by Honorius and helping her with money. He is not recorded to have taken any direct part in the conflict with John, but he could maintain the loyalty of Africa to the Theodosian house and could exercise influence by his control of the corn supplies. The other rising soldier who played a part in these events was Aetius, of whom we shall hear much more. He accepted the new Emperor and was appointed to the post of Steward of the Palace (*cura palatii*). When the news arrived that an eastern army was on its way to Italy, he was sent to Pannonia to obtain help for his master from the Huns. For this mission he was well qualified, as he had formerly lived among them as a hostage and was on friendly terms with their king.

Ardaburius had embarked at Salona, but his fleet was unfortunate, it was caught in a storm and scattered. The general himself, driven ashore near Ravenna, was captured by the soldiers of John. If the usurper had proceeded immediately against Aspar, he might have thwarted his enemies. But he

---

[1] This may be inferred from the issue of gold coins of Theodosius II. at Rome, which may probably be assigned (so de Salis) to 424–425. The Roman mint did not issue coins of John (for whose Ravenna coins see Cohen, viii. 207). The loyalty of Rome is also shown by an inscription of Faustus, Prefect of the City in 425, acknowledging the Caesarship of Valentinian (*C.I.L.* vi. 1677).

[2] Prosper, *sub* 423. He was consul in 424, and was not acknowledged in the east.

[3] Cp. Prosper, *sub* 422, and Hydatius. It is not quite clear whether Boniface seized the government of Africa without Imperial warrant, or, as seems more likely, he had received the appointment before his disobedience in refusing to go to Spain. The presence of an able military commander in Africa was urgently demanded by the hostilities of the Moors. See the discussion in Freeman, *Western Europe*, 305 *sqq.*

did not take prompt advantage of his luck.   He decided to wait for the arrival of the Hun auxiliaries whom Aetius had gone to summon to his aid.

Meanwhile Ardaburius employed the time of his captivity at Ravenna in forming connexions with the officers and ministers of the usurper and undermining their fidelity.   He then succeeded in sending a message to his son, who waited uneasily and expectantly at Aquileia, bidding him advance against Ravenna without delay.   Guided by a shepherd through the morasses which encompassed that city, the soldiers of Aspar entered it without opposition ;   some thought that the shepherd was an angel of God in disguise.   John was captured and conducted to Aquileia, where Placidia doomed him to death.   His right hand was cut off, and mounted on an ass he was exposed in the circus before his execution.   Castinus, the Master of Soldiers, was banished.[1]

When all was over, Aetius arrived in Italy with 60,000 Huns ; if he had come a few days sooner, the conflict would probably have had a different issue and the course of history would have been changed.   At the head of this large army, Aetius was able to make terms for himself with the triumphant Empress.   She was forced to pardon him and accept his services.   The Huns were induced by a large donation of money to return to their homes.

Placidia then proceeded with her children to Rome, where Valentinian III. was created Augustus on October 23, A.D. 425.[2] Theodosius had himself started for Italy to crown his cousin with his own hand, but fell ill at Thessalonica, and empowered the Patrician Helion, the Master of Offices, to take his place. It seems certain that Valentinian's sister Honoria was crowned Augusta, if not on the same occasion, soon afterwards.[3]

---

[1] The victory of Placidia must be placed in May or June.   For on July 9 she issued a law at Aquileia restoring some ecclesiastical privileges which had been abolished by John.   *Sirmondianae*, 6 ; also *C. Th.* xvi. 2. 46 and 47 ; xvi. 5. 62 and 63.   Cp. Seeck, *Regesten*, p. 5, on these laws.   Placidia and her son did not leave Aquileia before Aug. 6 (*C. Th.* xvi. 2. 47 and v. 64).   Philostorgius (xii. 13) says that John reigned for a year and a half, a rough figure but, if he was elevated in Sept. 423, pointing to May as the date of his fall.

[2] Socrates, vii. 24, *Chron. Pasch.*, *sub a.*   On the date compare Tillemont, *Hist. des Emp.* vi. 621, Clinton, *F.R.*, *sub a.*   Gold coins of Valentinian were issued in Constantinople, conjecturally in 426 : on the reverse two Emperors, both nimbate, one large, the other small, with the legend *Salus Reipublicae*.

[3] See below, p. 288.   Helion had acted for the Emperor in conferring

Ardaburius was rewarded for his successful conduct of the war by the honour of the consulship in A.D. 427. He and his son Aspar were the ablest generals Theodosius had, and their devotion to the Arian creed did not stand in the way of their promotion. Aspar received the consulship in A.D. 434, when he was again commanding an army in the interests of Placidia, this time against a foreign foe, not against a rebel ; [1] and we have an interesting memorial of the event in a silver disc, on which he is represented, a bearded man, with a sceptre in his left hand and a handkerchief in his raised right, presiding at the consular games.[2] It was a more than ordinary honour that was paid to Aspar, for he was consul for the West, not for the East,[3] and the designation may have been suggested by Placidia herself, who owed him much for his services in securing the diadem for her son.

§ 4. *The Empress Eudocia*

Twelve years passed, and the marriage arranged between the cousins, Valentinian and Licinia Eudoxia, was, as we saw, celebrated at Constantinople, whither the bridegroom went for the occasion (October 29, A.D. 437).[4] Now, if not before, a considerable part of the Diocese of Illyricum—Dalmatia and Eastern Pannonia certainly—were transferred from the sway of Valentinian to the sway of Theodosius.[5] This political trans-

the Caesarship at Thessalonica and had doubtless accompanied Placidia to Italy. A mutilated metrical inscription at Sitifis in Mauretania would refer to the elevation of Valentinian if de Rossi's restoration were near the truth (*C.I.L.* viii. 8481). It runs :

> Terra [*about* 16 *letters*] ni sidera regni
> ia]m de . . . ans armorum fulmina
> [co]ndit
> gra[. . . t]utela Valentinianu[s
> . . . . . . et Theodosius artem.

De Rossi proposed *fulgida conscendens*] *terra*[*e*]*ni s. r.* in 1, [*Placidiae*] *gra*[*ndis t*]*utela* in 3, and [*pace fruens doctam exerc*]*et* in 4 (very improbable). Cp. Bücheler's note in *Anth. Lat.* ii. 288.

[1] In Africa. See below, p. 248.

[2] It was found near Florence and is preserved there. The inscription round the disc is: *Fl. Ardabur Aspar vir inlustris com. et mag. militum*

et consul ordinarius. For a full description see W. Meyer, *Zwei ant. Elf.* pp. 6-7.

[3] The eastern consul of the year was Areobindus.

[4] *Chr. Pasch.*, and Prosper, *sub a.* Coins were issued in honour of the occasion : on the face a full-faced bust of Theodosius, on the reverse three figures, Theodosius in the centre joining the hands of his daughter and Valentinian, with legend *Feliciter Nubtiis.*

[5] Cassiodorus, *Var.* xi. 1. 9 (*Placidia*) *remisse administrat imperium . . . nurum denique sibi amissione Illyrici comparavit factaque est coniunctio regnantis divisio dolenda provinciis* ; Jordanes, *Rom.* 329 *datamque pro munere soceri sui totam Illyricum* (sic). The *totam* of Jordanes does not authorise us to suppose with Tillemont (*Hist. des Emp.* vi. 75) that the

action was part of the matrimonial arrangement, and was looked
upon as the price which Placidia paid for her daughter-in-law.
The new provinces were now controlled by the Praetorian Prefect
of Illyricum, and his seat was transferred for some years from
Thessalonica to Sirmium.[1]

After the departure of her daughter the Empress probably
felt lonely, and she undertook, in accordance with her husband's
wishes, a pilgrimage to Jerusalem to return thanks to the Deity
for the marriage of their daughter.[2] In this decision they
seem to have been confirmed by a saintly lady of high reputation, Melania by name, a Roman of noble family, who had been
forced into a repugnant marriage, and had afterwards, along
with her husband, whom she converted to Christianity, taken
up her abode at first in the land of Egypt, where she founded
monastic houses, and then at Jerusalem. She had visited
Constantinople to see her uncle Volusian, whom she converted
before his death, and she exercised considerable influence with the
Emperor and his household. The journey of Eudocia to Jerusalem (in spring, A.D. 438) was marked by her visit to Antioch,
where she created a sensation by the elegant oration which
she delivered, posing rather as one trained in Greek rhetoric
and devoted to Hellenic traditions and proud of her Athenian
descent, than as a pilgrim on her way to the great Christian
shrine. Although there was a large element of theological
bigotry both in Antioch and in Alexandria, yet in both these
cities there was probably more appreciation of Hellenic style
and polish than in Constantinople. The last words of Eudocia's
oration brought down the house—a quotation from Homer,

$$\text{ὑμετέρης γενέης τε καὶ αἵματος εὔχομαι εἶναι.}$$

---

cession included the provinces of
Noricum or even all Pannonia.
Dalmatia, Pannonia Secunda, and
Valeria were probably ceded, and no
more. Cp. Zeiller, *Les Origines chrét.
dans les prov. Dan.* pp. 6, 7.

[1] We learn this from a law of
Justinian (*Nov.* xi.): *cum enim in
antiquis temporibus Sirmii praefectura
fuerat constituta ibique omne fuerat
Illyrici fastigium tam in civilibus
quam in episcopalibus causis, postea
autem Attilanis temporibus eiusdem
locis devastatis Apraeemius praefectus
praetorio de Sirmitana civitate in*

Thessalonicam profugus venerat [c. A.D.
447, see below, p. 275]. This prefect
is otherwise unknown.

[2] See Socrates, vii. 47. The
following inscription, recorded as
existing in the church of St. Peter
ad vincula at Rome, seems also to
refer to the fulfilment of a vow for
Eudoxia's marriage:

Theodosius pater Eudocia cum coniuge
votum,
Cumque suo supplex Eudoxia nomine
solvit

(where *cum suo nomine* = *suo nomine*).
De Rossi, ii. 1, p. 110.

" I boast that I am of your race and blood." [1]   The city that
hated and mocked the Emperor Julian and his pagan Hellenism
loved and fêted the Empress Eudocia with her Christian Hellenism ; a golden statue was erected to her in the curia and one
of bronze in the museum. Her interest in Antioch took a
practical form, for she induced Theodosius to build a new
basilica, restore the thermae, extend the walls, and bestow other
marks of favour on the city.

Eudocia's visit to Aelia Capitolina, as Jerusalem was called,
brings to the recollection the visit of Constantine's mother
Helena, one hundred years before, and, although Christianity
had lost some of its freshness in the intervening period, it must
have been a strange and impressive experience for one whose
youth was spent amid pagan memories in the gardens of the
philosophers at Athens, and who in New Rome, with its museums
of ancient art and its men of many creeds, had not been entirely
weaned from the ways and affections of her youth, to visit,
with all the solemnity of an exalted Christian pilgrim, a city
whose memories were typically opposed to Hellenism, and whose
monuments were the bones and relics of saints. [2]   It was probably
only this religious side that came under Eudocia's notice ; for
Jerusalem at this period was a strange mixture of piety with
gross licence. We are told by an ecclesiastical writer of the
age that it was more depraved than Gomorrah ; and the fact
that it was a garrison town had something to do with this
depravity. But it drew pilgrims from all quarters of the world.

On her return from Palestine (A.D. 439) Eudocia's influence
at Court was still powerful. [3]   She seems to have been on terms
of intimate friendship with Cyrus of Panopolis, who held a very
exceptional position. He filled at the same time the two high

---

[1] Evagrius, *H.E.* i. 20. The verse
is an adaptation of *Iliad*, vi. 211. It
has been suggested that Eudocia's
oration consisted of a poem in
hexameters (Ludwich, *Eudociae frag-
menta*, p. 12).

[2] Of the relics which she received
(the bishop of Jerusalem plied a trade
in relics), especially remarkable were
the chains with which Herod bound
Peter. One of these she gave to her
daughter Eudoxia, who founded a
church in Rome (called originally
after herself, and in later times St.
Peter ad vincula), where it is still

preserved. Cp. above, p. 226, *n.* 2.
An account of Eudocia's visit to
Jerusalem will be found in the *Vita
Melaniae iunioris*. Melania met the
Empress at Sidon and acted as her
companion and cicerone.

[3] In this year, the 42nd of his
reign, Theodosius was consul for the
17th time, and the mint of Constantinople issued gold coins (1) of
the Emperor with a helmeted Rome
on the reverse and the legend IMP
xxxxii. cos xvii. PP, (2) of the Empress,
with Constantinople seated on the
prow of a vessel and the same legend.

offices of Praetorian Prefect of the East and Prefect of the city.[1]
He was a poet like his fellow-townsman Nonnus though of minor
rank ; [2] he was a student of art and architecture ; and he was
a " Hellene " in faith. It has been remarked that Imperial
officialdom was beginning to assume in the East a more distinctly
Greek complexion in the reign of Theodosius II., and Cyrus was
a representative figure in this transition. He used to issue
decrees in Greek, an innovation for which a writer of the following
century expressly blames him.[3]   His prefecture was popular
and long remembered at Constantinople, for he built and restored
many buildings and improved the illumination of the town, so
that the people enthusiastically cried on some occasions in the
Hippodrome, " Constantine built the city but Cyrus renewed it." [4]
He still held his offices in the autumn of A.D. 441,[5] but it cannot
have been long after this that he fell into disgrace. Perhaps
his popularity made him an object of suspicion ; his paganism
furnished a convenient ground for accusation. He was compelled
to take ecclesiastical orders and was made bishop of Cotyaeum in
Phrygia. His first sermon, which his malicious congregation
forced him to preach against his will, astonished and was
applauded by those who heard it :

" Brethren, let the birth of God, our Saviour, Jesus Christ be
honoured by silence, because the Word of God was conceived
in the holy Virgin through hearing only. To him be glory for
ever and ever. Amen." [6]

The friendship between Cyrus and the Empress Eudocia,

[1] That Cyrus held these offices
simultaneously is expressly stated by
John Lydus, *De mag.* ii. 12, and by
John Malalas, xiv. 361.   Malalas
says that he held them for four years.
It is probable that the source of this
record was Priscus, see *Chron. Pasch.*,
sub 439. We know from Theodosius,
Nov. 18, that he was Pr. Pr. Or. in
Nov. 439 ; and from *C.J.* viii. 11. 21,
that he was Pr. Urb. in Jan. 440.

[2] John Lydus, *ib.*, says contemptu-
ously that he knew nothing except
poetry. Some epigrams and short
poems are extant. The most interesting of these is *Anth. Pal.* ix. 136,
written before leaving the city in
exile :

Would that my father had taught me to
   tend his flock in the pastures,

Where sitting under the shade of elm-
   trees or rocks overhanging
Sweetly piping on reeds I would charm
   dull care with my music.
O Pierian maids, let us flee from the fair-
   built city
Forth to another land.   And there will
   I tell of the mischief
Wrought by the baleful drones to the
   bees who toil for the honey.

The first verse is imitated by Nonnus,
Dionys. xx. 372.

[3] John Lydus, *ib.*

[4] For the building of the sea walls
see above, Chap. III.

[5] *C.J.* i. 55. 10.

[6] The anecdote is told by John
Malalas, *ib.*   The right reading ὁ
τοῦ θεοῦ λόγος (for λόγῳ) is preserved in the corresponding passage
of Theophanes, A.M. 5937. For the
opening words cp. below, Chap. XI.
p. 349, *n.* 3.

who was naturally sympathetic with a highly educated pagan, suggests the conjecture that his disgrace was not unconnected with the circumstances which led soon afterwards to her own fall. We may conjecture that harmony had not always existed between herself and her sister-in-law, and differences seem to have arisen soon after her return from Palestine.[1] Discord was fomented by the arts of a eunuch, Chrysaphius Zstommas, who was at this time beginning to establish his ascendancy over the Emperor.[2] Pulcheria had enjoyed the privilege of having in her household the Chamberlain (*praepositus Augustae*) who was officially attached to the service of the reigning Empress. It would not have been unnatural if this arrangement had caused jealousy in the heart of Eudocia, and we are told that Chrysaphius urged her to demand from the Emperor that a High Chamberlain should also be assigned to her. When Theodosius decidedly refused, she urged, again at the suggestion of Chrysaphius, that Pulcheria should be ordained a deaconess, inasmuch as she had taken a vow of virginity. Pulcheria refused to be drawn into a contest for power. She sent her Chamberlain to Eudocia and retired to the Palace of Hebdomon.[3] When Chrysaphius had succeeded in removing one Empress from the scene, his next object was to remove the other, so that his own influence over the weak spirit of Theodosius might be exclusive and undivided. In accomplishing this end he was probably assisted by the orthodox party at court, who were devoted to Pulcheria and looked with suspicion on the Hellenic proclivities of her sister-in-law. The Emperor's mind was poisoned against his wife by the suggestion that she had been unduly intimate with Paulinus,[4] a

---

[1] They differed on the Eutychian controversy, but there were doubtless other causes of jealousy.

[2] These intrigues are related by Theophanes, A.M. 5940 = A.D. 447–448. But the chronology of Theophanes during these years is full of errors. We know from Marcellinus and other sources that Eudocia had retired to Jerusalem in 444. John Malalas tells the story of Eudocia's life consecutively without chronological indications.

[3] This story appears in a curious form in John of Nikiu (*Chron.* lxxxvii. 29-33), who thoroughly disliked Pulcheria.

[4] We have no means of knowing whether there was any truth in this charge, but it should be observed that in Marcellinus, *Chron.*, *sub* 421, the true reading is *Eudociam Achivam*, not *moecham* (found in one MS.), so that this writer does not, as Gülden-penning thinks (*op. cit.* p. 325), stigmatize her as unfaithful. Contemporary evidence for the charge of adultery has recently come to light in the *Book of Heraclides* of Nestorius (tr. Nau, p. 331). The ex-Patriarch writes, " the demon-prince of adultery, who had thrown the Empress into shame and disgrace, has just died." Cp. E. W. Brooks, *B.Z.*, 21, 94-95.

handsome man who had been a comrade of the Emperor in his boyhood.

This is probably the kernel of truth in the legend of Eudocia's apple which is thus told by a chronicler.[1]

It so happened that as the Emperor Theodosius was proceeding to the church on the feast of Epiphany, the Master of Offices, Paulinus, being indisposed on account of an ailment in his foot, remained at home and made an excuse. But a certain poor man brought to Theodosius a Phrygian apple,[2] of enormously large size, and the Emperor was surprised at it, and all his Court (senate). And straightway the Emperor gave 150 nomismata to the man who brought the apple, and sent it to Eudocia Augusta ; and the Augusta sent it to Paulinus, the Master of Offices, as being a friend of the Emperor.[3] But Paulinus, not being aware that the Emperor had sent it to the Empress, took it and sent it to the Emperor Theodosius, even as he entered the Palace. And when the Emperor received it he recognised it and concealed it. And having called the Augusta, he questioned her, saying, ' Where is the apple that I sent you ? ' And she said, ' I ate it.' Then he caused her to swear the truth by his salvation, whether she ate it or sent it to some one ; and she sware, ' I sent it unto no man but ate it.' And the Emperor commanded the apple to be brought and showed it to her. And he was indignant against her, suspecting that she was enamoured of Paulinus and sent him the apple and denied it. And on this account Theodosius put Paulinus to death. And the Empress Eudocia was grieved, and thought herself insulted, for it was known everywhere that Paulinus was slain on account of her, for he was a very handsome young man. And she asked the Emperor that she might go to the holy places to pray ; and he allowed her. And she went down from Constantinople to Jerusalem to pray.

Whatever may have been the circumstances it seems that Paulinus, Master of Offices, was sent to Cappadocia and put to death by the Emperor's command in A.D. 444.[4] It is credible that her former intimacy with Paulinus was used to alienate Theodosius from his wife, and she found her position so intolerable that at last she sought and obtained the Emperor's permission to withdraw from the Court and betake herself to Jerusalem (A.D. 443).[5] She was not deprived of Imperial honours and an

[1] John Malalas, xiv. p. 356.

[2] It may be observed that in Greek romances the apple was a conventional love-gift, and meant on the part of a woman who bestowed it on a man a declaration of love.

[3] He was brought up along with Theodosius and at his marriage acted as παράνυμφος, or " groomsman."

[4] This is the year to which the context in the passage of Nestorius

points, and is confirmed by *Chron. Pasch.* Marcellinus places the death of Paulinus in 440.

[5] Cedrenus and Zonaras place Eudocia's visit to Jerusalem in the 42nd year of Theodosius, " also 450 was ganz irrig ist," says Gregorovius (*Athenais*, p. 187). But the 42nd year is reckoned from 402 (not from 408) and = Jan. 10, 443 to Jan. 10, 444. This was the official reckoning of

ample revenue was placed at her disposal. In Jerusalem she kept such state and was so energetic in public works that the jealousy of Theodosius was aroused and he sent Saturninus, the commander of his guards, to inquire into her activities. Saturninus slew the priest Severus and the deacon John who were confidants of the Empress.[1] She avenged this act by permitting the death of Saturninus; the words of one of our authorities might lead us to suppose that she caused him to be assassinated,[2] but it has been suggested that officious servants or an indignant mob may have too hastily anticipated her supposed wishes. Then by the Emperor's command she was compelled to reduce her retinue.

The last sixteen years[3] of the life of this amiable lady were spent at Jerusalem where she devoted herself to charitable work, built churches, monasteries and hospices, and restored the walls of the city.[4] She was drawn into the theological storm which swept over the East in the last years of Theodosius, an episode which will claim our notice in another place. It is said that before her death she repeated her denial of the slander that she had been unfaithful to her husband.[5]

§ 5. *The University of Constantinople and the Theodosian Code*

The three most important acts of the reign of Theodosius II. were the fortification of the city by land and sea, which has already been described, the foundation of a university, and the compilation of the legal code called after his name. It would be interesting to know whether the establishment of a school for higher education in the capital was due to the influence of the young Empress, who had been brought up in the schools of

---

his regnal years as appears from the coins which were issued in this very year: reverse: a seated Victory holding a cruciger globe, star underneath, and buckler on the ground behind, with legend Imp. xxxxii cos xvii PP. This shows that the 42nd year fell between the 17th consulship 439 and the 18th, 444, and therefore fell in 443. At the same time were minted coins of Eudocia, Pulcheria, Valentinian and Eudoxia with the same reverse. See De Salis, *Coins of the Eudoxias,* and Sabatier, *Monn. byz.*

Pl. v. 1, vi. 1 and 11.

[1] Marcellinus, *Chron.,* *sub* 444.

[2] Besides Marcellinus, Priscus, speaking of the heiress of Saturninus, says: τὸν δὲ Σατορνῖλον ἀνῃρήκει ᾿Αθηναΐς (*fr.* 3, De leg. Rom. p. 146). See the discussion of Gregorovius, *op cit.* cap. xxiii.

[3] She died Oct. 20, 460. Cyrillus, *Vita Euthymii,* p. 74.

[4] Evagrius, i. 22; John of Nikiu, lxxxvii. 22, 23.

[5] *Chron. Pasch.,* *sub* 444.

Athens. The new university (founded February 27, A.D. 425) was intended to compete with the schools of Alexandria and the university of Athens, the headquarters of paganism—with which, however, the government preferred not to interfere directly —and thereby to promote the cause of Christianity. Lecture-rooms were provided in the Capitol. The Latin language was represented by ten grammarians or philologists and three rhetors, the Greek likewise by ten grammarians, but by five rhetors ; one chair of philosophy was endowed and two chairs of juris-prudence. Thus the Greek language had two more chairs than the Latin, and this fact may be cited as marking a stage in the official Graecisation of the eastern half of the Roman Empire.[1]

In the year 429 Theodosius determined to form a collection of all the constitutions issued by the " renowned Constantine, the divine Emperors who succeeded him, and ourselves." The new code was to be drawn up on the model of the Gregorian and Hermogenian codes,[2] and the execution of the work was entrusted to a commission of nine persons, among whom was Apelles, professor of law at the new university. Nine years later the work was completed and published, but during the intervening years the members of the commission had changed ; of the eight who are mentioned in the edict which accompanied the final publication only two, Antiochus and Theodorus, were among the original workers, and a constitution of A.D. 435, which conferred full powers on the committee for the completion of the work, mentions sixteen compilers.[3]

The code was issued conjointly by Theodosius and Valentinian, and thus expressed the unity of the Empire (February 15, A.D. 438). The visit of the younger Emperor to Constantinople on the occasion of his marriage with his cousin Eudoxia facilitated this co-operation. On December 23 of the same year, at a meeting of the Senate of Old Rome, the code which had been drawn up by the lawyers of New Rome was publicly recognised, and an official account of the proceedings on that occasion— *gesta in senatu Urbis Romae de recipiendo Codice Theodosiano—*

---

[1] *C. Th.* xiv. 9. 3, and vi. 21. 1. For the lecture-rooms in a portico in the Capitol see *C. Th.* xv. 1. 53.

[2] The Gregorian Code (c. A.D. 300) contained constitutions from Hadrian to A.D. 294 ; the Hermogenian those from 296 to 324.

[3] See *C. Th.* i. 1. 5, March 26, 429, i. 1. 6, Dec. 20, 435.

may still be read.   The Praetorian Prefect and consul of the
year, Anicius Acilius Glabrio Faustus, spoke as follows :

The felicity of the eternal Emperors proceeds so far as to adorn with
the ornaments of peace those whom it defends by warfare.   Last year
when we loyally attended the celebration of the most fortunate of all ceremonies, and when the marriage had been happily concluded, the most
sacred Prince, our Lord Theodosius, was fain to add this dignity also to
his world, and ordered the precepts of the laws to be collected and drawn
up in a compendious form of sixteen books, which he wished to be consecrated by his most sacred name.   Which thing the eternal Prince, our
Lord Valentinian, approved with the loyalty of a colleague and the affection of a son.

And all the senators cried out in the usual form, " Well
spoken ! " (*nove diserte, vere diserte*).   But instead of following
the course of the *gesta* in the Roman senate-house, it will be
more instructive to read the Imperial constitution which introduced the great code to the Roman world.

The Emperors Theodosius and Valentinian, Augusti, to Florentius,
Praetorian Prefect of the East.
Our clemency has often been at a loss to understand the cause of the
fact, that, when so many rewards are held out for the maintenance of arts
and (liberal) studies, so few are found who are endowed with a full knowledge of the Civil Law, and even they so seldom ; we are astonished that
amid so many whose faces have grown pale from late lucubrations hardly
one or two have attained to sound and complete learning.
When we consider the enormous multitude of books, the diverse
modes of process and the difficulty of legal cases, and further the huge
mass of imperial constitutions, which hidden as it were under a rampart
of gross mist and darkness precludes men's intellects from gaining a knowledge of them, we feel that we have met a real need of our age, and dis-
pelling the darkness have given light to the laws by a short compendium.
We selected noble men of approved faith, lawyers of well-known learning ;
and clearing away interpretations, we have published the constitutions
of our predecessors, so that men may no longer have to await formidable
Responses from expert lawyers as from an inner shrine, when it is really
quite plain what action is to be adopted in suing for an inheritance, or
what is to be the weight of a donation.   These details, unveiled by the
assiduity of the learned, have been brought into open day under the
radiant splendour of our name.
Nor let those to whom we have consigned the divine secrets of our
heart imagine that they have obtained a poor reward.   For if our mind's
eye rightly foresees the future, their names will descend to posterity linked
with ours.
Thus having swept away the cloud of volumes, on which many wasted
their lives and explained nothing in the end, we establish a compendious
knowledge of the Imperial constitutions since the time of the divine

Constantine, and allow no one after the first day of next January to use
any authority in the practice of law except these books which bear our
name and are kept in the sacred bureaux.   None of the older Emperors,
however, has been deprived of his immortality, the name of no author of a
constitution has fallen to the ground ; nay rather they enjoy a borrowed
light in that their august decrees are associated with us.   The glory of
the originators, duly refined (filed), remains and will remain for ever ;
nor has any brilliance passed thereby to our name except the light of
brevity (*nisi lux sola brevitatis*).

And though the undertaking of the whole work was due to our auspicious
initiation, we nevertheless deemed it more worthy of the imperial majesty
(*magis imperatorium*) and more illustrious, to put envy to flight and allow
the memory of the authors to survive perennially.   It is enough and more
than enough to satisfy our consciences, that we have unveiled the laws
and redeemed the works of our ancestors from the injustice of obscurity.

We further enact that henceforward no constitution can be passed in
the West (*in partibus occidentis*) or in any other place, by the unconquer-
able Emperor, the son of our clemency, the everlasting Augustus, Valentinian, or possess any validity, except the same by a divine pragmatica be
communicated to us.

The same precaution is to be observed in the acts which are promulgated by us in the East (*per Orientem*) ; and those are to be condemned as
spurious which are not recorded in the Theodosian Code, excepting special
documents in the official bureaux.

It would be a long tale to relate all that has been contributed to the
completion of this work by the labours of Antiochus, the all-sublime ex-
prefect and consul ; by the illustrious Maximin, ex-quaestor of our palace,
eminent in all departments of literature ; by the illustrious Martyrius,
count and quaestor, the faithful interpreter of our clemency ; by Sperantius,
Apollodorus, and Theodore, all respectable men and counts of our sacred
consistory ; by the respectable Epigenes, count and magister memoriae ;
by the respectable Procopius, count, and magister libellorum.   These
men may be compared to any of the ancients.

It remains, O Florentius, most dear and affectionate relative, for your
illustrious and magnificent authority, whose delight and constant practice
is to please Emperors, to cause the decrees of our August Majesty to come
to the knowledge of all peoples and all provinces.

Dated 15 February at Constantinople (438).[1]

The Code of Theodosius was superseded at the end of a hundred years by the Code of Justinian, and to the jurist it is less
indispensable than to the historian.   The historian must always
remember with gratitude the name of Theodosius and that of
Antiochus, if we may credit this minister with having originated
the idea of the work.   For the full record of legislation which it
preserves furnishes clear and authentic information on the social

---

[1] Theodosius II. *Nov.* 1.

conditions of the Empire, without which our other historical
sources would present many insoluble problems.[1]

The last ten years of the reign were unfortunate. The Illyrian
provinces suffered terribly from the depredations of the Huns,
and the payments which a weak government made to buy off
the invaders depleted the treasury.[2] The eunuch Chrysaphius,
having succeeded in removing from the Palace the rival influences of the Emperor's wife and sister, completely swayed the
mind of his sovran and seems to have controlled the policy of the
government. It is stated, and we can easily believe it, that
Theodosius at this time was in the habit of signing state papers
without reading them.[3]

The power of Chrysaphius remained unshaken [4] until a few
months before the Emperor's death, when he fell out of favour
and the influence of Pulcheria again re-asserted itself.[5] Theodosius died on July 28, A.D. 450, of a spinal injury caused by a
fall from his horse.[6]

§ 6. *The Reign of Marcian* (A.D. 450–457)

As Theodosius had no male issue and had not co-opted a
colleague, the government of the eastern half of the Empire
ought automatically to have devolved upon his cousin and
western colleague Valentinian III. But this devolution would
not have pleased Theodosius himself, and would not have been
tolerated by his subjects. And we are told that on his death-

---

[1] The object of the compilers of the
Code was to include all the laws,
whether edicts or rescripts, which they
could find, not to make a selection of
those which were still valid. One
might have thought that a record of
all imperial laws would have been carefully preserved in the eastern and
western chanceries, but it was not so.
Seeck's valuable investigation of the
sources of the Code (*Regesten der
Kaiser und Päpste*) shows that in
many cases there were no copies at
Constantinople, and the texts had
to be sought at provincial centres,
e.g. at Berytus. Of much legislation
there was probably no trace to be
found anywhere. But laws issued in
the west were more abundantly pre-

served than those in the east. It is
remarkable that though the Code
includes laws of Theodosius up to
437, it does not include laws of
Valentinian after 432.

[2] The gold paid to the Huns during
the eight years A.D. 443–450 exceeded
in value £1,000,000.

[3] Theophanes, A.M. 5942.

[4] He had an enemy in the Isaurian
Zeno, Master of Soldiers, who seems
to have threatened a revolt in A.D.
449. See John Ant. *fr.* 84 (*De ins.*),
and Priscus, *fr.* 5 (*De leg. Rom.*).

[5] Theophanes, *ib.*

[6] The accident happened near the
River Lycus not far from the city. See
John Mal. xiv. 366.

bed Theodosius indicated a successor. Among the senators who
were present on that occasion were Aspar, Master of Soldiers,
and Marcian, a distinguished officer who had served as Aspar's
aide-de-camp in more than one campaign. The Emperor said
to Marcian, " It has been revealed to me that you will reign
after me." [1] We may conjecture that this choice had been
arranged beforehand by Pulcheria and her brother. For Pulcheria agreed to become the nominal wife of Marcian, and thus
the Theodosian dynasty was formally preserved.[2]

Marcian was crowned in the Hebdomon by the Empress
(August 25),[3] and it is possible that on this occasion the Patriarch
Anatolius took part in the coronation ceremony.[4] The first act
of the new reign was the execution of Chrysaphius,[5] and it is
worthy of notice that Chrysaphius had favoured the Green
faction of the Circus, and that Marcian patronised the Blues.
His reign was a period of calm, all the more striking when it is
contrasted with the storms which accompanied the dismemberment of the Empire in the west. In later times it was looked
back to as a golden age.[6] The domestic policy of Marcian was
marked by financial economy, which was the more necessary,
as during the last years of his predecessor the treasury was
emptied by the large sums which were paid to the Huns.

Marcian refused to pay this tribute any longer, and at his
death he left a well-filled treasury.[7] He accomplished this, not
by imposing new burdens on the people, but by wisely regulating

---

[1] Marcellinus and *Chron. Pasch.*,
sub a.

[2] At the beginning of his reign
Marcian issued gold coins both of
himself and of Pulcheria with a side-
faced Victory holding a cross on the
reverse and the legend *Victoria Auggg*.
See Sabatier, *Monn. byz.* Pl. vi. 6
and 13. An inscription found in
Eastern Thrace (*C.I.L.*, iii. 14207)
describes Marcian as *serius in regnum
missus* (he was nearly 60 years old)
and applying prompt remedies (*celeri
medicina*) to restore a falling world.

[3] *Chron. Pasch.*, *sub a.*

[4] Theophanes, A.M. 5942, *ad fin.*
μεταστέλλεται (sc. Pulcheria) τὸν
πατριάρχην καὶ τὴν σύγκλητον καὶ
ἀναγορεύει αὐτὸν βασιλέα 'Ρωμαίων.
We are ignorant what was the

authority of Theophanes for intro-
ducing the Patriarch. See below, p.
317. According to John Malalas, xiv.
367, Marcian was crowned " by the
Senate "; according to John of Nikiu,
ed. Zotenberg, p. 472, and Zonaras,
xiii. 24, by Pulcheria; according to
Simeon, the Logothete, vers. Slav. ed.
Sreznevski, p. 50 (= Theodosius Mel.
p. 78 = Leo Gramm. p. 111) by Anatolius. This last tradition is accepted
by W. Sickel, *BZ.* vii. 517, 539.

[5] John Mal. xiv. 368. Marcellinus,
ib. Pulcheriae nutu interemptus est.

[6] Theoph. A.M. 5946. καὶ ἦν
ἐκεῖνα τὰ ἔτη κυρίως χρυσᾶ τῇ τοῦ
βασιλέως χρηστότητι. Cp. John Lydus,
De mag. iii. 42 (p. 132) Μαρκιανὸν τὸν
μέτριον.

[7] More than £4,500,000. John
Lydus, *ib.*

his expenditure. He alleviated the pressure of taxes so far as
Roman fiscal principles would permit. He assisted his subjects
from the exchequer when any unwonted calamity befell them.
One of his first acts was a remission of arrears of taxation.[1]
He confined the burdensome office of the praetorship to senators
resident in the capital.[2] He decreed that the consuls instead
of distributing money to the populace should contribute to
keeping the city aqueduct in repair.[3] He attempted to put an
end to the system of selling administrative offices.[4] Perhaps
the act which gave most satisfaction to the higher classes was
the abolition of the *follis*, the tax of seven pounds on the property
of senators.[5]

One of his enactments may perhaps be regarded as characteristic. Constantine the Great, in order to preserve the purity
of the senatorial class, had declared illegal the marriage of a
senator with a slave, a freed woman, an actress, or a woman of
no social status (*humilis*). Marcian ruled that this law should
not bar marriage with a respectable free woman, however poor,
or however lowly her birth might be, and professed to believe
that Constantine himself would have approved of this interpretation.[6] The Emperor's most confidential minister was
Euphemius, the Master of Offices, whose advice he constantly
followed.[7] While Marcian was not engaged in hostilities with
any great power, there were slight troubles in Syria with the
Saracens of the desert, and there was warfare on the southern
frontier of Egypt. Since the reign of Diocletian Upper Egypt
had been exposed to incursions of the Blemyes and the Nobadae.
For the purposes of strengthening the defences of the frontier
Theodosius II. divided the province of Thebais into two (upper
and lower), and united the civil and the military administration of the upper province in the same hands.[8] At the beginning of Marcian's reign Florus held this post and distinguished

---

[1] Marcian, *Nov.* 2 (A.D. 450).
[2] *C.J.* xii. 2. 1, A.D. 450.
[3] Marcellinus, *sub* 452.
[4] Theodore Lector, i. 2.
[5] *C.J.* xii. 2. 2. Cp. above, p. 50.
[6] Marcian, *Nov.* 4 (A.D. 454).
[7] Priscus, *fr.* 12, *De leg. gent.*
Palladius was Praet. Pref. of the
East during the greater part of the
reign (see *Novels*, and other laws in
C.J.).

[8] This arrangement was probably
made in the latter half of the reign.
The title of the governor was, as
elsewhere, *dux*; cp. a Leyden papyrus
in *Archiv f. Papyrusforschung*, i. 399,
κόμιτα καὶ δοῦκα τοῦ Θεβαικοῦ λιμίτου.
In this passage the barbarians are
mentioned τῶν ἀλιτηρίων βαρβάρων
. . . τῶν τε Βλεμύων καὶ τῶν Νουβάδων.
Cp. M. Gelzer. *Studien zur byz. Ver.
Ägyptens*, p. 10.

himself by driving the barbarians who were again annoying the province back into the desert.[1] The Blemyes expressed a desire to conclude a definite treaty with the Empire and for this purpose they sent ambassadors to Maximin, who seems to have been Master of Soldiers in the East. Terms were arranged, and it was conceded to the Blemyes that they might at stated times visit Philae in order to worship in the temple of Isis, in which the policy of the Emperors still suffered the celebration of old pagan rites. But we are told that when Maximin soon afterwards died the predatory tribes renewed their raids.

The act for which the reign of Marcian is best remembered by posterity is the assembling of the Fourth Ecumenical Council at Chalcedon. The decisions of this council gave deep satisfaction to the Emperor and Empress ; they could not foresee the political troubles to which it was to lead. Pulcheria died in A.D. 453.[2] By a life spent in pious and charitable works she had earned the eulogies of the Church, and she left all her possessions to the poor. Among the churches which claimed her as foundress may be mentioned three dedicated to the Mother of God. One was known as the church of Theotokos in Chalkoprateia,[3] so called from its situation in the quarter of the bronze merchants, not far from St. Sophia. The church of Theotokos Hodegetria,[4] Our Lady who leads to victory, which she built on the eastern shore of the city under the first hill, was sanctified by an icon of the Virgin which her sister-in-law sent her from Jerusalem. More famous than either of these was the church which she founded shortly before her death at Blachernae. This sanctuary was deemed worthy to possess a robe of the Virgin, brought from Jerusalen in the reign of Marcian's successor, who built a special chapel to receive it.[5]

---

[1] Jordanes, *Rom* p. 43 ; Priscus, *fr.* 11, *De leg. gent.* ; Evagrius, ii. 5. It was in these raids probably that the exiled Patriarch Nestorius was captured by the barbarians at Oasis, see Evagrius (i. 7) who quotes his letters. Fragments of a heroic poem on a war with the Blemyes, preserved on papyrus, are supposed by some to refer to the campaign of Florus. They have been edited most recently by A. Ludwich under the title of *Blemyomachia*, but it is very doubtful to what historical events they refer. All the names of persons are fictitious (Persinoos, etc.) with the possible exception of Germanus. Ludwich thinks that the hostilities described are imaginary and, on metrical grounds, he regards the poem as considerably prior to A.D. 450.

[2] Marcellinus, *sub a.*

[3] Theodore Lector, i. 5. See Bieliaev, *Khram Bog. Khalkopr*, p. 87, n. 2.

[4] Nicephorus Callistus, xiv. cap. 11. The picture was said to be the work of St. Luke.

[5] ἡ ἁγία σορός. Cedrenus, i. 614,

In later days the people of Constantinople put their trust in this precious relic as a sort of palladium to protect their city.

Marcian died in the first month of A.D. 457,[1] and with him the Theodosian dynasty, to which through his marriage he belonged, ceased to reign at New Rome.

[1] Sometime between 26th January and 7th February (Clinton, *F.R. sub a.*); possibly on 26th January; there is a lacuna in Theodore Lector, i. 12, where the date is mentioned.

CHAPTER VIII

THE DISMEMBERMENT OF THE EMPIRE IN THE WEST

§ 1. *Regency of the Empress Placidia. The Defence of Gaul* (A.D. 425–430)

DURING the first twelve years of the reign of Valentinian, the Empress Placidia ruled the West, and her authority was not threatened or contested. Unbroken concord with her nephew Theodosius, who considered himself responsible for the throne of his young relative, was a decisive fact in the political situation and undoubtedly contributed to her security. The internal difficulties of her administration were caused by the rivalries of candidates not for the purple but for the Mastership of Both Services, the post which gave its holder, if he knew how to take advantage of it, the real political power.

The man whom Placidia chose to fill the supreme military command was Felix, of whose character and capacities we know nothing. He remained in power for about four years (A.D. 425–429),[1] and, so far as we know, did not leave Italy. He did not attempt to play the active and prominent part which had been played by Constantius and by Stilicho. The Germans, who had penetrated into the Empire, were the great pressing problem, and in the dealings with them during these four years it is not the name of Felix that history records, but those of the two

---

[1] Flavius Constantius Felix was consul in 428, and we have portraits of him on the two leaves of his consular diptych. See Gori, *Thes.* i. p. 129. For a dedicatory inscription, in fulfilment of a vow, by him and his wife Padusia, see de Rossi, ii. 1, p. 149: Dessau, 1293. To Felix we must attribute the reorganisation of the defences of the Danubian provinces in A.D. 427–428 (for which we find evidence in the *Not. dig.*; see Seeck, *Hermes*, xi. 75 *sqq.*), after the Huns restored Valeria, see below, Chap. IX. § 2 *ad init.*

subordinate officers whom we have seen taking opposite sides in the struggle for the throne of Honorius—Boniface and Aetius.

Flavius Aetius was the son of Gaudentius, a native of Lower Moesia,[1] and an Italian mother. The career of his father, who fought with Theodosius the Great against the tyrant Eugenius, had been in the west, and Aetius had been given, in his child-hood, as a hostage to Alaric,[2] and some years later had been sent, again as a hostage, to the Huns, among whom he seems to have remained for a considerable time, and formed abiding bonds of friendship with King Rugila. This episode in his life had a considerable effect upon his career.

A panegyrical description of this soldier and statesman, on whom the fortunes of the Empire were to lean for a quarter of a century, has come to us from the pen of a contemporary.[3] He was " of middle height, of manly condition, well shaped, so that his body was neither too weak nor too weighty, active in mind, vigorous in limb, a most dexterous horseman, skilled in shooting the arrow, and strong in using the spear. He was an excellent warrior and famous in the arts of peace ; free from avarice and greed, endowed with mental virtues, one who never deviated at the instance of evil instigation from his own purpose, most patient of wrongs, a lover of work, dauntless in perils, able to endure the hardships of hunger, thirst, and sleeplessness."

That Aetius should take a German to wife was characteristic of the age in which an Imperial princess wedded a Goth and an Emperor was on the throne who had Frank blood in his veins. The lady was of royal Gothic family, " a descendant of heroes," [4] and they had a son, Carpilio, who was old enough in A.D. 425 to be delivered as a hostage to the Huns.[5]

It was to Aetius that the defence of Gaul was now entrusted ; he commanded the field army and soon received the title of

---

[1] Aetius was born at Durostorum (Silistria).

[2] This fact is known from Mero-baudes, *Carm.* iv. 46 *sqq.* :

> uix puberibus pater sub annis
> obiectus Geticis puer cateruis,
> bellorum mora, foederis sequester,
> intentas Latio faces remouit
> ac mundi pretium fuit pauentis ;

and *Pan.* ii. 129. The occasion may have been in 405–406, or perhaps after the first siege of Rome in 408. Cp. above, p. 180, *n.* 3.

[3] Renatus Profuturus Frigeridus, in Gregory of Tours, *H. Fr.* ii. 9. Mommsen, in his brief sketch of the career of Aetius, regards him as over-rated (*Hist. Schr.* i. 531 *sqq.*).

[4] *Heroum suboles*, Merobaudes, *op. cit.* ; Sidonius Apoll. *Paneg. in Maior.* 126 *sq.* Her father's name was Carpilio.

[5] Priscus, *fr.* 3 (*De leg. Rom.* p. 128) ; Cassiodorus, *Var.* i. 4. 11.

Magister Equitum.[1]   He had to defend the southern provinces
against the covetous desires of the Goths, and the north-eastern
against the aggressions of the Franks.   King Theoderic was
bent upon winning the Mediterranean coast adjacent to his
dominion, and Aetius established his military reputation by the
relief of Arles, to which the Goths laid siege in A.D. 427.[2]
Hostilities continued, but a peace was made in A.D. 430 confining
the Goths to the territories which had been granted to Wallia.
On this occasion the Roman government gave hostages to
Theoderic, and it has been suggested that at the same time the
Goths were recognised as an independent power, the Roman
governors were withdrawn from Aquitania Secunda and Novempopulana, and the Gallo-Roman inhabitants of those provinces
passed under the direct rule of Theoderic.[3]   It may be doubted
whether this change came about so early, but in any case the
attitude of the Visigoths towards the Imperial government for
the ensuing twenty years was that of an independent and hostile
nation.

The Salian Franks had been living for nearly seventy years
in the north-eastern corner of Lower Belgica, in the district
known as Thoringia, where they had been settled as Federates
by the Emperor Constantius II. and Julian.   In these lands
of the Meuse and Scheldt they seem to have lived peacefully
enough within the borders assigned to them by Rome.   They
were ruled by more than one king, but the principal royal
family, which was ultimately to extinguish all the others, was
the Merovingian.   They seemed to be the least formidable of
all the German peoples settled within the Empire, though they
were destined to become the lords of all Gaul.   The first step
on the path of expansion seems to have been taken by Chlodio,
the first of the long-haired Merovingian kings whose name is

---

[1] We are only told that Placidia
conferred on him the title of count
(Philostorgius, xii. 14).   For the new
post of *mag. eq. per Gallias* see Bury,
The Not. dig. (*J.R.S.* x.).

[2] Prosper, *sub* 425 ; *Chron. Gall.*
p. 658.   A success won in 430 over
Gothic forces near Arles, mentioned
by Hydatius, 92, may be the battle
of Mons Colubrarius recorded by
Merobaudes, *Pan.* i. 10 (Vollmer,
ad loc.).

[3] Schmidt (*op. cit.* i. 235) has

adduced arguments for this view—
among others the fact that Theoderic
made laws affecting relations between
Goths and provincials (referred to in
Euric's Code : *Leg. Vis. ant.* 277,
cp. Sidonius Apoll. *Epp.* ii. 1).   He
holds that in 453, after the accession
of Theoderic II., the Goths again
became foederati of the Empire (*ib.*
252).   But what exactly happened,
how the legal position was changed
he leaves very vague—inevitably, as
there is no clear evidence.

recorded. Taking advantage of the weakening of the Roman power, which was manifest to all, he invaded Artois. Aetius led an army against him and defeated him at Vicus Helenae, about A.D. 428.[1] But before his death Chlodio seems to have succeeded in extending his power as far as the Somme, crossing the Carbonarian Forest (the Ardennes) and capturing Cambrai.[2] This annexation was probably recognised by the Imperial government ; for the Salians remained federates of the Empire and were to fight repeatedly in the cause of Rome.

If the units of the field army with which Aetius conducted the defence of Gaul were up to their nominal strength, he had somewhat less than 45,000 men under his command. We do not know whether he had the help of the federate Burgundians in his operations against Visigoths and Franks. But it is certain that the most useful and effective troops, on whom he relied throughout his whole career in withstanding German encroachments in Gaul, were the Huns, and without them he would hardly have been able to achieve his moderate successes. Here his knowledge of the Huns, his friendship with the ruling family, and the trust they placed in him stood the Empire in good stead.

The prestige which Aetius gained in Gaul was far from welcome to the Empress Placidia, who never forgave him for his espousal of the cause of John. But now he was able to impose his own terms, and extort from her the deposition of Felix and his own elevation to the post which Felix had occupied. He was appointed Master of Both Services in A.D. 429, and it is said that he then caused Felix to be killed on suspicion of treachery.[3]

---

[1] Hélesmes (nord). The source is Sidonius Apoll. *Carm.* v. 212 *sqq.* Cp. Prosper, *sub a.* It is hardly to this campaign of Aetius that Merobaudes refers when he says (*Pan.* ii. 6 *sq.*) that the Rhine—

> Hesperiis flecti contentus habenis
> gaudet ab alterna Thybrim sibi crescere
> ripa,

words which point to some pacification on the Middle Rhine, apparently an arrangement with the Ripuarian Franks between Cologne and Mayence, the two rivers alluded to being the Moselle and the Main, and probably made at a later date.

[2] See Greg. Tur. *H. Fr.* ii. 9. His source was no doubt a Frank legend, and its historical value might be doubted, were it not borne out, so far as Chlodio's aggressive policy is concerned, by the incident related by Sidonius (last note).

[3] The brief notices we have of these events only excite our curiosity. Prosper says that Felix was created a Patrician and succeeded by Aetius in 429, and was slain by Aetius on suspicion of treachery in 430 along with his wife Padusia. John Ant. (*fr.* 85, *De ins.* p. 126) says that Felix was suborned by Placidia to kill Aetius. Hydatius (94) says that Felix was killed in a military riot.

It was, no doubt, the power of the Hunnic forces, which he could summon at his will, that enabled him to force the hand of the Empress. The one man whom she would have liked to oppose to him was Boniface, formerly her loyal supporter. Boniface had been for some time enacting the part of an enemy of the " Republic." We must now go back to follow the fatal course of events in Africa.[1]

§ 2. *Invasion of Africa by the Vandals* (A.D. 429–435)

Africa, far from the Rhine and Danube, across which the great East-German nations had been pouring into the Roman Empire, had not yet been violated by the feet of Teutonic foes. But the frustrated plans of Alaric and Wallia were intimations that the day might be at hand when this province too would have to meet the crisis of a German invasion. The third attempt was not to fail, but the granaries of Africa were not to fall to the Goths. The Vandal people, perhaps the first of the East-German peoples to cross the Baltic, was destined to find its last home and its grave in this land so distant from its cradle.[2]

We saw how the Vandals settled in Baetica, and how King Gunderic assumed the title of " King of the Vandals and the Alans." [3] He conquered New Carthage and Hispalis (Seville), and made raids on the Balearic Islands and possibly on Mauretania Tingitana.[4] He died in A.D. 428 and was succeeded by his brother Gaiseric, who had perhaps already shared the kingship with him.[5] About the same time events in Africa opened a new and attractive prospect to the Vandals.

After the restoration of the legitimate dynasty and the coronation of Valentinian,[6] the conduct of Count Boniface laid him open to the suspicion that he was aiming at a tyranny himself.

[1] In 430 and 431 Aetius was occupied in pacifying the Danubian provinces, Vindelicia (Sidon. Apoll. *Carm.* vii. 234), Raetia (*ib.* 233, Hydatius 93, *Chron. Gall.* p. 658), Noricum (Hydatius 93, 95, Sidon. *ib.*).

[2] For the difficult questions connected with the Vandal invasion of Africa and the part played by Boniface the most important modern discussions are those of Freeman, *op. cit.* ; Schmidt, in *Geschichte der Wandalen* ; Martroye, in *Genséric.*

[3] This remained the official style of all the Vandal kings in Africa.

[4] Hydatius, 86, 89.

[5] Cp. Martroye, *Genséric*, p. 103.

[6] For his adhesion to Placidia see above, p. 223. He seems to have gone to Ravenna immediately after the restoration and to have received the additional dignity of *comes domesticorum.* Cp. Augustine, *Ep.* 220 § 4 *nauigasti.* See Seeck, *Bonifacius*, in P.-W.

It had been a notable part of his policy, since he assumed the military command in Africa, to exhibit deep devotion to the Church and co-operate cordially with the bishops. He ingratiated himself with Augustine, the bishop of Hippo, and a letter of Augustine casts some welcome though dim light on the highly ambiguous behaviour of the count in these fateful years. Notwithstanding his professions of orthodox zeal, and hypocritical pretences that he longed to retire into monastic life, Boniface took as his second wife [1] an Arian lady, and allowed his daughter to be baptized into the Arian communion. This degeneracy shocked and grieved Augustine, but it was a more serious matter that instead of devoting all his energies to repelling the incursions of the Moors, he was working to make his own authority absolute in Africa.[2] So at least it seemed to the court of Ravenna, and Placidia—doubtless by the advice of Felix [3]—recalled him to account for his conduct. Boniface refused to come and placed himself in the position of an " enemy of the Republic." An army was immediately sent against him under three commanders, all of whom were slain (A.D. 427). Then at the beginning of A.D. 428 another army was sent under the command of Sigisvult the Goth, who seems to have been named Count of Africa, to replace the rebel.[4] Sigisvult appears to have succeeded in seizing Hippo and Carthage,[5] and Boniface, despairing of overcoming him by his own forces, resorted to the plan of inviting the Vandals to come to his aid.[6]

[1] *Ib.* Her name was Pelagia, Marcellinus, *Chron., sub* 432. There is no positive evidence for the opinion of Baronius that she was a relative of the Vandal king (*Ann. ecc., sub* 427).

[2] Augustine, *ib.* § 7. Prosper, *sub* 427. *Bonifatio cuius intra Africam potentia gloriaque augebatur.* He seems to have enjoyed a high military reputation (Olympiodorus, *fr.* 42), but the only exploit recorded, before his campaigns in Africa against the Moors (of which we know no details), is his defence of Marseilles against the Visigoths in A.D. 413.

[3] Prosper, *loc. cit.* Procopius (*B. V.* i. 3) makes Aetius act the perfidious part of instigating the Empress against Boniface, and at the same time secretly advising Boniface to defy her. But Aetius was at this time almost certainly in Gaul. Cp.

Freeman, *op. cit.* p. 337.

[4] Prosper, *loc. cit.*

[5] Cp. Augustine, *Collatio cum Maximino, P.L.* 42. 709 ; Possidius, *Vit. Aug.* c. 17. Maximin was an Arian bishop who had come with Sigisvult.

[6] Prosper, *loc. cit.*, places the calling of the Vandals in 427 before the arrival of Sigisvult : *exinde gentibus quae uti navibus nesciebant, dum a concertantibus in auxilium vocantur, mare pervium factum est, bellique contra Bonifatium coepti in Segisvultum comitem cura translata est.* The story in Procopius, *B.V.* i. 3 enables us to interpret the vague plural *a concertantibus* as referring to Boniface. I follow Martroye (*op. cit.* p. 87) in supposing that Boniface turned to the Vandals after the coming of Sigisvult. But it is of course possible that he took this step when the news

The proposal of Boniface was to divide Africa between himself and the Vandals, for whom he doubtless destined the three Mauretanian provinces, and he undertook to furnish the means of transport.[1] Gaiseric accepted the invitation. He fully realised the value of the possession of Africa, which had attracted the ambition of two Gothic kings. The whole nation of the Vandals and Alans embarked in May A.D. 429 and crossed over to Africa.[2] If the population numbered, as is said, 80,000, the fighting force might have been about 15,000.[3]

Their king Gaiseric stands out among the German leaders of his time as unquestionably the ablest. He had not only the military qualities which most of them possessed, but he was also master of a political craft which was rare among the German leaders of the migrations. His ability was so exceptional that his irregular birth—his mother was a slave [4]—did not diminish his influence and prestige. We have a description of him, which seems to come from a good source. " Of medium height, lame from a fall of his horse, he had a deep mind and was sparing of speech. Luxury he despised, but his anger was uncontrollable and he was covetous. He was far-sighted in inducing foreign peoples to act in his interests, and resourceful in sowing seeds of discord and

reached him that the expedition was being prepared. The invitation of Boniface is also recorded by Jordanes, *Get.* 167, 169 (following Cassiodorus).

[1] Procopius, *loc. cit.*, where it is said that a tripartite division was contemplated between Boniface, Gunderic, and Gaiseric. This would imply that Gunderic died after Boniface's negotiations began.

[2] Hydatius, 90. It is stated here that before he crossed to Africa, Gaiseric led an expedition against the Suevians who were plundering in Baetica or neighbouring regions. Martroye (p. 106) argues from this that Gaiseric intended to leave the non-combatant population in their Spanish home until his success in Africa was assured ; that he was ready to start in 428, and that the Suevian invasion forced him to postpone his departure till 429 ; and that as a matter of fact the mass of the Vandals remained in Spain till after the capture of Carthage, when the Visigoths conquered the country (Cassiodorus, *Chron., sub* 427, *a*

Gothis exclusa de Hispaniis). This hypothesis runs counter to the evidence. Hydatius, *ib.*, says that the Vandals embarked " with their families," and so Victor Vitensis, *Hist. Vand.* i. 1. The notice in Cassiodorus might have some importance if it were under a later year. As we know nothing of the circumstances, we have no means of conjecturing why Gaiseric found it imperative to attack the Suevians at this juncture. And in any case the natural inference from the notice of Hydatius is that the defeat of the Suevians belongs to 429.

[3] Victor Vit. *op. cit.* i. 2. This is to be preferred to the statement of Procopius, *B.V.* i. 5. See Schmidt, *Gesch. der Wandalen*, p. 37, and *B.Z.* xv. 620-621. Cp. also Martroye, *op. cit.* p. 104. The reason for numbering the people before the migration from Spain to Africa was obviously to find out how many vessels would be needed, and non-combatants as well as combatants had to be transported.

[4] Sidonius Apoll. *Carm.* 57 *famula satus.* Cp. Procopius, *B.V.* i. 3.

stirring up hatred." [1] All that we know of his long career
bears out this suggestion of astute and perfidious diplomacy.

The unhappy population of the Mauretanian regions were left
unprotected to the mercies of the invaders, and if we can trust
the accounts which have come down to us,[2] they seem to have
endured horrors such as the German conquerors of this age
seldom inflicted upon defenceless provinces. The Visigoths were
lambs compared with the Vandal wolves. Neither age nor sex
was spared and cruel tortures were applied to force the victims
to reveal suspected treasures. The bishops and clergy, the
churches and sacred vessels were not spared. We get a glimpse
of the situation in the correspondence of St. Augustine. Bishops
write to him to ask whether it is right to allow their flocks to
flee from the approaching danger and for themselves to abandon
their sees.[3] The invasion was a signal to other enemies whether
of Rome or of the Roman government to join in the fray. The
Moors were encouraged in their depredations, and religious
heretics and sectaries, especially the Donatists, seized the opportunity to wreak vengeance on the society which oppressed them.[4]

If Africa was to be saved, it was necessary that the Roman
armies should be united, and Placidia immediately took steps to
regain the allegiance of Boniface. A reconciliation was effected by
the good offices of a certain Darius, of illustrious rank, whom she
sent to Africa,[5] and he seems also to have concluded a truce with
Gaiseric,[6] which was, however, of but brief duration, for Boniface's
proposals were not accepted. Gaiseric was determined to pillage,
if he could not conquer, the rich eastern provinces of Africa.
He entered Numidia, defeated Boniface, and besieged him in
Hippo (May–June A.D. 430). The city held out for more than
a year.[7] Then Gaiseric raised the siege (July A.D. 431). New

[1] Jordanes, *Get.* 168 (after Cassiodorus).

[2] Possidius, *Vit. August.* 28, Victor Vit. *op. cit.* i. 1-3.

[3] Augustine, *Ep.* 228. Augustine
said that the bishop should let the
people flee, but not abandon his post,
so long as his presence was needed.

[4] See Martroye, *op. cit.* 113. The
devastation is described in general
terms in a letter addressed by the
bishop of Carthage to the Council of
Ephesus in summer of 431 (Mansi,
iv. 1207).

[5] See Augustine's letter to Darius,
congratulating him on his success,
Ep. 229 ; the reply of Darius, *Ep.* 230 ;
and Augustine's answer, *Ep.* 231.
Boniface seems to have given Darius
a hostage, *pignus pacis*, *Ep.* 229. 1
and 231. 7, who was probably the
Verimodus of 230. 6.

[6] *Ep.* 229. 2 *ipsa bella verbo occidere*,
to which Darius replies (230. 3) *si non
extinximus bella, certe distulimus.*

[7] For the siege see Possidius, *Vit.
August.* Augustine died at the beginning of the siege (August 28, A.D. 430).

forces were sent from Italy and Constantinople under the command of Aspar, the general of Theodosius ; a battle was fought, and Aspar and Boniface were so utterly defeated that they could make no further effort to resist the invader. Hippo was taken soon afterwards,[1] and the only important towns which held out were Carthage and Cirta.

Boniface returned to Italy, where Placidia received him with favour, and soon afterwards she deposed Aetius, who was consul of the year (A.D. 432), and gave his military command to the repentant rebel, on whom at the same time she conferred the dignity of Patrician.[2] Aetius refused to submit. There was civil war in Italy. The rivals fought a battle near Ariminum, in which Boniface was victorious, but he died shortly afterwards from a malady, perhaps caused by a wound.[3] His son-in-law Sebastian was appointed to the vacant post of Master of Both Services,[4] but did not hold it long. Aetius escaped to Dalmatia and journeyed to the court of his friend Rugila the king of the Huns. By his help, we know not how, he was able to reappear in Italy, to dictate terms to the court of Ravenna, to secure the banishment of Sebastian, and to obtain for himself reinstatement in his old office and the rank of Patrician (A.D. 434).[5]

In the meantime, during this obscure struggle for power, the Vandals were extending their conquests in Numidia. In spite of his wonderfully rapid career of success Gaiseric was ready to come to terms with the Empire. Aetius, who was fully occupied in Gaul, where the Visigoths and Burgundians were actively aggressive, saw that the forces at his disposal were unequal to

---

[1] Possidius, c. 28. Aspar seems to have remained in Africa for some time. He was the western consul in 434 and was at that time in Carthage (*Lib. de permissionibus, P.L.* 51, 841). See above, p. 225.

[2] See *Consularia Italica*, p. 301.

[3] Cp. Hyd. 99 with Prosper, *sub* 432. If John Ant., *ib.*, says that Boniface was out-generalled by Aetius, this may be taken to mean that Aetius succeeded in the end. The common source of John Ant. and Procopius *may* have been Priscus.

[4] Hyd. *ib.*

[5] See Prosper, *ib.*, *Chron. Gall., sub* 433, from which source we learn that "Goths were summoned by the

Romans to bring aid" against the Huns. Hydatius, 103. Sebastian found a refuge at Constantinople, where he remained for ten years (Hyd. 104, 129), and he is said to have been the commander of a pirate squadron which served Theodosius II. (see Suidas, *sub* Θεοδόσιος, a fragment ascribed by Niebuhr to Priscus, by Müller to John Ant., *F.H.G.* iv. *fr.* 194). Falling out of favour in A.D. 444 he went to the court of Theoderic the Visigoth, who would not receive him. Then he managed to seize Barcelona. Driven from there he went to the Vandals, and was put to death by Gaiseric (A.D. 450, Hyd. 144), and has come down to fame as a Catholic martyr.

the expulsion of the Vandals, and it was better to share Africa with the intruders than to lose it entirely. Gaiseric probably wished to consolidate his power in the provinces which he had occupied, and knew that any compact he made would not be an obstacle to further conquests. Hippo, from which the inhabitants had fled, seems to have been reoccupied by the Romans,[1] and here (February 11, A.D. 435) Trygetius, the ambassador of Valentinian, concluded a treaty with Gaiseric, on the basis of the *status quo*. The Vandals were to retain the provinces which they had occupied, the Mauretanias and a part of Numidia, but were to pay an annual tribute, thus acknowledging the over-lordship of Rome.[2]

§ 3. *End of the Regency and the Ascendancy of Aetius*

Aetius had now firmly established his power and Placidia had to resign herself to his guidance. Valentinian was fifteen years of age, and the regency could not last much longer. The presence of the Master of Soldiers was soon demanded in Gaul, where the Visigoths were again bent on new conquests and the Burgundians invaded the province of Upper Belgica (A.D. 435). Against the Burgundians he does not appear to have sent a Roman army ; he asked his friends the Huns to chastise them. The Huns knew how to strike. It is said that 20,000 Burgundians were slain, and King Gundahar was one of those who fell (A.D. 436). Thus came to an end the first Burgundian kingdom in Gaul, with its royal residence at Worms. It was the background of the heroic legends which passed into the German epic—the Nibelungenlied. The Burgundians were not exterminated, and a few years later the Roman government assigned territory to the remnant of the nation in Sapaudia (Savoy), south of Lake Geneva (A.D. 443).[3]

Narbonne was besieged by Theoderic in A.D. 436, but was relieved by Litorius,[4] who was probably the Master of Soldiers in Gaul. Three years later the same commander drove the

---

[1] Cp. Martroye, p. 128.

[2] Prosper, *sub a.* 435. Cp. Isidore, *Hist. Vandalorum*, in *Chron. min.* ii. p. 297. Procopius, *B.V.* i. 4. The king's son Huneric was sent as a hostage to Rome, but was soon released (apparently before 439).

[3] *Chron. Gall.* p. 660; Prosper, *sub* 435 ; Sidonius Apoll. *Carm.* vii. 234. The number of 20,000 is of course an exaggeration.

[4] Sidonius, *ib.* 244 *sqq.* Cp. Merobaudes, *Pan.* i. 9, l. 23 ; *Pan.* ii. l. 16.

Goths back to the walls of their capital Toulouse, and it is interesting to find him gratifying his Hun soldiers by the performance of pagan rites and the consultation of auspices. These ceremonies did not help him. He was defeated and taken prisoner in a battle outside the city.[1] Avitus, the Praetorian Prefect of Gaul, who had great influence with Theoderic, then brought about the conclusion of peace. In these years there were also troubles in the provinces north of the Loire,[2] where the Armoricans rebelled, and Aetius or his lieutenant Litorius was compelled to reimpose upon them the " liberty " of Imperial rule.

In A.D. 437 Aetius was consul for the second time, and in that year Valentinian went to Constantinople to wed his affianced bride, Licinia Eudoxia. Now assuredly, if not before, the regency was at an end, and henceforward Aetius had to do in all high affairs not with the Empress who distrusted and disliked him but with an inexperienced youth. Valentinian was weak and worthless. He had been spoiled by his mother, and grown up to be a man of pleasure who took no serious interest in his Imperial duties. He associated, we are told, with astrologers and sorcerers, and was constantly engaged in amours with other men's wives, though his own wife was exceptionally beautiful.[3] He had some skill in riding and in archery and was a good runner, if we may believe Flavius Vegetius Renatus, who dedicated to him a treatise on the art of war.[4] From the end of the regency

---

[1] Merobaudes, *Pan.* ii. 153 *sqq.*; Hydatius, 116, 117; Sidonius, *ib.* 299 *sqq.*

[2] John Ant. *fr.* 201. 2 (source probably Priscus); Merobaudes, *Pan.* ii. 8:

lustrat Aremoricos iam mitior incola saltus;

Sidonius, *Carm.* v. 210, mentions the defence of alarmed Tours, and vii. 246 relates that Litorius having subdued the Armoricans hurried his troops against the Goths. This suggests 438–439 as the date. There was another Armorican rebellion in 442; Aetius sent Goar, the veteran chief of the Alans now settled near Orleans, to punish the rebels, and Germanus bishop of Auxerre went to Ravenna to plead the Armorican cause. See Constantius, *Vita Germani*, ii. c. 8, and *Chron. Gall., ib.*

[3] Procopius, *B.V.* i. 3. 10. Perhaps the source was Priscus.

[4] *Epitome rei militaris*, iii. 26. This treatise throws little light on the warfare of the writer's own time. It is mainly antiquarian, and there are few references to contemporary conditions. The fleet of *lusoriae* guarding the Danube is mentioned (iv. 46). The disuse of coats of mail and helmets is noted, and frequent defeats of Imperial forces by Gothic archers are attributed to this (i. 20). Vegetius also says that the art of naval warfare is now less important than formerly *quia iamdudum pacato mari cum barbaris nationibus agitur terrestre certamen*, a remark which points to the conclusion that the book was composed before 440 when the Vandal navy began to show what it could do. That the Emperor to whom the book is dedicated was Valentinian was conjectured by Gibbon and virtually proved by Seeck (in *Hermes*, xi. 61 *sqq.*).

to his own death, Aetius was master of the Empire in the west,
and it must be imputed to his policy and arms that Imperial
rule did not break down in all the provinces by the middle of the
fifth century.

Of his work during these critical years we have no history.
We know little more than what we can infer from some bald
notices in chronicles written by men who selected their facts
without much discrimination. If we possessed the works of the
court poet of the time we might know more, for even from the
few fragments which have survived we learn facts unrecorded
elsewhere. The Spaniard, Flavius Merobaudes, did for Valentinian and Aetius what Claudian had done for Honorius and
Stilicho, though with vastly inferior talent. Like Claudian,
he enjoyed the honour of having a bronze statue erected to him
at Rome, in the Forum of Trajan.[1] His name was known and
appreciated at the court of Constantinople, for Theodosius
conferred upon him the rank of patrician.[2]

He celebrated the three consulships of Aetius,[3] and we have
part of a poem which he wrote for the second birthday of the
general's younger son Gaudentius.[4] We may be as certain as
of anything that has not been explicitly recorded, that he wrote
an ode for the nuptials of Valentinian and Eudoxia, and it is little
less probable that he celebrated the birth of their elder child
Eudocia, who was born in A.D. 438. But of all the poems he
composed for the court only two have partly been preserved,
both composed soon after the birth of the Emperor's younger
daughter Placidia.[5] One of these is a description of mosaic
pictures in a room in the Palace of Ravenna, representing scenes
from the Emperor's life. He and Eudoxia shone in the centre
of the ceiling like bright stars, and all around were scenes in

---

[1] *C.I.L.* vi. 1724, Sidonius *Carm.*
ix. 296. It was set up in A.D. 435, and
he refers to it in his prose work on the
second consulship of Aetius, written
in 437. *Pan.* i. 8. From this inscription we learn that he had seen
some service as a soldier : *inter arma
litteris militabat et in Alpibus acuebat
eloquium.* In another, but fragmentary, inscription (*C.I.L.* vi.
31983), his name appears as *Flavius
Merobaudes orator.*

[2] *Ib.* p. 9 *pro his denique nuper ad
honorem maximi nomen ille nascenti*

soli proximus imperator euexit (rightly
explained by Vollmer).

[3] That he celebrated the first is a
probable inference, see Vollmer, p. 20.
We have parts of his oration on the
second, and his poem on the third
(*Pan.* ii.).

[4] *Carm.* iv. Gaudentius was probably born about 440.

[5] *Carm.* i. ii. As Placidia was
already married to Olybrius when she
was taken to Carthage in 455 (see
below, p. 325) she can hardly have
been born later than in 440.

which he appeared with his mother, his sister, his children, and his cousin Theodosius.[1]

Like another more famous man of letters, his younger contemporary Sidonius, Merobaudes was called upon to fill a high office and to assist Aetius in the work of maintaining order in the provinces. We are told that he was appointed Master of Both Services and went to his native province of Baetica to suppress a rebellion of turbulent peasants (*bacaudae*), that he successfully accomplished this task but was recalled to Rome through the machination of his enemies (A.D. 443). His immediate predecessor in the command had been his father-in-law, Asturius.[2]

It must not be thought that Asturius and Merobaudes, in bearing the title " Master of Both Services," had succeeded to the post of Aetius and were supreme commanders of the army. Aetius had not resigned the supreme command ; he was still Master of Both Services. The command which Asturius and Merobaudes held, and which Sigisvult had held two years before,[3] was simply that of the *magister equitum praesentalis* under a new name. Under Stilicho, Constantius, and Felix the *magister equitum* had been subordinate to the *magister utriusque militiae*, and this arrangement undoubtedly continued still, but some time before A.D. 440 he received the same title as his superior, doubtless because it was found convenient to place legions as well as cavalry under his command. The superior Master of Both Services, the Emperor's principal statesman and director of affairs, is from this time forward generally designated as " the Patrician "—the Emperor's Patrician, the Patrician in a superlative sense.[4]

---

[1] See Bury, *Justa Grata Honoria* (see Bibl.).

[2] Our informant is the contemporary Spanish writer Hydatius (128), and his statement as to the office held by Asturius is confirmed by the consular diptych of that personage (A.D. 449), on which he is described as *ex mag. utriusq. mil.* See Meyer, *Zwei ant. Elfenb.* p. 56.

[3] Valentinian III., *Nov.* 6. 1 and *Nov.* 9 (March and June A.D. 440).

[4] *Id.* Nov. 9, *patricium nostrum Aetium.* Cp. John Ant. *fr.* 84 (*De ins.* p. 126) τῆς πατρικιότητος. So in *Cons. Ital.* p. 305 *Messianus*,

patricius Aviti. That Aetius continued to hold the Mastership is shown by Val. III. *Nov.* 17 (A.D. 445). In A.D. 446 the subordinate master was Vitus, who was sent to Spain against the Suevians who were ravaging the southern and eastern provinces.—A different view is taken by Sundwall (in *Weströmische Studien*), who thinks that Asturius, Merobaudes, and Vitus were Masters of Soldiers in Gaul. I cannot see why. They did not operate in Gaul but in Spain, and were surely sent direct from Italy with Italian troops, so that it seems perverse not to regard them as the successors

The position of Aetius in these years as the supreme minister was confirmed by the betrothal of his son to the Emperor's daughter Placidia,[1] an arrangement which can hardly have been welcome to Galla Placidia, the Augusta. With Valentinian himself he can hardly have been on intimate terms. The fact that he had supported the tyrant John was probably never forgiven. And it cannot have been agreeable to the young Emperor that it was found necessary to curtail his income and rob his privy purse in order to help the State in its financial straits.[2] Little revenue could come from Africa, suffering from the ravages of the Vandals, and in A.D. 439, as we shall see, the richest provinces of that country passed into the hands of the barbarians.

The income derived from Gaul must have been very considerably reduced, and we are not surprised to find the government openly acknowledging in A.D. 444 that ." the strength of our treasury is unable to meet the necessary expenses." In that year two new taxes were imposed, one on the senatorial class, and one on sales, expressly for the purpose of maintaining the army. New recruits were urgently wanted, and there was not enough money in the treasury to feed and clothe the existing regiments. Senators of illustrious rank were required to furnish the money for maintaining three soldiers, senators of the second class one, senators of the third class one-third; that meant 90, 30, and 10 solidi respectively, as the annual cost of a soldier was estimated at 30.[3] A duty of $\frac{1}{24}$th was imposed on sales— a siliqua in a solidus—of which the seller and the buyer each paid half.[4] The government would have done better if it had forced the rich senators of Italy to contribute substantial sums, as they could well have afforded to do, to the needs of the State.[5]

of Sigisvult. The *magistri equitum* in Gaul had indeed a mixed command, but the first of them who certainly bore the title *mag. ped. et equit.* or *mag. utr. mil.* was Avitus in 455 (Sidonius, *Carm.* vii. 377). Cassius is described as *mag. militum Galliarum* in *Vita Hilarii*, 6, 9, *P.L.* 50, but this may mean no more than *mag. equit.*—At a later date, we find beside Ricimer a second *mag. utr. mil.* in Italy, namely Flavius Theodobius Valila, in A.D. 471 (see *C.I.L.* vi. 32169, 32221).

[1] Prosper, *sub* 454. The son of Aetius was doubtless Gaudentius, and the princess must have been Placidia, as Eudoxia was betrothed to Huneric (see below, p. 256).

[2] *C. Th.* xi. 1. 36, A.D. 431. In later years the necessity was more imperative. For the condition of Africa see *Nov. Valent.* xii., xiii., and i. 1.

[3] *Nov. Valent.* vi. 3.

[4] *Nov. Valent.* xv.

[5] Sundwall, *Weström. Studien*, 158. He calculates that the state revenue from the land tax c. A.D. 450 was at most £4,800,000, as compared with 13 millions fifty years before. What-

§ 4. Settlement of the Vandals in Africa (A.D. 435–442)

The treaty of A.D. 435 was soon violated by Gaiseric. He did not intend to stop short of the complete conquest of Roman Africa. In less than five years Carthage was taken (October 19, A.D. 439).[1] If there was any news that could shock or terrify men who remembered that twenty years before Rome herself had been in the hands of the Goths, it was the news that an enemy was in possession of the city which in long past ages had been her most formidable rival. Italy trembled, for with a foe master of Carthage she felt that her own shores and cities were not safe. And, in fact, not many months passed before it was known that Gaiseric had a large fleet prepared to sail, but its destination was unknown.[2] Rome and Naples were put into a state of defence ; [3] Sigisvult, Master of Soldiers, took steps to guard the coasts ; Aetius and his army were summoned from Gaul ; and the Emperor Theodosius prepared to send help.[4] There was indeed some reason for alarm at Constantinople. The Vandal pirates could afflict the eastern as well as the western coasts of the Mediterranean ; the security of commerce was threatened. It was even thought advisable to fortify the shore and harbours of Constantinople.

Gaiseric, aware that Italy was prepared, directed his attack upon Sicily, where he laid siege to Panormus.[5] This city defied

---

ever may be thought about his figures, the proportion of the decline is hardly overstated. In this work Sundwall also illustrates the growing distinction between the highest senatorial class (illustres), and the two lower classes, and argues that while the members of the Roman senate in 400 were about 3000, in 450 they were about 2000. He pertinently points out that out of the not very large amounts which the senators paid in taxes, many of them got much back in the salaries of the high posts (Prefectures, etc.) to which they were appointed.

[1] Prosper, *sub a.*

[2] *Satis incertum est ad quam oram terrae possint naves hostium pervenire.* Valentinian, *Nov.* 9 (June 24, A.D. 440).

[3] Naples: for I think that we should refer to this year the following in-

scription found there (*C.I.L.* x. 1485) : *d.n. Placidus Valentin[ianus providen]tissimus omnium retr[o principum], salvo adque concordi [d.n. Fl. Theo]dosio invictissimo Au[g. ad decus nom]inis sui Neapolitana[m civitatem], ad omnes terra mari[que incursus] expositam et nulla [securitate] gaudentem, ingenti [labore adque] sumptu muris turrib[usq. munivit].*

[4] *Ib.* All these preparations are announced in this constitution, addressed to the Roman people, and intended to calm their fears. The Emperor had come to Rome before March 3, where steps were being taken to repair the walls (*Nov.* 3).

[5] He is said to have been invited by Maximin, bishop of the Arian communities in Sicily (Cassiodorus, *Chron., sub* 440), and he persecuted the Catholics while he was in the island (Hydatius, 120).

him, but it is possible, though not certain, that he occupied Lilybaeum.[1] His fleet, however, returned to Africa, perhaps on account of the considerable preparations which were on foot at Constantinople.[2] The government of Theodosius had made ready a large naval squadron which sailed in the following year (A.D. 441), with the purpose of delivering Carthage from the Vandals.[3] The expedition arrived in Sicily, and Gaiseric was alarmed. He opened negotiations, pending which the Imperial fleet remained in Sicilian waters. These diplomatic conversations were protracted by the craft of Gaiseric, and in the meantime an invasion of the Huns compelled Theodosius to recall his forces. The Emperors were thus constrained to make a disadvantageous peace.

By the treaty of A.D. 442 Africa was divided anew between the two powers. This division nearly reversed that of A.D. 435, and was far more advantageous to the Vandals. The Empire retained the provinces of Tripolitana, Mauretania Sitifensis, Mauretania Caesariensis, and part of Numidia ; while the Vandals were acknowledged masters of the rest of that province, of Byzacena, and of the Proconsular province or Zeugitana.[4] Mauretania Tingitana was probably not mentioned in the treaty.[5] It was part of the diocese of Spain, not of the diocese of Africa, and it is probable that the Vandals never occupied it effectively. In any case it now belonged to the Empire, which, since the departure of the Vandals, had been in possession of all Spain, except the Suevian kingdom in the north-western corner.

This settlement was an even greater blow to the Empire

---

[1] Cp. Pope Leo I., *Ep.* 3 (*P.L.* 54. 606) ; Martroye, p. 132.

[2] Prosper, *sub* 440, ascribes his return to danger from the threat of an attack on Carthage by Sebastian (the son-in-law of Boniface), invading Africa *ab Hispania*. Sebastian seems to have been in the service of Theodosius. Cp. above, p. 248.

[3] The Imperial fleet was under three generals, Areobindus, Ansila, and Germanus (Prosper, *sub* 441). Theophanes is evidently referring to the same expedition *sub* A.M. 5942 = A.D. 448–449. He says that the fleet of transports numbered 1100 (which has a suspicious resemblance to the number of Leo's armada in A.D. 468), and adds the names of two other generals.

[4] The sources for this division are Valentinian III., *Nov.* 33 and *Nov.* 18 ; Victor Vit. i. 4.

[5] The words of Victor, *Byzacenam Abaritanam atque Getuliam*, are obscure. Getulia seems to be the southern districts of Byzacena. The exact meaning of Abaritana (cp. Pliny, *N.H.* xvi. 36, 172) is unknown. It seems to be a district of the Proconsular province, as we find among bishops of that province in the reign of Huneric *Felix abaritanus* (*Notitia prov. et civ. Afr.* p. 63). Schmidt (*Gesch. der W.* 72) thinks Tingitana is meant, but this has not the least plausibility. Cp. Martroye, 135-136.

than that which necessity had imposed upon Constantius of settling the Visigoths in Aquitaine. The fairest provinces of Africa were resigned to barbarians who had an even worse reputation than the Goths. But it was worth while to attempt to secure that the settlement, such as it was, should be permanent. Aetius saw that the best policy was to cultivate good relations with Gaiseric and to give that ambitious and unscrupulous monarch no pretext for attacking Sicily, or Sardinia, or Italy itself. And so he prevailed upon Valentinian to consent to a betrothal between his elder daughter, Eudocia, and Gaiseric's son, Huneric. It is probable that this arrangement was considered at the time of the treaty, though it may not have been definitely decided.[1] But Huneric was already married. The Visigothic king Theoderic had bestowed upon him his daughter's hand. Such an alliance between Vandals and Goths could not have been welcome to Aetius ; it was far more in the interest of his policy to keep alive the hostility between these two peoples which seems to have dated from the campaigns of Wallia in Spain. The existence of the Gothic wife was no hindrance to Gaiseric, and a pretext for repudiating her was easily found. She was accused of having plotted to poison him.[2] She was punished by the mutilation of her ears and nose, and in this plight she was sent back to her father. The incident meant undying enmity between Visigoth and Vandal. Theoderic soon sought a new ally by marrying another daughter to Rechiar, king of the Suevians (A.D. 449).[3] Huneric was free to contract a more dazzling matrimonial alliance with an Imperial princess.

We are not informed whether in the treaty of A.D. 442 any provision was made for supplying Italy with the corn of Africa on which the Romans had subsisted for centuries. In the absence of evidence to the contrary, we may safely assume that, throughout the duration of the Vandal kingdom, the surplus of the corn production of Africa was consumed as of old in

---

[1] It was prior to 446, the year of the third consulship of Aetius, for Merobaudes refers to it in his poem on that occasion, *Pan.* ii. 27 *sqq.* :

nunc hostem exutus pactis proprioribus
    arsit
Romanam uincire fidem Latiosque
    parentes
adnumerare sibi sociamque intexere
    prolem.

In an earlier poem of Merobaudes (*Carm.* i. 17) the future marriage of the child princess is touched on.

[2] Jordanes, *Get.* 184.

[3] Hydatius, who mentions that in the same year he helped his son-in-law to capture Ilerda (140, 142).

Italy (except, perhaps, in the few years in which there were open hostilities); only now instead of being a tribute it was an export.[1] It was obviously to the interest of the Vandal proprietors to send the grain they did not want to Italian markets.

The Vandals themselves settled in Zeugitana, and made Carthage their capital. They appropriated the lands of the proprietors in this province, who, unless they migrated else-where, were probably degraded to the position of serfs. The Vandals, as Arians, had from the very beginning assumed a definitely hostile attitude to the Catholic creed. When Carthage was taken the Catholic clergy were banished, and all the churches of the city were given up to Arian worship. The independent attitude of the Vandals towards the Empire is reflected in their adopting a chronological era of their own, beginning on October 19, A.D. 439, the date of the capture of Carthage.

It is to be observed that the Vandals now held a position of vantage in regard to the Empire that none of the other Teutonic nations ever occupied. In relation to the foreign peoples of northern Europe, the front of the Roman Empire was the Rhine and the Danube. And so we may say that the Vandals had come round to the back of the Empire and were able to attack it from behind. Another exceptional feature in their position was that, in the language of a chronicler, the sea was made pervious to them : they created a fleet of small light cruisers and attacked the Empire by sea, as no other Teutonic people had done or was to do in the Mediterranean, though the Saxons and other men of the north used ships to harry it in the northern and western oceans. Thus they were able to follow in the track of the Carthaginians of old, and extend their dominion over the western islands.

Till after the death of Valentinian (A.D. 455) the naval expeditions of the Vandals seem to have been simply piratical,[2]

---

[1] A certain amount could be requisitioned in the old way from the Mauretanias so long as they remained in Roman hands. We may wonder how the African shipping corporations, whose offices are to be seen in the great square north of the theatre at Ostia (cp. Ashby, "Recent Excavations at Ostia," *J.R.S.* ii. (1912) 180), were affected by the changed circumstances.

[2] These depredations, which extended to the Aegean, are mentioned, A.D. 457, by Nestorius, *Book of Heraclides*, p. 331 : "Sicily, Rhodes, and many other great islands with Rome itself." Rome, however, was

though Gaiseric may have definitely formed the design of conquering Sicily. But soon after that year he seems to have occupied without resistance the two Mauretanian provinces which the Empire had retained under the treaty of A.D. 442, and to have annexed Sardinia, Corsica, and the Balearic Islands.[1] Sicily itself was to pass somewhat later under his dominion.

The military and diplomatic successes of Gaiseric encouraged and enabled him to encroach on the liberties of his people. Among all the ancient Germanic peoples, the sovran power resided in the assembly of the folk, and in the case of those which formed permanent states on Imperial soil, like the Franks and the Visigoths, it was only by degrees that the kings acquired great but not absolute power. In the Vandal state alone the free constitution was succeeded by an autocracy, without any intermediate stages. The usurpation by the king of unconstitutional powers occasioned a conspiracy of the nobles, and it was bloodily suppressed.[2] The old aristocracy seems to have been superseded by a new nobility who owed their position, not to birth, but to appointments in the royal service. It is probable that the assembly of the folk ceased to meet. Before his death Gaiseric issued a law regulating the succession to the throne,[3] thus depriving the people of the right of election, and the royal authority was so firmly established that his will was apparently accepted without demur. By this law the kingship was treated as a personal inheritance and was confined to Gaiseric's male descendants, of whom the eldest was always to succeed.

not attacked till 455. Other sources mention raids in Greece and southern Italy after 457 (Procopius, *B.V.* i. 5 ; Victor Vit. *Hist. pers.* i. 51).—There is no definite record that he troubled Sicily between 442 and 455. Pace (*I Barb. e Biz.* p. 12) thinks he did, and that the services which Cassiodorus performed in defending the coasts of Bruttii·and Sicily (Cassiod. *Var.* i. 4) are to be referred to that period. But they may be connected with the events of 440.

[1] Victor Vit. *op. cit.* i. 13.

[2] Prosper, *sub* 442. Cp. Schmidt, *op. cit.* 161.

[3] Procopius, *B.V.* i. 7. 29. Here it is not called a testament, but a law, *ib.* 9. 12 (*constitutio*, Victor Vit. *op. cit.* ii. 13). On this act cp. Schmidt, *ib.* 165. Gaiseric had already done

away with the sons and wife of his brother Gunderic (Victor, *ib.* 14). Neither Gaiseric nor his successor Huneric struck coins with their own names or busts (it is just possible that Huneric issued a bronze coin with his bust, but the attribution is uncertain). Gunthamund (484–496) struck silver, and all his successors silver and bronze, with names and busts. The Vandals seem to have made little use of a gold currency, and their gold coins are all of Imperial type. The large bronze coins, probably attributed to Gaiseric (issued perhaps, as Wroth suggests, about 435 when he captured Carthage), marked with XLII and XXI N(ummi), are remarkable as an anticipation of the *folles* of Anastasius (see below p. 444). See Wroth, *Coins of the Vandals, etc.* xvi. *sqq.*

The policy of Gaiseric differed entirely from that of the Goths in Gaul. He aimed at establishing a kingdom which should be free, so far as possible, from Roman influence, and he saw that, for this purpose, it was necessary above all to guard jealously the Arian faith of his people, and not expose them to the danger of being led away by the propaganda of the Catholics. He was therefore aggressively Arian, and persecuted the Catholic clergy.[1] He imposed the Arian creed on all persons who were in his own immediate environment. After the capture of Carthage he seized the Donatist bishop Quodvultdeus and other clergy, set them on board old and untrustworthy ships, and committed them to the mercy of the sea. They reached Italy safely. Throughout the proconsular province the bishops were expelled from their sees and stripped of their property. It was not till A.D. 454 that a new bishop was allowed to be ordained at Carthage, and some churches were reopened for Catholic worship. But after the death of Deogratias, at the end of three years, the old rigorous suppression was renewed; the sees were left vacant throughout the province, and the priests were forced to surrender their books and sacred vessels. The monasteries, however, were not suppressed. And the persecution was not general or ubiquitous. Particular persons were singled out and dealt with by the express order of the king. He did not give a free hand to his officers, and there were probably few cases of death or personal violence.

It was no less important for the ends of Gaiseric's policy to eliminate the power of the senatorial aristocracy. He did this by such drastic measures that a contemporary chronicler observed, " It is impossible to say whether his hostility to men or to God was the more bitter." He deprived of their domains the nobles of the proconsular province, and told them to betake themselves elsewhere. They were not to be suffered to remain lords of the soil to organise an opposition to the king, and gradually to recover political influence under his successors. If they remained in the land they were threatened with perpetual slavery. After the capture of Carthage most of the senators had been compelled to leave the shores of Africa, some sailing to Italy,

---

[1] The chief sources are Victor Vit. *Hist. pers.* bk. i. ; Prosper, *sub* 437, 439 ; Theodoret, *Epp.* 52, 53 (*P.G.* 83). The details are recounted in Martroye, *Genséric*, 328 *sqq.*

others to the East.[1] In the other parts of his realm Gaiseric does not appear to have adopted such extreme measures. He deemed it sufficient to make the royal capital and the central province safe.

§ 5. *Ravenna*

The Empress Galla Placidia, who had been supreme ruler in the west for about ten years, and for fifteen more had probably exercised some influence on the direction of affairs, died at Rome in A.D. 450.[2] But her memory will always be associated with Ravenna, where the Imperial court generally resided [3] and where she was buried in the mausoleum which she had built to receive her ashes.

Honorius had done one memorable thing which altered the course of history. He made the fortune of Ravenna. To escape the dangers of the German invasions he had moved his government and court from Milan to the retired city of the marshes, which amid its lagoons and islands could defy an enemy more confidently than any other city in the peninsula, and, as events proved, could hardly be captured except by a maritime blockade. Before Augustus it had been an obscure provincial town, noted chiefly for its want of fresh water, but had served as a useful refuge to Caesar before he crossed the Rubicon. Augustus had chosen it to be a naval station, and had supplied it with a good harbour, Classis, three miles from the town, with which he connected it by a solid causeway across the lagoons. But nothing seemed more unlikely than that it should overshadow Milan and vie with Rome as the leading city in Italy. Through the act of Honorius, which though conceived in fear turned out to be an act of good policy, Ravenna became the home of emperors, kings, and viceroys, and throughout the vicissitudes of four centuries of crowded history was a name almost as familiar as Rome itself in the European world.

Ravenna has no natural amenities. Here are the impressions the place produced on a visitor from Gaul not many years after

---

[1] See *Vita Fulgentii*, c. 1 ; Theodoret, *Epp.* 29-36; Prosper, *sub* 539.

[2] Nov. 27, Prosper, *sub a.*

[3] All the laws during her regency—they are not numerous—were issued from Ravenna. Valentinian lived both at Rome and at Ravenna ; during the last years of his reign, after his mother's death, almost entirely at Rome.

Placidia's death.[1] " The Po divides the city, part flowing
through, part round the place. It is diverted from its main
bed by the State dykes, and is thence led in diminished volume
through derivative channels, the two halves so disposed that
one encompasses and moats the walls, the other penetrates
and brings them trade—an admirable arrangement for commerce
in general, and that of provisions in particular. But the draw-
back is that, with water all about us, we could not quench our
thirst ; there was neither pure-flowing aqueduct, nor filterable
cistern, nor trickling source, nor unclouded well. On the one
side the salt tides assail the gates ; on the other, the movement
of vessels stirs the filthy sediment in the canals, or the sluggish
flow is fouled by the bargemen's poles, piercing the bottom
slime." " In that marsh the laws of everything are always the
wrong way about ; the waters stand and the walls fall, the towers
float and the ships stick fast, the sick man walks, and the doctor
lies abed, the baths are chill and the houses blaze, the dead
swim and the quick are dry, the powers are asleep and the thieves
wide awake, the clergy live by usury and the Syrian chants the
psalms, business-men turn soldiers and soldiers business-men,
old fellows play ball and young fellows hazard, eunuchs take to
arms and rough allies to letters."

In this description the writer remarks the presence of the
Syrian, a familiar figure to him in the cities of southern Gaul.
But it was not only oriental traders whom the new Imperial
residence attracted. It is probable that artistic craftsmen from
Syria and Anatolia came to embellish the city of Honorius and
Placidia, and to teach their craft to native artists. For it is
difficult otherwise to explain the oriental inspiration which so
conspicuously distinguishes the Ravennate school of art that it
has been described as " half-Syrian." [2]

It was indeed in the artistic works with which its successive
rulers enriched it that the great attraction of Ravenna lay and
still lies. Many of these monuments have perished, but many
have been preserved, and they show vividly the development
of Christian art in Italy in the fifth and sixth centuries, under
the auspices of Placidia, Theoderic, and Justinian, under the
influence of the East. Brick was generally the material of

---

[1] Sidonius Apollinaris, *Epp.* i. 5 (A.D. 467) and 8 (A.D. 468), Dalton's translation.
[2] Dalton, *Byz. Art*, p. 8.

these buildings, but their unimpressive exterior appearance was compensated by the rich decoration inside and the brilliant mosaics which shone on the walls. Ravenna is the city of mosaics. At Rome we have from the fourth and early fifth centuries fine examples of this form of pictorial art in the churches of S. Costanza and S. Pudenziana and S. Maria Maggiore,[1] but at Ravenna, in the days of Placidia, the art of painting with coloured cubes seems to enter upon a new phase and achieve more brilliant effects.[2]

No trace remains of the Imperial palace of the Laurelwood, but the churches of St. John the Evangelist and St. Agatha, the Oratory of St. Peter Chrysologus,[3] the Baptistery, and the little chapel dedicated to SS. Nazarius and Celsus which was built to receive the sarcophagi of the Imperial family, are all monuments of the epoch of Placidia.[4] The basilica of St. John was the accomplishment of a vow which the Empress had made to the saint when she and her two children were in peril of ship-wreck on the Hadriatic.[5] The story of their experiences was

[1] The Basilica Liberiana, built by Pope Liberius on the Esquiline in the fourth century, was dedicated by Pope Sixtus III. to St. Mary c. A.D. 432 and perhaps partly rebuilt. The dating of the mosaics has been much debated. Richter and Taylor contend that the mosaics of the nave are pre-Constantinian, in their *Golden Age of Classic Christian Art*. All previous studies of the Church have been superseded by Wilpert's magnificent work *Die röm. Mosaiken . . . vom iv. bis xiii. Jahrhundert* (see Bibliography), where the pictures can be studied in coloured reproductions. His conclusion is (vol. i. 412 *sqq.*) that the mosaics of the nave belong to the time of Liberius, those of the triumphal arch to that of Sixtus.

[2] The blue and gold backgrounds strongly contrast with the pale effects at Rome.

[3] He became archbishop of Ravenna in 433 and was succeeded by Neon either in 449 or 458. His monogram in mosaic survives in one of the arches in his chapel. The source for the early ecclesiastical history of Ravenna is Agnellus, *Lib. Pont.* (ninth century).

[4] For the architecture of the churches of this period Rivoira (*Lombardic Arch.* i. 21-39) supersedes

previous studies. Structurally the Ravennate architects represent the Roman traditions. It is in the decoration that the oriental influence reveals itself. For the mosaics and sculptures see Diehl, *Ravenne*; Dalton, *op. cit.*

[5] The dedicatory inscription is preserved (*Galla Placidia cum filio suo Placido Valentiniano Augusto et filia sua Iusta Grata Honoria Augusta liberationis periculum maris votum solve[ru]nt*; Agnellus, *ib.* p. 68. *C.I.L.* xi. 276). The incident may have occurred on the voyage from Italy to an Illyrian port in 423. But I conjecture that the same storm which dispersed the ships of Arda-burius, drove the Empress and her children back to the Dalmatian coast, and they then proceeded by land to Aquileia (see above, p. 223). As it is not likely that Placidia delayed the fulfilment of her vow, we may place the building and inscription in 426-427. Another inscription is recorded (De Rossi, ii. 1. 435), in which Honoria is associated with her mother and brother (and which must therefore be prior to 437) dedicating the church of Santa Crux in Hierusalem at Rome, and probably in fulfilment of the same vow (*Sanctae ecclesiae Hierusalem*

depicted on the pavement and the walls, but all the original decorations of the church have perished.[1] The Baptistery may have been begun in the lifetime of Placidia, but appears not to have been completed till after her death by the archbishop Neon. It is an octagonal building, with two tiers of round arches springing from columns, inside, crowned by a hemispherical dome, of which it has been observed that " the ancient world affords no instance of so wide a vault constructed of tapering tubes." [2] The mosaics of the Baptistery and of Placidia's mausoleum have been wonderfully well preserved. The mausoleum, constructed about A.D. 440, is in the form of a small Latin cross, of which the centre is surmounted by a square tower closed by a conical dome.[3] Here the artist in mosaics has achieved a signal triumph in the harmonious effects of his colours. The cupola is a heaven of exquisite blue, dotted with golden stars and arabesques, and in the midst a great cross of gold. Above the door and facing it are two pictures, one perhaps of St. Laurence, the other of the Good Shepherd, but not the simple Shepherd of the Catacombs, bearing a sheep on his shoulder.[4] Here he is seated on a rock in a meadow where six sheep are feeding, his tunic is golden, his cloak purple, his head, which suggests that of a Greek god, is surrounded by a golden halo.

Into this charming chapel Placidia removed the remains of her brother Honorius and her husband Constantius, and it was her own resting-place. The marble sarcophagus of Honorius is on the right, that of Constantius, in which the body of Valentinian III. was afterwards laid, on the left. Her own sarcophagus of alabaster stands behind the altar, and her embalmed body in Imperial robes seated on a chair of cypress wood could be seen through a hole in the back till A.D. 1577, when all the contents

---

Valentinianus Placidia et Honoria Augusti votum solverunt).
[1] The Ravennate school of builders were fond of the motive of arcading. The walls of both St. John and St. Agatha are externally decorated with blank arcades resting on a plinth (Rivoira, *ib.* 21-22). Again we find small arcades, springing from corbels between pilasters, on the Baptistery, the chapel of Chrysologus, and the church of St. Francesco (begun in A.D. 450), used to form a sort of fringe below the cornice (*ib.* 36-37).

[2] *Ib.* 39.

[3] Rivoira writes (*ib.* 28) : " So far as I am aware there is no record of churches or tombs older than this mausoleum having the form of a Latin cross, with rectangular extended arms and not mere apses opposite to one another, and starting directly from the central space." The portico in front of the mausoleum connected it with the basilica of the Holy Cross, which was built about 449.

[4] Cp. Diehl, *op. cit.* p. 50.

of the tomb were accidentally burned through the carelessness of children.[1]

The coins of the Empress show a conventional face, like those of her daughter and of the other Imperial ladies of the age. They do not portray her actual features, nor can we form any very distinct impression of her appearance from a gold medallion of which two specimens are preserved.[2]

[1] See Hodgkin, *Italy and her Invaders*, i. 888. — The surviving mosaics of the Placidian period, in the tomb and the baptistery, are only a small portion of the artistic work which then adorned the churches of Ravenna. Besides the mosaics of St. John, those of the cathedral (built in the early years of Honorius, before 410), St. Agatha, St. Laurence, the Holy Cross have disappeared. Cp. the list in Dalton, *op. cit.* 365. The mosaics of the palace may have been carried off to Aachen to adorn the palace of Charles the Great.

[2] Cp. Delbrück, *Porträts byz. Kais.* 375. The legend *salus reipublicae* suggests a date in the last years of Honorius.—On a stamped silver ingot, found north of Minden and now in the Hanover Museum, there is an impression of three Imperial heads, which have been supposed to be Valentinian III., Theodosius II., and Placidia. Babelon, *Traité des monnaies gr. et rom.* i. p. 887.

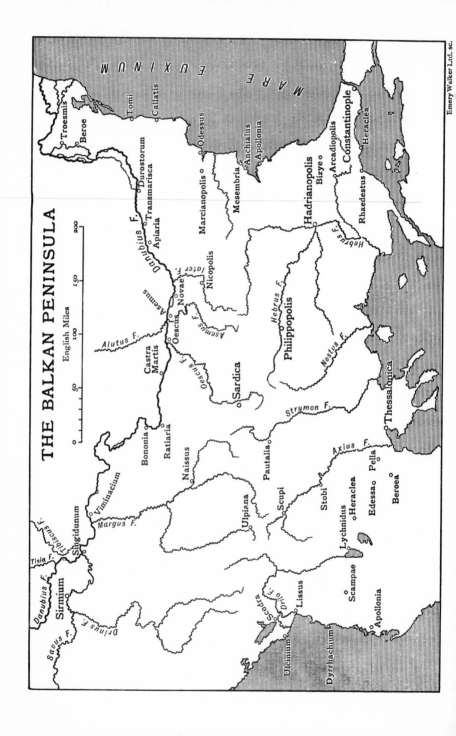

THE BALKAN PENINSULA

English Miles

Emery Walker Ltd. sc.

CHAPTER IX

THE EMPIRE OF ATTILA

§ 1. *The Geography of the Balkan Peninsula*

THE misfortunes of the Balkan Peninsula have been almost uninterrupted from the fourth century to the present day. In the fifth and sixth centuries their plight was almost unendurable. They suffered not only from the terrible raids of nomad savages who had come from beyond the Volga, but also from the rapacious cruelty of the Germans. From the reign of Valens to that of Heraclius the unhappy inhabitants might any morning wake up to find a body of barbarians at their gates. As we shall be concerned in these volumes with the successive invasions of Huns, Ostrogoths, Slavs, and Bulgars, it will be well for the reader to have a general idea of the conformation and geography of the peninsula.[1]

We may consider Mount Vitoš, and the town of Sardica, now Sofia, which lies at its base as the central point. Rising in the shape of an immense cone to a height of 7500 feet, Vitoš affords to the climber who ascends it a splendid view of the various intricate mountain chains which diversify the surrounding lands—a view which has been pronounced finer than that at Tempe or that at Vodena. In the group of which this mountain and another named Ryl, to southward, are the highest peaks, two

---

[1] The following works have been useful: Jireček, *Die Gesch. der Bulgaren* and *Die Heerstrasse v. Belgrad nach Constantinopel*; Evans, *Antiquarian Researches in Illyricum*, with good sketch maps; W. Tomaschek, *Haemus - halbinsel* (in *S.B.* of Vienna Acad. 1881); F. Kanitz, *Römische Studien in Serbien* (*Denksch.* of Vienna Acad., ph.-hist. Kl. xli., 1892); Kiepert, *Formae orbis antiqui*, Map xvii. *Illyricum et Thracia*; the maps in *C.I.L.* vol. iii. There is a good military map of Serbia, Montenegro, and Albania, attached to an article of O. Kreutzbruck v. Lilienfels, in Petermanns *Mitteilungen*, Nov. 1912.

rivers of the lower Danube system, the Oescus (Isker) and the Nišava have their sources, as well as the two chief rivers of the Aegean system, the Hebrus (Maritsa) and the Strymon (Struma).

From this central region stretches in a south-easterly direction the double chain of Rhodope, cleft in twain by the valley of the Nestos (Mesta). The easterly range, Rhodope proper, forms the western boundary of the great plain of Thrace, while the range of Orbelos separates the Nestos valley from the Strymon valley.

The Haemus or Balkan chain which runs from west to east is also double, like Rhodope, but is not divided by a large river. The Haemus mountains begin near the sources of the Timacus (Timok) and the Margus (Morava), from which they stretch to the shores of the Euxine. To a traveller approaching them from the northern or Danubian side they do not present an impressive appearance, for the ascent is very gradual; plateau rises above plateau, or the transition is accomplished by gentle slopes, and the height of the highest parts is lost through the number of intervening degrees. But on the southern side the descent is precipitous, and the aspect is imposing and sublime. This contrast between the two sides of the Haemus range is closely connected with the existence of the second and lower parallel range, called the Srêdna Gora, which runs through Roumelia from Sofia to Sliven. It seems as if a convulsion of the earth had cloven asunder an original and large chain by a sudden rent, which gave its abrupt and sheer character to the southern side of the Haemus mountains, and interrupted the gradual upward incline from the low plain of Thrace.

The chain of Srêdna Gora, which is not to be confused with the northern chain of Haemus, is divided into three parts, which may be distinguished as the Karadža Dagh, the Srêdna Gora, and the Ichtimaner. The Karadža Dagh mountains are the most easterly, and are separated from Srêdna Gora by the river Strêma (a tributary of the Maritsa), while the valley of the Tundža (Taenarus), with its fields of roses and pleasantly situated towns, divides it from Mount Haemus. Srêdna Gora reaches a greater height than the mountains to east or to west, and is divided by the river Topolnitsa from the most westerly portion, the Ichtimaner mountains, which connect the Balkan system with the Rhodope system, whilst at the same time they are the watershed between the tributaries of the Hebrus and those of the Danube.

There are eight chief passes across the Haemus range from Lower Moesia to southern Thrace. If we begin from the eastern extremity, there is the coast pass which a traveller would take who, starting from Odessus (Varna), wished to reach Anchialus. The next pass was one of the most important. It crossed the Kamcija at Pannysus, and through it ran the road from Trajan's Marcianopolis (near Provad, between Šumla and Varna) southward. Farther west were the two adjacent passes of Veregava and Verbits (together known as the Gylorski pass).[1] Passing over the Kotel and Vratniti passes, which seem to have been little used for military purposes in the period which concerns us, we come to the celebrated pass of Šipka which connects the valley of the Jatrus (Jantra) with that of the Tundža. Through it ran the direct road from Novae (Šistova) on the Danube to Beroe (Stara Zagora), Philippopolis, and Hadrianople.

From this pass eastward extend the wildest regions of the Balkans, which have always been the favourite home of outlaws —scamars, as they were called, or klephts—who could defy law in thick forests and inaccessible ravines, regions echoing with the songs and romances of outlaw life.

The traveller from Novae or Oescus (at Gigen, at the mouth of the river Isker) could also reach Philippopolis by the pass of Trojan, close to the sources of the river Asemus (Osma). Finally the long pass of Succi lay on the road from Sardica to Constantinople.

The journey from Singidunum to Constantinople along the main road was reckoned as 670 Roman miles. Singidunum (Belgrade), situated at the junction of the Save with the Danube, was the principal city of the province of Upper Moesia, and was close to the frontier between the eastern and western divisions of the Empire. The road ran at first along the right shore of the Danube, passing Margus (near the village of Dubravica, where the Margus or Morava joins the greater river), till it reached,

---

[1] Veregava is now called the Rish pass, and is to be identified with the Iron Gate of Greek historians. These routes became important in the eighth century when the Bulgarians had built their royal capital at Aboba, near Šumla; for they connected it directly with the towns of Marcellae (Karnobad) and Diampolis (Jambol on the Tundža).

ten miles from the Viminacium (close to Kostolats), an important station of the Danube flotilla. Here the traveller, instead of pursuing the eastward road to Durostorum (Silistria), turned southward and again reached the Morava at the town of Horreum Margi, one of the chief factories of arms in the peninsula. The next important town was Naissus (Niš), on the north bank of the Nišava, so strongly fortified that hitherto no enemy had ever captured it. To-day it is the junction of railways, in old days it was the junction of many roads. The Byzantium route continued south-eastward, passing Remesiana (Ak Palanka) to Sardica, the chief town of the province of Dacia Mediterranea, beautifully situated in the large oval plain, under the great mountains, Vitoš on the west and Ryl to the south. From here south-westward ran a road to Ulpia Pautalia (Küstendil) and Dyrrhachium. The traveller pressing to Constantinople, when he left the plain of Sardica, ascended to the pass of Succi in the Ichtimaner mountains. This pass was considered the key of Thrace and was strongly fortified. Descending from this defile the road followed the left bank of the Hebrus to Philippopolis (the chief city of the province of Thracia), standing on its three great syenite rocks, with a magnificent view of Mount Rhodope to the south-west. From Philippopolis to Hadrianople (the capital of the province of Haemimontus) was a journey of six days. On the way one passed the fort of Arzus, on a river of the same name (probably the Uzundža). Hadrianople lies at the junction of three rivers ; here the Tonzus (Tundža) from the north, and the Artiscus (Arda) from the south, flow into the Hebrus. Another journey of six days brought the traveller to the shore of the Propontis. He passed Arcadiopolis (Lüle Burgas) the ancient Bergule, which the Emperor Arcadius had renamed, on a tributary of the river Erginus.[1] He passed Drusipara (near Karištaran), from which a road led northward to Anchialus on the Black Sea. Then he came to Tzurulon (Corlu), and at last to Heraclea (the old Samian colony of Perinthus) on the sea, now a miserable village. Here the road joined the road from Dyrrhachium and Thessalonica, and the rest of the way ran close to the seashore, past Selymbria [2] and the fort of Athyras (near

---

[1] Not far away was the port of Vrysis, now Bunar Hissar.

[2] Arcadius renamed it Eudoxiopolis in honour of his wife, but the new name, like so many other names of the kind, soon fell out of use, though it appears in the *Synecdemus* of Hierocles.

Boyuk-Chekmedže) and Rhegium (at Kuchuk-Chekmedže), to the Golden Gate, which the traveller who tarried not on his way would reach on the thirty-first day after he had left Singidunum.[1]

When we turn to the western half of the Peninsula, the lands of Illyria and Macedonia, we find an irregular network of mountains, compared with which the configuration of Thrace is simple. In these highlands there are no great plains, and perhaps the first thing to be grasped is that the rivers which water them belong to the systems of the Black Sea and the Aegean, except in the south-west where the Drin and other smaller streams fall into the Hadriatic. Thus the line of water-shed between the western and eastern seas runs near the Hadriatic as far as Montenegro and then follows an irregular direction eastward to the range of Scardus (Šar Dagh), which divides the streams that feed the Drilo (Drin) from the western tributaries of the Vardar. The Alpine lands of Dalmatia, using this name in its ancient and wider meaning, are watered by the river Drinus (Drina) and other tributaries of the Save. They are inhospitable and were thinly inhabited and their chief value lay in their mineral wealth.[2] The principal roads connecting these highlands with the Hadriatic were those from Jader (Zara) to Siscia on the Save, and from Salona to Ad Matricem, which corresponds to the modern Sarajevo though it is not on the same site.

The Drina is the western boundary of modern Serbia which answers roughly to the ancient provinces of Moesia prima, Dacia mediterranea, and Dardania. In the centre of this country is the high range known as Kopaonik (mountain of Mines), which with the Yastrebac Planina and the Petrova Gora forms a huge triangle round which the two great branches of the river Morava flow in many curves and windings. The western branch is now known as the Ibar in its upper course and the eastern is sometimes called the Bulgarian Morava.[3]

The three places marked out to be the most important inland centres in Illyricum were Naissus, Scupi (Uskub), and Ulpiana. We have seen that the great road from Constantinople to

---

[1] From Aquileia the distance was calculated as 47 days. For a pilgrim to Jerusalem walking from Burdigala (Bordeaux) by Aquileia and Singidunum, the distance to Byzantium was 112 days. See the full description of the route in Jireček, *Die Heerstrasse.*

[2] Especially iron and gold. Statius uses *Dalmaticum metallum* as a name for gold (*Silvae*, i. 2. 154). For the whole subject of the Illyrian mine-fields see Evans, *op. cit.* iii. 6, *sqq.*

[3] Also known as the Binačka.

Singidunum and the west passed Naissus, which lay near the right bank of the western branch of the Margus. Another road connected Naissus directly with Ratiaria (Widin) on the Danube, while south-westward it was linked by a route passing over the Prepolać saddle with Ulpiana,[1] which was on the site of the modern village of Lipljan but corresponded in importance to Priština. This town was situated at the southern end of the Kossovo Polje, a plain about twenty miles long, famous as a battlefield in the later Middle Ages. Through this plain ran a road to Ad Matricem which passed Arsa, close to the modern Novipazar, and then turning westward continued its course by Plevlje and Goradža. Two other roads converged at Ulpiana, one from Scupi, which followed the course of the Lepenac, a tributary of the Vardar, and crossed the Kačanik Pass. The other road led to the Hadriatic : crossing the hills it emerged in the open country watered by the upper streams of the Drilo, and known as Metochia, from which it descended to Scodra (Scutari), whence the coast was reached either at Ulcinium (Dulcigno) or at Lissus (Alessio).

Scupi lay on the great road through the valley of the Vardar which brought Thessalonica into communication with the central districts of Illyricum and the Danube. From this centre Naissus could be reached not only by the Kačanik Pass and Ulpiana, but also by another road which skirted the mountains of Kara Dagh and followed the course of the western Margus. The most important station between Thessalonica and Scupi was Stobi, where a north-eastward road diverged to Pautalia and Sardica, while a cross-road connected Stobi with Heraclea (Monastir).

The land communication of Constantinople and Thessalonica with the ports on the Hadriatic was by the great Via Egnatia.[2] Westward of Thessalonica this road ran through western Macedonia and Epirus by Pella, Edessa (Vodena), Heraclea, Lychnidus (Ochrida), Scampae (El Basan), and Clodiana, where it diverged in a northerly direction to Dyrrhachium and in a southerly to Apollonia and Aulon (Valona).[3]

---

[1] Afterwards Justiniana secunda.

[2] See Tafel, De via mil. Rom. Egnatia.

[3] The provincial divisions of the Dioceses of Thrace and Dacia may here be enumerated. The D. of Thrace (which belonged to the Prefecture of the East) contained six provinces, two north and four south of the Haemus range. The northern were : (1) Lower Moesia—towns : Marcianopolis, Odessus, Durostorum, Novae, Nicopolis (Nicup) ; (2) Scythia (corresponding to the Dobrudža)—towns : Tomi (near Constanza), Callatis

Throughout the greater part of the peninsula, north of the Egnatian Way, Latin had become the general language when the Roman conquest was consolidated,[1] except in Thrace south of Mount Haemus and the southern towns of Macedonia near the coast-line, where the Greek tongue continued to be spoken.

§ 2. *The Hun Invasions of the Balkan Peninsula* (A.D. 441–448)

At the beginning of the reign of Theodosius an invasion of the peninsula by a host of Huns was a prelude and a warning. They were led by Uldin, who boasted that he could subdue the whole earth or even the sun. He captured Castra Martis,[2] but as he advanced against Thrace he was deserted by a large multitude of his followers, who joined the Romans in driving their king beyond the Danube. The Romans followed up their victory by defensive precautions. The strong cities in Illyricum were fortified, and new walls were built to protect Byzantium ; the fleet on the Danube was increased and improved. But a payment of money was a more effectual barrier against the barbarians than walls, and about A.D. 424 Theodosius consented to pay 350 lbs. of gold to King Rugila.

The tribes of the Huns were ruled each by its own chieftain, but Rugila seems to have brought together all the tribes into a

(Mangalia), Tropaeum (Adamclissi). The southern were : (3) south-eastern, *Europa*—towns : Selymbria, Heraclea, Arcadiopolis, Bizye ; (4) south-western, *Rhodope* — towns : Aenus, Traianopolis, Maroneia, Rusion ; (5) north-western, *Thrace*—towns : Philippopolis, Beroe ; (6) north-eastern, *Haemimontus*—towns : Hadrianople, Anchialus. The *D. of Dacia* contained five provinces : (1) *Upper Moesia*—towns : Singidunum, Viminacium, Margum ; (2) *Dacia ripensis*—towns : Bononia, Ratiaria, Castra Martis, Oescus (Gigen); (3) *Dacia mediterranea* — towns : Sardica, Naissus, Pautalia (Küstendil), Remesiana (Ak-Palanka); (4) *Dardania*—towns : Scupi, Ulpiana ; (5) *Praevalitana* — towns : Scodra, Lissus. The *D. of Macedonia* contained besides (1) *Thessaly*, (2) *Achaea*, (3) *Crete*, the provinces of (4) *Macedonia Prima*—towns : Thessalonica, Pella, Beroea, Edessa, (5) *Macedonia Secunda* (*Salutaris*)—towns : Stobi, Heraclea ; (6) *Old Epirus*—towns : Nicopolis, Dodona ; (7) *New Epirus*—towns : Dyrrhachium, Scampae, Apollonia, Aulon.

[1] That Latin prevailed in the central and northern provinces there are many indications. For instance, the bishop of Marcianopolis used it in his correspondence with the Council of Chalcedon. Priscus in describing his journey to the court of Attila (see below, p. 283) says that Latin was the language everywhere. Nicetas, bishop of Remesiana (in the fourth century), who converted the Thracian Bessi, was a Latin writer. The Emperor Justinian, a native of Dardania, speaks of Latin as his own language. The first traces of the development of Latin into Roumanian are found in the sixth century.

[2] On the Danube, near Oescus.

sort of political unity.[1] He had established himself between the
Theiss and the Danube. The treaty which the government of
Ravenna made with Rugila, when the Huns withdrew from Italy
in A.D. 425 after the subjugation of the tyrant John, seems to
have included the provision that the Huns should evacuate the
Pannonian province of Valeria which they had occupied for
forty-five years.[2] But soon afterwards a new arrangement was
made by which another part of Pannonia was surrendered to
them, apparently districts on the Lower Save,[3] but not including
Sirmium. We may conjecture that this concession was made by
Aetius in return for Rugila's help in A.D. 433.[4]

Rugila died soon after this,[5] and he was succeeded by his
nephews Bleda and Attila,[6] the sons of Mundiuch, as joint rulers.
Bleda played no part on the stage of history. Attila was a
leading actor for twenty years, and his name is still almost a
household word. He was not well favoured. His features,
according to a Gothic historian, " bore the stamp of his origin ;
and the portrait of Attila exhibited the genuine deformity of a
modern Kalmuck : a large head, a swarthy complexion, small,
deep-seated eyes, a flat nose, a few hairs in the place of a beard,
broad shoulders, and a short square body of nervous strength
though of a disproportioned form. The haughty step and de-
meanour of the king of the Huns expressed the consciousness of
his superiority above the rest of mankind, and he had the custom of
fiercely rolling his eyes as if he wished to enjoy the terror which
he inspired." [7] He was versed in all the arts of diplomacy, but

---

[1] About 430 there seems to have
been at least three Hun kings—
Rugila, his brother Mundiuch, and
Octar (probably another brother).
Socrates, vii. 30; Jordanes, *Get.* 105.

[2] Marcellinus, *Chron.*, *sub* 427.

[3] Priscus, *fr.* 5, *De leg. gent.* p. 579
τὴν πρὸς τῷ Σάῳ ποταμῷ Παιόνων
χώραν. I am sure that Mommsen and
others are wrong in assuming that the
province of Savia is meant. The words
can equally apply to the parts of
Pannonia Secunda west and north of
Sirmium, between the Save and
Drave, districts which (like Valeria)
were only separated by the Danube
from Hunland. I am inclined to
suspect that Valeria was again handed
over to the Huns at the same time.

[4] See above p. 248.

[5] According to Socrates, vii. 33 (cp.
Theodoret, *H.E.* v. 37), he was killed
by lightning in an invasion of Thrace.

[6] The indications are that Bleda was
older than Attila, cp. *Chron. Gall.*
(A.D. 434), p. 660 *Rugila rex Chunorum,
cum quo pax firmata, moritur cui
Bleda successit*; Marcellinus, *sub*
442, *Bleda et Attila.* Bleda is the
historical prototype of Blödel, as
Attila is of Etzel, in the Nibelungen
Lied.

[7] Gibbon, iii. p. 443, after Jordanes,
Get. 182. For Attila and his relations
and wars with the Empire the main
source was the History of Priscus. Of
this we have one long and a good
many small fragments ; but we have
a great deal of important matter
derived from Priscus, through Cassiodorus, in Jordanes.

the chief aim of his policy was plunder.   He was far less cruel
than the great Mongolian conqueror of the thirteenth century,
Chingiz Khan, with whom he has sometimes been compared ; he
was capable of pity and could sometimes pardon his enemies.

Attila had some reason for his haughty disdain if he could
trace his line of ancestry back for a thousand years and was
directly descended from the great chieftains of the Hiung-nu,[1]
whose names have been recorded by early Chinese writers.   And
if we accept this descent as a genuine tradition, we can infer
that he was not of pure Turkish blood.   Some of his forefathers
had married Chinese princesses, and there may also have been
an admixture of the blood of Indo-Scythians.[2]

At the beginning of the new reign several points of dispute
which had arisen between Rugila and Theodosius were settled.
The settlement was entirely to the advantage of the Huns.   The
Imperial government undertook to double the annual payment,
which was thus raised to 700 lbs. of gold ; not to receive Hun
deserters ; to surrender all those who had already deserted ; to
restore or pay a ransom for Roman prisoners who had escaped ;
not to form an alliance with any barbarian people at war with
the Huns ; and to place no restrictions on the trade between
the two peoples.   The prohibition of receiving fugitives from
Attila's empire was particularly important, because the
Roman army was largely recruited from barbarians beyond the
Danube.

During the early years of his reign, from A.D. 434 to 441, he
seems to have been engaged in extending his power in the east
towards the Caucasian Mountains.   But in A.D. 441 an irresistible
opportunity offered itself for attacking the provinces of Theodosius, for in that year the Imperial armies were engaged in
operations against both the Vandals and the Persians.

He condescended to allege reasons for his aggression.   He
complained that the tribute had not been regularly paid, and

---

[1] See above, Chap. IV. p. 101.

[2] The pedigree is preserved in John
of Thurócz, *Chronica Hungarorum*, in
Schwandtner's *Script. rer. Hung.* i.
p. 81, and has been discussed and
compared with Chinese records in the
interesting inquiry of Hirth, *Die
Ahnentafel Attilas.*   In this list
Bendegus or *Bendeguck* appears as

Attila's father, and Hirth gives reasons
for believing that it is the same name
as Mundiuch of the Greek sources.
He also seems to succeed in identifying
the names of some of the remoter
ancestors of the list with the names
of Hiung - nu chiefs (between 209
and 60 B.C.) mentioned in Chinese
documents.

that deserters had not been restored. When the Imperial government disregarded his complaints,[1] he appeared on the Danube and laid siege to Ratiaria. Here Roman ambassadors arrived to remonstrate with him for breaking the peace. He replied by alleging that the bishop of Margus had entered the land of the Huns and robbed treasures from the tombs of their kings, and he demanded the surrender of these treasures as well as of deserters. The negotiations broke down, and, having captured and plundered Ratiaria, the Hunnic horsemen rode up the course of the Danube to take the great towns on its banks. Viminacium and Singidunum itself were overwhelmed in the onslaught. Margus, which faces Constantia on the opposite side of the river, fell by treachery; the same bishop whom Attila accused as a grave-robber betrayed a Roman town and its Christian inhabitants to the cruelty of the heathen destroyer. Advancing up the valley of the Margus, the invaders halted before the walls of Naissus, and though the inhabitants made a brave defence, the place yielded to the machines of Attila and the missiles of a countless host. Then the marauders rode south-eastward and approached Constantinople. He did not venture to attack the capital, but he took Philippopolis and Arcadiopolis and the fort of Athyras.[2]

The strong fortress of Asemus on the Danube, in Lower Moesia,[3] won high praise for its valiant resistance to Hunnic squadrons, which separating from the main body had invaded Lower Moesia. They besieged Asemus, and the garrison so effectually harassed them by sallies that they were forced to retreat. A successful defence was not enough for the men of Asemus. Their scouts discovered the times when plundering bands were returning to the camp with spoils, and these moments were seized by the garrison, who unexpectedly assailed these small bodies of Huns and rescued many Roman prisoners.

The Imperial troops, which had been operating against the Persians and the Vandals, must have been available for operations against the Huns in A.D. 442 or 443, but it is not recorded

---

[1] Cp. Güldenpenning, op. cit. p. 341. The sources for these invasions of Attila in 441–448 are fragments of Priscus (De leg. gent., fr. 1-6; De leg. Rom., fr. 2-5; and fr. 2 in F.H.G., v. p. 25); Marcellinus; Chron. Pasch. (ultimate source: Priscus).

[2] Theophanes, A.M. 5942. Güldenpenning, ib. p. 344.

[3] Asamum near Nicopoli. The name is preserved in that of the river Osma, which flows into the Danube near the place. See C.I.L. iii. p. 141.

that Aspar or Areobindus took the field when they returned
from Persia and Sicily. We hear that a battle was fought in
the Thracian Chersonese and that Attila was victorious, and after
this a peace was negotiated by Anatolius (A.D. 443). The terms
were humiliating for the Emperor. Henceforward the annual
Hun-tribute of 700 lbs. of gold was to be trebled, and an additional
payment of 6000 lbs. was to be made at once. All Hun deserters
were to be surrendered to Attila, while Roman deserters were
to be handed over to the Emperor for a payment of ten solidi
a head.

Hitherto the realm of the Huns had been divided between
the two brothers, Bleda and Attila. Of Bleda's government
and deeds we hear nothing. We may conjecture that he ruled
in the east, from the Lower Danube to the Volga, and Attila
in the west. Soon after the Peace of Anatolius, Attila found
means to put Bleda to death and unite all the Huns and vassal
peoples under his own sway. For the next nine years (A.D.
444–453) he was the most powerful man in Europe.

The Illyrian and Thracian provinces enjoyed a respite from
invasion for three years. But in A.D. 447 the Huns appeared
again south of the Danube. The provinces of Lower Moesia
and Scythia, which had suffered less in the previous incursions,
were now devastated. Marcianopolis was taken, and the Roman
general Arnegisclus fell in a battle on the banks of the river
Utus (Wid). At the same time, another host of the enemy
descended the valley of the Vardar and advanced, it is said, to
Thermopylae.[1] Others approached Constantinople, and many
of its inhabitants fled from it in terror. So we are told by a contemporary, who says that more than a hundred towns were
taken, and that the monks and nuns in the monasteries near
the capital were slain, if they had not already fled.[2]

Attila was now in a position to enlarge his demands. A new
peace was concluded (A.D. 448) by which a district, along the
right bank of the Danube, extending from Singidunum eastward
to Novae, and of a breadth of five days' journey, should be left
waste and uninhabited, as a march region between the two
realms, and Naissus, which was now desolate, should mark the

---

[1] It was perhap in this invasion
that Sardica was destroyed. See
Priscus, *fr.* 3, *De leg. Rom.* p. 123.

[2] Callinicus, *Vit. Hypatii*, p. 108.
Callinicus wrote this life in 447–
450.

frontier.[1] But Attila continued to vex the government at Constantinople with embassies, complaints, and demands, and as the drain on the treasury was becoming enormous, the eunuch Chrysaphius conceived the base idea of bribing an envoy of Attila to murder his master. Edecon, the principal minister of Attila, accepted the money and returned to his master's residence, which was somewhere between the rivers Theiss and Körös, in company of a Roman embassy at the head of which was Maximin. But the plot was revealed to Attila. He respected the person of the ambassador, but he sent to Constantinople Orestes (a Roman provincial of Pannonia who served him as secretary) with the bag which had held the bribe tied round his neck, and ordered him to ask Chrysaphius in the Emperor's presence whether he recognised it. The punishment of the eunuch was to be demanded. The Emperor then sent two men of patrician rank, Anatolius (Master of Soldiers *in praesenti*) and Nomus (formerly Master of Offices), to pacify the anger of the Hun. Attila treated them haughtily at first, but then showed surprising magnanimity and no longer insisted on the punishment of Chrysaphius. He promised to observe the treaty and not to cross the Danube (A.D. 449-450).

Until the end of the reign of Theodosius the oppressive Hun-money was paid to Attila, but, as we saw, Marcian refused to pay it any longer. It seemed that the Illyrian provinces would again be trampled under the horse-hoofs of the Hun cavalry, though little spoil can have been left to take. But Attila turned his eyes westward, where there was hope of richer plunder, and the realm of Valentinian, not that of Marcian, was now to be exposed to the fury of the destroyer.

§ 3. *The Empire and Court of Attila*

Under the rule of Rugila and Attila the Hunnic empire had assumed an imposing size and seemed a formidable power. The extent of Attila's dominion has doubtless been exaggerated, but his sway was effective in the lands (to use modern names) of Austria, Hungary, Roumania, and Southern Russia. How

---

[1] Priscus, *fr.* 5, *De leg. gent.* It seems to have been in 447-448 that the Huns got possession of Sirmium (*id. fr.* 3, *De leg. Rom.* p. 133). The seat of the Praet. Prefect of Illyricum, which had been moved there in A.D. 437 (see above, p. 221), was now moved back to Thessalonica.

far northward it may have reached cannot be decided. The most important of the German peoples who were subject to Attila were the Gepids (apparently in the mountainous regions of northern Dacia [1]), the Ostrogoths (who had migrated westward from their old homes on the Euxine [2]), and the Rugians (somewhere near the Theiss [3])—all in the neighbourhood of the lands where the Huns themselves had settled. The Gepid king, Ardaric, was Attila's most trusted counsellor, and next to him, Walamir, one of the Ostrogothic kings. On these peoples he could rely in his military enterprises. Before A.D. 440 the Huns had made an incursion into the Persian empire, and such was the prestige of their arms and Attila's power eight years later that Roman officers talked of the chances of the overthrow of Persia and the possible consequences of such an event for the Roman world.

Attila indeed looked upon himself as overlord of all Europe, including the Roman Empire. Theodosius paid him a huge sum yearly, Valentinian paid him gold too ; were they not then his tributaries and slaves ? He dreamed of an empire reaching to the islands of the Ocean,[4] and he was soon to make an attempt to extend it actually to the shores of the Atlantic.[5] In his dealings with the Empire he had one great military advantage. We have already seen how the Imperial government depended on the Huns and on the Germans beyond the frontier for the recruiting of its armies. Without his Hunnic auxiliaries Aetius would hardly have been able to save as much of Gaul as he succeeded in saving from the rapacity of the German settlers. Attila was in a position to stop these sources of supply. He could refuse to send Hunnic contingents to help the Romans against their enemies ; he could forbid individual Huns to leave

---

[1] Cp. Schmidt, *Deutsche Stämme*, i. 306-307.

[2] *Ib.* 124.

[3] *Ib.* 327. The Scirians were also, no doubt, under Hun rule.

[4] Priscus, *fr.* 3, *De leg. Rom.* p. 141. Britain, as Mommsen suggests, is probably meant.

[5] Priscus says that Attila thought himself destined to be lord of the whole world by virtue of the accidental discovery of '' the Sword of Mars.'' A cowherd one day had seen a heifer limping, and following the tracks of blood that had dripped from her wounded foot found a sword on which she had trodden, and brought it to Attila. It was declared to be the Sword of Mars—that ἀκινάκης σιδήρεος to which the Scythians used to sacrifice animals and men (Herodotus, iv. 62). So the Alans used to fix a naked sword in the ground and worship it as the god of war (Amm. Marc. xxxi., 2. 23). See Jordanes, *Get.* 183, and Priscus, *fr.* 3, *De leg. Rom.* p. 142.

their country and enter Roman service ; and he could bring
pressure to bear on his vassal German kings to issue a similar
prohibition to their subjects. That he was fully conscious of
this power and made it a feature of his policy, is shown by his
stern insistence, in negotiating with Theodosius, that all Hun
deserters should be surrendered ; perhaps by the device of
keeping a strip of neutral territory south of the Danube in
order to make it more difficult for his own subjects to pass into
the Roman provinces ; and particularly by the fact that when
his empire was broken up after his death, the empire was
inundated by Germans seeking to make their fortunes in Roman
service.

Since their entry into Europe the Huns had changed in
some important ways their life and institutions. They were
still a pastoral people, they did not learn to practise tillage,
but on the Danube and the Theiss the nomadic habits of the
Asiatic steppes were no longer appropriate or necessary. And
when they became a political power and had dealings with the
Roman Empire—dealings in which diplomacy was required as
well as the sword—they found themselves compelled to adapt
themselves, however crudely, to the habits of more civilised
communities. Attila found that a private secretary who knew
Latin was indispensable, and Roman subjects were hired to
fill the post. But the most notable fact in the history of the
Huns at this period is the ascendancy which their German
subjects appear to have gained over them. The most telling
sign of this influence is the curious circumstance that some of
their kings were called by German names. The names of
Rugila,[1] *Mundiuch* (Attila's father), and *Attila* are German or
Germanised. This fact clearly points to intermarriages, but it
is also an unconscious acknowledgment of the Huns that their
vassals were higher in the scale of civilisation. If the political
situation had remained unchanged for another fifty years
the Asiatic invader would probably have been as thoroughly

[1] Priscus calls him Ruas (= Roas in
Jordanes) ; Rugas in Socrates and
Roilas in Theodoret (*H.E.* v. 37)
point to the form Rugila, which is
independently preserved in *Chr. Gall.*,
sub 433. Ruga and Rugila are
probably both right, the termination
-*ila* being hypocoristic. *Attila* (as
mean " little father." The deriva-
tion of Marquart (*Chron. der alttürk.
Insch.* p. 77) from the Hunnic name
of the Volga, Atil or Itil ('Αττίλας in
Menander, p. 8, *De leg. gent.*), should
be rejected.

Mr. H. M. Chadwick informs me) could

Teutonised as the Alans, whom the Romans had now come to class among the Germanic peoples.[1]

Of Attila himself we have a clearer impression than of any of the German kings who played leading parts in the period of the Wandering of the Nations. The historian Priscus, who accompanied his friend Maximin, the ambassador to Attila, in A.D. 448, and wrote a full account of the embassy, drew a vivid portrait of the monarch and described his court. The story is so interesting that it will be best to reproduce it in a free translation of the original.[2]

We set out with the barbarians, and arrived at Sardica, which is thirteen days for a fast traveller from Constantinople. Halting there we considered it advisable to invite Edecon and the barbarians with him to dinner. The inhabitants of the place sold us sheep and oxen, which we slaughtered, and we prepared a meal. In the course of the feast, as the barbarians lauded Attila and we lauded the Emperor, Bigilas remarked that it was not fair to compare a man and a god, meaning Attila by the man and Theodosius by the god. The Huns grew excited and hot at this remark. But we turned the conversation in another direction, and soothed their wounded feelings ; and after dinner, when we separated, Maximin presented Edecon and Orestes with silk garments and Indian gems. . . .

When we arrived at Naissus we found the city deserted, as though it had been sacked ; only a few sick persons lay in the churches. We halted at a short distance from the river, in an open space, for all the ground adjacent to the bank was full of the bones of men slain in war. On the morrow we came to the station of Agintheus, the commander-in-chief of the Illyrian armies (*magister militum per Illyricum*), who was posted not far from Naissus, to announce to him the Imperial commands, and to receive five of those seventeen deserters, about whom Attila had written to the Emperor. We had an interview with him, and having treated the deserters with kindness, he committed them to us. The next day we proceeded from the district of Naissus towards the Danube ; we entered a covered valley with many bends and windings and circuitous paths. We thought we were travelling due west, but when the day dawned the sun rose in front ; and some of us unacquainted with the topography cried out that the sun was going the wrong way, and portending unusual events. The fact was that that part of the road faced the east, owing to the irregularity of the ground. Having passed these rough places we arrived at a plain which was also well wooded. At the river we were received by barbarian ferrymen, who rowed us across the river in boats made by themselves out of single trees hewn and hollowed. These preparations had not been made for our sake, but to convey across a company of Huns ; for Attila pretended that he wished to hunt in Roman territory, but his intent was really hostile, because all the deserters

---

[1] Cp. Jung, *op. cit.* 210, 221. Gothic was the *lingua franca* in Central Europe. Cp. below, p. 283.

[2] Priscus in *Exc. de leg.* p. 123 *sqq.*

had not been given up to him. Having crossed the Danube, and proceeded with the barbarians about seventy stadia, we were compelled to
wait in a certain plain, that Edecon and his party might go on in front
and inform Attila of our arrival. As we were dining in the evening we
heard the sound of horses approaching, and two Scythians arrived with
directions that we were to set out to Attila. We asked them first to
partake of our meal, and they dismounted and made good cheer. On the
next day, under their guidance, we arrived at the tents of Attila, which
were numerous, about three o'clock, and when we wished to pitch our
tent on a hill the barbarians who met us prevented us, because the tent
of Attila was on low ground, so we halted where the Scythians desired. . . .
(Then a message is received from Attila, who was aware of the nature
of their embassy, saying that if they had nothing further to communicate
to him he would not receive them, so they reluctantly prepared to return.)
When the baggage had been packed on the beasts of burden, and we were
perforce preparing to start in the night time, messengers came from Attila
bidding us wait on account of the late hour. Then men arrived with an
ox and river fish, sent to us by Attila, and when we had dined we retired
to sleep. When it was day we expected a gentle and courteous message
from the barbarian, but he again bade us depart if we had no further
mandates beyond what he already knew. We made no reply, and prepared
to set out, though Bigilas insisted that we should feign to have some other
communication to make. When I saw that Maximin was very dejected,
I went to Scottas (one of the Hun nobles, brother of Onegesius), taking
with me Rusticius, who understood the Hun language. He had come
with us to Scythia, not as a member of the embassy, but on business with
Constantius, an Italian whom Aetius had sent to Attila to be that monarch's
private secretary. I informed Scottas, Rusticius acting as interpreter,
that Maximin would give him many presents if he would procure him an
interview with Attila ; and, moreover, that the embassy would not only
conduce to the public interests of the two powers, but to the private interest
of Onegesius, for the Emperor desired that he should be sent as an ambassador to Byzantium, to arrange the disputes of the Huns and Romans,
and that there he would receive splendid gifts. As Onegesius was not
present it was for Scottas, I said, to help us, or rather help his brother,
and at the same time prove that the report was true which ascribed to him
an influence with Attila equal to that possessed by his brother. Scottas
mounted his horse and rode to Attila's tent, while I returned to Maximin,
and found him in a state of perplexity and anxiety, lying on the grass
with Bigilas. I described my interview with Scottas, and bade him make
preparations for an audience of Attila. They both jumped up, approving
of what I had done, and recalled the men who had started with the beasts
of burden. As we were considering what to say to Attila, and how to
present the Emperor's gifts, Scottas came to fetch us, and we entered
Attila's tent, which was surrounded by a multitude of barbarians. We
found Attila sitting on a wooden chair. We stood at a little distance
and Maximin advanced and saluted the barbarian, to whom he gave the
Emperor's letter, saying that the Emperor prayed for the safety of him and
his. The king replied, " It shall be unto the Romans as they wish it to

be unto me," and immediately addressed Bigilas, calling him a shameless
beast, and asking him why he ventured to come when all the deserters
had not been given up.[1] . . .

After the departure of Bigilas, who returned to the Empire (nominally
to find the deserters whose restoration Attila demanded, but really to get
the money for his fellow-conspirator Edecon), we remained one day in
that place, and then set out with Attila for the northern parts of the
country. We accompanied the barbarian for a time, but when we reached
a certain point took another route by the command of the Scythians who
conducted us, as Attila was proceeding to a village where he intended to
marry the daughter of Eskam, though he had many other wives, for the
Scythians practise polygamy. We proceeded along a level road in a plain
and met with navigable rivers—of which the greatest, next to the Danube,
are the Drecon, Tigas, and Tiphesas—which we crossed in the monoxyles,
boats made of one piece, used by the dwellers on the banks : the smaller
rivers we traversed on rafts which the barbarians carry about with them
on carts, for the purpose of crossing morasses. In the villages we were
supplied with food—millet instead of corn, and mead ($\mu\acute{\epsilon}\delta o\varsigma$), as the
natives call it, instead of wine. The attendants who followed us received
millet, and a drink made of barley, which the barbarians call *kam*. Late
in the evening, having travelled a long distance, we pitched our tents on
the banks of a fresh-water lake, used for water by the inhabitants of the
neighbouring village. But a wind and storm, accompanied by thunder
and lightning and heavy rain, arose, and almost threw down our tents ;
all our utensils were rolled into the waters of the lake. Terrified by the
mishap and the atmospherical disturbance, we left the place and lost one
another in the dark and the rain, each following the road that seemed most
easy. But we all reached the village by different ways, and raised an
alarm to obtain what we lacked. The Scythians of the village sprang out
of their huts at the noise, and, lighting the reeds which they use for
kindling fires, asked what we wanted. Our conductors replied that the
storm had alarmed us ; so they invited us to their huts and provided
warmth for us by lighting large fires of reeds. The lady who governed
the village—she had been one of Bleda's wives—sent us provisions and
good-looking girls to console us (this is a Scythian compliment). We
treated the young women to a share in the eatables. but declined to take
any further advantage of their presence. We remained in the huts till
day dawned and then went to look for our lost utensils, which we found
partly in the place where we had pitched the tent, partly on the bank of
the lake, and partly in the water. We spent that day in the village drying
our things ; for the storm had ceased and the sun was bright. Having
looked after our horses and cattle, we directed our steps to the princess,
to whom we paid our respects and presented gifts in return for her courtesy.
The gifts consisted of things which are esteemed by the barbarians as not
produced in the country—three silver *phialai*, red skins, Indian pepper,
palm fruit, and other delicacies.

---

[1] Edecon had betrayed to Attila
the design which he and Bigilas had
formed against Attila's life. This was
the real reason of Attila's roughness
towards the latter.

Having advanced a distance of seven days farther, we halted at a village; for as the rest of the route was the same for us and Attila, it behoved us to wait, so that he might go in front. Here we met with some of the "western Romans," who had also come on an embassy to Attila—the count Romulus, Promotus governor of Noricum, and Romanus a military captain. With them was Constantius whom Aetius had sent to Attila to be his secretary, and Tatulus, the father of Orestes ; these two were not connected with the embassy, but were friends of the ambassadors. Constantius had known them of old in the Italies, and Orestes had married the daughter of Romulus.[1]

The object of the embassy was to soften the soul of Attila, who demanded the surrender of one Silvanus, a dealer in silver plate [2] in Rome, because he had received golden vessels from a certain Constantius. This Constantius, a native of Gaul, had preceded his namesake in the office of secretary to Attila. When Sirmium in Pannonia was besieged by the Scythians, the bishop of the place consigned the vessels to his (Constantius') care, that if the city were taken and he survived they might be used to ransom him ; and in case he were slain, to ransom the citizens who were led into captivity. But when the city was enslaved, Constantius violated his engagement, and, as he happened to be at Rome on business, pawned the vessels to Silvanus for a sum of money, on condition that if he gave back the money within a prescribed period the dishes should be returned, but otherwise should become the property of Silvanus. Constantius, suspected of treachery, was crucified by Attila and Bleda ; and afterwards, when the affair of the vessels became known to Attila, he demanded the surrender of Silvanus on the ground that he had stolen his property. Accordingly Aetius and the Emperor of the Western Romans sent to explain that Silvanus was the creditor of Constantius, the vessels having been pawned and not stolen, and that he had sold them to priests and others for sacred purposes. If, however, Attila refused to desist from his demand, he, the Emperor, would send him the value of the vessels, but would not surrender the innocent Silvanus.

Having waited for some time until Attila advanced in front of us, we proceeded, and having crossed some rivers we arrived at a large village, where Attila's house was said to be more splendid than his residences in other places. It was made of polished boards, and surrounded with a wooden enclosure, designed, not for protection, but for appearance. The house of Onegesius was second to the king's in splendour, and was also encircled with a wooden enclosure, but it was not adorned with towers like that of the king. Not far from the enclosure was a large bath which Onegesius—who was the second in power among the Scythians—built, having transported the stones from Pannonia ; for the barbarians in this district had no stones or trees, but used imported material. The builder of the bath was a captive from Sirmium, who expected to win his freedom as payment for making the bath. But he was disappointed, and greater trouble befell him than mere captivity among the Scythians, for Onegesius

---

[1] Romulus and his daughter were of Poetovio in Noricum.

[2] MSS. ἀρμίου or ἀσμίου τραπέζης.

Valesius amended ἀργυρίου. I conjecture ἀσήμου, plate or bullion. ἀσῆμι is used in modern Greek for silver plate.

appointed him bathman, and he used to minister to him and his family when they bathed.

When Attila entered the village he was met by girls advancing in rows, under thin white canopies of linen, which were held up by the outside women who stood under them, and were so large that seven or more girls walked beneath each. There were many lines of damsels thus canopied, and they sang Scythian songs. When he came near the house of Onegesius, which lay on his way, the wife of Onegesius issued from the door, with a number of servants, bearing meat and wine, and saluted him and begged him to partake of her hospitality. This is the highest honour that can be shown among the Scythians. To gratify the wife of his friend, he ate, just as he sat on his horse, his attendants raising the tray to his saddle-bow ; and having tasted the wine, he went on to the palace, which was higher than the other houses and built on an elevated site. But we remained in the house of Onegesius, at his invitation, for he had returned from his expedition with Attila's son. His wife and kinsfolk entertained us to dinner, for he had no leisure himself, as he had to relate to Attila the result of his expedition, and explain the accident which had happened to the young prince, who had slipped and broken his right arm. After dinner we left the house of Onegesius, and took up our quarters nearer the palace, so that Maximin might be at a convenient distance for visiting Attila or holding intercourse with his court. The next morning, at dawn of day, Maximin sent me to Onegesius, with presents offered by himself as well as those which the Emperor had sent, and I was to find out whether he would have an interview with Maximin and at what time. When I arrived at the house, along with the attendants who carried the gifts, I found the doors closed, and had to wait until some one should come out and announce our arrival. As I waited and walked up and down in front of the enclosure which surrounded the house, a man, whom from his Scythian dress I took for a barbarian, came up and addressed me in Greek, with the word Χαῖρε, " Hail ! " I was surprised at a Scythian speaking Greek. For the subjects of the Huns, swept together from various lands, speak, besides their own barbarous tongues, either Hunnic or Gothic,[1] or— as many as have commercial dealings with the western Romans—Latin ; but none of them easily speak Greek, except captives from the Thracian or Illyrian sea-coast ; and these last are easily known to any stranger by their torn garments and the squalor of their heads, as men who have met with a reverse. This man, on the contrary, resembled a well-to-do Scythian, being well dressed, and having his hair cut in a circle after Scythian fashion. Having returned his salutation, I asked him who he was and whence he had come into a foreign land and adopted Scythian life. When he asked me why I wanted to know, I told him that his Hellenic speech had prompted my curiosity. Then he smiled and said that he was born a Greek [2] and had gone as a merchant to Viminacium, on the Danube, where he had stayed a long time, and married a very rich

---

[1] That is, Hunnic and Gothic were the recognised languages of the Hun empire.

[2] Ἔφη Γραικὸς μὲν εἶναι τὸ γένος. Γραικός, not Ἕλλην, a Greek, not a Hellene, which would mean a pagan. Ἑλληνικός and ἑλληνίζειν were still used in their old sense ; and we even meet τὴν Ἑλλήνων φωνήν. Cp. below, p. 287, n.

wife. But the city fell a prey to the barbarians, and he was stript of his
prosperity, and on account of his riches was allotted to Onegesius in
the division of the spoil, as it was the custom among the Scythians for
the chiefs to reserve for themselves the rich prisoners. Having fought
bravely against the Romans and the Acatiri, he had paid the spoils
he won to his master, and so obtained freedom. He then married a
barbarian wife and had children, and had the privilege of eating at the
table of Onegesius.

He considered his new life among the Scythians better than his old
life among the Romans, and the reasons he gave were as follows : " After
war the Scythians live in inactivity, enjoying what they have got, and
not at all, or very little, harassed. The Romans, on the other hand, are
in the first place very liable to perish in war, as they have to rest their
hopes of safety on others, and are not allowed, on account of their *tyrants*,
to use arms. And those who use them are injured by the cowardice of
their generals, who cannot support the conduct of war. But the condition of the subjects in time of peace is far more grievous than the evils of
war, for the exaction of the taxes is very severe, and unprincipled men
inflict injuries on others, because the laws are practically not valid against
all classes. A transgressor who belongs to the wealthy classes is not
punished for his injustice, while a poor man, who does not understand
business, undergoes the legal penalty, that is if he does not depart this
life before the trial, so long is the course of lawsuits protracted, and so
much money is expended on them. The climax of the misery is to have
to pay in order to obtain justice. For no one will give a court to the
injured man unless he pay a sum of money to the judge and the judge's
clerks."

In reply to this attack on the Empire, I asked him to be good enough
to listen with patience to the other side of the question. " The creators
of the Roman republic," I said, " who were wise and good men, in order
to prevent things from being done at haphazard, made one class of men
guardians of the laws, and appointed another class to the profession of
arms, who were to have no other object than to be always ready for battle,
and to go forth to war without dread, as though to their ordinary exercise,
having by practice exhausted all their fear beforehand. Others again
were assigned to attend to the cultivation of the ground, to support both
themselves and those who fight in their defence, by contributing the
military corn-supply. . . . To those who protect the interests of the liti-
gants a sum of money is paid by the latter, just as a payment is made by
the farmers to the soldiers. Is it not fair to support him who assists and
requite him for his kindness ? The support of the horse benefits the
horseman. . . . Those who spend money on a suit and lose it in the end
cannot fairly put it down to anything but the injustice of their case. And
as to the long time spent on lawsuits, that is due to concern for justice,
that judges may not fail in passing correct judgments, by having to give
sentence offhand ; it is better that they should reflect, and conclude the
case more tardily, than that by judging in a hurry they should both injure
man and transgress against the Deity, the institutor of justice. . . . The
Romans treat their servants better than the king of the Scythians treats

his subjects. They deal with them as fathers or teachers, admonishing them to abstain from evil and follow the lines of conduct which they have esteemed honourable ; they reprove them for their errors like their own children. They are not allowed, like the Scythians, to inflict death on them. They have numerous ways of conferring freedom ; they can manumit not only during life, but also by their wills, and the testamentary wishes of a Roman in regard to his property are law." [1]

My interlocutor shed tears, and confessed that the laws and constitution of the Romans were fair, but deplored that the governors, not possessing the spirit of former generations, were ruining the State.

As we were engaged in this discussion a servant came out and opened the door of the enclosure. I hurried up, and inquired how Onegesius was engaged, for I desired to give him a message from the Roman ambassador. He replied that I should meet him if I waited a little, as he was about to go forth. And after a short time I saw him coming out, and addressed him, saying, " The Roman ambassador salutes you, and I have come with gifts from him, and with the gold which the Emperor sent you. The ambassador is anxious to meet you, and begs you to appoint a time and place." Onegesius bade his servants receive the gold and the gifts, and told me to announce to Maximin that he would go to him immediately. I delivered the message, and Onegesius appeared in the tent without delay. He expressed his thanks to Maximin and the Emperor for the presents, and asked why he sent for him. Maximin said that the time had come for Onegesius to have greater renown among men, if he would go to the Emperor, and by his wisdom arrange the objects of dispute between the Romans and Huns, and establish concord between them ; and thereby he will procure many advantages for his own family, as he and his children will always be friends of the Emperor and the Imperial family. Onegesius inquired what measures would gratify the Emperor and how he could arrange the disputes. Maximin replied : " If you cross into the lands of the Roman Empire you will lay the Emperor under an obligation, and you will arrange the matters at issue by investigating their causes and deciding them on the basis of the peace." Onegesius said he would inform the Emperor and his ministers of Attila's wishes, but the Romans need not think they could ever prevail with him to betray his master or neglect his Scythian training and his wives and children, or to prefer wealth among the Romans to bondage with Attila. He added that he would be of more service to the Romans by remaining in his own land and softening the anger of his master, if he were indignant for aught with the Romans, than by visiting them and subjecting himself to blame if he made arrangements that Attila did not approve of. He then retired, having consented that I should act as an intermediary in conveying messages from Maximin to himself, for it would not have been consistent with Maximin's dignity as ambassador to visit him constantly.

The next day I entered the enclosure of Attila's palace, bearing gifts to his wife, whose name was Kreka. She had three sons, of whom the eldest governed the Acatiri and the other nations who dwell in Pontic

---

[1] This passage is interesting as an illustration of the attitude of the higher classes in the Empire to slavery in the fifth century.

Scythia. Within the enclosure were numerous buildings, some of carved boards beautifully fitted together, others of straight, fastened on round wooden blocks which rose to a moderate height from the ground. Attila's wife lived here, and, having been admitted by the barbarians at the door, I found her reclining on a soft couch. The floor of the room was covered with woollen mats for walking on. A number of servants stood round her, and maids sitting on the floor in front of her embroidered with colours linen cloths intended to be placed over the Scythian dress for ornament. Having approached, saluted, and presented the gifts, I went out, and walked to another house, where Attila was, and waited for Onegesius, who, as I knew, was with Attila. I stood in the middle of a great crowd— the guards of Attila and his attendants knew me, and so no one hindered me. I saw a number of people advancing, and a great commotion and noise, Attila's egress being expected. And he came forth from the house with a dignified gait, looking round on this side and on that. He was accompanied by Onegesius, and stood in front of the house; and many persons who had lawsuits with one another came up and received his judgment. Then he returned into the house, and received ambassadors of barbarous peoples.

As I was waiting for Onegesius, I was accosted by Romulus and Promotus and Romanus, the ambassadors who had come from Italy about the golden vessels; they were accompanied by Rusticius and by Constantiolus, a man from the Pannonian territory, which was subject to Attila. They asked me whether we had been dismissed or are constrained to remain, and I replied that it was just to learn this from Onegesius that I was waiting outside the palace. When I inquired in my turn whether Attila had vouchsafed them a kind reply, they told me that his decision could not be moved, and that he threatened war unless either Silvanus or the drinking-vessels were given up. . . .

As we were talking about the state of the world, Onegesius came out; we went up to him and asked him about our concerns. Having first spoken with some barbarians, he bade me inquire of Maximin what consular the Romans are sending as an ambassador to Attila. When I came to our tent I delivered the message to Maximin, and deliberated with him what answer we should make to the question of the barbarian. Returning to Onegesius, I said that the Romans desired him to come to them and adjust the matters of dispute, otherwise the Emperor will send whatever ambassador he chooses. He then bade me fetch Maximin, whom he conducted to the presence of Attila. Soon after Maximin came out, and told me that the barbarian wished Nomus or Anatolius or Senator to be the ambassador, and that he would not receive any other than one of these three; when he (Maximin) replied that it was not meet to mention men by name and so render them suspected in the eyes of the Emperor, Attila said that if they do not choose to comply with his wishes the differences will be adjusted by arms.

When we returned to our tent the father of Orestes came with an invitation from Attila for both of us to a banquet at three o'clock. When the hour arrived we went to the palace, along with the embassy from the western Romans, and stood on the threshold of the hall in the presence of Attila. The cup-bearers gave us a cup, according to the national custom, that we might pray before we sat down. Having tasted the cup, we proceeded to take our seats ; all the chairs were ranged along the walls of the room on either side. Attila sat in the middle on a couch ; a second couch was set behind him, and from it steps led up to his bed, which was covered with linen sheets and wrought coverlets for ornament, such as Greeks [1] and Romans use to deck bridal beds. The places on the right of Attila were held chief in honour, those on the left, where we sat, were only second. Berichus, a noble among the Scythians, sat on our side, but had the precedence of us. Onegesius sat on a chair on the right of Attila's couch, and over against Onegesius on a chair sat two of Attila's sons ; his eldest son sat on his couch, not near him, but at the extreme end, with his eyes fixed on the ground, in shy respect for his father. When all were arranged, a cup-bearer came and handed Attila a wooden cup of wine. He took it, and saluted the first in precedence, who, honoured by the salutation, stood up, and might not sit down until the king, having tasted or drained the wine, returned the cup to the attendant. All the guests then honoured Attila in the same way, saluting him, and then tasting the cups ; but he did not stand up. Each of us had a special cup-bearer, who would come forward in order to present the wine, when the cup-bearer of Attila retired. When the second in precedence and those next to him had been honoured in like manner, Attila toasted us in the same way according to the order of the seats. When this ceremony was over the cup-bearers retired, and tables, large enough for three or four, or even more, to sit at, were placed next the table of Attila, so that each could take of the food on the dishes without leaving his seat. The attendant of Attila first entered with a dish full of meat, and behind him came the other attendants with bread and viands, which they laid on the tables. A luxurious meal, served on silver plate, had been made ready for us and the barbarian guests, but Attila ate nothing but meat on a wooden trencher. In everything else, too, he showed himself temperate ; his cup was of wood, while to the guests were given goblets of gold and silver. His dress, too, was quite simple, affecting only to be clean. The sword he carried at his side, the latchets of his Scythian shoes, the bridle of his horse were not adorned, like those of the other Scythians, with gold or gems or anything costly. When the viands of the first course had been consumed we all stood up, and did not resume our seats until each one, in the order before observed, drank to the health of Attila in the goblet of wine presented to him. We then sat down, and a second dish was placed on each table with eatables of another kind. After this course the same ceremony was observed as after the first. When evening fell torches were lit, and two barbarians coming forward in front of Attila sang songs they had composed, celebrating his victories and deeds of valour in war. And of the guests, as they looked at the singers, some were pleased with the verses, others reminded of wars were excited in their souls, while yet others, whose bodies were feeble with age and their spirits compelled to

---

[1] "Ελληνές τε καὶ 'Ρωμαῖοι. In using this expression Priscus had ancient times in his mind—times when the
Greeks were not 'Ρωμαῖοι but "Ελληνες, and when "Ελλην was not opposed to Χριστιανός.

rest, shed tears. After the songs a Scythian, whose mind was deranged, appeared, and by uttering outlandish and senseless words forced the company to laugh. After him Zerkon, the Moorish dwarf, entered. He had been sent by Attila as a gift to Aetius, and Edecon had persuaded him to come to Attila in order to recover his wife, whom he had left behind him in Scythia ; the lady was a Scythian whom he had obtained in marriage through the influence of his patron Bleda. He did not succeed in recovering her, for Attila was angry with him for returning. On the occasion of the banquet he made his appearance, and threw all except Attila into fits of unquenchable laughter by his appearance, his dress, his voice, and his words, which were a confused jumble of Latin, Hunnic, and Gothic. Attila, however, remained immovable and of unchanging countenance, nor by word or act did he betray anything approaching to a smile of merriment except at the entry of Ernas, his youngest son, whom he pulled by the cheek, and gazed on with a calm look of satisfaction. I was surprised that he made so much of this son, and neglected his other children ; but a barbarian who sat beside me and knew Latin, bidding me not reveal what he told, gave me to understand that prophets had forewarned Attila that his race would fall, but would be restored by this boy. When the night had advanced we retired from the banquet, not wishing to assist further at the potations.

§ 4. Attila's Invasions of Gaul and Italy, and the Fall of the Hun Empire (A.D. 450–454)

If the western provinces of the Empire had hitherto escaped the depredations of the Huns, this was mainly due to the personality and policy of Aetius, who had always kept on friendly terms with the rulers. But a curious incident happened, when Attila was at the height of his power, which diverted his rapacity from the east to the west, and filled his imagination with a new vision of power.

Of the court of Valentinian, of his private life, of his relations to his wife and to his mother we know no details. We have seen that he was intellectually and morally feeble, as unfitted for the duties of the throne as had been his uncles Honorius and Arcadius. But his sister Justa Grata Honoria had inherited from her mother some of the qualities we should expect to find in a granddaughter of Theodosius and a great-granddaughter of the first Valentinian. Like Placidia, she was a woman of ambition and selfwill, and she had inherited the temperament of her father which chafed against conventionality. We saw that she had been elevated to the rank of an Augusta probably about the same time that the Imperial title had been conferred on her brother.[1] During her girlhood and until Valentinian's marriage her position in the court was important, but when her nieces were born she had the chagrin of realising that henceforward from a political and dynastic point of view she would have to play an obscure part. She would not be allowed to marry except a thoroughly safe man who could be relied upon to entertain no designs upon the throne. We can understand that it must have irked a woman of her character to see the power in the hands of her brother, immeasurably inferior to herself in brain and energy ; she probably felt herself quite as capable of conducting affairs of state as her mother had proved herself to be. We can divine that she was a thorn in the side of Valentinian, but we are given no glimpse into the domestic drama played in the Palaces of Ravenna and Rome.

She had passed the age of thirty when her discontent issued in action. She had a separate establishment of her own, within the precincts of the Palace, and a comptroller or steward to manage it. His name was Eugenius, and with him s̄ ̄ had ar amorous intrigue in A.D. 449.[2] She may have been in love with him, but love was subsidiary to the motive of ambition. She designed him to be her instrument in a plot to overthrow her detested brother. The intrigue was discovered,[3] and her paramour was put to death. She was herself driven from the Palace, and betrothed compulsorily to a certain Flavius Bassus Herculanus, a rich senator of excellent character, whose sobriety assured the Emperor that a dangerous wife would be unable to draw him into revolutionary schemes.[4]

The idea of this union was hateful to Honoria and she bitterly

---

[1] See above, p. 224. For her coins (solidi with DN IVST GRAT HONORIA PF AVG) see Cohen, viii. 219 ; De Salis, *Numismatic Chronicle*, vii. 203 ; Bury, *Justa Grata Honoria*, p. 4. The early date of her coronation can be inferred from her coins as well as from the inscription, *C.I.L.* xi. 276 (above, p. 262).

[2] See Bury, *op. cit.*, where it is shown that the date commonly accepted for the affair with Eugenius, 434, is due to an error of the chronicler Marcellinus and is inconsistent with the story of Priscus and the evidence of Merobaudes. The error arose from the indictional dating : 449 was a 2nd indiction, and Marcellinus made the

entry inadvertently under 434, also a 2nd indiction. The sources for Honoria's life are Merobaudes, *Carm.* i. ; Priscus, *fr.* 2 ; 7, 8, *De leg. gent.* ; John of Antioch, *fr.* 84 *De insidiis* (based on, or transcribed from, Priscus) ; Jordanes, *Get.* 223-224, *Rom.* 328 (sources : Cassiodorus, *Gothic Hist.*, of which the source here was Priscus, and Marcellinus).

[3] Marcellinus says she was pregnant (*concepit*), which may or may not be true. He also says that she was sent to Constantinople, but this is inconsistent with the story of Priscus.

[4] *Fasti cons.*, *sub* 452 ; *C.I.L.* ix. 1371.

resented the compulsion. She must often have heard—-she had
perhaps been old enough to have some recollection herself—
of the breach between her mother and her uncle after her father's
death. In that crisis of her life Placidia had turned for help
to a barbarian power. Her daughter now decided to do likewise.
She despatched by the hands of a trustworthy eunuch, Hyacinthus,
her ring and a sum of money to Attila, asking him to come to
her assistance and prevent the hateful marriage. Attila was
the most powerful monarch in Europe and she boldly chose
him to be her champion.

The proposal of the Augusta Honoria was welcome to Attila,
and was to determine his policy for the next three years. The
message probably reached him in the spring of A.D. 550. She
had sent her ring to show that the message was genuine, but he
interpreted, or chose to interpret, it as a proposal of marriage.
He claimed her as his bride, and demanded that half the territory
over which Valentinian ruled should be surrendered to her.[1] At
the same time he made preparations to invade the western
provinces. He addressed his demand to the senior Emperor,
Theodosius, and Theodosius immediately wrote to Valentinian
advising him to hand over Honoria to the Hun. Valentinian
was furious. Hyacinthus was tortured, to reveal all the details
of his mistress's treason, and then beheaded. Placidia had
much to do to prevail upon her son to spare his sister's life.
When Attila heard how she had been treated, he sent an embassy
to Ravenna to protest ; the lady, he said, had done no wrong,
she was affianced to him, and he would come to enforce her
right to a share in the Empire. Attila longed to extend his
sway to the shores of the Atlantic, and he would now be able
to pretend that Gaul was the portion of Honoria.

Meanwhile Theodosius had died and we saw how Marcian
refused to pay the annual tribute to the Huns. This determined
attitude may have helped to decide Attila to turn his arms
against the weak realm of Valentinian instead of renewing
his attacks upon the exhausted Illyrian lands which he had so
often wasted. There was another consideration which urged

---

[1] His theory was that the subject
territory of the Empire was the
private property of the Emperors, in
this case of Constantius III. and
Honorius, and that the children male
or female had a claim to equal
portions. Attila's Latin secretaries
could have informed him that Roman
constitutional custom did not recognise such a principle.

him to a Gallic campaign. The King of the Vandals had sent
many gifts to the King of the Huns and used all his craft to
stir him up against the Visigoths. Gaiseric feared the vengeance
of Theoderic for the shameful treatment of his daughter,[1] and
longed to destroy or weaken the Visigothic nation. We are told
by a contemporary writer, who was well informed concerning
the diplomatic intrigues at the Hun court, that Attila invaded
Gaul " to oblige Gaiseric." [2] But that was only one of his
motives. Attila was too wary to unveil his intentions. It was
his object to guard against the possibility of the co-operation of
the Goths and Romans and he pretended to be friendly to both.
He wrote to Tolosa that his expedition was aimed against the
enemies of the Goths, and to Ravenna that he proposed to
smite the foes of Rome.[3]

Early in A.D. 451 [4] he set forth with a large army composed
not only of his own Huns, but of the forces of all his German
subjects. Prominent among these were the Gepids, from the
mountains of Dacia, under their king Ardaric, and the Ostrogoths
under their three chieftains, Walamir, Theodemir, and Widimir ; [5]
the Rugians from the regions of the Upper Theiss ; the Scirians
from Galicia ; the Heruls from the shores of the Euxine ; the
Thuringians ; [6] Alans, and others. When they reached the
Rhine they were joined by the division of the Burgundians who
dwelled to the east of that river and by a portion of the Ripuarian
Franks. The army poured into the Belgic provinces, took
Metz (April 7),[7] captured many other cities, and laid waste the

---

[1] See above, p. 256.
[2] Priscus, *loc. cit.*, Jordanes, *Get.*
184.
[3] Prosper, *sub* 451, Jord. *Get.* 185,
186. A minor matter on the Gallic
frontier also engaged Attila's attention.
There had been a struggle for kingship
among the Ripuarian Franks ; they
had appealed to him, and the claimant
against whom he decided appealed to
Aetius. The route which he chose for
the invasion of Gaul was perhaps
determined by this affair. When he
was already on the march he sent
another embassy to Ravenna, renewing
his demand for the surrender of
Honoria and transmitting her ring
as a proof of the betrothal (Priscus,
fr. 8).
[4] For his account of the Gallic cam-

paign Jordanes used Cassiodorus, and
the account of Cassiodorus was
derived from Priscus. This narrative,
doubtless abbreviated and distorted
in a reproduction at third hand, is
supplemented by Sidonius Apoll.
Carm. vii. and the Latin chroniclers
(Prosper, Marcellinus, etc.). Sidonius
intended to write a history of the
war, but only began it. Cp. *Epp.*
viii. 15.
[5] We are not told where precisely
the Ostrogoths were settled at this
period. Schmidt (*op. cit.* i. 124) conjectures with probability that, after
they came under the empire of the
Huns, they moved westward from
their old territory on the Black Sea.
[6] Sid. Apoll. *Carm.* vii. 323.
[7] Hydatius, 150.

land. It is not clear whether Aetius had really been lulled into security by the letter of Attila disclaiming any intention of attacking Roman territory. Certainly his preparations seem to have been hurried and made at the last moment. The troops which he was able to muster were inadequate to meet the huge army of the invader. The federate Salian Franks, some of the Ripuarians, the federate Burgundians of Savoy, and the Celts of Armorica obeyed his summons.[1] But the chance of safety and victory depended on securing the co-operation of the Visigoths, who had decided to remain neutral. Avitus, whom we have already met as a *persona grata* at the court of Tolosa, was chosen by Aetius to undertake the mission of persuading Theoderic. He was successful ; but it has been questioned whether his success was due so much to his diplomatic arts as to the fact that Attila was already turning his face towards the Loire.[2] There was a settlement of Alans[3] in the neighbourhood of Valence, and their king had secretly agreed to help Attila to the possession of that city. The objective then of Attila was Orleans, and the first strategic aim of the hastily cemented arrangement between the Romans and Goths was to prevent him from reaching it. The accounts of what happened are contradictory.[4] The truth seems to be that the forces of the allies—the mixed army of Aetius, and the Visigothic host under Theoderic, who was accompanied by his son Thorismud—reached the city before the Huns arrived, and Attila saw that he would only court disaster if he attempted to assault their strongly fortified camp. No course was open but retreat. Aetius had won a bloodless strategic victory (summer A.D. 451).[5]

---

[1] Also Saxons, which shows there were already some Saxon settlements north of the Loire, recognised by the government.

[2] Schmidt, *ib.* 246.

[3] Settled there by Aetius in A.D. 440 (Prosper).

[4] The narrative of Jordanes-Priscus implies that Orleans was not besieged by the Huns. Nor do I think that the words of Sidonius Apoll. *Ep.* 8, 15 *oppugnatio, inruptio nec direptio* (we must allow for rhetoric) imply that the enemy entered the city. But in this passage we may see the beginning of the ecclesiastical legend, which is expanded in the late *Vita*

Aniani. Bishop Anianus probably did much to keep up the hopes and spirits of the alarmed inhabitants. The arrival of the allies in time to save the city would be interpreted as an answer to his prayers. It was natural to magnify the danger and augment the services of the Church by representing the enemy as already within the gates.

[5] The date implied in the *Vita Aniani*, c. vii. p. 113 *octavodecimo kal. Iulias* = June 14, for the relief of Orleans probably preserves a true tradition. Clinton (*F.R.* i. 642), combining Isidore (*Hist. Goth.* p. 278) with Hydatius, puts the battle of

The Huns took the road to Troyes (Tricasses), and not very far from this town, in a district known as the Mauriac place,[1] they halted, and prepared to oppose the confederate army which was marching close upon their heels.[2] The battle, which began in the afternoon and lasted into the night, was drawn ; there was immense slaughter,[3] and king Theoderic was among the slain. Next day, the Romans found that Attila was strongly entrenched behind his wagons, and it was said that he had prepared a funeral pyre in which he might perish rather than fall into the hands of his foes. Thorismud, burning to avenge his father's death, was eager to storm the entrenchment. But this did not recommend itself to the policy of Aetius. It was not part of his design to destroy the Hunnic power, of which throughout his career he had made constant use in the interests of the Empire ; nor did he desire to increase the prestige of his Visigothic allies. He persuaded Thorismud to return with all haste to Tolosa, lest his brothers should avail themselves of his absence to contest his succession to the kingship. He also persuaded the Franks to return immediately to their own land. Disembarrassed of these auxiliaries, he was able to pursue his own policy and permit Attila to escape with the remnant of his host.

The battle of Maurica was a battle of nations, but its signifi-

Troyes after Sept. 27. Hodgkin conjectures that it was fought early in July (ii. 124). If the *Vita* is right, the battle may be placed about June 20.

[1] The battle has been vulgarly known as the battle of Châlons, because some of the sources (Jordanes, Hydatius) vaguely describe it as fought in the Catalaunian Plains, an expression which probably denoted nearly the whole of Champagne. That the scene was near Troyes and not near Châlons (Durocatalaunum) is shown by the more precise notices in *Chron. Gall.* p. 663 *Tricassis pugnat loco Mauriacos* and *Consul. Ital.* (Prosper Havn.) p. 302 *in quinto miliario de Trecas loco nuncupato Maurica in eo Campania.* (Cp. Greg. Tur. ii. 7 *Mauriacum campum*; and in the *Lex Burgundionum,* xvii. 1, the battle is called *pugna Mauriacensis.*) It has been thought that the Mauriac name may be preserved in Méry-sur-Seine, which is about 20 miles N. of Troyes,

and it may be that the battle was fought between Méry and Troyes. But Méry cannot be identified with Maurica of *Cons. Ital.* if the numeral *quinto* is right. Hodgkin (*ib.* 139-142) thinks that the claims of this locality (as against the neighbourhood of Châlons) are made more probable by the discovery in 1842 at Pouan, ten miles from Méry, of bones, weapons, and gold ornaments (including a ring inscribed *heva*). Peigné-Delacourt was confident that here was the grave of Theoderic. There is, however, no evidence for connecting the bones and ornaments with the battle of 451.

[2] Aetius was posted on the right wing, Theoderic on the left ; the Alans, whose treacherous designs were suspected, in the centre. On the other side, Attila was in the centre The action began with a struggle to gain possession of a hill, in which the Romans and Goths were successful.

[3] Jordanes gives the absurd figure of 165,000 for the fallen.

cance has been enormously exaggerated in conventional history. It cannot in any reasonable sense be designated as one of the critical battles of the world. The Gallic campaign had really been decided by the strategic success of the allies in cutting off Attila from Orleans. The battle was fought when he was in full retreat, and its value lay in damaging his prestige as an invincible conqueror, in weakening his forces, and in hindering him from extending the range of his ravages. But can the invasion and the campaign regarded as a whole be said to assume the proportions of an ecumenical crisis ? The danger did not mean so much as has been commonly assumed. If Attila had been victorious, if he had defeated the Romans and the Goths at Orleans, if he had held Gaul at his mercy and had translated— and we have no evidence that this was his design—the seat of his government and the abode of his people from the Theiss to the Seine or the Loire, there is no reason to suppose that the course of history would have been seriously altered. For the rule of the Huns in Gaul could only have been a matter of a year or two ; it could not have survived here, any more than it survived in Hungary, the death of the great king, on whose brains and personal character it depended. Without depreciating the achievement of Aetius and Theoderic we must recognise that at worst the danger they averted was of a totally different order from the issues which were at stake on the fields of Plataea and the Metaurus. If Attila had succeeded in his campaign, he would probably have been able to compel the surrender of Honoria, and if a son had been born of their marriage and proclaimed Augustus in Gaul, the Hun might have been able to exercise considerable influence on the fortunes of that country ; but that influence would probably not have been anti-Roman.

Attila lost little time in seeking to take revenge for the unexpected blow which had been dealt him. He again came forward as the champion of the Augusta Honoria, claiming her as his affianced bride,[1] and invaded Italy in the following year (A.D. 452). Aquileia, the city of the Venetian march, now fell before the Huns, and was razed to the ground, never to rise again ;

---

[1] After 452 we hear nothing more of Honoria. We are left to wonder whether she was compelled to marry Herculanus, who was consul in that year. A word in John of Antioch seems to hint that some grave punish- ment befell her. Recording her escape from death in 450 he says that " Honoria on that occasion (τότε) escaped from chastisement," suggest- ing that afterwards she was less lucky.

in the next century hardly a trace of it could be seen. Verona
and Vicentia did not share this fate, but they were exposed to
the violence of the invader, while Ticinum and Mediolanum
were compelled to purchase exemption from fire and sword.

The path of Attila was now open to Rome. Aetius, with
whatever forces he could muster, might hang upon his line of
march, but was not strong enough to risk a battle. But the
lands south of the Po, and Rome herself, were spared the presence
of the Huns. According to tradition, the thanks of Italy were
on this occasion due not to Aetius but to Leo, the bishop of
Rome. The Emperor, who was at Rome, sent Leo and two leading
senators, Avienus [1] and Trygetius, to negotiate with the invader.
Trygetius had diplomatic experience ; he had negotiated the
treaty with Gaiseric in A.D. 435. Leo was an imposing figure,
and the story gives him the credit for having persuaded Attila
to retreat. He was supported by celestial beings ; the apostles
Peter and Paul are said to have appeared to Attila and by their
threats terrified him into leaving the soil of Italy.[2]

The fact of the embassy cannot be doubted. The distinguished ambassadors visited the Hun's camp near the south
shore of Lake Garda. It is also certain that Attila suddenly
retreated. But we are at a loss to know what considerations
were offered him to induce him to depart.[3] It is unreasonable
to suppose that this heathen king would have cared for the
thunders or persuasions of the Church. The Emperor refused
to surrender Honoria, and it is not recorded that money was
paid. A trustworthy chronicle hands down another account
which does not conflict with the fact that an embassy was sent,
but evidently furnishes the true reasons which moved Attila
to receive it favourably. Plague broke out in the barbarian
host and their food ran short,[4] and at the same time troops
arrived from the east, sent by Marcian to the aid of Italy.

[1] For Gennadius Avienus, consul in
450, see Sidonius Apoll. *Epp.* i. 9.

[2] Pope Leo in his *Sermo in octavis
Apost. Petri et Pauli,* lxxxiv. (*P.L.* 54),
probably refers to this invasion, not
to that of the Vandals in 455 (see
Gregorovius, *Rome in the Middle Ages*,
i. 200). Was it, he asks, the circus
games or the protection of the saints
that delivered Rome from death ?

[3] Hydatius, 154. According to
Priscus (Jordanes, *Get.* 222) it was

Attila's own counsellors who decided
him to abandon the idea of marching
to Rome by reminding him that
Alaric had died a few weeks after its
capture. There may be something in
this. Attila's secretaries were doubtless open to bribes.

[4] It may be noted that in the winter
of 450–451 Italy suffered from a severe
famine. See *Novel* 32 of Valentinian
(Jan. 31, 451) *obscaenissimam famem
per totam Italiam desaevisse.*

If his host was suffering from pestilence, and if troops arrived from the east, we can understand that Attila was forced to withdraw. But whatever terms were arranged, he did not pretend that they meant a permanent peace. The question of Honoria was left unsettled, and he threatened that he would come again and do worse things in Italy unless she were given up with the due portion of the Imperial possessions.[1]

Attila survived his Italian expedition only one year. His attendants found him dead one morning, and the bride whom he had married the night before sitting beside his bed in tears.[2] His death was ascribed to the bursting of an artery, but it was also rumoured that he had been slain by the woman in his sleep.[3]

With the death of Attila, the Empire of the Huns, which had no natural cohesion, was soon scattered to the winds. Among his numerous children there was none of commanding ability, none who had the strength to remove his brothers and step into his father's place, and they proposed to divide the inheritance into portions. This was the opportunity of their German vassals, who did not choose to allow themselves to be allotted to various masters like herds of cattle. The rebellion was led by Ardaric, the Gepid, Attila's chief adviser. In Pannonia near the river Nedao another battle of the nations was fought, and the coalition of German vassals, Gepids, Ostrogoths, Rugians, Heruls and the rest, utterly defeated the host of their Hun lords (A.D. 454). It is not improbable that the Germans received encouragement and support from the Emperor Marcian.[4]

This event led to considerable changes in the geographical distribution of the barbarian peoples. The Huns themselves were scattered to the winds. Some remained in the west, but the greater part of them fled to the regions north of the Lower Danube, where we shall presently find them, under two of Attila's sons, playing a part in the troubled history of the Thracian provinces. The Gepids extended their power over the whole of Dacia (Siebenbürgen), along with the plains between the Theiss

---

[1] Jordanes, *Get.* 223.

[2] *Ib.* 254. Priscus doubtless is the source and there is no hint at foul play. Ildico was the name of the woman.

[3] Marcellinus, *sub* 454. In Teutonic legend the tradition that he was murdered by a woman was preserved, but the lady was Gudrun, the sister of the Burgundian king. Cp. Chadwick, *The Heroic Age*, 37, 156.

[4] The source for the battle is Jordanes, *Get.* 260. The Nedao cannot be identified.

and the Danube which had been the habitation of the Huns.[1] The
Emperor Marcian was deeply interested in the new disposition
of the German nations, and his diplomacy aimed at arranging
them in such a way that they would mutually check each other.
He seems to have made an alliance with the Gepids which proved
exceptionally permanent.[2] He assigned to the Ostrogoths settlements in northern Pannonia, as federates of the Empire. The
Rugians found new abodes on the north banks of the Danube,
opposite to Noricum, where they also were for some years federates
of Rome. The Scirians settled farther east, and were the northern
neighbours and foes of the Ostrogoths in Pannonia ; and the
Heruls found territory in the same vicinity—perhaps between
the Scirians and Rugians.[3] But from all these peoples there
was a continual flow into the Roman Empire, men seeking military service. In the depopulated provinces of Illyricum and
Thrace there was room and demand for new settlers. Rugians
were settled in Bizye and Arcadiopolis ;[4] Scirians in Lower
Moesia.[5]

The battle of the Nedao was an arbitrament far more momentous than the battle of Maurica. The catastrophe of the Hun
power was indeed inevitable, for the social fabric of the Huns and
all their social instincts were opposed to the concentration and
organisation which could alone maintain the permanence of their
empire. But it was not the less important that the catastrophe
arrived at this particular moment—important both for the German peoples and for the Empire. Although their power disappeared, at one stroke, into the void from which it had so
suddenly arisen, we shall see, if we reflect for a moment, that
it affected profoundly the course of history. The invasion of the
nomads in the fourth century had precipitated the Visigoths
from Dacia into the Balkan peninsula and led to the disaster of
Hadrianople, and may be said to have determined the whole
chain of Visigothic history. But apart from this special consequence of the Hun invasion, the Hun empire performed a
function of much greater significance in European history. It

---

[1] Jordanes, *Get.* 264. It is probable that they also had part of
Walachia, see Schmidt, *op. cit.* i. 308.

[2] Schmidt, 309.   Jordanes, *ib.*
They received the yearly payments
(*annua sollemnia*) granted to Federates,

and this arrangement lasted till the
fall of the Gepid power.

[3] Schmidt, 335.

[4] Jordanes, *ib.* 261. Cp. John Ant.
fr. 214 (*De ins.* p. 137).

[5] Jordanes, *ib.* 265.

helped to retard the whole process of the German dismemberment of the Empire. It did this in two ways : in the first place,
by controlling many of the East German peoples beyond the
Danube, from whom the Empire had most to fear ; and in the
second place, by constantly supplying Roman generals with
auxiliaries who proved an invaluable resource in the struggle
with the German enemies. The devastations which some of the
Roman provinces suffered from the Huns in the last years of
Theodosius II. and Valentinian III. must be esteemed a loss
which was more than set off by the support which Hunnic arms
had for many years lent to the Empire ; especially if we consider
that, as subsequent events showed, the Germans would have
committed the same depredations if the Huns had not been
there. This retardation of the process of dismemberment, en-
abling the Imperial government to maintain itself, for a longer
period, in those lands which were destined ultimately to become
Teutonic kingdoms, was all in the interest of civilisation ; for
the Germans, who in almost all cases were forced to establish
their footing on Imperial territory as *foederati*, and then by degrees
converted this dependent relation into independent sovranty,
were more likely to gain some faint apprehension of Roman
order, some slight taste for Roman civilisation, than if their
careers of conquest had been less gradual and impeded.

§ 5. *Deaths of Aetius* (454) *and Valentinian III.* (455)

The reward of Aetius for supporting Valentinian's throne for
nearly thirty years was that he should fall by Valentinian's
hand. One of the most prominent senators and ministers since
the later years of Honorius was Petronius Maximus.[1] He had
been twice Prefect of Rome, twice Praetorian Prefect of Italy ;
he had twice held the consulship ; and in A.D. 445 we find him
a Patrician. He had a distinguished pedigree, though we do
not know it ; perhaps he was connected with the great Anician
gens. But he probably owed his prestige and influence more to
his immense wealth than to his family or to his official career.

---

[1] He was *comes sacr. larg.* in 415–
417, and Prefect of the City in 420–421.
On laying down this office a statue was
erected to him by the Emperors, on
the petition of the senate and people,
in the Forum of Trajan, and there his
distinguished pedigree is referred to,
a proavis atavisque nobilitas (*C.I.L.*
vi. 1749). His first consulship was in
433, the second in 443.

He was a notable figure at Rome, " with his conspicuous way of life, his banquets, his lavish expense, his retinues, his literary pursuits, his estates, his extensive patronage." [1] In A.D. 454 he was approaching his sixtieth year. He bore personal enmity against Aetius and determined to oust him from power.

He discovered that the sentiments of Heraclius, a eunuch who had the Emperor's ear, were similar to his own. The two conspired together, and persuaded Valentinian that he would perish at the hands of Aetius unless he hastened to slay him first. [2]

Valentinian listened to this counsel and devised death against his powerful general. One day, when Aetius was in the Palace, laying some financial statement before the Emperor, Valentinian suddenly leaping from his throne accused him of treason, and not allowing him time to defend himself, drew his sword and rushed upon the defenceless minister, who was at the same moment attacked by the chamberlain Heraclius. Thus perished the Patrician Aetius (September 21, A.D. 454). A poet wrote his epitaph : [3]

> Aetium Placidus mactavit semivir amens ;

and it is said that some one afterwards boldly told the truth to Valentinian, " You have cut off your right hand with your left." Who was now to save Italy from the Vandals ?

Petronius Maximus assuredly was not the man for the task. It was his ambition to be " the Patrician " of the Emperor, but he reckoned without Heraclius. The eunuch persuaded Valentinian that, being well rid of the oppressive influence of Aetius, he would act foolishly if he transferred the power to Maximus. Bitterly disappointed, Maximus wove another murderous plot. He sought out two barbarians, Optila and Thraustila, who had been personal retainers of Aetius, had fought in his campaigns, and enjoyed the favour of the Emperor. [4] He urged these men to avenge their master, and the issue may be told in a chronicler's words :

" It seemed good to Valentinian to ride in the Campus Martius with a few guards accompanied by Optila and Thraustila and

---

[1] Sidonius, *Epp.* ii. 13, tr. Dalton.

[2] I follow John of Antioch (*fr.* 85, *ib.* p. 125), because I hold that he followed Priscus. That Maximus played a part in the fall of Aetius is confirmed by Marcellinus : *Valen-*

tinianus dolo Maximi patricii cuius etiam fraude Aetius perierat.

[3] Sidonius Apoll. *Carm.* vii. 359.

[4] Cp. Prosper, *sub a.* Gregory of Tours calls Optila *Occila bucellarius Aetii* (*H.F.* ii. 8).

their attendants. And when he dismounted and proceeded to practise archery, Optila and those with him attacked him.[1] Optila struck Valentinian on the temple, and when the prince turned to see who struck him dealt him a second blow on the face and felled him. Thraustila slew Heraclius. And the two assassins taking the Imperial diadem and the horse hastened to Maximus. They escaped all punishment for their deed." [2] The day of the murder was March 16, A.D. 455.

These two bloody deeds mark the beginning of a new disastrous period in the history of the western provinces. The strong man who might have averted the imminent danger from the Vandals, and the weak man whose mere existence held Italy, Gaul, and Spain together, were removed ; there was no general to take the place of Aetius, " the last of the Romans," [3] as there was no male member of the Theodosian house to succeed Valentinian. A chronicler speaks [4] of the Patrician Aetius as " the great safety of the western republic " (*magna occidentalis reipublicae salus*), the terror of king Attila ; " and with him the Hesperian realm fell, and up to the present day has not been able to raise its head." We can comprehend this judgment ; the death of Aetius was a grave event. He was the greatest of the three Romans who had been responsible for the defence of Italy and the western provinces since the fall of Stilicho, and he was to have no Roman successor. Two years after his death the supreme command of the Imperial forces would again pass into the hands of a Romanised German. But we must not leave out of sight the importance of the death of his master Valentinian without male offspring. A legitimate heir of the Theodosian house would have prevented some of the troubles which befell Italy in the following years.

---

[1] The scene of the attack was called the Two Laurels (Prosper ; *Chron. Pasch.*). There was a place of the same name on the Via Labicana. Cp. Holder-Egger in *Neues Archiv*, i. 270, and Hodgkin, ii. 198.

[2] John Ant. *ib.* p. 126. The story of Valentinian's adultery with the wife of Maximus may or may not be true. The Salmasian fragment,

attributed by Müller to John Ant. (*fr.* 200), belongs to some other writer. The story is also found in Procopius, *B.V.* i. 4.

[3] Procopius, *ib.*, where Aetius and Boniface are so described. The compliment to Aetius is weakened by the inclusion of Boniface.

[4] Marcellinus.

§ 6. *Christian and Pagan Speculations on the Calamities of the Empire*

An amazing sequence of events had surprised the Empire after the death of Theodosius the Great.   Provinces had been seized by barbarous invaders, and the very soil of Italy desecrated by German violence.   The sight of Rome herself stricken and insulted, no longer able to speak the language of a mistress but compelled to bargain with the intruders on her own territory, could not fail to make men ask, " What is the cause of these disasters ?   Civil wars there have been in the past, our frontiers have been crossed, our provinces invaded, but since the Gauls bore down on Rome nearly eight hundred years ago, the queen of the world has never been violated and plundered by a foreign enemy till now, and it hardly entered any man's dream that such a horror might some day come to pass."   In that age there was probably no one who held the view that political and social changes depend on the series of antecedent events and that sudden catastrophes are no exception.   It was in the will of heaven, the anger of divine tyrants, or the inscrutable operations of the stars, that men were prone to seek explanations of shocking or unexpected public calamities.

Pagan patriots had no difficulty in solving the problem.   " So long," they said, " as the gods under whose favour Rome won her Empire were supreme, so long as the traditions of the ancient religion were preserved, our empire flourished and was impregnable.   But now their temples are destroyed, impious hands have been laid on the altars, the worship of our divinities has been proclaimed a crime.   And what is the result ?   Has the alien deity, who has usurped their time-honoured prerogatives, conducted the state to new glory or even to its old prosperity.   On the contrary, the result of his supremacy is rapine and ruin. The Empire is inundated by a wild tide of rapacious savages, the dominions of Rome are at their mercy, her sword is broken, and her lofty walls have been scaled.   These are the gifts that Constantine and the religion of Galilee, which he embraced in a disastrous hour, have bestowed upon the world." [1]

---

[1] This point of view appears in the writings of pagan historians like Eunapius and Zosimus.

Similar arguments indeed had been urged long before. In
the third century pagans had made Christianity answerable for
plagues, droughts, and wars ; nature herself, they cried, had
changed, since the advent of this abominable religion. Two
African divines had replied to the charge. Cyprian the bishop
of Carthage declared [1] that the disasters of his day were signs
of the approaching end of the world, and the inference might
be drawn that they did not much matter in view of the vast
event so soon to happen. Arnobius of Sicca, half a century
later, in his *Seven Books against the Nations*, met the arguments
of the heathen by pointing out that before the appearance of
Christianity the world had been the scene of as great or rather
of greater calamities.

But in the early fifth century there was stuff for a more
telling indictment, and one to which the average Christian of
that age might find it hard to produce a convincing answer.
And the Christian himself might have his own difficulties. How,
he might wonder, is it compatible with a wise and just government of the universe that the godly who hold the right opinion
concerning the nature of the Trinity should suffer all these
horrors at the hands of barbarians, and that those barbarians
who believe in a blasphemous heresy, which places them as
much as the heathen outside the Christian pale, should triumph
over us and wrest our provinces from us.[2]

Such questionings evoked three books. Africa, Spain, and
Gaul each contributed an answer, one a work of genius, the other
two dull but remarkable each in its way.

The first, as it was the greatest, was Augustine's *City of God*.
Augustine had been deeply impressed by the capture of Rome by
Alaric, and he recognised that the situation of the world called

---

[1] See Cyprian, *Ad Demetrianum.*

[2] The Eunomian historian Philostorgius, who graphically described
the miseries which the provinces
suffered in the reigns of Arcadius
and Theodosius II., attributed the
calamities to the persecution of the
Eunomians. It seems likely that he
shared the view of those who saw in
these contemporary events the signs
of the end of the world predicted by
Jesus in the Gospels. This view is
reflected in a clearly contemporary
Apocalypse, preserved in Syriac and
translated by Arendzen, in *Journal
of Theological Studies*, 1901, 401 *sqq.*
(Cp. Bidez, *Proleg.* to his ed. of
Philostorgius, cxv. *sqq.*) How soon
the impression of great events may
grow faint is illustrated by the fact
that Socrates and Sozomen, who wrote
in the middle of the fifth century,
notice Alaric's capture of Rome as
if it were no extraordinary event ;
Theodoret does not even mention it.
We can see from the abridged notice
which has been preserved how
differently it struck Philostorgius
(xii. 3).

for a Christian explanation in reply to the criticisms of the pagans who made the new religion responsible for Rome's misfortunes. The motive and occasion of the work, which seems to have outgrown its original scope, may account for some of its defects.[1] It is one of the greatest efforts of Christian speculation, but the execution is not equal to the conception, and the fundamental conception itself was not original. The work consists of two distinct sections which might just as well have formed two independent treatises. The first section (Bks. i.-x.) is a polemic against pagan religion and pagan philosophies, in which it is shown that polytheism is not necessary to secure happiness either in this world or in the next. The most effective argument is that which had been already used by Arnobius : the miseries which we suffer to-day are no exception to the general course of experience, for we have only to read the history of Rome to find them paralleled or exceeded. The writer insists that earthly glory and prosperity are unnecessary for true happiness. These things were bestowed on Constantine the Great, but that was in order to prove that they are not incompatible with the life of a Christian. On the other hand, if the reign of Christian Jovian was shorter than that of the apostate Julian, and if Gratian was assassinated, these were divine intimations that glory and long life are not the true reward of Christian faith.[2] Such an argument was not likely to make much impression upon pagans.

But the answer of Augustine to the questions which were perplexing the world is not to be found in the first part of his work. He realised that any satisfactory solution of the problem must lie in discovering a harmony between the actual events of history and the general plan of the universe. The synthesis which he framed for the interpretation of history as part of a general scheme of things is an essay in that field of speculation which is known nowadays as the philosophy of history. It can hardly, however, be described as philosophical, for the premises

---

[1] It was composed in the years 413 to 426 and parts of it were published before it was completed. In reading Augustine it is always well to bear in mind that he was a Neoplatonist before he was a Catholic, and a Manichean before he was a Neoplatonist. The stages of his thought have recently been studied by P. Alfaric, *L'Évolution intellectuelle de Saint Augustin*, 1918. It is also well to remember that he was a rhetorician. His most interesting work *The Confessions* is marred for modern taste by its rhetoric.

[2] *De civ. Dei*, v. 25.

on which it is based are not derived from reason but from revelation.[1]

Augustine's conception is that the key to the history of the human race is to be found in the coexistence side by side of two cities or states which are radically opposed to each other in their natures, principles, and ends, the Civitas Dei and the Civitas Terrena. It may be observed that this conception was not original; Augustine derived it from his Donatist friend Tychonius. The origins of both these states go back to a time when man did not yet exist; the City of God was founded by the creation of the angels, the other city by the rebellion of the angels who fell. Since the sin of Adam the history of each of these cities, " intertwined and mutually mixed " (*perplexas quodam modo invicemque permixtas*), has been running its course. The vast majority of the human race have been and are citizens of the earthly city, of which the end is death. The minority who belong to the heavenly city are during their sojourn on earth merely foreigners or pilgrims (*peregrini*) in the earthly city. Till the conversion of the first Gentile to Christianity the members of the City of God belonged exclusively to the Hebrew race and its patriarchal ancestors; and Augustine determines the chief divisions of universal history by the great epochs of the Biblical record : the Flood, Abraham, David, the Captivity, and the birth of Christ.[2] This last event is the beginning of the sixth period, in which we are living at present ; and the sixth period is the last. For the periods of history correspond to the days of Creation, and as God rested on the seventh day, so the seventh period will witness the triumph of the heavenly City and the eternal rest of its citizens. To the question how long will the sixth period last, Augustine replies that he does not know.[3] In this connexion he tells us an interesting fact. An oracle was current among the pagans, and seems to have given them much consolation, that the Christian religion would disappear from the world at the end of 365 years. It was said that the disciple Peter had been able by his sorceries to impose upon the world the worship of Christ for this period, but at its termination the work of the wizard would dissolve like a dream.

---

[1] On its influence in later times see J. N. Figgis, *The Political Aspects of St. Augustine's City of God.*

[2] Augustine here depended on the chronological scheme worked out by Hippolytus, Sextus Julius Africanus, and Eusebius.

[3] *De civ. Dei*, xviii. 53 ; xxii. 30.

Augustine observes triumphantly, and perhaps with a certain relief, that more years than 365 had already elapsed since the Crucifixion, and that there was no sign of the fulfilment of the oracle.[1]

To a modern, and possibly also to an ancient, inquirer, Augustine's work would have been more interesting if he had seriously addressed himself to an historical study of the Babylonian and Roman Empires, which according to him were the two principal embodiments of the earthly City. But he entrenches himself and remains almost immovably fixed in his headquarters in Judaea, and the excursions which he makes into other regions are few and slight. Many of his notices of events in secular history are simply trivial.

Having completed his historical survey he devotes the last portion of his work to an exposition of the ultimate goal to which the world and the human race are travelling. He examines the question of the Last Judgment, expatiates on the fiery death which is the destiny of the earthly City, and ends with a discussion on the bliss which awaits the citizens of the City of God.

Among the thinkers of the Middle Ages the influence of Augustine's work went far and deep. But his fruitful conception was lodged in a somewhat dreary mansion. If the polemical section which he intends to be a preliminary defeat of the enemies of the City of God [2] had been omitted, the work would have gained in simplicity. But the main argument itself, although it has a definite architectural scheme,[3] is marred by diffuseness and digressions. Augustine did not possess the literary art or command the method of lucid exposition whereby the prince of Greek philosophers compels his readers to assist in the building of the City, " of which a model perchance is in heaven," with breathless interest from page to page and from section to section. There is at least one part which may hold the attention of the reader, fascinated by the very horror, the Book in which this arch-advocate of theological materialism and vindictive punishment expends all his ingenuity in proving that the fire

---

[1] *De civ. Dei*, xviii. 53, 54.

[2] Cp. *ib.* xi. 1.

[3] He indicates the design repeatedly in the work itself and in his *Retractationes*. Bks. xi.-xiv. deal with the *exortus* of the two cities and come down to Cain and Abel ; Bks. xv.-xviii. describe the *procursus*, and survey the historical growth of the *Civ. Dei* ; and the last four Books deal with the future and the *debiti fines* of the two cities.

of hell is literal fire and spares no effort to cut off the slenderest chance that the vast majority of his fellow-beings will not be tormented throughout eternity.

Augustine had produced a book which transcended in importance its original motive. But it is this motive which concerns us here. It was to teach the world to take a right view of the misfortunes which were befalling the Empire, and to place them in their true perspective. He says in effect to the pagans, " These misfortunes are nothing exceptional, they are simply part of the heritage of your City of sin and death." [1] To the Christians he said, " These things do not really concern you. Your interests are not affected by the calamities of a country in which you are merely foreigners." This theory might be consolatory, but if it were pressed to its logical conclusion it would assuredly be destructive of the spirit of patriotism ; and, though the author would doubtless have deprecated this criticism, he does not consider the secular duties of Christians towards the state of which they are citizens in the earthly sense.

He was conscious that his treatment of the history of Rome was casual and superficial, and he thought that a fuller development of his historical argument in reply to the pagans was desirable. He requested his friend Orosius, a Spanish priest, to supply this need. He said to Orosius, " Search the annals of the past, collect all the calamities which they record, wars, plagues, famines, earthquakes, fires, and crimes, and write a history of the world. Thus my general refutation of the charges of the unbelievers who impute to our religion the present misfortunes, which they allege to be unusual, will be proved abundantly by a long array of facts." [2] A work entitled *Histories to confute the Pagans* was the outcome of this request, and it may thus be regarded as a sort of supplement to the *City of God*.[3] Perhaps it deserves more than any other book to be described as the first attempt at a universal history, and it was probably the worst. But it had considerable vogue in the Middle Ages, and gave currency to the idea of four great monarchies, the

---

[1] It is to be observed that Augustine regarded the virtues of the pagans as vices, because *vera religio* was absent (xix. c. 25). Chrysostom seems to take a more lenient and human view,

Hom. 5, on *Ep. ad Rom.*, *P.G.* 60, 426 *sqq.*

[2] See Orosius, *Hist.*, *Prol.*

[3] The date of the work is A.D. 418.

Babylonian, Carthaginian, Macedonian, and Roman, corresponding to the four points of the compass.[1]

Fifteen or twenty years after the completion of Augustine's
work Salvian, a priest of Marseilles, wrote his treatise *On the
Government of God*,[2] dealing from a different point of view with
the same problem which had suggested the books of Augustine
and Orosius. Salvian addresses his discourse expressly to
Christians, for he has no hope that his arguments would
have any effect upon pagans.[3] He propounds the question :
How comes it that we Christians who believe in the true God
are more miserable than all men ? Is God indifferent to us ?
Has he renounced the business of governing the world ? If he
regards human affairs, why are we weaker and more unfortunate
than all other peoples ? Why are we conquered by the barbarians ? Salvian's answer is, We suffer these evils because we
deserve them. If, living in such vice and wickedness as we
do, we flourished and were happy, then indeed God might be
accused of not governing. In support of his argument the author
paints an appalling picture of the condition of the Empire.
His descriptions of the corruptness of the administration and
of the oppression of the poor by the rich furnish the modern
historian with an instructive commentary on those Imperial
laws which attempt to restrain the rapacity of public officials.
Salvian does not forget to dwell, with the zeal of a churchman,
on the general love of unedifying pleasures, the games of the
circus and licentious plays in the theatre, amusements of which
the average Christian was not less avid than the average pagan.

But, it might be objected, we, whatever be our faults, have
at least right theological beliefs, whereas the barbarians who
are permitted to overcome us are heathen or heretics. That is
true, replies Salvian ; in just one point we are better than
they ; but otherwise they are better than we. He then proceeds
to enlarge on the virtues of the barbarians, which he uses, somewhat as Tacitus did in the *Germania*, as a foil to Roman civilisation. Among the Germans, or even among the Huns, we do
not see the poor oppressed by the rich. If the Alamanni are

---

[1] *Hist.*, *Prol.* ii. 1. The number was
based on Daniel, chap. ii. Sulpicius
Severus (*Chron.* ii. 3) makes the four
kingdoms, the Chaldaean, Persian,
Macedonian, and Roman.

[2] *De gubernatione Dei.* It was
written not earlier than 439 and before
Attila's invasion in 451.

[3] iii. v.

given to drunkenness, if the Franks and Huns are perjured and perfidious, if the Alans are rapacious, are not all these vices found among us ?   On the other hand, the Vandals have put the provincials to shame by their high standard of sexual morality, and if the Saxons are ferocious and the Goths perfidious, both these peoples are wonderfully chaste.

There is no relief in Salvian's gloomy picture.   It must be accepted with the reserves with which we must always qualify the rhetoric of preachers or satirists when they denounce the vices of their age.   But the tone of despondency is genuine. He says that " the Roman Republic is either dead, or at least is drawing her last breath in those parts in which she still seems to be alive." [1]   He speaks as if this were a fact which was beyond dispute and to which men had already become accustomed. More than thirty years had elapsed since the news of the Goths at Rome had surprised Jerome in his retreat at Bethlehem and extorted the cry, *Quid salvum est si Roma perit ?*   Meanwhile the Romans had quickly recovered from the shock and had almost forgotten it.   The calamity of the provinces did not move them to alter their way of life or renounce their usual amusements.   And the one phrase that is worth remembering in Salvian's gloomy, declamatory book is the epigram on Rome, *Moritur et ridet.*

§ 7. *Modern Views on the Collapse of the Empire*

The explanations of the calamities of the Empire which have been hazarded by modern writers are of a different order from those which occurred to witnesses of the events, but they are not much more satisfying.   The illustrious historian whose name will always be associated with the "Decline" of the Roman Empire invoked " the principle of decay," a principle which has itself to be explained.   Depopulation, the Christian religion, the fiscal system have all been assigned as causes of the Empire's decline in strength.[2]   If these or any of them were responsible

---

[1] *De gubernatione Dei,* iv. 30.

[2] Gibbon, iv. chap. xxxviii. 173 *sqq.* Hodgkin, *Italy and her Invaders,* ii. 538 *sqq.*, enumerates as contributory causes Christianity, the destruction of the middle classes, and " barbarous finance." Seeley, "Roman Imperial-ism," in *Macmillan's Magazine,* August 1869, makes depopulation mainly responsible.   Over-taxation of the rich has sometimes been assigned as one of the causes of the " fall " of the Empire.   It has been pointed out above (p. 153) that under-taxation of the rich was rather the trouble.

for its dismemberment by the barbarians in the West, it may be asked how it was that in the East, where the same causes operated, the Empire survived much longer intact and united.

Consider depopulation. The depopulation of Italy was an important fact and it had far-reaching consequences.[1] But it was a process which had probably reached its limit in the time of Augustus. There is no evidence that the Empire was less populous in the fourth and fifth centuries than in the first.[2] The " sterility of the human harvest " in Italy and Greece affected the history of the Empire from its very beginning, but does not explain the collapse in the fifth century. The truth is that there are two distinct questions which have been confused. It is one thing to seek the causes which changed the Roman State from what it was in the best days of the Republic to what it had become in the age of Theodosius the Great—a change which from certain points of view may be called a " decline." It is quite another thing to ask why the State which could resist its enemies on many frontiers in the days of Diocletian and Constantine and Julian suddenly gave way in the days of Honorius. " Depopulation " may partly supply the answer to the first question, but it is not an answer to the second. Nor can the events which transferred the greater part of western Europe to German masters be accounted for by the numbers of the peoples who invaded it. The notion of vast hosts of warriors, numbered by hundreds of thousands, pouring over the frontiers, is, as we saw, perfectly untrue.[3] The total number of one of the large East German nations probably seldom exceeded 100,000, and its army of fighting men can rarely have been more than from 20,000 to 30,000. They were not a deluge, overwhelming and irresistible, and the Empire had a well-organised military establishment at the end of the fourth century, fully sufficient in capable hands to beat them back. As a matter of fact, since the defeat at Hadrianople which was due to the blunders of Valens, no very important battle was won by German over Imperial forces during the whole course of the invasions.

It has often been alleged that Christianity in its political effects was a disintegrating force and tended to weaken the power of Rome to resist her enemies. It is difficult to see that

[1] Seeck, *Untergang*, vol. i.   [2] Cp. above, Chap. III. § 4.
[3] Cp. above, Chap. IV. § 3.

it had any such tendency, so long as the Church itself was united. Theological heresies were indeed to prove a disintegrating force in the East in the seventh century, when differences in doctrine which had alienated the Christians in Egypt and Syria from the government of Constantinople facilitated the conquests of the Saracens. But, after the defeat of Arianism, there was no such vital or deep-reaching division in the West, and the effect of Christianity was to unite, not to sever, to check, rather than to emphasise, national or sectional feeling. In the political calculations of Constantine it was probably this ideal of unity, as a counterpoise to the centrifugal tendencies which had been clearly revealed in the third century, that was the great recommendation of the religion which he raised to power.[1] Nor is there the least reason to suppose that Christian teaching had the practical effect of making men less loyal to the Empire or less ready to defend it. The Christians were as pugnacious as the pagans. Some might read Augustine's *City of God* with edification, but probably very few interpreted its theory with such strict practical logic as to be indifferent to the safety of the Empire. Hardly the author himself, though this has been disputed.

It was not long after Alaric's capture of Rome that Volusian, a pagan senator of a distinguished family,[2] whose mother was a Christian and a friend of Augustine, proposed the question whether the teaching of Christianity is not fatal to the welfare of a State, because a Christian smitten on one cheek would if he followed the precepts of the Gospel turn the other to the smiter. We have the letter[3] in which Augustine answers the question and skilfully explains the text so as to render it consistent with common sense. And to show that warfare is not forbidden another text is quoted in which soldiers who ask " What shall we do ? " are bidden to " Do violence to no man, neither accuse any falsely, and be content with your wages." They are not told not to serve or fight. The bishop goes on to suggest that those who wage a just war are really acting *misericorditer*, in a spirit of mercy and kindness to their enemies, as it is to the true

---

[1] Cp. below, Chap. XI. § 2, on the political bearing of the law of 445 in favour of the Roman See.

[2] On the family of the Albini and Volusiani see Seeck, *Praef.* to Sym-

machus, p. clxxiv *sqq.* Augustine's correspondent was *comes rei priv.* in 408.

[3] *Epp.* 138, addressed to their common friend Marcellinus.

interests of their enemies that their vices should be corrected. Augustine's *misericorditer* laid down unintentionally a dangerous and hypocritical doctrine for the justification of war, the same principle which was used for justifying the Inquisition. But his definite statement that the Christian discipline does not condemn all wars was equivalent to saying that Christians were bound as much as pagans to defend Rome against the barbarians. And this was the general view. All the leading Churchmen of the fifth century were devoted to the Imperial idea, and when they worked for peace or compromise, as they often did, it was always when the cause of the barbarians was in the ascendant and resistance seemed hopeless.[1]

The truth is that the success of the barbarians in penetrating and founding states in the western provinces cannot be explained by any general considerations, It is accounted for by the actual events and would be clearer if the story were known more fully. The gradual collapse of the Roman power in this section of the Empire was the consequence of *a series of contingent events*. No general causes can be assigned that made it inevitable.

The first contingency was the irruption of the Huns into Europe, an event resulting from causes which were quite independent of the weakness or strength of the Roman Empire. It drove the Visigoths into the Illyrian provinces, and the difficult situation was unhappily mismanaged. One Emperor was defeated and lost his life ; it was his own fault. That disaster, which need not have occurred, was a second contingency.[2] His successor allowed a whole federate nation to settle on provincial soil ; he took the line of least resistance and established an unfortunate precedent. He did not foresee consequences which, if he had lived ten or twenty years longer, might not have ensued. His death was a third contingency. But the situation need have given no reason for grave alarm if the succession had passed to an Emperor like himself, or Valentinian I., or even Gratian. Such a man was not procreated by Theodosius and the government of the West was inherited by a feeble-minded boy. That

---

[1] The monastic movement was anti-social, but in the period in question it was young, and cannot have withdrawn so many young men from public service as to affect appreciably the strength of the State.

[2] It may be remembered that Valens would not wait for Gratian, who was hastening to his help.

was a fourth event, dependent on causes which had nothing to do with the condition of the Empire.

In themselves these events need not have led to disaster. If the guardian of Honorius and director of his government had been a man of Roman birth and tradition, who commanded the public confidence, a man such as Honorius himself was afterwards to find in Constantius and his successor in Aetius, all might have been tolerably well. But there was a point of weakness in the Imperial system, the practice of elevating Germans to the highest posts of command in the army. It had grown up under Valentinian I., Gratian, and Theodosius; it had led to the rebellion of Maximus, and had cost Valentinian II. his life. The German in whom Theodosius reposed his confidence and who assumed the control of affairs on his death probably believed that he was serving Rome faithfully, but it was a singular misfortune that at a critical moment when the Empire had to be defended not only against Germans without but against a German nation which had penetrated inside, the responsibility should have devolved upon a German. Stilicho did not intend to be a traitor, but his policy was as calamitous as if he had planned deliberate treachery. For it meant civil war. The dissatisfaction of the Romans in the West was expressed in the rebellion of Constantine, the successor of Maximus, and if Stilicho had had his way the soldiers of Honorius and of Arcadius would have been killing one another for the possession of Illyricum. When he died the mischief was done; Goths had Italy at their mercy, Gaul and Spain were overrun by other peoples. His Roman successors could not undo the results of events which need never have happened.

The supremacy of a Stilicho was due to the fact that the defence of the Empire had come to depend on the enrolment of barbarians, in large numbers, in the army, and that it was necessary to render the service attractive to them by the prospect of power and wealth. This was, of course, a consequence of the decline in military spirit, and of depopulation, in the old civilised Mediterranean countries. The Germans in high command had been useful, but the dangers involved in the policy had been shown in the cases of Merobaudes and Arbogastes. Yet this policy need not have led to the dismemberment of the Empire, and but for that series of chances its western provinces would not have been converted, as and when they were, into German kingdoms. It may be said that a German penetration of western Europe must ultimately have come about. But even if that were certain, it might have happened in another way, at a later time, more gradually, and with less violence. The point of the present contention is that Rome's loss of her provinces in the fifth century was not an " inevitable effect of any of those features which have been rightly or wrongly described as causes or consequences of her general ' decline.' " The central fact that Rome could not dispense with the help of barbarians for her wars (*gentium barbararum auxilio indigemus*) may be held to be the cause of her calamities, but it was a weakness which might have continued to be far short of fatal but for the sequence of contingencies pointed out above.

CHAPTER X

§ 1. *Leo I.* (A.D. 457–474)

It was always a critical moment when an Emperor died without a designated successor or a member of his family marked out to claim the diadem. Theodosius I. had created his sons Augusti ; Arcadius had co-opted his infant son ; Theodosius II. had designated Marcian as his successor just before his death, and Marcian's title was sealed by his marriage with the Augusta Pulcheria. On Marcian's death the Theodosian dynasty had come to an end, and the choice of a new Emperor rested with the army and the Senate. There was one obvious candidate, Anthemius, who was the grandson of the great Praetorian Prefect and had married Marcian's daughter Euphemia. He had held the office of Master of Soldiers in Illyricum, and had been consul in A.D. 455. But Marcian had not designated him as his successor, and though the Senate perhaps would have liked to elect him,[1] he was not favoured by the man of most authority in the army, the patrician Aspar, who with his father Ardaburius had distinguished himself thirty-five years before in the suppression of the usurper John. Being an Arian, as well as a barbarian, he could not hope to wear the Imperial diadem ; the only course open to his ambition was to secure the elevation of one on whose pliancy he might count. He chose Leo, a native of Dacia and an orthodox Christian, who was tribune of the Mattiarii,[2] a legion

[1] Sidonius, *Carm.* ii. 214 *quamquam te posceret ordo.* The poet asserts that he did not covet the throne, 210. From this poem we learn that he distinguished himself in defending Illyricum against the Ostrogoths under Walamir.

[2] Constantine Porph. *De cer.* i. p. 411. The Mattiarii seniores were under one *mag. mil. in praes.*, the Mattiarii iuniores under the other. In the former case they are associated with Dacians.

belonging to the troops which were under the control of a
Master of Soldiers *in praesenti*. Aspar doubtless held this post,
as Leo was his *domesticus*. The Senate was unable to reject the
general's nominee and (on February 7) Leo was crowned at the
Palace of Hebdomon. As there was no Augustus or Augusta
to perform the ceremony of coronation, this duty was assigned
to the Patriarch Anatolius, who had perhaps taken some part
in the coronation of Marcian.[1] We have a contemporary description of the ceremonies connected with Leo's elevation, though
the act of crowning is passed over.

The senators and officials, the Scholarian guards, the troops
which were present in the capital, and the Patriarch gathered
at the Campus in the Hebdomon. The military insignia, the
labara and the standards, lay on the ground. All began to cry,
" Hear, O God, we call upon thee. Leo will be Emperor. The
public weal demands Leo. The army demands Leo. The
palace expects Leo. This is the wish of the palace, the army,
and the Senate." Then Leo ascended the tribunal or raised
platform, and a chain was placed on his head, and another in
his right hand, by officers.[2] Immediately the labara were
collected, and all cried : " Leo Augustus, thou conquerest![3]
God gave thee, God will keep thee. A long reign ! God will
protect the Christian Empire." Then the Candidati closed round
him and held their locked shields over his head. At this stage
he must have retired into the palace where he put on the Imperial
robes and the actual coronation was performed.[4] He came forth
again bearing the diadem, and was adored by all the officials, in
order of precedence. Then he took a shield and spear and was
acclaimed anew. When the cries ceased, he replied, through
the mouth of the *magister a libellis*,[5] in the following words :

" Imperator [6] Caesar Leo, Victorious, Ever August (saith) :
Almighty God and your choice, most valiant fellow-soldiers,

See *Not. Dig.*, *Or.* vi. 42, v. 47. Leo's
Dacian origin is mentioned by Candidus, *F.H.G.* iv. p. 135 ; John Mal. xiv.
p. 369, says he was a Bessian. He
had the rank of count.

[1] See above, p. 236.

[2] *Campiductores*, army-guides. Perhaps they were attached to the legion
of the Lanciarii, for a καμπιδούκτωρ
τῶν λαγκιαρίων performed the same
office at the elevation of Anastasius
(Const. Porph. *op. cit.* p. 423). The

Greek word for the chain or torc is
μανιάκιν.

[3] Σὺ νικᾷς. But the Latin τοῦ βίγκας
(*tu vincas*) remained long a regular
acclamation in the Byzantine Hippodrome. We also meet the hybrid
σὺ βίγκας.

[4] This may be inferred from the
order of proceedings in the case of
the coronation of Anastasius.

[5] Ὁ λιβελλήσιος.

[6] Αὐτοκράτωρ.

elected me Emperor of the Roman State." All : " Leo Augustus, thou conquerest. He who chose thee will keep thee. God will protect his choice." Leo : " Ye shall have me as your master and ruler, who shared the toils which as your fellow-soldier I learned to bear with you." All : " Our good fortune ! The army accepts thee as Emperor, O conqueror. We all desire thee." Leo : " I have decided what donatives I shall give to the troops." All : " Pious and powerful and wise ! " Leo : " To inaugurate my sacred and fortunate reign, I will give five nomismata [about £3] and a pound of silver to each shield." [1] All : " Pious, lavish ! Author of honour, author of riches ! May thy reign be fortunate, a golden age ! " Leo : " God be with us ! " Then a procession was formed, and the Emperor returned to the city where more ceremonies awaited him.[2]

The danger which had threatened the Empire in the reign of Arcadius through the power of Gaïnas and his German faction was now repeated, though perhaps in a less openly menacing shape, and the interest and importance of Leo's reign lie in the struggle for ascendancy between the foreign and native powers in the State. To have averted this peril was Leo's one achievement. The position of Aspar, who, though an Alan and not a German, represented the German interest,[3] was extremely strong. He was Master of the Soldiers *in praesenti*, and his son Ardaburius was, if not already, at least soon after Leo's accession, Master of Soldiers in the East.[4] The Emperor, however, whom

---

[1] Καταβουκοῦλον, which should obviously be κατὰ βούκολον. The βούκολον was the centre of the *clipeus*. The Latin version mistranslates *pro singulis buccis* " to each mouth."

[2] This description is taken from an evidently contemporary document preserved in Constantine Porph. *De cerimoniis*, i. c. 91. There can, I think, be little doubt that Constantine found it in the ceremonial book (Κατάστασις) compiled by Peter the Patrician in the sixth century, from which we know that he derived other accounts of early ceremonies (see *ib.* cc. 84, 85). It is to be noted that the description of the actual ceremonies of A.D. 457 comes down only as far as the words κατὰ τάξιν, p. 412, l. 18 ; the rest of the piece is generalised (in

the present tense) so as to apply to any Emperor who is crowned in the Hebdomon Palace. It describes the return to the city, the halt at Hellenianae (near the Forum of Arcadius) and ceremonies there, a second halt at the Forum of Constantine, a third at St. Sophia, before the Great Palace is reached.

[3] His wife may have been an Ostrogoth, for Theoderic, son of Triarius, was her nephew (Theophanes, A.M. 5970).

[4] John Malalas, xiv. p. 369. For the character of Ardaburius, who in time of peace devoted himself to frivolous amusements — actors, jugglers, and stage entertainments,—see Suidas, *sub* 'Αρδαβούριος, where Priscus may be the source (cp. *F.H.G.* iv. p. 100).

Aspar hoped to use as a puppet, soon showed that he had a will of his own and would not be as amenable to his general's dictation as he had led the general to expect. But, though differences arose [1] and Aspar was unable always to have his own way, yet for at least six or seven years his influence was predominant. Leo had made two promises, to raise Aspar's son Patricius to the rank of Caesar,[2] thereby designating him as successor to the throne, and to give the Caesar one of his daughters in marriage.[3] The second arrangement could probably not be carried out immediately because the girl was too young, and Leo managed to postpone the fulfilment of the first. In the meantime he discovered a means of establishing a counterpoise to the excessive influence of the Germans.

In order to neutralise the fact on which Aspar's power rested, namely that the bulk and the flower of the army consisted of Germans and foreigners—who since the fall of the Hun Empire had begun again to offer themselves as recruits—he formed the plan of recruiting regiments from native subjects no less valiant and robust. He chose the hardy race of Isaurian mountaineers who lived almost like an independent people in the wild regions of Mount Taurus and were little touched by Hellenism. The execution of this policy, begun by himself and carried out by his successor, counteracted the danger that the Germans would prevail in the East as they were prevailing in the West.

[1] Cp. Candidus, p. 135. Brooks (*Zenon and the Isaurians*, 211-212) gives reasons for dating the incident, referred to here, to 459.

[2] The eastern consul in 459 was Patricius, but it is improbable that this was Aspar's son. We must rather identify him with Patricius, *magister officiorum*, to whom several undated laws of Leo are addressed (*C.J.* xii. 19. 9 ; 20. 3-5 ; 50. 22) and who played a public part after Leo's death. Ardaburius was raised to the rank of patrician (Marcellinus, *sub a.* 471), but the date is unknown. A third brother, Ermanaric, was perhaps consul in 465, as colleague of Leo's brother-in-law Basiliscus. At that time Severus was Emperor in the West, and, as Leo did not recognise him, both consuls belonged to the eastern realm.

[3] Of Leo's two daughters, Ariadne was born before, Leontia after, his accession. Brooks (*ib.*) thinks that Ariadne must have been betrothed to Patricius, because Leontia was too young, and because a marriage with the younger daughter would not have had the same significance. But Leo might have preferred to promise the infant —many things might occur before she was ripe for marriage ; and against the second objection might be set the fact that Leontia was born in the purple. We must also take into account that when Zeno married Ariadne we do not hear that Aspar complained that Leo had broken his promise. Leontia married Marcian (son of the western Emperor, Anthemius) whom we shall meet again ; Eustathius, *apud* Evagr. iii. 26.

Leo had recourse to Tarasicodissa,[1] an Isaurian chieftain, who came to Constantinople, and presently married his daughter Ariadne (A.D. 466 or 467),[2] having changed his uncouth name to Zeno. For about four years there was a struggle for ascendancy between the two factions. A new corps of Palace guards was formed, and we may conjecture that it was recruited from stalwart Isaurians, with the title of Excubitors.[3] The Excubitors are for many centuries to be an important section of the residential troops, and, when we meet them for the first time in the reign of Leo, they were, as we shall see, called upon to oppose the Germans.

When a great expedition sailed to Africa against the Vandals in A.D. 468,[4] Leo entrusted the command, not to Aspar or his son, but to Basiliscus, the brother of the Empress Verina. The commander's incompetence led to the failure of the enterprise. It was alleged, but the charge was probably false, that Aspar, sympathising with the Vandals, bribed Basiliscus to betray the fleet with the promise of making him Emperor.[5] In the following year Zeno was consul. It is possible that he had already been appointed Master of Soldiers *in praesenti*,[6] and in this capacity he took the field in Thrace apparently against an incursion of Huns.[7] Some of his soldiers, at the instigation of Aspar, con-

---

[1] Zeno's name is variously given as Tarasikodissa (Candidus, p. 135, who as an Isaurian should have known; cp. Στρακωδισσεων in the MS. of John Malalas), Arikmesios (Eustathius of Ephiphania, *ap.* Evagr. ii. 15), Traskalissaios (Theoph. A.M. 5974, perhaps an error for Τρασκωδισσαίον, cp. Agathias, iv. 29, Ταρασικωδίσαιος). He was a native of Rousoumblada in Isauria (Candidus, *ib.*; Ramsay, *Hist., Geography of Asia Minor*, p. 370). His mother's name was Lallis. Of his brother Longinus we shall hear much.

[2] Cp. Brooks, *op. cit.* 212, and Kulakovski, *Ist. Viz.* i. 352. Theophanes records the marriage under A.M. 5956 = A.D. 459, which is certainly wrong. 467 is the latest possible date, as Leo, son of Zeno and Ariadne, was six years old at the end of 474 (Michael Syr. ix. c. 5, ed. Chabot, vol. ii. p. 143.

[3] John Lydus, *De mag.* i. 16. Th number was 300.

[4] See below, p. 335.

[5] Hydatius, *Chron.* 247. According to this chronicler Aspar was consequently degraded from office and one of his sons put to death.

[6] John Mal. xiv. p. 375. This statement seems probably correct, for if Zeno was *mag. mil.* of the East he would have had no business to defend Thrace. The danger he ran with the Thracian army determined his transference to the eastern command. The statement of Theophanes (A.M. 5962) is certainly not decisive, but the date = A.D. 469, is probably right, and it seems probable that Zeno had been appointed to the East before the end of the same year. He continued to hold this post till the summer of 471 at least (see *C.J.* x. 3. 29, and Brooks, *op. cit.* 212, *n.* 17).

[7] The invasion of Huns under Attila's son Denzic is recorded in this year by Marcellinus. He was opposed by Anagast, *mag. mil.* in Thrace, and slain. *Chron. Pasch.* records this under 468.

spired to assassinate him, but forewarned of the plot he escaped
to Sardica. After this he was nominated Master of Soldiers in
the East, and left Constantinople for Isauria, where he suppressed
the brigand Indacus, one of the most dangerous and daring of
the Isaurian bandits.[1]

It was probably during the absence of his son-in-law in the
East that Leo was at length induced by Aspar to perform his old
promise of conferring the rank of Caesar upon his son Patricius
(A.D. 469–470).[2] Aspar is said (whether on this or some previous
occasion) to have seized the sovran by his purple robe and said,
" Emperor, it is not fitting that he who wears this robe should
speak falsely," and Leo to have replied, " Nor yet is it fitting
that he should be constrained and driven like a slave." [3] There
was great displeasure in Byzantium at the elevation of an Arian
to a rank which was a recognised step to the Imperial throne.
It appears that a deputation of clergy and laymen waited on the
Emperor, imploring him to choose a Caesar who was orthodox,
and the public dissatisfaction was expressed in the Hippodrome
by a riotous protest, in which monks played a prominent part.
Leo pacified the excited crowd by declaring that Patricius was
about to turn from his Arianism and profess the true faith.[4]
The new Caesar was soon afterwards betrothed to Leontia, the
Emperor's younger daughter.

Meanwhile Anagast, a German soldier who had been appointed
Master of Soldiers in Thrace, threatened to rebel. Messengers
from the court persuaded him to desist from his enterprise, and
he alleged that he had been instigated by Ardaburius, whose
letters he sent to the Emperor as evidence.[5] Having failed in
this attempt, Ardaburius endeavoured to gain over the Isaurian
troops in Constantinople [6] to his father's faction. These intrigues

[1] John Ant. *fr.* 90 (*Exc. de Ins.*
p. 130), and Suidas, *sub* 'Ινδακός
(source Priscus ?). The fortress of
Indacus was Cherris.

[2] Theophanes places this event in
or before 468 (A.M. 5961), Victor Tonn.
in 470, to which Brooks inclines.
I agree, for Aspar would have been
able to press Leo more effectively in
Zeno's absence.

[3] Zonaras, xiv. 1 (p. 122 ed. B.-W.).

[4] See *Vita Marcelli* in Simeon
Metaphrastes, *P.G.* 116. 74. Marcellus, archimandrite of the Sleepless
monks, led the protest. Theophanes

says that Leo created Patricius Caesar
διὰ τὸ ἑλκύσαι τὸν "Ασπαρα ἐκ τῆς
'Αρειανικῆς δόξης. Possibly Aspar was
converted.

[5] John Ant. *ib.* (date, consulship of
Jordanes = 470).

[6] These Isaurians were reinforced
by a body of their fellow-countrymen
who had descended on the island of
Rhodes. Many of these brigands had
been cut down there, but the remnant
escaped to Constantinople and were
received by Zeno. Brooks dates this
incident to 469 (*op. cit.* 213, and
C. Med. H. i. 470).

were betrayed to Zeno,[1] who, if he was still in the East, must have hastened back to the capital (A.D. 471). The destruction of Aspar and his family was now resolved upon. There was only too good reason to regard them as public enemies, but foul means were employed for their removal. Aspar and Ardaburius were slain in the palace by eunuchs ; [2] the Caesar Patricius was wounded, but unexpectedly recovered ; the third son Ermanaric happened to be absent and escaped.[3] From this act the Emperor received the name of Butcher (Makelles). It was an important act in the long struggle against the German danger in the East. But it inaugurated a period of Isaurian domination which was to involve the Empire in a weary civil war. This was the price which had to be paid for the defeat of the German generals who sought to appropriate the Empire.

But the German danger was not yet quite stamped out. The Gothic friends of Aspar were dismayed, and they determined to avenge him. Count Ostrys,[4] an officer of high rank who belonged to Aspar's faction, burst into the palace with an armed troop, but in an encounter with the new guards, the Excubitors, they were worsted. Ostrys fled to Thrace, taking with him Aspar's Gothic concubine. The Byzantine populace, with whom the powerful general, Arian as he was, probably had not been unpopular, cried, " A dead man has no friend save Ostrys." [5] The fugitive found a refuge in the camp of the Ostrogothic chief of German federate troops, Theoderic Strabo, Aspar's relative, who, as soon as he heard tidings of the murder, replied by ravaging Thrace. Whether he was deeply incensed or not, he saw an opportunity of stepping into Aspar's place, and when he made his peace with Leo in A.D. 473, he was appointed to the post of Master of Soldiers *in praesenti*, which Aspar had held. The career of Strabo will claim our attention later.[6]

---

[1] Candidus, *ib.* Zeno did not enter the city but remained at Chalcedon till after the murder, Theoph. A.M. 5964.

[2] Marcellinus, *sub* 471. The murder is branded by Damascius as treacherous (ἐδολοφόνησεν, *Vita Isidori* in Photius, *Bibliotheca*, 242, p. 340 ed. Bekker).

[3] Candidus, *ib.* Zeno is said to have assisted Ermanaric's escape to Isauria, where he married a daughter of an illegitimate son of Zeno. After Leo's death he returned to Constantinople (Theoph. *ib.*).

[4] Doubtless the same as the στρατηγός Ostryas mentioned by Priscus, *fr.* 2 (*De leg. gent.* p. 589), in connexion with the Hun invasion of 469. As στρατηγός means *mag. mil.*, it may be conjectured that Ostrys succeeded Zeno as *mag. mil. in praesenti* in that year (cp. above, p. 318, *n.* 6).

[5] John Mal. xiv. p. 371.

[6] Below, Chap. XII. § 5.

At this time it was a common practice for rich people to maintain in their service not only armed slaves but bands of free retainers, often barbarians. It was natural enough that this practice should grow up in provinces which were exposed to hostile depredations, as in Illyricum and in those parts of Asia Minor which were constantly threatened by the Isaurian free-booters. But it is noteworthy, in view of Leo's Isaurian policy, that in his reign Isaurians were themselves hired or retained by private persons and that the Emperor found it necessary to forbid this dangerous usage.[1]

Leo was a man of no education, but he seems to have possessed a good deal of natural good sense. The historian Malchus, who hated him for his religious bigotry, describes him as a sewer of wickedness and condemns his administration as ruinously rapa-cious.[2] This accusation is probably untrue and malicious. The financial methods of the Empire were so oppressive that the charge of rapacity might be brought against any Emperor, but Leo seems to have done nothing to make the system more rigorous, and to have followed in the steps of Marcian in adopting particular measures of relief and clemency as occasion offered.[3] He is reported to have said that a king should distribute pity to those on whom he looks, as the sun distributes heat to those on whom he shines, and he may at least in some degree have practised what he preached. An anecdote suggests that he encouraged petitions. His unmarried sister, Euphemia, resided in a house in the south-eastern corner of the Augusteum, close to the Hippo-drome. The Emperor used to pay her a visit with affectionate regularity every week. She erected a statue to him beside her house, and on its base petitioners used to place their memorials, which were collected every morning by one of the palace servants.[4]

One of the destructive conflagrations which have so often ravaged Constantinople occurred in A.D. 465 (September 2). The fire broke out close to the arsenal,[5] and it was said that it was

---

[1] *C.J.* ix. 12. 10 *omnibus per civitates et agros habendi bucellarios vel Isauros armatosque servos licentiam volumus esse praeclusam* (A.D. 468). See above, p. 43.

[2] Malchus, *fr.* 2a (*F.H.G.* iv. p. 114).

[3] Antioch was laid in ruins by an earthquake in Sept. 458 (cp. Clinton,

F.R., sub a.). Leo rebuilt the public edifices (John Mal. xiv. p. 369, Evagrius, ii. 12).

[4] The statue was hence called the Pittakes (from πιττάκια, letters). See *Patria*, p. 167 (cp. 65).

[5] Near the Gate of the Neorion, now Baghtsche Kapu.

caused by an old woman who was careless with her candle. Superstitious people believed that a malignant demon had assumed the shape of the old woman.[1] The fire spread eastward to the Acropolis, as far as the old temple of Apollo, and southward to the Forum of Constantine, whence it devastated the porticoes and buildings of Middle Street westward as far as the Forum of Taurus, and also pursued a southward course to the House of Amantius or Church of St. Thomas and to the Harbour of Julian.[2] It lasted three days. The Senate-house on the north side of the Forum of Constantine was destroyed,[3] and the Nymphaeum directly opposite to it, a building in which those who had not large enough houses of their own used to celebrate their weddings. Many magnificent private residences were burned down. It is said that Aspar ran about the streets with a pail of water on his shoulders, urging all to follow his example and offering silver coins to encourage them. There is no hint of the existence of a fire-brigade.[4] The Emperor, alarmed by the disaster, withdrew across the Golden Horn to the palace of St. Mamas and remained there for six months.

In his ecclesiastical policy Leo followed Marcian and faithfully maintained orthodoxy as established by the Council of Chalcedon. No memorable feat of arms distinguished his reign [5] to counterbalance the disastrous issue of his ambitious expedition against the Vandals, which will be recounted in another place. The Illyrian peninsula was troubled by the restlessness of the Ostrogoths, but the brunt of their hostilities was to be borne by Leo's successor. He died on February 3, A.D. 474, having co-opted as

---

[1] See Evagrius, ii. 13, the chief description of the fire (probably derived from Priscus, through Eustathius). Also Theodore Lector, i. 22 ; John Mal. xiv. 372 ; Zonaras, xiv. 1, 16.

[2] From here it spread to the Church of Homonoia of which the position is unknown.

[3] Cedrenus, i. p. 610 (source unknown), mentions the Σενάτον and Νυμφαῖον. The building in the Forum Tauri to which he refers may be the Basilica Theodosiana. The fire was described in the work of Candidus (cp. *F.H.G.* iv. p. 135), and Shestakov has tried to show that the accounts in Cedrenus and Zonaras are derived

from him (*Kandid Isauriski*, cp. Bibl. ii. 2, 13).

[4] In later times we hear of regular arrangements for extinguishing fires. See Michael, *Vita Theodori Studitae* in *P.G.* 99, p. 312 τὴν τῶν σιφώνων κατὰ τόπους παρασκευήν.

[5] Early in his reign a barbarian people, which invaded Pontus, was repelled and subjugated. We hear of this in a letter of bishops of Pontus to the Emperor (Mansi, vii. p. 600), and the same event seems to be referred to in other letters (*ib.* 581, 583). Tillemont thought these barbarians must be Huns (*Hist. des Empereurs*, vi. 367), but it seems to me more probable that they were the Tzani (for whom see below, p. 434).

Augustus (in October) his grandson Leo, an infant aged about six years.[1]

§ 2. *Maximus, Avitus, and Majorian* (A.D. 455–461)

If it was a critical moment at Constantinople at the death of Marcian, it had been a still more critical moment in Italy on the death of Valentinian III. two years before (A.D. 455). For not only was there no male heir of the house of Theodosius, but there was no minister or general of commanding influence, no Aetius or Aspar, to force a decision. Military riots were inevitable, a civil war was possible ; and we read that " Rome was in a state of disturbance and confusion, and the military forces were divided into two factions, one wishing to elevate Maximus, the other supporting Maximian (son of an Egyptian merchant) who had been the steward of Aetius." [2] A third possible candidate was Majorian, brother-in-arms of Aetius, with whom he had fought against the Franks,[3] and he had the good wishes of Eudoxia, the widowed Empress. If there had been time to consult the Emperor Marcian, we may conjecture that his influence would have been thrown into the scale for Majorian. But the money of Petronius Maximus [4] decided the event in his favour, just as Pertinax had won the Empire after the death of Commodus by

---

[1] For dates see John Mal. xiv. p. 376. The details of the coronation of Leo II. are preserved in a contemporary account which was probably included in a work of Peter the Patrician (Const. Porph. *De cer.* i. c. 94). After the coronation of the child the two Leos had to be distinguished as Λέων ὁ μέγας and Λέων ὁ μικρός, and this, I believe, must be the origin of the designation of Leo as " the Great " ; just as reversely Theodosius II. was called "the Small," because in his infancy he had been known as ὁ μικρὸς βασιλεύς to distinguish him from Arcadius (see above, p. 7). Leo never did anything which could conceivably earn him the title of Great in the sense in which it was' bestowed by posterity on Alexander or Constantine. — Coins issued at the beginning of Leo's reign show Marcian's head, the legend being merely altered to *Dn Leo Perpet Aug* ; and Pulcheria's coin stamp with

Victoria Augg (see above, p. 236) was used for Verina (*Ael Verina Aug*). Later coins of Leo have his portrait, a bearded man ; but his face is seen better on a medallion (Sabatier, *Pl.* vii. 1), for which an old stamp of the seventh quinquennalia of Theodosius II. was used (as the unaltered reverse shows).

[2] John Ant. *fr.* 85 (*De ins.* p. 127). His account deserves credit because he drew his information from the contemporary historian Priscus.

[3] Aetius, however, dismissed him from whatever post he held. Sidonius attributes this injustice to the influence of the wife of Aetius who was jealous of Majorian's growing fame (*Carm.* v. 126-294). Majorian retired to his country estate, but was recalled to military service after the Patrician's death, by Valentinian (*ib.* 305-308).

[4] The wealth of Maximus is noted by Sidonius Apollinaris, *Epp.* ii. 13.

bribing the Praetorian guards. He was elevated to the throne on March 17, A.D. 455.

Maximus endeavoured to strengthen himself on the throne by forcing Eudoxia to marry him, and if she had yielded willingly, it is possible that the Italians might have rallied round him and he might have reigned securely. But though he was a member of the noble Anician house, he was not like Marcian ; he was not one whom the Augusta could bring herself to tolerate even for cogent political reasons. If he was really related to the British tyrant Maximus, who had been subdued by Theodosius, the great-granddaughter of Theodosius had perhaps not forgotten the connexion ; but the widow of Valentinian must have known or suspected the instigator of her lord's murder.[1] In any case, the new Augustus was so hated and despised by Eudoxia that she was said to have taken the bold and fatal step of summoning Gaiseric the Vandal to overthrow the tyrant. There was indeed a particular reason for asking aid from Carthage, instead of appealing, as one might have expected her to do, to Constantinople. Maximus had not only forced her to wed him, but he also forced her daughter Eudocia to give her hand to his son Palladius whom he created Caesar. And Eudocia was the affianced wife of Huneric, the heir to the Vandal throne. The act of Maximus touched the honour of Gaiseric, and he would be likely to come to the rescue more promptly than Marcian. The story, therefore, of the appeal of the Empress to the Vandal is credible, though it is not certainly true.[2]

Petronius Maximus enjoyed the sweets of power for two months and a half, but he found them far from sweet. The man who as a private individual was so great a figure, " once made emperor and prisoned in the palace walls, was rueing his own success before the first evening fell." Formerly he used to live by the clock, but now he had to renounce his old regular life and his " senatorial ease." His rule was " from

---

[1] The favour he showed to the assassins is recorded by Prosper, *sub a.*

[2] Little is said of it by western writers (Hydatius, 167, refers to it as an evil rumour). The sources are John Ant. *loc. cit.*; Marcellinus, *Chron.*, *sub a.*, Procopius, *B.V.* i. 4 ; Evagrius, *H.E.* ii. 7. All these accounts are probably derived from Priscus, but it is evident from John Ant. (cp. οἱ δέ φασι) that Priscus did not tell the story as definitely true, but admitted the possibility that Gaiseric might have come of his own accord. The part played by the mysterious *Burgundio* in Sidonius, *Carm.* vii. 441 *sqq.*, is not clear. For Palladius see Prosper, *ib.*

the first tempestuous, with popular tumults, tumults of
soldiery, tumults of allies." An influential nobleman, who
was often with him, used to hear him exclaim, "Happy
thou, O Damocles, whose royal duresse did not outlast a single
banquet ! " [1]

In May it was known in Italy that Gaiseric had set sail.
There was consternation at Rome, and a considerable exodus
both of the higher and the lower classes. Maximus, when he
heard that the Vandals had landed, thought only of flight. He
was deserted by his bodyguard and all his friends, and as he
was riding out of the city, some one cast a stone and hit him
on the temple. The stroke killed him on the spot and the
crowd tore his body limb from limb (May 31).[2]

Three days later [3] Gaiseric and his Vandals entered Rome.
Whether they came entirely of their own accord or in answer
to a summons from the Empress, they were now bent only on
rapine. The bishop of Rome, Leo I., met them at the gates.
Although he did not succeed in protecting the city against
pillage, violence, and "vandalism," he preserved it by his
intervention from the evils of massacre and conflagration. For
fourteen days the enemy abode in the city, and plundered it
coolly and methodically.[4] The palace on the Palatine was
ransacked thoroughly. Precious works of art were carried off,
and many of the gilt bronze tiles which roofed the temple of
Jupiter Capitolinus were removed. The robbers added to their
booty the golden treasures which Titus had taken from the
temple of Jerusalem. When they had rifled the public and
private wealth of Rome, and loaded their ships, they returned
to Africa with many thousand captives, including the Empress
Eudoxia and her two daughters, Eudocia and Placidia.[5] It will
be remembered that the idea of an alliance between Gaiseric's
heir and a daughter of Valentinian had been suggested by
Aetius. This plan was now carried out. Huneric married

---

[1] Sidonius Apoll. *Epp.* ii. 13
(Dalton).

[2] His end is described by Prosper,
ib., and with more detail by John Ant.
ib. ; Jordanes, *Get.* 235, names Ursus,
a Roman soldier, as the assassin.

[3] Victor Tonn. *sub a.*

[4] *Secura et libera scrutatione*
(Prosper).

[5] For the sack of Rome see, besides
Prosper, Procopius, *B.V.* i. 5 (he
mentions that a ship laden with
statues was lost on the way to
Carthage). Gaudentius, son of Aetius,
was one of the captives. Cp. Grisar,
Hist. of Rome and the Popes (Eng.
tr.), i. 96-99 ; Martroye, *Genséric*,
158 *sqq.*

Eudocia. Her sister Placidia was already the wife of a distinguished Roman, Olybrius.[1]

But the question was, who was to be Emperor ? Rome was paralysed by the shock of the Vandal visitation, but Gaul intervened. Marcus Maecilius Flavius Eparchius Avitus, the man who had fought by the side of Aetius and at a great crisis had decided Theoderic the Visigothic king to march against the Huns, had been appointed by Maximus Master of Both Services in Gaul. It was important for the new Emperor to establish a friendly understanding with the Visigothic ruler, and no one was more fitted to bring this about than Avitus, the intimate friend of Theoderic I., and no less a *persona grata* to Theoderic II. He was, in fact, at Tolosa when the news of the death of Maximus arrived, and Theoderic persuaded him that he was the necessary man.[2] He was proclaimed Emperor by the Goths at Tolosa (July 9, or 10) ; five weeks later his assumption of the Imperial power was confirmed at a meeting of representative Gallo-Romans at Ugernum (Beaucaire), and he was formally invested at Arles with Imperial insignia.[3]

Towards the end of the year Avitus crossed the Alps to assert his authority in Italy and assume the consulship for A.D. 456. He was accompanied by a famous man of letters who was his son-in-law, Caius Sollius Apollinaris Sidonius, son and grandson of Praetorian Prefects of Gaul.[4] Sidonius had been born and educated at Lyons, and was now about twenty-five years of age. For a quarter of a century he was to play a considerable part in the relations between Gaul and Italy as well as in the internal affairs of Gaul. The poetical panegyric which he recited at Rome in honour of his father-in-law's consulship [5] marks the beginning of his public career ; his statue was set up in the Forum of Trajan. But the Emperor Avitus, who was so much at home at Tolosa, was not welcome at Rome, though he was acknowledged by Marcian. He was acceptable neither to the soldiers nor to the Senate, and his

---

[1] Priscus, *fr.* 10, *De leg. Rom.* ; Procopius, *B.V.* i. 4. Evagrius, *H.E.* ii. 7 blunders. See Clinton, *F.R.* ii. p. 127.

[2] Sidonius, *Carm.* vii. 517 *tibi pareat orbis, ni pereat.*

[3] *Ib.* 522-600. For dates see *Fast. Vind. pr.* p. 304, and Victor Tonn.

sub a. We have a portrait of Avitus on gold coins which show his side face, bearded ; on the reverse he is trampling on a captive.

[4] The father was Prefect in 448; the grandfather in 408.

[5] *Carm.* vii.

behaviour did not tend to make him popular, although his reign was distinguished by military successes by land and sea.

Both the Vandals and the Suevians had been alert to take advantage of the difficulties which followed Valentinian's death. Gaiseric had been extending his authority over those African provinces which had been left to Rome by the treaty of A.D. 442. The Emperor Marcian had sent an embassy to remonstrate with him on the sack of Rome and the captivity of the Imperial ladies ; Avitus sent an embassy warning him to observe the treaty. But Gaiseric was inflexibly hostile ; he defied both Marcian and Avitus ; and he sent a fleet of sixty ships to descend on Italy or Gaul. The general Ricimer, destined to be the leading figure in the West for about sixteen years, now makes his appearance on the scene. His mother was a daughter of the Visigothic king Wallia, and his father was a Sueve ; he had risen in Roman service, and Avitus appointed him Master of Soldiers.[1] He now went to Sicily with an army and a fleet ; a Vandal descent on that island was evidently expected, and was apparently attempted in the neighbourhood of Agrigentum. The enemy was forced to retreat, but Ricimer followed them and gained a naval victory in Corsican waters (A.D. 456).[2]

Theoderic II., who seems to have been chiefly responsible for the elevation of Avitus, had won the Gothic throne by murdering his brother Thorismund (A.D. 453).[3] He now showed his goodwill to the new Emperor by marching into Spain and making war upon the Suevians, who were perpetually harrying the Roman provinces. But, though he went in the name of Avitus and the Roman Republic, we cannot doubt that he was deliberately preparing for the eventual fulfilment of the ambition of the Goths to possess Spain themselves, by weakening the Suevic power. The king of the Suevians, Rechiar, was his brother-in-law, and to him Theoderic sent ambassadors calling upon him to desist from his raids into Roman territory. Rechiar defied him and invaded Tarraconensis, whereupon Theoderic led a host of Goths, reinforced by Burgundians, into Gallaecia, and defeated the Suevians in a battle on the river Urbicus, near Astorga (October 5, A.D. 456). The victor pushed on

---

[1] Sidonius, *Carm.* ii. 361 *sqq.*

[2] We have to combine Hydatius, 177, with Sidonius, *ib.* 367, and Priscus, *fr.* 7, *De leg. Rom.*

[3] There is an interesting account of Theoderic and the daily routine of his life in Sidonius, *Epp.* i. 2.

to Bracara, which he captured three weeks later, and his barbarous army committed all the acts of violence and rapine usual in sacks, short of massacre and rape. Sometime later Rechiar, who had fled, was captured at Portuscale (Oporto) and paid with his life for defying his brother-in-law.[1]   The battle of the Urbicus was an important event, for it shattered the power of the Suevians. Their kingdom indeed survived for 120 years, but it never recovered its old strength.

The crushing victory won by his German allies in Spain did not avail Avitus. Before the great battle was fought he had left Rome, virtually as a fugitive, on his way to Gaul, and was probably already a prisoner. The circumstances which led to his fall are thus related : [2]—

> When Avitus reigned at Rome there was famine in the city, and the people blaming Avitus compelled him to remove from the city of the Romans the allies from Gaul who had entered it along with him (that so there might be fewer mouths to feed). He also dismissed the Goths whom he had brought for the protection of Rome, having distributed among them money which he obtained by selling to merchants bronze stripped from public works, for there was no gold in the imperial treasury. This excited the Romans to revolt when they saw their city stripped of its adornments.
>
> But Majorian and Ricimer, no longer held in fear of the Goths, openly rebelled, so that Avitus was constrained—terrified on the one hand by the prospect of internal troubles, on the other hand by the hostilities of the Vandals—to withdraw from Rome and set out for Gaul.[3]

He was captured at Placentia by Ricimer and Majorian. He was deposed from the throne and elected bishop of the city which witnessed his discomfiture (October 17 or 18, A.D. 456), but died soon afterwards.[4]

A new Emperor was not immediately elected. A temporary cessation of a separate Imperial rule in the West occurred on several occasions during the twenty years which followed the death of Valentinian. One of these intervals occurred now. They are often called interregnums ; it is natural to say that from October A.D. 456 to April A.D. 457 there was an inter-

---

[1] Hydatius, 170-175.

[2] By John Ant. *fr.* 86, *De ins.*

[3] John Ant. *fr.* 86 (*De ins.* p. 128). This notice (doubtless derived from Priscus) is the sole authority for the vandalism of Avitus, which was probably the immediate motive of Majorian's measure for the preserva-

tion of public buildings.

[4] John Ant. *ib.* says he was starved or strangled. There is a different story in Gregory of Tours, *Hist. Franc.* ii. 11. For the date cp. *Cons. Ital.* p. 304. Avitus had armed men with him, and there was a battle at Placentia in which " his patrician " Messianus was slain, *ib.*

regnum in the West, and the expression represents the actual
situation. But we must not forget that in theory the phrase
is incorrect. Legally, Marcian was the sole head of the Empire
from the fall of Avitus to his own death at the end of January,
and Leo was the sole head of the Empire for three months after
the death of Marcian.[1]

The Master of Soldiers, Ricimer, whose prestige had been
established by his naval victory, now held the destinies of Italy
in his hands. He had succeeded to the post and the responsibilities of Stilicho, Constantius, and Aetius, but his task was
vastly more difficult. For while those defenders of the Empire
against the German enemies were supported by the secure
existence of an established dynasty, Ricimer had to set up
Emperors in whose name he could act. At the beginning of
A.D. 457 the situations in Italy and at Constantinople were
similar. In both cases the solution of the difficulty depended
on the action of a military leader of barbarian birth ; Aspar's
position was as that of Ricimer. Both were the makers of
Emperors, neither could aspire to be an Emperor himself. They
were Arians as well as barbarians.[2]

The legitimacy of any Emperor set up in Italy depended on
his being recognised as a colleague by the Emperor reigning at
Constantinople. Avitus had been recognised by Marcian, and
if the seat of his successor was to be firmly established it was
indispensable that he should obtain similar recognition. The
political importance of conforming to this constitutional necessity
was realised by Ricimer, and we may confidently assume that
after the fall of Avitus, he, acting probably through the Roman
Senate, communicated with the Emperor of the East. Marcian's
death postponed a settlement, but one of the early acts of Leo I.
was to nominate a colleague. That the suggestion of Majorian's
name came from Rome we can hardly doubt. Julius Valerianus
Majorianus was a thorough Roman and on that account most
acceptable to the Senators. He had been, we saw, the candidate

---

[1] Coins of Marcian minted in Italy
belong to this interval, and those of
Leo to the longer period between the
death of Majorian and the accession
of Anthemius (461–467). Cp. de Salis,
Coins of the Eudoxias, p. 215, who
holds that the custom of striking
coins at Italian mints in honour of
the eastern colleague ceased at the
beginning of the reign of Valentinian III.

[2] We have an inscription of Ricimer
recording that he decorated with
mosaics the Arian church of S. Agatha
in Rome in accordance with a vow.
Its date is later than 459, the year of
his consulship. De Rossi, ii. 1, p.
438 ; Dessau, 1294.

of Eudoxia after her husband's death. He was elevated to the
throne on April 1, A.D. 457.[1] At the same time Leo conferred
upon Ricimer the title of Patrician.

There were two tasks for the new Augustus to accomplish
if he was to make his seat on the throne secure and exercise
effective rule in the west. He had, in the first place, to quell
the opposition in Gaul. The fall of Avitus had aroused the
wrath both of his barbarian friends, Visigoths and Burgundians,
and of the provincials. Gallic Avitus had failed to conciliate
Italian goodwill; it was now to be seen whether Italian Majorian
would succeed in solving the reverse problem. There was little
love lost between the Romans and the trans-Alpine provincials,
and there was now a serious danger, such as had often occurred
before, that Gaul would attempt to dissociate itself politically
from Italy, and have an Emperor to itself.

There are indeed signs of a gradually widening rift between
Gaul and the rest of the Empire ever since the time of the
tyrants in the reign of Honorius. It has been observed [2] that
of the twenty-eight Praetorian Prefects of Gaul in the fifth
century whose names are recorded, we know that eighteen were
Gauls, and of the other ten none is known to be of Italian birth.
This points to the conclusion that the feeling in Gaul was such
that the central government considered it impolitic to appoint
any one to that post outside the circle of Gallic senators. The
loss of Africa probably accentuated the sectional feeling in both
Italy and Gaul, and from this point of view the elevation of
Avitus was a momentarily successful attempt of the Gallic
nobility to wrest from the Italians the political predominance
which had hitherto been theirs. It was the business of Majorian
to preserve for Italy her leading position and at the same time to
conciliate the Gallic nobility.

Majorian entered Gaul with an army composed mainly of
German mercenaries, and found the Burgundians in league with
the inhabitants of Lugdunensis Prima against himself.[3] Lyons,

---

[1] He had been created *magister
militum* in February (*Fast. Vind. Pr.*
p. 305). His address to the Senate
(*Nov.* 1 *de ortu imperii divi Maioriani*)
announces the inauguration of a new
era. Ricimer is thus mentioned : *erit
apud nos cum parente patricioque nostro
Ricimere rei militaris pervigil cura.*

[2] By   Sundwall   (*Weströmische
Studien,* p. 8), who has insisted
rightly on the importance of the
struggle for power between Gaul and
Italy.

[3] *Cons. Ital.* (Auct. Prosper, Havn.),
sub 457 ; Marius Avent. *sub* 456.

which had received a Burgundian garrison, was compelled to surrender and was punished for its rebellion by the imposition of heavier taxation. This burden, however, was soon remitted, through the efforts of Sidonius Apollinaris, who delivered an enthusiastic Panegyric at Lyons on the man who had helped to dethrone his father-in-law.[1] The Visigoths were besieging Arelate, but Majorian's general, Aegidius, drove back Theoderic from its walls and firm compacts were made between the two potentates.[2] The Burgundians were allowed peacefully to possess the province of Lugdunensis Prima.[3] Honours were freely distributed to the Gallic nobility.

Majorian had accomplished one task; the other was more difficult. It was indispensable for an Emperor, who had not the prestige of belonging to a dynasty, to win general confidence by proving himself equal to the great emergency of the time; he must " preserve the state of the Roman world." [4] The deliverance of Arelate was a good beginning. But the great emergency was the hostility of the Vandals who in their ships harried the Roman provinces and infested the Mediterranean waters. The defeats which Ricimer had inflicted on their fleet at Corsica did not paralyse their hostilities. The words of an historian indicate that Avitus in facing this danger had felt his inability to grapple with it : " He was afraid of the wars with the Vandals." [5]

Majorian prepared an expedition against Africa on a grand scale; his fleet numbered 300 ships and was collected off the coast of Spain. The hopes of all his subjects were awakened and their eyes fixed on his preparations. But a curious fatality attended all expeditions undertaken against the Vandals, whether they proceeded from Old Rome or from New Rome, or from both together. The expedition of Castinus had collapsed in A.D. 422, that of Aspar had failed in A.D. 431, the armament of Ardaburius did not even reach its destination in A.D. 441, and the expedition of Majorian came to naught in A.D. 460. Gaiseric ravaged the coasts of Spain and many of the Roman warships

---

[1] *Carm.* iv., v.

[2] Hydatius, 197, A.D. 459. Majorian was in Gaul in 458–459.

[3] Not including Lyons.

[4] Majorian, *Nov.* 1 *Romani orbis* *statum . . . propitia divinitate servemus.*

[5] See Priscus, *fr.* 13 (*De leg. gent.* p. 585), who is almost verbally followed by John Ant. *fr.* 87, p. 203.

were surprised and captured in the bay of Alicante.[1] Yet another expedition, and one on a grand scale, was soon to be fitted out and also to meet with discomfiture ; and more than seventy years were to elapse until the numerous failures were to be retrieved by the victories of Justinian and Belisarius.

This misfortune led to the fall of Majorian. He returned from Spain to Gaul, and after a sojourn at Arles [2] passed into Italy without an army. In Italy, and at Rome, he was probably popular ; [3] but now that he had proved himself unable to " preserve the state of the Roman world," Ricimer, who was thoroughly dissatisfied with him, could venture to take action against him. At Tortona Majorian was seized by Ricimer's officers, stripped of the purple, and beheaded (August 2, A.D. 461).[4] He had done at once too little and too much. An Emperor who was just strong enough to act with independent authority, but not strong enough to contend with the enemies of the State, was useless to Ricimer, who himself seemed resolved not to leave Italy, probably judging that the constant presence of a capable general with considerable forces was necessary against descents of the Vandals. There were other enemies too against whom he had to defend it. He had to fight against the Ostrogoths of Pannonia, and to repel an invasion of Alans. But the great foe was Gaiseric, who hated him as the grandson of King Wallia.

§ 3. *The War with the Vandals* (A.D. 461–468)

Nearly three and a half months passed before Majorian was succeeded by Libius Severus, a Lucanian, who was elected by the Senate at the instance of Ricimer and proclaimed at Ravenna (November 19, A.D. 461). He was not recognised at Constan-

---

[1] Marius Avent. *sub a.* 460 (where Elice = Alicante is misleadingly described as near New Carthage). Cp. Hydatius, 200, and see Martroye, *Genséric*, p. 192. Majorian made a " disgraceful treaty " with Gaiseric, John Ant. *ib.* Probably he ceded the Roman provinces in Africa (the Mauretanias and Tripolitana) which Gaiseric had recently seized.

[2] He celebrated games at which Sidonius Apollinaris was present (*Epp.* i. 11).

[3] During A.D. 458 Majorian had attempted much remedial legislation. He alleviated the public burdens by a remission of arrears (*Nov.* 2) and resuscitated the office of *defensor civitatis* (*Nov.* 3). He enacted a much-needed law for preserving the public buildings of Rome, to check the " disfigurement of the face of the venerable city " (*Nov.* 4). He also endeavoured to deal with the social evil of celibacy (*Nov.* 6).

[4] *Fasti Vind. pr.*, *sub a.* 464.

tinople. He reigned as a figurehead ; Ricimer was the actual
ruler.[1]

It might seem that at this juncture Italy might have received
another Augustus from Gaul, and that Aegidius, Master of Both
Services in Gaul [2] and friend of Majorian, might have crossed
the Alps to avenge his death. Aegidius acknowledged no allegiance to Ricimer's Emperor,[3] but he was fully occupied with the
defence of the Gallic provinces against the Visigoths, who
were attempting to extend their power northward and eastward.
We find him winning a battle at Orleans in A.D. 463,[4] and in
the following year he died.

Ricimer had an opponent in another quarter, the count
Marcellinus. In A.D. 461 this general was in Sicily, in command
of an army chiefly consisting of Hun auxiliaries ; he had probably
been posted there by Majorian to protect the island against the
Vandals. But the bribes of Ricimer prevailed upon the cupidity
of the Huns and induced them to leave the service of Marcellinus
and enter his own. Then Marcellinus, conscious that he could
not vie with Ricimer in riches, went to Dalmatia, where he
ruled under the authority of Leo, and perhaps with the title of
Master of Soldiers in Dalmatia.[5] On his departure Sicily was
ravaged by the Vandals and Moors, and a pacific embassy from

---

[1] His monogram appears on the
reverse of coins of Severus. There
were a good many issues of coins
during this reign. Perhaps one of the
earliest of the solidi of Severus was
that with the same reverse type which
appears on solidi of Petronius Maximus
and Majorian—an Emperor holding
a cross and a globe surmounted by a
Victory, with his right foot on a
dragon's head.—A bronze weight with
an inscription of Plotinus Eustathius,
Prefect of Rome, may belong to the
reign of Severus (*C.I.L.* x. 8072).
It illustrates the position of Ricimer,
whose name is associated with those of
Emperors : *salvis dd. nn. et patricio
Ricimere.* On another tablet, of the
Praet. Prefect Probianus, his name
does not appear with those of Leo
and Severus (Dessau, 811).

[2] Hydatius, 218. It was doubtless Maximus who first conferred
this higher rank and title on a
Gallic commander (Avitus), hitherto a
magister equitum. The change illus-

trates the political importance of Gaul
at this time. See above, p. 326.

[3] Priscus, *fr.* 14, *De leg. gent.*

[4] Cp. Hydatius, *ib.* ; Marius Avent.
sub a. Aegidius defeated Frederic,
brother of King Theoderic, near
Orleans. Before his death he was
negotiating with Gaiseric, the plan
being that the Vandals should attack
Ricimer in Italy while Aegidius was
making war on the Visigoths.

[5] Marcellinus had been a friend of
Aetius and after his murder had withdrawn to Dalmatia. The Gallo-
Romans offered him the Imperial
crown in 458 before they accepted
Majorian. (Procopius, *B.V.* i. 6 ;
Sidonius, *Epp.* i. 11. 6.) Damascius
in his *Vita Isidori* (Photius, *Bibl.* 242
p. 342) describes him as αὐτοδέσποτος
ἡγεμών of Dalmatia. I conjecture
that his title was *magister militum
Dalmatiae,* because after his death
his nephew Julius Nepos held this
exceptional title ; see *C.J.* vi. 61. 5
(A.D. 473).

Ricimer had no effect. But another embassy sent at the same time by the Emperor Leo induced Gaiseric to come to terms at last in regard to the ladies of the Theodosian house, whose deliverance from their captivity in Carthage Marcian had vainly endeavoured to secure. Eudocia, the bride of Huneric, was retained, but her mother Eudoxia and her sister Placidia were sent to Constantinople. In return, Gaiseric bargained for a certain share of the property of Valentinian III. as the dowry of Eudocia.[1] He had already occupied and annexed the Mauretanian provinces, as well as Sardinia, Corsica, and the Balearic islands.

This concession had its definite political purpose which was soon revealed. The Vandal monarch now came forward as the champion of the Theodosian house against Ricimer and his upstart Emperor. Placidia had married Olybrius, a member of the noble Anician gens, and Gaiseric demanded that Olybrius should succeed to the throne in Italy. Threatened on one hand by the Vandals, on the other by the ruler of Dalmatia, Ricimer and the obedient Senate solicited the good offices of Leo. He was asked to bring about a reconciliation with Gaiseric and with Marcellinus. Leo consented. One envoy prevailed on Marcellinus not to wage war against the Romans, the other returned from Carthage without result. Gaiseric claimed in his daughter-in-law's name all the private property possessed by her father in Italy, and also the inheritance of Aetius, whose son Gaudentius he retained a prisoner. In pursuance of these claims he led a great expedition against Italy and Sicily, ravaged the country districts and undefended towns. There was no efficient navy to oppose him at sea.

The elevation of Olybrius, which would have been a restitution of the Theodosian dynasty, might have seemed a hopeful solution of some of the difficulties of the situation, but the fact that he was Gaiseric's candidate and relative was a reason against accepting him. For a year and eight months after the death of Severus (August 15, A.D. 465),[2] no successor was appointed. Then Gaiseric made a raid on the Peloponnesus (A.D. 467) and Leo determined to take decisive steps and act in close conjunction

---

[1] A.D. 462. Hydatius, 216. Priscus, *fr.* 10 (in *De leg. Rom.*).

[2] *Fast. Vind. pr.*, *sub* 464. According to the Chronicle of Cassiodorus,

ut dicitur, Ricimeris fraude Severus Romae in palatio veneno peremptus est. If this is true, Ricimer had a hand in the death of no fewer than three, if not four, Emperors.

with the Italian government. Now that not only Italy and
Sicily were threatened, but the entire commerce of the Mediterranean, the forces of the east were to be united with those of
Italy and Dalmatia against the African foe. The first step was
to find a suitable man to invest with Imperial authority in the
west. The choice of Leo fell on the patrician Anthemius, who,
as the son-in-law of the Emperor Marcian, might be considered in
some sort a representative of the house of Theodosius, and his
pretensions might be set against those of Gaiseric's candidate, the
husband of Placidia. The support of Ricimer was secured by
an arrangement that he should marry the daughter of Anthemius.
The elder Placidia had married Athaulf, her granddaughter
Eudocia had married Huneric, both indeed under a certain
compulsion ; yet Anthemius afterwards professed to regard it
as a great condescension to have given his daughter to the
barbarian general. He arrived in Italy and was proclaimed
Emperor near Rome on April 12, A.D. 467.[1]

The expedition which was organised to overthrow the kingdom
of the Vandals was on a grand and impressive scale, but it ended
in miserable failure, due to lukewarmness and even treachery
both in the east and in the west.

The number of vessels that set sail from Constantinople
(A.D. 468) is said to have been 1113, and the total number of
men who embarked was calculated as exceeding 100,000. But
unfortunately Leo, under the influence of his wife Verina and his
friend Aspar, appointed as general a man who was both incompetent and untrustworthy, his wife's brother Basiliscus.
Aspar, it is said, was not over-anxious that Leo's position should
be strengthened by such an exploit as the subversion of the Vandal
kingdom ; he schemed therefore to procure the election of a
general whose success was extremely improbable.[2] The western
armament obeyed a more competent commander. Marcellinus

---

[1] *Cons. Ital.*, *sub a.* p. 305, Cassiodorus, *Chron.*, *sub a.* He was not
created Emperor or crowned until he
arrived in Italy, for he sent Heliocrates
to Constantinople to announce his
elevation and obtain formal recognition. Leo sent his image bound with
bay leaves (τὰ λαυρεάτα) to the cities
of the east with a command that it
should be honoured like his own, " that
all the cities may learn with joy that

the powers of both sections of the
Empire are united " (Peter Patricius,
in Constantine Porph. *De cer.* i. 87,
where the ceremony of the reception
of the ambassador of Anthemius is
described).

[2] Compare Hydatius, 247 *Asparem
degradatum   ad   privatam   vitam
filiumque eius occisum adversus Ro-
manum imperium, sicut detectique sunt,
Vandalis consulentes.*

assumed the direction of the Italian fleet.[1] But his participation in the enterprise alienated Ricimer, who was his personal enemy, and who seems to have been jealous of Anthemius already.

The plan of operations was that the eastern forces should be divided into two parts, and that the Vandals should be attacked at three points at the same time. Basiliscus himself was to sail directly against Carthage. Heraclius, another general, having taken up the forces of Egypt on his way, was to disembark in Tripolitana, and to march to Carthage by land. Marcellinus, with the Italian forces, was to surprise the Vandals in Sardinia, and sail thence to join the eastern armies at Carthage.

If the commander-in-chief had not been Basiliscus, and if the opponent had not been Gaiseric, the expedition might easily have succeeded. But Gaiseric, though physically the least, was mentally the greatest of the barbarians of his time. Even as it was, though Basiliscus had such a foe to cope with, success was within the grasp of his hand. The invaders were welcome to the Catholics of Africa, who were persecuted by their Arian lords. Marcellinus accomplished his work in Sardinia without difficulty ; Heraclius met no obstacle in executing his part of the scheme ; and the galleys of Basiliscus scattered the fleet of the Vandals in the neighbourhood of Sicily. On hearing of this disaster, Gaiseric is said to have given up all for lost ; the Roman general had only to strike a decisive blow and Carthage would have fallen into his hands. But he let the opportunity slip, and, taking up his station in a haven at some distance from Carthage, he granted to the humble prayers of his wily opponent a respite of five days, of which Gaiseric made good use. He prepared a new fleet and a number of fireships. The winds favoured his designs, and he suddenly bore down on the Roman armament, which, under the combined stress of surprise, adverse wind, and the destructive ships of fire, was routed and at least half destroyed. Basiliscus fled with the remnant to Sicily, to join Marcellinus, whose energy and resources might possibly have retrieved the disaster ; but the hand of an assassin, inspired perhaps by Ricimer, rendered this hope futile.[2] Heraclius, who had not reached Carthage when he heard of the defeat of the

---

[1] Marcellinus, *Chron.*, *sub a.* 468, where it is mentioned that Marcellinus was a pagan. He had received from Leo (we may assume) the title of Patrician.

[2] Marcellinus, *Chron.*

fleet, retraced his steps, and Basiliscus returned to Constantinople, where amid popular odium [1] he led a life of retirement at Heraclea on the Propontis, until he appeared on the scene of public life again after Leo's death.

The ill-success of this expedition, organised on such a grand scale that it might have seemed irresistible, must have produced a great moral effect. The Roman Empire had put forth all its strength and had signally failed against one barbarian nation. This event must have not only raised the pretensions and arrogance of the Vandals themselves, but increased the contempt of other German nations for the Roman power ; it was felt to be a humiliating disaster by the government at Constantinople, while the government in Italy was too habituated to defeat to be gravely affected.

The cost of the armament was immense. Leo had found in the treasury a reserve of 100,000 lbs. of gold (over £4,500,000).[2] This was exceeded by the expenses of equipping the ill-omened expedition,[3] and the consequence is said to have been that the treasury hovered on the brink of bankruptcy for more than thirty years.

§ 4. *Anthemius and Ricimer* (A.D. 467–474)

The conciliation of Gaul was a problem which was no less important for Anthemius than it had been for Majorian. The situation there had changed for the worse. The Visigothic crown had passed to Euric, who had murdered his brother Theoderic in A.D. 466. Euric was perhaps the ablest of all the Visigothic kings, and he aimed at extending his rule over all Gaul. The

[1] He was obliged to seek refuge in the sanctuary of St. Sophia.

[2] John Lydus, *De mag.* iii. 43.

[3] According to Procopius, *B.V.* i. 6, the total cost was 130,000 lbs. of gold ; according to Lydus, *ib.*, 65,000 lbs. of gold and 700,000 lbs. of silver, which (calculating the ratio of gold to silver as 1 : 18) would together amount to about 104,000 lbs. of gold. The statement of Lydus evidently rests on the same data as the interesting notice of the historian Candidus (*fr.* 4, in *F.H.G.* iv. p. 137). The chests of the Praetorian Prefects (East and Illyricum) contributed 47,000 lbs. gold, the treasury of the Sacred Largess, 17,000 lbs. gold : in all 64,000 lbs. ; while the 700,000 lbs. of silver were supplied partly ἐκ δημευσίμων (*i.e.* from confiscated property, and therefore from the treasury of the Private Estate) and partly by the treasury of Anthemius. It is unfortunate that we have not the story of the expedition given by the contemporary Priscus, whose work was the source of Theophanes, A.M. 5961, and indirectly (through Eustathius of Epiphania) of Procopius. Cp. Haury, *Proleg.* to his ed. of Procopius, ix. *sqq.*

Gallo-Romans felt themselves now in greater danger, and they looked to Anthemius for protection with an eagerness which they had not shown in the case of Majorian.   They sent a deputation to the new Emperor at Rome, both to petition him to remedy some administrative abuses and to stimulate him to take adequate measures for the defence of the Gallic provinces.   The most distinguished member of the deputation was Sidonius Apollinaris.[1]   The panegyrist of Avitus and Majorian was now called upon to compose a panegyric of a third Emperor, on the occasion of his consulship.[2]   It was publicly recited on the kalends of January A.D. 468.   The poet emphasised the fact that the elevation of Anthemius was a restoration of the unity of the Empire.   He hailed Constantinople in these words :

> Salve sceptrorum columen, regina orientis,
> orbis Roma tui,

and praised the Byzantine education of the new Augustus of the West.   He was rewarded by the Prefecture of Rome.   This appointment was much more than a recognition of his personal merit ;   it was intended to conciliate Gallo-Roman sentiment.[3]

The pleasure of Sidonius in holding this high office was somewhat marred by the sensational trial of Arvandus, the Praetorian Prefect of Gaul, with whom he was on terms of friendship. Arvandus had sunk deeply into debt and had peculated public funds.   His prosecution was decided by the Council of the Seven Provinces, and he was brought to trial before the Roman Senate. If malversation had been the only charge, he might have escaped through the influence of his friends, but he had been guilty of treasonable communications with the enemy, and there was clear proof of this in a letter in his own handwriting to King Euric, on which his accusers had managed to lay hands.   Sidonius did all he could to help him, but the confidence of Arvandus himself, who was unable till the last moment to believe that he could be condemned, refused the advice of his friends and frustrated their efforts to save him.   His confidence indeed was so strange that it has been conjectured that his communications with Euric

[1] In an interesting letter (*Epp.* i. 5) Sidonius describes his journey to Rome (in 467), where he arrived when the nuptials of Ricimer with Alypia were being celebrated, and the city was given over to rejoicing.

[2] *Carm.* ii.

[3] Cp. *Epp.* i. 9. Dalton has rightly pointed out that the whole affair was prearranged ;   the panegyric was a pretext, not the motive, of the appointment.

had been secretly prompted by Ricimer, and that he was trusting
in the protection of the Emperor's son-in-law.[1] He was condemned to death " and flung into the island of the Serpent of
Epidaurus (Island of the Tiber).   There," writes Sidonius, " an
object of compassion even to his enemies, his elegance gone, spewed
as it were by Fortune out of the land, he now drags out by benefit
of Tiberius' law his respite of thirty days after sentence, shudder-
ing through the long hours at the thought of hook and Gemonian
stairs, and the noose of the brutal executioner." [2]

Anthemius made large concessions to the Burgundians in Gaul
to ensure their aid against the Goths, but he was not successful
in resisting the aggression of Euric.[3]   In Italy he was not popular.
He was a Greek ; he was too fond of philosophy or thaumaturgy ;
he was inclined to paganism.[4]   His high standard of justice and
honest attempts to administer the laws impartially did not overcome the prejudices of the Italians, and the failure of the Vandal
expedition did not heighten his prestige.   His relations to Ricimer
gradually changed from mutual tolerance to distrust and hostility ;
the father-in-law regretted that he had given his daughter to a
barbarian ;   the son-in-law retorted with the epithets Galatian
and Greekling (Graeculus).   In this contest the Senate and
people of Rome preferred the Greek Emperor to the Suevian
patrician.[5]   The question of " Roman " or German ascendancy,
which had underlain the situation for fifteen years, was now clearly
defined.

As a result of these dissensions, Italy in A.D. 472 was practically divided into two kingdoms, the Emperor reigning at Rome,
the Patrician at Milan.   The venerated Epiphanius, bishop of
Ticinum, attempted in vain to bring about a reconciliation.   It
will be remembered that Gaiseric had wished to elevate to the
Imperial throne Olybrius, the husband of the younger Placidia.
At this time Olybrius was at Constantinople, and his Vandal
connexion made him a suspicious person in the eyes of Leo,
who is said to have planned a treacherous device to remove him.

---

[1] Martroye, *Genséric*, p. 234.

[2] Sidonius, *Epp.* i. 7, Dalton's
translation.   The sentence was not
carried out.   Seronatus, governor of
Aquitanica Prima, was less lucky.
Accused of oppression and treacherous relations with the Goths by the
people of Auvergne, he was executed.

Sidonius calls him a Catiline, *Epp.* ii. 1.

[3] His son Anthemiolus was a
commander in operations against the
Goths.   *Chron. Gall.* 649 (p. 664).

[4] Damascius (*Vita Isidori*, p. 208)
says that he cherished the hope of
restoring pagan idolatry.

[5] John Ant. *fr.* 93 (*loc. cit.* p. 131).

He sent Olybrius to Rome for the ostensible purpose of reconciling Anthemius and Ricimer. But he also sent a messenger to Anthemius with a letter instructing him to put Olybrius to death. Ricimer intercepted the letter, and Leo's stratagem led to the result which he least wished.[1] Ricimer invested Olybrius with the purple (April).

The army of Ricimer soon besieged Rome. Leo had overcome the power of Aspar ; was Anthemius to overcome the power of Ricimer ? In the camp of the besiegers was the Scirian soldier Odovacar, son of Edecon, destined soon to play a more memorable rôle in Italian history than Ricimer himself. The Tiber was guarded and supplies were cut off ; and the Romans pressed by hunger resolved to fight. An army under Bilimer, who was perhaps Master of Soldiers in Gaul, had come to assist them. The Imperial forces lost heavily in the battle, and Ricimer completed his victory by treachery.[2] Anthemius, when his adherents had surrendered to the barbarians, disguised himself and mingled with the mendicants who begged in the church of St. Chrysogonus.[3] There he was found by Gundobad, Ricimer's nephew, and beheaded (July 11, A.D. 472).[4]

But the days of Ricimer were numbered. He survived his father-in-law by six weeks,[5] and the last Emperor he created died two months later.[6] He is not an attractive figure, and it would be easy to do him injustice. Barred by his Arian faith as well as by his German birth from ascending the throne, Ricimer had the choice of two alternative policies—to maintain an

[1] This transaction is related by John Malalas, xiv. p. 374, and is quite credible. Cp. my note on *The Emperor Olybrius* in *E.H.R.*, July 1886. Olybrius had been consul in 464. He was descended from Sextus Petronius Probus, consul in 371. His grandson (by his daughter Juliana) was consul in 491, and married Irene, a niece of the Emperor Anastasius. That he was never recognised as Augustus in the East seems clear from the circumstances, and Stein (*Stud. z. Gesch. des byz. Reiches*, p. 176) has adduced confirmatory evidence.

[2] Ennodius, *Vit. Epiph.* p. 344 *sqq.*; John Ant. *fr.* 93 (*Exc. de ins.* p. 131); Paul. Diac. *Hist. misc.* 15. 4; Schmidt, *op. cit.* 262.

[3] This church, restored more than

once, still stands, near Sta. Maria in Trastevere.

[4] John Ant. *fr.* 209 (*F.H.G.* iv.), says " Gundobad, Ricimer's brother," and afterwards speaks of Gundibalos as his nephew. The fact is that Ricimer's sister married Gundioc, the Burgundian king, and their son was Gundobad, now in Roman service, but soon to succeed to a Burgundian throne.

[5] He died August 18, 472, from vomiting blood, John Ant. *ib.*

[6] Nov. 2, of dropsy, *ib.* The date in the *Paschale Campanum* (*Chron. min.* i. p. 306), borne out by an *Auctarium* to Prosper (*ib.* p. 492), is to be preferred to Oct. 23 of the *Fasti Vind. pr.* (*ib.* p. 306).

Imperial succession in Italy or to recognise the sole authority of the Emperor at Constantinople. It would probably have been repugnant to the ideas and traditions of his training to have cast off all allegiance to the Empire and created in Italy a government on German foundations, formally as well as practically independent. His choice of the first of the two policies was doubtless decided by public opinion and the influence of the Roman Senate, perhaps also by his own attachment to the system under which he was the successor of the great Masters of Soldiers, Stilicho and Aetius. But Italy had a taste of the other alternative in those sometimes long intervals between the puppet Emperors, when Leo was its only legitimate ruler. The success of Ricimer in maintaining this system for so many years was partly due to his diplomatic skill in dealing with Leo. But it worked badly. For it was based on the assumption that the Emperor was to be a nonentity like Honorius and Valentinian, and except in the case of Severus (whom Leo never acknowledged) circumstances hindered Ricimer from choosing a man who was suited to the rôle. In the matter of the expedition against the Vandals he had shown but lukewarm loyalty to the interests of the Empire, but Italy owed much to him for having defended her shores, and for having kept in strict control the German mercenaries on whom her defence depended. The events which followed his death will be the best commentary on the significance of his rule and enable us to appreciate his work.

§ 5. *Extension of German Rule in Gaul and Spain*

The accession of Euric to the Visigothic throne, which he won by murder, meant the breaking of the last weak federal links which attached the Visigoths to the Empire.[1] Euric was probably the ablest of their kings. He aimed at extending his power over all Gaul and Spain, and he accomplished in the eighteen years of his reign a large part of his programme. He was a fanatical Arian. " They say that the mere mention of the name of Catholic so embitters his countenance and heart that one might take him for the chief priest of his Arian sect rather than for the monarch of his nation." [2] The principal

---

[1] He sent an embassy to Constantinople (Hydatius 238). It has been conjectured that the purpose was to denounce the status of foederati and claim full sovranty (Schmidt, i. 260).

[2] Sidonius, *Epp.* vii. 6. 6.

hope of those Gallo-Romans of the south, who clung passionately
to the Roman connexion, lay in the Burgundian power, which
had itself in recent years made large encroachments on the
Imperial provinces. King Chilperic ruled in Lyons and Vienne
in the west, and at Geneva in the east ; the provinces of Lugdunensis Prima and Maxima Sequanorum were almost entirely
under his sway. His Arianism was not like that of Euric ;
he was tolerant and on friendly terms with Catholic bishops ;
he was glad to enjoy the breakfasts of Patiens, the rich and
hospitable archbishop of Lyons.[1] The higher clergy, who were
mostly men of means and good family, played prominent parts
in the politics of the time, and did a great deal to preserve the
Roman tradition.[2] In the north the Imperial cause depended
much on the attitude of the Salian Franks, who, under their
king Childeric, seem to have been consistently loyal to their
federal obligations. But in the Belgic provinces Roman civilisation was gradually declining.[3] The lands of the Moselle and
the Somme had never recovered from the shocks they had
experienced in the days of Honorius. As for north-western
Gaul, the province of the Third Lugdunensis, which was at this
time generally called Armorica, it seems since some years before
Valentinian's death to have been virtually independent.

The first important success that Euric won was a victory
over the Bretons on the Indre. This enabled him to seize Bourges
and the northern part of Aquitanica Prima, which, under their
king Riothamus, they had come to defend at the request of the
Emperor Anthemius. But he was unable to advance beyond
the Loire, which was bravely defended by a count Paulus.
Soon afterwards he laid siege to Arles, and defeated an Imperial
army which had advanced to relieve it under Anthemiolus, the
Emperor's son. Arles he appears to have occupied and then
to have marched up the valley of the Rhone, burning the crops,
and taking the towns of Riez, Orange, Avignon, Viviers and
Valence.[4] He did not hold these places, for he was not prepared
to go to war with the Burgundians, but he left the land ruined,
and the people would have starved if the archbishop Patiens

---

[1] Sidonius, *Epp.* vi. 12. 3.
[2] Among the prominent bishops
were, besides Patiens, Lupus of Troyes,
Fonteius of Vaison, Perpetuus of

Tours, Graecus of Marseilles, Leontius
of Arles, Faustus of Riez, Basilius of
Aix, and Sidonius himself.
[3] *Ib.* iv. 17. 2.   [4] *Ib.* vi. 12.

had not collected supplies of corn at his own expense, and sent grain carts through the ravaged districts.

Euric was determined to annex the rich country of Auvergne, and here he met a stout and protracted resistance, of which Ecdicius,[1] son of the Emperor Avitus, was the soul. He was supported by his brother-in-law, Sidonius Apollinaris, now bishop of Clermont, which held out for nearly four years against repeated sieges. But no help came either from Italy or from Burgundy, and finally the Emperor Julius Nepos arranged a peace with Euric, which surrendered Auvergne and recognised the conquests which the Goths had already made in Spain as well as in Gaul (A.D. 475).[2] The Gallic portion of the Gothic kingdom was now bounded by the Loire, the Rhone, and the Pyrenees, and seems to have included Tours.

Sidonius was taken prisoner and confined in fort Livia, near Carcassonne.[3] Here he employed his time in editing or translating the life of Apollonius of Tyana, by Philostratus, and was so well treated that the worst he had to complain of was that when he lay down to sleep " there were two old Gothic women established quite close to the window of my chamber who at once began their chatter—quarrelsome, drunken, and disgusting creatures." [4] He was finally released through the influence of Leo, the principal minister of Euric and his own good friend.

The peace lasted for little more than a year. Then Euric found a pretext for denouncing it, invaded Provence, and seized Arles and Marseilles. Then a new arrangement was made, and southern Provence, with the consent of the Emperor Zeno, was conceded to the Goths.[5]

Euric was now the most powerful of the German kings. His prestige spread far and wide. The Burgundians hastened to make peace with him. Ostrogoths, Heruls, Saxons, Franks were to be seen at Toulouse or Bordeaux paying court to him. Even the Persian king thought it worth while to send envoys

---

[1] He seems to have held the post of Master of Soldiers in Gaul, see Jordanes, *Get.* 45. Nepos created him patrician in 474 (Sidonius, *Epp.* v. 16).

[2] The negotiations were conducted by four south Gallic bishops (*ib.* vii. 6. 10), and also by Epiphanius, bishop of Ticinum (Ennodius, *Vit. Epiph.* 81) ;

but it is not clear whether or not two separate missions were sent to Euric.

[3] Sidonius was very bitter over the surrender of Auvergne, *ib.* vii. 7.

[4] *Ib.* viii. 3. 3.

[5] Procopius, *B.G.* i. 12. 20. Cp. Candidus, in *F.H.G.* iv. p. 136. Schmidt, *op. cit.* i. 267.

to his court.[1]   When he died in A.D. 484 the Spanish peninsula, except the Suevian kingdom in the north-west, was entirely under his dominion.[2]

For the Gallic provincials the change of masters probably made very little difference.   They and the Goths lived side by side, each according to their own law.   The Roman magnate had to surrender a part of his estates, but he could live with as much freedom and ease, and in just the same way, under the Goth as under the Emperor.   Some of these men were enlisted in the royal service, such as Leo of Narbonne ; Namatius, who commanded the Gothic fleet in the Atlantic to guard the coasts against Saxon pirates ;[3] Victorius, who was made governor of Auvergne.   Latin was the language of intercourse.   It is probable that very few provincials learned any of the German tongues which were spoken by their masters.   Syagrius, a man of letters, who lived much at the Burgundian court, mastered the Burgundian language, to the amazement of his friends.   Sidonius bantered him on his feat.   " You can hardly conceive how amused we all are to hear that, when you are by, not a barbarian but fears to perpetuate a barbarism in his own language.   Old Germans bowed with age are said to stand astounded when they see you interpreting their German letters ; they actually choose you for arbiter and mediator in their disputes.   You are a new Solon in the elucidation of Burgundian law.   In body and mind these people are as stiff as stocks and very hard to form ; yet they delight to find in you, and equally delight to learn, a Burgundian eloquence and a Roman spirit."[4]   In this connexion it is significant that the early German codes of law were composed in Latin.   The earliest that we know of was the code of Euric, of which some fragments are preserved ;[5] a little later come the Burgundian laws of Gundobad.   It is legitimate to guess that the Visigothic law-book was drawn up under the supervision of Euric's minister Leo, who was a notable jurist.

Sidonius gives us occasional glimpses of the life and habits

---

[1] Sidonius, viii. 9. 5.

[2] The capture of Caesaraugusta, the siege of Tarraco, and the capture of coast cities in A.D. 473 are recorded in *Chron. Gall.* pp. 664 - 665.   Cp. Isidore, *Hist. Goth.* 34.

[3] Sidonius, viii. 6.

[4] *Ib.* v. 5 (this and the other quotations are taken from Dalton's translation).   Syagrius was a great-grandson of Flavius Afranius Syagrius, who was Pr. Pr. of Gaul and consul in A.D. 382.

[5] Edited by Zeumer in the *Leges Visigothorum.*

of the Germans, who were then moulding the destinies of Gaul.
Writing to a friend, for instance, he describes the wedding of a
Burgundian princess : the bridegroom,[1] walking amid his guards
" in flame-red mantle, with much glint of ruddy gold, and
gleam of snowy silken tunic, his fair hair, red cheeks and white
skin according with the three hues of his equipment." The
chiefs who accompanied him were in martial accoutrement.
" Their feet were laced in boots of bristly hide reaching to the
heels ; ankles and legs were exposed. They wore high tight
tunics of varied colour, hardly descending to their bare knees,
the sleeves covering only the upper arm. Green mantles they
had with crimson borders ; baldrics supported swords hung
from their shoulders, and pressed on sides covered with cloaks
of skin secured by brooches. No small part of their adornment consisted of their arms ; in their hands they grasped
barbed spears and missile axes ; their left sides were guarded
by shields which flashed with tawny golden bosses and snowy
silver borders, betraying at once their wealth and their good
taste."

Sidonius confesses that he did not like Germans,[2] and it is
the society of his own fellows, the country gentlemen of southern
Gaul, among whom he had a wide acquaintance, that is mainly
depicted in his correspondence. The life of these rich members
of the senatorial class went on its even and tranquil way, little
affected by the process which was gradually substituting Teuton
for Roman power.[3] They had generally town mansions, as well
as country estates on which they lived, well provided with
slaves, and amusing themselves by hunting, hawking, and
fishing, ball games, and dice. But the remarkable feature of the
life of these Gallo-Roman magnates was that they did not confine
themselves to the business of looking after their domains and
the outdoor pursuits of country gentlemen, but were almost
all men of literary tastes and culture. There were many poets
and trained rhetoricians among them ; they circulated their
verses ; and mutually admired one another's accomplishments.
It is probable that in literary achievement Sidonius was considerably superior to his friends, but in any case his works show

---

[1] Sigismer, otherwise unknown.
Sidonius, iv. 20.
[2] *Ib*. vii. 14. 10.

[3] In Dalton's Introduction to his
translation of the Letters there is
an admirable account of this society.

us the sad decadence in style to which the tendencies of the rhetorical schools of the Empire, in Gaul as elsewhere, had brought literary prose. Of his epistolary style it is enough to say that it gains in a good modern translation. He could write good verses, occasionally approaching Claudian, and bad verses, which remind us of Merobaudes.

Of the last thirty years of Imperial rule in northern Gaul we know virtually nothing. Childeric, the principal king among the Salian Franks, seems to have loyally maintained the federal bond with the Empire.[1] The blue-eyed Saxons, who were at this time the scourge of the coasts of Gaul, in the west as well as in the north, had sailed up the Loire and seized Angers. We find Childeric aiding the Imperial commander Paul in his operations against this foe.[2] We have already seen Paul holding the line of the Loire against the Visigoths. We are not told his official rank or functions ; he is designated by the title of Count, but we may fairly assume that he had succeeded Aegidius as Master of Soldiers. His name and that of Syagrius are the only two recorded names of Roman functionaries who maintained Imperial authority in northern Gaul after the death of Aegidius. Syagrius was the son of Aegidius, and on him devolved the defence of Belgic Gaul in the last years of Childeric.[3]

Childeric died in A.D. 481 and was succeeded by his son Clovis (Chlodwig), who entered upon new paths of policy. He saw clearly that the Imperial power in Gaul was now negligible. The few provinces that were still administered in the name of the Augustus at Constantinople were cut off from the rest of the Empire by the kingdoms of the Visigoths and the Burgundians. It was evidently the destiny of Gaul to be possessed entirely by German rulers, and Clovis determined that the Franks should have their share. He took the field against Syagrius soon after his accession and defeated him near Soissons (A.D. 486).[4] The province of Belgica Secunda, with the important cities of Soissons

---

[1] He had fought with Aegidius against the Goths at Orleans (see above, p. 333).

[2] For the dealings with the Saxons see Gregory of Tours, *H.F.* ii. 18. 19. On their invasion and the *Litus Saxonicum* in Gaul see Lot, *Les Migrations saxonnes*, 6 and 13 *sqq.*

[3] We may conjecture that he owed his appointment either to Anthemius or to Julius Nepos, and that he succeeded Paul as Master of Soldiers. He is mentioned only by Gregory of Tours, unless, as some think, he is identical with the correspondent of Sidonius referred to above.

[4] Syagrius fled to Toulouse, but King Alaric gave him up to Clovis, who put him to death.

and Reims, immediately passed under his sway.[1] Of his subsequent advance westward to the Loire and the borders of penin-
sular Brittany we know nothing, probably because it was gradual
and easy.

The victory of Soissons completely changed the political
situation and prospects of Gaul. Two years before, when
Euric died, the destinies of the land seemed to depend on the
Goths and the Burgundians, and if any one had prophesied that
the whole land would ultimately be ruled by Gothic kings, few
outside Burgundy would have questioned the probability of
the prediction. Yet twenty years later the formidable power
which Euric had created was to go down before the Franks ;
afterwards it would be the turn of the Burgundians. The failure
of the Goths to fulfil their early promise was due above all to
their Arian faith, which deprived them of the support of the
Church. When Clovis embraced Christianity in its Catholic
form, ten years after the battle of Soissons, he made the fortune
of the Franks.

The part which the Church was able to play throughout the
critical age in which the country was passing from Roman to
Teuton lords depended on the fact that the Gallic episcopate
was recruited from the highly educated and propertied class.
The most public-spirited members of the senatorial families
found in the duties of a bishop an outlet for their energies. It
was these bishops who mediated between the German kings and
the Roman government, and after the Imperial power had
disappeared, helped to guide and moderate the policy of the
barbarian rulers towards the provincials, and to preserve in some
measure Gallo-Roman traditions. The study of the society
mirrored in the pages of Sidonius, himself a case in point, is an
indispensable preparation for the study of the France created
by Clovis, of which the early history is recorded by Gregory,
the bishop of Tours.

[1] For some years Clovis allowed
the Imperial administration to continue unchanged in this province.
See the letter which Remigius, archbishop of Reims, addressed to him
(*Epp. Austras.* 2, in *Epp. Mer. et Kar.
aevi*, vol. i.), which must be dated
after 496.

CHAPTER XI

THE existence of the State Church made a profound difference in the political and social development of the Empire. The old State religion of Rome was often used as an instrument of policy, but perhaps its main political value was symbolic. It involved no theory of the universe, no body of dogma to divide the minds of men and engender disputes. The gods were not jealous, and it was compatible with the utmost variety of other cults and faiths. For the Christian Church, on the contrary, a right belief in theological dogmas was the breath of its life, and, as such questions are abstruse and metaphysical, it was impossible to define a uniform doctrine which all minds would accept. As the necessity of ecclesiastical unity was an axiom, the government had to deal with a new problem, and a very arduous and embarrassing one, such as had not confronted it in the days before Constantine. Doctrine had to be defined, and heretics suppressed. Again, the Church, which once had claimed freedom for itself, denied freedom to others when it was victorious, and would not suffer rival cults. Hence a systematic policy of religious intolerance, such as the Greek and Roman world had never known, was introduced. Another consequence of the Christianising of the State was the rise to power and importance of the institution of monasticism, which was not only influential economically and socially, but was also, as we shall see, a political force. The theological controversies, the religious persecution, and the growth of monasticism, in the fifth century, will be reviewed briefly in this chapter.

§ 1. *The Controversies on the Incarnation*

The great theological controversy which rent Christendom in twain in the fourth century had been finally closed through the energy and determination of Theodosius the Great, and unity was for a short time restored to the Church. Theodosius had been baptized in Thessalonica in A.D. 380, and immediately afterwards he issued an edict, commanding his subjects to accept the orthodox faith of the Council of Nicaea.[1] He described it as the doctrine professed by the bishop of Rome and the bishop of Alexandria. Then he proceeded to hand over to the orthodox all the Arian churches in Constantinople, and to prohibit heretics from holding public worship in the city. In the meantime he had come to see that the best prospect of terminating discussion in the East would be by a Council which was not controlled either from Alexandria or from Rome. The Council which met at his summons in A.D. 381 at Constantinople was entirely eastern, and Meletius, the bishop of Antioch, presided. Seventy years later it came to be called an Ecumenical Council; in the West it was not recognised as such till the end of the fifth century. This assembly of eastern bishops ratified the doctrine of the Council of Nicaea, and declared that the Son is of the same substance with the Father. Theodosius, after a vain attempt to win over the Arians by a Council which he summoned two years later, proceeded to measures of suppression,[2] and Arianism gradually declined.

But, while the Arian heresy in itself led to no permanent schism in the Church,[3] new and closely related controversies soon agitated

---

[1] *C. Th.* xvi. 1. 2. On the doctrine of Nicaea Harnack (*History of Dogma*, iv. 49) observes: "One of its most serious consequences was that from this time forward Dogmatics were for ever separated from clear thinking and defensible conceptions, and got accustomed to what was anti-rational. The anti-rational —not indeed at once, but soon enough—came to be considered as the characteristic of the sacred."

[2] *C. Th.* xvi. 1. 4.

[3] Harnack, *ib.* 106 : " The educated laity in the East regarded the orthodox formula rather as a necessary evil and as an unexplainable mystery than as

an expression of their Faith. The victory of the Nicene Creed was a victory of the priests over the faith of the Christian people. The Logos-doctrine has already become unintelligible to those who were not theologians. . . . The thought that Christianity is the revelation of something incomprehensible became more and more a familiar one to men's minds." He refers to a quotation in Socrates, iii. 7, from Evagrius the Anchorite, who will have nothing to do with theological categories, and says σιωπῇ προσκυνείσθω τὸ ἄρρητον, " Let the mystery be adored in silence."

the eastern world and were destined to issue in lasting divisions. Once the divinity of Christ in the fullest sense was universally admitted, the question ensued how the union of his divine substance with his human nature is to be conceived. Was the Godhead mixed with humanity, or only conjoined ? Did Mary bear the flesh only or the Logos along with the flesh ? Did Christ's human nature survive the Resurrection ? In the fourth century, there was no definite doctrine, but the problem was disturbing the minds of some metaphysical theologians.

Apollinaris of Laodicea argued that the union of a perfect God into a perfect man was out of the question. For the result of such a union would be a monster, not a uniform being. He concluded that Christ was not a perfect man, and that he adopted human nature, determining it in such a way that it did not involve free will, which would be inconsistent with his Godhead. His flesh was taken up into the nature of the Logos and was thus divine, and the Logos shared in the suffering of the flesh. Further, Christ's mind was not human ; for, if he had had a human mind, he would have had a duplicate personality.

It has been said that this theory of Apollinaris expressed the belief entertained at heart by all pious Greeks.[1] But it was clear that it did not do justice to the humanity of Christ as depicted in the Gospels, and other theologians who, like Apollinaris himself, belonged to the school of Antioch, sought to render intelligible the union of a perfect God with a perfect man. According to Theodore of Mopsuestia, the union of the two natures was a contact which became more intimate at each stage of human growth, and the indwelling of the Logos in the man was not substantial, but of the same order as the indwelling of God, by grace, in any human being. Each nature was itself a person, and the Logos did not become man. It was the man only who suffered. And Mary was not, in the strict sense, the mother of God.

In the reign of Theodosius II. this insoluble problem raised a bitter controversy, which agitated the eastern world. When Sisinnius, Patriarch of Constantinople, died at the end of A.D. 427, the bishops, the clergy, and the monks could not agree on the appointment of a successor, and the nomination was com-

---

[1] Harnack, p. 155.

mitted to the Emperor ; who, seeing that no possible candidate among the ecclesiastics of Constantinople would be generally acceptable, chose Nestorius,[1] a monk of a convent at Antioch, who had a high reputation as a preacher. The eloquence of Nestorius was matched by his intolerance, and no sooner was he seated on the Patriarchal throne [2] than he began an energetic campaign against heresies. But his forcible language in condemning Apollinarian views, which he discovered to be rife among the local clergy, soon gave the Patriarch of Alexandria, who was the natural enemy of any Patriarch of Constantinople, a welcome opportunity of accusing him of heresy himself. The rivalry between these great sees, bitter since the Council of A.D. 381, when precedence over all sees except Rome had been granted to New Rome,[3] had been aggravated by the struggle between Theophilus and Chrysostom.

The Patriarch Cyril and the Alexandrines held that the two natures of Christ were joined in an indissoluble, " hypostatic " or personal union, yet remained distinct, but that the human nature had no substance independently of the divine ; that the Logos suffered without suffering, and that Mary is the mother of God inasmuch as she bare flesh which was united indissolubly with the Logos. Cyril's doctrine approached that of Apollinaris in so far as it denied the existence of an individual man in Christ, but was sharply opposed to it by its maintenance of the distinction of the two natures.

Nestorius leaned to the doctrine of Theodore of Mopsuestia, which was popular in Syria. He characterised as fables the statements that a God was wrapped in swaddling clothes and was nailed upon the cross, and he protested against the use of the designation " Mother of God " (*Theotokos*).

It is to be observed that in this controversy both parties agreed in condemning the theory of Apollinaris and in holding that there were two natures in Christ. The main difference between them concerned the formula by which the union of the two natures was to be expressed—Cyril maintaining a " natural

---

[1] The Emperor's difficulties are shown in his remarkable conversation with the abbot Dalmatius, recorded by Nestorius in the *Bazaar of Heraclides* ; see the extract in Bethune-Baker, *Nestorius and his Teaching*, p. 6, *n.* 3. He desired Dalmatius to choose, but Dalmatius refused.

[2] He was consecrated on April 10, 428.

[3] By the 3rd Canon of the Council : τὰ πρεσβεῖα τῆς τιμῆς μετὰ τὸν τῆς Ῥώμης διὰ τὸ εἶναι αὐτὴν νέαν Ῥώμην.

union " [1] and Nestorius a less intimate " contact." [2]   The truth may be that the view of Nestorius was not so very different from that of Cyril as Cyril thought.   It seems probable that the doctrine of two Persons, somehow joined together, which is commonly imputed to Nestorius, would have been repudiated by him.[3]   Cyril wrote to Theodosius, to Eudocia, to Pulcheria and her sisters, censuring the heretical opinion of Nestorius,[4] and stirred up the Egyptian monks, who were ever ready for a theological fray.   A heated correspondence ensued between the two Patriarchs, and both invoked the support of Celestine, the bishop of Rome.   Pope Celestine was no theologian.   He was guided by the political expediency of supporting Alexandria against Constantinople, and he evaded the real issue by bringing into the forefront of the controversy a minor point, namely the question whether Mary might properly be called the Mother of God.   On this particular point Nestorius was ready to yield, but he would not recant his doctrine at the bidding of a Roman synod.[5] Anathemas and counter-anathemas flew between Alexandria and Constantinople, and then the Emperor, by the advice of Nestorius,

---

[1] "Ενωσις φυσική or ὑποστατική. On the ambiguity of this phrase see Bethune-Baker, *op. cit.* 171 *sqq.* The term *hypostasis*, subsistence, is not quite synonymous with οὐσία, substance; the difference is thus explained by a Nestorian theologian : " We apply the term *hypostasis* to the particular substance, which subsists in its own single being, numerically one and separate from the rest " (Labourt, *Le Christanisme*, pp. 283- 284). Cp. Bethune-Baker, *op. cit.* 220 *sqq.* Nestorius maintained there were two natures, two substances, and two hypostaseis in Christ.

[2] Κατὰ συνάφειαν.

[3] See Bethune-Baker, *op. cit.* ch. vi. The main object of this book is to prove that Nestorius was orthodox and was not a " Nestorian." The dialogue of Nestorius, the *Bazaar of Heraclides*, or Πραγματεία ʽΗρακλείδου, recently discovered in a Syriac version, supplies the important evidence that Nestorius survived till the eve of the Council of Chalcedon and agreed with the *Dogmatic Epistle* of Pope Leo. Cp. Loofs' *Nestorius* (pp. 21, 22), which gives a clear and interesting account of the tragedy of Nestorius.

This theologian agrees with Bethune-Baker partially ; he concludes that Nestorius can be considered orthodox *according to the western interpretation* of the definition of Chalcedon (p. 100). On the meaning of the term πρόσωπον (person) see pp. 76 *sqq.*

[4] See Mansi, iv. 617, 680.   Cyril counted on theological differences in the Imperial family.   Theodosius and Eudocia were under the influence of Nestorius.   Theodosius saw through Cyril's tactics, and wrote him a sharp letter (*ib.* v. 1109).   Pulcheria took the other side.   She had quarrelled with Nestorius, who is said to have repeatedly rebuffed and insulted her. Nestorius describes her as " a bellicose woman, a queen, a young virgin, who quarrelled with me because I would not agree to her demand of comparing a person corrupted bʸ ᵉⁿ to the spouse of Christ " (*R. eraclides,* p. 89). It appears ᵗ he questioned her virtue. ᵗ ᵗᵉ grievances of Pulcheria against Nestorius are enumerated in a letter written after the death of Nestorius to a certain Cosmas of Antioch (*ib.* App. i. pp. 363-364).

[5] Held early in August 430.   It condemned the views of Nestorius.

summoned a Council on the neutral ground of Ephesus for
Whitsuntide A.D. 431. The two antagonists arrived in good
time, but John the Patriarch of Antioch was three weeks late.
Cyril, who was accompanied by fifty bishops, would not wait
for him ; and the supporters of the Alexandrian party met and
decreed the deposition of Nestorius, who refused to attend the
assembly. When John and the Syrian contingent arrived, a rival
but far less numerous Council was opened ; the commissioner
Candidian, Count of the Domestics, who represented the Emperor,
presided ; and Cyril was condemned and deposed. Then the
Roman legates appeared upon the scene, attended the assembly
of Cyril, and signed the decree against Nestorius.

The shameless proceedings of the satellites of Cyril and the
rabble whom they collected are graphically described by Nestorius,
whose house was guarded by soldiers to protect him from violence.
" They acted in everything as if it was a war they were conducting,
and the followers of the Egyptian and of Memnon (bishop of
Ephesus), who were abetting them, went about in the city
girt and armed with clubs, men with high necks, performing
strange antics with the yells of barbarians, snorting fiercely
with horrible and unwonted noises, raging with extravagant
arrogance against those whom they knew to be opposed to their
doings, carrying bells about the city, and lighting fires in many
places and casting into them all kinds of writings. Everything
they did was a cause of amazement and fear : they blocked up
the streets so that every one was obliged to flee and hide while
they acted as masters of the situation, lying about drunk and
besotted and shouting obscenities." [1] Such were the circumstances of the Third Ecumenical Council, which had gathered to
pronounce on the true doctrine of the natures of Christ.

The Emperor had at first resolved to reject the decree against
Nestorius, but afterwards he decided to carry out the rulings of
both assemblies. The two Patriarchs were deposed ; Nestorius
retreated to his old convent at Antioch. But at Constantinople
there was a strong ecclesiastical opposition to Nestorius ; the
clergy addressed a petition to the Emperor demanding justice

---

[1] *Book of Heraclides*, in Bethune-
Baker, p. 39 ; in Nau's version, p.
236. The antagonists of Nestorius
complained similarly of the violence
of the other faction and also of the
partiality of Candidian. The best and
fullest account of the whole proceedings is probably that of Tillemont,
Mémoires, xiv. 307 *sqq.*, allowing for
his prejudice against Nestorius.

for Cyril, and the monks, under the leadership of Dalmatius, excited the people.[1] The popular demonstrations were aided by Cyril's intrigues at court and a lavish distribution of bribes ; [2] Pulcheria doubtless threw her influence into the scale ; and the Emperor was compelled to yield and to permit Cyril to resume his Patriarchal seat. Cyril then sought to come to terms with Antioch, and a new formula was invented—" the unconfused union of two natures "—which could be accepted both by the Alexandrines and by moderate men of the Antiochian school. Cyril subscribed to this creed in A.D. 433. Good Nestorians retreated to Edessa, and here their theology was in the ascendant until the Emperor Zeno (A.D. 489) took measures to extirpate Nestorianism and succeeded in driving it beyond the frontier. The subsequent fortunes of the sect are connected with Persian and Saracen history.

It is clear that throughout the whole controversy personal dislike of Nestorius, who was not an amiable or courteous man, played a considerable part. He was permitted to remain peacefully in his monastery for a few years, notwithstanding the urgent request of Pope Celestine that such a firebrand should be removed from all contact with men. But at length the Emperor adopted harsh measures against him (A.D. 435).[3] He was denounced in an edict as sacrilegious, his books were condemned to the flames,[4] and he was banished at first to Petra and then to Oasis in Upper Egypt (A.D. 435). He seems to have died in A.D. 451.[5]

---

[1] Mansi, iv. 1453 ; 1428.

[2] A list of Cyril's presents to the chamberlains and some of the ministers at the court is preserved (printed in Nau, *op. cit.* p. 368). The most important persons to gain over were the Empress Eudocia and the Grand Chamberlain Chrysoretus, both of whom had been on the side of Nestorius. Two ladies-in-waiting, Marcella and Droseria, received each £2250 for " persuading " Eudocia. Paul, who was probably the *praepositus* of Pulcheria, received the same amount and a number of valuable household things (carpets, ivory chairs, etc.). Similar but more numerous presents were made to the Grand Chamberlain to buy off his opposition, and he was promised £9000 for his help. Hellen-iana, the wife of the Praetorian Prefect of the East, was presented with gifts of

the same kind and number, and was to receive £4500 if she enlisted her husband's help. And so on.

[3] It seems that John the Patriarch of Antioch, who had supported him at Ephesus, found his presence embarrassing and made representation at court. Pulcheria was believed to be responsible for the exile to Oasis. See Brière, " La Légende syriaque de Nestorius," in *Revue de l'orient chrétien* (1910), pp. 1-25.

[4] *C. Th.* xvi. 5. 66.

[5] He was for some time a prisoner among the Blemmyes. For the hardships he endured see Evagrius, i. 7. In the *Book of Heraclides*, which he wrote shortly before his death, he describes the proceedings of the Second Council of Ephesus (449), and he implies that the faith which he regarded as true had triumphed (at

The compromise of A.D. 433 was not final. The question was opened again by Dioscorus, who had succeeded Cyril (A.D. 444) in the see of Alexandria, and was jealous of the prestige of the theologians of Antioch. He set himself the task of destroying the Antiochian formula of " two natures or *hypostaseis* and one Christ." His views found a warm supporter at Constantinople in a certain Eutyches, the archimandrite of a monastery, who had been prominent in the agitation against Nestorius, and enjoyed the favour of the eunuch Chrysaphius.[1] Eutyches was charged with heresy ; the Patriarch Flavian [2] took up the matter and procured his condemnation at a local synod (A.D. 448). Eutyches appealed to Leo, the bishop of Rome ; and Dioscorus urged the Emperor to summon a general Council. Theodosius, guided by the counsels of Chrysaphius who hated Flavian, yielded to the wishes of Alexandria, and the Council met at Ephesus in August A.D. 449.

In the meantime Leo had come to the conclusion that the views of Eutyches were heretical, and he wrote in this sense to the Emperor and the Patriarch. He claimed that he was himself the person who should decide and define the dogma by virtue of the authority residing in the see of St. Peter ; there was no necessity for a General Council.[3] But the Council was called, and Leo sent three delegates, committing to them a Dogmatic Epistle or Tome addressed to Flavian in which he formulated the true doctrine : the unity of two hypostatic natures in one person, wherein the properties of both natures were preserved.[4] It was not explained how this union was possible, and a distinguished historian of dogma observes [5] that Leo left off at the point where the speculation of Cyril began.

Dioscorus presided at the Council. The letter of Leo was not read, and the Roman representative did not vote. Eutyches was declared orthodox, and Flavian was deposed as having gone

Chalcedon), and Dioscorus had been defeated. See Bethune-Baker, *op. cit.* 34-35, and *Journal of Theol. Studies*, ix. 601.

[1] Cp. Victor Tonn. *sub a.* 450.

[2] Nestorius had been succeeded by Maximian, 431, Proclus was elected in 434, Flavian in 446. There is a good article on Eutyches in the *Dict. of Chr. Biogr.*

[3] The collection of Pope Leo's letters (*P.L.* liv. ; Mansi, vi.) includes not only his own letters on the controversy to Theodosius, Pulcheria, Marcian, eastern ecclesiastics, etc., but also the correspondence of Galla Placidia and others with the Imperial family at Constantinople.

[4] Leo, *Ep.* 28 (*P.L.* liv. 755 *sqq.*).

[5] Harnack, *ib.* 207.

beyond the doctrine of the creed of Nicaea.[1]   Other more distinguished adherents of the Antiochian doctrine, including
Theodoret, bishop of Cyrrhus, a notable theologian, were also
deposed.   The result of the proceedings was to annul the compromise of A.D. 433 and to reinstate the Cyrillian doctrine of
the one incarnate nature of the God-Logos.   The voting of
many of the 115 bishops who signed the Acts was not free ; they
were overawed by the Imperial authorities and by the violence
of a noisy crowd of monks from Syria.   Yet it has been said,
perhaps with truth, that this Council more than any other
expressed the general religious feeling of the time, and would have
permanently settled the controversy in the East if extraneous
interests had not been involved.

The bishop of Rome denounced the " Robber Council,"
as he called it, and prompted Valentinian III. to propose to his
cousin Theodosius the convention of a new Council in Italy.
Theodosius replied that the recent Council had simply defended
the rulings of Nicaea and Ephesus against the innovations of
Flavian; no further action was called for; the Church was
at peace.   If the question had been simply doctrinal and no
political considerations had intervened, the decision of the
" Robber Council" might have been the last word in Eastern
Christendom.   But that Council had been a triumph for
Alexandria, and the prestige which Dioscorus acquired was a
menace not only to Old Rome—he promptly excommunicated
Leo—but also to New Rome.   This danger could not long be
ignored, and the death of Theodosius was followed by a change
of policy at Constantinople.

Marcian resolved to terminate the ecclesiastical despotism
which the Alexandrian bishops sought to impose upon the East,
and Anatolius, who through the influence of Dioscorus had
succeeded Flavian as Patriarch, did not scruple to lend himself
to a new policy and to subscribe the Dogmatic Epistle of Leo.
Marcian wrote to Leo agreeing to his request for a new Council,
but insisting that it should meet in the East.   Then the Pope
changed his tactics.   He claimed, as before, that his own Epistle
was sufficient to settle the whole matter, and did all he could
to prevent the meeting of a Council.[2]   But Marcian knew that,

[1] He was banished to Hypaepa in
Lydia, and died on his way thither in
consequence of ill-treatment.
[2] Leo, *Epp.* 82-86.

however wonderful Leo's Epistle might be, a Council would be indispensable to satisfy public opinion in the Eastern Churches, and he summoned a Council for the autumn (A.D. 451). Leo rather sulkily yielded.[1] In October an unusually large assembly of ecclesiastics [2] met at Chalcedon, and the presidency, which meant the right of first recording his vote, was given to the legate of the Pope.

It was the common object of Leo and of Marcian to procure the deposition of Dioscorus, and in this they succeeded, but not without exercising moral violence. Most of the bishops, including Anatolius who really agreed with Dioscorus, voted against their consciences and relinquished the formula in which they believed. But, while Leo desired that his epistle should be accepted as it stood, Marcian saw that a new formula, which should indeed take account of the Pope's statement, would be less unacceptable in the East. Accordingly the Council decreed that the true doctrine was contained in certain writings of Cyril [3] as well as in Leo's epistle ; and described Jesus Christ as complete in his humanity as well as in his divinity ; one and the same Christ in two natures, without confusion or change, division or separation ; [4] each nature concurring [5] into one person and one hypostasis.

The doctrine of the Fourth Ecumenical Council is still accepted as authoritative in the Churches of Christendom. It is interesting to learn the judgment of one of the most learned living theologians. The Council of Chalcedon, " which we might call the Robber and the Traitor Council, betrayed the secret of the Greek faith." " The disgrace attaching to this Council consists in the fact that the great majority of the bishops who held the same views as Cyril and Dioscorus finally allowed a formula to be forced upon them, which was that of strangers, of the Emperor and the Pope, and which did not correspond to their belief." [6] But the truth is that the definition of Chalcedon might be interpreted in different ways. To Leo and the Western Church it meant one thing; to the followers of Cyril another; to

[1] Ep. 89.
[2] About 600.
[3] Namely, his Synodal letters to Nestorius and the Orientals (Epp. 4, 17 ; 39).
[4] Ἐν δύο φύσεσιν ἀσυγχύτως κτλ.

Cp. Loofs, op. cit. 97.
[5] Συντρεχούσης.
[6] Harnack, ib. 196, 214. It is worth observing that the majority of the bishops of the Asiatic provinces absented themselves.

Antiochians and Theodoret, something different which Nestorius himself could have accepted.[1]

Politically, the Council was a decisive triumph for Constantinople and a final blow to the pretensions of the see of Alexandria. Marcian completed what Theodosius the Great had begun. Three successive Patriarchs, Theophilus, Cyril, and Dioscorus, had aimed at attaining to the supreme position in Eastern Christendom and at ruling Egypt like kings. Alexandria could never again claim to lead the Church in theology. But the defeat of Alexandria was accompanied by an exaltation of Byzantium which was far from acceptable to Rome. By the twenty-eighth Canon equal privileges with Rome were granted to the see of Constantinople, and all the episcopal sees of the Dioceses of Thrace, Asia, and Pontus were assigned to the jurisdiction of the Patriarch. The Roman legates protested against this Canon, and Leo refused to confirm it.[2]

Dioscorus was deposed by the Council, and was banished to Gangra. Feeling ran so high at Alexandria that the aid of soldiers was required to establish his successor Proterius.

In Egypt and Syria there was a solid mass of opinion loyal to the doctrine of one nature, and firmly opposed to the formula of Chalcedon. These Monophysites, as they were called, were far too numerous and earnest to be stamped out ; they ultimately created the national Coptic Church of Egypt. Throughout the reign of Leo I. the dispute over the meaning of the Incarnation led to scenes of the utmost violence in Alexandria and to occurrences hardly less scandalous in Antioch.

At Jerusalem the Monophysites obtained the upper hand after the Council of Chalcedon, and a reign of terror prevailed for some time. The episode derives interest from the association of the Empress Eudocia, who was living there in retirement, with the Monophysitic cause.[3] A monk named Theodosius,

---

[1] Loofs, *op. cit.* p. 99. Duchesne (*Hist. anc. de l'Église*, iii. 449) remarks : " Vive la doctrine de Flavien et de Léon ! Anathème à Nestorius ! C'est tout le concile de Chalcédoine."

[2] The change was bitterly felt by Ephesus, the premier see of Asia Minor, associated as it was with early apostolic history, the memories of Paul and Timothy, and of John the Evangelist, who was said to have died

and been buried there. The archbishop lost not only his independence but even his rank, for he was placed second to the metropolitan of Cappadocian Caesarea. It was hardly much consolation that he was allowed the title of " Exarch of the Diocese of Asia."

[3] See Cyrillus, *Vita Euthymii*, p. 64 *sqq.* Génier, *Vie de Saint Euthyme*, 209 *sqq.*

who was a zealous supporter of Dioscorus, gained the ear of the people, and the bishop of Jerusalem, Juvenal, when he returned from the Council, was forced to flee for his life, because he refused to renounce the doctrine which he had subscribed. Theodosius was ordained bishop, and methods of the utmost violence were adopted to coerce those who refused to communicate with him. He was supported by Eudocia, who had been a devoted admirer of Cyril and was led to believe that Cyril's doctrine was identical with that of Dioscorus and had been condemned at Chalcedon. The Emperor Marcian at length took strong measures ; Theodosius fled to Mount Sinai, and Juvenal was restored to his see.[1] Eudocia after some years began to feel doubts about her theology and she consulted the pillar saint, Simeon, who recommended her to seek the advice of Euthymius, abbot of the convent of Sahel, a few miles east of Jerusalem. An interview with the monk showed the Empress the error of her ways, and she died in the faith of Chalcedon.

The Christian religion, with its theology which opened such a wide field for differences of opinion, had introduced into the Empire dangerous discords which were a sore perplexity to the government. In some ways it augmented, in others it weakened, the power of the State to resist its external enemies. It cannot be maintained—as we have already seen—that it was one of the causes which contributed to the dismemberment of the Empire in the West by the Teutonic peoples ; and subsequently, the religious communion, which was preserved throughout political separation, helped the Empire to recover some of the territory it had lost. In the East, bitter theological divisions, consequent on the Council of Chalcedon,[2] facilitated the Saracen conquest of the provinces of Syria and Egypt, but afterwards, in the diminished Empire, the State religion formed a strong bond and fostered the growth of a national spirit which enabled the Imperial power to hold out for centuries against surrounding foes.

---

[1] The usurpation of Theodosius lasted for 20 months, A.D. 452–453. Evagrius, ii. 5. Theophanes, A.M. 5945.

[2] Gelzer (in Krumbacher, *G.B.L.*, p. 919) designates the decisions of Chalcedon, regarded from a political aspect, as a most grievous misfortune for the east-Roman empire.

§ 2. *The Controversy on Predestination, and the Growth of the Papal Power*

The subtle questions on the nature of the Incarnation, which were so hotly disputed by the Greeks and Orientals, created little or no disturbance in western Europe. But in the early years of the fifth century the western provinces were agitated by a heresy of their own, on a subject which had more obviously practical bearings, but involved no less difficult theological metaphysics. The Pelagian controversy concerned free will and original sin. Pelagius, probably a Briton of Irish extraction,[1] propagated the views that man possesses the power of choosing between good and evil, and that there is no sin where there is not a voluntary choice of evil ; that sin is not inherited ; that man can live, and some men actually have lived, sinless ; and that unbaptized infants attain to eternal life.[2] The controversy is memorable because these doctrines found their chief antagonist in Augustine and led him gradually to develop the predestinarian theories which had such a powerful influence on subsequent theology. He maintained that sin was transmitted to all men from Adam ; that man, by the mere gift of free will, cannot choose aright without the constant operation of grace ; that no man has ever lived a sinless life ; that infants dying unbaptized are condemned, as a just punishment for the sin which they inherited. As time went on, Augustine developed his theory, which raised the whole question of the origin of evil into a system which, while it professed to admit the freedom of the will, really annulled it. God, he said, decided from eternity to save some members of the human race from the consequence of sin ; he fixed the number of the saved, which can be neither increased nor diminished, and on these favoured few he bestows the gifts of grace which are necessary for their salvation. The rest perish eternally, if not

---

[1] Jerome, *Comm. in Jerem.*, *P.L.* xxiv. 680-682, 757-758. Cp. Bury, "The Origin of Pelagius," in *Hermathena*, xxx. 26 *sqq.* On the controversy, see Pelagius, *Letter to Demetrias, P.L.* xxxii. 1100; the numerous writings of Augustine on the subject, *P.L.* xlvii. ; Marius Mercator, *Commonitorium super nomine Caelestii, ib.* xlviii. ; Jerome's Three Books *Adversus Pelagrium*, and his *Letter to Ctesiphon* (*P.L.* xxii. 1152). A Commentary by Pelagius on the Pauline epistles existed in Ireland in the Middle Ages (Zimmer, *Pelagius in Ireland*, 1901). The Patriarch Nestorius wrote treatises against Pelagianism, of which Latin translations by Marius Mercator are preserved (*P.L.* xlviii.).

[2] Pelagius distinguished eternal life from the bliss of Paradise.

through their own transgressions, through the effects of original sin. This is not unjust, because there is no reason why God should give grace to any man ; by refusing to bestow it, he affirms the truth that none deserve it. Augustine allowed that in the eternal punishment which awaits all but the few there may be different degrees of pain.

Pelagius, along with his friend Caelestius whom he had converted to his views, went from Rome to Africa (A.D. 409). Leaving Caelestius there, he proceeded himself to Palestine. Caelestius stated his views before a council of African bishops at Carthage and was excommunicated (A.D. 412). Three years later a synod was held at Jerusalem, at which Pelagius was present, the question was discussed, and it was decided that it should be referred to Pope Innocent I. (A.D. 415), but some months later another synod at Diospolis acquitted Pelagius of heterodoxy. In the meantime Augustine was writing on the subject,[1] and the African bishops condemned the Pelagian doctrine and asked Innocent to express his approval.[2] A decision on the matter devolved upon Innocent's successor Zosimus, who was elected on March 17, A.D. 417, and the ear of this Pope was gained by Caelestius, who had come to Rome. Zosimus censured the African bishops for condemning Caelestius, and intimated that he would decide, if the accusers came and appeared before him. Then he received a letter from Pelagius, which convinced him that Pelagius was a perfectly orthodox Catholic.[3] But the African bishops were not convinced, and in defiance of the Pope's opinion, they condemned Pelagius and his teaching in a synod at Carthage (May 1, A.D. 418). Zosimus at last became aware that the doctrines of Pelagius were really heretical ; he was obliged to execute a retreat,[4] and he confirmed the findings of the African synod. Honorius issued a decree banishing Pelagius and Caelestius from Rome and inflicting the penalty of confiscation on their followers.[5] Although the views of the British heretic were crushed by the

---

[1] *De peccatorum meritis* ; *de natura et gratia* ; and *de perfectione iustitiae hominis* (A.D. 415).

[2] At the Synods of Carthage and Milevis (A.D. 416). Innocent replied (Jan. 417), condemning the heresy in strong language. The correspondence will be found in Innocent, *Epp.* 26-31, *P.L.* xx.

[3] Zosimus, *Epp.* 2 and 3 (*P.L.* xx.

649, 654).

[4] *Id.*, *Ep.* 12 (*ib.* 675). In this letter he says *quamvis patrum traditio apostolicae sedi auctoritatem tantam tribuerit ut de eius iudicio disceptare nullus auderet.*

[5] Cp. Maassen, *Gesch. der Quellen und der Lit. des kanonischen Rechts,* i. p. 316. Caelestius was condemned at the Council of Ephesus in 431.

arguments and authority of Augustine, they led to the formation of an influential school of opinion in Gaul [1] which, though condemning Pelagianism, did not accept the extreme predestinarian doctrines of the great African divine.

In the list of Roman pontiffs the name of Zosimus is not one which the Catholic Church holds in high esteem. His brief pontificate fell at a critical period, when the Roman see was laying the foundations of the supremacy which it was destined to gain by astute policy, and propitious circumstances, over the churches of western Europe. Zosimus, through his rashness and indiscretion, did as much as could be done in two years to thwart the purposes which he was himself anxious to promote. In the matter of Pelagius he committed himself to a judgment which shows that he was either unpardonably ignorant of the doctrine which had been challenged, or that he considered orthodox in A.D. 417 what he condemned as heterodox in A.D. 418 ; and he exposed himself to a smart rebuff from the bishops of Africa.[2] But his indiscretion in this affair was of less importance than the ill-considered policy on which he embarked on a question of administration in the Gallic Church, and which proved highly embarrassing to his successors.

The authority which the Roman see exercised in western Europe at this time, beyond its prestige and acknowledged primacy in Christendom, was twofold. Decrees of Valentinian I. and Gratian had recognised it as a court to which clergy condemned by provincial synods might appeal.[3] In the second place it was looked up to as a model, and when doubtful questions arose about discipline it was consulted by provincial bishops. The answers of the Popes to such questions were known as Decretals. They did not bind the bishops ; they were responses, not ordinances. Appellate jurisdiction and the moral weight of the Decretals were the principal bases on which the power of the Roman see was gradually to be built up.[4]

---

[1] Known as Semipelagians.

[2] In another African affair he also compromised himself. A priest of Sicca, deposed by his bishop, appealed to Rome. Zosimus, in demanding his reinstatement, based his action on a canon which he alleged to be Nicene. The African bishops were unable to discover it among the canons of the Council of Nicaea. It was really a canon of the Council of Sardica.

[3] *Epp. Impp. Pontt.*, ed. Günther, i. p. 58 = *P.L.* xiii. 587 ; it was provided that the appeal might also be addressed to a council of fifteen neighbouring bishops.

[4] It may be added that Roman excommunication was recognised as exclusion from Catholic communion. Boniface, *Ep.* 14, *P.L.* xx. 777. Cp. Babut, *Le Concile de Turin*, p. 75.

Zosimus entertained an idea of his authority which transcended these rights and anticipated the claims of his successors. Immediately after his election his ear was gained by Patroclus, the bishop of Arles, who desired to make his see an ecclesiastical metropolis of the first rank. In the three provinces of Viennensis, Narbonensis Prima, and Narbonensis Secunda, the bishops of Vienne, Narbonne, and Marseilles[1] were the metropolitans ; Arles was merely a bishopric in Narbonensis Prima. The idea of Patroclus was naturally enough suggested by the translation of the residence of the Praetorian Prefect of Gaul from Trier to Arles.[2] Zosimus determined to deprive the bishops of Vienne, Narbonne, and Marseilles of their metropolitan rights, and to invest the bishop of Arles with jurisdiction over the three provinces. He also proposed to establish the new Metropolitan of Arles as a sort of Roman vicar, apparently over the whole of Gaul.[3]

The bishop of Narbonne yielded with a protest to this revolutionary assumption of sovranty. But the bishops of Marseilles and Vienne defied Zosimus and brought the question before a council of the Milanese diocese which met at Turin (Sept. 22, A.D. 417).[4] The council at first decided against the pretensions of Arles, but finally compromised by dividing the Viennese province into two parts, of which the southern was to depend on Arles. Zosimus was not pleased, but deemed it prudent to concur. The bishop of Marseilles, who declined to yield, was excommunicated by a Roman synod, but remained quietly in his see. Thus a part of the Pope's plan was actually carried out, but the facts remained that the council of Turin had refused to recognise the supreme authority of Rome, and that Marseilles had resisted with impunity.

The indiscretions of Zosimus were a lesson for his successors.[5]

---

[1] Marseilles was an exception to the rule that the civil was also the ecclesiastical metropolis. The civil metropolis of Narbonensis II. was Aquae (Aix). Marseilles was in Narbonensis I.

[2] *C.* A.D. 413, cp. Mommsen, *Chron. Min.* i. p. 553. Patroclus was a friend of the Patrician, afterwards Emperor, Constantius, and doubtless had the support of his influence. Prosper, *sub* 412.

[3] See Zosimus, *Ep.* 1, *P.L.* xx.

642, addressed *universis episcopis per Gallias et septem provincias constitutis.*

[4] The difficulties about this Council, its date, and its importance, were first elucidated by Babut, *op. cit.* For the history of the struggle over the Arles see also Gundlach, *Der Streit der Bistümer Arles und Vienne,* 1890.

[5] After his death the bishops of Africa, in a letter to Pope Boniface, expressed a hope that they would not again be exposed to such arrogance, *non sumus iam istum typhum passuri,* *P.L.* xx. 752.

Moreover, they recognised that the establishment of such a large and powerful see as that which Zosimus called into being was likely to be a rival rather than a vassal of Rome. Their aim was to undo what Zosimus had done, and in accomplishing this they acted with greater circumspection and increased the authority of their see. Both Boniface and Celestine [1] did what they could to restrict the powers of the bishop of Arles. The first Narbonensis was withdrawn from his jurisdiction and restored to Narbonne.[2] But the situation was more difficult for Rome, because the monks of Lérins, whose influence was strong in southern Gaul, threw the weight of their interest into the scale of Arles. Their founder, Honoratus, had been elected to succeed Patroclus, and he was followed by his disciple Hilary, whose authority threatened to usurp that of Rome in the Gallic Church.[3] The conflict between Hilary and Leo I., who was elected in A.D. 440, is not edifying. An appeal to Rome (A.D. 444) gave the Pope a welcome opportunity of striking his opponent. He did not venture to excommunicate him, but he deprived him of the remnant of the province which Zosimus had created. This sentence could not be executed without the aid of the secular power. He had much influence with the Emperor and Galla Placidia, and he procured an edict, which was issued (July 8, A.D. 445) at the same time as his own decree.[4] Arles was deprived of its metropolitan dignity.[5]

But that edict of Valentinian III. did much more than settle in Rome's favour this particular question. It assigned to the Roman see that supremacy over the provincial churches which the Popes had been endeavouring to establish, but which the African synods and the council of Turin had refused to acknowledge.[6] It ordained that "the bishops of Gaul or any other province should take no decision contrary to the ancient rules of discipline without the consent and authority of the venerable Pope of the eternal city. They must conform to all the decrees

---

[1] Boniface, 418 – 422 ; Celestine, 422–432.

[2] By Boniface. For Celestine's attitude see his letter, *Ep.* 4, *P.L.* l. 429.

[3] Babut, *op. cit.* 147 *sqq.*

[4] Valentinian III., *Nov.* 17. Leo, *Ep.* 10, *P.L.* liv. 628. Cp. Tillemont, *Mém.* 15, 82 ; Babut, p. 172.

[5] Five years later, however, Leo restored this rank to Arles, giving it a part of the Viennese diocese. This was after Hilary's death.

[6] The unwillingness of leading churchmen at the beginning of the fifth century to admit the exorbitant claims of Rome is illustrated by Jerome's letter to Evangelus, *Ep.* 146, *P.L.* xxii. p. 1194; he observes, *orbis maior est urbe.*

of the Apostolic see. Bishops summoned before the tribunal of
Rome must be compelled to appear by the civil authorities."

It is the political bearing of this law that interests us here.
When many of the western provinces had wholly or partly passed
out of the Emperor's control, it was a matter of importance to
strive to keep alive the idea of the Empire and the old attachment
to Rome in the minds of the provincials who were now subject
to German masters. The day might come when it would be
possible to recover some of these lost lands, which the Imperial
government never acknowledged to be really lost, and in the
meantime a close ecclesiastical unity presented itself as a powerful
means for preserving the bonds of sentiment, which would then
prove an indispensable help. To accustom the churches in Gaul
and Britain, Spain and Africa to look up to Rome and refer their
disputes and difficulties to the Roman bishop was a wise policy
from the secular point of view, and it was doubtless principally
by urging considerations of this nature that Leo was able to
induce the government to establish the supremacy of his see.

It is important to bear in mind that the administrative
authority of the Pope, at this time, extended into the dominions
of the eastern Emperors. The lands included in the Prefecture
of Illyricum belonged to the Patriarchate of Rome, and constituted the Vicariate of Thessalonica, where the Pope's vicar,
who was entrusted with the administration, resided. Theodosius
II. wished to place this ecclesiastical province under Constantinople and published an edict with this intent, but the remon-
strances of Honorius induced him to retract it ; [1] and Greece,
Macedonia, and Dacia remained under the see of St. Peter till
the eighth century.

§ 3. *Persecution of Paganism*

Persecution was an unavoidable consequence of Constantine's
act in adopting Christianity. Two of the chief points in which
this faith differed from the Roman State religion were its exclu-
siveness and the vital importance which it assigned to dogma.
The first logically led to intolerance of pagan religions, the second
to intolerance of heresies, and these consequences could not be

---

[1] See above Chap. II. p. 64. A.D. 421, *C. Th.* xvi. 11. 45. Cp. Innocent,
Ep. 13. Gieseler, *Lehrbuch,* ii. 217.

averted when Christianity became the religion of the State. It might be suggested that Constantine would have done better if, when he decided to embrace it and favour its propagation, he had been content to deprive pagan cults of their official status and to allow Christianity to compete in a free field with its rivals, aided by the prestige which it would derive from the Emperor's personal adhesion and favour. But such a policy would have been an anachronism. A state, at that time, was unthinkable without a State cult, and if an Emperor became a Christian a logical result was that Christianity should be adopted as the official religion of the Empire, and a second that the old Roman policy of toleration should be thrown overboard. In an age of superstition this was demanded not merely in the interest of the Church but in the interest of the State itself. The purpose of the official cults in the pagan State was to secure the protection of the deities ; these were liberal and tolerant lords who raised no objection to other forms of worship ; and toleration was therefore a principle of the State. But the god of the new official religion was a jealous master ; he had said, " thou shalt have none other gods but me," and idolatry was an offence to him ; how could his protection and favour be expected by a state in which idolatry was permitted ? Intolerance was a duty, and the first business of a patriotic ruler was to take measures to extirpate the errors of paganism.

But these consequences were not drawn immediately. It must never be forgotten that Constantine's revolution was perhaps the most audacious act ever committed by an autocrat in disregard and defiance of the vast majority of his subjects. For at least four-fifths of the population of the Empire were still outside the Christian Church.[1] The army and all the leading men in the administration were devoted to paganism. It is not, therefore, surprising that Constantine, who was a statesman as well as a convert, made no attempt to force the pace. His policy did little more than indicate and prepare the way for the gradual conversion of the Empire, and was so mild and cautious that it has been maintained by some that his aim was to establish a parity between the two religions.

---

[1] Estimates, based on highly conjectural data, of the number of Christians vary from one-twentieth to one-sixth of the total population. See V. Schultze, *Der Untergang des gr.-röm. Heidentums*, i. p. 22 *sqq.*

He retained the title of Pontifex Maximus, and thereby the constitutional right of the Emperor to supervise the religious institutions. He withdrew the support of state funds from pagan rites, but made an exception in favour of the official cults at Rome. His most important repressive measure was the prohibition of the sacrifice of victims in the temples.[1] One reason for this measure was the dangerous practice of divination by entrails, often employed by persons who contemplated a rebellion and desired to learn from the higher powers their chances of success.

In some particular places cults were suppressed, but a pagan could still worship freely in the temples, could offer incense and make libations of wine, and might even perform sacrificial rites in a private house. The sons of Constantine [2] were indeed inclined to adopt a stringent policy, and their laws might lead us to suppose that there was something like a severe persecution. Constantius, in reaffirming the prohibition of sacrifices, menaced transgressors with the avenging sword.[3] But the death penalty was never inflicted, and there was a vast difference between the letter of the law and the practice. In the same edict was ordained the closing of temples " in all places and cities," but this order can only have been carried out here and there. Its execution depended on local circumstances, and on the sentiments of the provincial governors. In some places Christian fanatics took advantage of the Imperial decree to demolish heathen shrines, and the pagans were naturally apprehensive. When Julian visited Ilion, he inspected the antiquities under the guidance of Pegasius, who was " nominally a bishop of the Galilaeans," but really worshipped the Sun god.[4] He had taken orders and succeeded in becoming a bishop in order that he might have the means of protecting the heathen sanctuaries from Christian desecration.

When paganism was restored by Julian, it is probable that any temples which had been closed under the edict of Constantius were again reopened, and after his fall it would seem that they were allowed to remain open for worship, though sacrifices were regarded as unlawful.

---

[1] The law is not preserved, but is recorded by Eusebius, *Vita Const.* ii. 45, and referred to by Constantius, *C. Th.* xvi. 10. 2.

[2] Firmicus Maternus, in his *De errore profanarum religionum*, urged them to drastic measures.

[3] *C. Th.* xvi. 10. 4 (A.D. 342) *gladio ultore sternatur.*

[4] Julian, *Ep.* 78, ed. Hertlein.

The Emperors Valentinian I.[1] and Valens were consistently tolerant. The mysteries of Eleusis were expressly permitted, for the proconsul of Achaia told Valentinian that if they were suppressed the Greeks would find life not worth living.[2] But a new religious policy was inaugurated by Gratian and Theodosius the Great. Gratian abandoned the title of Pontifex Maximus ; he withdrew the public money which was devoted to the cults of Rome, and he ordered the altar of Victory to be removed from the Senate-house, to the deep chagrin of the senators. The fathers appealed to Valentinian II. to revoke this order, and to restore the public maintenance of the religious institutions of the capital ; but the moving petition of Symmachus, who was their spokesman, was overruled by the influence of Ambrose, the archbishop of Milan, who possessed the ear of Valentinian and of Theodosius.[3]

It remained for Theodosius to inflict a far heavier blow on the ancient cults of Greece and Rome. In the earlier years of his reign the extirpation of pagan worship does not seem to have been an aim of his policy. He was only concerned to enforce obedience to the laws prohibiting sacrifices, which had evidently been widely evaded. He decided on the closing of all sanctuaries in which the law had been broken. He entrusted to Cynegius, Praetorian Prefect of the East, a pious Christian, the congenial task of executing this order in Asia and Egypt. But otherwise temples were still legally open to worshippers.[4] It is to be particularly noted that the Emperor did not desire to destroy but only to secularise such buildings as were condemned, and the cases of barbarous demolition of splendid buildings which occurred in these years were due to the fanatical zeal of monks and ecclesiastics. Monks wrought the destruction of the great temple of Edessa, and the Serapeum at Alexandria, which gave that city " the semblance of a sacred world," [5] was demolished

[1] Ammianus Marc. xxx. 9 *inter religionum diversitates medius stetit.*

[2] Zosimus, iv. 3.

[3] Ambrose, *Epp.* i. 17 and 18 (*P.L.* xvi. 961 and 971). Symmachus, Relatio 3. Prudentius, *Contra Symmachum.* Gracchus, Prefect of Rome in 376, demolished a cave-temple of Mithras at Rome (Jerome, *Ep.* 107 *ad Laetam, P.L.* xxii. 868 ; Prudentius, *ib.* i. 561 *sqq.*).

[4] See Libanius, *Or.* xxx. § 8 (ed. Förster). This appeal which Libanius addressed to the Emperor on behalf of the temples was written in summer A.D. 388, as R. van Loy has satisfactorily shown (*B.Z.* xxii. 313 *sqq.*). The orator refers to the campaign conducted by Cynegius, who had recently died.

[5] Eunapius, *Vtia Aedesii,* p. 43.

under the direction of the archbishop Theophilus (A.D. 389),[1] who thereby dealt an effective blow to the paganism of Alexandria.

But Theodosius and his ecclesiastical advisers thought that the time was now ripe to make a clean sweep of idolatry, and in A.D. 391 and 392 laws were issued which carried to its logical conclusion the act of Constantine. We may conjecture that this drastic legislation was principally due to the influence of the archbishop of Milan. To sacrifice, whether in public or in private, was henceforward to be punished as an act of treason. Fines were imposed on any who should frequent temples or shrines ; and for worshipping images with incense, for hanging sacred fillets on trees, for building altars of turf, the penalty was confiscation of the house or property where such acts were performed.[2]

In the insurrection of A.D. 392 the restoration of paganism was a capital feature in the programme of the general Arbogastes and Eugenius the creature whom he crowned, and the lure attracted some distinguished adherents. For a short time the altar of Victory was set up in the Roman Senate-house. After the suppression of the revolt Theodosius visited Rome, attended a meeting of the Senate, and though his tone was conciliatory, his firmness compelled that body to decree the abolition of the ancient religious institutions of Rome.[3] Some of the pagan senators had Christian families,[4] and domestic influence may have reinforced the imperial will.

The last years of the fourth century mark an epoch in the decay of paganism. While the gods were irrevocably driven from Rome. itself, time-honoured institutions of Greece also came to an end. The old oracles seem to have been silenced at

---

[1] The account of Sozomen, vii. 15, is better than that of Socrates, v. 16, 17. See also Eunapius, *ib.* The pagans were not guiltless in this affair. They had attacked the Christians and fortified themselves in the buildings of the Serapeum ; but they had been provoked to this outbreak by Theophilus, who had paraded religious symbols, taken from a temple of Dionysus (which the Emperor had permitted him to convert into a church), through the streets in derision of the pagan cults.

The most unfortunate occurrence was the destruction of the library of the Serapeum (Orosius, vi. 15).

[2] *C. Th.* xvi. 10. 10 and 11 (391); 12 (392).

[3] A.D. 394. On the debate in the Senate see Zosimus iv. 59 ; Prudentius, *Contra Symm.* i. 415 *sqq.* ; Hodgkin, *Italy*, i. 580 *sqq.*

[4] *E.g.* Albinus, a pontifex. Jerome, *Ep.* 107 *ad Laetam* (*P.L.* xxii. 868). As to the small number of Christian senators cp. above, p. 164.

a much earlier date.   The "last oracle" of the Delphic god, said
to have been delivered to Julian, is a sad and moving expression
of the passing away of the old order of things.

> Tell the king on earth has fallen the glorious dwelling,
>   And the water springs that spake are quenched and dead.
> Not a cell is left the god, no roof, no cover ;
>   In his hand the prophet laurel flowers no more.[1]

The Olympian games were celebrated for the last time in A.D.
393, and the chryselephantine statue of Zeus, the greatest
monument of the genius of Pheidias, was removed soon afterwards from Olympia to Constantinople.[2]   The Eleusinian
mysteries ceased three years later in consequence of the injuries
wrought to the sanctuaries by the invasion of Alaric.[3]   The
legend that Athens was saved from the rapacity of the Goths
by the appearance of Athene Promachos and the hero Achilles
illustrates the vitality of pagan superstition.   Athens had fared
better than many other towns at the hands of the Emperors.[4]
Constantine, who ransacked Hellenic shrines for works of art
in order to adorn his new capital, spared Athens ; and in the
reign of Theodosius, when the Samian Hera of Lysippus, the
Cnidian Aphrodite of Praxiteles, the Athene of Lindos were
carried off, the Parthenon was not compelled to surrender the
ivory and gold Athene of Pheidias.   Soon after A.D. 429 this
precious work was ravished from the Acropolis,[5] but we do not
know its fate.   Nor do we know at what date the Parthenon
was converted into a church of the Virgin.[6]

The ordinances of Theodosius did not, of course, avail immediately to stamp out everywhere the forbidden cults.   Pagan
practices still went on secretly, and in some places openly,

---

[1] Swinburne's version. The original
is preserved in the *Vita S. Artemii*
(*A.S.* 20 Oct. viii.), § 35, p. 870 :

εἴπατε τῷ βασιλῆι, χαμαὶ πέσε δαίδαλος
  αὐλά·
οὐκέτι Φοῖβος ἔχει καλύβαν, οὐ μάντιδα
  δάφναν,
οὐ παγὰν λαλέουσαν · ἀπέσβετο καὶ
  λάλον ὕδωρ.

[2] Cedrenus i. 364 (*cp.* Moses of
Chorene, iii. 40) ; Clinton, *Fasti
Hellenici*, iii. p. xv.   A passage of
Julian (*Ep.* 35) seems to imply that
the Pythian, Nemean, and Isthmian
games were celebrated in his day.

[3] Eunapius (*Vita Maximi*) suggests
that the destruction was wrought by
a band of fanatical monks who accompanied the Gothic army.

Cp. *C. Th.* xv. 5. 4 for games at
Delphi (A.D. 424), and there is a
record that the Olympian games came
to an end in the reign of Theodosius
II. (*Scholia in Lucianum, Praec. Rhet.*
ed. Rabe, p. 174).

[4] Gregorovius, *Gesch. d. Stadt Athen*,
i. 26. 33.

[5] Marinus, *Vita Procli*, c. 30.

[6] Gregorovius, *ib.* 64, conjectures
in the reign of Justinian.

and the government, generally perhaps yielding to ecclesiastical
pressure, issued from time to time new laws to enforce the
execution of the old or to supplement them.[1] Arcadius, under
the influence of Chrysostom, issued an edict to destroy, not merely
to close, temples in the country and to use the material for public
buildings.[2] Chrysostom sent monks to Phoenicia to carry out
the work of destruction there, but the money required was
provided not by the state but by pious Christians, especially
women.[3] We have seen how bishop Porphyrius of Gaza secured
with the help of the Empress Eudoxia the demolition of the
temple of Marnas. As a rule the Emperors desired that the
ancient sanctuaries should be preserved and turned to other uses,
and we find them interfering to prevent destruction.[4] In many
country districts Christianity was only beginning to penetrate,
and for the eradication of heathenism there was much mis-
sionary teaching to be done, such as was carried on by Martin
in western Gaul, by Victricius, archbishop of Rouen, in
the Belgic provinces, and by Nicetas of Remesiana in the
Balkan highlands.[5]

Theodosius II. at one time professed to believe that no pagans
survived in his dominions,[6] but this sanguine view, if it was
seriously held, was premature, for in a later year he repeated
the prohibition of sacrifices and ordered anew the conversion
of temples into churches ; [7] and Leo I. legislated severely against
heathen practices.[8] It is to be observed that this persecution
differed in one important respect from the ecclesiastical perse-
cutions of later ages in western Europe. Only pagan acts were
forbidden ; *opinion as such was tolerated*, and no restrictions
were placed on the diffusion of pagan literature. Perhaps the
only exception was the edict of Theodosius II. shortly before
his death,[9] ordering the books of Porphyry, whose dangerous

[1] *C. Th.* xvi. 10. 13 (395); xvi. 10.
14 (396) abolishing some immunities
still enjoyed by old priesthoods.
[2] *Ib.* xvi. 10. 16.
[3] Theodoret v. 9.
[4] In southern Gaul, *C. Th.* xvi. 10.
15 ; in Africa, *ib.* xviii. (399).
[5] Sulpicius Severus, *Dialogus*, iii.
2. Vacandard, *Saint Victrice*, 1903.
Burns, *Life and Works of Nicetas of
R.*, 1905.
[6] A.D. 423, *C. Th.* xvi. 10. 22.

[7] A.D. 435, *ib.* 25.
[8] *C. Th.* i. 11. 8 ; subsequent laws
against Hellenism by Leo, Zeno, or
Anastasius (?), *ib.* 9. 10.
[9] A.D. 448, *ib.* i. 1. 3. The law
says, the books of Porphyry "or any
one else." The anti-Christian work
of Porphyry has perished, like those
of Celsus and Julian. There is a new
edition of the fragments by Harnack,
Porphyrius " Gegen die Christen "
1916 (*Abh.* of the Prussian Academy).

treatise *Against the Christians* had apparently shocked the Emperor or some of his advisers, to be burned. The same monarch had enacted that no Christian shall disturb or provoke Jews or pagans " living peaceably." [1] Indeed pagans could not be dispensed with in the civil service, and in the sixth century we still find them in prominent positions.[2] Hellenism largely prevailed in the law schools, and was no bar to promotion, though it might be made a pretext for removing an official who had fallen out of favour. An able pagan, Tatian, enjoyed the confidence of the fanatical Theodosius the Great, and was appointed Praetorian Prefect of the East ; and the same Emperor showed friendly regard towards spokesmen of the old religion like Libanius and Symmachus. The headquarters of unchristian doctrine, the university of Athens, was held in high esteem by Constantine and Constans,[3] and it continued throughout the fifth century unmolested as the home of a philosophy which was the most dangerous rival of Christian theology. Pagans also received appointments in the university of Constantinople.

In a hundred years the Empire had been transformed from a state in which the immense majority of the inhabitants were devoted to pagan religions, into one in which an Emperor could say, with gross exaggeration, but without manifest absurdity, that not a pagan survived. Such a change was not brought to pass by mere prohibition and suppression. It is not too much to say that the success of the Church in converting the gentile world in the fourth and fifth centuries was due to a process which may be described as a pagan transmutation of Christianity itself. If Christian beliefs and worship had been retained un-altered in the early simplicity of their spirit and form, it may well be doubted whether a much longer period would have sufficed to christianize the Roman Empire. But the Church permitted a compromise. All the religions of the age had common ground in crude superstition, and the Church found no difficulty in proffering to converts beliefs and cults similar to those to which they had been accustomed. It was a comparatively small

---

[1] *In quiete degentibus, C. Th.* xvi. 10. 24.

[2] A law issued at Ravenna in 408 excluded enemies of the Catholic faith from serving in the Palace, but was probably applied only temporarily. *C. Th.* xvi. 5. 42. In 416 persons polluted with errors of pagan rites were excluded from state service, *ib.* xvi. 10. 21, but this would not affect those who had not been found guilty of sacrificing.

[3] Gregorovius, *ib.* 28, 29.

matter that incense, lights, and flowers, the accessories of various
pagan ceremonials, had been introduced into Christian worship.
It was a momentous and happy stroke to encourage the introduction of a disguised polytheism.   A legion of saints and martyrs
replaced the old legion of gods and heroes, and the hesitating
pagan could gradually reconcile himself to a religion, which, if
it robbed him of his tutelary deity, whom it stigmatized as a
demon, allowed him in compensation the cult of a tutelary saint.
A new and banal mythology was created, of saints and martyrs,
many of them fictitious ; their bodies and relics, capable of
working miracles like those which used to be wrought at the
tombs of heroes, were constantly being discovered.   The devotee
of Athene or Isis could transfer his homage to the Virgin Mother.
The Greek sailor or fisherman, who used to pray to Poseidon,
could call upon St. Nicolas.   Those who worshipped at stone
altars of Apollo on hill-tops could pay the same allegiance to
St. Elias.   The calendar of Christian anniversaries corresponded
at many points to the calendars of Greek and Roman festivals.
Men could more easily acquiesce in the loss of the heathen celebrations connected with the winter solstice and the vernal
equinox, when they found the joyous celebrations of the Nativity
and the Resurrection associated with those seasons, and they
could transfer some of their old customs to the new feasts.   The
date of the Nativity was fixed to coincide with the birthday of
Mithras (*natalis Invicti,* December 25), whose religion had many
affinities with the Christian.   This process was not the result, in
the first instance, of a deliberate policy.   It was a natural
development, for Christianity could not escape the influence of
the ideas which were current in its environment.   But it was
promoted by the men of light and leading in the Church.[1]

A particular form of miraculous healing illustrates the way in
which Christianity appropriated pagan superstitions.   The same
dream-cures which used to be performed by Aesculapius or the
Dioscuri for those who slept a night in the temple courts were still
available ; only the patient must resort to a sanctuary of Saints
Cosmas and Damian,[2] the new Castor and Pollux, or of the arch-

---

[1] On the origins of the cult of saints
and martyrs see E. Lucius, *Die
Anfänge des Heiligenkults in der
christlichen Kirche,* 1904 ; P. Saintyves,
Les Saints successeurs des dieux, 1907 ;
J. Rendel Harris, *The Dioscuri in the*
Christian Legends, 1903, *Cult of the*
Heavenly Twins, 1906.

[2] Known as the *anargyroi,* physicians
who take no fee. For their miracles
see Zeumer, *De incubatione,* 69 *sqq.,*
where the whole subject is treated.

angel Michael [1] or some other Christian substitute. We have an interesting example of the method employed by ecclesiastical magnates in an incident which occurred in Egypt. Near Canopus there was a temple of Isis where such nocturnal cures were dispensed, and professing Christians continued to have recourse to this unhallowed aid. The Patriarch Cyril found a remedy. He discovered the bodies of two martyrs, Cyrus and John, in the church of St. Mark at Alexandria, and dislodging Isis he interred them, and dedicated a church to them, in the same place, where they freely exhibited the same mysterious medical powers which had been displayed by the great goddess.[2]

The more highly educated pagans offered a longer and more obdurate resistance to the appeals of Christianity than the vulgar crowd. Throughout the fourth and fifth centuries they retained higher education in their hands. The schools of rhetoric, philosophy, law, and science maintained the ancient traditions and the pagan atmosphere. In their writings, some pagans frankly showed their hostility to Christianity, others affected to ignore it. We saw how they threw upon this religion the responsibility for the invasion of the barbarians. But in general their attitude was one of resignation, and they found no difficulty in serving Christian Emperors and working with Christian colleagues.[3] This spirit of resignation is expressed in the most interesting piece we have of the poet Palladas of Alexandria, occasioned by the sight of a Hermes lying in the roadway.

At a meeting of ways I was ware of a bronze god prone at my feet,
And I knew him the offspring of Zeus, whom we prayed to of old, as was
   meet.
" Lord of the triple moon," I cried, " averter of woe,
Ever a lord hast thou been, and behold, in the dust thou art low."

---

[1] In his church at Sosthenion on the Bosphorus, Sozomen, ii. 3.

[2] See their Acts in *P.G.* lxxxvii. 3. 3424 *sqq.*

[3] There seems to have been much mutual tolerance between Christians and pagans in private life. Chrysostom exhorts to goodwill and friendliness toward Hellenes. " They are all children," he says, " and, like children, when we talk about necessary things they do not attend but laugh." *Hom.* 4 on *Ep.* i. *ad Corinth.*, *P.G.* lxi. 38.

In another sermon he describes a dispute between a Hellene and a Christian on the merits of Plato and Paul, the one asserting that Paul was rude and unlearned, the other that he was more learned and eloquent than Plato. Chrysostom's comment is that the Christian took a wrong line, and that the glory of the apostles lay in their rudeness and ignorance (*Hom.* iii. *ib.* 27). Elsewhere he disparages Socrates (*Hom.* 4, *ib.* p. 35), and Plato (*Hom.* 4 on *Acts*, *P.G.* 60, 50).

But at night with a smile on his lips the god stood by me sublime,
And said, " A god though I be, I serve, and my master is Time." [1]

Throughout the fifth century Athens was the headquarters of
what may be called higher paganism. The Stoic and Epicurean
schools had died out in the third century, and in the fourth the
most distinguished savants of the university like Proaeresius and
Himerius were sophists, not philosophers. But the Platonic
Academy continued to exist, independent of State grants, for
it had its own private property producing a revenue of more
than £600 a year.[2] Its scholarchs, however, were not men of
much talent or distinction, until the office was filled by Priscus,[3]
a Neoplatonist and a friend of Julian, after that Emperor's
death. Priscus inaugurated the reign of Neoplatonism at Athens ;
with him the revival of the university, as a centre of philosophic
study, began, and vastly increased under his successor Plutarch.
Towards the end of the fourth century, Synesius had spoken in
disparaging words of Athens and her teachers : her fame, he
said, rests with her bee-keepers. He was jealous for the reputation of Alexandria, and with good reason, for under Plutarch and
his successors Syrianus and Proclus Athens was to eclipse the
Egyptian city. These Platonists attracted students from all parts
of the East, and some who had begun their studies, like Proclus
himself, at Alexandria, completed them at Athens.[4]

The Athenian professors had always regarded themselves as
the champions of Hellenism, but when the Neoplatonic philosophy
became ascendant, the Hellenism of Athens was a more serious
danger. At this time Neoplatonism was the most formidable
rival of Christian theology among educated men of a speculative
turn of mind. Augustine recognised this ; we know how it
attracted him.[5] The Neoplatonists taught a system fundamentally differing from the current Christian theology as to the position which was assigned to the creator of the world. According

---

[1] *Anthol. Pal.* ix. 441.

[2] 1000 solidi or something more,
Damascius, *Vita Isidori*, § 158,
referring to the time of Proclus. That
the other professors were well paid from
the public σιτήσεις may be inferred
from Libanius, *Epp.* 1449.

[3] He was the pupil of Aedesius, the
most distinguished pupil of Iamblichus
who was himself a pupil of Porphyry.

[4] We know a good deal about

university life at Athens in the fourth
and fifth centuries. (See Hertzberg,
Gesch. Griechenlands, iii. *passim* ;
Sievers, *Das Leben des Libanius*, 42
sqq.) The principal sources for the
fifth are Olympiodorus, *fr.* 51 ; Marinus, *Vita Procli* ; Damascius, *Vita
Isidori* ; various articles in Suidas.

[5] He had studied Plotinus and
Porphyry in Latin translations. See
Angus, *Sources of De civ. Dei*, p. 268.

to Plotinus, Nous or Reason, the creator, emanated from and
was subordinate to the absolute One, and Soul again emanated
from Nous. His successors developed his principles by multiply-
ing and dividing the emanations, and the growth of the philosophy
culminated in the system which Proclus constructed by means
of a dialectic which Hegel himself has described as " extremely
tiring." [1] In all these phases, the Demiurge or Creator is sub-
ordinated to the One of which no divine attributes could be predicted, and thus an apparently impassable gulf was fixed between
the later Platonic philosophers and Christian theologians. There
was, indeed, at Alexandria another school of Platonism, which
held closer here and there to the teaching of Plato himself, and
men who were trained in this school found the transition to
Christian doctrine comparatively easy. We know something of
the system of Hierocles, a leading Platonist at Alexandria in the
fifth century.[2] In his system there was no One or any other higher
principle above God the creator and legislator, who was above,
and in no sense co-ordinate with, the company of sidereal gods ;
and he, like the Christian Deity, created the world out of nothing.
Some of the pupils of Hierocles became Christians. It is a curious
circumstance that Hierocles should have been condemned to exile
at Constantinople on grounds which are unknown to us.[3] It can
hardly have been for his teaching, seeing that the far more anti-
Christian Platonists, who had their stronghold at Athens, were
tolerated.

[1] *Gesch. der Philosophie*, 73-74, in
Werke, xv. The most recent treatment of the metaphysics of Proclus
will be found in Whittaker's *The
Neoplatonists*. Procopius, the famous
sophist of Gaza, wrote a refutation of
the theology of Proclus, which has
been preserved under the name of
Nicolaus of Methone (Ἀνάπτυξις
τῆς θεολογικῆς στοιχειώσεως Πρόκλου)
who simply transcribed Procopius, as
has been shown by J. Dräseke, *B.Z.*
vi. 55 *sqq.*

[2] See the instructive article of K.
Prächter, in *B.Z.* xxi. 1 *sqq.* Of the
works of Hierocles are preserved his
*Commentary on the Golden Words of
Pythagoras*, in Mullach, *Fr. phil.
graec.* i. 416 *sqq.*, and fragments Περὶ
προνοίας καὶ εἱμαρμένης in Photius, *Bibl.*
214, 251.

[3] Suidas, *sub* Ἱεροκλῆς : προσέκρουσε
τοῖς κρατοῦσι καὶ εἰς δικαστήριον ἀχθεὶς
ἐτύπτετο τὰς ἐξ ἀνθρώπων πληγάς . . .
φυγὴν δὲ κατακριθεὶς καὶ ἐπανελθὼν
χρόνῳ ὕστερον εἰς Ἀλεξάνδρειαν κτλ.
The source of Suidas was Damascius, *Vita Isidori*, see Photius, *Bibl.*
242 (p. 338). It may be noted
that in political philosophy the Neoplatonists held to Plato's theories.
The only attempt at original speculation in the field of political science in
this age is to be found in a tract Περὶ
πολιτικῆς ἐπιστήμης, much mutilated,
published in Mai (*Scriptores vet. nov.
coll.* ii. 571 *sqq.*) which has been
elucidated by Prächter in *B.Z.* ix.
621 *sqq.* It seems to have been
written by a Christian, *c.* A.D. 500,
who was influenced by Neoplatonism,
but did not swear by Plato, and made
much use of Cicero's *De republica*.

But the danger and offence of the later Neoplatonists did not lie in their mystical metaphysics, but in the theurgy and pagan practices to which they were almost always addicted. Proclus in his public lectures as scholarch confined himself, doubtless, to the interpretation of Plato in the Neoplatonic sense, and to problems of dialectic, but he reserved for his chosen disciples esoteric teaching in theurgy, and venerated the gods as beneficent beings worthy of worship, though occupying a subordinate place in the hierarchy of existences. He believed that by fasting and purifications on certain days it was possible to get into communication with supernatural beings, and he recognised the gods of other nations as well as those of Greece. He said that the philosopher should not confine himself to the religious rites of one city or people, but should be " a hierophant of the whole world." He was more scrupulous in observing the fasts of the Egyptians than the Egyptians themselves.[1] He had been initiated in the Eleusinian secrets by his friend Asclepigenia, the daughter of Plutarch,[2] who had learned them from the last priest of Eleusis, and in one of his writings he told how he had seen Hecate herself. Athens believed in his magical powers ; he was said to have constructed an instrument by which he could bring down rain.

The Hellenists, even in the days of Proclus, had not abandoned all hope of winning toleration for pagan worship. At any time some one might ascend the throne with Hellenic sympathies. The elevation of Anthemius in the West was a proof that this was not impossible, though Anthemius was able to do little to help the pagan interest. Proclus died in A.D. 485, and at that very time a former pupil of his was prominently associated with a rebellion [3] which, if it had been successful, might have been followed by some temporary relaxation of the severe laws against polytheism and pagan worship. This was to be the last flutter of a dying cause.

[1] Marinus, *Vita Procli*, c. 19. Six hymns of Proclus addressed to Greek gods are extant; others celebrated Isis, Marnas the god of Gaza, Thyandrites an Arabian deity (*ib.*).

[2] *Ib.* c. 28. The learned Asclepigenia married a rich landowner Archiadas, who was very generous to the university. Their daughter, the younger Asclepigenia, married Theagenes, the richest Greek of the day and notably public-spirited in the use of his wealth. He became Archon of Athens.

[3] See next Chapter, § 2.

§ 4. Persecution of Heresy

The persecution of heretics was more resolute and severe than the persecution of pagans. Those who stood outside of the Church altogether were less dangerous than those members of it who threatened to corrupt it by false doctrine, and the unity of the Catholic faith in matters of dogma was considered of supreme importance. " Truth, which is simple and one," wrote Pope Leo I., " does not admit of variety." [1] A modern inquirer is accustomed to regard the growth of heresies as a note of vitality, but in old times it was a sign of the active operation of the enemy of mankind.

The heresy which was looked upon as the most dangerous and abominable of all was that of the Manichees, which it would be truer to regard as a rival religion than as a form of Christianity.[2] It was based on a mixture of Zoroastrian and Christian ideas, along with elements derived from Buddhism, but the Zoroastrian principles were preponderant. This religion was founded by Manes in Persia in the third century, and in the course of the fourth it spread throughout the Empire, in the West as well as in the East. Augustine in his youth came under its influence. The fundamental doctrine was that of Zoroaster, the existence of a good and an evil principle, God and Matter, independent of each other. The Old Testament was the work of the Evil Being. Matter being thoroughly evil, Jesus Christ could not have invested himself with it, and therefore his human body was a mere appearance. The story of his life in the Gospels was interpreted mystically. The Manichees had no churches, no altars, no incense ; their worship consisted in prayers and hymns ; they did not celebrate Christmas, and their chief festival was the Bêma, in March, kept in memory of the death of their founder, who was said to have been flayed alive or crucified by Varahran I. They condemned marriage, and practised rigorous austerities.[3]

The laws against the Manichees, which were frequent and

[1] *Ep.* 172 *varietatem veritas, quae est simplex atque una, non recipit* (*P.L.* xx. p. 1216).

[2] The chief sources for Manichaeanism are : the *Acta Archelai*, and Alexander of Lycopolis (a Platonist, not a Christian), πρὸς τὰς Μανιχαίου δόξας (for the early stage of its development) ; Epiphanius, *De haer.* ; Augustine, *Contra Faustum* (and other treatises).

[3] They are accused of disgusting practices, Augustine, *De haer.* 46. Cp. Salmon's art. " Manicheans " in *Dict. Chr. Biog.* iii. 798.

drastic, began in the reign of Theodosius I. The heresy was insidious, because the heretics were difficult to discover; they often took part in Christian ceremonies and passed for orthodox, and they disguised their views under other names. Theodosius deprived them of civil rights and banished them from towns. Those who sheltered themselves under harmless names were liable to the penalty of death; and he ordered the Praetorian Prefect of the East to institute "inquisitors" for the purpose of discovering them.[1] This is a very early instance of the application of this word, which in later ages was to become so offensive, to the uses of religious persecution. When the government of Theodosius II., under the influence of Nestorius, made a vigorous effort to sweep heresy from the world, the Manicheans were stigmatised as men who had "descended to the lowest depths of wickedness," and were condemned anew to be expelled from towns, and perhaps to be put to death [2] (A.D. 428). Later legislation inflicted death unreservedly; they were the only heretics whose opinions exposed them to the supreme penalty.

Arcadius, at the beginning of his reign, reaffirmed all the pains and prohibitions which his predecessors had enacted against heretics.[3] In most cases, this meant the suppression of their services and assemblies and ordinations. The Eunomians, an extreme branch of the Arians, who held that the Son was unlike the Father, were singled out for more severe treatment and deprived of the right of executing testaments. This disability, however, was afterwards withdrawn, and it was finally enacted that a Eunomian could not bequeath property to a fellow-heretic.[4] Thus there was a certain vacillation in the policy of the government, caused by circumstances and influences which we cannot trace.

The combined efforts of Church and State were successful in virtually stamping out Arianism, which after the end of the fourth century ceased to be a danger to ecclesiastical unity. They were also successful ultimately in driving Nestorianism out of the Empire. The same policy, applied to the Monophysitic heresy,

---

[1] *C. Th.* xvi. 5. 7 (A.D. 381); 9 (A.D. 382). Further legislation under Arcadius and Theodosius II. will be found in the same title.

[2] The words *et ultimo supplicio*

tradendis, in *C.J.* i. 5. 5 are omitted in *C. Th.* xvi. 5. 65.

[3] *Ib.* 25.

[4] *Ib.* 27 (395); 58 (415).

failed. Marcian's law of A.D. 455 against the Eutychians was
severe enough.[1] They were excluded from the service of the
State ; they were forbidden to publish books criticising the
Council of Chalcedon ; and their literature, like that of the
Nestorians, was condemned to be burned. But in Syria, where
anti-Greek feelings were strong, and in Egypt, where national
sentiment was beginning to associate itself with a religious
symbol, all attempts to impose uniformity were to break down.

The severe measures taken by the State against the Donatists
in Africa were chiefly due to their own fanaticism. Donatism
was not properly a heresy, it was a schism, which had grown out
of a double election to the see of Carthage in A.D. 311, and the
question at issue between the Catholics and the Donatists was
one of church discipline. We need not follow the attempts of
Constantine and Constans to restore unity to the African church
by military force. The cause of the Donatists was not recommended by their association with the violent madmen known as
Circumcellions, who disdained death themselves, and inflicted
the most cruel deaths on their opponents. The schismatics
survived the persecution. At the death of Theodosius I. the
greater number of the African churches seem to have been in
their hands, and during the usurpation of Gildo they persecuted
the Catholics. When Augustine became bishop of Hippo, where
the Donatists were in a great majority, he set himself the task
of restoring ecclesiastical unity in Africa by conciliation.[2] He
and the Catholic clergy had some success in making converts,
but the fanatics were so infuriated by these desertions that
with their old allies the Circumcellions they committed barbarous
outrages upon the Catholic clergy and churches ; Augustine himself barely escaped from being waylaid. Such disorders
demanded the intervention of the secular power. Some injured
bishops presented themselves at Ravenna, and in A.D. 405 Honorius
condemned the Donatists to severe penalties by several laws
intended " to extirpate the adversaries of the Catholic faith." [3]

The Donatists rejoiced at the death of Stilicho whom they
regarded as the author of these laws, and disorders broke out
afresh.[4] When Alaric was in south Italy threatening Rome,

---

[1] *C.J.* i. 5. 8.
[2] The numerous writings against
the Donatists will be found in *P.L.* 43.

[3] *C. Th.* xvi. 6. 4 and 6 ; 5. 38
and 39.
[4] Augustine, *Ep.* cxi.

the Emperor revoked his decrees and soon afterwards, at the
request of the Catholics, he convoked a conference of the bishops
of the two parties which met at Carthage (A.D. 411) under the
presidency of Marcellinus, one of the " tribunes and notaries "
whom the Emperors employed for special services. Marcellinus
was empowered not only to act as chairman but to judge between
the rival claims. The appointment of a secular official to
adjudicate did not mean that the civil power claimed to settle
questions of doctrine. The controversy, which originally turned
on a dispute about facts, had throughout concerned the government not in its ecclesiastical aspect but as a cause of grave
disorders and disturbances. But the commission entrusted to
Marcellinus shows that the bishop of Rome was not yet recognised
as possessing the jurisdiction which in later times resided in his
see. At the end of the discussions, Marcellinus decided against
the Donatists ; they were allowed a certain time to come into
the Church.[1] Some were convinced, but others appealed to the
Emperor, who confirmed the decision of his deputy and enacted
a new law against the schismatics, imposing heavy fines on the
recalcitrants, and banishing the clergy.[2] Two years later they
were deprived of civil rights.[3] These strong measures, which
Augustine defended, alleging the text " Compel them to come
in," [4] broke the strength of the schismatics, and though the
Donatist sect continued to exist and was tolerated under the
Vandals, it ceased to be of importance.

It must be allowed that if the government had been perfectly
indifferent and impartial in matters of religion, it would have
had ample excuse for adopting severe measures of repression
against the fanatical sect who disturbed the peace of the African
provinces and persecuted their opponents. The penalties were
severe but they stopped short of death. It should be remembered to the credit of the Emperors that, in contrast with the
Christian princes of later ages, they never proposed, in pursuing
their policy of the suppression of heresy, to inflict the capital
penalty, except in the case of the Manichaeans, who were regarded
as almost outside the pale of humanity.[5] The same may be said

---

[1] For the proceedings of the conference see Mansi, iv. 51 *sqq.*

[2] A.D. 412.   *C. Th.* xvi. 5. 52.
Slaves and colons were to be beaten
out of their false religion (*a prava
religione*).

[3] A.D. 414.   *Ib.* 53 *perpetua
inustos infamia.*

[4] Augustine, *Ep.* cxiii.

[5] Diocletian had legislated against
Manichaeanism (A.D. 287) as destructive of morality.

for the leading and representative ecclesiastics, all of whom would have recoiled with horror if they could have foreseen the system of judicial murder which was one day to be established under the auspices of the Roman see.[1] Martin of Tours did all he could to stay the persecution of the Spanish bishop Priscillian, who, rightly or wrongly, was accused of heresies akin to Manichaeanism. Priscillian was put to death by the Emperor Maximus (A.D. 385), but he was tried before a civil tribunal for a secular offence.[2] It may well have been a miscarriage of justice, but, formally at least, he was not executed as a heretic.

Under the Christian Empire the Jews remained for the most part in possession of the privileges which they had before enjoyed.[3] The Church was unable to persuade the State to introduce measures to suppress their worship or banish them from the Empire. They were forbidden to possess Christian slaves,[4] and a law of Theodosius II. excluded them from civil offices and dignities.[5] But the legislator was perhaps more often concerned to protect them than to impinge upon their freedom.[6]

§ 5. Monasticism [7]

The same period, in which the Christian religion gradually won the upper hand in the Empire, witnessed a movement which was at first independent of the Church but was destined soon to become an important part of the ecclesiastical system.

[1] Chrysostom expresses his views on the repression of heretics in *Hom. 46 in Matth.* (*P.G.* xlviii. p. 477), where he comments on the parable of the tares. They should be silenced but not put to death.

[2] *Maleficium.* Sulpicius Severus, *Chron.* ii. 50 *nec diffitentem obscenis se studuisse doctrinis, nocturnos etiam turpium feminarum egisse conuentus nudumque orare solitum.* Babut, *Priscillien et le Priscilliénisme* (1909); Holmes, *The Christian Church in Gaul,* chapters viii., ix.

[3] A.D. 404. *C. Th.* xvi. 8. 15 confirms the privileges of the Jewish hierarchy. For the pressure put on Emperors by churchmen not to afford proper protection to the Jews against Christian fanatics cp. Ambrose, *Epp.* 40, 41. For the anti-Semitism of

Chrysostom see his eight homilies *Against the Jews* delivered at Antioch, *P.G.* xlviii. 843 *sqq.* He says that "demons inhabit their souls," p. 852. There is a virulent attack on the Jews in Rutilius Nam. *De reditu suo,* i. 382 *sqq.*

[4] *Ib.* ix. 4 (416); ix. 5 (423). Justinian extended this to pagans, Samaritans, and all heterodox persons (*C.J.* i. 10. 2).

[5] *C.J.* i. 9. 18 (439).

[6] Thus in 412, Christians were forbidden to disturb Jewish worship; and in 423 to burn or take away synagogues (*C. Th.* xvi. 8. 20 and 25).

[7] For the literature on early monasticism see *C. Med. H.* i. Bibliography to chap. xviii.; Bury, *App.* 3 to Gibbon iv.

The germs of asceticism had been implanted in Christianity from the very beginning, and the tendencies to a rigorous life of self-abnegation may have been stimulated by the example of the austerities of the Essenes, the Therapeutae, the monks of Serapis, and later by the influence of the semi-Christian Zoroastrian religion of the Manichees. Ascetic practices seem to have been a strong temptation to all men of an ardently religious temperament in these ages, whatever doctrines they might hold concerning the universe ; Julian the Apostate is an eminent example. For the Christian Church and State the consequences were far-reaching and could not have been anticipated. In the course of the fourth and fifth centuries a large and ever-growing number of men and women withdrew themselves from society, severed themselves from family ties, and embraced, whether in cells in the desert or in recluse communities in town or country, a life of celibacy, prayer, and fasting. Gradually regularised and organised by disciplines of varying degrees of rigour, monasticism established itself firmly as one of the most influential institutions of the Christian world, thoroughly consonant with the spirit of the time and richly endowed by the liberality of the pious.

We have not to follow the history of its growth, but the reader may be reminded that Christian monasticism originated *circa* A.D. 300 under the auspices of St. Anthony in Lower Egypt. At first it took the form of a solitary life in the desert, where ascetics lived independently of one another in neighbouring cells and devoted themselves to an otherwise idle existence of religious contemplation.[1] Another variety of monasticism was soon afterwards founded in Upper Egypt by Pachomius. In his monasteries near Tentyra (Denderah) and Panopolis (Akhmim) the brethren lived in common and performed all kinds of work. The Antonian ideal was approved by Athanasius, and his influence went far to spread it in the West. It was introduced into Palestine by Hilarion, and into Syria, where the rigours of the hermit assumed their most extreme and repulsive shape. There was originated the grotesque idea of living for years on the top of a high pillar. Simeon, the first of these

---

[1] The chief settlements were in the desert south of Alexandria, at Nitria (Wadi Natron) and Scete. At Nitria there were 5000 monks towards the end of the fourth century. The chief sources for Egyptian monasticism are Palladius, *Historia Lausiaca*, and Rufinus, *Historia monachorum*.

pillar-saints (*stylitae*),[1] had many followers, and such was the temper of the times that these abnormal self-tormentors, who could not have been more healthy in mind than in body, were universally revered and consulted as oracles.

The monastic movement engaged the attention of St. Basil, and awoke his enthusiasm. He came to the conclusion that monastic institutions, framed on right lines, would be useful to the Church, and he established a coenobitic community at Neocaesarea (about A.D. 360), and drew up minute regulations. The brethren were not required to take vows ; the asceticism of their life was not immoderate ; and they were expected to perform work in the fields. St. Basil's idea had an immediate success and he became the founder of Greek monasticism. Cloisters adopting his Rule [2] sprang up throughout Asia Minor, and in the following century in Palestine. But here there flourished also the lauras, or enclosures in which the monks lived an almost eremitical life in separate cells, and these institutions were numerous in the plain of the Jordan.[3] The most famous of the ascetics of Palestine were Euthymius, Sabas, and Theodosius.[4] Euthymius founded the laura of Sahel, to the east of Jerusalem, in A.D. 428 ; [5] Sabas founded in A.D. 483 the Great Laura on the Cedron, with a grotto which nature had moulded

[1] A.D. 388-459. Having lived at first in an enclosed cell at Antioch, he built a low pillar in 423, and gradually raised it till in 430 it was forty cubits high ; at the top it was three feet in circumference, according to Evagrius, i. 13. It was situated at the ruins known as Kalat Semian, house of Simeon, described by De Vogüé, *Syrie Centrale*, i. 141 *sqq.* Theodosius II. wrote a letter to him, asking him to descend from his column. On his death, his body was taken to Antioch with the honours of a state funeral, and Leo I. wished to have it transported to Constantinople (see Evagrius i. 13, 14 ; Theodore Lector ii. 41 ; *Vita Sim. Styl.* ed. Lietzmann). Daniel, an imitator of Simeon, set up a pillar four miles north of Constantinople, and lived on it for thirty-three years, in the reigns of Leo I. and Zeno. He was constantly frozen over with snow and ice, and his feet were covered with sores. Leo insisted on putting a shed over the top of the pillar. The saint descended from his perch in order to denounce the ecclesiastical policy of Basiliscus. The Patriarch Euphemius attended him in his last moments. See the *Vita Danielis*.

[2] The Rules will be found in his works, *P.G.* xxxi. 889 *sqq.*

[3] They are enumerated and located in Génier, *Vie de Saint Euthyme le Grand*, chap. i.

[4] The lives of Euthymius and Sabas were written by Cyril of Scythopolis in the sixth century. On Theodosius we have a brief sketch by the same writer and a panegyric by Theodore, bishop of Petrae, probably delivered in 530. (See Bibliography, i. 2, A.)

[5] Euthymius did much for the conversion of the Saracens, and founded the Parembole (to the east of his own laura), a large enclosure in which baptized Saracens were settled. They had their own bishop. The Parembole was ruined by the invasion of Al-Mundhar in the sixth century.

into the form of a church, and many others ; and Theodosius
his coenobitic monastery at the grotto of the Magi near Bethlehem
in A.D. 476. Sabas was appointed archimandrite of all the
lauras, and Theodosius of all the coenobia, in the diocese of
Jerusalem by the Patriarch Sallust (A.D. 494). It would seem
that the monks of the lauras were considered to have attained
to a higher grade of spiritual life than those who lived in convents,
which were regarded as a preparation in ascetic discipline.[1] As
Sabas and one of his disciples walked one day from Jericho to
the Jordan, they met a young and comely girl. " Did you
remark that girl ? " said the saint, " she is one-eyed." " No,
Father," said the disciple, " she had both her eyes." " You
are mistaken, my son, she is one-eyed." " No, Father, she has
two very fine eyes." " How do you know ? " " I looked at
her intently." " What about the commandment, ' Fix not your
eyes on her, neither let her take thee with her eyelids ' ? "[2] And
the saint sent the youth to a convent till he had learned better
to control his eyes and his thoughts.

The history of monasticism at Constantinople begins with the
abbot [3] Isaac, a Syrian, who in the reign of Theodosius I. founded
a convent in the quarter of Psamathia outside the Constantinian
Wall. He was a typical fanatical ascetic and was buried with
great pomp when he died.[4] He was succeeded by Dalmatius, an
active organiser, who founded new houses under his own authority. The community of the Akoimetoi or Sleepless was established at Gomon, near the northern entrance to the Bosphorus,
by one Alexander in the reign of Theodosius II., but his successor
John transported the monks to a new cloister at Chibukli, on
the Asiatic side of the straits opposite to Sosthenion,[5] where it
became famous under the next abbot Marcellus, who presided for
about forty years. Two other early foundations deserve notice.
The monastery of Drys, a suburb of Chalcedon, was established

---

[1] Cp. Génier, *op. cit.* p. 11.

[2] Cyril, *Vita Sabae*, xlvii. p. 251.

[3] *Archimandrite*, *i.e.* head of the
mandra or sheep-pen, often used
instead of ἡγούμενος, the usual term,
or ἀββᾶς. In later times archimandrite was confined to designate
authority over several monasteries ;
exarch was also used.

[4] In 407–408. He was an opponent

of Chrysostom. For the beginnings
of monasticism at Constantinople see
Pargoire's article in *Revue des questions
historiques*, lxv., 1899, where many
false traditions are exposed.

[5] *Vita Marcelli*, in Simeon Meta-
phastes, *P.G.* cxvi. p. 712. Cp. Pargoire, *Anaple et Sosthène*, p. 64. The
monks were called sleepless because
they maintained choral service con-
tinuously by relays.

by Hypatius, who enforced a very strict discipline, about A.D. 400. Hypatius enjoyed considerable influence. Theodosius II. used to visit him, and he was constantly consulted by the nobles and ladies of the capital.[1] The most famous of the monastic communities of Constantinople was founded by Studius, an ex-consul who had come from Rome,[2] in the reign of Leo I. He dedicated a small basilica to St. John the Baptist, which is still preserved as a mosque,[3] not far from the Golden Gate, and subsequently attached to it a monastery, in which he established some of the Sleepless brethren, who had belonged to the convent of Marcellus.[4] The Studite community was to become the largest and most influential in Constantinople.

Of the countries of western Europe, early monasticism spread most widely in Gaul. Martin of Tours was the pioneer ; he founded a monastery at Poictiers about A.D. 362. Some forty years later Cassian inaugurated monastic life at Marseilles, and Honoratus in the islands of Lérins off the coast of Provence. Both Cassian and Honoratus were under the direct influence of the theories of ascetic life which were practised by the Antonian monks of northern Egypt.[5] In the same period, monasteries both for men and for women—women already took their full share in the ascetic movement—were established at Rome and in Italian towns, and Augustine introduced monastic life in Africa. Spain, so far as our evidence goes, seems to have been little affected by the fashion before the sixth century.

We have no information that would enable us to conjecture the total number of the voluntary exiles from social life, who in the fifth century, whether in communities or lonely cells, mortified their bodies and their natural affections in order to assure themselves of eternal happiness. Ascetic enthusiasm was infectious, and the leading authorities of the Church, such as Jerome, Ambrose, Augustine, Chrysostom, all held up the monastic life as the highest spiritual ideal, and outdid each other in their

[1] See Callinicus, *Vita Hypatii*.

[2] Consul in 454. But an epigram on the church represents him as rewarded by the consulship for building it (*Anth. Graeca*, i. 4).

[3] Emir Ahor Jamissi. Described by van Millingen, *Byzantine Churches*, chap. ii.

[4] A.D. 462–463. Theodore Lector, i.

17 = Theophanes A.M. 5955. But the sleepless tradition was not maintained at Studion, and when we read of the Akoimetoi, the monks of the cloister on the Bosphorus are meant, not the Studites.

[5] Cassian's *Collationes* profess to reproduce the teaching of the monastic leaders of Nitria and Scete.

praises of celibacy and virginity.   But the Church and the State
soon found it necessary, in the interests of public order, to exercise control over the ascetics, who in the early period of the movement were each his own master and acknowledged no superior.
The towns were often troubled by the invasion of vagrant monks,
genuine or spurious, who formed a highly undesirable addition
to the idle and mendicant portion of the populace.[1] We have
seen again and again the turbulence of the monks, who, in their
religious zeal, were ready to commit any excess of violence and
transgression of decency.   Their fanaticism was responsible for
the useless destruction of pagan temples.   They played a leading
part in the disturbances at Alexandria which ended in the murder
of Hypatia.   They were the chief offenders in the scandalous
disorders which disgraced the Councils of Ephesus.   During the
first half of the fifth century, the bishops seem to have been
gradually acquiring some control over the cloisters, but the prevailing anarchy was definitely ended by the Council of Chalcedon.[2]
This assembly deplored the turbulence of the monks, and forbade
them to abandon their holy life.   It ordained that no one could
found a monastery without a licence from the bishop of the
diocese, and that no monk could leave his convent without the
bishop's permission.   Monastic communities were thus brought
under ecclesiastical control.

The estates of the monasteries gradually increased through the
donations of the rich and pious, and at the beginning of the sixth
century a pagan historian writes thus of the " so-called monks ": [3]
" They renounce legal marriages and fill their populous institutions in cities and villages with celibate people, useless either for
war or for any service to the State ; but gradually growing from
the time of Arcadius to the present day they have appropriated
the greater part of the earth, and on the pretext of sharing all
with the poor they have, so to speak, reduced all to poverty."
This is the exaggerated statement of a hostile observer, who had
been an official of the treasury ; but it testifies to the growing
popularity, wealth, and power of monastic institutions.

---

[1] An edict of 390 (Verona) commands monks to remain in " desert
places and vast solitudes," *C. Th.* xvi.
3. 1, but in 392 Theodosius withdrew
the prohibition of free entry into
towns (*ib.* 2).   Chrysostom excited
much resentment in monastic circles
by his endeavour to suppress the
monks who lounged about Constantinople.

[2] Canons 3, 4, 7, 16 (Mansi, vii.
371 *sqq.*). Cp. *C.J.* i. 3. 53.

[3] Zosimus, v. 23.

The ascetic spirit, which expressed itself in monasticism, affected the secular clergy also. The strict austerity of the Manichaean heretics was a certain challenge to the Church,[1] and in their extravagant praises of virginity some of the Christian fathers were barely able to stop short of the condemnation of marriage which was a tenet of the Manichees. The view that matrimony is a necessary evil naturally involved the question of the celibacy of the clergy. In this matter ecclesiastics were left free to follow the dictates of their own conscience, and no legislation was attempted, till a Roman council (about A.D. 384) summoned by Pope Siricius, forbade bishops, priests, and deacons to marry. "Celibacy," it has been said, "was but one of the many shapes in which the rapidly progressing sacerdotalism of Rome was overlaying religion with a multitude of formal observances."[2] Against the encroachments of this sacerdotalism, a protestant movement was led in Gaul by Vigilantius, who denounced celibacy, fasting, prayers for the dead, relics, and the use of incense; but it did not survive his death. By degrees, the celibacy of the clergy became the rule in the west. In the eastern provinces, where Roman influence was not preponderant, it was otherwise. Marriage after ordination was forbidden, but compulsory separation of clergy who were already married was not imposed except in the case of bishops.[3]

---

[1] Cp. Lea, *History of Sacerdotal Celibacy*, i. 33 *sqq.*

[2] Lea, *ib.* 66.

[3] Cp. Socrates, v. 22; *C.J.* i. 3. 45; Justinian, *Nov.* cxxiii. 12; *Concilium Trullanum*, Canons 13, 30 (Mansi, xi. 948, 956). Men who had been twice married were strictly excluded from holy orders.

CHAPTER XII

§ 1. *The Usurpation of Basiliscus* (A.D. 475–476)

THE new Emperor, Leo II., was a child of seven years, and the
regency naturally devolved on his father Zeno. But with the
consent of the Senate and the concurrence of the Empress Verina,
the child conferred the Imperial dignity on his father, in the
Hippodrome (February 9, A.D. 474) and died in the same year,
leaving to Zeno nominally as well as actually the sole power
(November 17).[1]

Zeno was not beloved.[2] He was unpopular both with the
Byzantine populace and in senatorial circles.[3] He was hated as
an Isaurian. If we remember the depredations of the Isaurians
in the reign of Arcadius, it is not surprising that they had an evil
name, and it is more than probable that the soldiers introduced
into the capital by Leo had not belied their reputation for rudeness and violence. Zeno's accession meant Isaurian ascendancy,

---

[1] See Candidus, p. 136 ; John Mal.
xiv. p. 376 ; Theodore Lector, i. 24,
27 ; Theophanes A.M. 5966, 5967.
The coronation in the Hippodrome
(instead of the Hebdomon) was an
innovation. We have coins of the
joint reign with *Dn Leo et Zeno Pp Aug*
and on the reverse the two Emperors
seated, Zeno on Leo's left ; and others
with different reverses. There are
also tremisses with *Dn Zeno et Leo
Caes* on the obverse. See Sabatier i.
Pl. vii. 15, 16, 17 ; Pl. viii. 13.

[2] He was married to Arcadia before
he married Ariadne, and by her had
a son, Zeno, of whom something more

will be heard. Zeno was a very fast
runner, according to a Ravenna
chronicler known as the Anonymus
Valesii (see below, p. 423, *n.* 1), who
had a marked liking for him. His
speed of foot was ascribed to a
peculiarity in his knee-caps ; *perhibent
de eo quod patellas in genucula non
habuisset, sed mobiles fuissent* (Anon.
Val. ix. 40). Fast running was an
Isaurian characteristic ; compare the
marvellous speed of Indacus (Suidas,
sub Ἰνδακός ; John Ant. in *F.H.G.*
iv. 617).

[3] Cp. Joshua Stylites, 12.

389

high places for the Emperor's fellow-countrymen, and more rude mountaineers in the capital.   Historians of the time vent their feelings by describing him as physically horrible and morally abominable,[1] and he was said to be a coward.[2]   His most trusted counsellor was the Isaurian Illus, who was, however, to prove a thorn in his side, and Trocundes, the brother of Illus, also rose into prominence.

The first year of the reign was crowded with anxieties. Vandals, Ostrogoths, Huns, and Arabs were all in arms against the Empire.   King Gaiseric must have been deeply displeased by the murder of the Arian Aspar, with whom he is said to have been on friendly terms.   After Leo's death, the Vandals descended on the western shores of Greece and captured Nicopolis.   Zeno was not prepared for war.   He sent to Carthage Severus, a man of high repute, who made a favourable impression on Gaiseric by refusing all his gifts.   The king made him a present of all the captives who had fallen to the share of the royal family and allowed him to redeem others from any Vandals who were willing to sell.   A perpetual peace was then concluded between the two powers (A.D. 474),[3] and was maintained for nearly sixty years. Meanwhile Zeno's coronation had provoked Aspar's Ostrogothic relative Theoderic Strabo to new hostilities in Thrace.   The Master of Soldiers in the Thracian provinces was captured and slain ; but Illus took the field and terminated the war.

If the Emperor was able to cope with foreign foes by negotiation or arms, his position amid a hostile court and people was highly precarious.   A formidable conspiracy was formed against him, of which the leading spirit was his mother-in-law, the Augusta Verina.[4]   She had concurred in Zeno's elevation, but she did not like him, and being a woman of energy and ambition she found it distasteful to fall into the background, overshadowed by her daughter, the Augusta Ariadne.   Her scheme was to raise to the throne and marry her paramour Patricius, who had formerly held the post of Master of Offices.   She engaged the co-operation of her brother Basiliscus, who had been living in retirement at

[1] Cp. Evagrius iii. 1 ; Malchus, *fr.* 16.   The prejudice of Malchus, who wrote under Zeno's successor, is undisguised.

[2] John Lydus, *De mag.* iii. 45, " he could not bear even the picture

of a battle."

[3] Malchus, *fr.* 3, Procopius, *B.V.* i. 7.

[4] The fullest sources for this conspiracy are Candidus, p. 136, and John Ant. *ib.*

Heraclea on the Propontis, and Basiliscus succeeded in seducing
the Isaurian brothers Illus and Trocundes to abandon their loyalty
to Zeno.[1]   When all the preparations were complete, the queen-
mother, with consummate skill, persuaded Zeno that his life
was in danger and that his only safety was flight.   Taking with
him a large company of Isaurians, and supplying himself with
treasure, he crossed over to Chalcedon (January 9, A.D. 475) and
fled to Isauria.[2]   Those who accompanied him were fortunate,
for, when the Emperor's flight was known, the populace indulged
in their inveterate hatred of the Isaurians by a colossal massacre.
Verina now hoped to reign as mistress of the palace, but she was
outwitted by her brother, who was himself ambitious of the
purple.   The choice of the ministers and Senate fell not on
Patricius but on Basiliscus, who was proclaimed and crowned
Emperor at the Hebdomon palace.   He immediately crowned his
wife Zenonis as Augusta, and conferred the rank of Caesar upon
his youthful son Marcus, whom he afterwards crowned Augustus.[3]
The circumstances of his elevation naturally led to a breach with
Verina, and, having good reason to fear her capacity for intrigue,
he took the precaution of putting Patricius to death.[4]

Basiliscus reigned for twenty months and in that time he
made himself extremely unpopular, chiefly by his ecclesiastical
policy.   He favoured the heresy of Monophysitism and issued a
decree against the Council of Chalcedon.   He and his wife had
fallen under the influence of Timothy Aelurus, the bishop of
Alexandria, who had come to Constantinople, and he went so far
as to withdraw the Asiatic sees from the control of the bishop of
Constantinople.[5]   Acacius, the Patriarch, was roused by this
injury to the rights of his see.   He draped St. Sophia in black
and appeared in mourning before a large sympathetic congregation.   Basiliscus left the city.

The Emperor had made another enemy in the Ostrogothic

---

[1] According to the text in John Ant.
Illus persuades Basiliscus, but it seems
probable that this is a textual error,
and that Basiliscus is really intended
to be the subject of ποιεῖται.

[2] See Brooks, *Emperor Zeno and
the Isaurians*, p. 217, *n.* 19.

[3] Theodore Lector, i. 29 and
Candidus, p. 136. That Marcus was
successively Caesar and Augustus is
borne out by the superscriptions of

the Encyclicals (in Zacharias Myt.
v. 2, cp. 3 *ad init.* ; Evagrius iii. 4,
5, 7).

[4] Candidus, *ib.* Verina then intrigued to bring back Zeno ; Basiliscus discovered her plots ; and it
might have gone hard with her, if
Armatus had not contrived to
conceal her.

[5] On ecclesiastical affairs see below,
§ 3.

Theoderic Strabo, who, as the enemy of Zeno, had supported his elevation, by bestowing a Mastership of Soldiers [1] on his relation Armatus, a young fop, who was the lover of the Empress Zenonis. Their love is described by a historian in a passage worthy of a romance.[2]

Basiliscus permitted Armatus, inasmuch as he was a kinsman, to associate freely with the Empress Zenonis. Their intercourse became intimate, and as they were both persons of no ordinary beauty they became extravagantly enamoured of each other. They used to exchange glances of the eyes, they used constantly to turn their faces and smile at each other ; and the passion which they were obliged to conceal was the cause of dule and teen. They confided their trouble to Daniel a eunuch and to Maria a midwife, who hardly healed their malady by the remedy of bringing them together. Then Zenonis coaxed Basiliscus to grant her lover the highest office in the city.

The preferment which Armatus received from his uncle elated him beyond measure. He was naturally effeminate and cruel. Theoderic Strabo despised him as a dandy who only cared for his toilet and the care of his body ; and it was said that in the days of Leo he had punished a number of Thracian rebels by cutting off their hands. When he was exalted by his mistress's husband, he imagined that he was a man of valour, and dressed himself as Achilles, in which guise he used to ride about and astonish or amuse the people in the Hippodrome. The populace nicknamed him Pyrrhus, on account of his pink cheeks, but he took it as a compliment to his valour, and became still more inflated with vanity. " He did not," says the historian, " slay heroes like Pyrrhus, but he was a chamberer and a wanton like Paris."

Basiliscus, perhaps soon after his elevation, had despatched Illus and Trocundes against Zeno, who, now in his native fortresses,[3] had resumed the life of an Isaurian chieftain. Basiliscus, however, failed to fulfil what he had promised to the two generals ; and they received letters from some of the leading ministers at

[1] According to John Mal. xv. 378, 379 (cp. *Chron. Pasch., sub a.* 478) he was *mag. mil. in praesenti* in 476. Otherwise Suidas (*sub* ᾿Αρμάτιος) στρατηγὸν ᾿Ιλλυριῶν, and otherwise again Theoph. A.M. 5969 στρατηγὸν ὄντα τῆς Θρᾴκης. As Suidas is probably copying either Malchus or Candidus, perhaps Armatus was at first *mag. mil.* in Illyricum and afterwards *in praesenti.* Shestakov has made it probable that the articles of Suidas ᾿Αρμάτος (and Βασιλίσκος)

which Müller (*F.H.G.* iv). assigned to Malchus, *fr.* 7, 8, come partly from Candidus (see his *Kandid Isauriski,* cp. *Bibl.* ii. 2 B).

[2] The passage is in Suidas and in *F.H.G.* iv. p. 117 is printed with the fragments of Malchus. But it is more probable that it comes from Candidus.

[3] The strongholds called Salmon (locality unknown), Zachariah Myt. v. 1.

the court, urging them to secure the return of Zeno. For the city was now prepared to welcome the restoration of the Isaurian, to replace the Monophysite, whose unpopularity was increased by the fiscal rapacity of his ministers.[1] Illus decided to change sides, and his resolution may have been reinforced by the fact that he had a certain hold over Zeno, having got into his power Longinus, Zeno's brother, whom he kept a prisoner in an Isaurian fortress. Accordingly, Zeno and Illus joined forces and started for Constantinople. When Basiliscus received news of this danger, he hastened to recall his ecclesiastical edicts and to conciliate the Patriarch and the people.[2] But it was too late. Armatus, the Master of Soldiers, was sent with all available forces to oppose the advancing army of the Isaurians, but secret messages from Zeno, who promised to give him the Mastership of Soldiers for life and to confer the rank of Caesar on his son, induced him to betray his master. He avoided the road by which Zeno was advancing and marched into Isauria by another way. This betrayal decided the fate of Basiliscus. Zeno entered the capital without resistance in August 476. Basiliscus was sent to Cucusus in Cappadocia and there beheaded; his wife and children shared his fate. The promise which had been made to Armatus was kept to the letter. His son was created Caesar at Nicaea. But immediately afterwards the Emperor, by the advice of Illus, caused him to be assassinated, and the Caesar was stripped of his rank and compelled to take orders.[3]

A deplorable misfortune, which occurred in the reign of Basiliscus, is said to have helped, as accidents in superstitious ages always help, to render his government unpopular. This was an immense conflagration,[4] which, beginning in the quarter of Chalkoprateia, spread far and wide, reducing to ashes the

[1] Especially of Epinicus who, then a favourite of Verina, had in Leo's reign filled the highest financial offices; and was appointed, apparently by Basiliscus, praetorian prefect. (Suidas, *sub nomine*, calls him ὕπαρχος τῆς πόλεως, but this seems inconsistent with what is said about his oppression of the provinces, καὶ τὰ ἔθνη καὶ τὰς πόλεις καπηλεύων κτλ., which are only appropriate to a praetorian prefect. The notice must come either from Malchus or from Candidus.) Cp. also Suidas, *sub* Βασιλίσκος (which appears

as Malchus, *fr.* 7, in *F.H.G.* iv. p. 116).
[2] See below, § 2.
[3] Evagr. iii. 24. Malchus, *ib.* The assassin was Onoulf, *Mag. Mil. per Illyr.*, a brother of Odovacar, who at this time was establishing his power in Italy. We have coins of Basiliscus, and of Basiliscus and Marcus together, and of Zenonis (Sabatier, i. Pl. viii. 14-20); the faces are all conventional.
[4] Cedrenus i. 618 = Zonaras xiv. 22-24. The ultimate source is evidently Malchus, see Suidas *s.v.* Μάλχος.

adjacent colonnades and houses. But more serious was the destruction of the Basilica, the library founded by Julian, which contained no fewer than 120,000 books. Among these rolls, the intestine of a serpent, 120 feet long, on which the *Iliad* and *Odyssey* were written in golden characters, is specially mentioned. The fire spread along Middle Street and destroyed the palace of Lausus, which contained among its splendours some of the most beautiful works of Greek plastic art, the Cnidian Aphrodite, the Lindian Athene, and the Samian Here.

§ 2. *The Revolts of Marcian and Illus* (A.D. 479–488)

For the first few years after the restoration of Zeno, Illus was all-powerful. He was consul in A.D. 478 ; he was appointed Master of Offices, and created a patrician. But he was bitterly detested by the two Empresses, Verina and Ariadne, who resented his influence with Zeno. Attempts on his life were made at Verina's instigation. Her favourite, the Prefect Epinicus, suborned a barbarian to assassinate him. The attempt failed ; the criminal confessed that the prefect had inspired his act ; and Zeno, having deprived Epinicus of his office, handed him over to Illus who sent him to a castle in Isauria.[1] Some time elapsed, and then, leaving the capital on a pretext, Illus visited Epinicus in his prison and elicited a confession that he had been instigated by the queen-mother. He then refused (towards the end of A.D. 479) to return to Constantinople unless Verina were surrendered to him. Zeno, to whom Illus was indispensable, complied ; she was sent to Tarsus where she was forced to become a nun and was confined by Illus in the castle of Dalisandus.[2] The presence of Illus was sorely needed, on account of Ostrogothic hostilities in Illyricum and Thrace,[3] and there was still a Gothic faction in the city. In his absence, Zeno had talked of taking the field himself, and there was much dissatisfaction at his failing to do so. He was

---

[1] John Ant. *fr.* 95 (*De ins.*). Cp. Brooks, *op. cit.* 218, *n.* 56 for date.

[2] Dalisandus, in the Decapolis of Isauria, is to be distinguished from Dalisandus in Lycaonia, see Ramsay, *Hist. Geog.* pp. 335, 366, with the map opp. p. 330.

[3] An earthquake on Sept. 25, 479, had done terrible damage to the walls of the city, and an Ostrogothic assault would have been a serious danger. Cp. Marcellinus, *sub* 480, Theoph. A.M. 5971, Brooks, *C. Med. H.* i. p. 476.

accused of cowardice, but the true reason probably was that he feared not the enemy but his own army.[1]

The treatment of Verina supplied a pretext to her son-in-law, Marcian, to attempt to overthrow Zeno (end of A.D. 479).[2] Marcian, who was son of Anthemius, the western Emperor, had married Leontia, Leo's younger daughter, and claimed that he had a better right to the throne than Zeno, because his wife had been born in the purple. This claim, according to the theory of the Imperial succession, was entirely futile, but it illustrates how the idea that children born in the purple had a natural title to the throne was beginning to grow. The barbarians in the city rallied round Marcian and his brother Procopius,[3] and the citizens were on their side. The brothers united their forces near the house of Caesarius, to the south of the Forum of Theodosius ;[4] and then one of them marched upon the palace, while the other attacked the house of Illus.[5] The Emperor nearly fell into their hands,[6] and during the day the rebels were victorious against the Imperial soldiers, on whose heads the citizens showered missiles from the roofs. But under the cover of night, Illus introduced into the city an Isaurian force from Chalcedon, and the next day Marcian's party was defeated. Marcian was ordained a priest and banished to Cappadocia ; Leontia fled to a convent.[7] Theoderic Strabo was in league with Marcian, but did not reach the city in time to help him.

It was perhaps not long after this that the Empress Ariadne entreated Zeno to recall her mother. Zeno told her to ask Illus. The Empress sent for Illus and implored him with tears to

---

[1] Cp. Brooks, *Emp. Zeno and the Isaurians*, p. 219. This article, to which I am under considerable obligations, has cleared up many difficulties in the chronology, and elucidated the whole story.

[2] Date in John Ant. *ib.* 3. This author and Eustathius (in Evagr. iii. 26) are the fullest sources.

[3] There was also a third brother Romulus (Theodore Lect. i. 37). The chief barbarian associate was Busalbos, an officer—perhaps commander of one of the legions of the troops *in praesenti*.

[4] Τὴν Καισαρίου οἰκίαν, to be identified with τὰ Καισαρίου (of which there was a curator), in Theophanes A.M. 6054 (A.D. 561–562). Evidently near the harbour of Caesarius, and this is

confirmed by its proximity to the Forum of Bous, which we can infer from the passage in Theoph.

[5] Κατὰ Ἰλλοῦ ἐν τοῖς λεγομένοις Οὐαράνου (John Ant.). I can find no trace of this locality elsewhere.

[6] The Stoa of the Delphax was attacked. This was evidently in the Palace, as indeed is expressly stated by Victor Tonn. *sub* 523 *intra palatium loco quod* δελφακα *graeco vocabulo dicunt.* Cp. Procopius, *B.V.* i. 21 ὅπη βασιλέως εἶναι στιβάδα ξυμβαίνει Δέλφικα τοῦτο καλοῦσι τὸ οἴκημα.

[7] Marcian escaped, and attacked Ancyra, but was defeated by Trocundes and imprisoned along with his wife in an Isaurian fortress.

release her mother. And Illus said, " Why do you want her ? Is it that she may set up another Emperor against your husband ? " Then Ariadne said to Zeno, " Is Illus to be in the Palace or I ? " and he replied, " Do what you can. I prefer you." She suborned Sporacius, one of the Scholarian guards, to assassinate Illus, and the attempt was made, on the occasion of a spectacle in the Hippodrome, as Illus was walking through the Pulpita behind the Kathisma. The assassin's sword, aimed at the head, cut off the minister's right ear, and he was hewn to pieces on the spot.[1] Illus did not believe Zeno's asseverations that he was ignorant of the plot, and when the wound was healed he requested the Emperor to allow him to go to the East for change of air. Zeno relieved him of the duties of Master of Offices and appointed him Master of Soldiers in the East. Illus proceeded to Antioch, taking with him a considerable number of friends and adherents (481–482), including Marsus and the pagan quaestor Pamprepius.[2] Soon afterwards the patrician Leontius seems to have been sent to Antioch demanding the release of Verina, but Illus won him over to his interests and he did not return to Constantinople.[3] The estrangement of the Emperor from his general was now complete, and a contest between the two Isaurians was inevitable. Illus and his party hoped to secure Egypt for their cause, and attempted, but without success, to take advantage of the ecclesiastical disputes which were at this time dividing Alexandria.[4] The hostilities of the Ostrogoths prevented Zeno from taking any measures before the end of A.D. 483, or the spring of 484. When his hands were at last free, he commanded Illus to surrender Longinus (Zeno's brother) who had been a prisoner for many years. Illus refused, and Zeno deposed him from his command of the eastern army and appointed John the Scythian in his stead. At the same time he expelled the friends of Illus from Constantinople, confiscated

---

[1] John Mal. xv. 387 *sqq.* For the position of the *Pulpita* cp. Theoph. A.M. 6024, p. 185, 10.

[2] Evagr. iii. 27. Brooks, 225-226, gives reasons for thinking that Evagr. (Eustathius) and John Mal. are mistaken in supposing that Leontius also accompanied Illus. Zeno grante I to Illus the special power of appointing dukes in the eastern provinces.

[3] See Joshua Styl. c. 14.

[4] See Asmus, " Pamprepios," in *B.Z.* xxii. 332 *sqq.* Pamprepius was sent to Alexandria, to combine measures with John Talaias who ascended the Patriarchal throne in 482, but in the same year (June) was deposed and succeeded by Peter Mongus, who was supported by Zeno. Peter organised an anti-pagan demonstration, and Pamprepius had to flee.

their property, and bestowed it upon the cities of Isauria. War ensued and lasted for about four years.

Illus had employed the two years which he spent at Antioch (482–484) in making himself popular and gaining friends. He counted, for the coming struggle, on the support of the orthodox adherents of the Council of Chalcedon, who had been displeased by an ecclesiastical decree (the *Henotikon*) in which Zeno had expressly declined to maintain the dogmas of that assembly (A.D. 481). He may also have hoped for some help from pagans. He was very intimate with the pagan philosopher Pamprepius, who had been appointed Quaestor through his influence, and had accompanied him to Antioch. Deciding not to assume the purple himself, Illus drew from his Isaurian prison the ex-tyrant Marcian, and proclaimed him Emperor. He proposed to make war on a great scale. He had sought the assistance of the Patrician and king Odovacar in Italy ; he had written to the Persian monarch Piroz and to some of the satraps of Roman Armenia. Odovacar refused ; the Persians and Armenians promised help when the time came. A great defeat which the Persians suffered at the hands of the Ephthalites (January, A.D. 484 ; Piroz was slain) rendered it impossible for them to fulfil their promise.

Zeno sent an Isaurian force against the rebels.[1] About the same time Illus changed his plans, and entered into an alliance with his old enemy the Empress Verina who was still languishing in an Isaurian fortress.[2] He brought her to Tarsus, arrayed her in imperial robes ; and it was decided to set aside Marcian,[3] and to proclaim as Emperor the patrician Leontius. Verina crowned him Emperor, and a proclamation in her name was sent through the provinces of the East and Egypt. In this document she claims that the Empire belongs to her, that it was she who conferred it upon Zeno, and that now, since his avarice is ruining the state, she has determined to transfer it to the pious Leontius.[4]

---

[1] Under Conon, a fighting parson (he was bishop of Apamea), and Linges, a bastard brother of Leo.

[2] The castle of Papirios, to which she had been removed (cp. Theodore Lector, i. 37). It seems to be the same as the fortress of Cherris (Brooks, *ib.* 228).

[3] We are not told why Illus desired the co-operation of Verina to

invest the rebellion with the prestige of legitimacy, and we may conjecture that he thought the association of the Empress with her son-in-law Marcian would be too dangerous a combination.

[4] See John Mal. *fr.* 35, *De ins.* p. 165. Brooks well notices that the insistence in this document on the piety of Leontius alludes to Zeno's heterodox *Henotikon* (*op. cit.* 227). Theophanes

The new Emperor was received at Antioch,[1] and the rebellion spread. The Isaurian troops which Zeno had sent were obviously unable to cope with it, and Zeno sought the help of Theoderic the Amal and his Ostrogoths. Theoderic, as Master of Soldiers *in praesenti*, joined the army of John the Scythian, and though he was recalled almost immediately, his followers seem to have remained and taken part in the campaign.[2] Rugian auxiliaries were also sent under the command of Aspar's son Ermenric. A battle was fought, the forces of Zeno were victorious, and Illus, Leontius, and Verina, with all their chief partisans, fled to the strong fortress of Cherris [3] in the Isaurian mountains (autumn, A.D. 484). The Empress died in a few days. The cause of Illus was now hopeless, but the fortress held out for nearly four years. It was taken by treachery (488), and Illus and Leontius were beheaded.[4]

The struggle between Illus and Zeno derives particular interest from the association of Illus with the prominent pagans who still flourished at Athens, Constantinople, and Alexandria. These men seem to have hoped that Illus, if victorious, would be able to secure public toleration for paganism.[5] It was im-

gives the date of the entry of Leontius into Antioch as June 27 ind. 7 (= 484). But a contemporary, Palchus the astrologer, gives the day of the coronation as July 19. See Cumont, " L'Astrologue Palchos," in *Revue de l'instruction publique en Belgique*, xl. p. 1206, and though Palchus was mistaken in placing the coronation at Antioch, his date must be accepted. If we correct *June* in Theoph. to *July*, Leontius entered Antioch only a week after the proclamation at Tarsus. The horoscope of Leontius given by Palchus was drawn incompletely by two astrologers, of whom one no doubt was Pamprepius. They inferred his success. Palchus shows that they overlooked certain data, which would have led them to a true prognostication. Leontius appointed Pamprepius as his Master of Offices. For this and other appointments see John Mal. in *De insidiis*, p. 165. For coins of Leontius minted at Antioch see Sabatier, i. Pl. viii. 22, 23.

[1] He was rejected at Chalcis, and at Edessa.

[2] The part played by Theoderic and the Ostrogoths is uncertain. Cp.

John Ant. *fr.* 214. 4 and 6 ; Brooks, 228.

[3] The fortress had been well supplied and strengthened by Zeno, as a place of refuge for himself in case of eventualities (Joshua Styl. c. 12). Art had assisted its natural strength. There was no path leading up to it save one so narrow that not even two persons could ascend at once (*ib.* c. 17).

[4] The protraction of the siege was partly due to the distraction of Theoderic's rebellion in 486, partly to the strength of the fortress. Illus made some proposals for peace about this time. But he had fallen into despondency, and occupied himself with reading, committing the command of the garrison to Indacus. It was Indacus who betrayed the fortress. (According to Theoph., the husband of the widow of Trocundes was sent by Zeno to the fortress and arranged the treachery. Source, Theodore Lector(?).) Pamprepius was put to death by his friends before the end of the reign, because he had falsely foretold success.

[5] The full significance of this element in the rebellion of Illus has been brought out by J. R. Asmus, in

possible, of course, to stamp the movement with a pagan character. If Illus had come forward as a new Julian, he would have had no following. But there is little doubt that he was personally in sympathy with the " Hellenes " ; he was a man with intellectual interests and was inclined to the Neoplatonic philosophy. His close intimacy with the pagan savant, Pamprepius of Panopolis, who shared his fortunes, proves this. Pamprepius, who is described as swarthy and ugly, went in his youth from Egypt to the university of Athens, where he studied under the philosopher Proclus and was appointed professor of grammar (literature and philology). A quarrel with a magistrate forced him to leave Athens, and he betook himself to Constantinople, where pagans of talent, if they behaved discreetly, could still find a place.[1] At the request of Illus he delivered a lecture, probably explaining the doctrines of Neoplatonism, and Illus procured his appointment as professor of grammar at the university. He established himself in the favour of Illus by the public recitation of a poem,[2] in reward for which he received a pension. But when Illus was absent in Isauria (A.D. 478), his enemies seized the opportunity to attack Pamprepius as a pagan and a sorcerer. He was banished from the city and retired to Pergamum ; but Illus summoned him to Isauria, and then brought him back in triumph, and procured his appointment to the high post of Quaestorship. Henceforward his fortunes were bound up with those of Illus, to whom he acted as confidant and adviser throughout the struggle for the throne. The pagans blamed Pamprepius for the failure of the movement, and represented him as a traitor to the cause of his chief. But we may take it as certain that this charge was false, and that he was slain not because he was suspected of treachery, but because his prophecies had not come true and he had proved himself a blind guide.[3]

his article on "Pamprepios" (*B.Z.* xxii. 320 *sqq.*). The principal evidence is in the fragmentary *Vita Isidori*, of Damascius (on which see Asmus, *ib.* xviii. 424 *sqq.*, and xix. 265 *sqq.*), and the art. of Suidas, Παμπρέπιος. There is an interesting statement in Zacharias, *Vita Severi*, p. 40, that pagans in Caria (at Aphrodisias) offered sacrifices to the gods and inquired of the entrails of the victims whether Leontius, Illus, and Pamprepius would be victorious over Zeno. One of these Carians was the distinguished physician and philosopher, Asclepiodotus, a pupil of Proclus.

[1] Ammonius of Alexandria seems to have taught philosophy at Constantinople in the reign of Zeno (cp. Asmus, "Pamprepios," p. 326).

[2] Perhaps the Ἰσαυρικά, mentioned by Suidas.

[3] See the conclusions of Asmus, *op. cit.*

The greater part of Zeno's reign had been troubled on the one hand by the hostile risings of the Ostrogoths, which have still to be described, and on the other by rebellion. In 488 both these troubles were terminated by the departure of the Goths from Italy and by the final suppression of Illus. The Emperor persisted in his policy of firmly establishing Isaurian pre-dominance. His brother Longinus, who had managed to escape from his prison,[1] was consul twice and *princeps* of the Senate.[2] Kottomenes had been appointed Master of Soldiers *in praesenti*, instead of Theoderic, in 484, and Longinus of Kardala at the same time became Master of Offices ; both these men were Isaurians.[3]

A modern historian who was perhaps the first to say a good word for Zeno, observes that " the great work of his reign was the formation of an army of native troops to serve as a counter-poise to the barbarian mercenaries " ; and goes on to remark that the man who successfully resisted the schemes and forces of the great Theoderic cannot have been contemptible.[4] And even from the pages of a hostile contemporary writer [5] we can see that he was not so bad as he was painted. He is said to have been in some respects superior to Leo, less relentless and less greedy. He was not popular,[6] for his ecclesiastical policy of conciliation did not find general favour, and he was an Isaurian. But he was inclined to be mild ; he desired to abstain from employing capital punishment. In the first year of his reign, Erythrius was Praetorian Prefect, a very humane man, who, when he saw that sufficient revenue could not be raised without severe oppression, resigned his office.[7] In fiscal administration Zeno

---

[1] In A.D. 485. Perhaps he had been set free by Illus, with the design of conciliating Zeno.

[2] It is possible that he was also created *mag. mil. in praes.*, and continued to hold this office in the first year of Anastasius ; see *C.J.* xii. 37. 16. Cp. John Mal. xv. p. 386. The dates of his consulships are 486 and 490.

[3] John Ant. *fr.* 98. Καρδάλων is the reading of the cod. Scorialensis, Καρδάμων of the Parisinus.

[4] Finlay, *History of Greece*, vol. i. p. 180.

[5] Preserved in Suidas *s.v.* Ζήνων (probably from Malchus).

[6] Yet the Ravenna chronicler known as the Anonymus Valesii

represents him as very popular : *Zeno recordatus est amore senatus et populi, munificus omnibus se ostendit, ita ut omnes ei gratias agerent. Senatu Romano et populo tuitus est ut etiam ei imagines per diversa loca in urbe Roma levarentur. Cuius tempora pacifica fuerunt* (9. 44). One would think that the writer was an Isaurian. Compare also 9. 40 : *in republica omnino providentissimus, favens gentis suae.*

[7] Suidas *s.v.* Ἐρύθριος = Malchus *fr.* 6. Erythrius seems to have succeeded Epinicus in 475 ; his tenure of office must have been very short. No extant constitutions are addressed to him. It is also possible that he was prefect in the last months of 476 after Zeno's restoration.

was less successful than his predecessors and his successor Anastasius. We are told that he wasted all that Leo left in the treasury by donatives to his friends and inaccuracy in checking his accounts. In A.D. 477 the funds were very low, hardly sufficient to supply pay for the army. But the blame of this may rather rest with Basiliscus, who, reigning precariously for twenty months, must have been obliged to incur large expenses, to supply which he was driven to extortion, and in the following years the Ostrogoths were an incubus on the exchequer ; while we must further remember that since the enormous outlay incurred by Leo's naval expedition the treasury had been in financial difficulties, which only a ruler of strict economy and business habits, like the succeeding Emperor Anastasius, could have remedied. Zeno was not a man of business, he was indolent and in many respects weak. Yet it is said that his reign would have been a good one but for the influence of the Praetorian Prefect Sebastian, who succeeded Erythrius, and introduced a system of selling offices.[1] Of Sebastian we otherwise hear very little.

By his first wife Arcadia, Zeno had a son,[2] of the same name, whose brief and strangely disreputable career must have been one of the chief scandals at the court. His father desired that he should be carefully trained in manly exercises, but unscrupulous young courtiers, who wished to profit by the abundant supplies of money which the boy could command, instructed him in all the vulgar excesses of luxury and voluptuousness. They introduced him to boys of his own age, who did not refuse to satisfy his desires, while their adulation flattered his vanity to such a degree that he treated all who came in contact with him as if they were servants. His excesses brought on an internal disease, and he died prematurely, after lying for many days in a senseless condition. After his death, Zeno seems to have intended to devolve the succession upon his brother Longinus, who enjoyed a vile reputation for debauchery.[3] We have already

---

[1] It is said that Sebastian used to buy for a small amount an office which Zeno bestowed on a friend, and then sell it to some one else for a much higher price, Zeno receiving the profit. He was Praetorian Prefect from 477 to 484. The decline of the Scholarian guards is attributed by Agathias (v.

15) to Zeno, who bestowed appointments on Isaurian relatives of no valour.

[2] Suidas, s.v. Ζήνων, probably from Malchus, see F.H.G. iv. 118.

[3] See Suidas s.v. Λογγῖνος (perhaps from Malchus).

seen how he was advanced to high posts of dignity. It is related that Zeno consulted a certain Maurianus, skilled in occult learning, who informed him that a silentiarius would be the next Emperor and would marry Ariadne. This prophecy was unfortunate for a distinguished patrician of high fame named Pelagius, who had once belonged to the silentiarii, for Zeno, seized with alarm and suspicion, put him to death.[1] The Emperor's unpopularity naturally made him suspicious, and he was in bad health. An attack of epilepsy carried him off on April 9, A.D. 491.

§ 3. *The Henotikon* (A.D. 481)

The doctrinal decrees of Chalcedon were the beginning of many evils for the eastern provinces of the Empire. Theological discord, often accompanied by violence, rent the Church, and the Emperors found it utterly impossible to suppress the Monophysite, as they had suppressed the Arian, faith. In Alexandria, the monks and the majority of the population were devoted to the doctrine of One Nature, and on the death of Marcian the smoulder-ing fire of dissatisfaction burst into flame. Timothy Aelurus,[2] an energetic Monophysite, was set up as a rival Patriarch ; Proterius was murdered in the baptistery (A.D. 457, Easter) and his corpse was dragged through the city. Timothy sent a memorial to the Emperor Leo demanding a new Council, and Leo formally asked for the opinion of the bishops of Rome, Constantinople, Antioch, and Jerusalem, and other leading dignitaries of the Church.[3] They condemned the conduct of Timothy and he was banished to the Chersonese.[4] At Antioch, the part of Timothy was played by Peter the Fuller, who during the reign of Leo was twice raised to the Patriarchal throne and twice ejected.[5]

---

[1] John Mal. xv. p. 390. Arcadius, the Praetorian Prefect, expressed such indignation at this that Zeno sought to slay him, but Arcadius sought refuge in St. Sophia and escaped with the confiscation of his property.

[2] Said to have been called Aelurus or Cat, because he used to creep at night into the cells of the monks at Alexandria to incite them against Proterius (Theodore Lector, i. 1). The view that he was a Herul (αἰλουρός

being a corruption of Ἔρουλος) is not probable.

[3] Fifty-five bishops, Simeon Stylites the younger, and two other monks.

[4] A.D. 460. He was succeeded by Timothy Salophaciolus (said to mean *white-capped*), who retired to a monas-tery in 475, when the other Timothy returned, and on his death was rein-stated in 477. He died in 482.

[5] Theodore Lector, i. 20 ; Liberatus, *Brev.* c. 18.

When Basiliscus ascended the throne, the Monophysite cause looked bright for a few months. Peter and Timothy were reinstated, and Basiliscus issued an Encyclical letter [1] in which he condemned the Council of Chalcedon and the Tome of Leo. But this declaration raised a storm in Constantinople which he was unable to resist. The monks were up in arms, and the Patriarch Acacius,[2] who was not a man of extreme views, found himself forced to oppose the Emperor's policy. Basiliscus hastened to retract, and he issued another letter, which was known as the Anti-encyclical. But the settlement of the ecclesiastical struggle did not lie with him. Zeno returned, and a new policy was devised for restoring peace to the Church. His chief advisers here were Acacius and Peter Mongus, who had been the right-hand man of Timothy Aelurus. The policy was to ignore the Council of Chalcedon, but not to affirm anything contrary to its doctrine ; and the hope was that the Monophysites and their antagonists would agree to differ, and would recognise that a common recognition of the great Councils of Nicaea and Constantinople was a sufficient bond of communion.

The *Henotikon*, a letter addressed by the Emperor to the Church of Egypt, embodied this policy (A.D. 481). It anathematises both Nestorius and Eutyches ; declares the truth, and asserts the sufficiency, of the doctrine of Nicaea and Constantinople ; and anathematises any who teach divergent doctrine " at Chalcedon or elsewhere." As the document was intended to conciliate all parties, it was a blunder to mention Chalcedon ; for this betrayed that the theological leanings of those who framed it were not favourable to the Chalcedonian dogma. The Monophysites gladly accepted it ; [3] interpreting it as giving them full liberty to denounce Chalcedon and the *Tome* of Pope Leo.

It is to be noted that Basiliscus by his *Encyclical* and Zeno by his *Henotikon* asserted the right of the Emperor to dictate to the Church and pronounce on questions of theological doctrine. They virtually assumed the functions of an Ecumenical Council. This was a claim which the see of Rome was not ready to admit except for itself. After the interchange of angry letters between

---

[1] A.D. 476. This Encyclical will be found in Evagrius, iii. 4 ; the Anti-encyclical, *ib.* 7 (cp. Zachariah Myt. v. 5) ; Zeno's Henotikon, *ib.* 14.

[2] Elected 471, as successor to Gennadius, who succeeded Anatolius in 458.

[3] Except an extreme party who were known as *Akephaloi* or " Headless."

Pope Simplicius and Acacius, a synod was held at Rome,[1] and Acacius and Peter Mongus, who was now Patriarch of Alexandria, were excommunicated.[2]

The general result of the *Henotikon* was to reconcile moderate Monophysites in Egypt and Syria, and to secure a certain measure of ecclesiastical peace in the East for thirty years [3] at the cost of a schism with the West. But the extreme Monophysites were not reconciled to the policy of Acacius and Peter.

§ 4. *The Rise of Odovacar and his Rule in Italy* (A.D. 473–489)

After the death of Olybrius, Leo was sole Roman Emperor for more than four months, and the Burgundian Gundobad, who had succeeded his uncle Ricimer as Master of Soldiers, directed the conduct of affairs in Italy. On March 5, A.D. 473, Glycerius, Count of the Domestics, was proclaimed Emperor at Ravenna " by the advice of Gundobad," [4] just as Severus had been proclaimed in the same city by the advice of Ricimer. Of this Augustus, whose reign was to be brief, one important public act is recorded. Italy was threatened by an invasion of Ostrogoths who, under the leadership of Widemir, began to move from Pannonia, but the diplomacy of Glycerius averted the storm, so that it fell on Gaul.

The election of Glycerius was not approved at Constantinople, and Leo selected another as the successor of Anthemius.[5] His choice was Julius Nepos, husband of the niece of the Empress, and military governor of Dalmatia, where he had succeeded his

[1] A.D. 484 under Felix II., successor of Simplicius. One of the Sleepless monks of Studion pinned the sentence of excommunication on the back of Acacius as he was officiating in St. Sophia. Acacius retorted the sentence on the Pope.

[2] After the death of Timothy Salophaciolus in 482, there was a struggle for the Patriarchal throne between Peter and John Talaias. Peter was supported by Zeno, and John, who was actually consecrated, betook himself to Rome and appealed to Simplicius.

[3] Nominally till A.D. 518, but after A.D. 512 the spirit of the Henotikon did not prevail in the East (see below, Chap. XIII. § 2). Various views are held by modern writers of the Henotikon. Gelzer praises it unreservedly ; Harnack considers it unfortunate, but admits that Zeno " simply did his duty " in issuing it (*op. cit.* p. 228).

[4] Cassiodorus, *Chron.*, *Gundibato hortante.* Marcellinus, *Chron.*, *Glycerius apud Ravennam plus praesumptione quam electione Caesar factus est* (this was the view at Constantinople). John Ant. *fr.* 92. For date see Anon. Cusp.

[5] John Ant. *ib.*

uncle, count Marcellinus.[1] We do not hear that any resistance
was offered to Nepos, who arrived in Italy, probably escorted
by eastern troops ; and it was not long before Gundobad,
whether perforce or voluntarily, retired to Burgundy where, in
the following year, he succeeded his father as one of the Burgundian kings.[2] Glycerius was deposed, and at Portus, the
town at the mouth of the Tiber, he was ordained bishop of
Salona.[3] Nepos was proclaimed Emperor and ruled at Rome
(June 24, A.D. 474). Once more two Augusti reigned in unison.

To the vacant post of Master of Soldiers, which carried with
it almost as a matter of course the title of Patrician, Orestes
was appointed. This was that Orestes who had been the
secretary of Attila, and he had married the daughter of a certain
count Romulus. Possessing the confidence of the German
troops he determined to raise his son to the Imperial throne.

We are told that Nepos, driven from Rome, went to Ravenna
and, fearing the coming of Orestes, crossed over to Salona. This
was on August 28, A.D. 475. The same year that saw the flight
of Zeno from Constantinople saw the flight of Nepos from
Ravenna. At Salona he lived for five years, and his Imperial
authority was still recognised in the East and in Gaul. But in
Italy the Caesar Julius was succeeded by the Caesar Augustulus,
for so the young Romulus was mockingly nicknamed, whom
his father Orestes invested with the Imperial insignia on October
31. These names, Julius, Augustulus, Romulus, in the pages
of the chroniclers, meet us like ghosts re-arisen from past days
of Roman history.[4]

It is important to remember that the position of Romulus
was not constitutional inasmuch as he had not been recognised
by the Emperor at Constantinople, in whose eyes Nepos was
still the Augustus of the West. For twelve months Orestes
ruled Italy in the name of his son. His fall was brought about
by a mutiny of the troops. The army, which the Master of
Soldiers commanded, seems to have consisted under Ricimer and

[1] His parents were Nepotianus and
a sister of Marcellinus.

[2] Cp. Schmidt, *op. cit.* i. 380-381.

[3] Anon. Val. *factus est episcopus* ;
Marcellinus, *Chron., in portu urbis
Romae ex Caesare episcopus ordinatus
est et obiit*, where the form of expression
suggests a doubt whether Glycerius

ever reached Salona.

[4] Am. Thierry made a similar
remark. "Ces rapprochements fortuits
présentaient dans leur bizarrerie je ne
sais quoi de surnaturel qui justifiait
la crédulité et troublait jusqu'aux
plus fermes esprits : on baissa la tête
et on se tut." (*Les Derniers Temps de
l'empire d'occident*, p. 258.)

his successors almost exclusively of East Germans, chiefly
Heruls, also Rugians and Scirians. According to the usual
custom,[1] they were quartered on the Italians. But they were
weary of this life. They desired to have roof-trees and lands of
their own, and they petitioned Orestes to reward them for their
services, by granting them lands and settling them permanently
in Italy on the same principle on which various German peoples
had been settled in other provinces. They did not demand the
exceptionally large concession of two-thirds of the soil which
had been granted by Honorius to the Visigoths ; they asked
for the normal grant of one-third which had been assigned, for
instance, to the Burgundians. But such a settlement in Italy
was a very different thing from settlement in Gaul or Spain,
and Orestes, notwithstanding his long association with Germans
and Huns, was sufficiently Roman to be determined to keep
the soil of Italy inviolate. He rejected the demand. The
discontented soldiers found a leader in the Scirian Odovacar,
one of the chief officers of Orestes.[2] Ticinum to which Orestes
retired was easily taken, and the Patrician was slain at Placentia (August 28, A.D. 476). "Entering Ravenna, Odovacar
deposed Augustulus but granted him his life, pitying his infancy
and because he was comely, and he gave him an income of six
thousand solidi and sent him to live in Campania with his
relatives." [3]

The soldiers had proclaimed Odovacar king.[4] But it was
not as king over a mixed host of various German nationalities
that Odovacar thought he could maintain his position in Italy.
The movement which had raised him had no national significance,
and if he retained the royal title of an East German potentate,
it was as a successor of Ricimer, Gundobad, and Orestes that
he hoped to govern the Italians. In other words, he had no
idea of detaching Italy from the Empire, as Africa and much
of Gaul and Spain had come to be detached. The legal position
was to continue as before.[5] But the system of Ricimer was to

---

[1] See above, p. 206.

[2] For the nationality of Odovacar
see John Ant. 93, Anon. Val. 45.
He was son of Edica, probably
identical with Edeco, who acted as
Attila's envoy to Byzantium in 448.
His brother was Onoulf (Malchus,
fr. 8, John Ant. *ib.*).

[3] Anon. Val. viii. 38.

[4] He is styled *rex Herulorum* in
Cons. Ital. (*Chron. Min.* i. p. 313,
cp. p. 309).

[5] He issued silver and bronze coins
in his own name at Ravenna, without
the title *rex*. The inscription was
FL(avius) ODOVAC. See Wroth, *Coins
of Vandals*, p. 30.

be abandoned. There were to be no more puppet Emperors
in the West; Italy was to be under the sovranty of the Emperor
at Constantinople, and its actual government was to be in the
hands of Odovacar, who as Master of Soldiers was to be a
minister of the Emperor, while he happened at the same time
to be king of the East Germans who formed the army.

With this purpose in view Odovacar made the deposition
of Romulus take the form of an abdication, and induced the
Roman Senate to endorse formally the permanent institution
of a state of things which had repeatedly existed in the days
of Ricimer. A deputation of senators, in the name of Romulus,
was sent to the Augustus at Constantinople to announce the
new order of things. Zeno had already recovered the throne,
from which Basiliscus had driven him, when the ambassadors
arrived and informed him that they no longer needed a separate
Emperor but that his sole supremacy would be sufficient; that
they had selected Odovacar as a man capable of protecting Italy,
being both a tried soldier and endowed with political intelligence.
They asked Zeno to confer upon him the rank of Patrician and
entrust him with the administration of Italy. They bore with
them the Imperial insignia which Romulus had worn (A.D. 477).[1]

At the same time messengers arrived from Nepos to congratulate Zeno on his restoration, to ask for his sympathy with
one who had suffered the same misfortune as he, and to crave
his aid in men and money to recover the throne. But for the
existence of Nepos, the situation would have been simple. Zeno
could not ignore his legal right, but was not prepared to support
it with an army. He told the representatives of the Senate
that of the two Emperors they had received from the East, they
had slain Anthemius and banished Nepos; let them now take
Nepos back. But he granted the other request. He sent to
Odovacar a diploma conferring the Patriciate, and wrote to
him, praising the respect for Rome and the observance of order
which had marked his conduct, and bidding him crown his
goodness by acknowledging the exiled Emperor. The fact that
Verina was the aunt of the wife of Nepos was a consideration
which helped to hinder Zeno from disowning him. Odovacar

---

[1] These details are preserved in a
valuable fragment of Malchus (*fr.* 10).
Candidus relates that after the death
of Nepos the Gallo - Romans (τῶν
δυσμικῶν Γαλατῶν) rejected the rule
of Odovacar and sent an embassy to
Zeno, but Zeno rather inclined to
Odovacar (*fr.* 1, p. 136, *F.H.G.* iv.).

did not acknowledge the claim of Nepos, and Zeno cannot have expected that he would.

The events of A.D. 476 have been habitually designated as the " Fall of the Western Empire." The phrase is inaccurate and unfortunate, and sets the changes which befell in a false light. No Empire fell in A.D. 476 ; there was no " Western Empire " to fall. There was only one Roman Empire, which sometimes was governed by two or more Augusti. If it is replied that the expression is merely a convenient one to signify what contemporary writers sometimes called the Hesperian realm (*Hesperium regnum*), the provinces which had been, since the death of Theodosius I., generally under the separate government of an Emperor residing in Italy, and that all that is meant is the termination of this line of western Emperors, it may be pointed out that A.D. 480 is in that case the significant date. For Julius Nepos, who died in that year, was the last legitimate Emperor in the West ; Romulus Augustulus was only a usurper. The important point to seize is that, from the constitutional point of view, Odovacar was the successor of Ricimer, and that the situation created by the events of A.D. 476 was in this respect similar to the situation in the intervals between the reigns of the Emperors set up by Ricimer. If, on the death of Honorius, there had been no Valentinian to succeed him, and if Theodosius II. had exercised the sovranty over the western provinces, and if no second Augustus had been created again before the western provinces had passed under the sway of Teutonic rulers, no one would have spoken of the " Fall of the Western Empire." Yet this hypothetical case would be formally the same as the actual event of A.D. 476 or rather of A.D. 480. The West came finally, as it had more than once come temporarily, under the sole sovranty of the Emperor reigning at East Rome.

The Italian revolution of A.D. 476 was, however, a most memorable event, though it has been wrongly described. It stands out prominently as an important stage in the process of the dismemberment of the Empire. It belongs to the same catalogue of chronological dates which includes A.D. 418, when Honorius settled the Goths in Aquitaine, and A.D. 435, when Valentinian ceded African lands to the Vandals. In A.D. 476 the same principle of disintegration was first applied to Italy. The settlement of Odovacar's East Germans, with Zeno's acquiescence, began the process by which Italian soil was to pass into the hands of Ostrogoths and Lombards, Franks and Normans. And Odovacar's title of king emphasised the significance of the change.

It is highly important to observe that Odovacar established his political power with the co-operation of the Roman Senate, and this body seems to have given him their loyal support throughout his reign, so far as our meagre sources permit us to draw inferences. At this time the senators who counted politically belonged to a few old and distinguished clans, possessing large estates and great wealth, particularly the Decii and the Anicii.[1] The leading men of these families received high honours and posts under Odovacar. Basilius, Decius, Venantius, and Manlius Boethius held the consulship and were either Prefects of Rome or Praetorian Prefects ; [2] Symmachus and Sividius were consuls and Prefects of Rome ; [3] another senator of old family, Cassiodorus, was appointed a minister of finance.[4] The evidence indicates that while it was Odovacar's policy to appoint only men of Roman families to the Prefecture of the City, he allowed the Prefect to hold office only for a year, so that no man might win a dangerous political importance.[5]

Yet the Roman nobility were now compelled to contribute more largely to the maintenance of the military forces which defended Italy. The greater part of the land belonged to them, and by the new settlement one-third of their estates was taken

[1] There is a useful genealogical tree in Sundwall, *Abh. zur Gesch. d. ausg. Römerthums*, p. 131, showing the relationships of the Decii who played a public part from 450 to 540.

[2] Flavius Caecina Decius Maximus *Basilius* iunior was consul in 480, Praet. Pref. 483 ; Caecina Mavortius Basilius *Decius* iunior, consul 486, Prefect of Rome, and then Praet. Pref. between 486 and 493 ; Fl. Decius Marius Basilius *Venantius*, consul and Prefect of Rome 484 ; Flavius Manlius Boethius, consul and Prefect of Rome for the second time in 487, and Praet. Pref. earlier. Cp. *C.I.L.* v. 8120.

[3] Quintus Aurelius Memmius Symmachus iunior, consul 485, Prefect of Rome probably in same year. Rufius Achillius Sividius, consul 488, and twice Prefect of Rome ; cp.

C.I.L. xii. 133. A bronze tablet of Symmachus (Dessau, 8955) combines the names of Zeno and Odovacar : *salvo d.n. Zenone et domno Odovacre.*

[4] First *com. r. pr.* afterwards *com. s. larg.* Petrus Marcellinus Felix Liberius began, under Odovacar, a career which was to be long and distinguished, but we do not know what posts he held (cp. Cass. *Var.* ii. 16). Those parts of the Imperial domains which were appropriated to the Emperor's private purse and were taken over by Odovacar, were placed under an official entitled *comes et vicedominus noster* ; and this post might be held by a German. See Marini, *Pap.* n. 82 (grant of land to count Pierius, A.D. 489). These patrimonial lands were chiefly in Sicily.

[5] Sundwall, *op. cit.* 181.

from the proprietors, and Odovacar's barbarian soldiers and their families were settled on them. It is not probable that the number of these soldiers exceeded 20,000 at the most, and it has been reasonably doubted whether this measure was actually carried out throughout the length and breadth of the peninsula.[1] We may suspect that the needs of the army were satisfied without a drastic application of the principle of partition. If the illustrious landowners had been mulcted on a large scale, it is hardly credible that they would have co-operated with the king as loyally as they seem to have done.

Soon after the government of Italy had passed into his hands, Odovacar's diplomacy achieved a solid success by inducing Gaiseric, who died in January, A.D. 477., to cede to him the island of Sicily. He undertook indeed to pay for it a yearly tribute, and the Vandal king reserved a foothold in the island, doubtless the western fortress of Lilybaeum.[2] The death of Julius Nepos has been mentioned. He was murdered by two of his retainers in his country house near Salona in May, A.D. 480. Odovacar assumed the duty of pursuing and executing the assassins, and at the same time established his own rule in Dalmatia.[3] The claims of Nepos, so long as he lived, had embarrassed the relations between Zeno and Odovacar ; Zeno's acquiescence in Odovacar's position and the wishes of the Senate had been ambiguous and reserved. The death of Nepos relieved the situation, and there was no longer any difficulty at Constantinople about acknowledging the western consuls whom Odovacar chose. But the relations between the Emperor and his Master of Soldiers in Italy were always strained, and in A.D. 486 there was an open breach.[4] Though Odovacar did not help the rebel Illus in his revolt, there were negotiations, and Zeno may have been suspicious and alarmed. Odovacar prepared an expedition into the Illyrian provinces, then pressed hard by the Ostrogoths, and Zeno averted it by instigating the Rugians to invade Italy.[5] Odovacar anticipated their attack by marching through Noricum and surprising them in the winter

---

[1] Cp. the remarks of Sundwall, 178, and 183, *n.* 4.

[2] Victor Vit. i. 4.

[3] Dalmatia had been under Constantinople since the reign of Valentinian III. (see above, p. 125), and we must suppose that when Nepos was

created Augustus in 474, Leo handed it over to him.

[4] In this year and 487 the names of the western consuls were not published in the East.

[5] John Ant. *fr.* 98, *Exc. de Ins.* p. 138.

season (end of A.D. 487) in their territory beyond the Danube.
Their king Feletheus and his queen were taken to Italy and
beheaded, and with the death of his son, against whom a second
expedition was sent, the Rugian power was destroyed.[1]

Of the internal government we know little. The Church was
unaffected by his rule ; [2] as an Arian he held aloof from ecclesiastical affairs. As to the working of the Roman administration
under a German ruler, acting as an independent viceroy, and
the limitations imposed on his power, we have abundant evidence
regarding Odovacar's successor, Theoderic, and when we come
to his reign the details will claim our attention.

§ 5. The Ostrogoths in Illyricum and Thrace (A.D. 477–488)

In the reign of Arcadius the Visigoths had seemed likely
to form a kingdom within the Illyrian peninsula, before they
invaded Italy and established their home in the west. We
shall now see how history repeated itself in the case of the
Ostrogoths, how they too almost settled in the lands of the
Balkans before they went westward to found a kingdom in Italy.[3]

It will be remembered that after the collapse of the Hunnic
power in A.D. 454 the Ostrogoths, over whom three brothers
ruled, Walamir, Theodemir, and Widemir, were allowed by the
Emperor Marcian to occupy northern Pannonia, as *foederati*.[4]
After some years they were provoked by the Emperor Leo,
who refused to pay an annual sum of 100 pounds of gold which
Marcian had granted them ; and they ravaged the Illyrian
provinces and seized Dyrrhachium. Peace was made in A.D.
461, the money grant was continued, and Theoderic,[5] the son

[1] Eugippius, *Vita Severini*, c. 44.
This source throws interesting light
on the derelict provinces of Noricum,
which for thirty years were exposed
to the depredations of the Rugians,
left unprotected by the Italian government, and virtually governed by St.
Severinus.

[2] Only once does he seem to have
intervened. When the clergy met to
elect a Pope in succession to Simplicius in March 483, the Praetorian
Prefect appeared on Odovacar's behalf,
because Simplicius had urgently implored the king not to allow a new Pope
to be elected without his consent.

[3] The chief sources for the events

of this section are fragments of
Malchus and of John of Antioch, and
the *Getica* of Jordanes.

[4] Jordanes, *ib*. 268, knew how it was
apportioned among the three brothers.
Theodemir's people were on the
Plattensee and eastward towards the
Danube.

[5] Theoderic may have been born
about 454–455. He is said to have been
eight years old when he was sent to
Byzantium. His mother seems to
have been a concubine treated with
the honours of a wife. Her name in
Anon. Val. xiv. 58, is Ereriliva, but
she was a Catholic and took the
christian name of Eusebia.

of Theodemir, was sent as a hostage to Constantinople where he had the advantage of a Roman training. His education, however, in letters appears not to have advanced very far, for it is said that he was never able to write. During these years his nation was engaged in wars with neighbouring German peoples.[1] They won a decisive victory over the Scirians which cost Walamir his life. His section of the Goths passed then under the rule of Theodemir, who had soon to resist a large combination of Scirians, Rugians, Gepids, and others. Both parties applied to the Emperor for support, and Leo, acting against the advice of Aspar who was friendly to the Ostrogoths, sent troops to help the Scirian league. In a sanguinary battle the Goths were victors (A.D. 469), and their predominance on the Middle Danube was established.[2] Leo then considered it politic to cultivate their friendship and he allowed Theoderic to return to his people. The young prince at once distinguished himself in a campaign against the Sarmatians who had recently occupied Singidunum, and the Goths appropriated the city.

The last act of Theodemir seems to have been an invasion of the provinces of Dacia and Dardania, in which his army advanced as far as Naissus.[3] Death befell him soon afterwards and Theoderic was elected as his successor in 471.[4] Soon after his accession (before 475) he seems to have led his people from their Pannonian homes to a new settlement in Lower Moesia, the same regions which had once been occupied by the Visigoths of Alaric.[5] There is no evidence that this change of habitation was sanctioned by the Roman Emperor ; but it does not seem to have been opposed at the time.

After the collapse of the Hunnic empire a large number of Ostrogoths had taken service in the Roman army, and formed the most important part of the German forces on whose support Aspar had maintained his power. We have already met their commander Theoderic (son of Triarius), called Strabo, "squinter," who was not of very distinguished descent but was related through

---

[1] As Gasquet (*L'Empire byz.* p. 67) observes, "what the barbarians hated most cordially was [not Romans but] other barbarians." Jordanes put it otherwise : the Ostrogoths made war *cupientes ostentare virtutem* (*ib.* 52).

[2] Priscus, *fr.* 17, *De leg. gent.* ; John Ant. *fr.* 90, *De ins.* ; Jordanes, *ib.* 278.

[3] Jordanes, *Get.* 282 - 286, where events belonging to later incursions of Theoderic are mixed up with this invasion of Theodemir.

[4] Anon. Val. xvii. 67. Theoderic celebrated his *tricennalia* in A.D. 500.

[5] He seems to have resided in Novae. Anon. Val. vi. 42.

marriage to the family of Theodemir.[1]   We may call him Strabo
to distinguish him from his more famous namesake.   We saw
the hostile attitude which he assumed towards Leo after the
death of Aspar.   The German troops gathered round him and
proclaimed him king.   He then sent an embassy to Leo, demanding for himself the post of Master of Soldiers *in praesenti* which
Aspar had held, and the inheritance of Aspar, and for his troops
grants of land in Thrace.   The Emperor was willing to appoint
him to the generalship, but refused the other demands.   Then
Strabo ravaged the territory of Philippopolis and reduced
Arcadiopolis by starvation.   These energetic proceedings extorted concessions from Leo ; he agreed to pay a yearly stipend
of 2000 lbs. of gold (= £90,000) to the Goths and to allot them a
district in Thrace, and he conferred the post of Master of Soldiers
in praesenti on Strabo, who was to fight for the Emperor against
all enemies except the Vandals, and " enemies " doubtless
included the Goths of Theoderic.[2]   He was, moreover, to be
recognised as king of the Goths.[3]

In the troubles that followed Leo's death, Strabo naturally
took the part of Basiliscus against his old foe, while Zeno was
supported by Theoderic.   After his restoration Zeno deprived
Strabo of his military post and bestowed it on Theoderic, whom
he also created a Patrician, confirming him in possession of
the lands which his people had seized in Lower Moesia and
promising him an annual stipend.   He even adopted him as a
son, according to the German right of adoption.

But there were no sincere feelings behind this favour and
friendliness.   The policy of the Emperor was to play off one
Goth against the other.   In the three following years (A.D. 477–
479) the relations between him and the two rivals shifted rapidly
through all the stages of possible combinations.   In the first
stage Zeno and Theoderic are combined against Strabo ; in the
second the two Theoderics join forces against Zeno ; in the third
Strabo and Zeno co-operate against Theoderic.

The drama began with an embassy from Strabo desiring
reconciliation.   The ambassadors reminded Zeno of the injuries

[1] John Ant. *fr.* 98, Theoderic is said
to be ἀνεψιός of Recitach son of
Strabo.   Schmidt (*ib.* 127, *n.* 3) conjectures that Theodemir's sister had
married Strabo's brother.

[2] Cp. Schmidt, *op. cit.* i. 136.
[3] His wish to be recognised as king
by the Emperor shows that he was
not of royal descent.   Dahn, *Kön. der
Germanen*, ii. 69.

which Theoderic had inflicted on the Empire, though he was called a Roman " general " and a friend. Zeno convoked the Senate, and it was concluded to be impossible to support the two generals and their armies, for the public resources were hardly sufficient to pay the Roman troops. The exchequer, it must not be forgotten, had not yet recovered from the failure of the Vandal expedition of the previous reign. As Strabo had always shown himself hostile at heart, was unpopular on account of his cruelty, and had assisted Basiliscus " the tyrant," it was determined to reject his offer. Yet, as Zeno for a time withheld a reply, three friends of Strabo in Constantinople, Anthimus a physician, and two others, wrote him an account of the course which matters were taking ; but the letters were discovered, the affair was examined by a senatorial commission of three persons, in the presence of the Master of Soldiers, and the three friends of the Goths were punished by flogging and exile.

Soon after this, probably in A.D. 478, the Emperor, perceiving that Strabo was becoming stronger and consolidating forces, and that Theoderic was hardly in a position to cope with him, deemed it wise to come to terms. He therefore sent an embassy proposing that the son of the chief should be sent to Byzantium as a hostage, and that Strabo himself should live as a private individual in Thrace, retaining what he had already secured by plunder, but binding himself to plunder no more. The chief refused, representing that it was impossible for him to withdraw now without paying the troops whom he had collected. Accordingly Zeno decided on war ; troops were summoned from the dioceses of Pontus, Asia, and the East, and it was expected that Illus would assume the command. It seems, however, that Illus did not take the field, for we find Martinianus, his brother-in-law, conducting a campaign against the Goths in the same year, and proving himself incompetent to maintain discipline in his own army. Then Zeno sent an embassy to Theoderic calling upon him to fulfil the duties of a Roman general and advance against the enemy. He replied that the Emperor and Senate must first swear that they will never make terms with the other Ostrogothic king. The senators took an oath that they would not do so unless the Emperor wished it, and the Emperor swore that he would not break the contract if it were not first violated by Theoderic himself.

Theoderic then moved southwards. The Master of Soldiers of Thrace was to meet him with two thousand cavalry and ten thousand hoplites at a pass of Mount Haemus ; when he had crossed into Thrace another force was to join him at Hadrianople, consisting of twenty thousand foot and six thousand horse ; and, if necessary, Heraclea (on the Propontis) and the cities in the neighbourhood were prepared to send additional troops. But the Master of Soldiers was not at the pass of Mount Sondis, and the Goths when they advanced farther fell in with the army of Strabo, and the antagonists plundered one another's flocks and horses. Then Strabo, riding near his rival's camp, reviled him as a traitor to desert his own countrymen, and as a fool not to see through the plan of the Romans, who wished to rid themselves of the Goths, without trouble on their own part, by instigating them to mutual destruction, and were quite indifferent which party won. These arguments produced a powerful effect upon Theoderic's followers, and the two leaders made peace (478). This is the second stage of alliance, which we noted above. It was not to last long.

The reconciled Ostrogothic chieftains then sent ambassadors to Byzantium. Theoderic, upbraiding Zeno for having deceived him with false promises, demanded the concession of territory to his people, a supply of corn to support his army till harvest time, and urged that, if these demands were not satisfied, he would be unable to restrain his soldiers from plundering, in order to support themselves. Strabo demanded that the arrangements he had made with Leo (in A.D. 473) should be carried out, that the payment he had been accustomed to receive in former years should be continued, and that certain kinsmen of his, who had been committed to the care of Illus and the Isaurians, should be restored. We are not informed what answer Zeno made to the elder Theoderic, or whether he made any ; to the son of Theodemir he replied, that if he consented to break with his namesake and make war upon him he would give him 2000 lbs. of gold and 10,000 lbs. of silver immediately, besides a yearly revenue of 10,000 nomismata, and the hand of a daughter of Placidia and Olybrius [1] or of some other noble lady. But his promises did not avail, and Zeno prepared for war, notifying his intention to accompany the army in person. This intention created great

---

[1] Probably Juliana, whom we afterwards find married to Areobindus.

enthusiasm among the soldiers, but at the last moment Zeno drew back, and they threatened a revolt, to prevent which the army was broken up and the regiments sent to their winter quarters.

When the army was disbanded, Zeno's only resort was to make peace on any terms with Strabo. In the meantime Theoderic, the son of Theodemir, was engaged in ravaging the fairest parts of Thrace in the neighbourhood of Mount Rhodope, which divides Thrace from Macedonia ; he not only ruined the crops, but oppressed the farmers or slew them. Strabo, when he received Zeno's message,—remarking that he was sorry that the innocent husbandmen, for whose welfare Zeno [1] did not care in the least, suffered from the ravages of his rival—concluded a peace on the conditions that Zeno was to supply a yearly payment sufficient to support thirteen thousand men ; that he was to be appointed to the command of two scholae and to the post of Master of Soldiers *in praesenti*, and receive all the dignities which Basiliscus had bestowed upon him ; that his kinsmen were to inhabit a city assigned by Zeno. The Emperor did not delay to execute this agreement ; Theoderic was deposed from the office of Master of Soldiers, and Strabo appointed in his stead (before end of 478). This marks the third stage in these changeful relations.

Theoderic, now threatened by the superior forces of Strabo, was in a difficult position. But he managed to escape across Mount Rhodope into Macedonia (perhaps with the Emperor's collusion), and the town of Stobi felt the full brunt of his wrath. Thence he turned his steps towards Thessalonica, and the inhabitants felt so little confidence in Zeno that they actually believed that the Emperor wished to hand their city over to the barbarians. A sedition broke out which ended in the transference of the keys of the city from the Praetorian Prefect of Illyricum to the archbishop, a remarkable evidence of the fact that the people looked on the ministers of the Church as defenders against Imperial oppression. These suspicions of the Emperor's intentions were undoubtedly unjust. Zeno sent Artemidorus and Phocas to Theoderic, who was persuaded by their representations to stay his army and send an embassy to Byzantium. Theoderic

---

[1] " Zeno *or Verina* " (Malchus, *fr.* 9, *De leg. Rom.*). This seems to show that Verina had a preponderant influence at this time.

demanded that a plenipotentiary envoy should be sent to treat with him. Zeno sent Adamantius, directing him to offer the Goths land in Pautalia (about Küstendil), and 200 lbs. of gold to supply food for that year, as no corn had been sown in the designated region. The motive of Zeno in choosing Pautalia was that if the Goths accepted it they would occupy a position between the Illyrian and Thracian armies, in which they might be more easily controlled.

Meanwhile Theoderic had proceeded by the Egnatian Way to Heraclea (Monastir), and had sent a message to one Sidimund,[1] an Ostrogoth who had been in the service of Leo and had inherited an estate near Dyrrhachium, where he was living peaceably. Theoderic induced him to make an attempt to take possession of that important city of New Epirus, and for this purpose Sidimund employed an ingenious device. He visited the citizens individually, informing each that the Ostrogoths were coming with Zeno's consent to take possession of the city, and advising him to move his property with all haste to some other secure town or to one of the coast islands. The fact that his representations were listened to and that he effected the removal of a garrison of two thousand men proves that he possessed considerable influence. Theoderic was at Heraclea [2] when the messenger of Sidimund arrived with the news that the plan had been successfully carried out ; and having burnt a large portion of the town because its inhabitants could not supply him with provisions, he set out for Epirus. He proceeded along the Egnatian Way, crossing the range of the Scardus mountains, and arrived at Lychnidus, which is now Ochrida. Built in a strong situation on the shore of Lake Ochrida, and well provided with water and victuals, Lychnidus defied the assault of the barbarians, who, unwilling to delay, hastened onwards, and having seized Scampae, the most important town between Lychnidus and Dyrrhachium, arrived at the goal of their journey.

It may be wondered whether at Dyrrhachium it entered the mind of Theoderic to ship his people across to the western peninsula and attack the Italian kingdom of Odovacar in the

[1] He was cousin of Aidoing, Count of the Domestics, and a friend of Verina ; and he belonged to the Amal family.

[2] It is worth noticing that a sister of Theoderic, as well as his mother and brother, accompanied him on his march ; she died at Heraclea and was buried there.

south. Adamantius, the ambassador who had been sent by
Zeno to treat with him, seems to have thought it more likely
that the Ostrogoths would employ vessels for the purpose of
plundering the Epeirot or Dalmatian coasts, for he sent a post
messenger to Dyrrhachium, to blame Theoderic for his hostile
advance while negotiations were pending, and to exhort him to
remain quiet and not to seize ships until he arrived himself.

Starting from Thessalonica, and passing Pella on the Via
Egnatia, Adamantius came to Edessa, the modern Vodena,
where he found Sabinian Magnus, and informed him that
he had been appointed Master of Soldiers in Illyricum. The
messenger, who had been sent to Dyrrhachium, returned in the
company of a priest, to assure Adamantius that he might proceed
confidently to the camp of Theoderic ; and, having issued a
mandate to collect all the troops available, the general and the
ambassador moved forward to Lychnidus. Here Sabinian [1]
made difficulties about binding himself by oath to restore the
hostages whom Theoderic was willing to deliver as a gage for
the personal safety of Adamantius. This produced a deadlock ;
Theoderic naturally refused to give the hostages. Adamantius
naturally refused to visit Theoderic.

Adamantius invented a simple solution of the difficulty,
which led to a striking scene. Taking with him a body of two
hundred soldiers he climbed by an obscure and narrow path,
where horses had never set hoof before, and reached by a circuitous route an impregnable fort, built on a high cliff, close to the
city of Dyrrhachium. At the foot of the cliff yawned a deep
ravine, through which a river flowed. A messenger was sent
to inform Theoderic that the Roman ambassador awaited him,
and, attended by a few horse-soldiers, the Ostrogoth rode to
the bank of the river. The physical features, the cliff, the
chasm, and the river, are sufficiently simple and definite to
enable us to call up vividly this strange scene. The attendants
of both Adamantius and Theoderic had retired beyond range
of earshot ; and standing on the edges of the ravine the
Ostrogothic king and the ambassador of the Roman Empire
conversed together.

---

[1] Sabinian was a strict disciplin-
arian, see Marcellinus, *sub a.* 479 :
disciplinae praeterea militaris ita op-
timus institutor coercitorque fuit ut
priscis Romanorum ductoribus compa-
retur.

"I elected to live," complained Theoderic, "beyond the borders of Thrace, far away Scythia-ward, deeming that if I abode there I should trouble no man, and should be able to obey all the behests of the Emperor. But ye summoned me as to war against Theoderic, and promised, firstly, that the Master of Soldiers in Thrace would meet me with his army, yet he never appeared ; secondly, ye promised that Claudius, the steward of the Gothic contingent, would come with the pay for my troops (ξενικῷ), yet I never saw him ; thirdly, ye gave me guides who, leaving the better roads that would have taken me to the quarters of the foe, led me by steep and precipitous rocky paths, where I wellnigh perished with all my train, advancing as I was with cavalry, waggons, and all the furniture of camp, and exposed to the attacks of the enemy. I was therefore constrained to come to terms with them, and owe them a debt of gratitude that they did not annihilate me, betrayed as I was by you and in their power."

"The Emperor," replied Adamantius, "bestowed upon you the title of Patrician, and created you a Master of Soldiers. These are the highest honours that crown the labours of the most deserving Roman officers, and nothing should induce you to cherish towards their bestower other than filial sentiments." Having endeavoured to defend or extenuate the treatment of which Theoderic complained, the envoy proceeded thus : "You are acting intolerably in seizing Roman cities, while you are expecting an embassy ; and remember that the Romans held you at their mercy, a prisoner, surrounded by their armies, amid the mountains and rivers of Thrace, whence you could never have extricated yourself, if they had not permitted you to withdraw, not even were your forces tenfold as great as they are. Allow me to counsel you to assume a more moderate attitude towards the Emperor, for you cannot in the end overcome the Romans when they press on you from all sides. Leave Epirus and the cities of this region—we cannot allow such great cities to be occupied by you and their inhabitants to be expelled—and go to Dardania, where there is an extensive territory of rich soil, uninhabited, and sufficient to support your host in plenty."

To this proposal Theoderic replied that he would readily consent, but that his followers, who had recently endured many hardships, would be unwilling to leave their quarters in Epirus,

where they had fully expected to pass the winter. He proposed a compromise, and engaged that if he were permitted to
winter at Dyrrhachium he would migrate to Dardania in the
ensuing spring. He added that he was quite ready to leave
the unwarlike mass of his Ostrogoths in any city named by Zeno,
and giving up his mother and sister as hostages, to take the field
against Strabo with six thousand of his most martial followers,
in company with the Illyrian army ; when he had conquered
his rival he expected to succeed to the post of Master of Soldiers
and to be received in New Rome as a Roman.[1] He also observed
that he was prepared, if the Emperor wished, " to go to Dalmatia
and restore Julius Nepos." Adamantius was unable to promise
so much ; it was necessary to send a messenger to Byzantium
to consult the Emperor. And thus the interview terminated.

Meanwhile the military forces, stationed in the Illyrian cities,
had assembled at Lychnidus, around the standard of Sabinian.
It was announced to the general that a band of the Ostrogoths
led by Theodimund, the brother of Theoderic, was descending
in secure negligence from Mount Candaira, which separates the
valley of the Genusus (Skumbi) from that of the Drilo. This
band had formed the rear of the Ostrogothic line of march,
and had not yet reached Dyrrhachium. Sabinian sent a few
infantry soldiers by a circuitous mountain route, with minute
directions as to the hour and place at which they were to appear ;
and himself with the rest of the army proceeded thither, after the
evening meal, by a more direct way. Marching during the night
he assailed the company of Theodimund at dawn of day. Theodimund and his mother, who was with him, fled with all speed
into the plain, and, having crossed a deep gully, destroyed the
bridge which spanned it to cut off pursuit. This act, while it
saved them, sacrificed their followers, who turned at bay upon
the Romans. Two thousand waggons and more than five
thousand captives were taken, and a great booty (A.D. 479).

After this the Emperor received two messages, one from
Adamantius announcing the proposals of Theoderic, the other
from Sabinian exaggerating his victory and dissuading from the
conclusion of peace. War seemed more honourable to Zeno
and the pacific offers were rejected, Sabinian was permitted to
continue the war, and for about a year and a half he held the

---

[1] Τὸν 'Ρωμαικὸν πολιτεύσοντα τρόπον. For Julius Nepos see above, p. 404.

Goths in check in Epirus.   But the active general was murdered by an ungrateful master,[1] and John the Scythian and Moschian were sent to succeed him.

The revolt of Marcian towards the end of A.D. 479 had given Strabo a pretext for approaching Constantinople to assist the government.   Having extorted money from Zeno, he received two of the conspirators in his camp and refused to surrender them.   He was then once more deprived of his dignities and declared an enemy of the republic.   He entered again into alliance with Theoderic and devastated Thrace.   Zeno invoked the aid of the Bulgarians of the Lower Danube, but they were defeated by Strabo, who then advanced on Constantinople (A.D. 481).

It was a surprise, and we are told that he would easily have captured the city if Illus had not set guards at the gates just in time.   He attempted to cross over to Bithynia, but was defeated in a battle on the water, and departed to Thrace.   Thence he set forth for Greece, with his son Recitach, his wife, and about 30,000 followers.   At a place called the Stable of Diomede, on the Egnatian Road, his horse threw him one morning on a spear which was standing point upwards, close to his tent.   The accident was fatal (A.D. 481).   Recitach succeeded him, and ruled in Thrace, " performing more outrageous acts than his father had performed." [2]   Three years later Recitach was slain by Theoderic, son of Theodemir, whom Zeno instigated to the deed.[3]

In 482 we find Theoderic—the name is no longer ambiguous— ravaging the provinces of Macedonia, and Thessaly, and capturing the town of Larissa.   He was no longer held in check by the able general Sabinian who had been murdered the year before.   The Emperor decided to make a new agreement.   Parts of Moesia and Dacia Ripensis were conceded to the Ostrogoths, and Theoderic was appointed Master of Soldiers (A.D. 483).[4]   In A.D. 484 he enjoyed the coveted distinction of giving his name to the year as consul, and he assisted Zeno against the rebel Illus. But a new breach soon followed.   He devastated Thrace (A.D. 486) and marched on Constantinople (A.D. 487).   Rhegium was occupied, Melantias was taken, and the capital once more

---

[1] For the fate of Sabinian see John Ant. *fr.* 97 ; for the date, 481, Marcellinus, *sub a.*

[2] John Ant. *fr.* 95.   Another account will be found in Eustathius, *fr.* 3 (*apud Evagrium*, iii. 25).

[3] Recitach had murdered his uncles, so that the act of Theoderic (who was related to Strabo) was an act of blood-vengeance.   John Ant. *fr.* 98.

[4] Marcellinus, *Chron.*, *sub a.*

threatened. But the intervention of his sister,[1] who was at
Zeno's court, induced him to retire to his headquarters in Moesia,
which he was soon to abandon for ever. The days of the Thracian
period of Theoderic's career were numbered.

§ 6. *Theoderic's Conquest of Italy* (A.D. 489–493)

We have seen that there had been friction between the
Emperor and his Viceroy in Italy, and that Odovacar had
thoroughly defeated the Rugians whom Zeno had stirred up
against him. The thought now occurred to Zeno or his advisers
that he might at once punish Odovacar and deliver the Illyrian
provinces from the menacing presence of the Ostrogoths by
giving Theoderic a commission to supersede the ruler of Italy.
Theoderic accepted the charge. A compact was made that
(in the words of a chronicler) " in case Odovacar were conquered,
Theoderic should, as a reward of his labours, rule in place of
Odovacar, until Zeno came himself." [2] The last condition is
simply a way of saying that Zeno reserved all the Imperial rights
of sovranty.

At the head of his people, numbering perhaps about 100,000,[3]
Theoderic set forth from Moesia in the autumn of A.D. 488.
Following the direct road to Italy, past Viminacium and Singidunum, he approached Sirmium, and here he was confronted by
a formidable obstacle. This town was in the possession of the
Gepids, who now blocked Theoderic's path. The place was taken
after fierce fighting, but the Goths passed on with their booty and
the Gepids reoccupied it. The winter, spring, and summer of the
following year were spent somewhere between Sirmium and the
Italian borders, and the causes of this delay are unknown.

It was not till the end of August (A.D. 489) that, having crossed
the Julian Alps, the Ostrogoths reached the river Sontius (Isonzo)
and the struggle for Italy began. Of this memorable war we
have only the most meagre outline. The result was decided
within twelve months, but three and a half years were to elapse

---

[1] Perhaps Amalafrida (Schmidt,
op. cit. i. 147, *n.* 4).

[2] Anon. Val. ii. 49. We may
conjecture that Theoderic, who had
been *mag. mil. in praes.* in the East

since 483, was now appointed *mag.
mil. in praes.* in Italy, to replace
Odovacar.

[3] Schmidt, *op. cit.* i. 152.

before the last resistance of Odovacar was broken down and
Theoderic was completely master of Italy.[1]

It was perhaps where the Sontius and the Frigidus meet that
Theoderic found Odovacar in a carefully fortified camp, prepared
to oppose his entry into Venetia. He had considerable forces,
for besides his own army he had succeeded in enlisting foreign
help.[2] We are not told who his allies were ; we can only guess
that among them may have been the Burgundians, who, as we
know, helped him at a later stage. The battle was fought on
August 28 ; Odovacar was defeated and compelled to retreat.
His next line of defence was on the Athesis (Adige), and he
fortified himself in a camp close to Verona, with the river behind
him.[3] Here the second battle of the war was fought a month
later (about Sept. 29)[4] and resulted in a decisive victory for
Theoderic. The carnage of Odovacar's men is said to have been
immense ; but they fought desperately and the Ostrogothic
losses were severe ;[5] the river was fed with corpses. The king
himself fled to Ravenna. The greater part of the army, with
Tufa who held the highest command, surrendered to Theoderic,
who immediately proceeded to Milan.[6]

Northern Italy was now at the feet of the Goth ; Rome and
Sicily were prepared to submit, and it looked as if nothing
remained to complete the conquest but the capture of Ravenna.
But the treachery of Tufa changed the situation. Theoderic
imprudently trusted him, and sent him with his own troops and
a few distinguished Ostrogoths against Odovacar. At Faventia
(Faenza) he espoused again the cause of his old master and
handed over to him the Goths, who were put in irons.

---

[1] The chief sources are Ennodius
(*Panegyricus* and *Vita Epiphanii*)
and the chronicle known as Anonymus
Valesianus, Part 2. The most recent
editor, Cessi, has shown (correctly, I
think) that it falls into two sections
of different authorship (1 = § 36-§ 77 ;
2 = § 78-§ 96). They are contrasted
by the fact that the first is highly
favourable to Theoderic, and the
second undisguisedly censorious. The
first was written before his death, the
second probably between 527 and
534 (Cessi, clxvi. *sqq.*). The conjecture of some that Maximian,
archbishop of Ravenna, was the
author, will not hold.

[2] Ennodius, *Pan.* p. 271, says
rhetorically *universas nationes*, and
*tot reges quot sustinere generalitas
milites vix valeret.*

[3] Ennodius (*ib.* 272) suggests that
Odovacar chose the position to render
flight impossible for his army.

[4] Sept. 29 or 30 (Hodgkin) seems
implied by Anon. Val. 50.

[5] *Caedis enormitas*, Ennod. p. 273 ;
ceciderunt populi ab utraque parte,
Anon. Val. *ib.*

[6] Anon. Val. 51, where it is said that
Tufa was appointed *mag. mil.* by
Odovacar and his chief men. If so,
Odovacar had usurped a right which
belonged to the Emperor.

Theoderic made Ticinum (Pavia) his headquarters during the winter, and it is said that one of his motives for choosing this city was to cultivate the friendship of the old bishop Epiphanius, who had great influence with Odovacar. In the following year Odovacar was able to take the field again, to seize Cremona and Milan, and to blockade his adversary in Ticinum. At this juncture the Visigoths came to the help of the Ostrogoths and sent an army into Italy. The siege was raised and the decisive battle of the war was fought on the river Addua (Adda), in which Odovacar was utterly defeated (Aug. 11, A.D. 490). He fled for the second time to Ravenna. It was probably this victory that decided the Roman Senate to abandon the cause of Odovacar, and accept Theoderic. It made him master of Rome, southern Italy, and Sicily.

The agreement that Zeno made with Theoderic had been secret and unofficial. The Emperor did nothing directly to break off his relations with Odovacar.[1] But Odovacar seems some time before the battle of the Addua to have courted a formal rupture. He created his son Thela a Caesar, and this was equivalent to denouncing his subordination to the Emperor and declaring Italy independent.[2] He probably calculated that in the strained relations which then existed between the Italian Catholics and the East, on account of the ecclesiastical schism, the policy of cutting the rope which bound Italy to Constantinople would be welcomed at Rome and throughout the provinces. The senators may have been divided on this issue, but the battle of the Addua decided them as a body to " betray " Odovacar,[3] and before the end of the year Festus, the princeps of the Senate, went to Constantinople to announce the success of Theoderic, and to arrange the conditions of the new Italian government.

Theoderic confidently believed that his task was now virtually finished. But the cause of his thrice-defeated enemy was not yet hopelessly lost. Tufa was still at large with troops at his command ; and other unexpected difficulties beset the conqueror. The Burgundian king Gundobad sent an army into

---

[1] This is shown by the fact that the western consul of 490, Flavius Probus Faustus, assuredly nominated by Odovacar, was acknowledged in the East. Sundwall (*Abh.* 187 *sqq.*) is right, I think, in his treatment of the political situation in these years.

[2] Sundwall would place the elevation of Thela at the beginning of 490. The fact is recorded by John Ant. *fr.* 99, *De ins.*

[3] John Mal. xv. p. 383 πολεμήσας (Th.) αὐτῷ (Od.) κατὰ γνώμην προδοσίαν τῆς συγκλήτου 'Ρώμης.

North Italy and laid waste the country.[1] Theoderic had not
only to drive the invaders out, but he had also to protect Sicily
against the Vandals, who seized the opportunity of the war to
attempt to recover it. Their attempt was frustrated and they
were forced to surrender the fortress of Lilybaeum as well as
all their claims to the island.[2]

It seems to have been in the same year that Theoderic
resorted to a terrible measure for destroying the military garrisons
which held Italian towns for Odovacar. The Italian population
was generally favourable to the cause of Theoderic, and secret
orders were given to the citizens to slaughter the soldiers on a
pre-arranged day. The pious panegyrist, who exultantly, but
briefly, describes this measure and claims Providence as an
accomplice, designates it as a " sacrificial massacre " ; [3] and
Theoderic doubtless considered that the treachery of his enemy's
army in surrendering and then deserting justified an unusual
act of vengeance. The secret of the plot was well kept, and
it seems to have been punctually executed. The result was
equivalent to another victory in the field ; and nothing now
remained for Theoderic but to capture the last stronghold of
his adversary, the marsh city of Honorius.

The siege of Ravenna lasted for two years and a half. The
Gothic forces entrenched themselves in a camp in the Pine-woods
east of the city, but were not able entirely to prevent provisions
from reaching the city by sea. Yet the blockade was not in-
effective, for corn rose to a famine price. One attempt was
made by Odovacar to disperse the besiegers. He made a sortie
at night (July 10, A.D. 491) with a band of Herul warriors and

---

[1] This episode is very obscure.
The sources are Ennodius, *Pan.* p.
276, *Vit. Epiph.* 369 *sqq.* ; *Hist.
Misc.* xv. 16 (cp. Cassiodorus, *Var.*
12, 28). Ennodius gives no clear
chronological indications. Hodgkin
places the event in 490, before the
battle of the Addua ; but the circumstances seem to point to a later date,
for Theoderic was apparently besieged in Ticinum till the arrival of the
Visigoths and could not have dealt
with the Burgundians.   Schmidt's
chronology is preferable (*op. cit.* i.
156).   The motive for Gundobad's
interference is intelligible ; he may
well have feared the enclosure of his

kingdom between a Visigothic power
on one side and an Ostrogothic on
the other.

[2] Cassiodorus, *Chron.*, *sub a.* 491.
Theoderic had also trouble with the
Rugians who had joined his expedi-
tion.   Having plundered Ticinum
they went over to Tufa, but then
quarrelled with him and returned to
Theoderic.   Cp. Ennod. *Pan. ib., Vit.
Epiph.* 361 *sqq.*

[3] *Nex votiva*, Ennodius, *Pan.* p.
275. This atrocious act is not mentioned by Anon. Val. It is discussed
by Dahn, *Kön. der Germ.* ii. 80 ;
Hodgkin, iii. 226.

attacked the Gothic trenches. The conflict was obstinate, but
he was defeated.[1] Another year wore on, and it appeared that
the siege might last for ever unless the food of the garrison
could be completely cut off. Theoderic managed to procure a
fleet of warships—we are not told whether they were built for
the occasion,—and, making the Portus Leonis, about six miles
from Ravenna, his naval base, he was able to blockade the two
harbours of the city (August, A.D. 492).[2] Odovacar held out
for six months longer, but early in A.D. 493 negotiations,
conducted by the bishop of Ravenna, issued in a compact
between the two antagonists (February 25) that they should
rule Italy jointly.[3] Theoderic entered the city a week later
(March 5).

The only way in which the compact could have been carried
out would have been by a territorial division. But Theoderic
had no mind to share the peninsula with another king, and
there can hardly be a doubt that, when he swore to the treaty,
he had the full intention of breaking his oath. Odovacar's
days were numbered. Theoderic, a few days after his entry
into Ravenna, slew him with his own hand in the palace of
Lauretum (March 15). He alleged that his defeated rival was
plotting against him, but this probably was a mere pretext.[4]
" On the same day," adds the chronicler, " all Odovacar's
soldiers were slain wherever they could be found, and all
his kin." [5]

In three years and a half Theoderic had accomplished his
task. The reduction of Italy cost him four battles, a massacre,
and a long siege. His capital blunder had been to trust Tufa

---

[1] *Consularia Italica*, p. 318.

[2] These harbours are now dry land,
and are marked, one by the Church of
S. Apollinare in Classe, the other by
that of S. Maria in Porto fuori.

[3] Procopius, *B.G.* i. 1; John Ant.
fr. 99 (*De ins.* p. 140).

[4] Anon. Val. 54 *dum ei Odoachar
insidiaretur*. In the other sources
which depend on the Ravennate
Annals (Anon. Cuspin., Cont. Prosperi
Havn. and Agnellus) there is no
mention of a plot, nor in John Ant. ;
but see Cassiodorus, *Chron.* (*Odoacrem
molientem sibi insidias*), and Procopius
B.G. i. 1 ἐπιβουλῇ ἐς αὐτὸν χρώμενον.

The plot was evidently part of the
official Ostrogothic account.

[5] " On the same day " is not quite
accurate. See John Ant. *ib.*, who
records that Odovacar's son, " whom
he had proclaimed Caesar," was
exiled to Gaul, but returning to Italy
was put to death. Sunigilda,
Odovacar's wife, was starved to
death. It is true that his brother was
slain on the same day. The name of
the son was Thela (Anon. Val.), and
Ὀκλάν in John Ant. is probably an
error for Θήλαν (as Mommsen conjectured). The statement that all
Odovacar's soldiers were killed is
doubtless an exaggeration.

after the victory of Verona. We may be sure that throughout
the struggle he spared no pains to ingratiate himself in the
confidence of the Italian population. But when his rival had
fallen, and when he was at last securely established, Theoderic's
first measure was to issue an edict depriving of their civil rights
all those Italians who had not adhered to his cause. This harsh
and stupid policy, however, was not carried out, for the bishop
Epiphanius persuaded the king to revoke it and to promise that
there would be no executions.[1]

Two more services were to be rendered to his country by
Epiphanius before his death. The war had a disastrous effect
on Italian agriculture.[2] Liguria had been devastated by the
Burgundians; King Gundobad had carried thousands into
captivity, and no husbandmen were left to till the soil and tend
the vineyards. Theoderic was prepared to ransom the captives,
and he charged Epiphanius with the office of persuading the
Burgundian king to release them. The bishop, notwithstanding
his infirm age, undertook the cold and difficult journey over the
Alps in March (A.D. 494), and was received by Gundobad at Lyons.
To the arguments and prayers of the envoy, Gundobad, who was
an excellent speaker, replied with the frank and cynical assertion
that war permits and justifies everything which is unlawful in
peace. " War ignores the bridle of moderation which you, as
a Christian luminary, teach. It is a fixed principle with belli-
gerents that whatever is not lawful is lawful when they are
fighting. The object of war is to cut up your opponent's strength
at the roots." He went on to say that a peace had now been
concluded—it had been sealed by the betrothal of a daughter
of Theoderic to Gundobad's son Sigismund,—and that if the
bishop and his companions would return to their homes he
would consider what it were best to do in the interests of his
soul and his kingdom. Epiphanius had gained his cause.
Gundobad set free all prisoners who were in his own hands,
without charge, and those who were the slaves of private
persons were ransomed. More than six thousand were restored
to Italy.[3]

The last public act of Epiphanius was to induce Theoderic

---

[1] Ennodius, *ib.* 362 *sqq.*

[2] *Ib.* 366, *uides universa Italiae loca
originariis uiduata cultoribus.*

[3] *Ib.* 370 *sqq.*   Ennodius accompanied Epiphanius on this embassy.

to grant a reduction of the taxation of Liguria. " The wealth,"
he urged, " of a landed proprietor is the wealth of a good ruler." [1]
Theoderic remitted two-thirds of the taxes for A.D. 497. Epiphanius caught a chill in the cold marsh air of Ravenna and
died on his return home.[2] He had played a considerable and
beneficent part in Italian politics for nearly thirty years.

---

[1] *Boni imperatoris est possessoris opulentia, ib.* 379.
[2] A.D. 497, at the age of 58.

CHAPTER XIII

THE REIGN OF ANASTASIUS I. AND THE VICEROYALTY OF
THEODERIC

§ 1. *The Elevation of Anastasius* (A.D. 491) *and the Isaurian War*

On the evening of the day after Zeno's death, the Senate, the ministers, and Euphemius the Patriarch assembled in the palace, and a crowd of citizens and soldiers gathered in the Hippodrome (December 10, 491).[1] Ariadne,[2] wearing the Imperial cloak, and accompanied by the Grand Chamberlain Urbicius, the Master of Offices, the Castrensis, the Quaestor, and others, but not by the Patriarch, then entered the Kathisma of the Hippodrome to address the people. She was warmly acclaimed. " Long live the Augusta! Give the world an orthodox Emperor." Her speech was delivered by the Magister a libellis, who stood on the steps in front of the Kathisma. " Anticipating your request, we have commanded the illustrious ministers, the sacred Senate, with the approval of the brave armies, to select a Christian and Roman Emperor, endowed with every royal virtue, who is not the slave of money, and who is, so far as a man may be, free

---

[1] The following description is taken from the contemporary document preserved in Constantine Porph. *De cer.* i. 92. Cp. above, p. 316, *n.* 2.

[2] Ariadne is represented on five diptychs belonging to the later part of the reign : namely, those of (1) Clementinus, cons. 513, at Liverpool ; (2) Anthemius, cons. 515, one leaf, at Limoges ; (3) Anastasius, cons. 517, in Bibl. nationale ; (4) same, one leaf, at Verona ; (5) same, one leaf, at Berlin ; the other at South Kensington. With

the help of these, by comparing the character of the head-dress, Delbrück has identified three female marble heads found in Italy as Ariadne's : (1) the head in the Lateran Museum, vulgarly known as St. Helena, on a bust which does not belong to it ; (2) a head in the Palazzo dei Conservatori at Rome, found in 1887 near S. Maria dei Monti ; (3) a head found at Rome but now in the Louvre. He considers them as probably Byzantine work. See his *Porträts byz. Kais.*

from every human vice." *People* : " Ariadne Augusta, thou
conquerest ! O heavenly king, give the world a Basileus who
is not avaricious ! " *Ariadne* : " In order that the choice may
be pure and pleasing to God, we have commanded the ministers
and the Senate, the vote of the army concurring, to make the
election, in the presence of the Gospels, and in the presence of
the Patriarch, so that no one may be influenced by friendship
or enmity, or kinship, or any other private motive, but may
vote with his conscience clear. Therefore, as the matter is
weighty and concerns the welfare of the world, you must acquiesce
in a short delay, till the obsequies of Zeno, of pious memory,
have been duly performed, so that the election may not be
precipitate." *People* : " Long live the Augusta ! Cast out the
thieving Prefect of the City ! May all be well in thy time,
Augusta, if no foreigner is imposed on the Romans ! " [1] *Ariadne* :
" We have already anticipated your wishes. Before we came
in, we appointed the illustrious Julian to the office of Prefect."
People : " A good appointment ! Long live the Augusta."
After a few more words, Ariadne withdrew to the palace,[2] and
the ministers held a council in front of the Delphax to consult
about the election. Urbicius proposed that the choice should
be left to Ariadne, and the Patriarch, who was present, was
sent to summon her. She chose Anastasius, a silentiary, and
the Master of Offices sent the Counts of the Domestics and
Protectors to fetch Anastasius from his house. He was kept
that night in the Consistorium ; notices were issued for a
silentium [3] to be held on the morrow ; and the funeral of Zeno
was performed.

Anastasius was a remarkable and well-known figure in Constantinople. He held unorthodox opinions, partly due, perhaps,
to an Arian mother and a Manichaean uncle,[4] and he was
possessed by religious enthusiasm, which led him to attempt to
convert others to his own opinions. He did this in a curiously
public manner. Having placed a chair in the church of St.
Sophia, he used to attend the services with unfailing regularity

---

[1] Εἰ οὐδὲν ξένον αὔξει τὸ γένος τῶν
'Ρωμαίων. Probably the unpopular
Prefect of the City was an Isaurian.
[2] Εἰς τὸν Αὐγουστέα (so read for
αὐγουσταῖον), *De cer.* p. 421, l. 7.—The
delphax seems to have been in the
palace, but adjoining the Hippodrome.

Ebersolt (*Grand Palais*, p. 66) thinks
it was an isolated building. See
above, p. 395.
[3] Σιλέντιον καὶ κοβέντον (= *conventus*), see above, p. 24, *n.* 2.
[4] Theodore Lector, ii. 7 ; Theoph.
A.M. 5983.

and give private heterodox instruction to a select audience from his cathedra. By this conduct he offended the Patriarch Euphemius, who by Zeno's permission expelled him from the church and removed his chair of instruction ; [1] but he was well thought of by the general public on account of his piety and liberality. It even appears that he may have at one time dreamt of an ecclesiastical career, for he was proposed for the vacant see of Antioch.[2] The Patriarch was highly displeased at the Empress's choice of Anastasius, whom he stigmatised as unworthy to reign over Christians. His objections were overruled by the Senate and the Empress, but before he consented to take part in the coronation ceremony he insisted that the new Emperor should be required to sign a written declaration of orthodoxy. This was agreed to.

The officials dressed in white gathered in the Consistorium [3] on the following day (April 11), and were received ceremonially by Anastasius. The Patriarch was present, and now, if not before, he must have obtained the Emperor's signature to the declaration, which was lodged in the archives of St. Sophia under the care of the treasurer. Anastasius then left the Consistorium and ascended the steps of the portico [4] of the triklinos of the Nineteen Akkubita. Here at the request of the senators he took a public oath that he would distress no person against whom he had a grudge, and that he would govern conscientiously. Then he proceeded to the triklinos of the Hippodrome, put on the Imperial tunic, girdle, leggings, and red boots,[5] and entered the Kathisma, in front of which stood the troops, the standards lying on the ground. When he had been raised on a shield, and the torc placed on his head, the standards were raised, and he was acclaimed. Then he returned to the triklinos, when the Patriarch covered him with the Imperial cloak and crowned him. Reappearing in the Kathisma, he addressed the people, promising a donation of 5 nomismata and a pound of silver to

[1] See Theophanes, A.M. 5982.

[2] In 488, when Palladius was elected. Compare A. Rose, *Kaiser Anastasius I.* (p. 13), who translates συνεψηφίσθη in Theophanes rightly.

[3] Not, it is expressly noticed, in the Arma (p. 422). Αἱ πύλαι τοῦ ἄρματος are mentioned in a seventh-century document, Const. *De cer.* p. 628. Ebersolt (*Le Grand Palais*, 63) thinks

that the Arma was a dépôt of arms, near the Tribunal of the 19 Akkubita.

[4] The space in front of the Portico was the Tribunal of the 19 Akkubita. For details see Ebersolt, 62.

[5] Στιχάριν διβητήσιν αὐρόκλαβον, ζωνάριν, τουβία, καμπάγια βασιλικά (p. 423).

each soldier—the same amount which had been given by Leo I.
Among the enthusiastic acclamations with which he was greeted
we may notice, " Reign as thou hast lived ! Thou hast lived
piously ! reign piously ! Restore the army ! Reign like
Marcian ! " and " Cast out the informers ! "

A few weeks later Anastasius married Ariadne (May 20).
His accession was undoubtedly a welcome change to Byzantium.
He was a man of tall stature and remarkable for his fine eyes,
which differed in hue.[1] He is described as intelligent, well-
educated, gentle, and yet energetic, able to command his temper,
and generous in bestowing gifts.[2] A bishop of Rome wrote to
him, " I know that in private life you always strove after
piety." [3]

The first task imposed upon the new Emperor was to put an
end to the unpopular predominance of the Isaurians, which
had lasted for over twenty years. The choice of Anastasius
had disappointed and alarmed the Isaurians, who had looked
forward to the succession of Longinus. A riot in the Hippodrome
soon gave Anastasius a pretext for driving them out of the city.
During a spectacle at which the Emperor was present, the people
clamoured against Julian, the Prefect of the City, who had
done something which public opinion disapproved. Anastasius
ordered his guards to intimidate the rioters, who then set fire
to the Hippodrome, and pulled down and insulted the bronze
statues of the Emperors. Not a few were slain in the tumult.[4]
The Emperor found it politic to replace Julian by his own brother-
in-law Secundinus, but he attributed the disturbance to the
machinations of the Isaurians. He expelled them all from the
city. He forced Zeno's brother Longinus to take orders and
banished him to the Thebaid. He confiscated Zeno's property,
even selling his Imperial robes. He naturally withdrew the
large allowances which Zeno had made to his fellow-countrymen,
amounting to 1400 lbs. of gold.[5] A revolt had already broken
out in Isauria,[6] and the rebels were now reinforced by the exiles

[1] Hence called Dikoros. John
Mal. xvi. p. 392 describes his personal
appearance.
[2] John Lydus, *De mag.* i. 47.
Zacharias Myt., well disposed to him
as a Monophysite, says (vii. 1) " he
was powerful in aspect, vigorous in
mind, and a believer."
[3] Gelasius, in Mansi, xiii. 30.

[4] John Ant. *fr.* 100 (*De ins.* p. 141).
For date, Marcellinus, *sub* 491.
[5] John Ant. *ib.* p. 142. Evagrius
(iii. 35) says 5000 pounds. His
account of the war (from Eustathius ?)
is very inaccurate.
[6] John Ant. *ib.* p. 141 ἤδη ἀγγελ-
θείσης τῆς κατὰ [τὴν] χώραν αὐτῶν ἀπο-
στάσεως.

from Constantinople, among them Longinus of Kardala.[1] Their total force is said to have numbered 100,000, and included Romans as well as Isaurians. The leaders in command were Linginines and Athenodorus.[2] They were met at Cotyaeum in Phrygia by an Imperial army under John the Scythian and John the Hunchback,[3] and were completely defeated, Linginines being slain. This battle shattered the power of the Isaurians irretrievably. But the defeated leaders did not submit, and, just as in the case of the struggle between Illus and Zeno, warfare was carried on in the Isaurian mountains for several years before all the rebels were captured and killed.[4] It was not till A.D. 498 that the last of them, Longinus of Selinus, was taken and done to death by torture at Nicaea.

The Emperor settled large colonies of Isaurians in Thrace.[5] The brief ascendancy of this people was now over for ever, but it was not to be regretted, for it had served the purpose of averting the far more serious peril of a German ascendancy, which might have brought upon the East the fate of Italy. Henceforward the foreign elements in the army were kept well in control by a preponderance of native troops.

It was fortunate for the Empire that the Isaurian struggle was over before a serious war broke out with Persia, which will

[1] The ex-Master of Offices.

[2] A man of wealth. (In Evagrius he is called Theodorus.) There was also a second leader of the same name. Linginenes (John Ant.) = Λογγινίνης ὁ χωλός (John Mal. p. 393) = Libingis (Marcellinus). He was the *comes Isauriae*. Other prominent leaders were Conon, the fighting bishop, and Longinus of Selinus. The number of their forces is probably much exaggerated.

[3] John the Hunchback (ὁ κυρτός) was Master of Soldiers *in praesenti* (John Mal. p. 393) and we may suppose that John the Scythian was still Master of Soldiers in the East. (Otherwise Theophanes A.M. 5985.) Another general was the patrician Diogenianus, kinsman of the Empress (John Mal. *ib.*). Justin (afterwards Emperor) took part in this battle. The number of the army given by John Ant. (2000) is corrupt. There were both Hunnic and Gothic auxiliaries.

[4] The chronology has been elucidated by Brooks, *op. cit.* 235 *sqq.* :—

A.D. 493. Claudiopolis besieged by Diogenianus ; his army blockaded by the Isaurians, and relieved by John the Hunchback ; bishop Conon slain.

494–497. Isaurians hold out in their fortresses, and are furnished with provisions by Longinus of Selinus, from the seaport of Antioch (not far from Selinus).

497. Longinus of Kardala and Athenodorus captured by John the Scythian, and their heads exposed on poles at Constantinople (cp. Evagrius, *ib.* and Marcellinus, *sub* 497).

498. Longinus of Selinus and two others who were holding out at Antioch captured. (Evagrius, *ib.* and Marcellinus, *sub* 498.)

The year 497 was reckoned as the last of the war (cp. Marcellinus, and Theodore Lector, ii. 9).

The two Johns who conducted the war were rewarded by the consulship (498 and 499).

[5] Theoph. A.M. 5988. Cp. Procopius Gaz. *Panegyr.* c. 10.

be described in another chapter. But there was fighting from time to time with other enemies. The Blemyes troubled Egypt,[1] the Mazices attacked Libya,[2] the Tzani overran Pontus.[3] The Saracens of the desert invaded Euphratesia, Syria, and Palestine in 498, but were thoroughly defeated. Another raid four years later was followed by a treaty of peace.[4] In A.D. 515 Cappadocia was laid waste by an irruption of the Sabeiroi who came down from the region of the Caucasus.[5] But a more dangerous foe than any of these were the Bulgarians beyond the Danube.

After the disruption of the Hunnic empire in A.D. 454, a portion of the Huns had occupied the regions between the mouths of the Danube and the Dniester, where they were ruled by two of the sons of Attila. During the reign of Leo and Zeno, they sometimes raided the Roman provinces and some-times supplied auxiliaries to the Roman armies.[6] They were kept in check by the Ostrogothic federates, but the departure of Theoderic from Italy had left the field clear for their devastations in Thrace and Illyricum, which throughout the reign of Anastasius suffered severely. These Huns now come to be known under the

---

[1] See Joshua Styl. c. 20.

[2] John Ant. *fr.* 74 (*Exc. de virt. et vit.* p. 205). Probably during the Prefecture of Marinus, which seems to have begun in 512.

[3] Theodore Lector, ii. 19, perhaps in 505 or 506.

[4] (1) The Saracens of Hira, under Naman, who were vassals of Persia, overran the Euphratesian province and were defeated at Bithrapsas by Eugenius, the military commander in that province. Theoph. A.M. 5990. (2) The Saracens of Ghassan, of whom Harith was chief, overran Palestine and were defeated by Romanus, Dux of Palestine, *ib.* Cp. Evagr. iii. 36; John of Nikiu, c. 89. (3) In 502 Phoenicia, Syria, and Palestine were overrun again by the bands of Harith, who retreated so quickly that Romanus could not reach them. Theoph. A.M. 5994. For the treaty see *id.* A.M. 5995 and Nonnosus in *F.H.G.* iv. p. 179. For these Saracens see above, Chap. IV. § 1.

[5] Marcellinus, *sub a.*; John Ant. 103, *Exc. de ins.* p. 146 (from which it appears that this was a second

incursion); John Mal. xvi. p. 406. The Emperor then fortified the larger villages of Cappadocia, and remitted the taxes of the provinces which had suffered, for three years. The Sabeiroi were a Hunnic people (Οὖννοι Σαβήρ) who lived north of the Caucasus, near the Caspian. Cp. Procopius, *B.P.* ii. 29, *B.G.* iv. 3 and 11; above p. 115.

[6] For the relations of the Empire to the Huns see Priscus, *fr.* 18 *Exc. de leg. gent.* p. 587 (where we learn that they were ruled by two of Attila's sons, Dengisich and Ernach), and *fr.* 20; Marcellinus and *Chron. Pasch.*, *sub a.* 469, where the defeat of the Huns and the slaying of Dengisich, whose head was brought to Constantinople, by Anagastus, *mag. mil.* of Thrace, is recorded (cp. John Ant. *fr.* 89, *Exc. de ins.* 205, where the date is 468, but perhaps the same event is not referred to. The text seems to be corrupt). In 480 Zeno called on the Huns (Bulgarians) to support him against the Ostrogoths, John Ant. *fr.* 211. 4. We have seen that Huns were employed by Anastasius against the Isaurians (p. 433, *n.* 3).

name of Bulgarians.[1] But we must distinguish these Bulgarians, who were also known as Unogundurs, from two other great Hunnic hordes who will presently come upon the scene of history : the Kotrigurs who lived between the Dnieper and the Don, and the Utigurs who lived to the south of the Don. These latter peoples were to disappear in the course of time ; the Unogundurs were to be the founders of Bulgaria.

The Bulgarians were undoubtedly the foes who invaded the Empire in A.D. 493, defeated a Roman army, and killed Julian, Master of Soldiers.[2] The next recorded incursion was in A.D. 499, when Aristus, Master of Soldiers in Illyricum, lost more than a quarter of his army of 15,000 men in a battle against the Bulgarians.[3] Their depredations were repeated three years later (A.D. 502), and on this occasion their progress was unopposed.[4] Anastasius had determined to secure at least the immediate neighbourhood of the capital against the raids of the barbarians, and for this purpose he built a Long Wall,[5] the line of which can still be traced, from the Propontis to the Black Sea, at a distance of about 40 miles west of Constantinople. The southern extremity was just to the west of Selymbria, and the northern between Podima and Lake Derkos. The fortification consisted of a stone wall about 11 feet thick, without earthworks or ditch, and traces of round towers projecting about 31 feet in front

---

[1] See Marquart, *Die Chronologie der alttürkischen Inschriften*, p. 77. (Cp. also Zeuss, *Die Deutschen*, etc., 710 *sq.*) The national Bulgarian tradition began the series of their kings with Avitochol, who may well be identical with Attila, and the second is Irnik, in whom we can hardly refuse to recognise Ernach (Attila's favourite son). Cp. Bury, *The Chronological Cycle of the Bulgarians*, *B.Z.* xix. p. 135.

[2] Marcellinus, *sub a.* (*Scythico ferro*).

[3] *Id. sub a.* The scene of the battle was *iuxta Tzurtam fluvium.* The Roman army was accompanied by 520 wagons laden with arms. In the following year Anastasius encouraged the Illyrian troops by sending them a donative (*id. sub* 500).

[4] *Id. sub a.*, Theoph. A.M. 5994.

[5] The building is recorded in *Chron. Pasch.*, apparently under Indiction 15 = 3rd consulship of Anastasius, that

is A.D. 507. There are two entries under this year, (1) a demonstration in the circus, in favour of raising Areobindus to the throne ; (2) the building of the Wall. Now (1) is recorded much more fully by Marcellinus under Ind. 5 = cons. of Paulus and Muscianus = 512 ; and all the dates between Ind. 15 and Ind. 6 have fallen out of our text. Hence it was inferred by Ducange that these two entries belong to Ind. 5. Rightly, but there is a deeper error, due not to the scribe but to the chronicler. The building of the Wall is lauded in the *Panegyric* of Procopius (c. 21), and that oration cannot be dated later than 502 (as C. Kempen has shown in the Preface to his text). My view is that the date of the Wall is 497, which corresponded to an Ind. 5 ; and that the mistake arose through entering the notice under the Ind. 5 of the following cycle. Cp. above, p. 289, *n.* 2.

have been found. The length of the wall was 41 miles, and it corresponds roughly to the modern Turkish fortifications known as the Chatalja Lines, though the extreme points were further west.[1] We do not hear of another invasion till A.D. 517, when a host of barbarian cavalry laid waste Macedonia, Epirus, and Thessaly, penetrating as far as Thermopylae.[2] The consequences of the devastations of Germans and Huns for more than a hundred years was the depopulation of the Balkan provinces, the decline of its agricultural produce, and a considerable diminution of the Imperial revenue.[3]

§ 2. *Church Policy*

If the elevation of Anastasius had been popular, his popularity did not continue. His reign was frequently troubled by seditions in Constantinople, which were in many cases provoked by his ecclesiastical policy. His purpose was to maintain the Henotikon of Zeno ; his personal predilections were Monophysitic. We are ignorant of the cause of the sedition which broke out in A.D. 493, but it was evidently serious, as the statues of the Emperor and Empress were dragged through the city.[4] The relations between Anastasius and the Patriarch Euphemius, who had been opposed to his elevation, were strained. Euphemius was devoted to the doctrine of Chalcedon, and had been planning a campaign against the Patriarch of Alexandria, first Peter, and then his successor Athanasius, both of whom anathematised the Council of Chalcedon and the Tome of Leo. Without the Emperor's knowledge he wrote a letter to Felix, the bishop of Rome, invoking his aid. The Patriarchs of Alexandria and Jerusalem informed

---

[1] This account of the Wall is taken from C. Schuchhardt, *Die Anastasius Mauer bei Constantinopel und die Dobrudscha-Wälle*, in the *Jahrbuch des k. d. arch. Instituts*, xvi. 107 *sqq.* (1901). The dimensions given by Evagrius, iii. 38, and in Suidas (whose source is doubtless John Ant.), *sub* Ἀναστάσιος and *sub* Τεῖχος disagree with each other, and are all inaccurate. The settlements of Heruls " in the lands and cities of the Romans " recorded by Marcellinus, *sub* 512, were evidently designed to strengthen the depopulated lands of the Illyrian peninsula.

[2] Marcellinus, *sub a.*, *Getae equites*.

I suspect that these are Bulgarians, whom elsewhere this chronicler calls Bulgares. Otherwise they must be Slavs, who are often designated as *Getae*. A thousand pounds of gold was sent to redeem the captives, but it was insufficient, and many were put to death.

[3] Cp. the undated law of Anastasius in *C.J.* x. 27. 2, 10 ἐν Θρᾴκῃ γὰρ ἐπειδὴ οὐκ εἰς ὁλόκληρον εἰσφέρεται τὰ δημόσια διὰ τὸ προφάσει τῶν βαρβαρικῶν ἐφόδων ἐλαττωθῆναι τοὺς γεωργούς, καὶ μὴ ἀρκεῖν τὴν ἐν εἴδεσι συντέλειαν τοῖς κατ' αὐτὴν ἱδρυμένοις στρατιώταις.

[4] Marcellinus, *sub a.*

the Emperor that Euphemius was a heretic ;[1] and a council was
held at Constantinople which confirmed the Henotikon and
deposed Euphemius (A.D. 496).[2] This led to a disturbance, and
the people, rushing to the Hippodrome, supplicated the Emperor
in vain to restore the Patriarch. Macedonius was appointed
to the Patriarchal throne. He seems to have held much the
same opinions as Euphemius, but he did not scruple to sign the
Henotikon.[3]

A serious riot in the Hippodrome occurred in A.D. 498. The
Prefect of the City had thrown into prison some members of the
Green faction for the not uncommon offence of stone-throwing.
The Greens demanded their release, and when the Emperor
summoned the Excubitors to suppress them, there was a great
uproar. Stones were thrown at the Kathisma, and one of these
nearly hit Anastasius. The man who had thrown it was hewn
in pieces by the Excubitors, and then the Greens set fire to the
Bronze Gate of the Hippodrome. The fire spread not only to
the Kathisma but also, in the other direction, to the Forum of
Constantine. Many offenders were punished, but a new Prefect,
Plato, was appointed.[4]

The pagan festival of the Brytae, which was celebrated with
dancing,[5] repeatedly caused sanguinary riots among the demes,

---

[1] That is, a Nestorian.

[2] Zacharias Myt. vii. 1. A copy
of the letter to Felix was procured
by Anastasius through his apocri-
siarius at Rome and was sent to the
Emperor. Other than purely ecclesiastical reasons entered into the
quarrel between Anastasius and Euphemius. Anastasius suspected the
Patriarch of secret intrigues with
the Isaurian leaders. See Theodore
Lector, ii. 9-12 (who records an
attempt on the Patriarch's life in
St. Sophia). The same writer says
that the Emperor endeavoured to
recover from Euphemius the signed
declaration of orthodoxy which he
had made at his coronation, *ib.* 8.
Euphemius was banished to Euchaita.

[3] Theodore, ii. 13. The Monophysite
Zacharias (vii. 7) says that Macedonius
" omitted no intrigue of heart [*sic*]
to conceal his opinions." He had
been a monk of the Akoimetoi, " of
whom there were about one thousand
and who lived luxuriously in baths
and in other bodily indulgences . . .

and were adorned with the semblance
of chastity, but were inwardly like
whited sepulchres, full of all uncleanness. . . . And he used to celebrate
the memory of Nestorius every year,
and they used to celebrate it with
him." Perhaps there was some
foundation for this attack ; the
Akoimetoi may have made a habit of
personal cleanliness. Orthodox writers
describe Macedonius as an ascetic.

[4] John Mal. xvi. p. 394 (and
Excerpta de ins. p. 168) = *Chron.
Pasch. sub a.* The deposed Prefect
was perhaps Secundinus. The succession of Prefects of the City in this
reign seems to have been : Julianus
491 ; Secundinus 491 ; Plato 498 ;
Helias (John Ant. *fr.* 103, p. 142) ;
Constantius Tzurukkas (already in
501, Marcellinus, *sub a.*) ; Plato, 512
[Marcellinus, *sub a.*].

[5] John Ant. *ib.* Suidas *sub
Maïoumâs*, a passage which does not
prove that the Maïumas (in May) was
identical with the Brytae. Combining
Marcellinus with Joshua Styl. p. 35,

and in one of these disturbances (A.D. 501) a bastard son of the Emperor was killed, and the Emperor forbade its celebration for the future throughout the Empire, thereby " depriving the cities of the most beautiful dancing." He had already abolished the practice of contests with wild beasts (A.D. 499).[1]

In A.D. 511 the Patriarch Macedonius, who no longer concealed his adhesion to the Council of Chalcedon, met the same fate as his predecessors. The Monophysites represented him as plotting against the Emperor, while the orthodox asserted that he was deposed because he declined to give up the profession of orthodoxy signed by the Emperor at his coronation. In any case, Anastasius had begun to move in the Monophysitic direction so far as to abandon the neutral spirit of the Henotikon. The position of Macedonius was not strong, because by signing the Henotikon he had alienated the orthodox monks of the capital. Seeking to win back their confidence he did not scruple to denounce Anastasius as a Manichean. He was deposed by a local council in August, A.D. 511, was forced to surrender the document with the Emperor's signature, and was banished to Euchaita. Timothy, an undisguised Monophysite, was elected in his stead.

A distinguished Monophysite monk, Severus of Sozopolis, had, a few years before, arrived at Constantinople with a company of two hundred fellow-heretics and had been received with honour by Anastasius.[2] He caused scandal and disturbances by holding services in which the Trisagion (" Holy, holy, holy, Lord God of Hosts ") was chanted with the Monophysitic addition

---

we may infer that the date of the second riot, when Constantius was Prefect, was in 501, and the previous riot under Helias (John Ant.) in 500 (or 499). The edict prohibiting the feast was in 502 (Joshua). See further, John Mal. *ib.* The date of Theophanes, A.D. 504-505, must be rejected. More than 3000 were killed, acc. to Marcellinus, *sub* 501. Procopius Gaz. *Pan.* 16 probably refers to the licentiousness of the Brytae.—On the celebration of the festival of Brumalia (Nov. 24–Dec. 17) in the fifth and sixth centuries—notwithstanding its condemnation by the Church, John Lydus, *De mens.* iv. § 158—see J. R. Crawfurd, *De Bruma et Brumalibus festis*, in *B.Z.* xxiii.

375 *sqq.*

[1] Priscian, *Pan.* 223 *sqq.*; Procopius Gaz. *Pan.* 15.

[2] In A.D. 508. Severus was brought up as a pagan, studied rhetoric at Alexandria and law at Berytus. He was baptized shortly before 490, and soon afterwards became a monk in the monastery of Peter the Iberian not far from Gaza. The cause of his visit to Constantinople was the persecution of Monophysite monks in Palestine by one Nephalius. He remained in the capital for three years. For his life we have two Syriac biographies by Zacharias and John ; and some of his letters have been edited and translated by Brooks (see Bibliography).

"Who wast crucified for us," which had been introduced at
Antioch fifty years before. The new Patriarch Timothy inter-
polated this heretical phrase into the liturgy in St. Sophia.
Anastasius, supported by the counsels of Marinus, Praetorian
Prefect of the East,[1] determined to defy the religious sentiment
of the people of Byzantium. On Sunday, Nov. 4 (A.D. 512),[2]
the orthodox multitude in the Church drowned with their shouts
the chanting of the heretical priests, and there was such a disturbance that Marinus and Plato, the Prefect of the City, interfered with armed force. Some were slain and others imprisoned.
On the following day there was a more sanguinary conflict in
the court of a church, and on Tuesday (Nov. 6) the orthodox
congregated and formed a camp in the Forum of Constantine.
The rioting now assumed the dimensions of a revolt. The
general Areobindus was the husband of Juliana Anicia, who was
the granddaughter of Valentinian III.,[3] and thus a member of
the Theodosian house. The people proclaimed him Emperor
and pulled down the statues of Anastasius. Celer, the Master
of Offices, and Patricius, Master of Soldiers *in praesenti*, who were
sent to pacify them, were driven off with showers of stones;
the house of Marinus was burnt. On the next day the Emperor
sent heralds to the people proclaiming that he was ready to
abdicate, and appeared in the Kathisma of the Hippodrome
without his crown. He was greeted with demands that Marinus
and Plato should be thrown to the beasts. But in some extraordinary way he succeeded in calming the tumult. The crowd
begged him to put on his crown and promised good behaviour.

It was unfortunate for the peace of the East that Anastasius
was not indifferent in questions of religious doctrine. His
reason prompted him to enforce the Henotikon and to lean to
neither party in his ecclesiastical measures. He honestly
endeavoured to carry out this policy up to the year A.D. 511–512,
but he was growing old, and, despairing of maintaining peace

[1] See Zacharias Myt. vii. 9.

[2] The date depends on Marcellinus,
sub a., whose account is the fullest.
It is to be supplemented by *Chron.
Pasch.*, under the wrong year 507, and
Evagrius, iii. 44.

[3] Daughter of Placidia and Olybrius.
There is a remarkable portrait of the
princess (who died in 527) in the
Vienna MS. of the work of Dioscorides
on plants, which was written for her.
She sits on a throne between the figures
of Megalopsychia and Phronesis.
The desire of the foundress (Πόθος
τῆς φιλοκτίστου) offers her the book,
and the gratitude of the Arts kneels
below her. See Kraus, *Gesch. d. christl.
Kunst*, i. 460 ; Dalton, *Byz. Art*, 460.

between the extreme parties, he threw himself into the arms of his Monophysite friends. It is to be observed that neither all the orthodox nor all the Monophysites demanded at this time a repudiation of the Henotikon ; for the Monophysites could argue that it condemned the doctrines of Chalcedon, the orthodox that it did not.[1] The middle party, of whom Flavian of Antioch was the most prominent, sought to act more or less in the true spirit of the act of Zeno and leave the doctrine of Chalcedon severely alone. In the capital the difficulty of preserving peace was aggravated by the agitation of the Sleepless Monks of the monastery of Studion, who were uncompromising opponents of the Henotikon, and remained in communion with the Church of Rome. Some vain attempts had been made to end the schism. Pope Anastasius II., in his brief pontificate,[2] desired to conclude it by a concession which was almost equivalent to a partial acceptance of the Henotikon. He sent to Constantinople two bishops proposing to withdraw the demand of his predecessors that the name of Acacius should be expunged from the roll of Patriarchs. On account of this policy he is one of the Popes for whom the Catholic Church has little good to say, and Dante found for him a suitable place in hell.[3] His successors obstinately refused to heal the breach.[4]

Far more significant than the deposition of Macedonius, who had never approved of the Imperial policy, was the deposition of the Patriarch of Antioch, the moderate Flavian,[5] and the election of the Pisidian Severus, whom we have already met as the leading theologian of the Monophysites and bitter foe of Chalcedon (A.D. 512).[6] On the occasion of his enthronement at Antioch, Severus anathematised the doctrinal decisions of that Council, and he determined to make his own Patriarchate as

---

[1] Those Monophysites who would not accept the Henotikon were known as the Akephaloi.

[2] A.D. 496–498.

[3] *Inferno*, xi. 8.

[4] See below, p. 464.

[5] At a synod held at Antioch. Zach. Myt. vii. 10.

[6] The other most prominent Monophysite leader was Xenaias, bishop of Hierapolis, at whose instance a synod was held at Sidon in A.D. 512. Flavian's moderate policy at this

synod enabled Xenaias to report to Anastasius that he was a heretic, and his ejection (not without violence) followed. Zach. Myt. vii. 10. Severus was " a confidant and friend " of Probus, the nephew of Anastasius (*ib.*). The influence of his nephew may well have counted for something in the old Emperor's change of policy ; and the influence of Marinus counted too. If (see below, p. 470) I am right in placing the elevation of Marinus to the Pr. Prefecture in A.D. 512, this too may have some significance.

Monophysitic as that of Egypt. A synod at Tyre (A.D. 513)[1] condemned Chalcedon and confirmed the Henotikon, which was interpreted in the Monophysite sense. The triumphant party were ready for extreme measures, and the Emperor had to warn the Duke of Phoenicia Libanensis that he would countenance no bloodshed in dealing with recalcitrant bishops. But the general proceedings of the Monophysites, under the guidance of Severus, during the next few years, seem to have amounted to a persecution.

The reply to the revolution in the Emperor's policy was soon to come in the shape of a rebellion in Thrace.[2]

§ 3. *Financial Policy*

Anastasius was a conscientious ruler, and one of the great merits of his government was the personal attention which he paid to the control of the finances. A civil servant, who belonged to the bureau of the Praetorian Prefect, and began his career in this reign, asserts that the careful economy of Anastasius and his strictures in supervising the details of the budget saved the State, which ever since the costly expedition of Leo I. against the Vandals had been on the brink of financial ruin.[3]

The economy of the Emperor enabled him to abolish the tax on receipts, known as the Chrysargyron, which weighed heavily on the poorest classes of the population.[4] This act (May, A.D. 498) earned for him particular glory and popularity. The reception of the edict in the city of Edessa illustrates the universal joy which the measure evoked. " The whole city rejoiced, and they all put on white garments, both small and great, and carried lighted tapers and censers full of burning incense," and praising the Emperor went to a church and celebrated the eucharist. They kept a merry festival during the whole week and resolved to celebrate this festival every year.[5]

---

[1] *Op. cit.* vii. 12.
[2] See below, § 4.
[3] John Lydus, *De mag.* iii. 45.
[4] *C.J.* xi. 1; Procopius Gaz. *Paneg.* 13; Priscian, *Pan.* 149 *sqq.* (*argenti relevans atque auri pondere mundum*); Theodore Lector, ii. 53. The hardship of the tax is described by Zosimus, ii. 38. For date cp. Brooks, *C. Med. H.* i. 484; Stein,

in *Hermes*, lii. 578.
[5] Joshua Styl. xxxi. p. 22. The amount raised by the tax at Edessa (every four years) was 140 lbs. of gold. Anastasius is said to have burned all the documents relating to the collection of this tax, so as to place a difficulty in the way of its revival. See Procopius and Priscian, *locc. citt.*, and Evagrius, iii. 39, where it is

The consequent loss of revenue suffered by the fisc was made good by an equivalent contribution from the revenue of the Private Estates.[1] The Imperial Estates seem to have received considerable additions in this reign, principally from the confiscation of the property of Zeno and the Isaurian rebels. In consequence of this increase, Anastasius found it expedient to institute a new finance minister, with similar functions to those of the Count of the Private Estates, who was to administer the recently acquired domains and all that should in future be acquired by the crown. This minister was designated by the title of Count of the Patrimony.[2]

Perhaps the most important financial innovation introduced by Anastasius was in the method of collecting the *annona*. He relieved the town corporations of the responsibility for this troublesome task,[3] and assigned it to officials named *vindices*, who were probably appointed by the Praetorian Prefect. The appointments seem to have been given by auction to those who promised most,[4] so that this reform was equivalent to a revival of the old system of farming the revenue. Opinion was divided as to the effects of this change. On one hand it was said that the result was to impoverish the provinces ;[5] on the other, that it was a great relief to the farmers.[6] One of the abuses which the measure may have been intended to remove was the unfair advantage enjoyed by the richer and more influential landowners, whom the curial bodies were afraid to offend. Under the new system, however, inequality of treatment could

---

mentioned that the Emperor consulted the Senate. According to Cedrenus (that is, John Skylitzes, whom he transcribed), the hardships of the tax were brought to the attention of Anastasius by a deputation of monks from Jerusalem, and by a tragedy composed by Timotheus of Gaza (i. p. 627). Timotheus was a grammarian, and he wrote zoological books on Indian animals, of ǀwhich excerpts are preserved (see Krumbacher, *Gesch. d. byz. litt.* pp. 631, 633, 582). It is to be noted that the abolition of the Chrysargyron gave special satisfaction to the Church, because the tax, which fell on the earnings of prostitutes, implicitly gave a legal recognition to vice (see Evagr. *ib.*).

[1] Ἐκ τῶν ἰδίων αὐτοῦ, John Mal. xvi. p. 398.

[2] *C.J.* i. 34. 1. The Greek title was κόμης τῆς ἰδικῆς κτήσεως (in this constitution the *Comes rer. priv.* is called κόμης τῆς ἰδικῆς περιουσίας).

[3] See above, p. 59. The chief source is John Lydus, iii. 46, 49. Cp. John Mal. p. 400 ; Evagr. iii. 42.

[4] Lydus, iii. 49.

[5] So Lydus (*ib.*), who belonged to the anti-Marinus faction. Evagrius, *ib.*, says ὅθεν κατὰ πολὺ οἵ τε φόροι διερρύησαν τά τε ἄνθη τῶν πόλεων διέπεσεν.

[6] Priscian, *Pan.* 193-195 :

agricolas miserans dispendia saeva relaxas ;
curia perversis nam cessat moribus omnis,
nec licet iniustis solito contemnere leges.

be secured in another way, by bribing the *vindices*. Anastasius hoped perhaps to mitigate this danger by strengthening the hands of the *defensores* and bishops, who were expected to protect the rights of subjects against official oppression. Those who condemned the new policy said that the *vindices* treated the cities like hostile communities.[1]

The originator of this revolutionary measure was an able financier of Syrian birth, named Marinus, who seems to have been the most trusted adviser of Anastasius, throughout the latter part of his reign. He began his career as a financial clerk under the Count of the East,[2] and attained to the post of head of the tax department of the Praetorian Prefect.[3] In this capacity he gained the ear of the Emperor, and ultimately was elevated to the Praetorian Prefecture. The reform was probably carried out during his tenure of that post, but the date and duration of his Prefecture are a little uncertain.[4] The immediate result of the new method of collecting the taxes was a considerable increase of the revenue and also of the private income of the Praetorian Prefect.[5]

It is not clear whether the reform of Marinus meant that the actual tax-collectors, who had hitherto been members of the town communities, were replaced by government officials. It seems more probable that the change consisted in placing the local collectors under direct government control. They received their instructions from the vindex, and the provincial governor, who remained responsible for the taxation of the province, communicated with the vindex and not with the corporation of decurions. The new system was not permanent. Though it was not completely done away with, it was considerably modified in the following reigns. In some places the vindex survived,

---

[1] John Lydus, *ib.*

[2] John Lydus, iii. 36. He was a scriniarius (or logothete, John Mal. xvi. 400 ; cp. Stein, *Studien*, p. 149). The *scriniarii* were clerks who kept the tax accounts. Originally, according to Lydus, they had no recognised place in the hierarchy of the civil service. They were incorporated in it by Theodosius the Great, and towards the end of the fifth century they became a very important body. The *rationales* of the financial ministries were recruited from them ; and

scriniarii sometimes rose to be Praetorian Prefects. John Lydus looked down upon them as mere accountants. They had not the liberal education of the Scholastici. Marinus is highly praised by his fellow heretic Zacharias of Mytilene (vii. 9).

[3] John Mal. xvi. 400.

[4] See Appendix to this chapter.

[5] John Lydus, iii. 49 γίνεται μὲν πολύχρυσος εἴπερ τις ἄλλος ὁ βασιλεὺς καὶ μετ' αὐτὸν ὁ Μαρῖνος καὶ ὅσοι Μαρινιῶντες ἁπλῶς.

but in most of the provinces he disappeared, and there was probably a return to the old methods.[1]

Other revenue questions occupied the anxious attention of the government at this period. The practice of converting the annona into money payments seems to have been considerably enlarged.[2] But the problem of sterile lands appears now· to have become more acute than ever. This grave difficulty perpetually solicited the care and defied the statesmanship of the Imperial government. Farms were constantly falling out of cultivation through the impoverishment of their owners or the deficiency of labour. The heavy public burdens, aggravated by the oppression of officials, reduced many of the small struggling farmers to bankruptcy. This would have meant a considerable loss to the revenue, in the natural course of things, and the problem for the government was to avoid this loss by making others suffer for the unfortunate defaulters. For this purpose the small properties of the free farmers of a commune were regarded as a fiscal unity, liable for the total sum of the fiscal assessments of its members ; [3] and when for any cause one property ceased to be solvent, the others were required to make good the deficiency. This addition to their proper contributions was known as an *epibole*.[4] In the case of larger estates, which were not included in a commune, if one part became unproductive, the whole estate remained liable for the tax as originally estimated.[5] But a difficulty arose when parts of such an estate were sold or when it was divided among several heirs. Notwithstanding the division it was still treated as a fiscal unity, and if one of the proprietors became insolvent the government was determined that the deficiency should be made good by other portions of the original estate.[6] But there was a considerable difference of opinion as to the apportionment of the epibole in such a

---

[1] The local survival of the vindex is shown by Justinian, *Nov.* 128 §§ 5 and 8; 38 τοὺς ὀλεθρίους μισθωτὰς οὓς δὴ βίνδικας καλοῦσι. There is clear evidence in the *Novels* of Justinian that the local authorities shared in the collection of the taxes. Probably the system differed in different provinces. The term πολιτευόμενοι refers to municipal authorities. Cp. *Nov.* 130 § 3, p. 263 ; 128 § 5 εἴτε ἄρχοντες εἴτε πολιτευόμενοι, εἴτε ἐξάκτορες εἴτε βίνδικες εἴτε κανονικάριοι

[2] (special emissaries sent by the Praetorian Prefect) ; *ib.* § 16 σιτῶναι and διοικηταί are appointed by the municipalities.

[2] This seems to be the meaning of the χρυσοτέλεια τῶν ἰούγων introduced by Anastasius, John Mal. xvi. 394 ; Evagrius, iii. 42. Cp. *C.J.* x. 27. 2.

[3] These lands were hence called ὁμόκηνσα.

[4] *Adiectio sterilium.*

[5] Called ὁμόδουλα.

[6] *C. Th.* xiii. 11. 9.

case. Should the whole estate be liable, or should the sterile property be annexed, along with its obligations, to the productive land in its immediate neighbourhood ? The former solution would have assimilated the treatment of these estates to that of the lands of the communes. It is not clear what method was applied before the sixth century. We only know that the epibole in the two cases was not the same. In the reign of Anastasius an attempt seems to have been made to break down the distinction, and to have been successfully opposed by the Praetorian Prefect Zoticus (A.D. 511–512).[1] Perhaps he defined the general method of dealing with sterile lands which was developed in the following reign by the Praetorian Prefect Demosthenes (A.D. 520–524).[2] The most important points in this ruling were, that the provincial governor was empowered to decide in each case on whom the epibole should fall; that the unproductive land, with all that appertained to it, including the colons, should be transferred to those who were made liable for its burdens ; and that this liability should be determined not by proximity, but by the history of the property.

[1] Justinian, *Nov.* 168, seems to be a fragment of a praetorian edict of Zoticus. It lays down that the ἐπιβολή only concerns property included in the census, and therefore does not apply to houses (in towns) as only farms and agricultural lands (χωρία) are included in the census. For the tendency to assimilate ὁμόκηνσα and ὁμόδουλα see an additional fragment in Kroll's note *ad loc.* A law of Anastasius lays down that the lands of the Imperial patrimony are not to be treated on the same principle as ὁμόκηνσα, which must mean that they are to be treated as ὁμόδουλα (*C.J.* i. 34. 2).

[2] The edict of Demosthenes, addressed to the governor of Lydia, περὶ ἀπόρων ἐπιβολῆς, is extant in the collection of Justinian's *Novels* (166). The general tenor of the edict is : If a farm or a whole complex of property is sold by its proprietor (A), or on his death passes either to his children or to heirs who are outsiders (B) ; and if the purchasers or heirs should similarly alienate ; and if the alienated land should become unproductive, then the ἐπιβολή is to fall on the property of the last purchaser or inheritor (C), not on all those who formerly possessed it. But if the last acquirer (C) is insolvent, then the burden must fall on those from whom he immediately acquired it (B). If they are insolvent, then the epibole shall be imposed on the original proprietor (A). Those on whom the epibole falls, whether few or many, shall bear it in proportion to the value of their fertile possessions. It seems evident that this edict was provoked by a particular case which the governor of Lydia referred to the Prefect. On the subject of the ἐπιβολή, see Zacharia, *Gesch. d. gr.-röm. Rechts,* ed. 3, 228 *sqq.* ; Monnier, *Études de droit byzantin,* 345 *sqq.,* 514 *sqq.,* 642 *sqq.* ; Panchenko, *O tainoi istorii Prokopiia,* 138 *sqq.* I think we may fairly infer from the evidence (see last note) that the principle which governed the epibole in the case of ὁμόκηνσα was that of proximity. See further Justinian, *Nov.* 128 §§ 7, 8. A remission of the epibole is mentioned in Joshua Stylites, c. 39, where Wright's translation has erroneously " two folles."

The result of the economical policy of Anastasius and his financial reforms was that he not only saved the State from the bankruptcy which had threatened it, but, at his death, left in the treasury what in those days was a large reserve, amounting to 320,000 pounds of gold (about £14,590,000).[1] His strict control of expenditure made him extremely unpopular with the official classes whose pockets suffered, and his saving policy, which probably included a great reduction of the expenses of the court, did not endear him to the nobles and ladies accustomed to the pageants and pleasures of Byzantine festivals. He was accused of avarice and stinginess, vices for which the men of Dyrrhachium, his native place, had a bad repute.[2] This accusation was unjust, and can be refuted by the admissions of one of the writers who report it.[3] Personally Anastasius was generous and open-handed ; he seldom sent any petitioners empty away ; and several instances of his liberality to individuals are recorded. His "parsimonious resourcefulness," stigmatised by his successor Justin,[4] was entirely in the interests of the State ; and the general tenor of his policy was to finance the Empire by economy in expenditure, and not to increase, but rather to reduce, the public burdens.[5] This feature of his administration corresponded to his character. Though resolute and energetic, he was distinguished, like Nerva, by his mildness.

> Et mitem Nervam lenissima pectora vincunt.[6]

If he had not held heretical opinions, historians would have had little but praise for the Emperor Anastasius.

It remains to mention his useful monetary reform. For a long time past the general public had suffered great inconvenience through the bad quality of the copper money in circulation. It consisted of coins of very small denomination with no marks of value. Anastasius introduced a large copper follis, equivalent

---

[1] Procopius, *H.A.* 19, where he is described as " the most provident and economical of all Emperors."

[2] John Lydus, *De mag.* iii. 46, quotes malicious verses which were placed on an iron statue of the Emperor in the Hippodrome.

[3] *Ib.* 47 μεγαλόδωρος.

[4] *C.J.* ii. 7. 25 *parca posterioris subtilitas principis.*

[5] His remission of arrears is recorded by John Ant. *fr.* 100 (*Exc. de ins.* p. 141), where it is also implied that confiscations of property were infrequent during his reign. The land taxes were remitted constantly in Mesopotamia during the Persian war (Joshua Styl. pp. 55, 63, 71, 75).

[6] Priscian, *Pan.* 47. John Lydus, who did not approve of his policy in some respects, describes him as ἐπιεικής, κρείττων ὀργῆς, ἀγαθός (iii. 47).

to forty sesterces, with smaller coins of the value of twenty, ten, and five sesterces, each clearly marked by a letter showing the value.[1] This mintage was a great practical benefit, and must have been highly appreciated by the poorer citizens.

He was always ready to spend money on useful public works. Besides the Long Wall of Thrace, he constructed a canal in Bithynia connecting the Gulf of Nicomedia with Lake Sophon, and thus realised an old project of the younger Pliny. Liberal sums were always forthcoming to repair injuries caused by war, to assist towns which were damaged by earthquake, to cleanse harbours, to build aqueducts or baths.[2]

§ 4. The Rebellion of Vitalian [3] and the Death of Anastasius (A.D. 513-518)

Partly through his religious policy and partly through his public economy Anastasius failed to secure the goodwill of various classes of his subjects ; his unpopularity increased in the later years of his reign ; and it was not surprising that an ambitious soldier should conceive the hope of dethroning him. Vitalian held the post of Count of the Federates, who were stationed in Thrace, and these troops now consisted chiefly of

[1] M, K, I, and E. See Wroth, *Imperial Byz. Coins*, I. xiii., xiv. ; lxxviii.-ix. This type of bronze coinage remained current till the last quarter of the seventh century. The reform is noted in two texts, (1) the difficult and much discussed passage in Marcellinus, *Chron.*, *sub* 498, and (2) John Mal. xvi. p. 400, which has been generally overlooked. From Malalas we learn that John the Paphlagonian, *comes s. larg.*, carried out the reform : ἅπαν τὸ προχωρὸν κέρμα τὸ λεπτὸν ἐποίησε φολλερά προχωρεῖν εἰς πᾶσαν τὴν Ῥωμαικὴν κατάστασιν ἕκτοτε. For προχωρὸν we should, I think, read προχωροῦν (an inspection of the unique Oxford MS. suggests that this was originally written. πρόχειρον is another possibility). Perhaps a participle has fallen out. But the passage means, " He converted all the small copper currency into *follera* which circulated henceforward in the Empire." Marcellinus says that the Romans called the new coins *Terentiani*, the Greeks

follares—which corresponds to φολλερά. The following table will show the relations of the chief gold, silver, and copper coins :

1 nomisma, or solidus (gold) = 12 miliaresia (silver).
1 milaresion = 2 keratia (siliquae) silver.
1 keration = 6 M folles or follera (copper).
1 M follis = 2 K coins (oboloi).
1 K coin = 2 I coins (dekanumia).
1 I coin = 2 E coins (pentanumia).

There were two small gold coins, the semissis = ½ nomisma and the tremissis = ⅓ nomisma. Roughly speaking the miliaresion corresponds to our shilling, the keration to sixpence, the follis to a penny.

[2] Cp. John Mal. xvi. p. 409 ; John Lydus, iii. 47 ; Joshua Styl. p. 69. For the canal see Anna Comnena, x. 5.

[3] The best and fullest source is John of Antioch, *fr.* 103 (*Exc. de ins.* p. 143 *sqq.*) ; to be supplemented by John Malalas, xvi. 402 *sqq.* ; .Marcellinus, *Chron.*, *sub* 514, 515 ; Evagrius, iii. 43 ; Theophanes, A.M. 6005, 6006, 6007.

Bulgarians.[1] The immediate pretext for his revolt was the conduct of Hypatius, the Master of Soldiers in Thrace, whom the Federates regarded as responsible for depriving them of the provisions to which they were entitled. But Vitalian claimed to be more than merely the leader of aggrieved soldiers.[2] He pretended to represent the religious discontent, to voice orthodox indignation at the new form of the *Trisagion*, and to champion the cause of the deposed Patriarch Flavian who was his personal friend, and the deposed Patriarch Macedonius. Vitalian was a man of exceptionally small stature and afflicted with a stammer ; his enemies acknowledged his courage and cunning in war.

Hypatius seems to have been unpopular with the army. In A.D. 513 [3] Vitalian, by stratagem, compassed the death of two of the chief officers of the general's staff ; gained over to his side the Duke of Lower Moesia ; and then, capturing Carinus, a trusted friend of Hypatius, granted him his life on condition that he should help him to seize Odessus. Hypatius, unable to cope with the situation, withdrew to Constantinople. The rebel reinforced his Federate troops by a multitude of rustics, and, at the head of 50,000 men (it is said), advanced to Constantinople, hoping that the populace of the capital would rally to him as the champion of orthodoxy.

The Emperor commanded bronze crosses to be set up over the gates of the city, with inscriptions setting forth his own view of the cause of the rebellion.[4] He reduced by one-quarter the tax on the import of live stock for the inhabitants of Bithynia and Asia, in order to secure the loyalty of these provinces. The military authorities made what arrangements they could to meet the sudden crisis. When Vitalian occupied the suburbs and appeared before the walls, Patricius, Master of Soldiers *in praesenti*, who had won distinction in the Persian war and

---

[1] His father Patriciolus also held the office of Count of the Federates (acc. to Theoph.), and he took part in the Persian war. He was a native of Zaldaba in Lower Moesia. It is possible that the family was of Gothic descent (Zacharias Myt. vii. 13). For the Federates see below, vol. ii. chap. xvi. § 1.

[2] Acc. to Zach. Myt., he had a personal reason for hatred of Hypatius (*ib.*).

[3] The outbreak of the rising is generally placed in A.D. 514 (cp. Marcellinus). But the evidence in Wright, *Catalogue Syn. MSS. Brit. Mus.* 333, adduced by Brooks (*C. Med. H.* i. 485) shows that the true date is 513, and there is nothing inconsistent with this in John Ant.

[4] The object of the manifesto was doubtless to show that Vitalian's championship of orthodoxy was only a pretext.

had considerably helped the advancement of Vitalian, was sent to confer with the rebel. Vitalian explained the purpose of his resort to arms. He was determined to rectify the injustices committed by Hypatius, and to obtain the ratification of the orthodox theological creed. He and his chief officers were invited into the city to discuss the matters at issue. He refused to accept the invitation himself, but his chief officers went on the following day and had an audience of the Emperor. Anastasius won them over by gifts and promises that the soldiers would receive all that was due, and by undertaking that the Church of Rome would be allowed to settle the religious questions in dispute. Vitalian had no option but to yield to the unanimous opinion of his officers, and he returned with his army to Lower Moesia to bide his time and mature new schemes.

The Emperor deposed the unpopular Hypatius and appointed in his stead Cyril, an officer of some experience, who immediately proceeded to Lower Moesia, perhaps with the purpose of capturing Vitalian by guile. But Vitalian was on the alert, and Cyril was assassinated. This act made it clear that the rebel was still a rebel, and a decree of the Senate was passed, in old Roman style, that Vitalian was an enemy of the Republic. Alathar, a soldier of Hunnic origin, was appointed to succeed Cyril, but the supreme command of the Imperial army was assigned to another Hypatius, a nephew of the Emperor. This army, said to have been 80,000 strong, gained an inconsiderable victory (autumn, A.D. 513), which was soon followed by serious reverses.[1] Hypatius then fortified himself behind a rampart of wagons at Acris, on the Black Sea, near Odessus. In this entrenchment the barbarians attacked him, and, assisted by a sudden darkness, which a superstitious historian attributed to magic arts, gained a signal victory. The Romans, driven over precipices and into ravines, are said to have lost about 60,000 men. Hypatius himself ran into the sea, if perchance he might conceal himself in the waves, but his head betrayed him. Vitalian preserved him alive as a valuable hostage.[2] This victory enabled him to pay his barbarian allies richly, and placed him in possession

---

[1] Julian, a clerk in the bureau of the *Magister memoriae*, was carried about in a cage until he was ransomed. We need not doubt that the numbers both of the army and of the losses are grossly exaggerated.

[2] Alathar was captured also and other officers. Vitalian paid ransoms to the Bulgarians who had taken them.

of all the cities and fortresses in Moesia and Scythia. The Emperor sent ambassadors with ten pounds of gold to ransom his nephew, but they were captured at Sozopolis (Sizeboli), which at the same time fell into the rebels' hands.

In the meantime a tumult, attended with loss of life, occurred at Constantinople, because Anastasius forbade the celebration of festivities in the evening on account of disorders in the Hippodrome. Among others the Prefect of the Watch was slain. This disturbance may have helped to dispose the Emperor to consider a compromise, when shortly afterwards (A.D. 514) Vitalian, flushed with victory, appeared in the neighbourhood of the capital. He had collected in the Thracian ports a fleet of 200 vessels. These he sent to the Bosphorus, and marching himself along the coast occupied the European shores of the Straits. A certain John,[1] who seems to have been Master of Soldiers *in praesenti*, was sent to Sosthenion (Stenia) to treat with him. Conditions were arranged. Vitalian was appointed to the post of Master of Soldiers in Thrace, and Hypatius was liberated for a ransom of 9000 pounds of gold.

But the most important provision of the contract was that measures should be taken to establish peace in the Church by the convocation of a general Council, and it was agreed that a Council should be held at Heraclea in the following year.[2] Vitalian expressly insisted that Rome should be represented, and it was arranged that both he and the Emperor should communicate with Pope Hormisdas.[3] The date of the Council was

---

[1] He was known as son of Valeriane. This designation by the mother's name is very unusual. John Ant. *ib.* p. 146.

[2] Victor Tonn. *Chron., sub* 514. Theoph. A.M. 6006.

[3] We have the letters of Anastasius to Hormisdas: *Coll. Avell., Ep.* 109 (Dec. 28, 514) and *Ep.* 107 (Jan. 12, 515), of which the latter arrived at Rome first ; the replies of Hormisdas, *Ep.* 110 (July 8) and *Ep.* 108 (April 4), his letter to Anastasius sent by the bishops who did not leave Rome till August, *Ep.* 115 (Aug. 11), and the Indiculus of instructions to the bishops as to their behaviour, 116. In this document the Pope's correspondence with Vitalian is mentioned (p. 514), but it has not been preserved. The bishops returned to Rome, before

the end of the year, with a letter from the Emperor to the Pope, containing a profession of faith and alleging that if he yielded on the question of Acacius, bloodshed would be the consequence, *Ep.* 125. In July 516 he again wrote to Hormisdas, in the interests of unity, and at the same time to the Roman Senate, asking it to exert its influence with the pontiff, *Epp.* 111, 113 ; he was told that the restoration of unity entirely rested with him, *Epp.* 113, 114. In 517 there was a further interchange of letters, *Epp.* 126, 127 (cp. 128, 129, 130), and finally Anastasius angrily broke off the correspondence, saying that he might put up with insult, but he would not tolerate being ordered, *Ep.* 138 (July 11).

fixed for July 1, A.D. 415, but it never met. Delegates indeed were sent from Rome and arrived at Constantinople late in the year, but as the Pope adopted an uncompromising attitude in regard to the condemnation of the memory of Acacius, and as the Emperor held that it was unjust that living persons should be excluded from the Church on account of the dead,[1] no conciliation could be effected. A fruitless correspondence between Hormisdas and Anastasius ensued.

The Emperor appears to have also promised Vitalian that the bishops who had been driven from their sees should be restored,[2] but it is not clear whether this measure was intended to depend on the decisions of the Council. As the Council did not meet, and as the bishops were not restored, Vitalian was convinced that the Emperor had no intention of fulfilling his part of the bargain, and it was probably in the later months of the same year that he assembled his fleet anew, and reappeared with his army on the banks of the Bosphorus,[3] whence he occupied Sycae, the region of the city, on the north side of the Golden Horn, which was in later times called Galata. It is surprising to find that the command of the Imperial forces was committed to Marinus, the Emperor's influential adviser, who had hitherto been employed only in civil affairs. This exceptional arrangement was due to the attitude of the two Masters of Soldiers *in praesenti*, Patricius and John, who were personal friends of Vitalian and his father. They hesitated to take command on the ground that if they were defeated they would be suspected of treason. The great financier, however, was equal to the crisis. The issue was decided by a naval battle at the mouth of the Golden Horn, in which the ships of the rebel were completely routed.[4] It is related that this victory was achieved by the use of a chemical compound, similar to the

[1] *Ep.* 125, p. 539.

[2] Victor and Theophanes, *locc. citt.*

[3] The fullest account of the events of this year is given by John Malalas (and is summarised by Evagrius). His story does not completely tally with that of John Ant., who does not say a word about Marinus.

[4] The place is designated as opposite the Church of St. Thecla in Sycae, in the part of the Golden Horn ὅπου λέγεται τὸ Βυθάριν, John Mal. 405 (περὶ τὰ καλούμενα Βυθάρια, Evagrius,

iii. 43). I know no other mention of the Βυθάρια. John Ant.'s account is different. He says that a fast vessel commanded by Justin (Count of the Excubitors, afterwards Emperor) engaged with one of the enemy's ships off Chrysopolis and captured the crew, and that this success caused the flight of the other rebel ships. This is incredible as an account of the naval action ; the exploit of Justin can only have been one incident.

Greek fire of later days, which, projected upon the enemy's ships, set them on fire.[1] Marinus then landed his forces at Sycae, slew the rebels whom he found there, and in the evening took up a position on the shores of the Bosphorus.[2] In the night Vitalian fled with all the troops that were left to him and reached Anchialus, where he seems to have remained undisturbed during the next three years. The Emperor made a solemn procession to Sosthenion, which Vitalian had made his head-quarters, and in the church of St. Michael, for which that place was noted, offered thanks to the archangel for the deliverance. All the rebels did not escape as easily as Vitalian. Tarrach, one of his henchmen, whom he had employed to assassinate Cyril, was burned at Chalcedon, and two others who happened to be taken were put to death.

The Empress Ariadne died in this year.[3] Anastasius survived her by three years. He died at the age of eighty on the night of July 8–9, A.D. 418.[4] He had no children and made no provision for the succession, though it was probably his intention to designate one of his three nephews, Probus, Pompeius, or Hypatius.[5] His last months seem to have been troubled by new hostilities on the part of Vitalian, but the details are unknown to us.[6]

---

[1] This compound, according to John Mal., was supplied to Marinus by an Athenian man of science named Proclus (not to be confounded with the famous Neoplatonist who had died in A.D. 485), and Proclus is said to have refused a reward of 400 lbs. of gold.

[2] The meaning of *Anaplûs*, which occurs in our sources (John Ant., John Mal., Evagr.), and has caused some difficulty, has been elucidated by Pargoire (*Anaple et Sosthène*, in *Izv. russk. arkh. Inst. v Kplie*, iii. 60 *sqq.*). In these passages the 'Ανάπλους designates the whole European shore of the Bosphorus, or at all events the whole southern strip from Stenia southwards. But it is also found, in other texts, with two more restricted local meanings, designating points on the European shore corresponding to (1) Kuru Chesme and Arnaut Keui (see Marcellinus, *Chron.*, *sub* 481) and (2) Rumili Hissar. The first of these places was also called

Hestiae, where there was a Church of St. Michael, built by Constantine, not to be confounded with that of Sosthenion (= Laosthenion), now Stenia, north of Rumili Hissar.

[3] Marcellinus, *Chron.*, *sub a.*

[4] This date (which is given in Cyril, *Vita S. Sabae*, p. 354) follows from the fact that Justin was elected on July 9 (John Mal. xvii. p. 411 = *Chron. Pasch.*, *sub a.*) and that Anastasius died during the previous night (Peter Patr. apud Const. Porph. *De cer.* i. 93). This agrees with the length of the reign of Anastasius given by Marcellinus, *sub a.* Therefore the date of Theophanes (*Chron.*, *sub a.*), April 9, is false. See Tillemont, *Hist. des Empereurs*, vi. 586.

[5] Cp. Anon. Val. 13.

[6] Cyril, *op. cit.* p. 340 συνεχόμενος ὑπὸ τῶν Βιταλιανοῦ βαρβαρικῶν ὀχλήσεων. This was soon after the death of the Patriarch Timotheus, that is after April 5, A.D. 518. See Andreev, *Konstantinopol'skie Patriarkhi*, p. 168.

§ 5. *Italy under Theoderic*

The rule of the Patrician Theoderic in Italy, if we date it from the battle of the Adda in A.D. 490, lasted thirty-six years. In its general constitutional and administrative principles it was a continuation of the rule of Odovacar. One of the first things Theoderic had to do was to settle his own people in the land, and this settlement was exactly similar to that which had been carried out by his predecessor. The Ostrogoths for the most part replaced Odovacar's Germans, who had been largely killed or driven out, though some of them who had submitted were permitted to retain their lands. The general principle was the assignment of one-third of the Roman estates to the Goths ; [1] but the commission which carried out the division was under the presidency of a senator, Liberius, so that we may be sure the senatorial domains were spared so far as possible.

For six years the Emperor Anastasius hesitated to define his attitude to Theoderic,[2] but Theoderic carefully refrained from taking any measures that were incompatible with the position of a viceroy or that would render subsequent recognition difficult. At length they came to terms (A.D. 497), and a definite arrangement was made which determined the position of Italy and the

---

[1] A different view is maintained by Dumoulin (*C. Med. H.* i. 447). He thinks that the lands assigned to the Germans both by Odovacar and by Theoderic were one - third of the State lands (*ager publicus*). It may be doubted whether the number of the Ostrogothic army exceeded 25,000. Hodgkin (iii. 202) puts it at 40,000, and the number of the whole nation at 200,000. This figure seems too high.

[2] We saw that Theoderic, after his victory in 490, sent Flavius Festus, the chief of the Roman Senate, as an ambassador to Zeno (above, p. 424). While Festus was still at Constantinople, Anastasius succeeded and refused to recognise Theoderic. A second embassy was sent in 492, led by another distinguished senator, Flavius Anicius Probus Faustus Niger (*C.I.L.* vi. 32,195), consul in 490, whom Theoderic had appointed Master of Offices. The result of the negotiations of Faustus was a partial recog-

nition, as was shown by the fact that Anastasius permitted two western consuls to be nominated in 494. But Anastasius suspected Theoderic's intentions, and there was a breach. Faustus returned to Italy in 494. Then at the end of 496 (after the death of Pope Gelasius and the election of Anastasius II.) Festus was again sent, and succeeded in concluding the definite arrangement of 497. The whole course of these negotiations has been ably examined by Sundwall (*Abh.* 190 *sqq.*), who makes it probable that they were closely affected by the ecclesiastical schism, and that the Synod of Rome held in May 495 by Gelasius and the intransigent attitude of the Italian bishops made it difficult for Anastasius to come to terms with the Senate, as the Senate itself was divided on the ecclesiastical question. That Theoderic depended mainly on the support of the Senate for regularising his position comes out very clearly in these transactions.

status of the Ostrogothic kingdom. Theoderic still held the office of Master of Soldiers which Zeno had conferred upon him. Anastasius confirmed him in this office and recognised him as Governor of Italy on certain conditions, which in their general scope must have corresponded to the arrangement which Zeno had made with Odovacar. These conditions determined the constitutional position of Theoderic.

Under this arrangement Italy remained part of the Empire, and was regarded as such officially both at Rome and at Constantinople. In one sense Theoderic was an independent ruler, but there were a number of limitations to his power, which implied the sovranty of the Emperor and which he loyally observed.[1]

The position of the Ostrogothic king as a deputy comes out in the fact that he never used the years of his reign for the purpose of dating official documents. It comes out in the fact that he did not claim the right of coining money except in subordination to the Emperor.[2] It comes out, above all, in the fact that he did not make laws.[3] To make laws, *leges* in the full sense of the term, was reserved as the supreme prerogative of the Emperor. Ordinances of Theoderic exist, but they are not *leges*, they are only *edicta* ; and various high officials, especially the Praetorian Prefect, could issue an edictum. Nor was this difference between law and edict, in Theoderic's case, a mere difference in name. Theoderic did promulgate general edicts, that is, laws which did not apply only to special cases, but were of a general kind permanently valid, and which if they had been enacted by the Emperor would have been called laws. But the Praetorian Prefect had the right of issuing a general

[1] The following account is based on Mommsen's *Ostgotische Studien* in *Hist. Schr.* iii. p. 362 *sqq.*

[2] Under Theoderic, and under Odovacar before him, gold coins minted at Ravenna and Rome bore the name and types of the contemporary Emperors. Odovacar struck silver and bronze coins with his own name and portrait (the thick moustache is realistic). Theoderic's silver coins have the Emperor's bust on the obverse and his own monogram on the reverse. The bronze have the Imperial bust on the obverse. The only known coin on which Theo-

deric's bust appears is a large triple solidus, obviously struck for some particular occasion. Only one specimen is extant. It has been supposed that the bust, which is almost a half-length figure, was copied from an actual statue or mosaic picture of Theoderic. We know that such figures existed. See Wroth, *Catalogue of the Coins of the Vandals, etc.* xxxi.-xxxii. Theoderic's coinage is " singularly neat and even elegant " (*ib.*).

[3] In Procopius this is expressly asserted both of Theoderic and of his successors by representatives of the Goths. *B.G.* ii. 6. p. 176.

edict, *provided it did not run counter to any existing law.* This
meant that he could modify existing laws in particular points,
whether in the direction of mildness or of severity, but could
not originate any new principle or institution. The ordinances
of Theoderic, which are collected in his code known as the *Edictum
Theoderici,* exhibit conformity to this rule. They introduce no
novelties, they alter no established principle. We are told that,
when Theoderic first appeared in Rome, he addressed the people
and promised that he would preserve inviolate all the ordinances
of the Emperors in the past.[1] Thus in legislation, Theoderic
is neither nominally nor actually co-ordinate with the Emperor.
His powers in this department are those of a high official, and
though he employed them to a greater extent than any Praetorian
Prefect could have done, on account of the circumstances of
the case, yet his edicts are qualitatively on the same footing.

The right of naming one of the consuls of the year, which
had belonged to the Emperor reigning in the West, was transferred by the Emperors Zeno and Anastasius to Odovacar and
Theoderic.[2] From A.D. 498 forward Theoderic nominated one
of the consuls. On one occasion (A.D. 522) the Emperor Justin
waived his own nomination and allowed Theoderic to name
both consuls—Symmachus and Boethius. But in exercising
this right the Ostrogothic king was bound by one restriction.
He could not nominate a Goth ; only a Roman could fill the
consulship. The single exception corroborates the existence of
the rule. In A.D. 519 Eutharic, the king's son-in-law, was consul.
But it is expressly recorded that the nomination was not made
by Theoderic ; it was made by the Emperor, as a special favour.[3]

The capitulation which excluded Goths from the consulship
extended also to all the civil offices, which were maintained under
Ostrogothic rule, as under that of Odovacar.[4] There was still
the Praetorian Prefect of Italy, and when Theoderic acquired
Provence, the office of Praetorian Prefect of Gaul was revived.
There was the Vicarius of Rome ; there were all the provincial
governors, divided as before into the three ranks of consulars,

---

[1] Anon. Val. 66. Compare Cassiodorus, *Var.* i. 1 ; xi. 8 *ad init.* The
general conservatism of Theoderic is
emphasised in *Var.* iii. 9 *propositi
quidem nostri est nova construere sed
amplius vetusta servare.* Cp. i. 25.
[2] For the details of the arrange-

ments as to the consulate see
Mommsen, *op. cit.* 226 *sqq.*
[3] Cassiodorus, *Var.* viii. 1.
[4] It is to be noted that in most of
his appointments to important offices
Theoderic communicated his intentions to, or consulted with, the Senate.

correctors, and *praesides*. There was the Master of Offices. There were the two great finance ministries.[1] There was the Quaestorship of the Palace.[2] It may be added that Goths were also excluded from the honorary dignity of Patricius. Under Theoderic no Goth bore that title but Theoderic himself, who had received it from the Emperor.

The Roman Senate, to which Goths on the same principle could not belong, continued to meet and to perform much the same functions which it had performed throughout the fifth century. It was formally recognised by Theoderic as possessing an authority similar to his own.[3]

If all the civil offices were reserved for the Romans, in the case of military posts it was exactly the reverse. Here it was the Romans who were excluded. The army was entirely Gothic ; no Roman was liable to military service ; and the officers were naturally Goths.[4] Theoderic was the commander of the army, as Master of Soldiers, for, though he did not designate himself by the title, he had retained the office, and no Master of Soldiers was appointed, subordinate to himself.[5] Though the old Roman troops and their organisation disappeared, it has been shown that the military arrangements were based in many respects on practices which had existed in Italy under Imperial rule.

The various disabilities of the Ostrogoths which have been described depended on the fact that they were not Roman

---

[1] A *comes patrimonii* was instituted, Odovacar's *vicedominus* (see above, p. 409), under another name. Goths were eligible for this post.

[2] All the *officia* or staffs of subordinate officials were maintained. In the State documents of Cassiodorus, *officium nostrum* means the staff of the Master of Offices. Both this minister and the Praetorian Prefect resided at Ravenna, but had representatives at Rome who, like themselves, were *illustres*.

[3] *Parem nobiscum reipublicae debetis adnisum*, Cassiod. *Var.* ii. 24.

[4] The chief officers were called priors or counts.

[5] Mommsen has illustrated this point by certain measures taken after Theoderic's death. His successor, Athalaric, was out of the question as commander of the forces, and the regent Amalasuntha appointed Tuluin, a Gothic warrior, and Liberius, a Roman, who was Praet. Prefect of Gaul, to be *patricii praesentales*. This involved two deviations from rule. Tuluin as a Goth was debarred from the dignity of patrician, and Liberius, as a Roman, from a military command. The office was simply that of *mag. mil.* ; the modification of the title illustrates the fact that the Mastership of Soldiers had become closely associated with the kingship through its long tenure by Theoderic. But I question whether Mommsen is right in assuming that Theoderic simply continued throughout his reign to hold the Mastership conferred on him by Zeno in 483. That was a Mastership in the East. I conjecture that Zeno had appointed him *mag. utriusque militiae* in Italy before he set out (cp. above, p. 422), and that this was confirmed by Anastasius.

citizens. They, like the Germans settled by Odovacar, had legally the same status as mercenaries or foreign travellers or hostages who dwelled in Roman territory, but might at any time return to their homes beyond the Roman frontier. The laws which applied only to Roman citizens, for instance those relating to marriage and inheritance, did not apply to them. But what may be called the *ius commune*, laws pertaining to criminal matters and to the general intercourse of life, applied to all foreigners who happened to be sojourning in Roman territory ; and thus the Edict of Theoderic, which is based on Roman law, is addressed to Goths and Romans alike. The status of the Goths reminds us of a fundamental restriction of Theoderic's power. He could not turn a Goth into a Roman ; he could not confer Roman citizenship ; that power was reserved to the Emperor.

Their quality, as foreign soldiers, determined the character of the courts in which the Ostrogoths were judged. The Roman rule was that the soldier must be tried by a military court, and military courts were instituted for the Goths. But here Theoderic interfered in a serious way with the rights of the Italians. All processes between Romans and Goths, to which-ever race the accuser belonged, were brought before these military courts. A Roman lawyer was always present as an assessor, but probably no feature of the Gothic government was so unpopular as this. Like the Emperor, Theoderic had a supreme royal court, which could withdraw any case from a lower court or cancel its decision, and this tribunal seems to have been more active than the corresponding court of the Emperor. It is indeed in the domain of justice, in contrast with the domain of legislation, that the German kings in Italy sharply asserted their actual authority.

Besides being Master of Soldiers in regard to the Ostrogothic host, Theoderic was likewise the king of his people. He did not style himself *rex Gotorum* ; like Odovacar, he adopted the simple title of *rex*. This indefinite style was hardly due to the circumstance that the foreign settlers in Italy were not all Ostrogoths, that the remnant of Odovacar's Germans, and notably the Rugians,[1] acknowledged his kingship. It was perhaps in-tended also to express his actual, as distinguished from his

---

[1] Procopius, *B.G.* iii. 2.

constitutional, relation to the Roman population. While the Roman citizens were constitutionally the subjects of the Emperor, of whom the Patrician Theoderic was himself a subject and official, they were actually in the hands of Theoderic, who was their real ruler. To designate this extra-constitutional relation, the word *rex*, which had no place in the constitutional vocabulary of Rome, was appropriate enough. It served the double purpose of expressing his regular relation to his German subjects, and his irregular relation, his quasi-kingship, to the Romans of Italy.[1]

The continuity of the administration of Odovacar with that of Theoderic was facilitated by the fact that some of the Roman ministers of Odovacar passed into the service of the Ostrogothic ruler, and probably the mass of the subordinate officials remained unchanged. For instance, the first Praetorian Prefect of Italy under Theoderic was Liberius (A.D. 493–500), who had been one of the trusted ministers of Odovacar. Cassiodorus—father of the famous Cassiodorus whose writings are our chief authority for Theoderic's reign,—who had held both the great financial offices under Odovacar, continued to serve under Theoderic, and in the early years of the sixth century became Praetorian Prefect.[2]

The constitutional system of administration which Theoderic accepted and observed was not a necessity to which he reluctantly

---

[1] In an inscription commemorating his draining of the Pomptine marshes he is given the Imperial title of *semper Augustus*. He is there styled *d. n. gloriosissimus adque inclytus rex, victor ac triumfator semper Aug., bono reipublicae natus, custos libertatis et propagator Romani nominis, domitor gentium*, *C.I.L.* x. 6850. In one inscription he is mentioned along with an Emperor, probably Anastasius : *salvis domi[no . . .] Augusto et gl[oriosissimo rege] Theoderico, C.I.L.* vi. 1794. He never wore the diadem.

[2] The thoroughly Roman character of the Italian kingdom is clear. There are one or two points in which Germanic influence has been suspected. (1) The *saiones* were marshals or messengers whom the king employed to intimate his commands. They might summon the Gothic soldiers to arms or recall a Roman official to a sense of duty. The office of *saio* may be a German institution, or there may be nothing German about it but the name. The functions of these officials correspond to those of the *agentes in rebus*, who also existed in Italy at this time, though, as Mommsen has shown, they were called *comitiaci*. They may have served as a model for the institution of the *saiones*. (2) By an Imperial law of A.D. 393 any person who considered his personal safety in danger might apply for special protection, *tuitio*, and a judge was bound to assign a civil officer (*apparitor*) to protect him. *Tuitio* is very prominent in Ostrogothic Italy ; it was granted by the king himself, and was one of the methods by which he preserved peace and order among the two races. The quickening of this Roman custom, and its special association with the king, may have been partly due to the Germanic idea of the king's duty of protection (*munt*).

or lukewarmly yielded. It was a system in which he seems to have been a convinced believer, and he threw his whole heart and best energies into working it. His object was to civilise his own people in the environment of Roman civilisation (*civilitas*). But he made no premature attempt to draw the two classes of his subjects closer, by breaking down lines of division. They were divided by religion and by legal status. So far as religion was concerned, the king was consistently tolerant, unlike the rulers of the Vandals and the Franks. His principle was : " We cannot impose religion because no one can be compelled to believe against his will "—a maxim which might well have been pondered on by Roman emperors.[1] So extreme was his repugnance to influencing the creed of his fellow-creatures that an anecdote was invented that he put to death a Catholic deacon for embracing Arianism to please him. If there is any foundation for the story, there must have been other circumstances ; but it is good evidence as to his religious attitude ; if it was entirely invented, it proves his reputation.[2]

And just as he accepted the duality of religion, he accepted the dual system by which Goths and Romans lived side by side as two distinct and separate peoples. He made no efforts to bring about fusion, his only aim was that the two nations should live together in amity. But little love was lost between them. The rude German barbarians despised the civilised Italians, and the Ostrogothic kingdom was overthrown before fusion could begin ; but the development in Visigothic Spain, under similar conditions, makes it probable that fusion would have ensued, if the Ostrogothic power had endured. It says much for Theoderic's authority and tact that he was able to hold an equal balance between the two peoples, and to attain so nearly in practice to the difficult ideal which he set before him :

Tros Tyriusque mihi nullo discrimine agetur.

After his death the concealed impatience of the Goths under his philo-Roman policy was soon to burst out and hurry them to disaster.

Although he aimed at maintaining peaceful relations with the Emperor throughout his long reign, this concord was

---

[1] *Religionem imperare non possumus, quia nemo cogitur ut credat invitus.* Cassiodorus, ii. 27.

[2] To the Jews also he extended toleration and protection. Cassiodorus, *loc. cit.*

threatened more than once, and there were even actual hostilities. A campaign which Theoderic undertook against the Gepids, in order to recover Sirmium and adjacent districts of the Prefecture of Italy which this people had occupied, led to a collision with the Imperial troops (A.D. 504–505). The events are obscure.[1] It would seem that the Gepids yielded with little resistance, in consequence of internal dissensions. But the expedition which Theoderic sent against them aroused the suspicions of Anastasius. At this time the central provinces of the Balkan peninsula were exposed to the depredations of a Hun, named Mundo, who had organised a band of brigands. The government sent the Master of Soldiers, Sabinian, to capture him, and Sabinian was supported by a formidable force of allied Bulgarians. Mundo appealed for help to the Ostrogothic general Pitzias, who was engaged in completing the occupation of the territory which he had won from the Gepids. Our informants do not explain why he should have made the brigand's cause his own, or regarded Sabinian's movements as a threat to the Goths ; but he marched into Dacia and won a decisive victory over the Bulgarians. Mundo also inflicted a severe defeat on Sabinian at Horrea Margi.[2] The key to this episode probably is that Anastasius viewed with alarm the Gothic occupation of the important frontier town of Sirmium ; he preferred that it should be in the hands of the Gepids rather than in those of his viceroy.[3] After the defeat of Sabinian, he must have acquiesced in Theoderic's restoration of the Prefecture of Italy to its old limits, for no further hostilities followed.[4]

These operations in the region of the Save were probably connected with an attempt to make his authority felt in the Pannonian province. Of the conditions in Noricum and Pannonia

---

[1] The sources are Ennodius, *Pan. Theod.* 277-280 ; Cassiodorus, *Chron.*, *sub* 504; Marcellinus, *Chron.*, *sub* 505 ; Jordanes, *Get.* 300-301 ; Cassiodorus, *Var.* viii. 10. 4 ; *Or.* p. 473. There are difficulties in reconciling them. Cp. Hodgkin, iii. 438 *sqq.* ; Schmidt, *Gesch. der deutschen Stämme*, i. 310.

[2] The place is given by Marcellinus, who says nothing of Ostrogoths or Bulgarians, and by Jordanes, who does not mention Bulgarians. From Ennodius one might infer that the battle was fought in two sections ;

he passes lightly over *Sabiniani ducis abitionem turpissimam.*

[3] The words of Ennodius are important : *per foederati Mundonis adtrectationem Graecia est professa discordiam, secum Bulgares suos in tutela deducendo.* It is to be observed that Mundo is described as an ally of the Ostrogoths. We are told nothing of his subsequent fortunes.

[4] Ennodius, *loc. cit., ad limitem suum Romana regna remearunt.* For the organisation of Sirmian Pannonia by Theoderic see Cass. *Var.* iii. 23, 24.

at this time we have no clear idea. But we know that about the year 507 Theoderic settled a portion of the Alamannic people in Pannonia, perhaps in Savia. The remnant of this people, after their defeat by Clovis (perhaps in A.D. 495), had wandered southward into Raetia to escape the sword or the yoke of the victor. Clovis requested Theoderic to surrender them, and we possess Theoderic's reply. He deprecated the Frank king's desire to push his victory further. " Hear the counsel," he wrote, " of one who is experienced in such matters. Those wars of mine have been profitable, the ending of which has been guided by moderation." He took the Alamanni under his protection and gave them a home within the borders of his kingdom.[1]

In his relations with foreign powers, Theoderic acted as an independent sovran. The four chief powers with which he had to reckon were the Visigoths, the Burgundians, the Franks, and the Vandals. It was natural that he should look for special co-operation from the Visigoths, who were a kindred folk. But his policy at first was not to draw the Visigoths into a close intimate alliance, which might seem a threat to the other powers. He sought to form bonds of friendship with all the reigning houses, by means of matrimonial alliances. If he wedded one of his daughters to the Visigothic king, Alaric II., the other married Sigismund (A.D. 494), who became king of the Burgundians after his father Gundobad's death. Theoderic himself took as his second wife a Frankish princess, sister of Clovis. And his own sister married Thrasamund, king of the Vandals (A.D. 500). Thus he formed close ties with all the chief powers of the West.[2] One object of this policy was doubtless to maintain the existing order of things, to preserve peace in western Europe,

---

[1] See Cassiodorus, *Var.* ii. 41 and cp. iii. 50, where we see the Alamanni, on their way from Raetia to Pannonia, passing through Noricum. The date of both these letters is 507. Also Ennodius, *Paneg.* c. xv. (this work belongs to the same year). Cp. Mommsen, *Preface* to Cassiod. pp. xxxiii.-xxxiv. ; Dahn, *Kön. der Germ.* ix. 1. p. 64. Parts of Noricum and Raetia were occupied about the year 500 by Marcomanni and Quadi coming from Bohemia, driven westward by the Slavs ; they were now known under the name of Bajuvarii, Bavarians (cp. Jordanes, *Get.* 280).

Thus was founded Bavaria.

[2] His niece married Hermanfrid, king of the Thuringians. He adopted as a son the king of the Heruls (Cassiodorus, *Var.* iv. 2). He gave Lilybaeum to his sister Amalafrida when she married Thrasamund, acc. to Procopius, *B.V.* i. 8, 11, whose statement is illustrated by an inscription on a boundary stone near that town marking the *fines inter Vandalos et [Go]thos, C.I.L.* x. 7232. Amalafrida Theodenanda (Dessau, 8990) seems to be a different person from Theoderic's sister, perhaps her daughter.

and secure Italy against attack.   But we can hardly be wrong
in thinking that it was also the purpose of Theoderic to secure
his own position in Italy, in relation to the Imperial power.
He could hardly fail to foresee that the day might come when
Anastasius or one of his successors might decide to bring Italy
under his immediate government or to deal with himself as
Zeno had dealt with Odovacar.   To meet such a danger, it
would be much to have behind him the support of the western
powers.   As the centre and head of a system, linking together
the German royalties, he would be in a far stronger position in
regard to his sovran at Constantinople than Odovacar had been
standing alone.

The family alliances of Theoderic did not avail to hinder war.
He could not avert the inevitable struggle between the Franks
and the Visigoths in Gaul.   No moment in his reign caused him
perhaps more anxiety than when Clovis declared war upon
Alaric.   Theoderic did what he could.   We have the three
letters which he wrote at this crisis to Alaric, to Gundobad, and
to Clovis himself.[1]   It was in vain.   Theoderic promised armed
help to his son-in-law.   But for some reason he was unable to
render it.   It would seem that he had calculated that the
Burgundians would not side with the Franks, and that they cut
him off so that he could not reach Aquitaine in time to intervene
in the struggle.   On the field of Vouillé (near Poictiers) the
Visigothic king fell and Aquitaine was annexed to the dominion
of the Franks (A.D. 507).   But in the following years the generals
of Theoderic conducted campaigns in Gaul.   They succeeded in
rescuing Arles and in saving Narbonensis for the Visigothic
kingdom.   They wrested Provence from Burgundy and annexed
it to Italy.   At the same time the personal power of Theoderic
received another extension.   The heir of Alaric was a child,
and the government of his realm was consigned to Theoderic,
who was his grandfather and most powerful protector.   For
the rest of his life Theoderic ruled Spain and Narbonensis.
Thus no inconsiderable part of the western section of the old
Roman Empire was under his sway : Spain, Narbonensis, and
Provence, Italy and Sicily, the two provinces of Raetia, Noricum,
part of Pannonia, and Dalmatia.

---

[1] Cass. *Var.* iii. 1, 2, 4.   He also wrote a circular letter to the kings
of the Thuringians, Heruls, and Varni, *ib.* 3.

Thus the war in Gaul involved Theoderic, in spite of his relations to the royal houses, in hostilities against both the Franks and the Burgundians. The Burgundian alliance does not seem to have led to any close intimacy. Gundobad remained an Arian till his death (A.D. 516), but he took good care to remain on friendly terms with Anastasius. His son Sigismund, Theoderic's son-in-law, who succeeded him, had been converted to Catholicism[1] by Avitus, the bishop of Vienne, and appears to have been completely in the hands of Avitus and the Catholic clergy. He looked to the Emperor as his overlord, and addressed him in almost servile terms.[2] Theoderic was alarmed at the prospect of political intimacy between Burgundy and Constantinople, and he would not allow Sigismund's messengers to travel through Italy to the East.[3] The strained relations between the courts were shown by the circumstance that the consulship of Eutharic was not accepted in Burgundy as the date of A.D. 519.[4] Theoderic probably placed his hopes in his grandson Sigeric, who, though he had been converted to the Catholic creed, was not on good terms with his father. His mother was dead, and Sigismund had taken a second wife. We know nothing authentic of the breach between father and son, but the end was that Sigeric was put to death by his father's orders (A.D. 522).[5] Theoderic prepared for war to avenge his grandson, but it was the Franks, not the Ostrogoths, who were to punish Sigismund. It was not to their mind that Theoderic should have a free hand in Burgundy, and moving more quickly, they captured Sigismund and his family and subdued a part of the kingdom. An Ostrogothic force arrived afterwards and annexed the district between the Isère and the Durance to Theoderic's realm (A.D. 523).[6]

The war between the Franks and Visigoths seems to have led to friction between Theoderic and the Emperor. In that struggle Clovis posed as the champion of Catholic orthodoxy, going forth to drive the Arian heresy from the confines of Gaul,

---

[1] Avitus, *C. Arianos*, p. 2. The letters and works of Avitus, and the *Vita* of Caesarius, bishop of Arles, throw some general light on the history of Burgundy during the first quarter of the sixth century.

[2] Avitus, *Epp.* 93 and 94. He writes for instance : *vester quidem est populus meus et plus me servire vobis*

quam illi praesse delectat.

[3] *Ep.* 94.

[4] *C.I.L.* xii. 1500.

[5] Marius Avent., *sub a.* A legend grew up that his stepmother, whom he had insulted, accused him of treason, Gregory of Tours, *H.F.* iii. 5.

[6] Cassiodorus, *Var.* viii. 10. 8. Cp. *Vita Caesarii*, i. 60.

and all the sympathies of the Gallo-Roman Church were with
the Franks. The Emperor afterwards showed his approbation
of the Merovingian king by conferring upon him the honorary
consulship.[1] Theoderic meanwhile was supporting the Visigoths, and we may conjecture that his Gallic policy was disapproved by Anastasius, who (A.D. 508) despatched a squadron
of a hundred ships to ravage the coasts of Apulia.[2]

The ecclesiastical relations between Rome and Constantinople
affected the political situation in Italy, more or less, throughout
the reign of Theoderic.[3] This was partly due to the fact that
the great Roman families were now all Christian, and many of
the senators held strong opinions on the subject of the schism
which the Henotikon of Zeno had provoked. Festus had taken
advantage of his political mission to Constantinople in A.D. 497
to attempt to heal the schism. He told the Emperor that he
had hopes of inducing the Pope Anastasius to sign the Henotikon. But when he returned to Italy the Pope was dead.[4]
Festus, however, only represented the opinion of part of the
Senate. There was a marked division in the views of the
senators, of whom an influential section were opposed to any
compromise on the theological question. This difference of
opinion led to a bitter struggle over the election of a new Pope.
Two men were elected on the same day (November 22, A.D. 498),
Laurentius, the candidate of Festus and the party of reconciliation, and Symmachus, supported by the orthodox, who were
prepared to make no concessions. Two rival Popes were
enthroned in Rome, each upheld by strong and determined
partisans, and for years the city was disturbed by sanguinary
tumults.[5] An appeal was made to Theoderic to decide between

---

[1] Gregory of Tours, *Hist. Fr.* ii. 38
*ab Anastasio imperatore codecillos de
consulato accepit . . . et ab ea die
tamquam consul aut augustus est
vocitatus.* The expression *tamquam
consul* seems to be equivalent here to
ex consule, the official title of honorary
consuls (*augustus* seems to be a
mistake of Gregory; if Clovis did
assume it, it certainly was not conferred on him). In the *Lex Salica*
(ed. Behrend, p. 125) Clovis is called
proconsul. Mommsen has suggested
that this is a mistake for *praecelsus*.
It is possible that Gregory has con-

fused consulship with proconsulship,
and that Anastasius really conferred
an honorary proconsulship. This,
perhaps, is less likely.

[2] Marcellinus, *Chron., sub a.* The
ships carried 8000 soldiers.

[3] This has been best elucidated by
Sundwall, *op. cit.*, which I have used
much in what follows. Pfeilschifter's
Theod. und die Kathol. Kirche is
indispensable.

[4] Died November 19, 498.

[5] Cp. Theodore Lector, ii. 17. The
most prominent supporter of Symmachus was Faustus.

the two claimants. It is a remarkable episode in the history of the Church that such a question should be referred to an Arian. As the tranquillity of Italy was in peril, the ruler could not stand aloof, and he consented to give a decision. He was conscious of his obligations to Festus, but the clergy, especially the clergy of North Italy, were as a body adherents of Symmachus, and it was in favour of Symmachus that Theoderic decided (A.D. 499).

But the matter was not finally settled by the king's arbitrament. The behaviour of Symmachus was aggressive and uncompromising,[1] and charges were brought against him, which were submitted to a synod held two years later. He was acquitted and recognised as the legitimate bishop of Rome,[2] but his conduct alienated Theoderic, and no steps were taken to remove or suppress Laurentius, who continued to maintain his papal pretensions at Rome for the next few years. But in A.D. 505 there was a revulsion of feeling. The adherents of Laurentius were chiefly men who considered the maintenance of close relations with the Imperial court a fundamental interest of Italy. But their Italian sentiments were aroused by the incidents connected with Sirmium. Here their sympathy was with Theoderic, and it seems highly probable that the hostilities between the troops of Anastasius and those of his viceroy in Dacia were partly at least responsible for a general change of opinion in favour of Symmachus.[3] This made the position of Laurentius impossible, and he was obliged to retire before the end of A.D. 506.

Thus ten years after the settlement which had been arranged between Theoderic and the Emperor, the policy of the Gothic ruler had brought it about that Italy presented a united front, and the influence of Constantinople now reached its lowest point. The Church and the Senate were united against the East on the ecclesiastical question. In the spring of A.D. 507 Ennodius, one of the leading dignitaries of the Italian Church,

---

[1] He addressed a letter to the Emperor, to which the Emperor after some delay replied by a manifesto, and Symmachus rejoined in a rather violent Apologetic, which will be found in Thiel, *Epp. R. Pont.* p. 700 *sqq.*

[2] The date of the Synodus Palmaris

was probably early summer 502: Sundwall, *op. cit.* p. 206. Its enemies called it the *Synodus absolutionis incongruae*, and it was defended in a pamphlet by Ennodius, *Libellus pro Synodo*, 287 *sqq.*

[3] Sundwall, p. 212.

pronounced his Panegyric on the Arian king.[1]   But this situation was only momentary.   Hitherto Theoderic had followed
the example of Odovacar in basing his government on close
co-operation with the great Roman families, members of which
were chosen to fill the highest civil posts, especially the Prefecture
of Rome and the Praetorian Prefecture of Italy.   But from
this time forward we can mark the beginning of a new policy.
Probus Faustus Niger, who had been the leading champion of
Symmachus in the conflict over the Papal throne, is indeed
Prefect of Italy from A.D. 507–512, but we find new men, who
do not belong to the senatorial circle, appointed Prefects of
the City.[2]   It was apparently the aim of Theoderic to diminish
his dependence on the Senate.   At Ravenna he had gathered
round him a circle of other ministers of provincial origin who
were devoted to his interests.   To such were entrusted the
financial offices ; from such were generally selected the Master
of Offices and the Quaestor.

Of Theoderic's acts and policy throughout the rest of the
reign of Anastasius we know very little.   He looked with favour
on the vain attempts of Vitalian to restore the unity of the
Church, and was ready to co-operate with Pope Hormisdas to
bring it about.[3]   It would be a mistake to read into his *Edict*,
which was probably issued in A.D. 512, any design of diminishing
the power or prestige of the senatorial classes.[4]   Throughout
the provinces Romans and Goths alike were constantly attempting to encroach upon the lands of their neighbours ; many acts
of violence occurred ;[5] and the principal object of the Edict seems
to have been to put an end to these illegalities and disorders.

---

[1] Sundwall, pp. 42-43, has fixed the date.

[2] Agapitus, 507-509, followed by Artemidorus, and then Argolicus. Sundwall, p. 215.

[3] Hormisdas succeeded Symmachus in 514. It may be mentioned here that it was in these two pontificates that the Scythian monk Dionysius Exiguus worked at Rome under the auspices of the Roman Church, translating into Latin the " Apos-tolical Canons " and the Canons of the great Councils. This collection, to which he added the Canons of the Council of Sardica and the African Councils, became authoritative, and

protected the chancery of the church of Rome (where Greek was little known) from being imposed upon by forgeries. Dionysius also established the custom of dating events from the Nativity, and introduced the cycle of 532 years (= 28 solar cycle × 19 lunar cycle), invented by Victorius of Aquitaine for the computation of Easter. For his works see *P.L.* 67. Maassen, *Gesch. der Quellen u. der Litt. des Canonischen Rechtes*, vol. i.

[4] See Gaudenzi's article in *Zeit-schrift der Savigny-Stiftung*, vii. 1, 1886.

[5] Cassiodorus, *Var.* viii. 27. Lécrivain, *Le Sénat*, 178 *sqq.*

The relations between Ravenna and Constantinople were never cordial. Italians who were banished from Italy by Theoderic were treated with marked favour at the Byzantine court, and received posts in the Imperial service. We learn this fact from Priscian, the distinguished African grammarian, who, leaving the realm of the Vandals, had settled in Constantinople and sympathised with the national feeling of the Italians against Gothic rule.[1] The presence of these exiles, who, we may be certain, maintained a frequent correspondence with their friends in Rome, is a circumstance which must not be lost sight of in studying the relations of Theoderic with the Emperor and with the Roman Senate.

It is remarkable that Theoderic, who was educated at Constantinople and was imbued with sincere admiration for Greek and Roman civilisation, was illiterate. It is recorded that he was unable to write his own name. He caused a gold stencil plate to be pierced with the four letters *legi* (I have read), so that he could sign documents by drawing a pen through the holes.[2]

Theoderic chose Ravenna, the city of Honorius and Placidia and Valentinian, as his capital. The Emperors who reigned in the days of Ricimer had seldom resided in the palace of the Laurelwood (Lauretum), but Odovacar had made it his home. Theoderic built a new palace in another part of the city, and erected beside it a new church dedicated to St. Martin, in which his Arian Goths worshipped. Of the palace only a wall, if any-

---

[1] Priscian, *Paneg. in Anastas.* vv. 242 *sqq.* V. 265 expresses the hope that Gothic rule will not last long :

utraque Roma tibi nam spero pareat uni.

Priscian was a friend of Symmachus, to whom he dedicated three minor works (Sandys, *Hist. Class. Scholarship*, i. p. 258). Cp. Usener, *Anecd. Holders*, 26.

[2] Anon. Val. 79, where, however, it seems to be implied that at the end of ten years he had learned to write the four letters. If there is any truth in this we must suppose that the letters were arranged in an elaborate monogram, which would explain the use of a stencil plate, without having recourse to the inference of the chronicler that Theoderic was unable

to write at all. The same device was adopted by the illiterate Emperor Justin, according to Procopius (*H.A.* 6). In Anon. Val. *loc. cit.*, *quattuor litteras* legi *habentem* has manuscript authority and is read by the latest editor, Cessi ; cp. the passage of Procopius (γραμμάτων τεττάρων, ἅπερ ἀναγνῶναι τῇ Λατίνων φωνῇ δύναται). The old reading was *regis*, and Valesius inserted THEOD. after *habentem*. But the signature THEOD or THEODORICUS has more than four letters. A. J. Evans (*Antiquarian Researches in Illyricum*, Part III. pp. 22, 23), with the text of Valesius before him, thought that a monogram of *Theodoricus* is meant such as is found on coins and on an engraved gem, apparently a seal of an official of Theoderic.

thing, remains. But the church, one of the fine works of the
Ravennate school of architecture, still stands. It was afterwards dedicated to St. Apollinaris, and is known as San Apollinare
Nuovo.[1] Of the mosaic pictures which adorn the nave only
those which are aloft near the roof,—scriptural scenes,—and
the figures between the windows, belong to Theoderic's reign ;
the decoration of the church was not completed till thirty years
after his death.[2] We may assume that it was he who built
the Arian baptistery which survives as S. Maria in Cosmedin.
It is interesting to learn that near the State factories at the port
of Classis he drained a portion of the marshes and planted an
orchard.[3]

Ravenna has another famous memorial of Theoderic, the
round mausoleum which he built for himself. It was " covered
by a cupola consisting of a single piece of Istrian limestone, the
circumference of which is provided with twelve handles, intended,
without doubt, to lift by means of ropes and drop into its place
this wonderful inverted basin." [4] We must suppose that the
body of the king once lay in the sepulchre which was designed
to receive it. What befell it is a matter for conjecture ; we only
know that three hundred years later the tomb had long been
empty.[5]

Under the rule of Theoderic, Italy is said to have enjoyed
peace, prosperity, and plenty, such as she had not known for
many a long year. His success was due not only to his political
and military capacity, but also to his rigorous though humane
ideal of justice. The praises of Italian panegyrists are borne

[1] See Rivoira, *Lombardic Architecture*, i. 40 *sqq.* The Corinthian
capitals in the nave and the ambo
are of Byzantine workmanship. The
palace of Theoderic is represented in
the mosaics. The round campanile
belongs to the ninth century (*ib.*
45).

[2] Cp. Dalton, *Byz. Art*, 350. See
below, vol. ii. p. 285.

[3] *Rex Theodericus . . . fabricis suis
amoena coniugens, sterili palude siccata,
hos hortos suavi pomorum fecunditate
ditavit. C.I.L.* xi. 10 ; Jordanes,
Get. 151.

[4] Rivoira, *ib.* 54. He remarks on
the ability displayed in the construction of the building and its excellent
proportions. Internally it is shaped

like a cross with equal arms, and must
have been inspired by some Roman
sepulchral edifice. Rivoira acknow-
ledges the impulse given by Theoderic
to art. Many public works were
carried out by his direction, *e.g.* the
restoration of the aqueducts of
Ravenna, of the walls of Rome, and
of the Theatre of Pompey ; the
construction of baths at Verona.
Literature as well as art flourished
under Theoderic. Cassiodorus, Boethius, and Ennodius were the most
distinguished writers, but they do
not exhaust the list.

[5] This is recorded by Agnellus
(who wrote in the ninth century),
Lib. Pont. (in *Scr. r. Lang.*) p. 304.
The sarcophagus was a porphyry urn.

out by the verdict of one who was afterwards employed in active hostility against Theoderic's successors. If a Ravennate chronicler asserts that the king " did nothing wrong " (*nihil perperam gessit*),[1] the historian Procopius makes a statement, hardly less unqualified, in regard to the justice of the administration, and dwells on the deserved devotion which his subjects entertained towards him.[2] The peace and plenty of his times are illustrated with vivid hyperboles in an Italian chronicle.[3] " Merchants from divers provinces used to throng to him. For so perfect was the public order that if a man wished to leave his silver or gold in his field, it was respected as much as if it were within the walls of a town. This was shown by the fact that he built no new gates for any town in all Italy, nor were the gates of any town ever closed. Any one could go about his business at any hour of the night just as if it were day. In his time sixty modii of wheat cost a solidus, and thirty amphoræ of wine were sold for the same price." [4] If this cheapness of provisions was normal, it would be one of the most convincing signs of the prosperity of Italy under Theoderic's government. But notwithstanding the improvement in their material conditions and in their general security, we can hardly believe that the Italians, with the barbarians settled in their midst, regarded themselves as steeped in felicity.

[1] Anon. Val. 60.

[2] The encomium of Procopius will be found in *B.G.* i. 1.

[3] Anon. Val. 72, 73. The laudatory notices in this chronicler were perhaps inspired by the Panegyric of Ennodius. See Dumoulin's article in *Revue historique*, 1902.

[4] Thus a modius of wheat (= about 2 gallons) cost $2\frac{1}{2}$d., or a bushel cost 10d. and a quarter 6s. 8d. As the Roman amphora was nearly 6 gallons, a gallon of wine cost less than 1d. The price of wheat in Julian's time was between $\frac{1}{10}$th and $\frac{1}{15}$th of a solidus for a modius (*Misopogon*, 369), *i.e.* about a shilling. In the sixth century 16 artabae of Egyptian wheat were sold for two solidi (*Pap. Cairo*, i. 67062). An artaba is generally reckoned = $3\frac{1}{3}$ modii, but at this time it was equated with 3 modii (see tables in *Pap. Cairo*, ii. 67138), so that the price was $\frac{1}{24}$th solidus = about 6d. a modius. On the other hand, in the accounts of Ammonius (*ib.*) we find 25 art. sold for $99\frac{1}{2}$ keratia, or 1 art. for $\frac{1}{6}$th solidus and 1 modius for $8\frac{1}{3}$d. (or somewhat more if the solidus was equated with 22 instead of 24 keratia).

APPENDIX

ON THE PRAETORIAN PREFECTS OF THE EAST UNDER ANASTASIUS

There are considerable difficulties as to the succession of the Praet. Prefects in this reign. The evidence will be found collected in Borghesi, *Les Préfets de Prétoire*, i. 370 *sqq.*, but his results are not clear or satisfactory. The dates in *C.J.* are our main guide. The following seem to be fairly certain : Matronianus, A.D. 491, July (*C.J.* vii. 39. 4 ; i. 22. 6) ; Hierius, A.D. 494 (John Mal. xvi. p. 392) –496, Feb. 13 (*C.J.* vi. 21. 16) ; Euphemius, A.D. 496, April 1–Aug. 21 (*ib.* x. 16. 13 ; x. 19. 9) ; Polycarpus, A.D. 498, April 1 (*ib.* v. 30. 4) ; Constantine, A.D. 502, Feb. 15–July 21 (*ib.* iii. 13. 7-6, 20. 18) ; Appion, A.D. 503 (John Mal. xvi. p. 398) ; Leontius, A.D. 503–504 (John Lyd. iii. 17) ; Constantine again, A.D. 505 (*C.J.* ii. 7. 22, but the month *Iul.* is wrong ; Krüger suggests *Ian.*) ; Eustathius, A.D. 505, April 19–506, Nov. 20 (*ib.* i. 4. 19 ; ii. 7. 23) ; Zoticus, A.D. 511–512 (Cyrillus, *Vita S. Sabae*, pp. 290, 294 ; this agrees with the chronological indications in John Lyd. iii. 27 ; from whom we also learn that Zoticus held office for little more than a year) ; Sergius, A.D. 517, April 1–Dec. 1 (*C.J.* v. 27. 6 ; ii. 7. 24). The Prefects of uncertain date are Armenius, Arcadius, Leontius (*ib.* xii. 50. 23 ; xii. 37. 7 ; vii. 39. 6), and Marinus. As to Leontius, he held office after 500 (cp. *ib.* vii. 39. 5, and John Lyd. iii. 17). For the Prefecture of Marinus we have the limits 498 (John Lyd. iii. 36) and 515, in which year he was ex-Pr. Pr. (John Mal. xvi. pp. 403, 405, 407). He was influential with Anastasius in the Prefecture of Zoticus (Cyrillus, *loc. cit.*), and it is to be noted that Zacharias of Mytilene (vii. 9), speaking of him as the Emperor's friend and confidant, describes him as a *chartularius* (A.D. 511). The people of Constantinople held him as partly responsible for the ecclesiastical measures which caused the riot of Nov. 512, and his house was burnt down (Marcell. *Chron.*, *sub a.*). On the whole, I would conjecture that he became Prefect in that year, having succeeded Zoticus. It does not follow from John Lyd. *loc. cit.* (as Borghesi supposes) that he immediately succeeded Polycarpus. In the latter part of his reign, Anastasius appointed only Scholastici (ῥήτορες, λογικοί) to the Prefecture (John Lyd. iii. 50 ; Priscian, *Pan.* 246-251), in accordance with the old tradition of the civil service. For the training of the scholasticus cp. Macarius, *Hom.* 15, 42, in Migne, *P.G.* xxxiv. 604.— Marinus is meant by the Μαριανός who is mentioned in Justinian, *Nov.* 96 § 15, as is evident from the context. He was Praetorian Prefect again under Justin in A.D. 519 (*C.J.* v. 27. 7 ; ii. 7. 25).— There is a slight difficulty about Appion, though John Malalas (source : Eustathius of Epiphania) says expressly that the patrician

Appion was appointed ἔπαρχος πραιτωρίων ἀνατολῆς and sent to
the East on the outbreak of the Persian War. This seems to har-
monise with Joshua Styl. lv. p. 44, who states that Appion the hyparch
was at Edessa in May 503. But it would be very strange for a
Praet. Prefect to proceed himself to the seat of war to supervise the
commissariat, and we should naturally take hyparch to mean the
officer called prefect of the camp, ὁ τοῦ στρατοπέδου ἔπαρχος
(Procopius, *B.V.* i. 11), both here and *ib.* lxx., where we learn that
Calliopius became hyparch in May 404, an office which he occupied
till 506, *ib.* xcix. We cannot suppose Calliopius to have been
Praet. Prefect, as the post was held by Constantine and Eustathius
in 505–506, and it is a little difficult to interpret hyparch differently
in the two cases. But we have to take into consideration the
statement of John Lyd. iii. 17 that Anastasius was "moved with
anger against Appion," ἀνδρὸς ἐξοχωτάτου καὶ κοινωνήσαντος αὐτῷ
τῆς βασιλείας ὅτε Κωάδης ὁ Πέρσης ἐφλέγμαινε, Λεοντίου τὴν
ἐπαρχότητα διέποντος. This seems to mean that Appion was
Praet. Pref. at the outbreak of the Persian War, but fell into dis-
favour and was succeeded by Leontius, and establishes the Prefecture of Appion. I am inclined to think that Joshua's Appion was a
different person.

CATALOGUE OF DOVER BOOKS

Social Sciences

SOCIAL THOUGHT FROM LORE TO SCIENCE, H. E. Barnes and H. Becker. An immense survey of sociological thought and ways of viewing, studying, planning, and reforming society from earliest times to the present. Includes thought on society of preliterate peoples, ancient non-Western cultures, and every great movement in Europe, America, and modern Japan. Analyzes hundreds of great thinkers: Plato, Augustine, Bodin, Vico, Montesquieu, Herder, Comte, Marx, etc. Weighs the contributions of utopians, sophists, fascists and communists; economists, jurists, philosophers, ecclesiastics, and every 19th and 20th century school of scientific sociology, anthropology, and social psychology throughout the world. Combines topical, chronological, and regional approaches, treating the evolution of social thought as a process rather than as a series of mere topics. "Impressive accuracy, competence, and discrimination . . . easily the best single survey," Nation. Thoroughly revised, with new material up to 1960. 2 indexes. Over 2200 bibliographical notes. Three volume set. Total of 1586pp. 5⅜ x 8.

T901 Vol I Paperbound **$2.50**
T902 Vol II Paperbound **$2.50**
T903 Vol III Paperbound **$2.50**
The set **$7.50**

FOLKWAYS, William Graham Sumner. A classic of sociology, a searching and thorough examination of patterns of behaviour from primitive, ancient Greek and Judaic, Medieval Christian, African, Oriental, Melanesian, Australian, Islamic, to modern Western societies. Thousands of illustrations of social, sexual, and religious customs, mores, laws, and institutions. Hundreds of categories: Labor, Wealth, Abortion, Primitive Justice, Life Policy, Slavery, Cannibalism, Uncleanness and the Evil Eye, etc. Will extend the horizon of every reader by showing the relativism of his own culture. Prefatory note by A. G. Keller. Introduction by William Lyon Phelps. Bibliography. Index. xiii + 692pp. 5⅜ x 8. T508 Paperbound **$2.49**

PRIMITIVE RELIGION, P. Radin. A thorough treatment by a noted anthropologist of the nature and origin of man's belief in the supernatural and the influences that have shaped religious expression in primitive societies. Ranging from the Arunta, Ashanti, Aztec, Bushman, Crow, Fijian, etc., of Africa, Australia, Pacific Islands, the Arctic, North and South America, Prof. Radin integrates modern psychology, comparative religion, and economic thought with first-hand accounts gathered by himself and other scholars of primitive initiations, training of the shaman, and other fascinating topics. "Excellent," NATURE (London). Unabridged reissue of 1st edition. New author's preface. Bibliographic notes. Index. x + 322pp. 5⅜ x 8. T393 Paperbound **$2.00**

PRIMITIVE MAN AS PHILOSOPHER, P. Radin. A standard anthropological work covering primitive thought on such topics as the purpose of life, marital relations, freedom of thought, symbolism, death, resignation, the nature of reality, personality, gods, and many others. Drawn from factual material gathered from the Winnebago, Oglala Sioux, Maori, Baganda, Batak, Zuni, among others, it does not distort ideas by removing them from context but interprets strictly within the original framework. Extensive selections of original primitive documents. Bibliography. Index. xviii + 402pp. 5⅜ x 8. T392 Paperbound **$2.25**

A TREATISE ON SOCIOLOGY, THE MIND AND SOCIETY, Vilfredo Pareto. This treatise on human society is one of the great classics of modern sociology. First published in 1916, its careful catalogue of the innumerable manifestations of non-logical human conduct (Book One); the theory of "residues," leading to the premise that sentiment not logic determines human behavior (Book Two), and of "derivations," beliefs derived from desires (Book Three); and the general description of society made up of non-elite and elite, consisting of "foxes" who live by cunning and "lions" who live by force, stirred great controversy. But Pareto's passion for isolation and classification of elements and factors, and his allegiance to scientific method as the key tool for scrutinizing the human situation made his a truly twentieth-century mind and his work a catalytic influence on certain later social commentators. These four volumes (bound as two) require no special training to be appreciated and any reader who wishes to gain a complete understanding of modern sociological theory, regardless of special field of interest, will find them a must. Reprint of revised (corrected) printing of original edition. Translated by Andrew Bongiorno and Arthur Livingston. Index. Bibliography. Appendix containing index-summary of theorems. 48 diagrams. Four volumes bound as two. Total of 2063pp. 5⅜ x 8½. The set Clothbound **$15.00**

THE POLISH PEASANT IN EUROPE AND AMERICA, William I. Thomas, Florian Znaniecki. A seminal sociological study of peasant primary groups (family and community) and the disruptions produced by a new industrial system and immigration to America. The peasant's family, class system, religious and aesthetic attitudes, and economic life are minutely examined and analyzed in hundreds of pages of primary documentation, particularly letters between family members. The disorientation caused by new environments is scrutinized in detail (a 312-page autobiography of an immigrant is especially valuable and revealing) in an attempt to find common experiences and reactions. The famous "Methodological Note" sets forth the principles which guided the authors. When out of print this set has sold for as much as $50. 2nd revised edition. 2 vols. Vol. 1: xv + 1115pp. Vol. 2: 1135pp. Index. 6 x 9. T478 Clothbound 2 vol. set **$12.50**

Literature, History of Literature

ARISTOTLE'S THEORY OF POETRY AND THE FINE ARTS, edited by S. H. Butcher. The celebrated Butcher translation of this great classic faced, page by page, with the complete Greek text. A 300 page introduction discussing Aristotle's ideas and their influence in the history of thought and literature, and covering art and nature, imitation as an aesthetic form, poetic truth, art and morality, tragedy, comedy, and similar topics. Modern Aristotelian criticism discussed by John Gassner. lxxvi + 421pp. 5⅜ x 8.   **T42 Paperbound $2.00**

INTRODUCTIONS TO ENGLISH LITERATURE, edited by B. Dobrée. Goes far beyond ordinary histories, ranging from the 7th century up to 1914 (to the 1940's in some cases.) The first half of each volume is a specific detailed study of historical and economic background of the period and a general survey of poetry and prose, including trends of thought, influences, etc. The second and larger half is devoted to a detailed study of more than 5000 poets, novelists, dramatists; also economists, historians, biographers, religious writers, philosophers, travellers, and scientists of literary stature, with dates, lists of major works and their dates, keypoint critical bibliography, and evaluating comments. The most compendious bibliographic and literary aid within its price range.

Vol. I. THE BEGINNINGS OF ENGLISH LITERATURE TO SKELTON, (1509), W. L. Renwick, H. Orton. 450pp. 5⅛ x 7⅞.   **T75 Clothbound $4.50**

Vol. II. THE ENGLISH RENAISSANCE, 1510-1688, V. de Sola Pinto. 381pp. 5⅛ x 7⅞.   **T76 Clothbound $4.50**

Vol. III. AUGUSTANS AND ROMANTICS, 1689-1830, H. Dyson, J. Butt. 320pp. 5⅛ x 7⅞.   **T77 Clothbound $4.50**

Vol. IV. THE VICTORIANS AND AFTER, 1830-1940's, E. Batho, B. Dobrée. 360pp. 5⅛ x 7⅞.   **T78 Clothbound $4.50**

EPIC AND ROMANCE, W. P. Ker. Written by one of the foremost authorities on medieval literature, this is the standard survey of medieval epic and romance. It covers Teutonic epics, Icelandic sagas, Beowulf, French chansons de geste, the Roman de Troie, and many other important works of literature. It is an excellent account for a body of literature whose beauty and value has only recently come to be recognized. Index. xxiv + 398pp. 5⅜ x 8.   **T355 Paperbound $2.25**

THE POPULAR BALLAD, F. B. Gummere. Most useful factual introduction; fund of descriptive material; quotes, cites over 260 ballads. Examines, from folkloristic view, structure; choral, ritual elements; meter, diction, fusion; effects of tradition, editors; almost every other aspect of border, riddle, kinship, sea, ribald, supernatural, etc., ballads. Bibliography. 2 indexes. 374pp. 5⅜ x 8.   **T548 Paperbound $1.85**

MASTERS OF THE DRAMA, John Gassner. The most comprehensive history of the drama in print, covering drama in every important tradition from the Greeks to the Near East, China, Japan, Medieval Europe, England, Russia, Italy, Spain, Germany, and dozens of other drama producing nations. This unsurpassed reading and reference work encompasses more than 800 dramatists and over 2000 plays, with biographical material, plot summaries, theatre history, etc. "Has no competitors in its field," THEATRE ARTS. "Best of its kind in English," NEW REPUBLIC. Exhaustive 35 page bibliography. 77 photographs and drawings. Deluxe edition with reinforced cloth binding, headbands, stained top. xxii + 890pp. 5⅜ x 8.   **T100 Clothbound $6.95**

THE DEVELOPMENT OF DRAMATIC ART, D. C. Stuart. The basic work on the growth of Western drama from primitive beginnings to Eugene O'Neill, covering over 2500 years. Not a mere listing or survey, but a thorough analysis of changes, origins of style, and influences in each period; dramatic conventions, social pressures, choice of material, plot devices, stock situations, etc.; secular and religious works of all nations and epochs. "Generous and thoroughly documented researches," Outlook. "Solid studies of influences and playwrights and periods," London Times. Index. Bibliography. xi + 679pp. 5⅜ x 8.
          T693 Paperbound $2.75

A SOURCE BOOK IN THEATRICAL HISTORY (SOURCES OF THEATRICAL HISTORY), A. M. Nagler. Over 2000 years of actors, directors, designers, critics, and spectators speak for themselves in this potpourri of writings selected from the great and formative periods of western drama. On-the-spot descriptions of masks, costumes, makeup, rehearsals, special effects, acting methods, backstage squabbles, theatres, etc. Contemporary glimpses of Molière rehearsing his company, an exhortation to a Roman audience to buy refreshments and keep quiet, Goethe's rules for actors, Belasco telling of $6500 he spent building a river, Restoration actors being told to avoid "lewd, obscene, or indecent postures," and much more. Each selection has an introduction by Prof. Nagler. This extraordinary, lively collection is ideal as a source of otherwise difficult to obtain material, as well as a fine book for browsing. Over 80 illustrations. 10 diagrams. xxiii + 611pp. 5⅜ x 8.   **T515 Paperbound $3.00**

WORLD DRAMA, B. H. Clark. The dramatic creativity of a score of ages and eras — all in two handy compact volumes. Over ⅓ of this material is unavailable in any other current edition! 46 plays from Ancient Greece, Rome, Medieval Europe, France, Germany, Italy, England, Russia, Scandinavia, India, China, Japan, etc. — including classic authors like Aeschylus, Sophocles, Euripides, Aristophanes, Plautus, Marlowe, Jonson, Farquhar, Goldsmith, Cervantes, Molière, Dumas, Goethe, Schiller, Ibsen, and many others. This creative collection avoids hackneyed material and includes only completely first-rate works which are relatively little known or difficult to obtain. "The most comprehensive collection of important plays from all literature available in English," SAT. REV. OF LITERATURE. Introduction. Reading lists. 2 volumes. 1364pp. 5⅜ x 8.
Vol. 1, T57 Paperbound **$2.50**
Vol. 2, T59 Paperbound **$2.50**

MASTERPIECES OF THE RUSSIAN DRAMA, edited with introduction by G. R. Noyes. This only comprehensive anthology of Russian drama ever published in English offers complete texts, in 1st-rate modern translations, of 12 plays covering 200 years. Vol. 1: "The Young Hopeful," Fonvisin; "Wit Works Woe," Griboyedov; "The Inspector General," Gogol; "A Month in the Country," Turgenev; "The Poor Bride," Ostrovsky; "A Bitter Fate," Pisemsky. Vol. 2: "The Death of Ivan the Terrible," Alexey Tolstoy "The Power of Darkness," Lev Tolstoy; "The Lower Depths," Gorky; "The Cherry Orchard," Chekhov; "Professor Storitsyn," Andreyev; "Mystery Bouffe," Mayakovsky. Bibliography. Total of 902pp. 5⅜ x 8.
Vol. 1 T647 Paperbound **$2.25**
Vol. 2 T648 Paperbound **$2.00**

EUGENE O'NEILL: THE MAN AND HIS PLAYS, B. H. Clark. Introduction to O'Neill's life and work. Clark analyzes each play from the early THE WEB to the recently produced MOON FOR THE MISBEGOTTEN and THE ICEMAN COMETH revealing the environmental and dramatic influences necessary for a complete understanding of these important works. Bibliography. Appendices. Index. ix + 182pp. 5⅜ x 8.
T379 Paperbound **$1.35**

THE HEART OF THOREAU'S JOURNALS, edited by O. Shepard. The best general selection from Thoreau's voluminous (and rare) journals. This intimate record of thoughts and observations reveals the full Thoreau and his intellectual development more accurately than any of his published works: self-conflict between the scientific observer and the poet, reflections on transcendental philosophy, involvement in the tragedies of neighbors and national causes, etc. New preface, notes, introductions. xii + 228pp. 5⅜ x 8.
T741 Paperbound **$1.50**

H. D. THOREAU: A WRITER'S JOURNAL, edited by L. Stapleton. A unique new selection from the Journals concentrating on Thoreau's growth as a conscious literary artist, the ideals and purposes of his art. Most of the material has never before appeared outside of the complete 14-volume edition. Contains vital insights on Thoreau's projected book on Concord, thoughts on the nature of men and government, indignation with slavery, sources of inspiration, goals in life. Index. xxxiii + 234pp. 5⅜ x 8.
T678 Paperbound **$1.65**

THE HEART OF EMERSON'S JOURNALS, edited by Bliss Perry. Best of these revealing Journals, originally 10 volumes, presented in a one volume edition. Talks with Channing, Hawthorne, Thoreau, and Bronson Alcott; impressions of Webster, Everett, John Brown, and Lincoln; records of moments of sudden understanding, vision, and solitary ecstasy. "The essays do not reveal the power of Emerson's mind . . . as do these hasty and informal writings," N.Y. Times. Preface by Bliss Perry. Index. xiii + 357pp. 5⅜ x 8.
T477 Paperbound **$1.85**

FOUNDERS OF THE MIDDLE AGES, E. K. Rand. This is the best non-technical discussion of the transformation of Latin pagan culture into medieval civilization. Covering such figures as Tertullian, Gregory, Jerome, Boethius, Augustine, the Neoplatonists, and many other literary men, educators, classicists, and humanists, this book is a storehouse of information presented clearly and simply for the intelligent non-specialist. "Thoughtful, beautifully written," AMERICAN HISTORICAL REVIEW. "Extraordinarily accurate," Richard McKeon, THE NATION. ix + 365pp. 5⅜ x 8.
T369 Paperbound **$2.00**

PLAY-MAKING: A MANUAL OF CRAFTSMANSHIP, William Archer. With an extensive, new introduction by John Gassner, Yale Univ. The permanently essential requirements of solid play construction are set down in clear, practical language: theme, exposition, foreshadowing, tension, obligatory scene, peripety, dialogue, character, psychology, other topics. This book has been one of the most influential elements in the modern theatre, and almost everything said on the subject since is contained explicitly or implicitly within its covers. Bibliography. Index. xlii + 277pp. 5⅜ x 8.
T651 Paperbound **$1.75**

HAMBURG DRAMATURGY, G. E. Lessing. One of the most brilliant of German playwrights of the eighteenth-century age of criticism analyzes the complex of theory and tradition that constitutes the world of theater. These 104 essays on aesthetic theory helped demolish the regime of French classicism, opening the door to psychological and social realism, romanticism. Subjects include the original functions of tragedy; drama as the rational world; the meaning of pity and fear, pity and fear as means for purgation and other Aristotelian concepts; genius and creative force; interdependence of poet's language and actor's interpretation; truth and authenticity; etc. A basic and enlightening study for anyone interested in aesthetics and ideas, from the philosopher to the theatergoer. Introduction by Prof. Victor Lange. xxii + 265pp. 4½ x 6⅜.
T32 Paperbound **$1.45**

Americana

THE EYES OF DISCOVERY, J. Bakeless. A vivid reconstruction of how unspoiled America appeared to the first white men. Authentic and enlightening accounts of Hudson's landing in New York, Coronado's trek through the Southwest; scores of explorers, settlers, trappers, soldiers. America's pristine flora, fauna, and Indians in every region and state in fresh and unusual new aspects. "A fascinating view of what the land was like before the first highway went through," Time. 68 contemporary illustrations, 39 newly added in this edition. Index. Bibliography. x + 500pp. 5⅜ x 8.   **T761 Paperbound $2.00**

AUDUBON AND HIS JOURNALS, J. J. Audubon. A collection of fascinating accounts of Europe and America in the early 1800's through Audubon's own eyes. Includes the Missouri River Journals —an eventful trip through America's untouched heartland, the Labrador Journals, the European Journals, the famous "Episodes", and other rare Audubon material, including the descriptive chapters from the original letterpress edition of the "Ornithological Studies", omitted in all later editions. Indispensable for ornithologists, naturalists, and all lovers of Americana and adventure. 70-page biography by Audubon's granddaughter. 38 illustrations. Index. Total of 1106pp. 5⅜ x 8.   **T675 Vol I Paperbound $2.25**
T676 Vol II Paperbound $2.25
The set $4.50

TRAVELS OF WILLIAM BARTRAM, edited by Mark Van Doren. The first inexpensive illustrated edition of one of the 18th century's most delightful books is an excellent source of first-hand material on American geography, anthropology, and natural history. Many descriptions of early Indian tribes are our only source of information on them prior to the infiltration of the white man. "The mind of a scientist with the soul of a poet," John Livingston Lowes. 13 original illustrations and maps. Edited with an introduction by Mark Van Doren. 448pp. 5⅜ x 8.
T13 Paperbound $2.00

GARRETS AND PRETENDERS: A HISTORY OF BOHEMIANISM IN AMERICA, A. Parry. The colorful and fantastic history of American Bohemianism from Poe to Kerouac. This is the only complete record of hoboes, cranks, starving poets, and suicides. Here are Pfaff, Whitman, Crane, Bierce, Pound, and many others. New chapters by the author and by H. T. Moore bring this thorough and well-documented history down to the Beatniks. "An excellent account," N. Y. Times. Scores of cartoons, drawings, and caricatures. Bibliography. Index. xxviii + 421pp. 5⅝ x 8⅜.   **T708 Paperbound $1.95**

THE EXPLORATION OF THE COLORADO RIVER AND ITS CANYONS, J. W. Powell. The thrilling first-hand account of the expedition that filled in the last white space on the map of the United States. Rapids, famine, hostile Indians, and mutiny are among the perils encountered as the unknown Colorado Valley reveals its secrets. This is the only uncut version of Major Powell's classic of exploration that has been printed in the last 60 years. Includes later reflections and subsequent expedition. 250 illustrations, new map. 400pp. 5⅝ x 8⅜.
T94 Paperbound $2.25

THE JOURNAL OF HENRY D. THOREAU, Edited by Bradford Torrey and Francis H. Allen. Henry Thoreau is not only one of the most important figures in American literature and social thought; his voluminous journals (from which his books emerged as selections and crystalliza-tions) constitute both the longest, most sensitive record of personal internal development and a most penetrating description of a historical moment in American culture. This present set, which was first issued in fourteen volumes, contains Thoreau's entire journals from 1837 to 1862, with the exception of the lost years which were found only recently. We are reissuing it, complete and unabridged, with a new introduction by Walter Harding, Secretary of the Thoreau Society. Fourteen volumes reissued in two volumes. Foreword by Henry Seidel Canby. Total of 1888pp. 8⅜ x 12¼.   **T312-3 Two volume set, Clothbound $20.00**

GAMES AND SONGS OF AMERICAN CHILDREN, collected by William Wells Newell. A remarkable collection of 190 games with songs that accompany many of them; cross references to show similarities, differences among them; variations; musical notation for 38 songs. Textual dis-cussions show relations with folk-drama and other aspects of folk tradition. Grouped into categories for ready comparative study: Love-games, histories, playing at work, human life, bird and beast, mythology, guessing-games, etc. New introduction covers relations of songs and dances to timeless heritage of folklore, biographical sketch of Newell, other pertinent data. A good source of inspiration for those in charge of groups of children and a valuable reference for anthropologists, sociologists, psychiatrists. Introduction by Carl Withers. New indexes of first lines, games. 5⅜ x 8½. xii + 242pp.   **T354 Paperbound $1.75**

GARDNER'S PHOTOGRAPHIC SKETCH BOOK OF THE CIVIL WAR, Alexander Gardner. The first published collection of Civil War photographs, by one of the two or three most famous photographers of the era, outstandingly reproduced from the original positives. Scenes of crucial battles: Appomattox, Manassas, Mechanicsville, Bull Run, Yorktown, Fredericksburg, etc. Gettysburg immediately after retirement of forces. Battle ruins at Richmond, Petersburg, Gaines'Mill. Prisons, arsenals, a slave pen, fortifications, headquarters, pontoon bridges, soldiers, a field hospital. A unique glimpse into the realities of one of the bloodiest wars in history, with an introductory text to each picture by Gardner himself. Until this edition, there were only five known copies in libraries, and fewer in private hands, one of which sold at auction in 1952 for $425. Introduction by E. F. Bleiler. 100 full page 7 x 10 photographs (original size). 224pp. 8½ x 10¾. T476 Clothbound **$6.00**

A BIBLIOGRAPHY OF NORTH AMERICAN FOLKLORE AND FOLKSONG, Charles Haywood, Ph.D. The only book that brings together bibliographic information on so wide a range of folklore material. Lists practically everything published about American folksongs, ballads, dances, folk beliefs and practices, popular music, tales, similar material—more than 35,000 titles of books, articles, periodicals, monographs, music publications, phonograph records. Each entry complete with author, title, date and place of publication, arranger and performer of particular examples of folk music, many with Dr. Haywood's valuable criticism, evaluation. Volume I, "The American People," is complete listing of general and regional studies, titles of tales and songs of Negro and non-English speaking groups and where to find them, Occupational Bibliography including sections listing sources of information, folk material on cowboys, riverboat men, 49ers, American characters like Mike Fink, Frankie and Johnnie, John Henry, many more. Volume II, "The American Indian," tells where to find information on dances, myths, songs, ritual of more than 250 tribes in U.S., Canada. A monumental product of 10 years' labor, carefully classified for easy use. "All students of this subject . . . will find themselves in debt to Professor Haywood," Stith Thompson, in American Anthropologist. ". . . a most useful and excellent work," Duncan Emrich, Chief Folklore Section, Library of Congress, in "Notes." Corrected, enlarged republication of 1951 edition. New Preface. New index of composers, arrangers, performers. General index of more than 15,000 items. Two volumes. Total of 1301pp. 6⅛ x 9¼. T797-798 Clothbound **$12.50**

INCIDENTS OF TRAVEL IN YUCATAN, John L. Stephens. One of first white men to penetrate interior of Yucatan tells the thrilling story of his discoveries of 44 cities, remains of once-powerful Maya civilization. Compelling text combines narrative power with historical significance as it takes you through heat, dust, storms of Yucatan; native festivals with brutal bull fights; great ruined temples atop man-made mounds. Countless idols, sculptures, tombs, examples of Mayan taste for rich ornamentation, from gateways to personal trinkets, accurately illustrated, discussed in text. Will appeal to those interested in ancient civilizations, and those who like stories of exploration, discovery, adventure. Republication of last (1843) edition. 124 illustrations by English artist, F. Catherwood. Appendix on Mayan architecture, chronology. Two volume set. Total of xxviii + 927pp.

Vol I T926 Paperbound **$2.00**
Vol II T927 Paperbound **$2.00**
The set **$4.00**

A GENIUS IN THE FAMILY, Hiram Percy Maxim. Sir Hiram Stevens Maxim was known to the public as the inventive genius who created the Maxim gun, automatic sprinkler, and a heavier-than-air plane that got off the ground in 1894. Here, his son reminisces—this is by no means a formal biography—about the exciting and often downright scandalous private life of his brilliant, eccentric father. A warm and winning portrait of a prankish, mischievous, impious personality, a genuine character. The style is fresh and direct, the effect is unadulterated pleasure. "A book of charm and lasting humor . . . belongs on the 'must read' list of all fathers," New York Times. "A truly gorgeous affair," New Statesman and Nation. 17 illustrations, 16 specially for this edition. viii + 108pp. 5⅜ x 8½.
T948 Paperbound **$1.00**

HORSELESS CARRIAGE DAYS, Hiram P. Maxim. The best account of an important technological revolution by one of its leading figures. The delightful and rewarding story of the author's experiments with the exact combustibility of gasoline, stopping and starting mechanisms, carriage design, and engines. Captures remarkably well the flavor of an age of scoffers and rival inventors not above sabotage; of noisy, uncontrollable gasoline vehicles and incredible mobile steam kettles. ". . . historic information and light humor are combined to furnish highly entertaining reading," New York Times. 56 photographs, 12 specially for this edition. xi + 175pp. 5⅜ x 8½. T964 Paperbound **$1.35**

BODY, BOOTS AND BRITCHES: FOLKTALES, BALLADS AND SPEECH FROM COUNTRY NEW YORK, Harold W. Thompson. A unique collection, discussion of songs, stories, anecdotes, proverbs handed down orally from Scotch-Irish grandfathers, German nurse-maids, Negro workmen, gathered from all over Upper New York State. Tall tales by and about lumbermen and pirates, canalers and injun-fighters, tragic and comic ballads, scores of sayings and proverbs all tied together by an informative, delightful narrative by former president of New York Historical Society. ". . . a sparkling homespun tapestry that every lover of Americana will want to have around the house," Carl Carmer, New York Times. Republication of 1939 edition. 20 line-drawings. Index. Appendix (Sources of material, bibliography). 530pp. 5⅜ x 8½. T411 Paperbound **$2.25**

Teach Yourself

These British books are the most effective series of home study books on the market! With no outside help they will teach you as much as is necessary to have a good background in each subject, in many cases offering as much material as a similar high school or college course. They are carefully planned, written by foremost British educators, and amply provided with test questions and problems for you to check your progress; the mathematics books are especially rich in examples and problems. Do not confuse them with skimpy outlines or ordinary school texts or vague generalized popularizations; each book is complete in itself, full without being overdetailed, and designed to give you an easily-acquired branch of knowledge.

TEACH YOURSELF ALGEBRA, P. Abbott. The equivalent of a thorough high school course, up through logarithms. 52 illus. 307pp. 4¼ x 7. T680 Clothbound **$2.00**

TEACH YOURSELF GEOMETRY, P. Abbott. Plane and solid geometry, covering about a year of plane and six months of solid. 268 illus. 344pp. 4½ x 7. T681 Clothbound **$2.00**

TEACH YOURSELF TRIGONOMETRY, P. Abbott. Background of algebra and geometry will enable you to get equivalent of elementary college course. Tables. 102 illus. 204pp. 4½ x 7. T682 Clothbound **$2.00**

TEACH YOURSELF THE CALCULUS, P. Abbott. With algebra and trigonometry you will be able to acquire a good working knowledge of elementary integral calculus and differential calculus. Excellent supplement to any course textbook. 380pp. 4¼ x 7. T683 Clothbound **$2.00**

TEACH YOURSELF THE SLIDE RULE, B. Snodgrass. Basic principles clearly explained, with many applications in engineering, business, general figuring, will enable you to pick up very useful skill. 10 illus. 207pp. 4¼ x 7. T684 Clothbound **$2.00**

TEACH YOURSELF MECHANICS, P. Abbott. Equivalent of part course on elementary college level, with lever, parallelogram of force, friction, laws of motion, gases, etc. Fine introduction before more advanced course. 163 illus. 271pp. 4½ x 7. T685 Clothbound **$2.00**

TEACH YOURSELF ELECTRICITY, C. W. Wilman. Current, resistance, voltage, Ohm's law, circuits, generators, motors, transformers, etc. Non-mathematical as much as possible. 115 illus. 184pp. 4¼ x 7. T230 Clothbound **$2.00**

TEACH YOURSELF HEAT ENGINES E. DeVille. Steam and internal combustion engines; non-mathematical introduction for student, for layman wishing background, refresher for advanced student. 76 illus. 217pp. 4¼ x 7. T237 Clothbound **$2.00**

TEACH YOURSELF TO PLAY THE PIANO, King Palmer. Companion and supplement to lessons or self study. Handy reference, too. Nature of instrument, elementary musical theory, technique of playing, interpretation, etc. 60 illus. 144pp. 4¼ x 7. T959 Clothbound **$2.00**

TEACH YOURSELF HERALDRY AND GENEALOGY, L. G. Pine. Modern work, avoiding romantic and overpopular misconceptions. Editor of new Burke presents detailed information and commentary down to present. Best general survey. 50 illus. glossary; 129pp. 4¼ x 7. T962 Clothbound **$2.00**

TEACH YOURSELF HANDWRITING, John L. Dumpleton. Basic Chancery cursive style is popular and easy to learn. Many diagrams. 114 illus. 192pp. 4¼ x 7. T960 Clothbound **$2.00**

TEACH YOURSELF CARD GAMES FOR TWO, Kenneth Konstam. Many first-rate games, including old favorites like cribbage and gin and canasta as well as new lesser-known games. Extremely interesting for cards enthusiast. 60 illus. 150pp. 4¼ x 7. T963 Clothbound **$2.00**

TEACH YOURSELF GUIDEBOOK TO THE DRAMA, Luis Vargas. Clear, rapid survey of changing fashions and forms from Aeschylus to Tennessee Williams, in all major European traditions. Plot summaries, critical comments, etc. Equivalent of a college drama course; fine cultural background 224pp. 4¼ x 7. T961 Clothbound **$2.00**

TEACH YOURSELF THE ORGAN, Francis Routh. Excellent compendium of background material for everyone interested in organ music, whether as listener or player. 27 musical illus. 158pp. 4¼ x 7. T977 Clothbound **$2.00**

TEACH YOURSELF TO STUDY SCULPTURE, William Gaunt. Noted British cultural historian surveys culture from Greeks, primitive world, to moderns. Equivalent of college survey course. 23 figures, 40 photos. 158pp. 4¼ x 7. T976 Clothbound **$2.00**

Orientalia

ORIENTAL RELIGIONS IN ROMAN PAGANISM, F. Cumont. A study of the cultural meeting of east and west in the Early Roman Empire. It covers the most important eastern religions of the time from their first appearance in Rome, 204 B.C., when the Great Mother of the Gods was first brought over from Syria. The ecstatic cults of Syria and Phrygia — Cybele, Attis, Adonis, their orgies and mutilatory rites; the mysteries of Egypt — Serapis, Isis, Osiris, the dualism of Persia, the elevation of cosmic evil to equal stature with the deity, Mithra; worship of Hermes Trismegistus; Ishtar, Astarte; the magic of the ancient Near East, etc. Introduction. 55pp. of notes; extensive bibliography. Index. xxiv + 298pp. 5⅜ x 8.
T321 Paperbound **$2.00**

THE MYSTERIES OF MITHRA, F. Cumont. The definitive coverage of a great ideological struggle between the west and the orient in the first centuries of the Christian era. The origin of Mithraism, a Persian mystery religion, and its association with the Roman army is discussed in detail. Then utilizing fragmentary monuments and texts, in one of the greatest feats of scholarly detection, Dr. Cumont reconstructs the mystery teachings and secret doctrines, the hidden organization and cult of Mithra. Mithraic art is discussed, analyzed, and depicted in 70 illustrations. 239pp. 5⅜ x 8.
T323 Paperbound **$2.00**

CHRISTIAN AND ORIENTAL PHILOSOPHY OF ART, A. K. Coomaraswamy. A unique fusion of philosopher, orientalist, art historian, and linguist, the author discusses such matters as: the true function of aesthetics in art, the importance of symbolism, intellectual and philosophic backgrounds, the role of traditional culture in enriching art, common factors in all great art, the nature of medieval art, the nature of folklore, the beauty of mathematics, and similar topics. 2 illustrations. Bibliography. 148pp. 5⅜ x 8.
T378 Paperbound **$1.50**

TRANSFORMATION OF NATURE IN ART, A. K. Coomaraswamy. Unabridged reissue of a basic work upon Asiatic religious art and philosophy of religion. The theory of religious art in Asia and Medieval Europe (exemplified by Meister Eckhart) is analyzed and developed. Detailed consideration is given to Indian mechanical aesthetic manuals, symbolic language in philosophy, the origin and use of images in India, and many other fascinating and little known topics. Glossaries of Sanskrit and Chinese terms. Bibliography. 41pp. of notes. 245pp. 5⅜ x 8.
T368 Paperbound **$1.75**

BUDDHIST LOGIC, F.Th. Stcherbatsky. A study of an important part of Buddhism usually ignored by other books on the subject: the Mahayana buddhistic logic of the school of Dignaga and his followers. First vol. devoted to history of Indian logic with Central Asian continuations, detailed exposition of Dignaga system, including theory of knowledge, the sensible world (causation, perception, ultimate reality) and mental world (judgment, inference, logical fallacies, the syllogism), reality of external world, and negation (law of contradiction, universals, dialectic). Vol. II contains translation of Dharmakirti's Nyayabindu with Dharmamottara's commentary. Appendices cover translations of Tibetan treatises on logic, Hindu attacks on Buddhist logic, etc. The basic work, one of the products of the great St. Petersburg school of Indian studies. Written clearly and with an awareness of Western philosophy and logic; meant for the Asian specialist and for the general reader with only a minimum of background. Vol. I, xii + 559pp. Vol. II, viii + 468pp. 5⅜ x 8½.
T955 Vol. I Paperbound **$2.50**
T956 Vol. II Paperbound **$2.50**
The set **$5.00**

THE TEXTS OF TAOISM. The first inexpensive edition of the complete James Legge translations of the Tao Te King and the writings of Chinese mystic Chuang Tse. Also contains several shorter treatises: the T'ai Shang Tractate of Actions and Their Retributions; the King Kang King, or Classic of Purity; the Yin Fu King, or Classic of the Harmony of the Seen and Unseen; the Yu Shu King, or Classic of the Pivot of Jade; and the Hsia Yung King, or Classic of the Directory for a Day. While there are other translations of the Tao Te King, this is the only translation of Chuang Tse and much of other material. Extensive introduction discusses differences between Taoism, Buddhism, Confucianism; authenticity and arrangement of Tao Te King and writings of Chuang Tse; the meaning of the Tao and basic tenets of Taoism; historical accounts of Lao-tse and followers; other pertinent matters. Clarifying notes incorporated into text. Originally published as Volumes 39, 40 of SACRED BOOKS OF THE EAST series, this has long been recognized as an indispensable collection. Sinologists, philosophers, historians of religion will of course be interested and anyone with an elementary course in Oriental religion or philosophy will understand and profit from these writings. Index. Appendix analyzing thought of Chuang Tse. Vol. I, xxiii + 396pp. Vol. II, viii + 340pp. 5⅜ x 8½.
T990 Vol. I Paperbound **$2.25**
T991 Vol. II Paperbound **$2.25**

CATALOGUE OF DOVER BOOKS

EPOCHS OF CHINESE AND JAPANESE ART, Ernest T. Fenollosa. Although this classic of art history was written before the archeological discovery of Shang and Chou civilizations, it is still in many respects the finest detailed study of Chinese and Japanese art available in English. It is very wide in range, covering sculpture, carving, painting, metal work, ceramics, textiles, graphic arts and other areas, and it considers both religious and secular art, including the Japanese woodcut. Its greatest strength, however, lies in its extremely full, detailed, insight-laden discussion of historical and cultural background, and in its analysis of the religious and philosophical implications of art works. It is also a brilliant stylistic achievement, written with enthusiasm and verve, which can be enjoyed and read with profit by both the Orientalist and the general reader who is interested in art. Index. Glossary of proper names. 242 illustrations. Total of 704 pages. 5⅜ x 8½.
T364-5 Two vol. set, paperbound **$5.00**

THE VEDANTA SUTRAS OF BADARAYANA WITH COMMENTARY BY SANKARACHARYA. The definitive translation of the consummation, foremost interpretation of Upanishads. Originally part of SACRED BOOKS OF THE EAST, this two-volume translation includes exhaustive commentary and exegesis by Sankara; 128-page introduction by translator, Prof. Thibaut, that discusses background, scope and purpose of the sutras, value and importance of Sankara's interpretation; copious footnotes providing further explanations. Every serious student of Indian religion or thought, philosophers, historians of religion should read these clear, accurate translations of documents central to development of important thought systems in the East. Unabridged republication of Volumes 34, 38 of the Sacred Books of the East. Translated by George Thibault. General index, index of quotations and of Sanskrit. Vol. I, cxxv + 448pp. Vol. II, iv + 506pp. 5⅜ x 8½.
T994 Vol. I Paperbound **$2.00**
T995 Vol. II Paperbound **$2.00**

THE UPANISHADS. The Max Müller translation of the twelve classical Upanishads available for the first time in an inexpensive format: Chandogya, Kena, Aitareya aranyaka and upanishad, Kaushitaki, Isa, Katha, Mundaka, Taittiriyaka Brhadaranyaka, Svetarasvatara. Prasna — all of the classical Upanishads of the Vedanta school—and the Maitriyana Upanishad. Originally volumes 1, 15 of SACRED BOOKS OF THE EAST series, this is still the most scholarly translation. Prof. Müller, probably most important Sanskritologist of nineteenth century, provided invaluable introduction that acquaints readers with history of Upanishad translations, age and chronology of texts, etc. and a preface that discusses their value to Western readers. Heavily annotated. Stimulating reading for anyone with even only a basic course background in Oriental philosophy, religion, necessary to all Indologists, philosophers, religious historians. Transliteration and pronunciation guide. Vol. I, ciii + 320pp. Vol. II, liii + 350pp.
T992 Vol. I Paperbound **$2.25**
T993 Vol. II Paperbound **$2.25**
The set **$4.50**

Prices subject to change without notice.

Dover publishes books on art, music, philosophy, literature, languages, history, social sciences, psychology, handcrafts, orientalia, puzzles and entertainments, chess, pets and gardens, books explaining science, intermediate and higher mathematics, mathematical physics, engineering, biological sciences, earth sciences, classics of science, etc. Write to:

Dept. catrr.
Dover Publications, Inc.
180 Varick Street, N.Y. 14, N.Y.